ALSO BY

MELVILLE J. HERSKOVITS

◇◇◇◇◇◇◇◇◇◇◇

The Economic Life of Primitive Peoples

Life in a Haitian Valley

The American Negro

Trinidad Village
[WITH FRANCES S. HERSKOVITS]

THESE ARE BORZOI BOOKS PUBLISHED BY

ALFRED · A · KNOPF

MAN

AND HIS WORKS

MAN

AND HIS WORKS

THE SCIENCE OF

CULTURAL ANTHROPOLOGY

MELVILLE J. HERSKOVITS

NEW YORK: ALFRED·A·KNOPF

1950

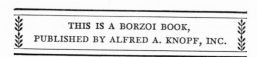

THIS IS A BORZOI BOOK,
PUBLISHED BY ALFRED A. KNOPF, INC.

PUBLISHED SEPTEMBER 1948
SECOND PRINTING, FEBRUARY 1949
THIRD PRINTING, NOVEMBER 1949
FOURTH PRINTING, SEPTEMBER 1950

To

My Students,

FROM WHOM I HAVE LEARNED

MANY THINGS

Each fresh start on
the never-ending quest of *Man as he ought to be* has been
the response of theory to fresh facts about *Man as he is.* . . .
Meanwhile, the dreams and speculations of one thinker after
another—even dreams and speculations which have moved
nations and precipitated revolutions—have ceased to command men's reason, when they ceased to accord with their
knowledge.

—SIR JOHN MYRES, "The Influence of Anthropology on the Course of Political Science,"
Univ. of California Pub. in History, vol. 4
(1916), no. 1, pp. 75–6

Preface

ANTHROPOLOGY is a young science, as the scholarly disciplines go, but the comprehension of man and his works which it has yielded has been of far-reaching significance. Its materials have underscored and documented the need to grasp the similarities that underlie the many different ways of life of human groups that must be understood if, in an age of expanding communications, adjustment between nations is to be achieved. This adjustment can only be reached, however, if mankind is considered in the broadest view, with a respect for differences and with a minimum of that militant centering on self and group, called ethnocentrism, that has been so great a bar to the creation of a functioning world society. And only anthropology, among the sciences, takes this broad view.

As a scientific discipline, anthropology has amassed an impressive body of materials, and has reached substantial conclusions about the nature, processes and functioning of human groups and their modes of existence. It is these conclusions, and such of the factual materials as are necessary to document them, that form the core of this book. It is hoped that a unified treatment of the entire field of anthropology will be of aid in giving insight into the kind of world we live in, and why it is that kind of world.

As in all science, the theories of anthropology have gained incisiveness and breadth from controversy. This process, which has led to the collection of more comprehensive data and the consequent development of new hypotheses to explain them, is thus an integral part of our account. Yet the discussion of theory is but an instrument to understanding, and that is why the core of agreement among anthropologists concerning the nature of the materials with which they deal is given more attention than the controversies that led to the resolution of differing points of view. Where controversy, past or present, is reviewed, I have tried to discuss the points at issue within the framework of the historic facts, and in all cases to present differing positions fairly, and as part of the stream of the prevailing intellectual currents. In the last third of the book, where I develop my own view and advance hypotheses to answer certain problems in the study of culture, I have endeavored to build on accepted methods and theories, and have in this way grounded my position in the discoveries of those who have preceded me, and in the work of my colleagues in the field of our common concern.

In writing this book, I have had primarily in mind the students in institutions of higher learning, who follow formal courses in anthropology. I have, however, not forgotten the many persons who, having completed their

ix

Preface

formal education in institutions where anthropology was not yet offered, wish in their mature years to learn about the subject. Happily, more and more colleges and universities are recognizing the kind of contribution anthropological teaching and research can make, and are adding courses in the field, taught by professionally trained anthropologists, to their curricula.

In its organization, the book moves from a discussion of the nature of culture, its materials, and structure, to a consideration of the processes of change that characterize it, and the general principles that govern cultural change. From a pedagogical point of view, it strives first to give the student a grasp of the phenomenon we call culture, then to afford him a sense of the range of variety in which it manifests itself, and finally to orient him in the body of theory that underlies the materials of the preceding chapters. In practical terms, I would suggest that shorter courses of an introductory nature use the first two-thirds of the book, leaving the final sections to be taken up in subsequent classes devoted to theory. However, where time permits, as when year courses are offered, the entire book can be used to give the student a comprehensive overview of anthropological science. The theoretical sections are not elementary, but my own teaching experience has convinced me that we tend to underrate the ability of students to handle theoretical materials. I have found that they are stimulated when they have to reach for ideas, and that, given the opportunity, they do surprisingly well.

I have centered my discussion of anthropology about the concept of culture because, like many of my fellow anthropologists, I believe it is the concept which gives the discipline as a whole its orientation. This preoccupation with culture is present no matter what particular aspect of human existence may be the immediate field of an anthropologist's interest. Students of prehistory, for example, are concerned basically with how man came to be a culture-building animal, and why. Physical anthropologists, aside from their purely anatomical concerns, seek to understand the relationship between physical type and culture. Comparative linguists are occupied with the problem of the function of speech as the instrument whereby man voices and transmits in the symbolism of language the conceptual and value systems that make up his culture. Hence, in approaching anthropology from the point of view of culture, we take into account all the many phases of our discipline—the "anthropological sciences," as they are sometimes called.

It is a privilege to express my thanks to the many persons who have helped me in the preparation of this book—some of them, far more than they know. Among them I may name my colleagues A. I. Hallowell, W. R. Bascom, R. A. Waterman, and Francis L. K. Hsü, who have criticized and evaluated many points of fact and theory advanced here; E. A. Haggard, who devised the term "enculturation" when I was in need of a word to describe the manner in which an individual achieves continuing competence

Preface

in his culture; W. M. Krogman, Robert and Linda Braidwood, Carl Voegelin, W. N. Fenton, Marshall Dimock, and Leslie Lipson, who gave expert advice on individual chapters; Frances S. Herskovits, who read and criticized the entire manuscript; and Justine M. Johnson, who made the fine drawings that illustrate the textual material. I also acknowledge with thanks the individuals and organizations who aided me in gathering many of the photographs I have used—F. Weidenreich and the American Museum of Natural History, New York; Kaj Birket-Smith and the Royal Ethnographic Museum of Copenhagen; F. Eggan, J. Stewart and W. Bennett; the Chicago Museum of Natural History and the members of its ethnographic staff, P. Martin, W. Hambly, D. Collier and G. I. Quimby; William Beebe and Miss Jocelyn Crane; H. W. Krieger and the U. S. National Museum; and C. E. Fuller. In the background are the organizations that have contributed to the support of my research program which, carried on over two decades, has furnished the basis for the inductions that have led to many of the hypotheses advanced in this book; and my friends in various parts of Africa and the New World who have taught me about their ways of life. Most of all, however, I am indebted to the numerous students who, over the years, have provided me with continuous stimulation to think through my ideas about the nature and functioning of culture. It is with a profound sense of gratitude that I have dedicated this book to them.

MELVILLE J. HERSKOVITS

Evanston, Illinois
14 November, 1947

Contents

I. *Introductory*

    1. Anthropology, the Science of Man   3

II. *The Nature of Culture*   15

    2. The Reality of Culture   17
    3. Culture and Society   29
    4. Culture and the Individual   43
    5. The Problem of Cultural Relativism   61
    6. The Ethnographer's Laboratory   79

III. *The Materials of Culture*   95

    7. The Evolution of Mankind   97
    8. The Prehistoric Development of Culture   114
    9. Physical Type and Culture   133
    10. Habitat and Culture   153

IV. *The Structure of Culture*   167

    11. Culture-Trait and Culture-Complex   169
    12. Culture-Areas: the Spatial Dimension   183
    13. The Pattern Phenomenon   201
    14. The Integration of Culture   214

V. *The Aspects of Culture*   227

    15. The Universals in Human Civilization   229
    16. Technology and the Utilization of Natural Resources   241
    17. Economics and the Fulfilment of Wants   266
    18. Social Organization: the Structure of Society   289
    19. Education and the Sanctions of Custom   310
    20. Political Systems: the Ordering of Human Relations   327
    21. Religion: the Problem of Man and the Universe   347

Contents

22. Religion: the Control of the Universe 361
23. The Aesthetic Drive: Graphic and Plastic Arts 378
24. Folklore 414
25. Drama and Music 427
26. Language, the Vehicle of Culture 440

vi. *Cultural Dynamics* 459

27. Cultural Origins and Cultural Evolution 461
28. Conservatism and Change in Culture 479
29. Discovery and Invention as Mechanisms of Cultural Change 492
30. Diffusion and the Reconstruction of Cultural History 505
31. Acculturation: Cultural Transmission in Process 523
32. Cultural Focus and Reinterpretation 542

vii. *Cultural Variation* 561

33. The Significance of Variation in Culture 563
34. Cultural Drift and Historic Accident 580
35. Classification and Process in the Study of Culture 595
36. Cultural Law and the Problem of Prediction 608

viii. *Summary* 623

37. A Theory of Culture 625
38. Anthropology in a World Society 642

Bibliographies

1. Literature Cited 659
2. A List of Selected Titles 674

INDEX ..... *follows page* 678

Illustrations

FIGURES IN TEXT

FIGURE		PAGE
1	Peck-order of pigeons.	34
2	The development of the human foot, from lemuroid and simian types of feet through gibbon, chimpanzee, and gorilla to man.	100
3	Basic skeletal structure of a quadruped, upright brachiating figure, and erect form.	102
4	Skulls of gorilla, sinanthropus and homo sapiens (Chinese), showing differences in height and length of skull.	111
5	Increase of facial angle from anthropoids through hominids to homo.	112
6	The "Sorcerer" of the cave of Trois Frères, Ariège, France.	115
7	Core, flake and blade tools.	119
8	The prehistory of Western Europe.	120
9	Cave at Drachenloch.	122
10	Line drawing showing superimposition of cave paintings of the Magdalenian period.	125
11	Painted pebbles of the Azilian (Mesolithic) period.	127
12	Distribution curves of Swedish and Kajji noses.	135
13	Nose, 37 mm. wide.	135
14	Distribution curves from homogeneous and heterogeneous populations.	140
15	Culture-areas of North and South America.	187
16	Culture types of South America.	189
17	Culture-areas of Africa.	191
18	Eskimo spear thrower.	242
19	Eskimo compound bow; Sauk and Fox simple bow.	243
20	Agricultural implements.	250
21	Bow-drill.	254

Illustrations

FIGURE   PAGE

22   *Simple loom used with twilling stick.*   257

23   *Loom with treadle.*   258

24   *Simple shuttle; spool shuttle.*   259

25   *Details of basketry-making techniques: weaving; twining; coiling.*   261

26   *Kinship under matrilineal descent system.*   297

27   *Relationships between Nuer lineages.*   302

28   *Ashanti political organization.*   336

29   *Nuer political segmentation.*   339

30   *Yurok-Karok basketry design elements.*   383

31   *Lace figures (ñanduti) from Paraguay.*   384

32   *Mural engravings of elk, Middle Aurignacian, France.*   386

33   *Aurignacian drawings of horses from cavern of Altamira, Spain.*   386

34   *Aurignacian drawing of elephant on cave-wall, Santander, Spain.*   387

35   *Mammoth, from cave-wall in the Dordogne, France; Aurignacian.*   387

36   *Wooly rhinocerous, Font-de-Gaume, Dordogne, France; Aurignacian.*   388

37   *Magdalenian engravings on stone, showing superimposition of figures.*   389

38   *Mural engraving of mammoth, Magdalenian, cave of Font-de-Gaume, France.*   390

39   *Stag and salmon, engraved on reindeer horn; Magdalenian, France.*   390

40   *Moose, engraved on reindeer horn. Magdalenian, France.*   391

41   *Torres Straits "crocodile-arrows and derivatives," as arranged in a presumed developmental series.*   392

42   *The "Venus" of Willendorf, Austria; Aurignacian epoch.*   393

43   *Aurignacian figure carved in low relief, from Laussel, Dordogne.*   394

44   *Aurignacian figurine in ivory, known as the "Venus" of Lespugue (Haute-Garonne, France).*   395

45   *Engraving of reindeer herd on wing-bone of an eagle; Upper Magdalenian, France.*   395

46   *Herd of horses, engraved on stone; Upper Magdalenian, Vienne, France.*   396

47   *Alaskan Eskimo needlecases.*   396

48   *Transformation of designs painted on calabash dishes, Oaxaca, Mexico.*   397

49   *Analysis of forms of Admiralty Island wooden bowls.*   399

Illustrations

FIGURE   PAGE

50 *Analysis of rests of Admiralty Island wooden bowls.*   400

51 *Analysis of shapes of wooden bowls from Tami Island.*   401

52 *Marquesan carved figure and an African figure.*   402

53 *Designs on Benin container.*   403

54 *Stylizations of human and animal forms woven by Cayapa Indians of Ecuador.*   406

55 *"Girl Pushing a Baby Carriage." Drawing by a scientifically trained adult.*   407

56 *"Girl Pushing a Baby Carriage." Drawing by a scientifically trained adult.*   407

57 *Two drawings, "Man on Horseback," by scientifically trained adults.*   408

58 *Basic double-curve motifs in Northeastern Algonkian art.*   408

59 *Elaboration of two basic double-curve Northeastern Algonkian motifs.*   409

60 *Elaboration of Northeastern Algonkian double-curve motif on Penobscot cradle-board.* 410

61 *Design on Sauk and Fox Indian rawhide box before folding.*   411

62 *Sauk and Fox Indian rawhide box, folded.*   412

63 *Fringe from legging, Thompson Indians, British Columbia.*   413

64 *Modification of stone celt into carved human figure, Mexico.*   504

65 *Diagram to illustrate basis of age-area concept.*   519

66 *BaTswa ladle.*   557

PLATES

PLATE   FACING PAGE

1a *Stages in the restoration of* pithecanthropus erectus.   76

1b *Comparison of molars of* gigantopithecus blacki, *male gorilla,* sinanthropus pekinensis, *and modern man.*   77

2a *Evolutionary changes in the skull, lateral view.*   108

2b *Evolutionary changes in the skull, front view.*   108

2c *Evolutionary changes in the skull, rear (occipital) view.*   108

3a *Upper Palaeolithic skulls.*   109

3b *Lateral view of skulls of gorilla,* sinanthropus, *and modern man, showing tendency of human skull to assume globular form.*   109

Plates

PLATE   FACING PAGE

4a Terraced valley, showing method of cultivating rice in the Philippines.   236

4b Close-up of rice terraces.   236

5 Sailing chart used by Marshall Islanders.   237

6a Inca masonry; wall of fortress above Cuzco, Peru.   268

6b Inca masonry; pre-Spanish walls still used as house-walls in Cuzco.   268

7 Pueblo pot, showing design resulting from even pinching of clay on preceding coil.   269

8a Yoruba masked dancer, showing manner of wearing mask.   372

8b Closer view of Yoruba masked dancer.   372

8c Yoruban mask in position customarily exhibited.   372

9a Bush-Negro tray used for winnowing rice.   373

9b Dahomean brass figures.   388

10 Bronze heads from Ife, Western Nigeria.   389

11a Bison painted in polychrome on the cave ceiling of Altamira, Santandar, Spain.   404

11b Wild boar, from the cavern at Altamira, Santandar, Spain.   404

12a Admiralty Island bowl.   405

12b Maori bone carving.   405

12c Maori carving, showing tattooing designs.   405

13 Carved ivory container from Benin, West Africa.   420

14 Dahomean appliqué cloths.   421

15 Ceremonial carved wooden statues from New Ireland.   428

16a Eskimo ivory implements from Point Barrow, Alaska.   429

16b Ceremonial jade adze from Hervey Island.   429

17 Bush-Negro comb, clothes-beater, and tray.   460

18 Indians of Papory River, Colombia, doing basketry work.   461

PART I

INTRODUCTORY

CHAPTER 1

Anthropology, the Science of Man

THE science of Anthropology is divided into two broad fields. One is concerned with the physical form of man, the other with his learned behavior.
They are called, respectively, *physical* and *cultural anthropology*. Physical
anthropology is, in essence, human biology. Physical anthropologists study
such problems as the nature of racial differences; the handing down of bodily
traits from one generation to the next; the growth, development, and decay
of the human organism; the influences of the natural environment on man.

Cultural anthropologists, on the other hand, study the ways man has devised to cope with his natural setting and his social milieu; and how bodies of
custom are learned, retained, and handed down from one generation to the
next. Students of culture are thus concerned with understanding how a given
way of achieving a given end—organizing family relationships, making a
fish-trap, or accounting for the creation of the world—can vary widely from
one people to another, and yet help each of them attain adjustment in the
business of living. They seek to determine how established forms of tradition
change with the passage of time, whether by reason of internal developments, or because of contact with foreign ways; and how an individual born
into a given society absorbs, uses, and influences the customs which make up
his cultural heritage.

In addition to the study of man's physical type and his cultural behavior,
anthropology also includes *prehistoric archaeology* and, as a specialized subdivision of cultural anthropology, *comparative linguistics*. The prehistoric
archaeologist investigates and analyzes those aspects of the study of man
that throw light on the early development of the human race, during that
period of a half-million years or more before the discovery of writing.

The linguistic anthropologist deals with the many varieties of that uniquely
human attribute, speech. He sets down the phonetic systems, the vocabu-
laries, and grammatical structures of unwritten languages. He seeks to discover the unities that underlie the great variety of ways of speech he deals
with, and to understand how differently men can express the same ideas and
the same emotions. As an anthropologist, however, he also treats language as
an aspect of culture, and frames his problems so as to contribute to the comprehension of the nature and functioning of human tradition. That is why

Introductory

questions about the influence of language habits on behavior and thought, of the "meaning of meaning," have come to bulk large in the work of the linguistic anthropologist.

When we consider the diversity of this subject-matter, we may well ask, what is the unity of anthropology? The answer lies in the paramount fact that anthropology, in centering its attention on man, takes into account all phases of man's existence, biological and cultural, past and present, combining these varied materials into an integrated attack on the problem of human experience. Unlike the disciplines that deal with more restricted aspects of the human being, anthropology emphasizes the principle that life is not lived by categories, but as a continuous stream. In practice, no anthropologist today studies all the divisions of his subject. But it is at the core of anthropological thinking that each problem investigated be recognized as only one manifestation of one segment of man's complex existence, and that it be studied with full consciousness of its wide implications. The physical anthropologist, for example, recognizes the influence of social convention on mating as a factor in determining the physical type of a people. The linguistic anthropologist is alert to the social significance of speech forms. The prehistorian makes his contribution to the understanding of how basic technological devices used by men to underwrite their social life were developed, and how the present races of mankind evolved. The cultural anthropologist is continuously aware that human traditions and ways of life are the expression of behavior based on the learning process, and thus in the broadest sense are derived from man's biopsychological makeup.

It has been stated that when all its subdivisions are taken into account, anthropology, in its totality, is to be thought of as one of the most highly specialized of the sciences, and yet at the same time one of the broadest. Physical anthropology is the more specialized aspect; cultural anthropology the one that ranges widely. In the former—anthropology as a biological science—the anthropologist, as human biologist, is interested in *homo sapiens* alone. He studies a single form out of the vast range of creatures that claim the attention of the general biologist. Though such matters as racial classification, or questions concerning the processes of heredity are problems of biological science wherever studied, the restriction of its field to man makes of human biology a comparatively narrow specialty.

Cultural anthropology, on the other hand, has a far wider breadth of interest than its related fields in the social sciences and the humanities, each of which takes up some one segment of human activity. The cultural anthropologist generally studies peoples who are outside the stream of European cultural history, and attempts, insofar as he can, to investigate a given body of custom as a whole. Or, if he concentrates on any one aspect of that culture, he takes as a primary objective the analysis of the interrelation of that aspect with the other phases of the life of the people. In considering the whole culture, he studies its technology and its economic life, its social and political institutions, its religion, folklore, and art. Moreover, he analyzes these aspects not only as each is to be distinguished from the others, but as all form a functioning system which adapts the people to their setting. In this, it is apparent

4

that the anthropologist differs from the economist, the political scientist, the sociologist, the student of comparative religions, or of art or literature.

A similar wide field of interest characterizes the anthropological linguist and the prehistorian. The linguist takes all languages as his province, though in practice he concentrates on unwritten tongues, studying them as cultural as well as purely linguistic phenomena. The prehistorian, who, in digging an archaeological site, finds evidence appertaining to the physical type and the cultural achievements of the people who lived there, must, in assessing these remains, not only integrate such different materials, but also employ skills developed to meet the special problems of the geologist and the palaeontologist.

The comprehensive definition of anthropology as "the study of man and his works" is thus justified because anthropology centers its attention on man, whether the focus of concern is broad or narrow. The great range of its subject matter has made it essential for anthropology to develop special techniques and objectives to provide a unity to its aims and methods. This very range gives it almost an "organic" relationship to many kinds of disciplines, but it is a relationship that differs in degree of intimacy as well as in kind from that which exists among these other disciplines. It will be of substantial aid to us in understanding the nature of anthropological science to explore its relation to other disciplines somewhat further.

2

WE MAY begin this analysis by recalling some relevant facts about the historical development of science. It is a truism that science, like charity, begins at home, if merely because economy of effort and immediacy of return is achieved through working with what is near at hand. In the social sciences, in particular, problems of an immediate nature that called for solution were self-evident and pressing points of attack. As a result, practical issues have been prominent in the interests of social scientists, and the general principles advanced by them have been based largely on the study of materials from a single country or, at most, a series of countries with similar historical backgrounds and bodies of tradition.

It was only after the great epoch of discovery and European expansion into the Near and Far East, the Americas and Africa, that it became apparent that other modes of behavior, other forms of linguistic expression, other ways of worshiping the gods than those known to ourselves, existed among peoples living in these newly visited regions of the world. The impact of this knowledge of new civilizations had far-reaching results. This is to be seen, for example, in the political philosophy of Rousseau, whose concept of the social contract still finds its repercussions in the thought and action of our day.

More often than not, speculations and theories were based on misconception rather than fact, for much of the information about the peoples of the far places consisted principally of day-by-day accounts given by chance observers. We shall see how difficult it is to reach out of our own background

Introductory

and, without systematic training, understand the motives, the aims, the values of another people. This skill, which lies at the very methodological heart of the science of cultural anthropology, developed late. For though by then, the other social science disciplines had their established techniques that were admirably adapted to the analysis of problems of our own culture, they were not adequate for the study of broader, cross-cultural topics.

It must be made clear that the problems attacked by the anthropologist interested, for example, in the economic life of some small, remote, nonliterate people do not differ in kind from the problems that concern economists in general; and the same holds true when political organization, religion, art, or forms of literary expression are studied. The problems indeed, may be identical. It is the methods employed in studying them that differ. Such questions as the nature of the state, the function of the family, the place of symbolism in design, the meaning of words, or the relationship between man and the forces of the universe are no different *as problems,* when studied in Patagonia or on the Zambesi, in Illinois or in the Arctic.

The student occupied with our own culture enjoys certain advantages that arise out of the nature of his materials. He has little language difficulty to cope with, and he can utilize written documents. Most important of all, the sanctions that validate the subject of his study, the things we take for granted, are known to him before he begins his work. The anthropologist, on the other hand, must have recourse to special techniques for getting such of these facts, conceptions, and attitudes as he can reach. Some of them may, of course, elude him completely, since written documents cannot, in the nature of the case, be drawn on among nonliterate peoples. He must struggle with unwritten languages, often quite unstudied, and difficult to a degree that is not readily grasped by those who have not attempted to cope with them. At the same time, he must discover and relate to his observations the sanctions that give meaning to the forms of behavior he records.

To understand the economic life of a society in which tradition dictates waste, rather than the accumulation of goods, as the surest road to prestige, the anthropologist must reorient his thinking considerably. Or, again, where the symbolism of an art stands between the student and comprehension of the forms of aesthetic expression of the people he is studying, he must laboriously analyze designs before he can even get to his problem. In another field, many an anthropologist has had to enquire from a series of women which one of them had actually given birth to the child who called them all "mother," before he could disentangle sociological from biological parenthood. Indeed, this single difficulty presented to early students of social structures one of their knottiest problems.

Though in this book we are most concerned with cultural anthropology, it is nonetheless important that we realize how the human biologist, the linguistic anthropologist, and the prehistorian, no less than the student of custom, are to be differentiated by this factor of specialization in method from those working in related disciplines.

The difference in the controls that can be exerted over his data marks off the physical anthropologist from the general biologist. The general biologist can employ laboratory techniques that are forbidden the student of human biology. The student of general genetics, working with the fruit fly, *drosophila melanogaster*, can count a numerous new generation every nine days. He who would study human genetics must work with a creature as long lived as himself, who, moreover, produces very few offspring in each mating, and customarily gives birth to only one individual at a time. The student of human growth finds that to follow the development of an individual requires years, rather than the relatively short period needed for the lower forms to mature. But a greater handicap is the simple fact that, of all biologists, the physical anthropologist alone deals with a creature that has a voice in determining whether or not he is going to be studied at all! Here, then, as in the instance of cultural anthropologists, the problems studied by human and general biologists differ but slightly; it is by the methods they employ that they are primarily to be distinguished.

The student of human prehistory studies problems closely related to those of palaeontology and geology, but he must, in addition, be equipped with his own special methods. On occasion a palaeontologist will find his knowledge of an entire extinct species restricted to a single bone, a unique fossil; but this is commonplace for the student of human evolution, for whom the find of a whole skull, to say nothing of a series of complete skeletons, is most unusual. The establishment of chronology through the study of geological strata is standard practice for the student of the earth sciences. The prehistoric archaeologist must, however, go on to infer an entire civilization from the fragments of artifacts he is able to recover from the earth. He must correlate these with the physical type of the early humans who produced them if skeletal material is associated with the cultural remains; with the flora and fauna that are indicated in the site; and with the data that tell not only when these people lived, but the environmental conditions to which they had to adapt their ways of life.

The anthropological linguist is similarly faced with special problems of method that must be solved before he can successfully attack the questions all linguists consider. Like other linguists he is interested in forms of speech, phonetic patterns and the consistency of their use, dialectic variation, the relation of one language to another, the symbolism in languages. But the anthropological linguist must treat these matters in terms of speech-forms cast in molds entirely unfamiliar to him—far more different from his own language than the degree to which Russian, let us say, differs from French.

He must, first of all, reduce the speech he hears to systematic phonemic forms, transcribing such sounds as the "clicks" of the Bushmen and Hottentots, or incorporate into his system the use of different sounds spoken at different pitch, the grammatically "significant" tones that are rare in Indo-European tongues. He must be prepared for genders not based on sex, but on movement, or tenses that refer to duration of time rather than points in time. He must at times even determine what the language he is studying regards as a word! It is apparent that such tasks as these, the detecting of the regularity that marks every language but lies concealed in the hubbub of everyday conversation, require methods quite different from those used in studying speech-systems which have been reduced to writing.

3

WE HAVE, thus far, seen that, despite the diversity of its interests, the unity of anthropological science derives from its central concern with the rounded study of man. Through its concentrated attack on the fundamental question of the nature of man and his works, anthropology has become the synthesizing discipline we must recognize it to be. This brings us once again to the question of its relation to the other fields of scholarship with which it has problems in common, or from which it has borrowed methods for the study of its special problems.

Most bodies of subject-matter fall into one of the three or four principal categories into which all knowledge is divided, the Exact and Natural Sciences, the Humanities, and the Social Sciences. Not so anthropology, for the science of man defies delimitation even in terms of such broad divisions as these. This is not strange; for man is obviously a creature of many facets. Those who would understand him must be prepared to disregard conventional boundaries as they pursue their problems in whatever fields these may lead. How true this is may be seen from the fact that, of all the disciplines, it is only anthropology that participates in the work and planning of the three organizations in the United States that encourage research in the principal areas of knowledge we have named.

Let us suppose, for example, that an anthropologist undertakes to study a people who inhabit an island in the South Seas, or an Indian tribe, or an African community. Insofar as he is concerned with their physical form and racial affiliation, he is working on a biological problem. But if he analyzes the patterns of selection in mating, or the effects of a particular form of diet, he must take into account the factor of tradition, which we know can deeply influence genetic and physiological endowment. He must understand their reaction to their habitat—that is to say, the fact that they inhabit an island, or a mountain valley, or a tropical forest will have many implications in shaping their way of life, so that the anthropologist here encounters the kind of problem treated by human geographers.

When our student investigates their language, his research is in the field of the humanities, as it is later, when he collects the texts of their myths and tales, or records their music, or analyzes the style of their art, or films their dances, or seeks to know those value-systems and concepts of the universe that go to explain life and give it meaning, and thus constitute their philosophy. But this same student is a social scientist when his problem is an analysis of their kinship system, or their economy, or when he investigates how their rulers govern, or describes the institutionalized forms of their religious life.

In doing all these he remains the anthropologist, for all his researches are conducted against the backdrop of the total culture. Nor need he work in remote areas, for near at home, too, life is lived along the continuum of time. Men and women move with little awareness from one aspect of their lives to another, regardless of how the student separates these aspects for purposes of study.

Cultural anthropology has wider affiliations with other disciplines than does any other phase of anthropological science. Because it treats of the "works" of man in all their great variety, it has experienced greater difficulty even in standardizing its nomenclature than any other branch of the discipline. On the continent of Europe, indeed, it is not called anthropology at all. There the term anthropology is reserved for the study of physical type. In the United States cultural anthropology is customarily divided into *ethnology* and *ethnography*, the first being the comparative study of culture and the investigation of the theoretical problems that arise out of the analysis of human custom, the second the description of individual cultures. Some students in England and the United States give it the name "social anthropology." When this term is employed, "ethnology" becomes the description of individual cultures, which we shall call ethnography, while to "social anthropology" is assigned something of the role we give ethnology.

We will not be confused by differing usages of this kind, if we keep in mind the ultimate aims of anthropological science and its branches; and if we consider the materials treated rather than the names of categories to which they are assigned. Controversy over such differences in terminology is to be regarded as the healthy growing-pains of a young discipline, striving to realize and describe its own potentialities.

Among the social sciences, cultural anthropology is most often identified with sociology, with which it has much in common, historically, as well as in subject-matter and theoretical interests. Social institutions and the problems of the integration of the individual into his society are obviously of great importance in the study of man. In assessing the relationship between the two disciplines, however, it must be remembered that the definition of what constitutes sociology differs substantially in continental Europe and England, and in the United States, to mention only two areas. Thus, an English study of the political institutions of native Africa, offered as "an attempt to bring into focus one of the major problems of African sociology," involves a use of the word "sociology" that rings strange in American ears. On the other hand, the interest of sociologists in the United States in the problems of adjustment and integration of groups in their own society, and their utilization of statistical techniques, is not in accord either with the English tradition or that of continental Europe, which lays stress on social philosophy. But when questions of the development and functions of institutions, general principles of human group behavior, and problems of social theory are involved, sociology and cultural anthropology march together with a give and take that is solidly rooted in the past, and has proved mutually helpful.

The geographers have stressed the interaction between habitat and culture more than have anthropologists, who have tended to take the natural setting for granted. As we shall see when we analyze the relationship between habitat and culture, this has been due, in a measure, to extravagances of

Introductory

some geographers in ascribing to the natural setting a degree of influence in shaping culture that anthropologists found easy to refute. This fact, however, in no way minimizes the problem, as anthropologists are more and more coming to understand. For just as man is a member of the biological series, a fact that must never be forgotten in studying his modes of life, so the fact that he lives in a setting that exists independently of him, and out of which he derives the raw stuff for the material objects he uses in getting a living, must also be continuously held in mind.

Active recognition of the problems common to anthropology and other social sciences like economics and political science has been relatively slight. Communication between anthropologists and economists is steadily increasing, however, especially since the recognition by anthropologists of the need to record as fully as possible the economic mechanisms of the societies they study. Only a certain flexibility in defining what is to be included under the rubric "economic" is needed to make available much obscured and unrecorded materials on the economic aspects of a culture. The economists, on their part—particularly those interested in economic institutions—are discovering that a comparative analysis of the different ways in which men solve the problems of carrying on the "ordinary business of life" reveals relationships and mechanisms hitherto overlooked.

This holds equally for the study of political institutions. Here, however, the matter of definition is technically more difficult. Non-European peoples have often devised controls that, despite their functional efficiency, differ so markedly in outer form from the political institutions of Euroamerican and other historical societies as almost to defy recognition. A system of regulating conduct such as is found among some Plains Indian tribes, for example, where certain degrees of cousinship permit public joking at the expense of a person who has transgressed accepted custom, can only be tenuously defined as political; or we may take the instance of a social group among whom such an institution as chieftainship is unknown. On the other hand, an understanding of the entire range of political institutions which, among native peoples, includes such complex systems as those of Africa and Polynesia, points the way toward a deeper comprehension of the nature, meaning and functioning of governmental forms in human groups everywhere.

The many common elements between cultural anthropology and the humanistic disciplines have as yet not been fully exploited. This is partly because the phases of cultural anthropology related to the humanities employ techniques which require special preparation to master, as in linguistics or music; and because of the existence of a long-standing tradition whereby the comparative study of social institutions has received far more attention than have other aspects of culture. This emphasis in marking off the study of society from the study of culture, has tended to ignore the broader, more inclusive base for generalizing about human social life that a rounded, balanced study of all aspects of culture provides.

Comparative religion, a field which, with varying emphasis may be accounted as a social science or one of the humanities, has been mutually well explored. Students of religion have drawn heavily on anthropological ma-

terials. Their work, in turn, has yielded theoretical reference points which have given direction to anthropological field-workers in the collection of their data. The relationship has been especially close and the interchange continuous where questions bearing on the sources of the great historic religions—Christianity, Judaism, Mohammedanism, Buddhism—have been probed. All of these, it has been found, contain concepts of the Universe and ritual practices to be encountered in many parts of the world today that lie outside the area where these historic religions are predominant. Moreover, anthropology has been able to throw light on such problems as the relationship between religion and magic, which holds special interest because of the widespread practice of magic in the literate societies of the world.

In the humanities, strictly speaking, the tie between anthropological linguistics and the study of written languages, especially of Indo-European stock, needs only to be mentioned to become apparent. In the field of art, students have in recent years sought knowledge of the widest possible range of aesthetic expression among all peoples of the earth. Creative artists have visited many non-European art provinces for stimulation and study. In the art galleries, African wood-carvings take their place with French modernist paintings and sculpture, on whose style they have had so profound an influence. Art students analyze Navaho sand-paintings, or Peruvian pottery and textiles in much the same way that they study the classical forms of our own past. The field of the social role of art, which is a kind of a no-man's-land between art and sociology, has been brought to the fore by students of primitive cultures. They have not only reproduced exotic art-forms and explained their symbolism, but in integrating all manifestations of the culture that produced them, have sought the meaning of the art to the people, the drives that actuate the artist, and the functioning of the art in its society.

The literary forms with which the anthropologist deals are known as folklore. Its analysis proceeds on much the same lines as does the study of any literature. Problems of style, narrative sequences, devices to heighten suspense or reach a climax; of the variation in a tale as it has moved from one people to another, and the way in which this reflects mutations in literary patterns; problems of origin and of the spread of tales, are all familiar to those who deal with written literature. Here we also move into the field of drama, one that has been far too neglected by anthropologists and students of the drama alike. Yet all these art-forms are universals in human experience, and the failure to study them in any society deprives us of valuable materials, and inhibits proper perspective.

Comparative musicology is another field that, though related to the conventional study of music in its techniques and problems, has yet to be accorded full recognition. Both because it widens the horizons of the musician and student of music, and because it gives to those whose concern is with the social life of man a tool of precision and reliability, a significant contribution is to be looked for from it. All people make music, and they make music in obedience to patterns to which they give little conscious thought—as little as men give to the grammatical or phonetic systems of the languages they speak. Mechanical recording of melodies and rhythms of peoples in all

Introductory

parts of the world has provided an accurate instrument with which to test problems of cultural stability, of individual variation in performance, of reworking of old melodies in a new cultural setting. These recorded songs, furthermore, provide students of music and composers with thematic and rhythmic materials that bring to them all the advantages that a knowledge of exotic art-forms has given to students of art.

Since human biology is essentially a specialized form of general biology, the closeness of the relationship between physical anthropology and the study of other living beings is apparent. In the analysis of the evolution of man, however, palaeontology plays an important role, while the line between anatomy and physical anthropology is so fine that they have traditionally shared in many problems. Certainly in conventional studies of the human form, especially in the analysis of racial differences, anatomy is essential—so much so that physical anthropology is often studied and taught in departments of anatomy. It has been said, with good reason, that no one can specialize in physical anthropology without prior training in anatomy—to which some have added the need for medical training, as well.

The study of human genetics, another branch of physical anthropology, requires knowledge of the findings of geneticists in general. The physical anthropologist also must be able to use mathematical tools, since biometrics, the statistical analysis of data from living creatures, is of critical significance here. In all this, however, the human biologist remains an anthropologist, employing the aids given him by these other disciplines, but carrying the common problems into the total area of human living.

The affiliation of prehistoric archaeology with the earth sciences is intimate. The critical point in any archaeological work is the relation of a find in time to other remains. To this only geology can provide an answer, that at some later date may be confirmed by study of the extinct animal forms found in association with human skeletal remains, or in a deposit of artifacts. For example, the critical question that had to be answered in dating the worked stone "points," discovered at Folsom, New Mexico, imbedded in the vertebrae of an extinct species of bison, was the geological stratum in which the remains lay. The archaeologist could tell us that the points differed from others previously recovered. The palaeontologist could identify the bison skeleton as that of an extinct form. But to the questions: When did the form become extinct? When were the points made? only the collaboration of the geologist could yield an answer.

Still other disciplines are called on by the archaeologist in solving his problems. Botany, for example, has been responsible for the brilliant achievement of the technique called dendrochronology, whereby the date of a ruin is established by intensive scrutiny of the pattern of tree-rings on the remains of wood in dwellings and implements. This delicate method, it may be pointed out, was developed by an astronomer in search of an answer to the problems of climatological cycles! Thus the archaeologist benefits by utilizing the findings of many specialties, though his aim, to write the whole story of the development of man and his civilizations, is the characteristic mark of his craft.

Anthropology, the Science of Man

4

A FACT of some importance emerges from our discussion of the interrelationships between anthropology and its sister disciplines. We have seen that anthropology, as a specialized biology, has drawn significantly on the exact and natural sciences out of which, in a very real sense, it has developed. In its relation to the humanities and the social sciences, however, anthropology is essentially the contributor, the synthesizing agent. This is as true of method as of objectives. To illustrate, the methods of anthropology used in studying human physical type are refinements of techniques already applied in such older disciplines as anatomy and statistics, in this case adapted to the narrowed field in which physical anthropology specializes. The same principle applies also to prehistory, when this branch of anthropology is considered in terms of the methods it employs that come from related fields. When its relationship to the social sciences and the humanities is analyzed, however, we find that it is the older disciplines that are the more restricted in scope, and have the more specific methods of attack. Anthropology thus brings to these disciplines a wider frame of reference within which surer generalizations can be erected, together with methods that represent radical departures from earlier techniques.

This brings us to three disciplines that stand in a relationship to anthropology, actual or potential, that is peculiarly close. As a dynamic field of investigation that would understand the whole development of man, and study the many varieties of culture that are the result of changes over long periods of time, anthropology is _historical_. As a science that seeks to understand the mainsprings of social behavior, and the role of culture in making for human adjustment, it is _psychological_. Finally, as a discipline that considers the nature and range of the value-systems by which all men live, the meaning of the goals they erect to guide their activities, their explanations of the universe, and the relations between institutions and those who live in accordance with them, it is _philosophical_.

This is not the place to develop the relationships between anthropology and these disciplines as this has been done for the others. They are too fundamental, too complex and, especially in their philosophical implications, as yet too little examined to permit more than an underscoring of the significance of their mutual contributions. In a sense, much of the remainder of this book will be germane to this point, since our approach to an understanding of the cultures that have been evolved by man will be in terms of many concepts and findings of these disciplines. Like anthropology, these three disciplines are concerned with syntheses of broad areas of human experience. All of them thus have a common point of departure and common objectives that give added meaning to the results of cross-disciplinary cooperation between them.

Thus, in still different terms, we once more express the fundamental unity of anthropological science and its primary contribution to knowledge. The comprehensive approach of anthropology to the study of man that arises

Introductory

out of the diversity of its materials, and the analysis of them achieved through the utilization of the special methods it has developed, must always be held in mind. In depicting man in the round, so to speak—conceiving him at once as a biological animal, a speaking animal, a culture-building animal, in all the great variety of his present physical types and his cultural achievements, both today and during the millenia he has inhabited the earth—anthropology affords perspective not only in time but also in terms of the possible range of human behavior. It widens the world stage on which man has played his many roles, projecting our view beyond the scope of written history and into societies where conventions, never dreamed of in our culture, regularize and give meaning to behavior. In making possible this broadening of our perspective, we are permitted to peer out over the rim of our own culture and then to look back at our way of life with an objectivity not otherwise to be gained.

PART II

THE NATURE OF CULTURE

CHAPTER 2

The Reality of Culture

MAN lives in many dimensions. He moves in space, where the natural environment exerts a never ending influence on him. He exists in time, which provides him with an historic past and a sense of the future. He carries on his activities as a member of a society, identifying himself with his fellows and cooperating with them in maintaining his group and assuring its continuity.

But man is not unique in this. All animals must take time and space into account. Many forms live in aggregates where the necessity of adjusting to their fellows is an ever-present factor in their lives. What marks off man, the social animal of our concern, from all of these, is *culture*. This propensity to develop cultures cements into a unified whole all the forces that play on man, integrating for the individual the natural setting in which he finds himself, the historic past of his group, and the social relations he must assume. Culture brings all these together and thus affords man a means of adjusting to the complexities of the world into which he is born, giving him the sense, and sometimes the reality, of being its creator as well as a creature of it.

Definitions of culture are numerous. There is general agreement that culture is learned; that it allows man to adapt himself to his natural setting; that it is greatly variable; that it is manifested in institutions, thought-patterns and material objects. One of the best early definitions was given by E. B. Tylor, who described culture as, "that complex whole which includes knowledge, belief, art, morals, law, custom, and any other capabilities and habits acquired by man as a member of society." [1] One synonym for culture is *tradition*, another is *civilization;* but their use has come to be weighted with implications of different kinds or different qualities of customary behavior.

A short and useful definition of culture is: *Culture is the man-made part of the environment.* Implicit in this is the recognition that man's life is lived in a dual setting, the natural habitat and his social "environment." The definition also implies that culture is more than a biological phenomenon. It includes all the elements in man's mature endowment that he has acquired from his

---

[1] E. B. Tylor, 1874, p. 1.

group by conscious learning or, on a somewhat different level, by a conditioning process—techniques of various kinds, social and other institutions, beliefs, and patterned modes of conduct. Culture, in short, can be contrasted with the raw materials, outer and inner, from which it derives. Resources presented by the natural world are shaped so as to meet existing needs; while inborn traits are so molded as to derive out of inherent endowment the reflexes which are preponderant in the overt manifestations of behavior.

It is scarcely necessary to differentiate the concept of culture used as a tool in the study of man, from the popular meaning of the term "cultured." Yet for those unfamiliar with anthropological usage, the application of the concept "culture" to a digging-stick or a cooking recipe necessitates some readjustment in thinking. A popular concept of culture comes within the terms of what may be called a boarding-school definition, and is the equivalent of "refinement." Such a definition implies the ability of a person who has "culture" to manipulate certain aspects of our civilization that bring prestige. In reality, these aspects are principally the possession of those persons who have the leisure to learn them.

For the scientist, however, a "cultured person," in the popular sense, commands but a specialized fragment of our culture, sharing more than he suspects with the farmer, the bricklayer, the engineer, the ditch-digger, the professional man. The rudest economy, the most frenzied religious rite, a simple folktale, are all equally a part of culture. The comparative study of custom shows us this very clearly. In small isolated groups, where the economic base is narrow, and technical knowledge is slight, there is no room for the social stratification that must be present if a person, "cultured" in the popular sense, is to have the economic resources essential for his support while he devotes himself to his avocations.

2

THOSE who would comprehend the essential nature of culture must resolve a series of seeming paradoxes that are not to be ignored. These paradoxes can be phrased in many ways, but may be stated here as follows:

1. *Culture is universal in man's experience, yet each local or regional manifestation of it is unique.*
2. *Culture is stable, yet culture is also dynamic, and manifests continuous and constant change.*
3. *Culture fills and largely determines the course of our lives, yet rarely intrudes into conscious thought.*

How fundamental are the problems raised by these formulations, and how difficult it is to reconcile their seeming contradictions, will not become fully apparent until their many implications have been probed—a point that will be reached only at the end of this book. Here we will consider them as they bear on the immediate question of the reality of culture.

1. The fact that man is often spoken of as a "culture-building animal" is a

The Reality of Culture

recognition of the universality of culture; that it is an attribute of all human beings, no matter where they live or how their manner of living may be ordered. This universality can be described in quite specific terms. All cultures, at least when viewed objectively, possess a restricted number of aspects into which they are conveniently to be divided for study. To document such a simple statement requires many pages, and will occupy an entire section of this book where these aspects will be taken up, one by one. But we may, at this point, scan these aspects briefly so as to grasp how the concept of the universality of culture is extended to include all those broad subdivisions of human experience it invariably comprehends.

In the first place, all people have some way of getting a living. This is achieved by the technological equipment they use to wrest from their natural environment the means of sustaining life and carrying on their daily activities. They have some way of distributing what they thus produce, an economic system that allows them to make the most of those "scarce means" that require them to economize. All peoples give formal expression to the institution of the family or various kinds of broader kinship structures, and to associations based on other than blood ties. No people live in complete anarchy but are everywhere found to have devised some kind of political control. None is without a philosophy of life, a concept of the origin and functioning of the universe and how the powers of the supernatural world are to be manipulated to achieve desired ends—in short, a religious system. With song and dance and tale, and graphic and plastic art-forms to give aesthetic satisfaction, language to convey ideas, and a system of sanctions and goals to give meaning and point to living, we round out this summary of these aspects of culture which, like culture as a whole, are attributes of all human groups, wherever they may live.

Yet, as is known to anyone who has had contact with persons of a different way of life from his own, even with a group living in another part of his own country, no two bodies of custom are identical in detail. This is why it can be said that every culture is the result of the particular experiences of the population, past and present, who live in accordance with it. In other words, every body of tradition must be regarded as the living embodiment of its past. It follows that a culture cannot be understood unless its past is taken into account as fully as possible, using every available device—historic sources, comparisons with other ways of living, archaeological evidence—to probe its background and development.

In reality, then, our first paradox is to be resolved by accepting both of its terms. What this means is that the universality of culture is an attribute of human existence. Even its division into a series of aspects is proved by all we know of the most diverse ways of life, in all parts of the globe, wherever cultures have been studied. On the other hand, it is equally susceptible of objective proof that no two cultures are the same. When observations of this fact, gained from present-day investigation, are translated into the dimension of time, it means that each culture has had a development unique to itself. The universals in culture, we may thus say, provide a framework within which the particular experiences of a people are expressed in the particular forms taken by their body of custom. And, at this point, we may let this first of our paradoxes rest, leaving the explanation of why it can be met in this way for later chapters.

2. When we weigh cultural stability against cultural change, we must, first of all, recognize that the evidence in hand proves beyond doubt that culture is dynamic; that the only completely static cultures are dead ones. We have but to look at our own experience to see how change comes upon us, frequently so softly that we never suspect it until we project the present on the past. The instance of a photograph of ourselves, perhaps only a few years old, which amuses us because of the difference in the style of clothing from what we wear now makes the point. Nor is it to be thought that this tendency to change our ways is unique to our own culture. The same phenomenon is to be studied among any people, no matter how few in number, how isolated, or how simple their customs. Change may only be manifest in small details of their culture, such as a variation on an accepted pattern of design, or a new method of preparing an accepted foodstuff. But some change will always be apparent if such people can be studied over a period of time, if remains of their culture can be excavated from the earth, or if their ways can be compared with those of some neighboring, related group whose culture is like theirs in general, yet varies in detail.

Though cultural change is ubiquitous, and its analysis is thus fundamental in the study of human group life, it must not be overlooked that, as in any aspect of the study of culture, it exists in terms of setting and background, and not in absolute terms, by and of itself. This is how we escape from our second apparent dilemma, and rest comfortably on both its horns. Culture is *both* stable and everchanging. *Cultural change can be studied only as a part of the problem of cultural stability; cultural stability can be understood only when change is measured against conservatism.* Furthermore, both terms are not only relative in the large, but must also be considered in relation to each other. The conclusions reached concerning permanence and change in a given culture are dependent to a very considerable extent on the stress laid by the particular observer of that culture on its conservatism or its flexibility. Perhaps the basic difficulty arises from the fact that there are no objective criteria of permanence and change.

The matter is one of immediate importance, since it is almost an article of faith that Euroamerican culture is more receptive to change than any other, and that this receptivity explains its preeminence. How relative such a point of view is, may be seen from the expressions of opinion of those who variously hold that this hospitality to change is to be regarded as something desirable, or is to be deplored. Contemporary patterns of thought hold change in material aspects of our civilization to be, on the whole, good. On the other hand, change in such intangible elements in our culture as the moral code, family structure, or underlying political sanctions, are frowned upon or denounced. As a result, technological developments are so emphasized in our minds that the changes in this area of our life symbolize for us a tendency to change in our culture taken as a whole. Our culture is then differentiated from others on this basis of receptivity to technological change, so that its stability, in contrast to its propensity to change, is minimized.

3. Our problem in resolving the third paradox, that culture fills our lives, yet we are largely unconscious of it, differs somewhat from the preceding paradoxes in that more is involved than just a weighing of possible alternatives. Here we are confronted with basic psychological and philosophical questions. We must seek to understand the psychological problem of how human beings learn their cultures and function as members of society, and to find an answer to the philosophical question that asks whether culture is thus a function of human mentality, or exists by and of itself.

Essentially we must here face the issue that, while culture, a human attribute, is restricted to man, culture as a whole, or any individual culture, is more than any individual human being can grasp or manipulate. A case can thus be cogently made for studying culture as though it were independent of man; to create, as White has called it, a science of "culturology." Yet an equally strong case can be made for conceiving culture as having no more than psychological reality, existing as a series of constructs in the mind of the individual. Philosophically, here is but another instance of the age-old clash between realism and idealism, a clash that defines a fundamental cleavage of concept and approach to the nature of the world and of man. Bidney has shown that each of these positions, if pursued to the exclusion of the other, creates a logical fallacy that can be met only by an eclectic approach to the problem they pose. As he phrases it, "Neither natural forces nor cultural achievements taken separately or by themselves can serve to explain the emergence and evolution of cultural life." [2] Both points of view, however, hold much that is essential to an understanding of culture, so that it is important for us to consider the arguments advanced by the proponents of each, before attempting to answer the question of the nature of culture.

3

THERE is little doubt that culture *can* be studied without taking human beings into account. Most of the older ethnographies, descriptions of the ways of life of given peoples, are written solely in terms of institutions. Most diffusion studies—those which give the geographic spread of a given element in culture—are presented without any mention of the individuals who use the objects, or observe given customs. It would be difficult even for the most psychologically oriented student of human behavior to deny the value of such research. It is essential that the structure of a culture be understood first of all, if the reasons why a people behave as they do are to be grasped; unless the structure of custom is taken fully into account, behavior will be meaningless.

The argument for the objective reality of culture—granting for the moment that it is possible and even essential to study custom as though it had

---

[2] D. Bidney, 1944, p. 44.

objective reality—turns on the point that culture, being extra-human, "super-organic," is beyond the control of man and operates in terms of its own laws. In considering this position, we are, in essence, analyzing one of the several determinisms that have been advanced to explain the nature of culture—in this instance, *cultural determinism.*

Let us examine the statement that "any culture is more than any individual human being can grasp or manipulate," since it is crucial for the position we are now considering. Our own culture will do as well as any other. At the present time, many millions of people in our society, in given situations of their everyday life, behave in certain predictable ways, within describable limits. To illustrate: we can count on the word "yes" to mean an affirmative answer to a question; on our farms, women will not do the plowing except under exceptional circumstances; in the songs we sing, melody is more important than rhythm; our families, in the main, will be composed of father, mother and children rather than of a man, several wives, and their offspring. Now, however given to change our culture may be, "yes" has meant the affirmative for many centuries; plowing has for countless decades been recognized as the work of men; and so with a vast number of items. But of the people who have behaved in terms of these conventions, it is apparent that no person who two hundred years ago used the vocable "yes" to mean the affirmative or lived in a monogamous union then, is alive today.

Those who hold that culture exists by and of itself emphasize this fact that traditional ways of life continue generation after generation, without reference to the span of existence of any given person. Such an argument is undeniably impressive. We can almost envisage two entities—the everchanging group made up of human beings who enter it at birth, live their lives, and die; and the solid body of custom that flows on, its identity intact, the changes it experiences developing out of its own historic past. That interrelationships exist between people and culture, not even the most confirmed determinist would deny, just as those who hold culture to exist only as ideas in the minds of individuals who live it will grant the need to study its institutionalized forms. It cannot be too strongly stressed, therefore, that we are considering emphases and weightings rather than exclusive alternatives. With this reservation in mind, the fact that a cultural continuum exists, despite the constantly changing personnel whose behavior defines the culture, constitutes an argument for holding for the construct of culture as an entity in its own right.

Not only when considered in the large, over the centuries, can culture be shown to be more than men; within a given group, at a given moment in its history, no individual member of a society is competent in all details of the ways of life of his group. More than this, no individual, though he be a member of the smallest tribe, with the simplest culture, knows his cultural heritage in its entirety. To take but the most obvious example, one nevertheless so important that we shall give it detailed attention later, we need go no further than the fact of sex differences in accepted modes of behavior. Not only is an economic division of labor between men and women everywhere present, but we find in most cultures that the activities of men differ from those of the women in the nature of their preoccupations within the family, in their religious activities, or in the types of aesthetic satisfactions they find in their culture. Sometimes this is a matter of habituation—that in West Africa women should make pottery and men sew cloth is neither more nor less rational than that, among ourselves, men are the potters and women the seamstresses. Or the division may be one consciously imposed and penalized if transgressed, as with unauthorized manipulation of the supernatural among the Australian aboriginees, or the wearing of women's clothes by men in our own society.

In populations of considerable size, where a high degree of specialization exists and a class structure marks off one element in society from another, it is beyond the capacity of any one person to know his culture in its entirety. Both the Chinese peasant of the nineteenth century and the Mandarin scholar ordered their lives according to the dictates of a common culture. But both went their separate ways, each following his particular mode of life, and probably not concerned with questions of how their lives differed. Not only where urban and rural components exist in a society, but when priests are set off from laity, rulers from commoners, industrial specialists such as East African native iron-workers or Polynesian canoe-builders from those who follow other trades, the individual, to an even greater degree, is seen to know only a segment of his total culture. This is true despite the fact that the individual's total culture describes the basic orientations in terms of which his group, considered as a whole, regularize their day-to-day conduct.

Culture, viewed as more than man, forms the third term in the progression of inorganic, organic, and superorganic that was first formulated by Herbert Spencer as a conceptual frame to his evolutionary scheme. More than half a century later, the word *superorganic* was used by Kroeber to stress the fact that, just as culture and biological endowment are phenomena of a different order, so culture must be regarded as existing by and of itself, playing on the lives of human beings, who themselves are passive instruments under its sway. "Mohammedanism—a social phenomenon," says Kroeber, "in stifling the imitative possibilities of the pictorial and plastic arts, has obviously affected the civilization of many peoples; but it must also have altered the careers of many persons born in three continents during a thousand years." Or, again, "Even within one nationally limited sphere of civilization, similar results are necessarily bound to occur. The natural logician or administrator born into a caste of fishermen or street sweepers is not likely to achieve the satisfaction in life, and certainly not the success, that would have been his lot had his parents been Brahmins or Kshatriyas; and what is true formally of India holds true substantially for Europe."[3]

Much more documentation of his position is now at hand than existed when Kroeber wrote his paper. But the examples he cited there still illustrate well a point he originally brought forward. Darwin's discovery of the concept of evolution, paralleled by Wallace, who was working on the other side of the globe, is one of the most striking of these examples. Of Darwin, Kroeber

---

[3] A. L. Kroeber, 1917, pp. 204-5.

says, "No one can sanely believe that the distinction of Darwin's greatest accomplishment, the formulation of the doctrine of evolution by natural selection, would now stand to his credit had he been born fifty years sooner or later. If later, he would have been infallibly anticipated by Wallace, for one thing; by others, if an early death had cut off Wallace." The case of Gregor Mendel's work in heredity, lost sight because, according to this point of view, our culture was not ready for it, is equally well known. We need but recall how, published in 1865, it was ignored until 1900, when three students, independently, within a few weeks of each other, discovered the discovery of Mendel, and a new turn was given to biological science.

Other examples of this kind given by Kroeber include the independent discovery of the telephone by Alexander Bell and Elisha Gray, of oxygen by Priestly and Scheele, of the nebular hypothesis by Kant and Laplace, of the prediction of the existence of Neptune, within a few months, by Adams and Leverier. Some of the volumes Kroeber predicted would be written to pile instance upon instance of multiple discoveries, such as the detailed analysis of the social inevitability of medical discoveries by Stern or the discussion by Gilfillan of how direct were the progressions that led to the development of the steamboat, have since actually been published. All these later works, as anticipated, only strengthen the conclusion reached by Kroeber in his first paper, that, "The march of history, or as it is the current custom to name it, the progress of civilization, is independent of the birth of particular personalities; since these apparently averaging substantially alike, both as regards genius and normality, at all times and places, furnish the same substratum for the social. . . . The concrete effect of each individual upon civilization is determined by civilization itself. . . . The mind and the body are but facets of the same organic material or activity; the social substance—or unsubstantial fabric, if one prefers the phrase—the thing that we call civilization, transcends them for all its being rooted in life."

The study of women's dress styles made by Kroeber and Richardson, based on an earlier exploratory study of the subject by Kroeber,[4] is one of the most careful analyses of change in a specific element of culture that has been made. From various fashion guides, these students computed measurements and calculated ratios for certain traits in the female dress pattern, year by year, from 1787 to 1936. For the period 1605 to 1787 they gathered the same information for such years as data were available. The traits they analyzed were length and width of skirt, position and diameter of the waist, and length and width of the decolletage. In these traits they found changes in regular sequence, exhibiting a periodicity in the swings from large measurements to small that would seem to transcend the operation of any factors due solely to chance. Yet what, we may ask, is the significance of the activities of the Paris dress designers, who, from year to year, make it their business to invent new modes, and who have, to a high degree, perfected techniques of inducing the acceptance of change in women's dresses? It is

---

[4] Kroeber, 1919; Kroeber and Richardson, 1940.

precisely because the element of conscious planning, conscious choice by individuals, bulks so large in this phenomenon that it was selected for study as a test case. It is because of this, too, that the results cannot but be impressive as evidence of how man is swept on by the historic stream of his culture, apparently to be carried wherever it is bound, whether he desires it or not.

4

THE case for the psychological reality of culture rests largely on the undesirability of dividing human experience so that man, the organism, is conceptually set off from those aspects of his behavior that make up the "superorganic" elements in his existence. Any culture observed over the years, it is true, is seen to have a vitality that transcends the life of any member of the group that manifests it. Yet, on the other hand, without man, culture could not exist. Therefore, to objectify a phenomenon that can have no manifestation except in human thought and action is to argue a separate existence for something that actually exists only in the mind of the student.

A parallel is to be drawn between the "superorganic" conception of culture and the hypothesis of the group mind which, in earlier years, was favored by certain psychologists and made famous by such men as Le Bon and Trotter. The group mind—or the crowd mind, as it is sometimes called—was conceived as something more than the reactions of all the individuals composing, let us say, a mob. The question raised in this instance concerning the seat of this group mind, since it was held to be more than the sum of the reactions of individuals composing the group, led to its rejection as not susceptible to the kind of proof required by scientific method.

The clearest definition of culture in psychological terms states: *culture is the learned portion of human behavior.* Essential here is the word "learned," for it is recognized by all students that whatever forms susceptible of objective description may compose a culture, they must be learned by succeeding generations of a population if they are not to be lost. Otherwise, it would be necessary to assume that not only is man an animal equipped with an innate culture-building drive, but with drives so specific as to orient his behavior along invariable lines, as with the lower forms where limited drives guide reactions in predictable ways. This, indeed, was the view taken by the "instinct" psychologists. These students postulated one instinct after another to account for reactions that were later found not to be instinctive at all. They were, rather, found to be reactions so effectively assimilated that they had become automatic. It was thus impossible to tell whether these reactions were learned, or had resulted from innate endowment.

The arguments of the instinctivist school carried conviction because human beings actually do learn their cultures well, and by means of a process that is as pervasive as it is thorough. One device that we tend to stress when we use the word "education" is directed learning. But most culture, among all groups, is acquired by a process that is variously termed habituation, or imitation, or perhaps best, unconscious _conditioning_, which relates this form of learning to the other types, where conscious conditioning (training) is applied.

This process can be extraordinarily subtle. Thus, though a human being must periodically, for organic reasons, refrain from activity, the manner in which he will take his rest is culturally determined. In a culture where people sleep on mats spread on the ground, it is intolerable for them to sleep in beds on soft mattresses. The reverse is equally true. Where wooden headrests are used, down pillows become oppressive. Should circumstances force readaptation, then a process of relearning, or _reconditioning_, must be gone through to accommodate one's bodily structure to the new circumstances.

Language offers an endless variety of instances of how meticulously speech is conditioned. Regional differences, such as the broad _a_ of Boston as against the flat one of Cleveland; or status differences, as in the speech of the London cockney when contrasted to that of the upper-class Londoner, afford excellent examples. Some forms are so slightly shaded that they are never heard, except by a trained, sensitive ear, as in the transmutation, in Chicago, of the flat middlewestern _a_ in such a word as _cab_ into _keb_, with a short _e_. Other examples, such as motor habits characteristic of tribe, locality, nation, or class—in walking, or in the manner of sitting down—are but two more of the many instances that might be cited to show how, without giving any thought to the process and without conscious teaching, man learns his culture.

The effectiveness, then, with which techniques, accepted modes of behavior, and various beliefs are handed down from one generation to the next gives to culture the degree of stability that permits it to be regarded as something that has an existence of its own. Yet it must be emphasized that what is handed down is never so rigid a prescription of behavior as to leave no choice to the individual. One of the primary factors in cultural change, as we shall see, is the variation in any given mode of behavior that every society accepts. Thus most people in our own culture habitually rest by sitting on chairs. But some chairs are soft and others hard, some rock and some do not, some have straight backs and some are rounded. We do not ordinarily sit cross-legged at low tables, however, nor on small stools, nor relax by standing on one leg.

Does not, however, the conception of behavior as conditioned by tradition, again argue that man is but a creature of his culture? The answer to this lies in the factor of permitted variation in behavior that every people manifest. In every culture there is always room for choice, even, it must be stressed, among the simplest, most conservative groups. For even though it can be established that much of man's behavior is automatic, yet we do not thereby conclude that man is an automaton. When some aspect of his culture that he has always taken for granted—a belief about a particular deity, perhaps, or the validity of a certain way of doing business, or some item of etiquette— is challenged, his defense may be but a rationalization. Yet, especially when what has been challenged is incapable of objective proof, he makes his defense with a degree of emotion that eloquently bespeaks his feeling.

This signifies that culture is *meaningful*. Though behavior may be automatic, and sanctions taken for granted, yet any accepted form of action or belief, any institution in a culture, "makes sense." Herein lies the principal argument of those who hold for culture as a summation of the beliefs, habits, points of view of people, rather than a thing in itself. *Experience is culturally defined*, a definition which implies that culture has meaning for those who live in accordance with it. Even for material goods definition is essential. An object such as a table figures in the life of a people only as it is recognized as such. To a member of an isolated New Guinea tribe it would, of itself, be as incomprehensible as the symbolism of his designs would be to us. Only after explanation, definition, and awareness of function give meaning does an object come to life culturally.

The point of view advanced by the philosopher Ernst Cassirer is significant in this connection. His discussion of symbolism in language as the agent that permits man to carry on effectively as a culture-building animal shows brilliant insight into the problem of the distinction between man as a member of the biological series, and as the creator and inheritor of culture. "Man," he writes, "lives in a symbolic universe. Language, myth, art and religion are parts of this universe. They are the varied thread which weave the symbolic net, the tangled web of human experience. . . . No longer can man confront reality immediately; he cannot see it, as it were, face to face. Physical reality seems to recede in proportion as man's symbolic activity advances. Instead of dealing with the things themselves man is in a sense constantly conversing with himself. He has so enveloped himself in linguistic forms, in artistic images, in mythical symbols or religious rites that he cannot see or know anything except by the interposition of this artificial medium. His situation is the same in the theoretical as in the practical sphere. Even here man does not live in a world of hard facts, or according to his immediate needs and desires. He lives rather in the midst of imaginary emotions, in hopes and fears, in illusions and disillusions, in his fantasies and dreams. 'What disturbs and alarms man,' said Epictetus, 'are not the things, but his opinions and fancies about the things.' "[5]

Human behavior, indeed, has been defined as "symbolic behavior." Working back from this factor of symbolism, then, it is apparent that by the use of symbols man gives meaning to his life. Through this he culturally defines his experience, which he orders in terms of the ways of life of the group into which he is born and, through the learning process, grows to become a fully functioning member of it.

5

MUST we choose between the view that culture is an entity in its own right, moving irrespective of man, and the one that holds that culture is but a manifestation of the human psyche? Or is it possible to reconcile these two points of view?

So deeply do the conditionings of the individual lodge in human behavior,

---

[5] E. Cassirer, 1944, p. 25.

so automatic are his responses, so smooth the historic line to be traced when changes in a given culture are followed over a period of years, that it is difficult not to treat of culture as a thing outside man, dominating him, carrying him along whether he desires it or not to a destiny he can neither shape nor see. It is difficult, indeed, even to speak or write of culture without implying this. Yet, as we have seen, when culture is closely analyzed, we find but a series of patterned reactions that characterize the behavior of the *individuals* who constitute a given group. That is, we find *people* reacting, *people* behaving, *people* thinking, *people* rationalizing. Under these cir- cumstances, it becomes clear that what we do is to reify, that is, objectify and make concrete, the discrete experiences of individuals in a group at a given time. These we gather into a totality we call their culture. And, *for purposes of study,* this is quite proper. The danger point is reached when we reify similarities in behavior that only result from the similar conditioning of a group of individuals to their common setting, into something that exists outside man, something that is *superorganic.*

   This does not mean that we are to deny the usefulness, for certain an- thropological problems, of studying culture *as if* it had an objective existence. There is no other way in which we can attain an understanding of the range of variation to be found in the types of sanctioned behavior that achieve the ends all men do achieve. But we must not allow the recognition of a methodological need to obscure the fact that we are dealing with a construct —and that, as in all science, we erect this construct as a guide in our thinking and as an aid to analysis.

CHAPTER 3

Culture and Society

IN THE study of man and his works, it is necessary to distinguish the concept "culture" from its companion term "society," since failure to do this can seriously confuse our thinking. *A culture is the way of life of a people; while a society is the organized aggregate of individuals who follow a given way of life.* In still simpler terms *a society is composed of people; the way they behave is their culture.* Can we, however, thus separate man as a social animal from man as a creature who has culture? Is not social behavior actually cultural behavior? Indeed, have we not seen that the ultimate reality in the study of man is man himself, rather than the evanescent ideas, the intangible institutions, even the material objects that have arisen as a result of man's association in the aggregates we term societies? Let us consider these three points, briefly, in succession.

In stating that man is a social animal who lives only in organized aggregates, we touch on an aspect of his existence that, as we shall see, is shared by many other creatures in the biological world. Except for a few instances whose significance is not entirely clear, man is the only creature that has achieved culture—that is, whose ways of meeting the demands of life are cumulative and much more varied than are those of any other species in the biological series. Once we phrase the matter in this way—man shares with many other social animals the propensity to live in aggregates, but is the sole culture-building animal—a distinction between the two terms "society" and "culture" is at once apparent. Consequently, as a step in achieving understanding, the two must be considered separately as well as in their interrelationships.

Much the same argument enters when we consider our second question, whether social behavior is not also cultural behavior. Here, too, when we say that man is a social animal, that he shapes his relations with his fellows in accordance with social institutions, we must recognize that, however fundamental, this is not the whole story. Social institutions may be broadly interpreted to include economic and political orientations as well as those based on kinship and free association. But only with difficulty can they be extended to include such aspects of human behavior as religion, the arts, and languages, to say nothing of the unspoken sanctions that underlie all conduct. Social organization is the technical anthropological term for that basic aspect of human group life which comprises the institutions that provide a setting for all other kinds of behavior, both social and individual. To recognize the fact that man, a social animal, in interacting with his fellows does provide a setting for these other types of institutions, thus means that the sanctioned patterns of behavior can be differentiated from the motives out of which they have arisen.

Yet, in the final analysis, are not *people*—society—the reality rather than their ways of life? Are not these latter intangibles merely inferences from behavior that is to be observed when we visit a community of Eskimos, of Africans, of Frenchmen—when we follow the comings and goings of the people, seeing how they react to each other, studying the pattern of these reactions, and thus charting the institutions that channel this behavior? This, indeed, is the case; and the process of observing people, termed field research, is the tool by which ethnography obtains its primary data.

The concept "society" as used in this sense is, nonetheless, subject to all the reservations that must be held in mind when the concept "culture" is used. Just as any culture was seen to be a reification of individual behavior, so any human society is similarly reified out of the succession of human beings who compose a group. The point will be remembered that culture is more than any individual who lives in it, if only because the artifacts, the institutions, the sanctions that comprise it persist long after the death of any given member of the group that follows this way of life. In the same fashion, no society is made up of the same people for very long. Births and deaths constantly change its personnel. When a whole generation has passed, its composition is entirely different than it was. All that links it to the past are the patterns of behavior that have been handed down to the people who now comprise it. It is apparent that, in assuming *social* continuity, the same methodological departures from reality must be called into play as when we assume the continuity of culture.

The study of society is important for us because it is essential that we understand how the fact that man lives in aggregates affects his behavior. We must take into account not only the social institutions man has created to permit human societies to function, but also the drives that cause him to set up these aggregates, and the manner in which the individual is integrated into the society into which he is born. It is these latter points that will be considered in this chapter, since they bear most importantly on the relationship between society and culture. In a later section of this book, where culture in its various manifestations are to be considered, we shall describe some of the institutions that make up the patterns of human social life.[1]

2

To HOW great a degree man shares his propensity for social living with other animal forms is not generally realized. The systematic study of animal sociology is quite new. Allee, who has perhaps treated the subject most comprehensively, tells why it developed so slowly. In 1878 the French

---

[1] Chapters 17–20, below.

scientist, Espinas, published a work, *Des Sociétés Animales,* in which he affirmed, "that no living being is solitary, but that, from the lowest to the highest, each is normally immersed in some sort of social life." [2] Granting Espinas' statement was more sweeping than the facts justify, it was nonetheless important because "the scientific world was then . . . under the spell of the idea that there is an intense and frequently very personal struggle for existence so important and far reaching as to leave no room for so-called softer philosophies." [3]

In a later reaction against this philosophy of the fang and claw, Kropotkin stressed mutual aid as a factor in evolution. "Two aspects of animal life impressed me most during the journeys which I made in my youth in Eastern Siberia and Northern Manchuria," says Kropotkin. "One of them was the extreme severity of the struggle for existence which most species of animals have to carry on against an inclement Nature; the enormous destruction of life which periodically results from natural agencies; and the consequent paucity of life over the vast territory which fell under my observation. And the other was, that even in those few spots where animal life teemed in abundance, I failed to find—though I was eagerly looking for it—that bitter struggle for the means of existence, *among animals belonging to the same species,* which was considered by most Darwinists (though not always by Darwin himself) as the dominant characteristic of struggle for life, and the main factor of evolution." A lecture Kropotkin heard in St. Petersburg in 1880, delivered by the Russian zoologist Kessler, stimulated the formulation of his later ideas, for Kessler, as Kropotkin reports it, held, "that besides the *law of Mutual Struggle* there is in Nature the *law of Mutual Aid,* which, for the success of the struggle for life, and especially for the progressive evolution of the species, is far more important than the law of mutual contest." [4] And so Kropotkin went to work collecting examples of mutual aid among animals, and then, in the manner of his day, among "savages," and "barbarians," in the mediaeval city, and "amongst ourselves."

Kropotkin's data have for many reasons proved inacceptable to those trained in later times, especially because of what Zuckerman [5] terms their "purely anecdotal" quality. The aspect of his findings that has stood up under later investigation was the demonstration of how extensive is cooperation among members of the same species, and how far down in the biological scale these patterns of social behavior reach. Ants and bees have long been renowned for their social qualities—the "social insects," they are called—as have the wolf-pack and the bison herd. Later work, indeed, has not only shown that there are many other species that habitually form societies; it has also been demonstrated that non-social species, such as the ladybird beetles or male midges, collect in aggregates to hibernate, or to await the coming of the females in mating season. Animals likewise may form part of a wider ecological community that includes not only all the different species that

[2] W. C. Allee, 1938, p. 25.
[3] *Ibid.,* p. 26.
[4] P. Kropotkin, 1916, pp. 1–3.
[5] S. Zuckerman, 1932, pp. 10, 11.

inhabit a given region, but also the plant life. As Allee puts it, "The growing weight of evidence indicates that animals are rarely solitary; that they are almost necessarily members of loosely integrated racial and interracial communities, in part woven together by environmental factors, and in part by mutual attraction between the individual members of the different communities, no one of which can be affected without changing all the rest, at least to some slight extent." [6]

How important social life can be to animals is to be seen from an experiment conducted by this same student whereby goldfish, singly and in groups of ten, were exposed to fixed amounts of colloidal silver until they expired. Those exposed in groups of ten survived significantly longer than those exposed singly, because they shared a dose that not only would have killed, and did more quickly kill any one of them when alone, but permitted them to survive longer when together because they were found to secrete a slime that rendered the poison less toxic. White mice were shown to grow faster in small groups than those left to develop in isolation or when overcrowded. Where these mice had skin lesions in the region of the head that could only be treated by licking, the isolated mice went uncured until transferred to a cage where their fellows could treat them. The fact that they were able to huddle together when the temperature was lowered promoted their growth, since they could keep each other warm and thus use the energy they would otherwise have to employ for this purpose to give to the growth-process.[7] As for the larger forms, the importance of social life to such an animal as the chimpanzee has been stated by Köhler: "It is hardly an exaggeration to say that a chimpanzee kept in solitude is not a real chimpanzee at all." [8]

When we study animal societies, we find many analogies to human aggregates. It is hardly necessary to refer again to the social insects for parallels. Even if the more romantic allusions that have been made to them are discounted, resemblances between them and human groupings are strikingly sufficient. The mechanisms of dominance and submission operative in them, the factors of competition and cooperation within a group and between groups, the complexity of their social relationships, all contribute significantly to their successful functioning. What is perhaps not realized is how equally complex relationships, based on similar mechanisms, have been found in other animal groupings.

The most dramatic exemplification of dominance and submission has been uncovered in the research of Schjelderup-Ebbe on birds of various sorts. Among these creatures, he found, "There exists . . . a definite order or precedence or social distinction" which, he maintains, has "proved to be founded upon certain conditions of despotism." [9] This is what has come to be known as the *peck-order*. The "despotism" he describes comes after the animal has passed chickdom. As chicks, though there is competition for food, for example, there is no pecking. Later, however, their "spirit of competi-

---

[6] *Op. cit.*, p. 38.
[7] Allee, *op. cit.*, *passim*.
[8] W. Köhler, 1925, p. 293.
[9] T. Schjelderup–Ebbe, 1935, p. 949.

tion," which is regarded by this student as instinctive, "begins to turn into envy," especially when they must compete against other members of the flock who are older, stronger and better established. Old thus dominate young, males dominate females. Such other factors as the time of the year, illness—which may reduce a strong "despot" to weakness and thus expose him to the pecks of the others—and the degree of acquaintance the animals have with one another, are also operative.

The peck-order of barn-yard fowl has been most carefully analyzed. In studying this problem each individual bird is identified by a marker so that its contacts with every other member of the flock can be recorded. Sometimes the results show that more than one bird has power, or a bird that dominates most of the others submits to one that is relatively weak because, let us say, at the first encounter of these two the dominant bird was ill and the other, ordinarily weaker, was able to prevail. In one flock of 18 ducks of the same sex studied by Schjelderup-Ebbe the pecking hierarchy was clear:

1 bird	pecked	17	others	
1 "	"	16	"	
1 "	"	15	"	
1 "	"	14	"	
1 "	"	13	"	
1 "	"	12	"	
1 "	"	11	"	
1 "	"	10	"	
2 birds	"	8	"	
1 bird	"	7	"	
1 "	"	6	"	
2 birds	"	5	"	
2 "	"	3	"	
1 bird	"	1	other	
1 "	"	0	"	[10]

The fate of the lowest ranking birds is not pleasant to contemplate. "They spend time in out-of-the-way places, feed after others have fed, and make their way around cautiously, apparently with an eye out to avoid contacts. The lowest ranking birds may appear lean, and their plumage is somewhat more rumpled because they have less time to arrange it." [11]

It is not to be assumed that this kind of dominance is the rule in all social aggregates. Even the social orders found among birds seem to vary from species to species. Allee asserts that the peck-order of the common chicken is far more rigid than in any other species studied by him, and gives the findings of himself and his associates on the relationships within a flock of pigeons, as an example of what might be termed feathered democracy. His diagrams indicate the relationships between the females lowest in the social order, contacts being noted before mating (A); during the entire period of observation (B); and after mating (C). Before mating, two female pigeons

[10] Op. cit., pp. 965–6.
[11] Allee, op. cit., p. 182.

designated BY and BB (not shown on the charts) dominated the others, and afterwards RY joined them; but the relationships among these three was never a clear one. As for the others:

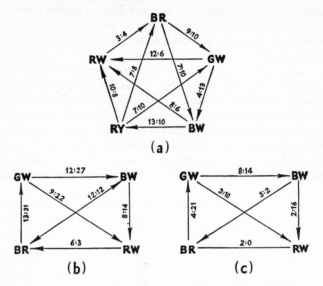

(a)

(b) (c)

Fig. 1 *Peck-order of pigeons (after Allee, 1938).*

The diagrams are to be read in this manner: in A, BR was observed to peck GW 10 times and was pecked 9 times by her when she retreated. GW pecked BW 13 times, but lost in 4 encounters. BR won 10 and lost 7 times to BW, and so on. Allee concludes that, in such flocks, "It frequently becomes difficult to decide which bird stands higher in the social order." Though "social hierarchy among chickens is based on an almost absolute peck-right which smacks strongly of the despotism of which Schjelderup-Ebbe writes, these other birds have an organization based on peck-dominance rather than on absolute peck-right." That is, though "one becomes fairly sure which bird . . . will dominate in the larger number of their contacts . . . the result of the next meeting between two individuals is not to be known with certainty until it has taken place." [12]

3

GROUPINGS of animals, then, are *organized*, though the degree and type of organization varies. Among some, it is so loose and so sporadic that one may use the designation "society" only with extreme reservation. Among many others, however, not only in its organization but in its functioning, it is, in every sense of the word, a social unit. For, like human societies, such aggregates constitute unified groupings whose members, both in their internal and external relations, have a sense of "belonging" by identifying themselves with

[12] Allee, *op. cit.,* pp. 186–9, *passim.*

a given locality, recognizing their fellow-members as such, and reacting against strangers.

Carpenter's report on the social life of the howler monkeys studied on Barro Colorado Island in 1932, as summarized by Yerkes,[13] may be quoted: "The howler clan is not primarily familial. It provides for reproduction, as also for all other activities and ecological relations which are essential to the life of the individual and of the species. Apart from the acceptance occasionally of a 'complemental' male, it is a closed society which repels the advances of members of other clans although it may permit primates of other genera to mingle with it on its feeding grounds without molestation or special attention. The clan exhibits such functionally important subgroups as female and nursing infant; female, infant and juveniles; play, defense, directing and retrieving groups; and assemblages about oestrus and parturient females. Such transient social groupings are obviously specialized as to social function and in manifestly important ways supplement the activities of the clan."

Membership in a social group rests on acceptance by at least a number of its members, which in turn means that each individual undergoes a process that adjusts him to his fellows in his associations with them. In most cases, acceptance is achieved merely by the circumstance of being born into the group and of growing to maturity under its shelter. Yet not only is the infant brought to maturity, but his relations to his fellows are defined for him. After his second field study of primates, in this case the gibbon, Carpenter reports, "The integration of primates into groups is believed to be a complex process involving mutually reciprocal patterns of naturalistic behavior which are modified and made specific by learning or conditioning. Almost every phase of behavior of which a primate is capable enters to some degree into the determination of its 'gregariousness' and the qualities of its complex social behavior." [14]

Relationships between individuals, in all societies, change with age, with strength, with obligations assumed, and with status achieved. The modifications in the behavior of the hamadryad baboon mother, which contrasts with her prematernal behavior, as described by Zuckerman, makes the point. Thus, while a female baboon is usually dominated by the males, and in many situations behaves with extreme passivity, as when males are struggling for her, after the birth of an offspring, she snatches up her baby at the first sign of danger, or of fighting between males, and moves to a place of safety with it.[15]

Experimentation has not proceeded far enough to determine to what extent the individual in animal societies follows instinctive drives in achieving integration into his group, or is aided by what Yerkes and Yerkes call "social stimulation" to enlarge on inborn tendencies. There is ample evidence, however, that anthropoid apes can be taught to eat substances foreign to their normal diet, to take but one instance, which may also be true of some mon-

[13] C. R. Carpenter, 1934; R. M. and A. W. Yerkes, 1933, p. 982.
[14] C. R. Carpenter, 1940, p. 199.
[15] S. Zuckerman, op. cit., pp. 237, 260.

keys. The factor of imitation probably enters in such cases, even though there is reason to believe that monkeys and apes are not as imitative as popular ideas would hold. Yet it is to be noted that most of the observations that have been made of this aspect of anthropoid and monkey behavior have come out of experimental situations, or where the animals have been in captivity. To what extent this tendency would function in the wild cannot be stated.

One important factor in all social life is the identification of the individual with his group. This means that the outsider, until he is accepted, leads a life of considerable hardship. Most studies of bird societies comment on this, telling how, until a newcomer has established his place in the peck-order, he is fair game for the other members of the group in which he has been placed. Köhler has given a most vivid description of this process in his classic study of chimpanzees. His group, he says, was "a vaguely organized community" of individuals *"used to each other."* He continues:

One day, a newly-bought chimpanzee arrived, and at first was put, for purposes of the sanitary control, in a special cage a few metres away from the others. She at once aroused the greatest interest on the part of the older animals, who tried their best with sticks and stalks put through the bars to indicate at least a not too friendly connexion with her; once even a stone was thrown against the wire-netting at the newcomer. . . . When the new-comer, after some weeks, was allowed into the large animals' ground in the presence of the older animals, they stood for a second in stony silence. But hardly had they followed her few uncertain steps with staring eyes than Rana, a foolish but otherwise harmless animal, uttered their cry of in-dignant fury, which was at once taken up by all the others in frenzied excitement. The next moment the new-comer had disappeared under a raging crowd of as-sailants, who dug their teeth into her skin, and who were only kept off by our most determined interference while we remained. Even after several days the eldest and most dangerous of the creatures tried over and over again to steal up to the stranger while we were present, and ill-treated her cruelly when we did not notice in time. She was a poor, weak creature, who at no time showed the slightest wish for a fight, and there was really nothing to arouse their anger, except that she was a stranger.[16]

The sequel is of equal interest.

Sultan, who had played less part in the above-mentioned assault, was the first to be left alone with the newly-arrived female. He at once began to busy himself with her, . . . but she was really very shy after her bad treatment. However, he went on trying to make friends, . . . until at last she gave way to his invitations to play, to his embraces, and—rather shyly—to his childish sexual advances. When the others came near and he was any distance away, she called him anxiously to her. . . . Whenever she was frightened, they at once put their arms round each other. Two other female apes, however, likewise soon broke away from the muttering group, and played with the new-comer . . . until at last only Chica and Grande, who up till now had shown no friendship for each other, united by a mutual aver-sion . . . led their own life in distant spots of the stockade, away from the new-comer and the renegades.[17]

[16] W. Köhler, *op. cit.*, p. 301. Reprinted by permission.
[17] *Ibid.*, pp. 301–2.

Culture and Society

Some of the reasons why societies are formed have been indicated in the preceding pages, where it has been shown how animal aggregates can achieve survival in a manner not possible for individuals. The degree to which their communal organizations are dictated by biophysical reasons, as suggested by Zuckerman's derivation of family life and social structure out of the oestrous cycle (the rutting season) of the female, the need to care for the young, and the conditioned grooming reflex, or whether other factors enter, need not concern us here. What we do know is that the tendency to live in societies is one that man shares with other animals, and that many of the basic social institutions found among mankind also characterize the life of subhuman aggregates.

4

HUMAN and infrahuman societies have much in common both in form and function. The localization of the group, the fact of differentiations within it on the basis of age, or size, or some other trait, its cooperative aspect, the identification of the members of what has been called the "in-group" as against those outside it, are all true of human as well as animal aggregates. Such functions as care of the young, protection against predatory forms, the integration into the life of the community of those born into the society or received as adults from outside, similarly characterize them all.

What differentiates human societies from others is that, though man is but one among many social animals, he is the only animal that has culture. The statement of the difference as phrased by Zuckerman is particularly cogent. "Cultural phenomena may not, in the last resort, prove to be absolutely different from physiological events. But there is a significant distinction between the physiological responses of the animal and the cultural behavior of man. The effective stimuli involved in the behavior of animals are mainly inherent in immediate physical events, which are in no way the by-products of the activities of pre-existing animals of the same species. Man, on the other hand, amasses experience through speech, and the effective stimuli underlying human behaviour are largely products of the lives of pre-existing people. The environment within which human beings live is mainly the accumulation of activities of previous generations. Culture, in this sense, is an essentially human phenomenon." [18]

This same position has also been taken by Schneirla, who points out that, among ants, "The learning process is stereotyped and rote in character, and as a process is limited to the individual and the given situation," so that unlike human societies, where knowledge is cumulative, "the special learning of each society dies with it." Because of this, Schneirla concludes, we must "recognize the existence of a qualitatively different process of individual socialization on the human level, influenced very differently by psychological factors according to cultural pattern and social heritage, rather than in

[18] S. Zuckerman, *op cit.*, p. 19. See also A. L. Kroeber, 1928.

dependence upon the direct function of hereditary organic agencies as on the insect level." [19]

These statements express from other points of view the uniquely human quality of culture, or, as we have phrased it, the fact that man is the only culture-building animal. Here, equally, are other expressions of the distinction we have drawn between society, an aggregate of individuals, and culture, the body of learned behavior in accordance with which their lives are lived. Yet this is not enough. We must draw still a further distinction between the processes involved when an individual is integrated into his society, as against what occurs when he learns the customary ways of thinking and acting that make up the culture that distinguishes his society from other human groupings.

The process by means of which an individual is integrated into his society is called *socialization*. It involves, in human no less than animal aggregates, the adaptation of the individual to the fellow-members of his group, the achievement of a position in relation to them that give him status and assign to him the role he plays in the life of the community. He passes through various stages in accordance with the degree of maturity he attains, each stage commonly distinguished by certain permitted and prohibited forms of behavior, such as playfulness in the young, or the manipulation of power among the elders. As sexual maturity is reached and the procreative drives come into play, he again participates in a family grouping, but now as parent, protector and teacher. He will also figure as a member of certain groupings not based on kinship at all but on sex differences; or as are constituted when some members prey on other creatures; or in clusters, such as Carpenter has described for the howling monkeys.

Because man alone has the ability to develop and transmit learned behavior, however, his social institutions exhibit a variety and a degree of complexity that the social forms of no other *single species* of animal possess. By his ability to communicate with his fellows in the symbolic and conceptual forms of speech, he alone has been able to ring the innumerable variations on even such a basic social structure as the family, or the local group, that we shall find when we later make a comparative study of the social institutions of mankind. If we consider the group life of any given species of infrahuman animals, we find that their social structures are far more uniform and thus much more predictable than are those of man. For each of their generations learns but behavior common to all its contemporaries, whereas man builds on the experience of all who have gone before him.

For animals and man alike, *conditioning*, in its broadest sense, is the essence of the process involved. Animals can, of course, learn; countless experiments have shown that canaries brought up among other birds will vary their song, or that cats can be brought up to play with rats rather than to kill them. Yet in one of the most often cited experiments of this latter kind, that of Kuo, where cats were even conditioned to be afraid of rats,

---

[19] T. C. Schneirla, 1946, pp. 390–9.

nine of the twenty kittens reared in isolation from rat-killing cats themselves became rat-killers.[20] The temptation to anthropomorphize on the basis of studies such as this is strong. It is only such explanations as that of Kuo, who refers the tendency of the cat to kill rats to its bodily structure, its habits of clawing, and the like, that escape this. Yet conscious learning cannot be discarded as a factor, and for kittens brought up under normal circumstances the example of the mother cat is of appreciable importance.

That older animals teach their young is recognized far beyond the limits of scientific inquiry. Such a tale as the following, from Dutch Guiana, shows how recognition of the factor of teaching and learning among animals can be expressed in homely form:

Kitten and little Rat were great friends. Every day they went to play together. But Rat did not know that he was Cat's favorite food, and Kitten did not know that Rat was his favorite food. But one day, when little Rat came home, his mother asked him, "With whom do you play?" He said, "With friend Kitten." And at the same time, when Kitten went home, his mother asked him, said, "With whom do you play?" He said, "With little Rat." Then Rat's mother said to him, "You must not play with Kitten any more, because you are his favorite food." And at the same time, too, mother Cat was saying to Kitten, "You stupid fellow, don't you know that he is your tidbit? When you play with him, you must strike him." The next day, no sooner did they come out on the street than Kitten called to friend Rat, said, "Aren't you coming to play with me any more?" At once little Rat answered him, "Yes, brother. There are wise people in your village, and there are wise people in my village, too! [21]

The socialization of men is understandably more complex than that of animals because human social institutions, as expressions of man's culture-building ability, take on such varied and changing forms. This means, moreover, that the process of socialization is only a part of the process by means of which men adjust themselves to their fellows in working with the total body of traditions—economic, social, technological, religious, aesthetic, linguistic—to which they fall heir. It is here that learning takes on a special significance that must be fully grasped if its all-important role in shaping the way of life of a people is adequately to be appreciated.[22]

5

THE aspects of the learning experience which mark off man from other creatures, and by means of which, initially, and in later life, he achieves competence in his culture, may be called *enculturation*. This is in essence a process of conscious or unconscious conditioning, exercised within the limits sanctioned by a given body of custom. From this process not only is all adjustment to social living achieved, but also all those satisfactions that, though

---

[20] Z. Y. Kuo, 1930.
[21] M. J. and F. S. Herskovits, 1936, p. 281.
[22] For statements of the psycho-cultural approach to this problem, see N. E. Millar and J. Dollard, 1941.

they are of course a part of social experience, derive from individual expression rather than association with others in the group.

Every human being goes through a process of enculturation, for without the adaptations it describes he could not live as a member of society. It is comparable to the broadest condition of achieved adjustment, termed *homeostasis* by the psychologists, which is essential in the life of any creature, human or infrahuman, and concerns the physiological as well as the psychological aspects of the organism.

Like any phenomenon of human behavior, the process of enculturation is a most complex one. In the earliest years of an individual's life, it is largely a matter of conditioning to fundamentals—habits of eating, sleeping, speaking, personal cleanliness—whose inculcation has been shown to have special significance in shaping the personality and forming the habit patterns of the adult in later life. Yet the enculturative experience is not terminated at the close of infancy. As an individual continues through childhood and adolescence to achieve adult status, he is continuously exposed to this process of learning, which can be said to end only with his death.

The difference between the nature of the enculturative experience in the early years of life and later is that the range of conscious acceptance or rejection by an individual continuously increases as he grows older. By the time he has reached maturity, a man or woman has been so conditioned that he moves easily within the limits of accepted behavior set by his group. Thereafter, new forms of behavior presented to him are in the main those involved in culture change—new inventions or discoveries, new ideas diffused from outside his society about which, as an individual, he has to "make up his mind" and thus play his role in reorienting his culture.

In truth, we are here touching on one of the most fundamental aspects of the enculturative process, an aspect whose full significance will be probed when we take up such a problem as the relation of the individual to culture, or the question of conservatism and change in culture, the reconciliation of which, it will be recalled, involved the resolution of one of our apparent dilemmas in the understanding of culture. However, the basic principle involved is clear: *The enculturation of the individual in the early years of his life is the prime mechanism making for cultural stability, while the process, as it is operative on more mature folk, is highly important in inducing change.*

It is because of the earliest conditionings that, as we have pointed out, "human beings learn their cultures so well that most behavior rarely rises to the level of consciousness." In our earliest years we are being continuously conditioned to conformity. Little choice is vouchsafed us, whether through the exercise of techniques of punishment and reward, as in the inculcation of the moral code of society; or by imitation, as in learning motor habits such as the gestures, or the cadences of speech. Infantile protest, such as occurs when a child refuses to learn to speak, is not absent, as the findings of psychiatrists and other students of child behavior testify. But such protests are individual ones, laid against the restraints placed on the infant's freedom of behavior. It is significant that the infantile protest is not rationalized. It cannot be, for the linguistic—that is, the symbolic—equipment of the child, to say nothing of the infant, does not permit this.

In other words, learning, at the earliest stages of human existence, by inculcating in the new member of society the enculturative disciplines essential for him to function as a member of his social group, contributes to social stability and cultural continuity. As the individual grows older, these early conditionings become so effective that they settle into the routines of daily behavior. Then the continuing enculturation to which he is exposed is in very large measure a reconditioning process, that lies on the conscious level. A man or woman knows the ways of behavior that are traditionally acceptable to his group in a given situation—in one society, that he must step off a path and turn his back on a passing elder to show respect, in another, that the thing to do with the property of a dead person is to burn it.

But should he have contact with another people who hold that respect is shown by facing a superior rather than by turning away from him, then even with the greatest freedom of choice, an alternative has been presented that must be grappled with, if only because it is a medium of intercourse with this strange folk. If he accepts the new mode for himself he may meet with resistance at home. But unless prevented from carrying on the new way of showing respect, his persistence will make of him a center from which a possible deviation from the sanctioned form of polite behavior radiates, and his fellows will be continuously faced with making the choice he has already made.

The resistances to revisions in economic behavior called into play by the spread of Euroamerican culture over the world, demonstrate how this process works. The destruction of property of the dead, or any other form of destruction of property is in our culture frowned on. Great pressure has been brought by administrators of native peoples whose concept of what to do with property does not envisage its destruction, to force change in such customs. Whether they have succeeded or not, the psychological processes of the natives in making an adjustment to this dictum is of a different order than the early conditioning process to which these same individuals were exposed as infants.

The enculturative experience of later life, however, is only intermittent. It thus presents a further contrast to the continuous conditioning to which the infant and young child are exposed. Nor do these enculturative situations, for the adult, cover as many segments of culture as for the young. The adult knows his language, the systems of etiquette that regulate behavior, how to face the supernatural, the musical forms of his culture—all things that the child must learn. For the adult, enculturation has been completed *except* where new situations must be met, new choices made; his culture, in the main, has been learned so well that he need give it little thought. He projects the decisions he must reach in his daily round against the background of knowledge his culture has provided him. This permits an adult human being to react to the stimuli presented to him by his culture most effectively, most efficiently, and with a minimum of need to traverse ground already covered. Enculturation is thus the process which permits most behavior to be carried on *below the level of conscious thought*. In nontechnical language, it can be taken for granted in the manner we accept without questioning even such complex manifestations of our own culture as automobiles, electricity, and symphony orchestras, to say nothing of the art of writing or such a fundamental technological device as the wheel.

CHAPTER 4

Culture and the Individual

THE concept of enculturation affords us a tool to bridge the gap between culture as a thing that exists by and of itself, and culture as the total behavior of the individuals through whom it is manifest. We have seen that, in the process of enculturation, an individual learns the forms of conduct acceptable to his group. He does this so well that his thoughts, his values, his acts rarely conflict with those of the fellow-members of his society. In consequence, the life of the group can be reified into a series of institutions, capable of objective description as though they existed independently of the people who live in accordance with them.

This is the way most ethnographic studies of culture are presented. It is possible, for example, to state that in East Africa cattle will be prized as tokens of status and wealth and not killed for food, or that in certain South American Indian cultures a man takes to his hammock when a child is born to his wife, there to be treated as an invalid while the woman goes about her work. Observation in the field will, in a general way, confirm this fact. Yet statements of this kind are but summations of the characteristic and thus predictable behavior of *people* in these situations. It is an East African man who swells with pride as he contemplates his cattle, or envies his neighbor who has a larger herd; it is a South American Indian woman who carries on her work after childbirth while her man is being petted in his hammock. In short, the individual must never be lost sight of in considering the institution.

In the course of the enculturative experience of the individual, he tends to be molded into the kind of a person his group envisages as desirable. Complete success is never achieved; some persons are more pliant than others, some resist the enculturative discipline more than their fellows. Yet by and large, all become sufficiently alike so that, as one travels over the earth, one finds that just as cultures differ from each other, so people seem to differ from one society to the next.

Here lies the core of one of the critical problems in the study of culture— how enculturation affects the development of individual personalities. Does the process of growing up in a given society tend to encourage aggressive drives, so that successful competition within the group and warfare with other groups bring the greatest rewards to an individual? Or are gentler procedures held desirable, so that the most cooperative individual is best adjusted within the group, and diplomacy and compromise rule in contact with outsiders? Are inconsistencies in sanctioned behavior within a society the sources of frustration, or are institutions harmoniously blended so that an individual can live an adjusted life with a minimum of inner conflict?

How deep-seated the reactions to influences of this sort can be is to be perceived when we give a moment's thought to two conflicting patterns in the United States. On the one hand, the American is born into a society whose ideology is based on the concept of equality of opportunity, typified by such a commonly stated article of faith as, "Every boy has a chance to become president;" or by the prominence of the success story in popular literature; or as a favorite theme for motion pictures. Yet the handicaps posed by economic or social class lines, by the circumstance of ethnic or racial origin—to name but two of the most prominent contradictions to the expressed ideal—cannot be denied. To untold persons who have been indoctrinated with the concept of equality of opportunity, these contradictions present a conflict between ideals and experience that produces at best a tortured cynicism, and at worst the psychoses that result from the frustrations the individual has experienced.

The relation between culture and the individual, as seen in terms of the enculturative process, yields a profound sense of the plasticity of the human organism. Here we see how broad is the range of possible behavior permitted by man's biological heritage. From this, too, we derive the principle that any human being can master any culture, even in its subtlest aspect, provided he has the opportunity to learn it. Mead's analysis of what were presented to be the biologically determined "puberty crises" of adolescent girls is to the point.[1] For many years students of child psychology maintained that the emotional instability of the adolescent girl was inevitable, since it was caused by the physiological changes that occur at this period of life. Yet in a South Seas society, where some of the inhibitions imposed by Euroamerican conventions of sexual behavior do not exist, these "crises" were found to be absent. The only conclusion to be drawn from such findings is that such emotional reactions are culturally, not biologically, determined. The human organism is sufficiently plastic so the enculturative experience can direct it toward a stormy or calm passage through this "critical" period.

But it must not be concluded that the individual is solely a passive element in the process. In his early enculturation, it is true, a person is mainly the recipient of attention which ensures his adaptation to the patterns of proper behavior sanctioned by his group. Yet the sense of security that comes to him from the care he receives during his infancy, or the insecurity he feels under neglect, the degree to which he experiences a rigorous training in the exercise of physiological functions or is permitted freedom—such differences in the development of the individual may, in turn, have far-reaching consequences for society. The infant whose sense of security is invaded by a feeling that he is not accepted will grow up compensating for this de-

---

[1] M. Mead, 1928.

ficiency. He may seek to impose his will on his fellows, by whatever means he finds at hand, until he becomes a tyrant like the Zulu chief Chaka.[2] Many instances of this type, whose influence was good no less than evil, can be drawn from the history of almost any group. The theory which holds that the history of a people is shaped by the dominant personalities who appear from time to time—the "great man" theory of history—derives from such facts. This theory is now discredited because it oversimplified a complicated process. But we can see how much it drew, all unwittingly, on the results of interaction between an individual and his group, as this was determined by his experience in the course of his adjustment through enculturation to its standards of conduct, its system of values, its institutionalized forms of behavior.

It will be remembered that in the opening pages of this book the closeness of the relationship between anthropology and psychology was stressed. This suggests that we should reconsider the formula that anthropology is concerned with groups, psychology with individuals—a formula long accepted, and still heard. Under this formula culture was studied by anthropologists as a series of institutions, without reference to the place or function of the individual. Psychologists were held to be interested in individual human beings, whose mental processes were to be analyzed with but little, if any, reference to the cultural setting in which they were found.

It is a middle ground of common concern, long neglected, that we treat here. Such fundamental processes as motivation and adjustment cannot be separated from the situations in which they take place. They cannot be studied without reference to individuals who are motivated and who must make their adjustments. But while individuals respond to approval, seek security, strive to conform to accepted modes of behavior, or reach preeminence, their culture dictates what they must do to achieve these ends, and perpetuates a tradition that motivates conduct in obtaining them. Our interest here, in short, is in the *psychology of culture*, which is preeminently the study of the individual as he is enculturated to the established norms of behavior already present in his society when he becomes a member of it.

2

THE schools of psychology that have most stimulated the study of the individual in his cultural setting are behaviorism, the Gestalt or configurational approach, and psychoanalysis. Other influences can, of course, be found. In the period antedating 1920, various anthropologists, such as Franz Boas, A. A. Goldenweiser, C. G. Seligman, W. H. R. Rivers, and others stressed the importance of taking psychology into full account. The behavioristic school, which emphasized the principle of the conditioned response, provided anthropologists with conceptual and methodological tools they were quick to grasp and use. Boas spoke of ethnography as a "behavioristic disci-

---

[2] T. Mofolo, 1931.

pline," while Wissler's work, *Man and Culture,* based its psychological arguments on the tenets of this school.

To what an extent the behavioristic point of view has been absorbed into the anthropological approach toward culture, is to be seen in our discussion of enculturation in the preceding chapter. In vast proportion, the learning process *is* a conditioning process, or, in later years, one of reconditioning. If this were not so, human beings could not function in the system of relationships that mark the course of their lives. They could not function at all, indeed, for their time would be spent in assessing each situation an individual might meet, instead of responding to a given set of circumstances, "without thinking," as we say.

The example of our reaction to the problem of crossing a busy street offers a case in point. It is a dangerous business, when viewed objectively. We recognize its dangers when we have to pilot a partially enculturated child who must negotiate the passage. Adults thread their way through traffic with but little thought unless they travel to countries where they must cross streets where traffic moves on the left, let us say, rather than the right, or vice versa. Only in such situations is the effectiveness of cultural conditioning realized and the efficiency and freedom with which it endows us grasped.

It is worthy of note that anthropologists never accepted the postulates of instinctivist psychology. From the first, it was apparent to them that to refer the differences found in human behavior to *instincts* was quite incompatible with the variation in customs mankind exhibits. The concept of *automatic* responses to situations deriving from the conditioning of each individual member of a social group to similar stimuli arising out of a common culture was, however, recognized as valid. This, it was felt, explained satisfactorily the immediacy with which every human being typically responds to a given situation in a manner acceptable to his group. We shall return to this fact many times in the pages of this book, for no discussion of the nature and processes of culture, or of the manner in which it fills the life of the individual, is possible without this basic term of reference.

Gestalt or configurational psychology which followed and, in a sense, grew out of behaviorism has been less specifically employed by anthropologists despite its considerable influence on their thinking. The core of its position lies in the stress it places on the essential unity of any human experience. This point was established by its telling attacks on earlier concepts that broke down the continuity of psychological states into disparate elements. This point of view was particularly congenial to an anthropology that was increasingly realizing the integration of every culture. Moreover, anthropology was laying more and more stress on the artificiality of attempts to divide a culture into sub-units without taking this integration into full account, however necessary such a device might be in furthering the study of problems such as economics, art, or religion. Gestalt, or later "field-theory" psychology, through the work of Lewin and of Brown underscored the importance of perceiving that the differentiation of the individual from his culture, leads inevitably to a distorted perspective on behavior. To be effective, all those elements which, at a given moment or in a given segment of time, figure in the total setting of an individual or of a group, must be taken into account. In this, of course, the culture in terms of which the life of the subject is lived takes a place of the greatest importance.

The writings of Sigmund Freud and his disciples have had a profound influence on the anthropological study of the individual in his culture. Insistence by Freud and his followers on the effective role of the experiences of the first years of life in shaping the human personality have stimulated studies by anthropologists of the life of the child and the training of the infant in nonliterate societies. Freud's refusal to accept the taboo on any discussion of sex that permeated Euroamerican nineteenth and early twentieth century thinking resulted in a recognition by anthropologists of the importance of sex habits in non-European cultures and the inclusion of their study in programs of research. The light thrown by the Freudians on the problem of motivation has stimulated a reexamination of many forms of behavior that represent rephrasings, "rationalizations," of objectives whose real character would not earlier have been admitted.

Freud's writings were accepted by anthropologists only slowly. One reason for this was the emphasis laid by him on dream symbolism. Enthusiastic disciples of Freud, attempting to impress on native thinking a symbolism derived from the conventions of late nineteenth century Vienna, where Freud worked, documented the inacceptability of such interpretations. Anthropologists, however, had had too long experience with this sort of argument, for the study of many cultures had taught them that no specific form of any institution has universal scope.

Interestingly enough, the one book in which Freud purported to use anthropological materials, *Totem and Taboo*, did most to make anthropologists hostile to Freudian psychology. "The work," says Seligman, one of the first to realize the potential contribution of psychoanalysis to anthropology, "may be said to have irritated anthropologists rather than stimulated them; yet irritation doubtless has a useful aspect which cannot be ignored." [3] Freud had found, in probing the human psyche, that the attraction a mother holds for her son, named the Œdipus complex after the Greek drama *Oedipus Rex*, was paralleled, on the level of the unconscious, by a dual attitude toward the father. This was well documented in Freud's analytical materials, as arising out of infantile jealousy of the father's relationship to the mother; a jealousy, however, by no means untempered, since many bonds of affection existed at the same time between father and son. As a result of these findings, Freud advanced one of his most valuable concepts, that of *ambivalence*, whereby at any given moment one may, at the same time, be attracted to any given person or object and be repelled by it; loving and at the same time hating it.

Struck by the implications of this mechanism for an understanding of the human mind, Freud turned to other cultures for materials to test its universality and to probe its origins. But without firsthand knowledge of any society but his own, without even knowing what studies of nonliterate

[3] C. G. Seligman, 1932, p. 197.

peoples might throw light on his problem, he turned to secondary sources, compilations by writers trained and untrained. Furthermore, he did not seek comparative materials in these works, but evidences of origins, a quest now recognized as beyond the possibility of attainment.

The competition between a man and his sons, he held, arose out of a situation that he believed to have existed in the earliest days of man's life on earth. In the *urfamilie*, the primaeval family, the "Old Man" by right of brute force, ruled unquestioned, and all the women of the horde were his. As his sons grew older, they rebelled, and one day combined forces to murder their progenitor. Moreover, they made of his body a cannibalistic feast so as mystically to take his power for themselves. Returning to the women, now available to them, they held to their pact not to reveal what they had done. Their food, they said, had been an animal that was from then on to be so sacred that it must not be eaten. Hence the phenomenon of ambivalence in the human mind, manifested in the wider social scene by the totemic symbols of many peoples, since the totem is a symbol at once sacred and loved, and yet tabooed and thus to be avoided.

B. Malinowski's chief contribution to the psychology of culture was his demonstration that Freud's findings reflected the time and place he worked, and that in the setting of certain types of family relationships, the Œdipus complex, as Freud enunciated it, did not exist.[4] Malinowski, a brilliant field-worker, studied the natives of the Melanesian Trobriand Islands. Here the family structure is of the familiar type where descent is counted on the side of the mother, so that a child does not belong to his father's family at all. Malinowski, indeed, asserted that the Trobriand Islanders possess no knowledge of the role of the male in procreation, though this has been disputed. The point is not critical, however, for since the child belongs to his mother's family and not his father's, it is the mother's elder brother who directs the boy's life, thus releasing the father to be a friend and playmate. With the uncle as the "surrogate for society," as he has been termed, the one who punishes, who thwarts the child as the father does in Euroamerican families, Malinowski found many examples in unconsciously phrased statements, and in the dreams of these people, of reactions of the Œdipus variety directed against the mother's brother, but none against the father.

The significance of this demonstration was not that it invalidated an important element in the Freudian system. Rather, it came increasingly to be realized that it gave this system a wider significance than it could otherwise have. Freud's postulate that the personality structure is dynamic and not fixed, the result of the total experience of the individual, was seen to be basically sound. Malinowski's findings merely underscored the fact that the forms of personality disorders and their compensating mechanisms discovered by Freud to exist in certain circles of Viennese society at the end of the nineteenth century could not validly be expanded into universals. Realization of the need to strike deep into the memories of infancy in un-

---

[4] B. Malinowski, 1927.

derstanding the human personality, as we have observed, led to studies of children in various societies as a key to the problem. But these studies, it came to be recognized, could only be made in their full cultural context. No reaction of any human being could be understood without reference to its cultural framework. By the same token, the nature of many culturally sanctioned forms of behavior had also to be referred back to the common experiences of those who acted in accordance with them.

It is here that psychoanalysis joins behaviorism in establishing the unity of human experience, and thus forces the conclusion that culture cannot, in fact, be separated from people. Sapir, preeminent in this movement in anthropology, and one of the first to stress the importance of studying the individual in relation to his culture, has phrased the point tellingly: "In spite of the oft asserted impersonality of culture, . . . far from being in any real sense 'carried' by a community or a group as such, . . . [it is] discoverable only as the peculiar property of certain individuals, who cannot but give these cultural goods the impress of their own personality. . . . Culture is not, as a matter of sober fact, a 'given' at all. It is so only by a polite convention of speech. As soon as we set ourselves at the vantage point of the culture-acquiring child, . . . everything changes. Culture is then not something given but something to be gradually and gropingly discovered." [5]

3

THREE approaches to the study of the interaction between the individual and his cultural setting may be distinguished. The first, or *cultural configurational* approach, seeks to establish the dominant integrative patterns of cultures which encourage the development of certain personality types. The second, or *modal personality* approach, lays emphasis on the reactions of the individual to the cultural setting into which he is born. The aim of those who employ this method is to discern the typical personality structures which on the basis of common experience are to be found in a given society. The third, or *projective* approach, employs the various "projective" methods of analysis, especially the Rorschach series of ink blots to establish, by induction, the range of personality structures in a given society.

These three approaches represent no more than differing emphases on different aspects of the same problem, represented by the utilization of different methods of study. They are, in fact, so closely interrelated that for a student to frame his research in terms of a single one of them is the exception rather than the rule. They are perhaps best described as successive steps taken in the development of concern with the psycho-anthropological problem of the role of the individual in culture and the impact of culture on the human personality. The differences between them may be briefly phrased as follows: 1. *The cultural configurational approach is essentially ethnological.* The reference here is always to institutions, to the cultural

---

[5] E. Sapir, 1934, pp. 412–4.

patterns that set the framework within which the predominant personality structures, as manifested by the group, develop. 2. *The modal personality approach lays its stress on the individual.* It derives from the application of psychoanalysis to the comparative study of broad problems of social adjustment. It represents a development out of the conceptual and methodological scheme of Freud. The contrasts between these two approaches may be said to arise out of their sources, the first from conventional ethnology, the second from orthodox Freudianism. 3. *Both the individual and culture figure where projective techniques are used.* Here the technique employed is the outstanding factor. The use of a standardized test to which all results can be referred provides a methodological tool to assess the personality structures of the individual members of a given group in terms of their enculturation to the institutions and values of their culture.

The cultural configurational attack is most often thought of as exemplified in the writings of R. Benedict and M. Mead, though one of its earliest and its most concise statements is that of E. Sapir, the source from which most anthropological study of the problem of the individual in his culture has stemmed. "The socialization of personality traits may be expected to lead cumulatively to the development of specific psychological biases in the cultures of the world," he wrote. "Thus Eskimo culture, contrasted with most North American Indian cultures, is extraverted; Hindu culture, on the whole corresponds to the world of the thinking introvert; the culture of the United States is definitely extraverted in character, with a greater emphasis on thinking and intuition than on feeling; and sensational evaluations are more clearly evident in the cultures of the Mediterranean area than in those of Northern Europe." [6] Though he states here that "such psychological characterizations of culture . . . in the long run . . . are inevitable and necessary," Sapir later gave over this approach as his interest moved from the classification of whole cultures in psychological terms to the dynamics of personality formation.

The contribution of Mead derives principally from her field researches in the Southwest Pacific.[7] One result of her first field study, made in Samoa, we have already had occasion to discuss. In Manus, an island off the New Guinea coast, she related the social conditioning of the individual to the sharp breaks between childhood and adult patterns of behavior, and described the tensions induced by the need to adjust to such sharply differing situations. Later she studied the personality types of men and women in three New Guinea societies. Here the conclusion reached was that it was culture that molded what had previously been held to be biologically determined patterns of dominance and submission between the sexes. In all these researches, individuals, it is true, were studied. But whether children or adults, the observations of their behavior were cast in terms of the overall patterns of the cultures in which they lived. The individual was conceived as the resultant of the socio-cultural forces to which he was subject, and thus disappeared in the group.

---

[6] E. Sapir, 1933, p. 87.
[7] M. Mead, 1939.

Culture and the Individual

The tendency to submerge the individual in studying differing psychological "sets" of different cultures also characterized the work of Benedict.[8] She drew on her own field research among the Zuñi Indians of the American Southwest, on Mead's researches, on those of Boas among the Kwakiutl Indians of British Columbia, and on Fortune's study of the inhabitants of Dobu in outlining the traits of the cultures which are used to exemplify the types she describes. These types she names Apollonian, which in broad terms can be equated with Sapir's introvertive, and Dionysian, the equivalent of the extraverted. The Zuñi Indians are given as an example of the first type. Their restraint in personal relations, submergence of the individual in the group, their slowness to anger, the absence of hysteria in their religious rites, are some of the traits held to mark them off as having this type of culture. On the other hand, the passion of the Kwakiutl and the suspicions of the Dobuans, the extravaganza of the rites that mark the economic waste of the Kwakiutl potlatch as a psychological adjustment to a frustrating situation, and the use of garden-magic in Dobu to extend the personality and establish the ego, are characteristics that cause these cultures to be classified as Dionysian.

The researches of Benedict and Mead were pioneer work. They were among the first to relate culture to the individual in accordance with a broad conceptual scheme, and to hint how considerably the enculturative experience could be expected to influence the character of persons who made up societies having different ways of life, and varied goals. The integrative nature of this process, wherein the human materials of thought and action were assimilated ever more closely to a prevailing body of traditions, was also stressed. Finally the role of custom in focussing behavior and attitudes so as to influence personality structures was clearly indicated.

On analysis, however, like all pioneer effort, this position proved to have the defects of its virtues. It was pointed out that, in stressing cultural types, the variation in individual behavior, within the limits of the sanctions set by a culture, was lost sight of. The question was raised whether all the institutions of any culture could be expected to be in accord with the overall pattern as provided by the Apollonian-Dionysian equation, or any other similar typological scheme. In the process of assigning cultures to these classifications, it was asked, must not the assumptions made by the observer and the selectivity of his observations as influenced by these assumptions dominate his judgment?[9] Papers by Li An-che on Zuñi, by Boas on the Kwakiutl, by Fortune on the Arapesh documented these reservations.[10] Li, a Chinese anthropologist, whose own physical traits made him inconspicuous among the Indians, found them, as people, to be quite different from the picture of themselves they had presented to white students. Boas observed how, among the Kwakiutl, the chief who indulged in the frenzied boasting of the potlatch could also, within his family, debase himself before the child who would one day be his successor. And Fortune pointed out that in one

[8] R. Benedict, 1934.

[9] For a discussion of the methodological problem involved here, see Chapter 35 below.

[10] Cf. Li, 1937, pp. 62–9; F. Boas, 1936, p. 267; R. F. Fortune, 1939, pp. 36–8.

of the New Guinea tribes studied by Mead, the Arapesh, the conception that there is little aggression shown either by males or females required modification in the light of materials indicating that this people had well-established patterns of warfare.

The influence of the cultural configurationist point of view is, however, to be seen in the next development in this field, wherein, as has been indicated, certain psychoanalytic concepts were used to account for the differences in the personalities of peoples living in societies where different ways of life prevail. The Kardiner-Linton postulate of the "basic personality structure," held to prevail in each society, may be regarded as an extension and refinement of the Benedict-Mead hypothesis. Basic personality structure, it is true, is conceived as a norm and not treated as a type, and is derived from the emphasis laid on the study of the individual. Yet stress placed on the varied influences that differing institutions of different cultures exert in the process of personality formation shows how this earlier work made available to the psychoanalyst, Kardiner, a sense of the possible variation in human institutions as a primary factor in explaining why peoples differ.[11]

The initial statement of the basic personality concept was made in a volume by Kardiner, to which Linton contributed a foreword and reports of his ethnographic researches in Madagascar and the Marquesan Islands. These provided the materials from which the hypothesis derived. Our discussion of it here will follow its exposition in this volume. Though more cultures have been studied from the point of view set forth there, little alteration has been made in the underlying theoretical postulates, except that its use as a tool to aid in historical analysis, as well as in understanding the personality orientations in a given culture at a given moment, has been explored.

The concept of culture, derived by Kardiner, is of interest. "Whenever we find . . . organized collections of human beings, we find some habitual regularity and organization of interrelations among the various individuals; we find also organized ways of dealing with the outer world in order to derive from it satisfactions essential to life; furthermore, we find organized ways of dealing with the processes of birth, growth, development, maturity, decline and death, with due regard for differences in age and sex. Whenever there is a persistence or transmission of these organized methods, we have a *culture*."[12] This total mode of life is envisaged as a series of institutions. An institution is defined as "any fixed mode of thought or behavior held by a group of individuals" which can be communicated, is generally accepted, and the violation of which causes disturbance. It is the reaction of the individual to the institution that produces the resultant behavior we call the personality. Institutions are classified as primary and secondary. The primary institutions arise out of the "conditions which the individual cannot control"—food, sex, various training disciplines. The secondary ones are derived from the satisfaction of needs and the release of tensions created by the primary institutions, and are exemplified by the deity that, for a people,

[11] Cf. A. Kardiner, 1944, p. 7.
[12] A. Kardiner, 1939, p. 5.

resolves the anxieties created by their need for assurance of a continued food supply. What distinguishes this approach from its predecessor is thus its dynamic character, since the basic personality structure is derived from a consideration of the institutions and their effect on people in one culture after another.

The data employed to document this hypothesis were those derived from the probing, by Kardiner, of various field-workers so as to cause them to bring out of their field experience materials which, when organized, would throw light on the personalities of the peoples they had studied. Such materials every field-worker has, but rarely publishes—casual observations of nursing practices, how a man behaved in a quarrel, the playthings of children, gossip about why a couple in the village failed to make the customary adjustment in marriage. The stress laid on the institutions centering about the food-quest and social structure, as well as on sex customs, represented a distinct advance over the conventional psychoanalytic preoccupation with data restricted to this last category. Objections, however, were raised to the slighting of elements in culture not related to its socioeconomic problems, such as aesthetic aspects, or the phases of religion concerned with other matters than the food quest and family continuity.

The study carried on by Du Bois in the island of Alor was designed to provide comprehensive field data that could be used to test the basic personality hypothesis. The assumptions underlying this research make clear the extension of the Kardiner position it represents: "First, there is a psychic substructure, perhaps physiologically determined, which is common to mankind. Second, this may be further elaborated by individual, innate personality trends. Third, these potentialities are acted upon by common cultural pressures and result in central tendencies to which the term *modal personality* has been assigned." [13] To achieve this, techniques of "psycho-cultural synthesis" are used—"cultural analyses, combined with the better established psychological processes of the analytical school."

The facts gathered from the Melanesian Alorese who were the subjects of the study indicate how this synthesis was sought. Details of infant care, early and late childhood, adolescence, marriage, sex, and the psychological aspects of religion were studied in addition to the more general ethnographic research into the customs of the people. Eight autobiographies were obtained, four of men and four of women, and these persons were encouraged to recount their dreams when meeting with the ethnographer at daily sessions. Children's drawings were collected, Porteus maze tests, and free association tests administered, and thirty-seven Rorschach protocols were recorded. On the basis of these data, Kardiner evaluated the personalities of the subjects in the light of their cultural setting, and these conclusions were checked by independent evaluation of the Rorschach tests by an expert in Rorschach analysis. That the correspondence in these independent evaluations of a field-worker's data, gathered to study the culture-personality equation, were as numerous as they proved to be, indicates that fruitful

---

[13] C. Du Bois, 1944, p. 5.

cooperation between anthropology and psychiatry is to be expected in further research. It also points toward the advisability of cross-disciplinary training to make it possible for the same individual to carry on the various phases of research and analysis demanded by this method of psycho-cultural synthesis.

It is here that the use of the Rorschach and perhaps other "projective" techniques will prove to be most effective. Hallowell has made the most consistent use of this method, and we may with profit cite his exposition of its usefulness in the study of individuals in different cultures, wherein he summarizes the nature of the test, how it is employed, and its potential contribution to this problem.[14] As described by Hallowell, the "raw data for personality appraisal in the Rorschach technique are obtained from the verbal responses the subject gives to a standard series of ten representationally indefinite but symmetrically structured ink-blots, presented to him one by one in a set order. Five of the blots are entirely black, but with variegated tonal values, three are in colors, and two combine black with red. . . . By means of an initial suggestion that he say what they might be, the subject is motivated to invest the stimulus fields successively set before him with representational values, rather than to see them as meaningless forms or empty designs. Whatever he says is written down by the administrator of the test." These ink-blots, which were standardized after much experimentation, permit through this process of interpretation—much after the manner we may see a horse's head in a cloud of the summer sky—that the subject express himself in ways of his own choosing. That is, "it is *he* who projects meaning into objectively meaningless forms; it is *he* who gives few or many answers, selects the whole card or a part of it for interpretation, makes use of the color or ignores it. . . ." This is why such tests are called *projective*. It is this process of projecting meaning into forms otherwise meaningless that permits the investigator, through analyzing the results, to reach his conclusions as to the personality structure of the individuals he is studying.

The question that immediately arises is whether the interpretation derived from subjects in the Euroamerican cultural scene can be applied to those who live in other cultures. It was even held questionable whether the tests could be administered to such persons at all, in the light of language and other difficulties. This has been answered by the fact that it has been successfully administered among many different peoples. Hallowell himself gave it to 151 Saulteaux Indians. It has been used among a number of other Indian groups, while Moroccans, Alorese (as mentioned), Fijians, Mexican Indians, and Sikhs have all taken it.

The possibility of employing standard interpretations to the protocols obtained from individuals outside Euroamerican culture has been heightened by the results of the independent evaluation of Rorschach tests, and descriptions of personalities, arrived at on the basis of Du Bois' data, and Hallowell's use of standard interpretations for the Saulteaux responses. A

---

[14] A. I. Hallowell, 1945b, pp. 198–9.

statement by Oberholzer, the Rorschach expert, who analyzed Du Bois' materials, makes the point. "The psychological meaning and significance of Rorschach's experimental factors have proved true for Europeans and Americans. I consequently applied these principles to a few Alorese and checked the results with the ethnographer's statements concerning the psychological background of these individuals. Many hours were spent assigning rank order to subjects for personality traits. The ethnographer worked from her knowledge of the individuals; I worked blind from the Rorschach materials. The degree of coincidence between our ranking was so high it left no doubt that the principles of the test could be applied cross-culturally." [15]

From the cross-cultural applicability of this method, a picture not only of the characteristic personality structures of different groups may eventually be expected, but a knowledge of the variation in such structures within each society as well. This is especially important since, given a sense of variability in psychological responses, we shall have a surer grasp on the problem of what constitutes normal and abnormal behavior. These are only two of the questions to which, as is pointed out by Hallowell, tests such as the Rorschach can make their contribution. "It is not a substitute for other methods of approach," he states in summary, "but it nicely supplements them." It, and others of its type, are thus an important addition to the battery of techniques which must be brought to bear on the problem of the interaction between the individual and the situation in which he finds adjustment or maladjustment.

4

It is apparent from the foregoing discussion that the attention which is given to the problem of the individual in his culture represents a major advance in the study of man. But it is equally apparent that the work done in this field represents only a beginning, and that methods, no less than documentation, are in their infancy. Let us briefly summarize what has been done, outline what needs to be done, and list some of the cautions experience suggests as anthropology treads the difficult path toward understanding this phase of its study of man.

That the problem has been well stated, and its significance clearly recognized, is itself a great gain for anthropological science. The fact that the life of man is one, that "culture" is a construct which describes the similar modes of conduct of those who make up a given society, that, in the final analysis, behavior is always the behavior of individuals however it may lend itself to summary in generalized terms, are some of the ways in which this realization is to be phrased. Although it makes the studying of culture even more complex than earlier researches have indicated, this only encourages us to feel that it is a clear step in the direction of reality.

It is a further gain that the problem is being attacked by the use of various

---

[15] C. Du Bois, op. cit., p. 589.

methods, and that its statement and the terminology applied to it are under continuous refinement. The ascription of personality _types_ to given cultures has given way to the study of the _range_ of personalities in a society. The concept of _basic_ personality has come to be thought of as _modal_ personality. And there has been the further recognition that even within a culture, characteristic personality sub-types may develop from the differing situations of the life of persons who play different roles in a given group. This is what Linton terms _status personalities,_ defined as "status-linked response configurations." [16]

An instance of how terminology and approach are undergoing refinement is to be had in the conceptual scheme for the study of the individual in culture advanced by Kluckhohn and Mowrer. These students distinguish, in the first place, "determinants" of behavior in the biological make-up of the individual, his physical environment, his social setting, and the culture in which he participates. Such determinants, they point out, are always present in human experience, and all personality structures must respond to them. In addition, however, other factors are in operation which cut across them. These other factors include, first of all, such universal experiences as birth, death, and the training for life in a social unit which give the human personality its broad configurations. Every person, moreover, is a member of a community, whence communal components of his personality are derived. He plays a role in his society in accordance with his status, which creates a role component. Finally, he is like no other member of his society, or even, perhaps, like no other human being anywhere, which gives him idiosyncrasies that mark him off from all other individuals. The table on the following page, drawn up by these students, illuminates the complexity of the problem, while suggesting a broadening of concept and terminology.

This table demonstrates the need, however, for the study of the individual in culture by other methods, in addition to the dominant psychiatric-psychoanalytic techniques that have been used in most studies. The great advance achieved by means of the concepts and methods of psychiatry and psychoanalysis has been indicated; yet it would be unrealistic not to recognize that they are techniques devised to be applied to individuals, and to achieve therapeutic ends. To adapt them to the study of societies composed of adjusted as well as maladjusted individuals involves a reorientation that has by no means been reached. The need for such a reorientation is to be seen in the classification of entire cultures in psychopathological terms such as paranoid or schizoid. It is to be seen in the description of behavior norms in terms of concepts derived from the study of neurotic states. It is to be seen in the extraordinary stress laid on analyzing cultures in terms of the frustrations they impose, and the comparative neglect of the channels to adjustment offered by every way of life.

A classification of the range of adjustment in a non-European group, given by Hallowell for his Saulteaux subjects on the basis of their Rorschach protocols, effectively makes the point we have just raised. Among these

---

[16] R. Linton, 1945, p. 130.

Culture and the Individual

DETERMINANTS	Universal	Communal	Role	Idiosyncratic
Biological	Birth, death, hunger, thirst, elimination, etc.	"Racial" traits, nutrition level, endemic diseases, etc.	Age and sex differences, caste etc.	Peculiarities of stature, physiognomy, glandular make-up, etc.
Physical-environmental	Gravity, temperature, time, etc.	Climate, topography, natural resources, etc.	Differential access to material goods, etc.	Unique events and "accidents" such as being hit by lightning, etc.
Social	Infant care, group life, etc.	Size, density, and distribution of population, etc.	Cliques, "marginal" men, etc.	Social "accidents" such as death of a parent, being adopted, meeting particular people, etc.
Cultural	Symbolism, taboo on incest and in-group murder, etc.	Traditions, rules of conduct and manners, skills, knowledge, etc.	Culturally differentiated roles	Folklore about accidents and "fate," etc.

people, who have to make extraordinarily severe adjustments because of frustrations induced by contact with the whites, the percentages were:

Well adjusted	10.7%
Adjusted	33.3%
Poorly adjusted	44.1%
Maladjusted	11.7%

In comparison, fifty percent of the Inland Indians who had had least contact with whites, were found to fall into the categories of "adjusted" and "well adjusted." Among those with most contacts, sixty percent were poorly adjusted or maladjusted, and this group also included the more extreme cases of failure to adapt.[18] From the point of view of the problem of understanding the interaction between the individual and his total setting, it is apparent that emphasis on the study of processes of adjustment is as essential as it is to discover the circumstances that make for maladjustment.

5

WHETHER the anthropologist can study the problem of personality in primitive societies without himself having been psychoanalyzed has been much discussed. One has not heard as much of whether the practising psycho-

---

[17] C. Kluckhohn and O. H. Mowrer, 1944, p. 4.
[18] A. I. Hallowell, 1945b, p. 208.

analyst concerned with cross-cultural studies must have first-hand experience of societies where sanctions, goals, systems of motivations and control are entirely different from his own. The fact is, however, that only a few of the psychoanalysts who have shown concern with the theoretical implications of these problems, have themselves conducted field research to test their hypotheses among groups outside the orbit of Euroamerican culture. This is almost as true, moreover, of students whose approach to the psychology of culture is that of academic psychology as it is of those who utilize the techniques and concepts of the analytic school.

One suggestion that has been advanced seems to offer a common-sense resolution of the difficulty which inheres in work on a problem that lies so broadly athwart two fields of science. "Some sort of immediate compromise" should be reached, it is stated, "in which anthropologist and psychologist will be willing each to learn as much as possible from the other and to define some of his problems and methods accordingly." [19] To the extent that some anthropologists have worked in psychological laboratories or have undergone analyses, and that some psychologists, especially in the more academic tradition, have tested their hypotheses in field research, this "immediate compromise" is being approached. Examples of this latter category, such as the studies by Dennis on Hopi children or by Campbell on the Negroes of the Virgin Islands may be cited. Yet much more cross-disciplinary research of this, and other kinds is needed, as can be seen from such a list of cross-disciplinary problems as that given by the psychologists Goodenough and Anderson. [20]

How illuminating field experience can be is to be seen from the following paragraph, taken out of a psychoanalyst's report of his initial experience with an Indian tribe: "When I asked F to tell me how she happened to become a shaman [i.e., a healer by the exercise of supernatural powers], she quickly and seriously said, 'This cost twice a dollar.' Anyone not prepared for the Yurok mentality could easily mistake this request for what it would mean among other Indian tribes, namely, an attempt to capitalize on what seems most interesting to the white man. Here, however, one receives the impression of a superindividual eagerness, a wish not for money but for the establishment of a certain ritual atmosphere. Like all activities of a higher importance, doctoring is highly paid among the Yurok: in American money, F receives as much as a psychiatrist (but has to return the fee when she is unsuccessful). Once the sanctity of the situation was established, a more intense level of Yurok experience opened up: F's seeming interest in money abruptly and surprisingly changed into 'pity and terror.' Soon she shed tears in recording how she was forced to become a doctor. However, we do well to restrain our sympathy until we understand more of the magic function of tears in Yurok culture." [21]

It is of importance also that the initial attack on the study of the individual in culture, from the point of view of the total configuration of the

---

[19] F. C. Bartlett, 1937, p. 402.

[20] F. L. Goodenough and J. E. Anderson, 1947, pp. 8–13.

[21] E. M. Erikson, 1943, p. 262.

Culture and the Individual

body of customs in which he lives, not be laid aside. Opler phrases this view as follows: "Out of the ethnologist's sojourn in the field are emerging two orders of problems and two sets of interests. One deals with total cultural patterns, those generalized and inclusive statements which any member of the group, whatever his own behavior and personality, would have to admit represent the traditions and recognized usages of his people. The other interest is that which . . . seeks to learn the relationship between the larger pattern of the culture and the world of intimate meanings, attachments and behavior patterns each individual builds up for himself." [22] The approach of cultural orientation is too fruitful to be lost through an exclusive emphasis on the study of the individual.

It is through a comprehension of these orientations that the importance of culturally sanctioned continuities and discontinuities in the process of growing up emerge. Such contrasts in our own culture, between the responsibility of the adult for his act and the lack of responsibility of the child, represent a patterned discontinuity that is by no means found in all cultures. It sets the stage for a difficult adjustment that each individual member of our society must make. Similarly, dominance of a father over his children, which is also the rule among ourselves, is to be contrasted to conventions where father and children are on a plane of relative equality. Growing up in a situation of father-child equality makes for no such discontinuity as exists in the father-dominance equation. This difference we would expect to find reflected in the personalities of those who live in the psychological atmosphere of the one type of society as against the other. [23]

How a study of the cultural setting may disclose psychological mechanisms that direct individual behavior, and channel aggressions through disciplined avenues of expression is to be seen in such an institution as the *apo* rite practised by the Ashanti of the Gold Coast, West Africa. During the *apo* ceremony, it is not only permitted, but held imperative that those in power hear the derision, reproaches, and imprecations of their subjects for the injustices they have committed. This, the Ashanti believe, assures that the souls of the rulers will not suffer harm by reason of the repressed ill will of those they have angered, which otherwise would cumulatively have the power to weaken, and even to kill them. The effectiveness of this obviously Freudian mechanism in releasing repressions calls for no elaboration. It clearly throws much light on how institutionalized forms of behavior correct imbalance in the development of the individual personalities involved. [24]

In a comparable manner, the concept of *fiofio* held by the Negroes of Dutch Guiana reveals the type of adjustment these people make to certain tensions that are always set up by group life. In this case, an unresolved quarrel between kindred or intimates is believed to exert its influence long after the fact of its occurrence has been erased from conscious thought. Let one party to the quarrel accept a gift or favor from the other, and illness or some misfortune will befall one or both of them. Only when, after con-

[22] M. E. Opler, 1938, p. 218.
[23] R. Benedict, 1938.
[24] R. S. Rattray, 1923, pp. 151–69.

59

sultation with a diviner, the cause has been revealed and the public cere-monial retraction, termed *puru mofo* ("withdraw from the mouth"), has been performed will the evil be removed. Otherwise, death is believed to result. "To have honest dislikes is natural enough and, says the native, these do a man no harm; it is only when quarrels are masked in surface friendli-ness and an ancient grudge is harboured that it is dangerous to make an exchange of belongings or accept any gesture of affection." [25]

Such socially sanctioned mechanisms that permit the release of inhibi-tions and the resolution of conflicts, are the means whereby the adjustment of the individual is, to a considerable degree, attained. They are aspects of those consenses of belief and behavior which, as elements in culture, con-stitute the matrix within which the personality structures of individuals develop, and in which they must function.

---

[25] M. J. Herskovits, 1934, p. 82.

CHAPTER 5

The Problem of Cultural Relativism

ALL peoples form judgments about ways of life that are different from their own. Where systematic study is undertaken, comparison gives rise to classification, and scholars have drawn many schemes for classifying ways of life. Moral judgments have been drawn regarding the ethical principles that guide the behavior and mold the value-systems of different peoples. Their economic and political structures, and their religious beliefs have been ranked in order of complexity, efficiency, desirability. Their art, music, and literary forms have been weighed.

It has become increasingly evident, however, that evaluations of this kind stand or fall with the acceptance of the premises from which they derive. But this is not the only reason. Many of the criteria on which judgment is based are in conflict, so that conclusions drawn from one definition of what is desirable will not agree with those based on another formulation.

A simple example will illustrate this. There are not many ways in which the primary family can be constituted. One man may live with one woman, one man may have a number of wives, one woman may have a number of husbands. But if we evaluate these forms on the basis of how they fulfil their function of perpetuating the group by assuring that the children are reared to adulthood, it is clear that they meet the pragmatic test. By the very fact of their existence, they prove that they perform their essential tasks. Otherwise, the societies wherein they function would not survive.

Such an answer will, however, by no means satisfy all those who have undertaken to study the problem of cultural evaluation. What of the status of the plural spouse, the moral questions inherent in the practice of monogamy as against polygamy, the adjustment of children raised in households where, for example, the mothers must compete in behalf of their offspring for the favors of a common husband? If monogamy is held to be the desired form of marriage, the responses to these questions are not conjectural. But when we consider these questions from the point of view of those who live in societies other than our own, the possibility of alternative answers, based on different conceptions of what is desirable, becomes clear.

Let us consider, for example, the life of a plural family in such a West African culture as that of Dahomey.[1] Here, within a compound, live a man

---

[1] Cf. M. J. Herskovits, 1938b, vol. I, pp. 137–55, 300–51.

and his wives. The man has his own house, as has each of the women, in consonance with the basic principle of African procedure that two wives cannot successfully inhabit the same quarters. The children of each wife live with their mother. Each wife in turn spends a native week of four days with the common husband, cooking his food, washing his cloths, sleeping in his house during this interval, and then making way for the next wife. Her children, however, remain in their mother's hut. With pregnancy, she drops out of this routine, and ideally, in the interest of her child's health and her own, does not resume her visits to her husband until the child has been born and weaned. This means a period of from three to four years, since infants are nursed two years and longer.

The compound, made up of these households, is a cooperative unit. The women who sell goods in the market or make pottery or have their gardens contribute to its support. This aspect, though of great economic importance, is secondary to the prestige that attaches to the larger unit, a prestige in which all its members share. This is why one often finds a wife not only urging her husband to acquire a second spouse but even aiding him by loans or gifts to make this possible. Since a woman's earnings are hers to dispose of and women as traders in the market enjoy high economic position in this polygamous society, there is an appreciable number who command substantial means in terms of the general economy, and can thus help a husband, if it is desired, to sustain the expenses incident upon each marriage.

That tensions arise between the women who inhabit a large compound goes without saying. Thirteen different ways of getting married have been recorded in this society, and in a large household those wives who are married in the same category tend to unite as against all others. Competition for the regard of the husband is also a factor, though this is as often in the interest of the children as for personal advantage. Rivalries are especially sharp when several wives try to influence the choice of an heir in favor of their own sons. Yet all the children of the compound play together, and the strength of the emotional ties between the children of the same mother more than compensates for whatever stresses may arise between brothers and sisters who share the same father but are of different mothers. Cooperation, moreover, is by no means absent among the wives. Many common tasks are performed in friendly unison, and there is solidarity in the interest of women's prerogatives, or where the status of the common husband, the father of their children, is threatened.

We may now return to the criteria to be applied in drawing judgments concerning polygamous as against monogamous families in the light of this portrayal of the Dahomean plural family. The family structure of Dahomey is obviously a complex institution. If we but consider one aspect of it, the many possible lines of personal relationships between the many individuals concerned, we see clearly how numerous are the ramifications of the reciprocal rights and obligations and, consequently, of areas of both security and conflict. Its effectiveness is, however, patent. It has, for untold generations, performed its function of rearing the young; more than this, the very size of the group gives it economic resources and a resulting stability that might well be envied by those who live under different systems of family organization. Moral values are always difficult to establish, but at least in this society marriage is clearly distinguished from casual sex relationships and from prostitution, which is also known to the Dahomeans. It is differentiated from them in its supernatural sanctions and in the prestige it confers, to say nothing of the economic obligations toward spouse and prospective offspring explicitly accepted by one who enters on a marriage.

Numerous problems of adjustment do present themselves in an aggregate of this sort. The clash of personalities is not to be underestimated where persons of different individual background are brought into such close and continuous contact. It does not call for much speculation to understand the plaint of the head of one large compound when he said, "One must be something of a diplomat if one has many wives." Yet the sly digs in proverb and song, and the open quarreling, are of no greater stress than that of any small rural community where people are also thrown closely together for long periods of time. Quarrels between co-wives are not greatly different from disputes over the back fence between neighbors. And Dahomeans who know European culture, when they argue for their system, stress the fact that it permits for the individual wife a spacing of her children that is in accord with the best precepts of modern gynecology.

Thus polygamy, when looked at from the point of view of those who practise it, is seen to hold values that are not apparent from the outside. A similar case can be made for monogamy, however, when it is attacked by those who are enculturated to a different kind of family structure. And what is true of a particular phase of culture such as this, is also true of others. Evaluations are *relative* to the cultural background out of which they arise.

2

THE principle of *cultural relativism* derives from a vast array of factual data, gained from the application of techniques in field study that have permitted us to penetrate the underlying value-systems of societies having diverse customs. This principle, briefly stated, is as follows: *Judgments are based on experience, and experience is interpreted by each individual in terms of his own enculturation.* In adducing this principle we touch on many fundamental questions that philosophers have long raised. The problem of value is one such question. Those who hold for the existence of fixed values will find materials in societies other than their own which necessitate extensive reinvestigation of their assumptions. Or, again, are there absolute moral standards, or do moral standards effectively channel conduct only insofar as they are in consonance with the orientations of a given people at a given period of their history? We even approach the problem of the ultimate nature of reality itself. Cassirer, in the passage we have quoted [2] holds that

---

[2] See p. 27, above.

reality can only be experienced through the symbolism of language. Is reality, then, not defined and re-defined by the ever-varied symbolisms of the innumerable languages of mankind?

Answers to problems such as these, in terms of the known facts that lead to a cultural relativistic position, represent one of the most profound, albeit one of the little explored contributions of anthropology to the analysis of man's place in the world. When we reflect that such intangibles as right and wrong, normal and abnormal, beautiful and plain are absorbed from infancy, as a person learns the ways of the group into which he is born, we see that we are dealing here with a process of first importance. Even the facts of the physical world are discerned through the enculturative screen, so that the perception of time, distance, weight, size, and other "realities" is mediated by the conventions of any given group.

No culture, however, is a closed system, a series of rigid molds to which the behavior of all members of a society must conform. In stressing the psychological reality of culture, it was made plain that a culture, as such, can *do* nothing. It is, in its very nature, but the summation of the behavior and habitual modes of thought of the persons who, at a given time and in a given place, make up a particular society. These persons, as individuals, though by learning and habit they conform to the ways of the group into which they have been born, nonetheless vary in their reactions to the situations of living they commonly meet. They vary, too, in the degree to which they desire change, as whole cultures vary. It is difficult for us, living in a culture where change is prized, to see the values in attitudes that stress stability as a desired end. This is but another way in which we see that the summation of behavior we call culture is flexible, not rigid, and holds many possibilities of choice within its larger framework. To recognize the values held to by a given people in no wise implies that they are a constant factor in the lives of succeeding generations of the same group. As Dewey has phrased it, "Whatever are the native constituents of human nature, the culture *of a period and group* is the determining influence in their arrangement."[3]

How the ideas of a people mediate their approach even to the physical world can be made plain by a few examples. Indians living in the southwestern part of the United States think in terms of *six* cardinal points rather than four. In addition to north, south, east and west, they include the directions "up" and "down." From the point of view that the universe is three-dimensional, these Indians are entirely realistic. Among ourselves, even in aeroplane navigation, where three dimensions must be coped with in a way not essential to those who keep to the surface of the earth, we separate direction from height in instruments and in our thinking about position. We operate, conceptually, on two distinct planes. One is horizontal ("We are traveling ENE"). One is vertical ("We are now cruising at 8000 feet"). It is rare even to hear "We are cruising ENE at 8000 feet" except in a pilot's

---

[3] J. Dewey, 1939, p. 18. (italics inserted)

report to headquarters where these and other psychologically disparate facts are given.

Or take a problem in the patterning of sound. We accept the concept of the wave-length, tune pianos in accordance with a mechanically determined scale, and are thus conditioned to what we call true pitch. Some persons, we say, have absolute pitch; that is, a note struck or sung at random will immediately be given its place in the scale. "That's B flat." A composition learned in a given key, when transposed, will deeply trouble such a person, though those who are musically trained but do not have true pitch will enjoy such a transposed work, if the *relation* of each note to every other has not been disturbed. Let us assume that it is proposed to study whether this ability to identify a note is an inborn trait, found among varying but small percentages of individuals in various societies. The difficulty of probing such a question appears immediately once we discover that but few peoples have fixed scales, and none other than ourselves has the concept of true pitch! Those living in cultures without mechanically tuned and true instruments are free to enjoy notes that are as much as a quarter-tone "off" as we would say. As for the patterned progressions in which the typical scales and modal orientations of any set of musical conventions are set, the number of systems, each of which is consistent within its own limits, is infinite.

The principle that judgments are derived from experience which is the result of the enculturative process, has a sure psychological foundation. This has been best expressed by Sherif in his development of the hypothesis of "social norms." His experiments are critical and fundamental, and his accessory concept of the "frame of reference," the background to which experience is referred, has become standard in social psychology. Because of its importance for an understanding of cultural differences, the work he did in testing his hypothesis that "experience appears to depend always on *relations*" may be briefly indicated.

The subjects were introduced into a dark room where a dim light, the duration of which was mechanically controlled, appeared and disappeared when an electric key was pressed. Some subjects were brought into the room, first alone and later as members of groups, while others were exposed to the group situation before they were tested individually. Though the light was a fixed one, the autokinetic response to a situation like this is such that the subject perceives movement where there is none, since being in a room that is perfectly dark, he has no fixed point from which to judge motion. The phenomenon is well known, and by no means restricted to the experimental laboratory. It occurs "whenever a visual stimulus object lacks a spatial frame of reference."

When the subject was seated and pressed his key, the stationary light was exposed for two seconds, after which the subject reported how far it seemed to him the light had moved—for he did not know it was fixed. One hundred judgments were obtained from each subject *individually*. These conclusively demonstrated that individuals subjectively establish "a range of extent and a point (a standard or norm) within that range which is peculiar to the individual" when no objective standard is available to them, and that in repetitions of the experiment the established range is retained.

In the group situation, where two and three individuals experienced this stimulus simultaneously, judgments of the extent of movement by the light were spoken by each subject. The effect of this was gradually cumulative, so that the diversity of individual ideas about the distance the light was presumed to have moved became gradually less. This was more marked when the subject began in the group situation, than when he first worked by himself. But each group established a norm peculiar to itself. The conclusion reached was stated as follows: "When a member of a group faces the same situation subsequently, *alone,* after once the range and norm of his group have been established, he perceives the situation in terms of the range and norm that he brings from the group situation."

The general principle that was advanced on the basis of these results, and those of many other psychological experiments that have a bearing on this problem, may be given in the words of Sherif: "The psychological basis of the established social norms, such as stereotypes, fashions, conventions, customs, and values, is the formation of common frames of reference as a product of the contact of individuals. Once such frames of reference are established and incorporated in the individual they enter as important factors to determine or modify his reactions to the situations he will face later—social, and even non-social, at times, especially if the stimulus field is not well structured" [4]—that is, if the experience is one for which precedents in accustomed behavior are lacking.

Numerous instances of how these norms vary are to be found in the anthropological literature. They are so powerful that they can flourish even in the face of what seems to the outsider an obvious, objectively verifiable fact. Thus many peoples have conventions of relationship that, while recognizing the role of both father and mother in procreation, count descent on but one side of the family. In such societies, it is common for incest lines to be so arbitrarily defined that "first cousins" as we would say, on the mother's side, call each other brother and sister and regard marriage with one another with horror. Yet marriage within the same degree of biological relationship on the father's side may be held not only desirable, but sometimes mandatory. This is because two persons related in this way are by definition not considered blood relatives.

The very definition of what is normal or abnormal is relative to the cultural frame of reference. As an example of this, we may take the phenomenon of possession as found among African and New World Negroes. The supreme expression of their religious experience, possession, is a psychological state wherein a displacement of personality occurs when the god "comes to the head" of the worshiper. The individual thereupon is held to be the deity himself. He often exhibits a complete transformation in his personality; facial expression, motor behavior, voice, physical strength, and the character of

---

[4] M. Sherif, 1936, pp. 32, 92–106.

his utterances are startlingly different from what they are when he is "himself."

This phenomenon has been described in pathological terms by many students whose approach is non-anthropological, because of its surface resemblance to cases in the records of medical practitioners, psychological clinicians, psychiatrists, and others. The hysteria-like trances, where persons, their eyes tightly closed, move about excitedly and presumably without purpose or design, or roll on the ground, muttering meaningless syllables, or go into a state where their bodies achieve complete rigidity, are not difficult to equate with the neurotic and even psychotic manifestations of abnormality found in Euroamerican society.

Yet when we look beneath behavior to meaning, and place such apparently random acts in their cultural frame of reference, such conclusions become untenable. For *relative to the setting in which these possession experiences occur, they are not to be regarded as abnormal at all,* much less psychopathological. They are *culturally* patterned, and often induced by learning and discipline. The dancing or other act of the possessed persons are so stylized that one who knows this religion can identify the god possessing a devotee by the behavior of the individual possessed. Furthermore, the possession experience does not seem to be confined to emotionally unstable persons. Those who "get the god" run the gamut of personality types found in the group. Observation of persons in New World Negro groups who are interested in this religion and frequent the cults, yet who, in the idiom of worship "have nothing in the head" and thus never experience possession, seems to show that they are far less adjusted than those who do get possessed. Finally, the nature of the possession experience in these Negro cultures is so disciplined that it may only come to a given devotee under particular and seemingly arbitrary circumstances. In West Africa and Brazil the gods come only to those who have been designated in advance by the priest of their group, who lays his hands on their heads. In Haiti, for an initiate not a member of the family group giving a rite to become possessed at a ceremony, is considered extremely "bad form" socially and a sign of spiritual weakness, for this is taken as evidence that the god has not been properly propitiated, and is therefore not under the control of his worshiper.

The terminology of psychopathology has been readily applied to these states of possession. Such designations as hysteria, autohypnosis, compulsion, have come to rest easily on the tongue. Employed solely as descriptive terms, their use in technical analysis of the possession phenomenon may be of some utility. But the connotation they carry of psychic instability, emotional imbalance, departure from normality recommends the use of other words that do not invite such a distortion of cultural reality. For in these Negro societies the interpretation given behavior under possession—the meaning this experience holds for the people—falls entirely in the realm of understandable, predictable, *normal* behavior. This behavior is known and recognized by all members as something which may come to any one of them. and is to be welcomed not only for the psychological security that derives from assurances of oneness with the powers of the universe it affords, but also for the status, economic gain, aesthetic expression, and emotional release it vouchsafes the devotee.

3

THE primary mechanism that makes for the evaluation of culture is *ethnocentrism*. Ethnocentrism is the point of view that one's own way of life is to be preferred to all others. Flowing logically from the process of early enculturation, most individuals have this feeling about their own culture, whether they verbalize it or not. Outside the stream of Euroamerican culture, particularly among nonliterate peoples, this is taken for granted rather than phrased in any precise terms. In this form, ethnocentrism is to be viewed as a factor making for individual adjustment and social integration. For the strengthening of the ego in terms of an identification with one's own group, whose ways are implicitly accepted as best, is all-important. It is when, as in Euroamerican culture, ethnocentrism is rationalized and made the basis of programs of action detrimental to the well-being of other peoples that it gives rise to serious problems.

The ethnocentrism of nonliterate peoples is best illustrated in their myths, folk-tales, proverbs, and linguistic habits. It is manifest in many tribal names whose meaning in their respective languages signifies "human beings." The inference that those to whom the name does not apply are outside this category is, however, rarely, if ever, explicitly made. Yet this gives the greater significance to the deeply rooted attitudes toward one's own group as against all others that such usages reflect. When the Suriname Bush-Negro, shown a flashlight, admires it and then quotes the proverb, "White man's magic isn't black man's magic," he is merely reaffirming his faith in his own culture. He is pointing out that the stranger, for all his mechanical devices, would be lost in the Guiana jungle without the aid of his Bush-Negro friends, at ease amidst its dangers.

A myth of the origin of human races, told by the Cherokee Indians of the Great Smoky Mountains gives another instance of this kind of ethnocentrism. These Indians, of course, know whites and Negroes. Like all Indians, they are brown-skinned, and, as in all mythologies, the acts of supernatural beings once performed are irrevocable. As in most mythologies, also, man is the supreme achievement of the Creator, who in this instance went about creating him by first fashioning and firing an oven and then, from the dough he had prepared, shaping three figures in human form. He placed the figures in the oven, and waited for them to get done. But his impatience to see the result of this, his crowning experiment in the work of creation, was so great that he removed the first figure too soon. It was sadly underdone—pale, an unlovely color. But for better or worse, there it was, and from it are descended the white people. His second figure had fared well. The timing was accurate, the form all he had envisaged. Richly browned, it pleased him in every way, this figure that was to be the ancestor of the Indians. He so admired it, indeed, that he neglected to take out of the oven the third form, until he smelled it burning. He threw open the door, only to find this last one charred and black. It was regrettable, but there was nothing to be done; and this was the first Negro.[5]

This is the more usual form that ethnocentrism takes among many peoples—a gentle insistence on the good qualities of one's own group, without any drive to extend this attitude into the field of action. With a point of view such as this, the objectives, sanctioned modes of behavior, and value systems of peoples with whom one's own group comes into contact can be considered in terms of their desirability, then accepted or rejected without any reference to absolute standards. For there are ways of culture that are good for one group and not necessarily good for another; what another group may feel is not good is not of necessity bad for yet a fourth. That differences in the manner of achieving commonly sought objectives may be permitted to exist without a judgment being entered on them, involves a reorientation in thought for those of us who are in the Euroamerican tradition, because in this tradition, a difference in belief or behavior too often implies something is worse, or less desirable, and must be changed.

The assumption that the cultures of nonliterate peoples are inferior to our own is the end-product of a long series of developments in our intellectual history. It is not often recalled that the concept of progress, that strikes so deep into our thinking, is relatively recent. It is, in fact, a unique product of our culture. It is a part of the same historic stream that developed the scientific tradition, and that developed the machine.

It was the controls provided by science and the machine technology that gave Europe and America the final word in debates about cultural superiority. "He who makes the gun-powder wields the power," runs a Dahomean proverb. There is no rebuttal to an argument, backed by cannon, advanced to a people who can defend their position with no more than spears or bows and arrows, or even a flint-lock gun. Technological superiority, of itself, carries considerable conviction even though it is not as convincing as we sometimes think. Anyone can see that an automobile can fulfil its function of traversing distance more effectively and with less expenditure of effort than a man on horseback or on foot. What we too often fail to recognize is that superiority of this demonstrable kind will not necessarily convince a person from another culture that an art foreign to his own is also preferable, or that monotheism is better than polytheism. He may even continue to use a hoe long after the plow has been made known to him, just because he prefers this less efficient instrument. He may, of course, wonder about these foreign conventions if they are urged on him often enough, and with enough force. If he fails to find a satisfactory answer to his questions, demoralization first, and eventually deculturation sets in. Acceptance of European beliefs and values, coupled with the withholding of opportunity to achieve an equitable way of life under them—the most common form, over the world,

---

[5] This unpublished myth was told Dr. F. M. Olbrechts of Brussels, Belgium in the course of field-work among the Cherokee. His having made it available is gratefully acknowledged.

of the contradictory situation that ensues on the imposition of Euroamerican controls—induces bewilderment, despair, and cynicism.

With the possible exception of technological aspects of life, the proposition that one way of thought or action is better than another is exceedingly difficult to establish on the grounds of any universally acceptable criteria. Let us take food as an instance. Food is needed by the human organism, and no people who do not provide adequate foodstuffs for themselves can survive. Cultures are equipped differently for the production of food, so that some peoples eat more than others. The point is, however, that even when on the subsistence level, there is no people who do not hold certain potential foodstuffs to be unfit for human consumption. Milk, which figures importantly in our diet, is rejected as food by the peoples of southeastern Asia. Beef, a valued element of the Euroamerican cuisine, is regarded with disgust by Hindus. Nor need compulsions be this strong. The thousands of cattle that range the East African highlands, as we shall see, are wealth to be preserved, and not to be consumed as food. Only the cow that dies is eaten —a practice that, though abhorrent to us, has apparently done no harm to those who have been following it for generations.

Totemic and religious taboos set up further restrictions on available foodstuffs, while the refusal to consume many otherwise edible and nourishing substances is simply based on the circumstance of enculturative conditioning. So strong is this conditioning that food consumed unwittingly in contravention of it may induce such physiological reactions as vomiting and illness. All young animals provide succulent meat, but the religious abhorrence of the young pig by the Mohammedan is no stronger than the secular rejection of puppy steaks or colt chops by ourselves. Ant larvae, insect grubs, locusts —all of which have caloric values and vitamin content—when roasted or otherwise cooked, or even when raw, are regarded by many peoples as delicacies. We never eat them, however, though they are equally available to us. On the other hand, some of the same peoples who feed on these with gusto regard substances that come out of tin cans as unfit for human consumption.

4

CULTURES are most often evaluated by the use of the designations "civilized" and "primitive." These terms have a deceptive simplicity, and attempts to document the differences implied in them in order to draw precise definitions have proved to be of unexpected difficulty. The distinctions embedded in this set of opposed terms are, however, of special importance for us. "Primitive" is the word commonly used to describe the peoples with whom anthropologists have been traditionally most concerned, the groups whose study has given cultural anthropology most of its data.

The word "primitive" came into use when anthropological theory was dominated by an evolutionary approach that equated living peoples, outside the stream of European culture, with the early inhabitants of the earth.

The Problem of Cultural Relativism

These early inhabitants, or primaeval men—the first human beings—may justifiably be regarded as "primitive" in the etymological sense of the word. It is quite another matter to call present-day peoples by the same term. In other words, *there is no justification for regarding any living group as our contemporary ancestors.*

The conception implicit in such usage pervades our thinking more than we realize. It colors many of the judgments we draw about the way of life of native peoples with whom the expansion of European and American controls have brought us into contact. When we speak or write of the living customs of American Indian or African or South Seas peoples in the past tense, we imply that their customs are in some way earlier than our own. We are treating their cultures as though they were unchanging when, as we have seen, one of the basic generalizations about culture is that no body of custom is static. No matter how conservative a people may be, we find on investigation that their way of life is not the same as it was in earlier times. If, then, we recognize the universality of cultural change, understand that all existing groups of men are descended from a single source, and think of the hundreds of thousands of years our common ancestors have lived on earth, we can but conclude that the past of all groups reaches back for untold generations. During this time, as remains of the past dug from the earth give ample evidence, continuous, though perhaps slow change was the rule. Hence we must conclude that no group that exists today lives either as its ancestry, or our own, lived.

With the passage of time, the word "primitive" has gathered other connotations that are evaluative rather than descriptive. Primitive peoples are said to have simple cultures. They are believed to be childlike, naive, or unsophisticated. One widely accepted hypothesis, that we will consider shortly, holds that primitive peoples are unable to appraise reality except in terms of a special kind of mental process. Perhaps as a summation of all these, it is asserted that primitive cultures are inferior in quality to the historic civilizations. Such terms as "savage" or "barbarous" are applied to them in this sense, deriving from a presumed evolutionary sequence of "savagery," "barbarism," and "civilization."

One example, out of the many that might be cited to make this point, can be taken from the extended investigation into the nature and processes of change in civilization by the historian A. J. Toynbee. Defining a civilization as "a field of study which appears to be intelligible within its own limits," and being concerned with the "base-line" of "the modern Western national community," he speaks of those peoples outside this line as the "external proletariat," whose contacts with a "civilization" tend to debase it. In the United States, the "external proletariat" was the Indian. The powerful influence exerted by the Indian in modifying the ways of life of the American frontiersmen, through the "barbarization" of European custom, as he terms it, astonishes Toynbee. "When we remind ourselves of the initial disparity— and this in spiritual culture as well as in corporate physical strength—between the incomers from Europe who have built this new nation up and the American aborigines whom they have swept from their path, . . . we shall be more astonished than ever at the strength of the influence exerted by a barbarism which was continually 'on the run' upon an invading civilization . . . which was animated by the 'driving-power,' and backed by the weight, of the whole body social of Western Christendom in its European homeland." Or again, in speaking of the influence of the "barbarians of West Africa" on modern art, Toynbee says, "This triumph of a Negro art in the northern states of America and in the western countries of Europe represents a much more signal victory for Barbarism than the progressive barbarization of the Hellenic image and superscription on the staters of King Philip's mintage in the course of the long and slow journey of this Hellenic coin-type from the banks of the Strymon to the banks of the Thames in Ultima Thule. To the layman's eye the flight to Benin [a center of African art] and the flight to Byzantium seem equally unlikely to lead the latter-day Western artist to the recovery of his lost soul." [6]

For all the philosophical grounding and immense scholarship in the massive work from which these citations are taken, it is apparent that assertions such as these but document the biases of the writer. We shall see that borrowing, a basic mechanism of cultural interchange, results inevitably from any contact of peoples. Quite as often as not a dominant group are deeply influenced by the customs of those over whom they rule. What was the "initial disparity in spiritual culture" that matched the power of guns and bullets brought to bear by the "incomers from Europe" against the Indians? Evidence is vast that the portrayal of the savage as a creature living in anarchism, without moral restraint, without sensibilities, is a vulgar caricature. What happened in America does not "astonish" the scientific student of culture. The mutual borrowing by colonists of Indian customs, by Indians of European custom should be taken for granted, despite disparity in size of the groups and their power and even capacity to survive under attack.

Some of the characteristics widely held to distinguish "primitive" or "savage" ways of life are open to serious question. What, for example, is a "simple" culture? The aboriginal Australians, customarily held to be one of the most "primitive" peoples on earth, have a kinship terminology and a method of counting relationship based on it so complex that for many years it defied the attempts of students to analyze it. It puts to shame our own simple series of relationship terms, where we do not even distinguish between paternal and maternal grandparents, or older or younger brother, and call literally dozens of relatives by the same word, "cousin." The natives of Peru, before the Spanish conquest, made tapestries of finer weave, dyed in colors less subject to deterioration, than any of the deservedly vaunted Gobelin tapestries. The world-view of the Africans, which has so much in common with the esteemed Hellenic world-view, the epic myths of the Polynesians, impress their complexities on all who take the trouble to become acquainted with them. These, and untold other examples, show that "primitive" folk do not have ways of life that are necessarily simple. Such instances also demonstrate that "primitive" peoples are neither childlike, nor naive,

---

[6] A. J. Toynbee, 1934–9, vol. V, pp. 373, 479–80, 482.

nor unsophisticated, to cite favored adjectives that are often used by those who have either had no first-hand experience with such peoples, or have not taken the trouble to come to know them through reading contemporary accounts of their ways of life.

That "primitive" peoples fail to distinguish between reality and the supernatural, as the theory concerning their presumed "prelogical mentality," put forward by the French philosopher L. Lévy-Bruhl [7] would hold, is similarly proved untenable by the facts. For the facts about many cultures demonstrate that there is no people who *at times* fail to think in terms of objectively provable causation, and none who also, *at times,* do not indulge in explanations that relate a fact to an *apparent* cause. What the comparative study of culture, based on first-hand contact with many peoples, has taught is that all peoples think in terms of certain premises that are taken largely for granted. Whatever the chain of reasoning employed, the logic is dictated by these assumptions. Granting the premises, the logic is inescapable.

In developing the theory of primitive mentality, much is made of the prevalence of magic, or of beliefs called totemism, wherein a kinship group acknowledges descent from a common animal or plant ancestor, whose name they take. Students who have studied this latter phenomenon in the field are not impressed with the argument that such beliefs keep the natives from drawing clear-cut distinctions between an animal and those who believe they are related to it. Furthermore, most of the life of any people is lived on a plane where ideas of causation, or explanations of the universe enter but rarely. In these homely aspects of life, what we would call a "hard-headed sense of reality" is manifested. Thus, except for the names, the following passage from the autobiography of a Navaho Indian, telling of the last illness of the narrator's father, rings entirely familiar to ears accustomed to the reasoning of a mechanistic tradition:

Old man Hat said, "I don't think I'll get well. I don't think I'll live long. That's how I feel about myself, because of the way I look now. I look at myself, and there's nothing on me, no flesh on me any more, nothing but skin and bones. That's why I don't think I'll live long. . . . About eating, you know I can't eat anything that's hard, only things that are soft, something I can swallow. But I don't take much, only two or three swallows. But I drink plenty of water." Choclays Kinsman said, "Even though you're that way, my older brother, you'd better keep eating all the time. By doing that it'll give you strength. If you don't you'll surely get weak. Even though you're so weak now and not able to eat, try to eat and swallow something. Somehow or other you might get over your illness. If you quit eating food, then you'll sure be gone." That's what he said, and then he left, and I went out with the herd.[8]

We readily recognize the common sense reasoning in this passage. Let us look to another instance where the explanation of a phenomenon is based on a premise at variance with what we regard as scientific fact. We take as our instance a widely spread West African belief that the youngest child is sharper of wit than his older brothers and sisters. This belief is based on the

---

[7] L. Lévy-Bruhl, 1923, 1926.
[8] W. Dyk, 1938, p. 269.

observation that children tend to resemble their parents, and the fact, further observed, that as a man or woman grows older, he grows in experience. These facts may seem unrelated to us, but not to the West African. He observes that when a first child is born, its parents are younger and therefore less knowledgeable than when its later brothers and sisters appear on the scene. He reasons that greater age permits them to pass on to their younger, and especially their youngest child, a surer, more alert awareness. Such a child is thus expected to surpass his older siblings in astuteness. The *logic* of this reasoning is impeccable. It is with the *premises* that we must differ, if we would challenge the conclusion.

In truth, it must be recognized that all human beings, ourselves included, think "prelogically" at times. The pattern of scientific thought, of reasoning from objectively controlled causes to their effects, on which we pride ourselves, is followed by no more than relatively few persons in our culture. Nor do these persons think logically all the time. On special occasions, when they are actually at work in their laboratories, they employ the rigorous logic of science. But outside it, quite other categories of reasoning come into play, as when a scientist thinks in terms of "luck" in social ventures, or pays homage to some symbolic representation of power or grace.

The assumption that all those called "primitives" or "savages" have many characteristics in common when they are contrasted to "civilized" peoples, is another expression of the tendency to evaluate cultures. In actuality, the range of behavior among all those many peoples termed "primitive" is much greater than among those few called "civilized." Thus in the economic area of life, we find "primitive" peoples with money economies like "civilized" ones, others who practise barter, and still others who are economically self-sufficient and do not trade at all. Numerous marriage forms and family types, including monogamy, are found in "primitive" societies. Some have totemism, but more do not. Some have a clan system, many do not. Some count descent through both parents, as we do; some count it only on the father's side; some count it on the mother's. And so we could continue with institutions of all kinds, and much customary behavior, meeting always with variety. Whatever the word "primitive" means, then, it comprehends no unity of custom, tradition, belief or institution.

In anthropological works, the words "primitive" or "savage"—the latter being used mainly as a synonym for "primitive" by English writers—do not have the connotation they possess in such a work as Toynbee's, or in other non-anthropological writings. As for the word "barbaric" most anthropologists do not employ it at all. Anthropologists merely use the word "primitive" or "savage" to denote peoples outside the stream of Euroamerican culture, who do not possess written languages. By reiterating this meaning, it was hoped that all other connotations might be sloughed off, and that it would no longer convey such meanings as simple, or naive, or serve as a catch-all to describe, except in the single matter of absence of writing, such differing civilizations as those of the Siberian reindeer herders or the Lunda empire of the Congo.

Several terms to replace "primitive" have been suggested. "Non-historic," which is one of these, has not found much acceptance. It implies that absence of written history is the equivalent of having no history at all, which, of course, cannot be said of any people who exist in time. "Pre-literate" has found more favor, but the objection to be raised here is that the prefix *pre-* carries a meaning of time that infers prediction. It is, in essence, a carry-over of the "contemporary ancestor" concept since it implies that peoples without written languages are at a stage antecedent to the one in which, presumably, they will devise, or at least acquire, writing. The third form, *nonliterate*, simply describes the fact that these peoples do not have written languages. It is sometimes confused with "illiterate," but the use of this latter word should be guarded against, since it carries a distinct connotation of inferiority in ability or opportunity, or both. Nonliterate, because it is colorless, conveys its meaning unambiguously, and is readily applicable to the data it seeks to delimit, is thus to be preferred to all the other terms we have considered. It will be employed consistently in this book from this point onward.

The question that inevitably comes to mind is whether any single criterion such as the presence or absence of writing is adequate to describe the many peoples it seeks to comprehend. Its adequacy has been indicated by its demonstrated usefulness, though it is evident that no one characteristic is ideally satisfactory for designating entire cultures. It is to be recognized that commonly certain other characteristics go with an absence of writing. Nonliterate peoples are found on observation to be relatively more isolated, to have smaller numbers, and to be less addicted to rapid change in their sanctioned modes of behavior than those that have writing. In recent generations, moreover, Euroamerican culture has had to be set off not only from nonliterate cultures, but from the literate cultures outside Europe and America as well, because of the presence in European and American culture of a technology based on power machinery and the scientific tradition. But it must be recognized that none of these differences, except perhaps this last, is as clearly manifest as is the presence or absence of writing.

5

BEFORE we terminate our discussion of cultural relativism, it is important that we consider certain questions that are raised when the cultural relativistic position is advanced. "It may be true," it is argued, "that human beings live in accordance with the ways they have learned. These ways may be regarded by them as best. A people may be so devoted to these ways that they are ready to fight and die for them. In terms of survival value, their effectiveness may be admitted, since the group that lives in accordance with them continues to exist. But does this not mean that all systems of moral values, all concepts of right and wrong, are founded on such shifting sands that there is no need for morality, for proper behavior, for ethical codes? Does not a relativistic philosophy, indeed, imply a negation of these?"

To hold that values do not exist because they are relative to time and place, or to deny the psychological validity of differing concepts of reality, is to fall prey to a fallacy that results from a failure to take into account the positive contribution of the relativistic position. For cultural relativism is a philosophy which, in recognizing the values set up by every society to guide its own life, lays stress on the dignity inherent in every body of custom, and on the need for tolerance of conventions though they may differ from one's own. Instead of underscoring differences from absolute norms that, however objectively arrived at, are nonetheless the product of a given time or place, the relativistic point of view brings into relief the validity of every set of norms for the people whose lives are guided by them, and the values these represent.

As a philosopher who has studied the problem of cultural relativism has phrased it: ". . . Virtue is not something which the individual can possess or enjoy independently of his relation to his fellows. A man can become and can be truly a man only in and through his participation in a culture. The inner harmony which constitutes his virtue must belong to the larger harmony of his life with others. The standards of virtue everywhere must accordingly be relative to culture, and this applies as fully to our own distinctions of right and wrong, good and bad, as it does to the standards of any primitive people." Even in the apparent dilemma posed by the fact that science, a unique mode of reaching objectively ascertainable truth, seemingly transcends the boundaries of any cultural convention, the force of the cultural setting, we are told, must be accorded full weight in making possible the achievements of scientific research. "If the scientific mode of thought can sustain itself only through continuous growth and self-regeneration, it can survive only in a social order permeated by its own philosophic faith and itself capable of cultural transcendence. Physical science deprived of these conditions must eventually wither like a plant cut at the roots." [9]

It is essential, in considering cultural relativism, that we differentiate absolutes from universals. *Absolutes* are fixed, and, in so far as convention is concerned, are not admitted to have variation, to differ from culture to culture, from epoch to epoch. *Universals,* on the other hand, are those least common denominators to be extracted, inductively, from comprehension of the range of variation which all phenomena of the natural or cultural world manifest. If we apply the distinction between these two concepts in drawing an answer to the points raised in our question, these criticisms are found to lose their force. To say that there is no absolute criterion of value or morals, or even, psychologically, of time or space, does not mean that such criteria, in differing *forms,* do not comprise universals in human culture. We shall see, in a later section, how certain values in human life are everywhere accorded recognition, even though the institutions of no two cultures are identical in form. Morality is a universal, and so is enjoyment of beauty, and some standard for truth. The many forms these concepts take are but products of the particular historical experience of the societies that manifest them. In each, criteria are subject to continuous questioning, continuous

---

[9] Grace A. deLaguna, 1942, pp. 161–6.

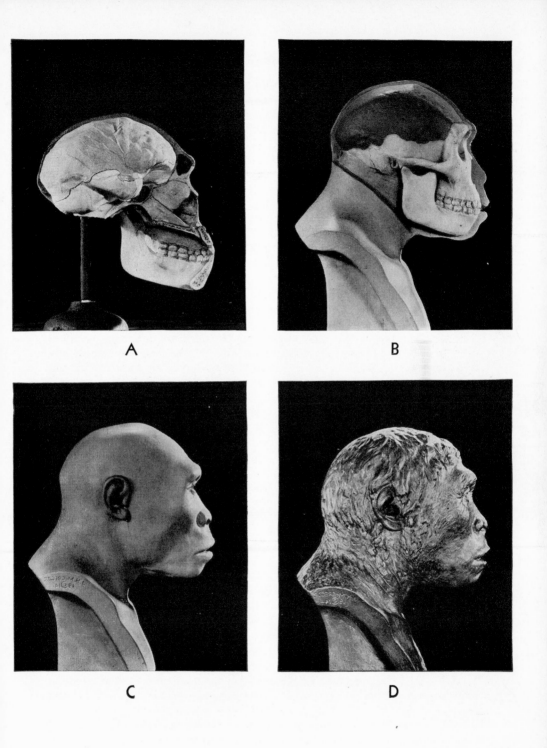

PLATE 1a *Stages in the restoration of* pithecanthropus erectus *by J. H. McGregor.*
(A) *Half-skull and brain;* (B) *skull with flesh modeled on one side;* (C) *half-skull with flesh modeled on;* (D) *complete restoration. See* page 98. [*Photographs courtesy American Museum of Natural History, New York*]

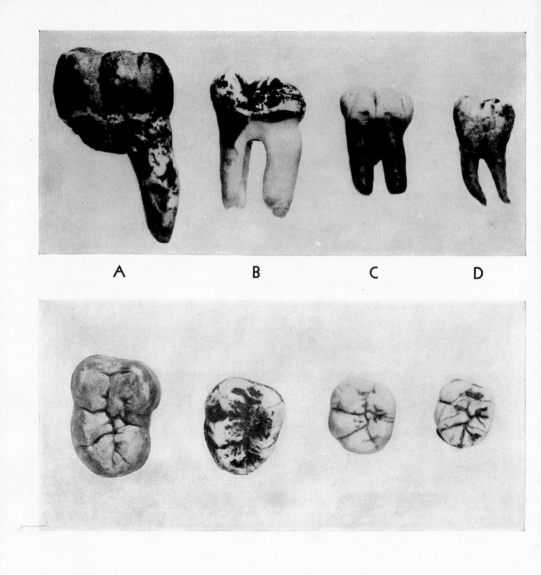

PLATE 1b (A) *Third lower molar of* gigantopithecus blacki *compared with* (B), *same tooth of male gorilla,* (C) *first lower molar of* sinanthropus pekinensis, *and* (D) *the same tooth of modern man. Upper, lateral; and lower, occlusal orientation. See page 104.* [Photographs courtesy F. Weidenreich and American Museum of Natural History, New York; cf. also F. Weidenreich, 1946, figs. 57 and 58]

change. But the basic conceptions remain, to channel thought and direct conduct, to give purpose to living.

It will later become apparent how dynamic culture can be. Whether by invention from within or borrowing from without, cultures continuously change, not only in their totality, but in each of their aspects. Change may be resisted, or changes may be welcomed. In this process, the individual changes his attitude toward the intangibles in culture no less than toward the material objects of his world. The morals, the world-view of one age are not identical with those of the next, as only a cursory study of our own history demonstrates. Yet the validity of each, for its time, is such as too often to make change difficult to envisage for the man who lives at that time.

In a similar manner, we can dispose of the contention that cultural relativism negates the force of the codes that prevail at a given time in a given culture. Everywhere, man seemingly always sets up goals for himself, and ideals toward which he strives. Because these are subject to change, or differ from people to people, does not make them any the less effective within a particular society during the period they prevail. Each people, having standards, not only inculcate them in the young so that each generation is enculturated to the value-systems of its predecessors, but they see to it that transgressions of accepted codes are punished. Law, no less than education, is one of the universals of culture, in each society stabilizing sanctioned modes of behavior, and stressing their values. Yet every culture knows the rebel, which means that man's experience encompasses cultural change as well as cultural stability.

The point may be put in a somewhat different way. *Cultural* relativism must be sharply distinguished from concepts of the relativity of individual behavior, which would negate all social controls over conduct. The existence of integrative moral forces has been remarked in every human society. Conformity to the code of the group is a requirement for any regularity in life. Yet to say that we have a right to expect conformity to the code of our day for ourselves does not imply that we need expect, much less impose conformity to our code on persons who live by other codes. The very core of cultural relativism is the social discipline that comes of respect for differences—of mutual respect. Emphasis on the worth of many ways of life, not one, is an affirmation of the values in each culture. Such emphasis seeks to understand, and to harmonize goals, not to judge and destroy those that do not dovetail with our own. Cultural history teaches that, important as it is to discern and study the parallelisms in human civilizations, it is no less important to discern and study the different ways man has devised to fulfil his needs.

That it has been necessary to consider questions such as have been raised, in discussing cultural relativism, itself reflects an enculturative experience wherein absolutes are stressed. These questions could only be asked by those who were trained in a culture such as our own, where the prevalent system of morals is not only consciously inculcated, but its exclusive claim to excellence emphasized. There are not many cultures, for example, where a rigid dichotomy between good and evil, such as we have set up, is insisted upon. Rather it is recognized that good and evil are but the extremes of a continuously varied scale between these poles that produces only different degrees of greyness. We thus return to the principle enunciated earlier, that "judgments are based on experience, and experience is interpreted by each individual in terms of his enculturation." In a culture where absolute values are stressed, the relativism of a world that encompasses many ways of living will be difficult to comprehend. Rather, it will offer a field-day for value-judgments based on the degree to which a given body of customs resembles or differs from those of Euroamerican culture.

It is not chance that a philosophy of cultural relativism, of which only the barest sketch has been given here, has had to await the development of adequate ethnographic knowledge. As long as the customs of peoples could not be studied in terms of their context of values, they of necessity had to be evaluated in terms of the ethnocentrism of the appraiser. But with effective techniques and a broad range of data, the humility reflected in the tolerance of the cultural relativistic position and its breadth of approach, becomes possible. Employing the field methods of the scientific student of man, and with an awareness of the satisfactions the most varied bodies of custom yield, this position gives us a leverage to lift us out of the ethnocentric morass in which our thinking about ultimate values has for so long bogged down. With a means of probing deeply into all manner of differing cultural orientations, of reaching into the significance of the ways of living of different peoples, we can, however, turn again to our own culture with fresh perspective, and an objectivity that can be achieved in no other manner.

◇◇◇◇◇◇◇◇◇◇◇◇◇◇

CHAPTER 6

The Ethnographer's Laboratory

THE field is the laboratory of the cultural anthropologist. To carry on his field-work, he goes to the people he has elected to study, listening to their conversation, visiting their homes, attending their rites, observing their customary behavior, questioning them about their traditions as he probes their way of life to attain a rounded view of their culture or to analyze some special aspect of it. In this, he is the ethnographer, the collector of data, which, in its wider ethnological significance, he will later, on his return from the field, analyze, and relate to other materials.

Traditionally, the anthropologist has carried on field studies among peoples who are outside the historic stream of Euroamerican or other literate cultures. That is, his researches have concerned those nonliterate, "primitive" peoples who, as we have seen, possess no written language and thus have no recorded history. This convention strikes deep and ranges widely in anthropological thought. For example, many Chinese anthropologists formerly took as their primary responsibility the study of such nonliterate inhabitants of China as the Lolo, leaving to others, in the main, the study of the ways of life of literate Chinese communities. The same division of labor has been established in the Philippines.

Often nonliterate peoples live in the far places of the earth, and to reach them the student may on occasion have to cope with difficulties of transportation, or disease, or physical harm. But this aspect of the cultural anthropologist's work, like its "romantic" elements that appeal to laymen who, baffled by the complexities of Euroamerican machine culture, would escape from the problems of everyday life that confront them, has been greatly overstressed. In the main, field-work is like all scientific routines. While intensely stimulating, it makes vigorous demands on the patience, the perseverance, and the sense of humor of the scientist.

The anthropologist studies the peoples among whom he works because from them he can obtain data that will throw light on the essential problems of the nature and functioning of culture, and of human social behavior. It is only in this way that, as a scientific student of man, he can establish the controls that are the essence of the scientific method, and that the exact or natural scientist sets up in his laboratory. Our data must be sought out over the face of the earth, for only by so seeking them can we study such problems as the effect of climate, race, innate psychic endowments or other factors on human culture, its range of variation in form, its processes of change. It was indeed only after a broad base of descriptive data had been achieved that we were able to discern the primacy of culture in shaping behavior, one of the most important achievements of our science.

That anthropologists study the wide range of peoples they do, does not, however, mean that cultural anthropology can be defined as the science which studies "primitive" peoples. As we have observed, this is, in a sense, the result of the historical development of science in our culture, just as is the preoccupation of physical anthropologists with questions of human, rather than general biology. Anthropologists came to study non-European peoples because the need for comparative materials was increasingly felt. There were few anthropologists and many such peoples—the number of nonliterate societies still unstudied is vast—and because it was soon recognized that method was paramount in studying them, the identification of cultural anthropology with this particular body of data that could best be studied by the use of its special methods came to be made.

But "the study of man and his works," if it is to live up to its mandate, cannot be expected to rest content with a delimitation of this sort. Any stream of investigation has a way of spilling over the retaining walls of definition. As a result, in seeking answers to problems, the need to follow data wherever they may lie has in recent years brought about the increasing utilization of the methods of anthropology in the study of literate folk, at home as well as in the far places. The first break in the retaining wall came in the 1920's, when the analysis of an American mid-west community by the sociologists Robert and Helen Lynd was prefaced with an introduction by the anthropologist Clark Wissler,[1] in which he pointed out that this work was an application of anthropological method to a community that was a unit in our literate, mechanized society. The controversy which ensued as to the validity of this assertion need not concern us here; the fact is that the experiment established a trend that has been increasingly felt.

Today anthropologists often study literate groups, employing many of the same techniques and the same concepts that figure in their study of non-Euroamerican societies. Only one point need be made here concerning this development. It is significant that it occurred only after the methodology developed during field-work among nonliterate peoples, and hypotheses arising out of the comparative study of their institutions permitted the study of our own ways of life in terms of these methods and hypotheses, with the realization that ours is but another one of the great variety of human cultures.

The relativistic point of view regarding cultures that differ from one's own expressed in the preceding chapter is essential to the ethnographer who is to carry on field research successfully. This cannot be too heavily stressed. A basic necessity of ethnographic research is the exercise of scientific detachment, which in turn calls for a rigid exclusion of value-judgments. Just as the

---

[1] R. S. and H. M. Lynd, 1929, p. vi.

The Ethnographer's Laboratory

chemist devotes himself to understanding the elements he is analyzing and their behavior in relation to each other, so the student of culture as such, must observe, describe, and analyze the traditions of the people he is studying as essential steps to comprehension. To do this is not easy, and requires special training for a person from our society. For, as we have seen, it is the essence of our particular kind of ethnocentrism that we judge, evaluate, and attempt to shape what differs from our own ways into the pattern that seems to us the only correct and, indeed, the only possible one. The anthropologist in the field, however, must accommodate himself to understanding ways of obtaining a living that never include a machine technology, and sometimes know neither agriculture nor domesticated animals. What is more difficult, he must adjust his reactions to grasp, in terms of the values of the people he is studying, customs as repugnant to his personal experience as infanticide, head-hunting, various "unpleasant" dietary and sanitary habits, and the like.

2

DESCRIPTIONS of actual methods used by anthropologists in the field are rare in the literature. Since, as we have seen, it is in its method that cultural anthropology makes one of its most important contributions to science, and since it is a basic postulate of scientific procedure that the means whereby a given body of materials is obtained be stated clearly and specifically, it is of interest to analyze this omission. The ethnographer's difficulty in describing his method arises out of the difference in the materials he deals with, and those dealt with by the laboratory scientist. There is little apparatus for the student of human culture to describe. The success of his work, in very great measure, depends on his sensitivity to the situations he encounters, on the interplay between his personality and the personalities of the natives with whom he must deal, rather than his skill in manipulating test-tubes or balances or incubators. Any report he can phrase must of necessity be anecdotal. It would, ideally, have to run with the presentation of his data, since each item of his materials is gathered under circumstances that differ from those in which every other item was obtained. It would, in short, almost require another book.

Let us see how this works out by citing a passage from such a book, written as an experiment in presenting method through describing the experiences of the ethnographers in gathering the data that are also given. The particular passage we quote introduces a chapter which tells how information regarding the kinship structure of these people, the Saramacca tribe of Bush Negroes who live in the forests of Dutch Guiana in northern South America, that would conventionally appear in the section of a monograph entitled "Social Organization," was gathered:

We were aroused early after our night of stories. The women were moving about, getting their morning meal before daybreak came to give them light for their harvesting. There was much they had to do. Late that afternoon they would be returning to their villages, for the next day was sacred to the Earth Mother, and

81

The Nature of Culture

no work could be done in the fields. Today, added to the round of harvesting were the preparations for the return to their village. The rice that had been cut during the week would have to be carried there for drying and winnowing, and yams and peanuts and beans were to be brought in. . . .

Soon our men, too, began to stir, and, as we came out of our hammocks, Bayo and Angita entered the clearing. They were just now returning from the dance at Pa'aba. . . . With Angita was a man we had not seen before, holding a small child by the hand.

"This is Awingu, my brother-in-law," said Angita in explanation. "His eyes trouble him. I brought him to you for medicine."

After an exchange of courtesies demanded by the visit, we turned to the child. "Is this your child, Awingu?" we asked.

His answer came promptly. "No, he is not my child. He is my wife's child. I made him."

Here was a fine distinction. He made him, but the child was not his.

Just then our cook came up with a small present for the child, but, since he would not take it from his hands or ours, Angita gave it to him.

"Thank you, father," he said to Angita.

Angita looked down affectionately at the youngster. "Two, three years more, Awingu, and he will be ready to go and live with his father at Gankwe. Do you remember your father at Gankwe? It was he who showed you how to make a gun from a reed. And you made it well. . . ."

There appeared, then, to be yet another father, for it was clear that Angita was not speaking of himself when he referred to the Gankwe father who had showed the child how to make a play gun.

All this, in itself, however confusing to a visitor, is by no means an unusual phenomenon. Different peoples have their own sanctions for establishing kinship and their own designations for relationships. In the city we had been told many tales of the manner of life of these Negroes of the bush. And the "matriarchate," as the custom of counting descent through the mother was termed, had often come up when these people were being discussed.

"Among them only the mothers count, because among savages, who can tell who the real father is? That is why a child calls many men 'father,'" we had heard variously explained and elaborated.

Yet here was a man who said without hesitation, "No, he is not my child. He is my wife's child. I made him." And the very next instant the child called Angita father, and Angita referred to still another man as the father who would in a few years take the child with him to live and train him for manhood.

Any number of questions came to our minds, but at daybreak a stranger coming to the planting ground of a village not his own is the least willing of talkers.

"This is not your child, Awingu," we took the occasion to remark when we were saying goodbye, "Yet he seems to like you very much."

"*Ma, tye! Ma Neng'e!*—Mother of all Negroes! What would you have? I am his father!"

The man showed by his amused expression that this was a story to carry back to his village. Only the politeness due a stranger kept Awingu and Angita from laughing aloud at this strange question. But Awingu was a thoughtful fellow. "Tell me," he said, after a while, "in your white man's country, don't children care for their fathers?" [2]

---

[2] M. J. and F. S. Herskovits, 1934, pp. 124–6.

The Ethnographer's Laboratory

The discussion then continues with a description of how, on various occasions, three different women claimed the man named Angita, who was a fine wood-carver, as a son, and how social reality resolved this biological impossibility and thus yielded further understanding of Bush-Negro kinship:

Later that day, when our boat found itself abreast of the dugout which Angita was poling, we lost no time in questioning him.

"Angita," we called, "is the woman who gave us the rice your mother?"

He nodded.

"But what of Tita, who said she was your mother, too?"

He was a quick-witted lad, and he saw at once what we had in mind. He said with a laugh, "You are asking about my true, true mother, the one who made me? It is not this one, and it is not Tita, who made me. It is Kutai."

"But who are the other two?"

"They are her sisters." [3]

By such devious ways the ethnographer obtains fact after fact. As digested after his return from the field, the experience would be presented in his monograph as no more than such a generalized statement as, "The social organization of the Bush Negroes is unilateral, descent being counted on the maternal side, with controls within the family exercised by the mother's eldest brother. Kinship nomenclature is classificatory, mother and mother's sisters being called by the term 'mother,' father and father's brothers being called 'father.' Biological parents have no distinguishing appelation, being identified by a child as the parent 'who made him.'"

In 1922 B. Malinowski's early work, *The Argonauts of the Western Pacific*, first gave explicit expression to the necessity for including a statement of field procedure in a report of the results of field work. He enunciated the following principles of ethnographic method: That the student must, first of all, "possess real scientific aims, and know the values and criteria of modern ethnography;" that he should, "in the main, . . . live . . . right among the natives;" and finally, that "he has to apply a number of special methods of collecting, manipulating and fixing his evidence." In this, he was verbalizing his own procedure, and unwittingly describing the technique of many other ethnographers of whose procedures he could not be aware since they had never been published. The uncompromising character of his second tenet did, however, represent a real departure from the usage of many earlier students of culture who, even though they went to the field, were content to remain in an island capital, a missionary compound, an official rest-house, and question natives, technically termed "informants," about ways of life that were spread before them at their doorsteps to be observed, if they would but go and look at them.

This was the doctrine of the "participant observer," which aroused considerable discussion. Malinowski was generalizing his statement of method from experience gained with a single society. Here customs were such that participation in their life was permitted, though even in his case there was

---

[3] *Ibid.*, pp. 127–8.

never complete acceptance of him. This is how he phrases it. "It must be remembered that as the natives saw me constantly every day, they ceased to be interested or alarmed, or made self-conscious by my presence, and I ceased to be a disturbing element in the tribal life which I was to study, altering it by my very approach, as always happens with a new-comer to every savage community. In fact, as they knew that I would thrust my nose into everything, even where a well-mannered native would not dream of intruding, they finished by regarding me as part and parcel of their life, a necessary evil or nuisance, mitigated by donations of tobacco." [4]

It is apparent that even here, whatever the adaptation to his presence that was achieved, the stranger remained a foreign element in the minds of the people, and an element that might, so to speak, induce a state of indigestion in the body politic. In other societies, where participation in the life of the people by an outsider is regarded with disfavor, this participant observer technique cannot be applied. Where a tradition of rank based on a class structure exists, the place assigned the ethnographer may be such that serious modifications of this method are necessary. Recent aggression by a colonial government may make for resentment among the natives against anyone of European origin, and still different procedures may be called for.

A useful rule to apply in field-work is something like the following: *See as much as you can, participate whenever you are permitted to do so, and compound your experiences by discussing them formally and informally with natives as widely as you are able.* Such a rule recognizes that there are as many situations to be met in carrying on field-work as there are peoples. Certainly there is no single method.

This point is well illustrated by a report of field work by Evans-Pritchard among the Nuer of East Africa, which followed research by the same student among the Azande, another tribe living in the same general area:

Since among the Nuer my tent was always in the midst of homesteads or wind-screens and my inquiries had to be conducted in public, I was seldom able to hold confidential conversations and never succeeded in training informants capable of dictating texts and giving detailed descriptions and commentaries. This failure was compensated for by the intimacy I was compelled to establish with the Nuer. As I could not use the easier and shorter method of working through regular informants I had to fall back on direct observation of, and participation in, the everyday life of the people. From the door of my tent I could see what was happening in camp or village and every moment was spent in Nuer company. Information was thus gathered in particles, each Nuer I met being used as a source of knowledge and not, as it were, in chunks supplied by selected and trained informants. Because I had to live in such close contact with the Nuer I knew them more intimately than the Azande, about whom I am able to write a much more detailed account. Azande would not allow me to live as one of themselves; Nuer would not allow me to live otherwise. Among Azande I was compelled to live outside the community; among Nuer I was compelled to be a member of it. Azande treated me as a superior; Nuer as an equal. [5]

---

[4] B. Malinowski, 1922, pp. 6–8.
[5] E. E. Evans-Pritchard, 1940, p. 15.

The Ethnographer's Laboratory

As is apparent from this citation, the ethnographer is only one factor in the field situation. The ideal method is therefore not always the one he can employ. The group under study must always be taken into account, since it is their preconceptions, their prejudices, their fears that dominate the scene. This factor of the native's attitude is one toward which the ethnographer cannot direct too sensitive a concern. It is the essence of the human element in his study, and is to be handled with the greatest delicacy possible. He achieves this by exhibiting an honesty of purpose that is manifest in his every act. He plays fair, and shows restraint. He does not go where he is not welcome. He asks permission before intruding into a house, or attending a rite of any kind. He realizes that, though the rituals of death and the beliefs concerning the dead they reveal are important for his research, the death of a member of a family causes deep grief among the surviving relatives, and he remains away from the funeral unless he is wanted there. If he is wise, he knows that, by exercising these restraints, he will, in the long run, gain in the respect and confidence of the people, and his materials will ultimately be the richer for this sensitivity. Above all, in living in a community, he will respect the place assigned to him by that community.

The following statement, which indicates how important this can be in West African and New World Negro cultures, makes explicit the point raised in the final sentences of the excerpt from the report on the Nuer cited earlier:

There is no tradition more deeply shared [among these Negro societies] than that of the importance of valuing individual identity in the scheme of things. Implicit in this is a sense of dignity that does not permit a man to escape the dictates set by any caste lines that may be drawn. The ethnographer, . . . especially if he be a white man, has what has been called a high degree of social visibility, and any attempt to live according to the canons of native life would forthwith expose him to the thrusts of a deadly weapon in the hands of the Negro, the weapon most destructive of that mutual respect that is the basis for all free and friendly intercourse between two human beings, whatever their race—ridicule. In Negro culture the white student must be content to remain what he actually is, an observer. He can and must be, if his work is to be of real worth, a sympathetic observer, and given patience, tact and sincerity, he will form warm friendships among the native folk after he comes to know them well, so that as a friend it will not be denied him to share with them their inner values.[6]

It is thus necessary that the ethnographer pitch his tent, or find a house, where he can be as close to the people he studies as they will permit. But it is their reactions, not his wishes, that will dictate how close he can come to them, and how much he can participate in their lives in making his observations. As a scientist he will arrange these observations in his notes and his published reports in accordance with his concept of culture and the nature of his problem. The conditions under which he obtained them, if not published, should at least be in his notes, where they can be referred to if questions of method arise in discussing a moot point. In this, he will follow a basic precept of scientific method, and in this way advance the techniques employed in his own discipline.

[6] M. J. Herskovits, 1937, p. 323.

85

3

ARRIVED at his destination, settled in his village, the initial problem that faces the ethnographer is how to get at his materials. It is a problem always paramount for any student of man. Whether he is among natives of a South Seas island or working in a middle-western American community, to achieve entree into the group is at once the most difficult and most important step in his research. Here again there is no single rule that can govern his procedure. It may be possible to come with an introduction from someone, either a member of the group or a friendly outsider, who will vouch for the ethnographer to someone of position and prestige, and thus gain for him initial cooperation. This is the optimum situation; the other end of the scale is when the student must make his way alone, perhaps even without the aid of an interpreter, and break down indifference and hostility.

The question is one of establishing workable human relations, and is difficult even under the most favorable conditions. We have all had the experience of finding ourselves in a strange community; of walking the streets alone, in a setting that differs only little from our accustomed one, but with a feeling of wanting to know what is happening here, who these people we brush by may be—of being an outsider. If we project ourselves into a situation where the physical environment differs from ours, where the language is incomprehensible, the food, the clothing, the houses, the very physical type of the people is strange, we can gain some insight into the initial problems the ethnographer must meet. Such a simple experience as walking through a public market in a tropical capital can be disturbing. The experience has not *sorted itself out*. The student feels merely the strangeness of a scene to which his own past offers no clues as to proper behavior, or to comprehension of the behavior of others. Is this argument that is witnessed a forerunner of violence, or only the usual way of bargaining? Is the laughter of that market-woman directed toward himself, or is she laughing at what her neighbor has just said to her?

It is this *sorting out process* that is crucial to success in field-work, and it applies to people no less than to cultural behavior. To the newly arrived ethnographer, personalities in the community are blurred, and only later do individuals emerge. Customary habits are meaningless when an act that is observed cannot be projected to its intended end, as it can be later when some degree of familiarity with the ways of life of the people has been attained. At this point, the student begins to make friends—and to be disliked as well as liked. Field experience soon teaches that no matter how different in physical type or cultural tradition a people may be, there will always be some individuals among them for whom he will have a warm personal regard, and with whom his relationships will be close and meaningful. But there will also be those who will baffle him, and whom he will come perhaps to dislike. And these reactions in any situation will be mutual. They are, above all, not to be feared or avoided, for they have much to teach the ethnographer of the personality of these individuals, and the tensions in the

86

group. Often, too, the man or woman whose confidence is the most difficult to gain, has valuable insights to give the student. Moreover, negative reactions may test his patience but they are of value in the notebook.

How information is obtained depends, once more, on the kind of study being conducted, the kind of people being studied, the kind of life they lead. No exclusive use of observation as against report is desirable, nor should entire reliance be placed on an informant. One must, first of all, be seen. To walk through the village or into the countryside is an aid in the first days of residence in a community. Curiosity will bring inhabitants to one's dwelling, contact will be established. In some Indian societies, and elsewhere where the people have had continuous experience with Euroamerican culture, a native can be induced to come for a stated number of hours a day to "talk," at the going rate for whatever kind of labor he has been accustomed to perform. In societies where such contact has not been experienced, observation and casual conversation may, for many weeks, be the only sources of information. But informants are essential if any rounded knowledge of the culture is to be had. Field-trips are not of indefinite duration, and not every happening in the repertory of a culture will occur even during an extended period of field-work. In a small community a birth, a wedding, a funeral may not take place during the ethnographer's stay, or he may not be permitted to witness it if it does occur. Yet an account of such important rites, and the conditions that introduce variants of these rites, must be included in a full description of any culture.

The answer to difficulties of this kind lies in the use of an informant. The very best use of an informant is to discuss with him events that have been witnessed, preferably those that were visited in his company. In time he can be relied upon to give descriptions of those typical events in the life of the people that have not been witnessed, that occur in the winter, for example, when field-work has had to be carried on during the summer. Eventually, where the rapport between informant and ethnographer is close, the work becomes almost a collaboration, the informant furnishing leads and going to men of repute in his own family and outside it for answers to questions that have arisen in their discussions, or that the ethnographer has posed.

Because every culture presents many facets, and different people in the same society view their common ways of life differently, it goes without saying that reliance on one informant is never advisable, even though it is inevitable that one or two persons will figure more in this capacity than others. For example, if a rite is described separately by several informants, and then is visited three or four different times, it will be found that only in outline do all these agree.[7] This shows us the extent to which the factor of variation in culture, whose significance will become apparent later in this book, must continuously be taken into account in field-work.

Of equal importance is the realization that an informant gives more than information of happenings. From him one obtains points of view, expressions of opinion that reveal the value systems, the bases of judgments, the socially

---

[7] See below, Chap. 33.

The Nature of Culture

accepted motivations that inspire or explain behavior. This is another reason why observation is never of itself sufficient. There are many persons who come to know and enjoy the rites of native peoples near whom they live, or whom they visit for the purpose. It is instructive to inquire of them the meaning to the people of the rituals they can describe so well in outer form. They are invariably at a loss for an answer. Behavior, in short, of itself rarely enough reveals its motivating drive even in our own culture; it never does this in a strange culture.

For many years it was an axiom of field-work that only the elders could give the student a "true" picture of a culture. Today we know better. Culture is as culture does, and the range of accepted variation in behavior permits, where it does not require, men to behave differently from women, young people from those who are older. The best procedure is thus to talk to both men and women, young and old; to observe a wide range of persons in as many situations as possible. In one West African community, the names and roles of the gods of a given pantheon as told by the chief-priest proved to differ in many respects from the account given by a new cult-initiate and this, in turn, differed from that of a lay person. Yet all these were "true" as far as the tellers were concerned. The principle that, to understand a culture, exoteric information is as important as esoteric—that what is of common knowledge is as significant as what is held secret—was enunciated many years ago. But the challenge to uncover what is secret is hard to resist, and the value of the commonplace has only recently come to be recognized.

The use of as many informants as possible to supplement observation is important for checking information, whether for omissions, distortions, or untruths. It must be remembered that individuals in all societies exhibit traits of discursiveness, and of reticence. Distortions may arise out of fear or caution, or even forgetfulness of everyday patterns so ordinary as not to be worth mentioning. One of the most skilled ethnographers has expressed it in this way: "Although distinctive customs were often pointed out to me lest I fail to observe them, on the other hand customs that were lapsing were not mentioned, merely from indifference. Such *costumbres* or *creencias* were the ways or beliefs of only a few old men or of some of the women, not worth noticing. In a conservative, secretive community the social detective learns much from the efforts to conceal. In Mitla I was to learn that in social as in personal life the idea that there is nothing important to conceal may result in almost complete concealment." [8] One person will remember what another has forgotten. Or, where a society enjoins reticence, one will reveal what another feels must be left unsaid. A well-directed question will elicit explanations that, on another occasion, the same individual will avoid by a skilful parry. The result of inquiry among as many persons as possible will be a many-sided body of materials. Such a method will, if carefully employed, give depth to comprehension, and enhance the insight with which generalizations on the sanctioned forms of behavior are drawn.

---

[8] E. C. Parsons, 1936, pp. 14–15.

The Ethnographer's Laboratory

4

THOUGH not many anthropologists have recounted in specific terms how they went about their research on particular field-trips, certain procedures that have been advanced by field-workers as methodological devices have come to be recognized as useful techniques of field-work. Like the method whereby the ethnographer becomes a participant observer, which we have already taken into account, these methods have arisen empirically, out of trial-and-error field research. As with the participant observer method, too, it must be recognized that none of these techniques is universally applicable. The usefulness of each varies with the situation in which the field researcher finds himself, with the type of culture he is studying and with his particular problem.

The oldest of these methods is what may be termed the *Notes-and-Queries* approach. This takes its name from the title of a publication, initially prepared by a committee of the Royal Anthropological Institute for the British Association for the Advancement of Science, which sponsored the first edition that appeared in 1875. The work has since undergone two revisions. It is a comprehensive questionnaire, covering all phases of material and non-material culture, aimed at permitting the person in contact with "primitive" peoples to amass the greatest possible range of materials. It is based on the following assumptions: that the civilizations of nonliterate peoples are in danger of extinction and we must obtain as much information about them as we can while they are still in existence; that there are not enough trained anthropologists to do this; that, therefore, the services of untrained persons, such as colonial officers, missionaries, traders and travelers must be utilized with the greatest possible effectiveness.

The notes-and-queries method, followed by one without anthropological training, results in the gathering of many facts, but yields little information either about how these facts are interrelated in the total cultural matrix, or about the human element involved in the daily life of a people. In the hands of the trained anthropologist, who as scientist organizes his data about a conceptual scheme that guides his research, and in terms of hypotheses that frame his problem, *Notes and Queries* is a helpful check on points he may have overlooked. Are the coiled baskets he has watched being made oriented in a clockwise or counterclockwise direction? Is the house of the dead destroyed after death, or is it deserted and allowed to fall to ruin? What implements are actually employed by the wood-carver? Such details, called to mind by looking through such a questionnaire as this, need only a few questions, or even a glance at some object, to fill in a gap in the materials already in the notebook. Such questions, moreover, may furnish clues to entire areas of life, perhaps not even found in the questionnaire, that would otherwise have remained unstudied.

Another special technique that has been effectively employed is the *genealogical method*. This method is associated with the name of W. H. R. Rivers, who first worked it out while a member of the famous Torres Straits Expedition, organized by the eminent English anthropologist A. C. Haddon at the end of the last century.[9] This method has proved useful because, despite its simplicity, it lays bare a broad range of information concerning the social structures and other institutions of the people being studied. In using it, only the simplest kinship terms are employed—father, mother, child, husband and wife. The informant is asked the *name* of those who stand in these relationships to him, after making it clear that biological kin are meant, and not those, such as cousins, who in what is called the classificatory system would be termed "brothers" or "sisters." He is asked what he calls each, what each calls him, and thus the kinship terminology is built up. Then, using the given name of each of these persons, the process is repeated and the system extended.

Rivers, in the paper where he described and evaluated the method he had already successfully employed in the Torres Straits area of Melanesia and among the Todas of India, indicates some of the objectives that can be attained by its use. By recording "the social condition" of each person, the "locality to which each . . . belongs," a sense of class lines and local groupings, how these are represented in marriage alliances, and the lines that draw localities together or hold them apart, is achieved. Clan organization is clearly shown, and whether descent is counted on the side of the father or mother, or both. This, in turn, reveals how incest lines are drawn. In addition to showing "systems of relationships," and the methods used in "the regulation of marriage," to quote Rivers' own terms, he points out other kinds of data which the use of this method may gather. The "laws regulating descent and the inheritance of property," the "mode of succession of chiefs" and "the study of migrations" are named by him in the area of social structure. He feels it is also useful in studying magic, religion and religious rituals, name-types and the taboos on names, while it also reveals such demographic and biological data as sex ratios and groupings among whom the problems of heredity can be investigated.

"The genealogical method," Rivers states, "makes it possible to investigate abstract problems on a purely concrete basis. It is even possible by its means to formulate laws regulating the lives of people which they have probably never formulated themselves, certainly not with the clearness and definiteness which they have to the mind trained by a more complex civilization." Instead of asking the informant to generalize about what a hypothetical person would call his elder brother's younger daughter, one merely takes the term actually used by someone who has an elder brother who has more than one daughter. If the term is fixed, it will always appear the same. If not, the range of usage will emerge in the differences found in the listings.

As with other techniques, this genealogical one is not everywhere effective or workable. In some societies, as Rivers himself states, an obstacle may be "the existence of a taboo on the names of the dead, and this can sometimes only be overcome with difficulty." "In my own experience," he continues, "I

---

[9] W. H. R. Rivers, 1910, *passim*.

The Ethnographer's Laboratory

have been compelled in consequence of this taboo to obtain the pedigrees in secret and from persons not of the family in question." Among groups where enumeration of any kind is feared, whether for magical or political reasons, the attempt to obtain genealogies would arouse suspicion and set up resistances. Finally, this method is far more applicable to studies of small isolated settlements of a Melanesian island or an American Indian tribe than the great aggregates of Indonesia or Africa, where the complexity of marriage lines, and other interrelationships, is such as to make it difficult, if not impossible, to achieve the satisfactory sampling of the population needed to justify pertinent inductions.

Village mapping may be thought of as an extension and as a special form of the genealogical method. Here not only are the relationships of every individual in a community to every other person recorded, but the ecological setting and the lines along which physical contact takes place are indicated. Ideally, each dwelling, each communal building, each storage-pit or other accessory structure, every public open place where groups collect, every shrine, each field or industrial center, such as a forge or where pottery is made, is located. Once again, the inapplicability of this method to larger settlements is apparent. Yet where it can be applied, it is equally evident that, when coupled with genealogies, it can yield a great deal of information concerning the life of a group.

A question often raised when methods of field investigation are under discussion concerns *the use of the native language.* That those going into the field should be linguistically equipped to render in accurate phonetic transcription the names of peoples and places and deities, titles of various sorts, critical texts such as invocations or words to songs, is accepted as a minimum requirement. This was one of the principal contributions to field methodology of the American anthropologists, who under the leadership of F. Boas amassed an impressive body of textual materials in native Indian languages. But work of this kind does not equip the student to carry on a conversation, or to understand a conversation of others that is overheard. Here is encountered the full play of idiom, of imagery, of nuance in thought patterns, of elision and elliptical expression. The ethnographer must be very sure of his command of the tongue in which he proposes to carry on his research or he will but skim the surface of the thought processes about him, too often misinterpreting what is told him or what he hears.

A happy medium is found in the "pidgin" dialects that have sprung up in many parts of the world. Usually these are relatively easy to learn, and sufficiently rich as to be usable in questioning informants or carrying on casual conversation. Among peoples where such a dialect exists it is a rare, remote village where someone is not to be found who speaks it. These dialects are often derived from Indo-European tongues, such as Melanesian pidgin, Negro-English, or Negro-French. But even where this is not the case, as in Swahili (Bantu-Arabic), or Chinook (Northwest coast of North America), these "jargons" are simpler to handle than the complicated languages of the peoples who speak hybrid tongues as accessory to their native forms.

The other alternative is the interpreter. The use of an interpreter presents many problems. The interpreter has to be won over by the ethnographer; he must not only be made to understand what is at issue, but must be enthusiastic about the work. This is a reaction not difficult to communicate if it is felt by the student. Translation is at best a difficult task, and especial care must be had that questions to be transmitted are phrased clearly, passed on correctly, and the replies properly rendered. An interpreter can become a most valuable informant, and will often expand on a reply or himself proffer significant information. The independent use of more than one interpreter is essential, since this insures a more adequate check on the materials transmitted and gives a sense of the range of belief and behavior in the culture.

Ideally, one makes use of any linguistic device that is at hand. A pidgin dialect is spoken if one exists. At the same time, every attempt is made to master the native language to the greatest degree possible. This does not mean that interpreters are not also to be employed, for they, too, can be of aid. Competence should move forward on all fronts. A knowledge of a key word in the native language may be a check on the validity of the interpreter's performance. A question in pidgin may clear up a moot point which the use of the native language alone would not clarify. As one field-worker put it, "I used an interpreter until I found myself discussing my problems with him in his language. Then I felt I could go on by myself." In the final analysis, the objective is to record the data as adequately as possible. Whatever contributes to this end justifies the techniques that are employed.

Biographies and *autobiographies* of natives are valuable aids in ethnographic research. They reveal many things about a culture. Most of all, they afford a corrective to exclusive preoccupation with institutions. Cultural behavior is institutionalized, but the range of accepted variation in individual conduct must be analyzed if the institution and the culture are to be seen in perspective. Intangibles such as values, goals, and other motivating drives come out in such documents, as does the play of differing personalities within a society.

We have already illustrated the homely processes of thought by a passage from one of these autobiographies. There are a considerable number of such works, some brief and some extensive. All of them merit careful study. The same is true of biographical materials, especially where, as in the treatment of the Zulu ruler Chaka, the author of the biography is himself a member of a tribe related to that of his subject. Here, in short, is another tool that permits us to penetrate the life of the individual in his cultural setting, at hand for the student who would assess to the fullest the function and meaning of culture.

5

POINTS of detail in field-method need not concern us here. Matters such as when notebooks may be used and when they are best left behind, how notes should be organized and whether they should be reworked in the field, the use of the field diary, the employment of still and motion picture cameras, and of recording instruments—these are the affair of the specialist, and are

The Ethnographer's Laboratory

increasingly presented in technical monographs where reports of research are offered. One of the most elaborate accounts of field techniques used in studying a specific problem has been written by Mead, in connection with her presentation of the data she collected among the Arapesh of New Guinea.[10] Such matters are the equivalent of the test-tubes and microscopes of the student who works in the laboratories of the physical and natural sciences. Their importance is clear, in terms of the more fundamental considerations that arise out of how the research worker conceives his problem, and his basic approach toward its solution.

In ethnographic field-work, this conception and this approach derive from the fact that the problem is essentially a human one. This is why honesty of purpose is so important, for the ethnographer is being observed far more intensely by the people he has come to study than he can ever observe them, and a false step is soon detected. This, too, is why the greatest sensitivity is essential. Even where opposition to his investigation develops, alertness to the values of a people, the ability to give way gracefully at the right moment, a feeling for canons of conduct and politeness can resolve a difficulty and win an ultimate advantage. Here, too, a sense of humor is of great usefulness, for it gives perspective when horizons seem to press irritatingly close about one.

With honesty, sensitivity and humor, then, field-work, for all its difficulties and frustrations, becomes an exciting adventure. There are few ethnographers who do not talk with affection of their friends among the people with whom they have worked. They look back on their periods of field study with a feeling that here has been an experience that more than any other has brought breadth and comprehension, not only of a particular culture, but of human culture as a whole. There is no logical reason why the student of comparative culture, who never leaves his study, should not make a contribution to the understanding of the nature of cultural institutions. But results from this type of analysis have in the main proved unsatisfactory where there has been no contact with the living reality of culture, with people who behave in ways that are never baffling when seen in their total setting.

---

[10] M. Mead, 1940, pp. 325–38, especially pp. 336–8.

PART III

THE MATERIALS OF CULTURE

leave out

The Evolution of Mankind

WHERE the human form first appeared, and when, is still under investigation. Concerning the locality in which this took place there is more speculation than fact, some holding for northern India, some for Africa, some for other regions. The earliest forms, however, have been recovered from sites in the Far East that reach from Java to Choukoutien, near Peking. The first of these sites yielded to Eugene Dubois, one of the early students of palaeo-anthropology, the famous *Pithecanthropus Erectus,* or the Java ape-man which in the terminology of the 1890's was held to be the "missing link" between man and ape. The passage of time, however, brought discoveries that taught us that no such simple formulation could explain the complexities of the problems of human development.

One of the most dramatic of these problems was posed when some enormous teeth were discovered in Chinese apothecary shops in Hong Kong, where they awaited use as medicine in accordance with the Chinese custom of grinding fossils to employ in this manner. What could these teeth, whose form indicated they were human molars, signify? Several times the size of the largest molars of living or fossil men, did they imply that man in the earliest days had been gigantic in proportion? Or could they have grown in jaws more in size like those of present-day human beings; and, if so, what appearance would such a creature have presented?

Yet here they are—and they epitomize the difficulties in archaeological research that pose its greatest challenge and give it its greatest fascination. No branch of anthropology requires more of inference, or the weighing of imponderables; in short, of the exercise of the scientific imagination, than prehistory. No matter how appealing an hypothesis, or how logical it may seem, one specimen taken out of an undisturbed place in the ground may disprove it. From the positive point of view, the existence of a human or protohuman type, hitherto unrecognized, must be assumed on the basis of equally fragmentary remains, as in the case of these great teeth.

What constitutes the greatest aid to the student in reconstructing the prehistoric development of man's physical type is that human morphology, like other phenomena in the natural world, has a certain order of regularity that can be counted on. A given bone, or complex of skeletal elements such as a skull or a spine or an extremity, will differ from species to species. The limits

97

of variation within a given species, however, are relatively slight. The relation of form to function, moreover, is such that even in different species the way in which one element is mortised into the whole is so consistent that much information can be gained from even a part of a single bone. Thus we do not attribute tallness to a form that has a short thigh-bone, while one that is curved tells us its owner had a stooping rather than an upright posture.

The regularity of the evolutionary process is also a factor of the greatest importance in telling the tale of human development. This regularity is attested in the work of the palaeontologists who have described for many animal forms the evolution they went through, in the same way the palaeo-anthropologist does for man. One of their most notable achievements is in reconstructing the process by which the horse, a small three-toed quadruped, evolved into the large-hoofed form known to us today. In the same way these students, and those concerned with the development of man, have been able to fill in many gaps in the evolution of primate forms that lived before the appearance of human and protohuman types.

By utilizing the logic of structure and the logic of evolutionary development, it has been possible for palaeoanthropologists to achieve what seems to the uninitiated almost miracles in reconstructing the characteristics of the earlier, extinct forms of mankind. No one claims perfection for these reconstructions, least of all those who have made them. They are always subject to revision on the discovery of more precise data than were at hand when a given one was made. Yet with the complete skulls, let us say, of Neanderthal man, it is possible to lay on clay replicas of the muscles that, under the logic of structure, must have been of a given length and thickness; and then, over this reconstructed musculature to place another covering that represents the skin. Or with more fragmentary remains, such as a part of a jaw-bone, it is possible, using both logical systems, and taking into account not only the bone itself but the period when a given creature lived, to achieve the same result, though in these instances the skull itself must first be "restored."

Certain cautions must always be kept in mind when looking at such restorations. The first example we have cited will have far greater chances of being a correct approximation than the second, since the more completely the underlying skeletal materials are available, the more certain we will be that basic structure is correct. In restorations from partial materials, too, those parts of the skeleton closest to the recovered bones will be handled more surely than those where the skeletal base is hypothetical. We must recognize, moreover, that certain "soft parts"—fleshy protuberances like the nose and ears—must always be guess work. When they disintegrate, they leave no clues as to what their shape had been. The same is true with hair, for the manner in which hair is reconstructed is especially liable to trick the unwary observer. In some of the earlier restorations, only the fully human types were represented as clean-shaven, with hair parted. The psychological effect of the contrast of these forms with the unkempt earlier protohumans is one that parallels the transparent, though unconscious, ethnocentrism—in this case, anthropocentrism—of those who made them! Despite the difficulties and reservations, the usefulness of such restorations is appreciable. For they make it possible for those unaccustomed to looking at skulls, or evaluating differences in skeletons, to understand, along broad lines, the development of *homo sapiens,* the species to which all living mankind belongs.

2

A CENTURY before Darwin, it was realized that the similarities between man and certain animal forms were so great that they could not be overlooked in setting up classifications of animal types. Linnaeus, therefore, grouped man, the great apes, and the monkeys in a single order, called *primates*. Within this order, New and Old World forms are to be distinguished. In the New World, evolution went no farther than certain small monkey forms. This is why there is no question of the New World origin of man, since in the New World there was nothing from which he could have evolved. Furthermore, all man's closest relatives, the anthropoid apes, today exist in the areas where man has lived longest. Gorilla and chimpanzee are found in Africa, orangutan and gibbon in Malaysia.

That man represents the end-result of a process of change characteristic of all living creatures is today beyond dispute. This process of change is what is meant when the word evolution is used. It occurs as the result of the variations which every living form exhibits. The importance of this factor of variability has been recognized since the time of Darwin. It is the variants a form produces that offer the possibility of change, and have been the instruments through which all living types and the many more extinct ones were enabled to appear as time slowly moved through the millenia life has existed on earth.

When we study the relationship between man and other forms, we base our investigation not only on palaeontological evidence but on the similarities in structure and functioning of the living representations of related types. No one can read such demonstration as has been given by Gregory[1] in tracing the bones of the face, item by item, from the fish, through intermediate types, to man, without being impressed at how widespread in the animal world these resemblances are found to be. Students have described many similarities between man and his closest primate relations, the great apes.[2] That none of these forms has a tail, that they alone have the vermiform appendix, that they have similar blood-types, have almost the same structure of uterus and placenta, are omnivorous, having the dental equipment to chew either meat or herbivorous foods, have stereoscopic vision, and possess the opposable thumb, indicate how numerous these resemblances are. Above all, however, we find that only man and the anthropoid apes share the tendency to upright posture and bipedal locomotion. Though man is the only true biped, and the apes employ their arms to assist them in walking, yet only man and the great apes have posterior extremities that can be put to such use.

---

[1] 1929, *passim.*
[2] One of the most detailed of these is Schultz, 1936.

The attainment of upright posture was fundamental in bringing about the changes which made of man the erect, speaking, tool-using, culture-building creature he has become. So important was this that it is said man became human through the use of his feet. We cannot here debate the question

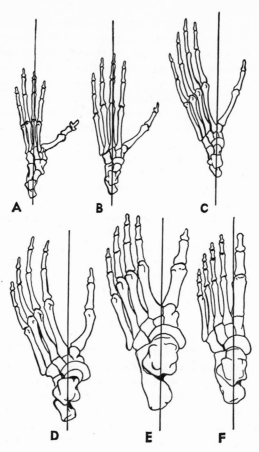

FIG. 2 *The development of the human foot, from (A) lemuroid and (B) simian (macaque) types of feet through (C) gibbon, (D) chimpanzee, and (E) gorilla to (F) man. The terrestrial adaptations of gorilla and human feet are seen in the more massive development of the heel and the increased development of the inner border of the foot, with a shortening of the toes (after Morton, 1927, fig. 3).*

whether or not the forms which preceded man began the march toward erect posture by coming out of the trees to lead a terrestrial rather than an arboreal life. The play of cause and effect is much too obscure, much too complex to permit any conclusive answer. It is difficult to envisage a 400-pound gorilla leaping from branch to branch in the forest. On the other hand, it is quite possible that a period of arboreal life did encourage the development of upright posture by shifting the axis of support to a line between the great toe and the rest of the foot. What is important here is to trace the consequences that followed when man's anterior extremities came exclusively to function as grasping organs, and his legs and feet came to be his only means of support and locomotion.

Morton, who has made the most intensive study of the evolution of the foot, has given a diagram which demonstrates how the human organ differs from that of his two nearest related forms, the chimpanzee and the gorilla.[3] The critical element here is the great toe, that in man is firm and fixed, and has lost most of the opposability which in the other primates permits it to be employed as we and they use the thumb. This rigidity is essential to upright posture. Without the great toe we could not stand erect, and those who in accidents or otherwise have lost this organ actually do experience considerable difficulty in walking. The great toe of the gorilla and chimpanzee give them stance in the approximations of upright posture they achieve. But because their great toes are not rigid they soon tire, and resume their characteristic position in which they support themselves with their arms.

With this assumption of upright posture, concomitant changes in many other parts of the body took place. It is not a question of whether these were the *only* changes that might have occurred. The point is that those which are to be observed, that comprise the outstanding differences between men and the forms closest to them, are in accordance with the operation of certain principles of physics that, had they been violated in the process, upright stance would have been rendered impossible.

If we depict, as on the next page, the basic skeletal structure of a quadruped, of an upright brachiating form, and of an erect type in simplest diagrams, we can reduce this structure to the following elements: the head, two girdles—one at the shoulder and the other at the hip—to which the extremities are attached, and which are related to the vertebral column. It is apparent from these simple diagrams that in the quadruped and semi-upright forms, the head must be attached to the rest of the body by a much stronger musculature than in the erect figure, where the skull benefits from having its support directly beneath it, and therefore can be kept in balance by relatively light muscles. Conversely, the posterior girdle, the pelvis, in the quadruped is not much more than something to which the hind legs are attached, while in an erect animal it must support the organs of the torso. In all this, the semi-upright forms will be intermediate. One further point must be made here before we explore the implications of these simple principles. We have used the term "musculature," and spoken of heavier or lighter muscles needed in a given area of the body to retain and accommodate the head or other parts. Most muscles attach themselves to bones at roughened places. The harder the work which the muscle must perform, the rougher the place of attachment and the heavier the bone. How important this fact was in shaping the human form will become at once apparent.

When man stood up on his feet, the femur (thigh-bone) became straighter

---

[3] D. J. Morton, 1927, p. 179, fig. 3.

and longer, and the articulations between the bones of the leg and foot underwent alterations at knee and ankle and thus allowed more effective adjustment to erect posture. The ridge or crest at the back of the human femur also became emphasized to allow for the stronger musculature that was necessary for walking and bending. The pelvis broadened and flattened, to become a kind of basin for the support not alone of the internal organs that were now above it, but also of the upper girdle, arms and head, that press down upon it. The triple curvature of the spine made the vertebral

Fig. 3   *Basic skeletal structure of a quadruped, upright brachiating type, and erect form, highly stylized to show balance of head in* homo.

column a kind of spring-like structure that cushioned, for the head, the shock the entire body experiences with walking. Though less change is apparent in the anterior girdle, it also broadened and flattened into the human scapulae, the forearm lengthened in proportion to the total length of the body, and the thumb and fingers became specialized as grasping organs.

The changes in the head and face were profound. It is a matter of conjecture whether the heavy jaw of the anthropoids became lighter because man was relieved of the need to use his teeth as grasping and fighting organs, or because the need for a heavy jaw to balance the cranium passed when the skull was balanced atop the spinal column. The fact remains that the jaw did become much lighter, and the teeth, especially the canines, became smaller. The jaw-bone, or mandible, is attached to the skull by the muscles by which it is moved, and its lighter character meant that it could be manipulated by lighter muscles. In this way there was more room inside it for the tongue, while the bones of the skull could become thinner, when they were not called upon to provide the rugged surfaces that heavy muscles require as points of attachment. The significance of this is apparent when we compare the smooth vault of the human skull with that of the gorilla skull, with its bony crest to which the muscles that operate the mandible are attached. Finally, with a change in the center of gravity, and the lighter bones of the skull, brains of a size distinctive of man alone could develop.

It must be emphasized again that the process so briefly sketched here leaves entirely aside the problem of why the changes occurred that resulted in *homo sapiens*. One scholar will argue that these came about from need, another from chance, another from the physical forces involved, another from selection. The data do not reveal the causes. But they are emphatic that these, and many other alterations in detail, not given here, do exhibit a pattern of consistency down the ages that is discernible when man is compared with other living forms. This consistency is best seen in tracing the evolutionary process by means of which the early hominid forms, far more like their primate relatives than any living human being, gradually assumed the characteristics we recognize as marking present-day man. The concomitants of a gradual assumption of upright posture are manifested in the direction of the changes in brain-size, in the development of the teeth and jaw, in the differing cross-section of the femur, and in all those other characteristics we have discussed, as man sloughed off anthropoid traits and assumed his present-day form.

Though many forms antecedent to present-day man have been recovered, the broad evolutionary trend we now propose to describe can be encompassed by naming those that are accepted by palaeoanthropologists as marking off the principal steps in the process. We may do this in spite of the fact, too, that the more the discoveries, the more complexly woven the strands of the tapestry of human development are found to be. Unlike the belief of the early twentieth century, it is now recognized that these types form a developmental series many of whose members were coexistent, instead of belonging to different species or even genera that, through mutation or some other process, arose one after the other. Weidenreich, in discussing some of the earliest forms, maintains that Java man differed from Peking man no more than an Australian aborigine living today differs from an Arab. The question whether *Homo sapiens* is quite different from Neanderthal man, or is rather a descendant of the Neanderthals, is no longer seriously debated. Ashley Montagu speaks of "the earliest neanthropic men, who were identical in almost every respect with Europeans of today, the men of Předmost of the late Aurignacian . . ."[4]

3

WE SHALL here first consider the forms that derive from the Far East, and then those that have been recovered from Africa and Europe. While they cannot be placed with finality in their geological order, it is evident that most specimens thus far recovered from sites in the Far East are, in their

---

[4] M. F. Ashley Montagu, 1945, p. 105.

morphological structures, closer to the anthropoids than are those from Europe and Africa. The geological horizon from which all these forms derive is the Pleistocene, though one European form, the so-called Piltdown man, was at first referred by some students to the late Pliocene. There is no question, however, that from the beginning of the Pleistocene period of the Quaternary epoch until the present, the earth has continuously had a protohuman or human population. Man, that is, can be said to have been on earth for a matter of some million years, more or less—it being always understood that dates of this kind, when applied to geological time periods, are tentative in the extreme.

Work in the Far East was interrupted by the outbreak of the second phase of World War II, so that to place the individual remains in chronological order is a task for the future. The order given here, which follows that of their morphological sequence as indicated by Weidenreich, must be regarded as tentative and subject to such revision as further study or later discoveries may call forth. There can be no doubt, however, that these Far Eastern finds, considered together, have already changed some of the fundamental conceptions held as to the evolutionary sequence out of which present-day man appeared. They will now be named, and some indication given of when and where they were found, by whom, and of what they consisted.

1. *Gigantopithecus blacki* (*"Gigantanthropus"*), is represented only by the great molars, found in a Chinese apothecary shop in Hong Kong, of which mention has already been made. The first tooth was acquired in 1935 by von Koenigswald, a Dutch colonial officer who discovered many other finds that will be mentioned here. Later two more teeth were recovered in other apothecary shops of the same city. Initially considered the dentition of a giant anthropoid, the name first indicated above was given it. However, closer examination suggested that they had belonged to a hominid and not an anthropoid form. The second name has been urged by Weidenreich as a more appropriate one, "if only the iron rule of scientific nomenclature" would permit the change.

2. *Meganthropus palaeojavanicus.* One and perhaps two mandibles belonging to a giant early form were recovered in 1939 and 1941 by von Koenigswald in the Sangiran district of central Java.

3. *Pithecanthropus robustus,* found in 1938, also by von Koenigswald, at Trinil, Java, where the original *pithecanthropus* discovery was made. This form, of which a skull cap and upper jaw have been recovered, was first regarded as a large *pithecanthropus* male, but after the discovery of the *gigantopithecus* teeth it was given this name by Weidenreich better to denote its place in the evolutionary sequence.

4. *Pithecanthropus erectus* was the first hominid form to be recovered from Java. For almost three decades it was the only early form from the Far East, and served as a constant challenge to students of early man. It was discovered by Dr. Eugene Dubois, a Dutch physician, in 1891–92, and received its name "erect ape-man of Java" because its discoverer felt its characteristics marked it as a form midway between apes and living man, some-

thing in the nature of a "missing link." Since the two series of *pithecanthropus* remains named above were discovered by von Koenigswald (in 1938 and 1939), its position, as determined by considerations of comparative morphology, has been revised to give it a later place in the human evolutionary series than these giant types. Besides the three skull parts, the remains now in hand consist of a mandible, six femora (not accepted as belonging to *pithecanthropus*) and two teeth (likewise of questionable affiliation).

5. *Homo modjokertensis,* found in 1936. This is a juvenile skull, which complicates its assignment to a place in the palaeoanthropological series, since the younger the individual, the more generalized its traits and the more difficult its identification. Weidenreich believes that its place in the evolutionary scale cannot be determined "without a thorough investigation, but also in this case the answer will probably remain doubtful because of the infantile character of the specimen." [5]

6. *Sinanthropus pekinensis,* first found in 1929, by W. C. Pei, reopened the whole problem of early man in the Far East. As the years passed, fresh discoveries were made of this type which, well documented by the finds, became as important as *pithecanthropus* for the understanding of the story of human evolution. Portions of the skulls of fourteen individuals, including entire calvaria, or brain-cases, facial bones of six individuals, and long bones and teeth that give us parts of almost forty more have been recovered from the cave at Choukoutien where this rich store of materials came to light. Its relationship to *pithecanthropus* has been remarked from the first, and it is quite likely that the two forms existed at about the same period of the Pleistocene.

The conclusions to be drawn from this earliest group of Far Eastern finds lead to a considerable alteration in the conventional picture of the early stages of human evolution. Thus the questions raised in the opening pages of this chapter concerning early gigantism, seem to require an affirmative answer. The conclusion of Weidenreich, who has gone far more exhaustively into the study of this group than any other scholar, is: "The hominids of the Sino-Malayan fauna, as far as they are known at present, represent a fairly continuous line proceeding from small types to gigantic ones in the following sequence: *Pithecanthropus erectus* (Skulls I, II, III), *Pithecanthropus robustus* (Skull IV), *Meganthropus palaeojavanicus, Gigantopithecus blacki.* As to their morphological characters, each larger type seems to be more primitive [i.e., nearer the anthropoid form] than the next smaller one. In other words, gigantism is a primitive character which has the tendency to diminish as evolution advances." [6] He continues further: "It is definite that *Sinanthropus pekinensis* represents about the same evolutionary stage as *Pithecanthropus erectus.* His relation to *Pithecanthropus robustus, Meganthropus,* and *Gigantopithecus* is therefore similar to that of *Pithecanthropus erectus. Gigantopithecus* as a South Chinese ancestral form of *Pithecanthropus* may also be the ancestral form of *Sinanthropus.* When the *Pithecanthropus* line extended southward from South China in Java, another branch may

[5] F. Weidenreich, 1945a, p. 388.
[6] F. Weidenreich, 1945b, p. 124.

have extended northward to North China and given origin to *Sinanthropus,* but in this case no intermediate forms so far have been discovered." [7]

That these gigantic beings existed over a period of time that caused them to overlap the smaller types, makes another alteration in the common point of view about early man essential. For it introduces a factor of contemporaneity of forms at different stages of evolution to a far greater extent than had been earlier granted. Indeed, to carry the argument farther, it means that *racial differentiation may have been a commonplace in human experience even as early as this.* Such speculations obviously open fascinating possibilities for revision of our conceptions of the types and varieties of men who inhabited the earth in the distant days when our earliest forerunners lived.

4

BEFORE considering the Euro-African group of fossil forms, we must note two other Javanese finds, which existed later than those we have discussed, and are in their morphological characters farther along the evolutionary scale.

7. *Homo soloensis* is represented by a series of skulls found near the Solo River, at the village of Ngandong, in 1931. The correspondences of this find with *pithecanthropus* and *sinanthropus* materials are too numerous to permit it to be sharply differentiated from them, yet there are too many differences to allow it to be placed in the same category with them. It is classed by Weidenreich as "an enlarged *Pithecanthropus* type on the way to an advanced form." He adds, "The fact that the geological level in which the Ngandong skulls were found is higher than that of the Trinil specimen also fits into this morphological picture." [8] The final Far Eastern type, probably from a still more recent horizon, is:

8. *Homo wadjakensis* (Wadjak man). The two skulls of this form were found in 1891 by E. Dubois, the discoverer of *pithecanthropus,* but not published until 1920. They have greater cranial capacity than the earlier types, and take their importance from their resemblance to the skulls of the modern aboriginal Australian, whose ancestors they have been claimed to be. This, however, is so controversial that it would be pointless to explore it here. The difficulties in assigning these skulls arises from the fact that they were badly crushed when recovered, while their discovery was announced so long after they were found that further investigation at the site was rendered impossible.

Turning now to the west, we find, first of all, a form on whose position, nature, even validity, there is little agreement. As MacCurdy has stated: "The prehistoric archaeologist sometimes uncovers strange bedfellows; no other discovery is quite so remarkable in this respect as the assemblage from

---

[7] *Loc. cit.*

[8] F. Weidenreich, 1943, p. 274.

The Evolution of Mankind

Piltdown. Nature has set many a trap for the scientist, but here at Piltdown she outdid herself in the concatenation of pitfalls left behind." [9]

9. *Eoanthropus dawsoni* (*Piltdown Man*), was discovered in Sussex, England, in 1911–12 by Mr. Charles Dawson. Later finds, made some two miles from Piltdown in 1915, were held to validate the original remains. The great difficulty in evaluating the materials is that the cranial fragments, which if found alone would have been named those of a modern man, lay near half of a lower jaw that was essentially anthropoid, most like that of a chimpanzee. The difficulty of reconciling jaw and skull, as belonging to the same individual, which those who defend the appellation *eoanthropus* ("dawnman") insist on doing, leaves its authenticity open to question pending further evidence. Some scholars have suggested that it be given the name of *homo sapiens fossilis* (*dawsoni*). They lay emphasis on the human character of the skull and its antiquity as evidenced by the age of the deposit in which it reposed, tactfully rejecting the anthropoid mandible. Weidenreich, however, dismisses the entire find as "an artificial combination of fragments of a modern-human braincase with orang-utan-like mandible and teeth." He terms it a "chemaera" that should be "erased from the list of human fossils." [10] Whatever the merits of the controversy, if the position of those who prefer to think of this form as *homo sapiens fossilis* is adhered to, the existence of "types of *homo sapiens* . . . not only . . . contemporaneously with Neanderthal man but . . . already flourishing even before his appearance on the scene" [11] will have to be postulated.

10. *Africanthropus njarasensis* is also a controversial form, though the dispute in this case concerns its place in the evolutionary series rather than any question of its validity. It was found in 1935, in Tanganyika, East Africa, in a Pleistocene deposit, by a Norwegian, Kohl-Larsen. The find consisted of many fragments of several skulls. These were reconstructed by Weinert, who related the reconstructed form to the *pithecanthropus-sinanthropus* group. Needless to say, if this were true it would be a fact of the first order of importance. Granting the validity of the reconstruction, however—which by no means all students do—the most that can be said is that this is morphologically an early type, that lived during the Pleistocene epoch, and that is transitional in the sense that it shares some traits with the Far Eastern early group, but more with the later Neanderthals.

11. *Homo heidelbergensis,* though discovered in 1907, has taken on a new importance with time. It consists only of a large and very heavy mandible —so heavy that it most probably would have been classified as that of an ape had not the teeth also been preserved. These, and the manner in which they are set in the jaw (the "dental arch") are, however, so definitely human that the classification of this type as *homo* was required. Whether or not it is to be regarded as ancestral to Neanderthal man cannot be said, though this claim has been raised, and has been justifiably argued on the basis of certain

---

[9] G. G. MacCurdy, 1924, vol. I, p. 333.

[10] 1943, p. 220.

[11] M. F. Ashley Montagu, 1945, p. 98.

traits of this jaw-bone and the teeth. The disparity between teeth and jaw. and the massiveness of this bone, make us think at once of the Far Eastern forms. With other finds that combine traits morphologically earlier and later, it indicates that such protohuman types as are represented by Heidelberg Man and the Far Eastern group may have been much more widely distributed than has otherwise been assumed.

We now reach the immediate forerunner of modern man, *homo neanderthalensis,* or Neanderthal man. The type had many variations which, following the usage of a number of students, we may call by the name Neanderthals. This is because no single find can be regarded as typical for the considerable number of representatives that have been discovered in localities not only widely dispersed over Europe, but in North and southeast Africa, Palestine, and central Asia. They are too numerous to allow us to describe them individually. Rather, following Weidenreich, we may distinguish them as more or less falling into four sub-groups, on the basis of a scale that takes into account the degree of resemblance to anthropoid forms or to modern man.

12a. The "Rhodesian group," is represented only by the find from Broken Hill, Northern Rhodesia, in southeastern Africa. Of all the Neanderthals it lies nearest the anthropoids. Like many others, it has been a subject for controversy, but since its affiliation with the Neanderthal group has in some measure been recognized by most students, it may be regarded as a transitional form, related more closely to the Neanderthal than to any other type.

12b. The forms termed "Mousterian" by Morant or "Spy group" by Weidenreich, including the skulls found at La Chapelle, La Quina, Spy, Neanderthal, Gibraltar, Krapina and Le Moustier, to name the outstanding instances.

12c. The "Ehringsdorf group," which besides the Ehringsdorf skull comprehends that from Tabun, from Steinheim, and others.

12d. The group closest in type to modern man, including the Skhūl Mount Carmel finds of McCown and Keith, and the Galilee skull. These remains are particularly important, for it was their discovery in the late 1920's that forced the conclusion that the transition from Neanderthal to *homo sapiens* was gradual, and not due to the clash of two species that resulted in the extinction of the less advanced. As it has been put: "The combination of definite neoanthropic (i.e., modern) with paleoanthropic features in human types which antedate the Neanderthals of western Europe . . . raises perplexing questions regarding the definition of *Homo neanderthalensis,* the relationship of the two types, and the origin of the neoanthropic type." [12]

Neanderthal remains were first found in 1848, at Gibraltar. Their real significance was not recognized until much later, and this particular specimen was not studied in detail until 1936. The find that gave the type its name was recovered in 1856, in a cave of the Neanderthal ravine near Düsseldorf, Germany. It was recognized as a new species and named in 1864, though the dispute over whether this was a pathological example of modern man or an

---

[12] J. H. McGregor, 1938, p. 68.

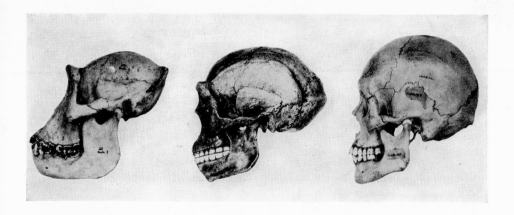

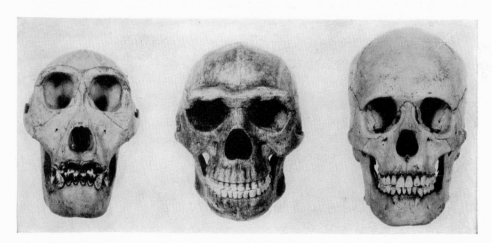

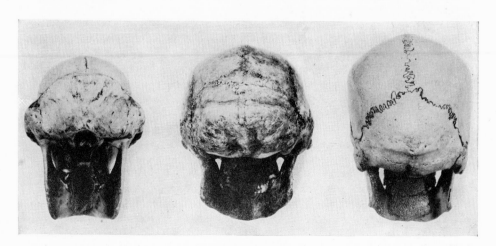

PLATE 2a *Evolutionary changes in the skull. Left to right, female gorilla, female of* sinanthropus pekinensis, *modern man (male) from North China. Lateral view. See page 105.*
PLATE 2b *Same skulls as in Pl. 2a, front view. See page 105.*
PLATE 2c *Same skulls as in Pl. 2a, rear (occipital) view. See page 105. [Photographs courtesy F. Weidenreich and American Museum of Natural History, New York; cf. also F. Weidenreich, 1946, figs. 9, 32, and 33]*

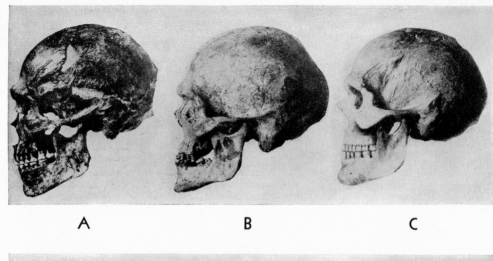

A   B   C

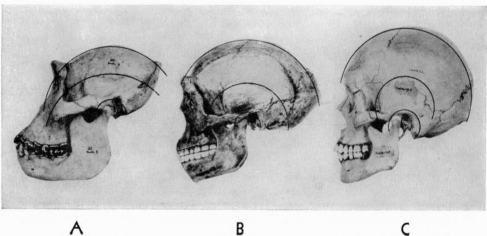

A   B   C

PLATE 3a *Upper Palaeolithic skulls, lying structurally between Palestine finds and modern man. (A) Male, from Předmost, (B) male, from Beni-Segoual (Algiers), and (C) male from Obercassel. See page 110.*

PLATE 3b *(A) Gorilla, (B) sinanthropus and (C) modern skulls in lateral view, with circles at identical levels, showing tendency of human skull to assume globular form. See page 111. [Photographs courtesy F. Weidenreich and American Museum of Natural History, New York; cf. also F. Weidenreich, 1946, figs. 36 and 42]* early human type went on for many years. The large number of comparable remains that came to light as time passed finally provided a definite answer to this question. Today, with parts of more than one hundred individuals at hand, long bones as well as skulls, the type is well enough known so that not only have reconstructions been made of its head, but the entire body of both male and female Neanderthal have been sculptured.

The career of this form on the earth was a long one. The earliest examples of it that can be dated by the geological strata from which they were recovered are about 100,000 years old, the latest some 25,000 years. The span of time during which the Neanderthal types lived was thus far greater than the period which has elapsed since the most recent specimen died. It is therefore apparent why the line of division between the Neanderthals and their successors, the Cro-Magnon men, is to be loosely drawn. The best opinion now holds that crossing between neoanthropic man and *homo sapiens* was not only possible, but probably occurred to a considerable degree. This hypothesis is borne out by the fact that in museum and laboratory skull collections, specimens of present-day individuals appear with distinct neoanthropic traits—traits that have all unwittingly been carried by persons whose physical characteristics while living were not measurably distinct from the others among whom they lived. It is now beyond dispute that the first *sapiens* type to appear, Cro-Magnon men, was for long generations a contemporary of the Neanderthal types who, on the basis of comparative morphology are to be thought of as their immediate ancestors.

What kind of creatures were these Neanderthals? Even taking into full account the variation in the many specimens of this type we have, he manifests a sufficient degree of homogeneity so that he can be described in terms of average values, much after the manner in which living races are described. Neanderthal man was short, about five feet three inches tall. He was somewhat stooped, and walked with semi-flexed knees, which means that he did not attain a posture that was completely upright. He was heavy-set, with a short, thick neck. Whether he was hairy, as restorations depict him, or not, cannot be said, since hair, like soft parts, completely disappears with the passage of time. He had a large head, characterized by a rugged skull, a low forehead, marked brow-ridges and a heavy, chinless jaw. His nose was broad, and the orbits of the eye were large; in the skull these orbits are set deeply. On first glance there is a temptation to associate his receding forehead with small brain-size, but this is not justified by the facts. The capacity of his cranium, which varies between 1220 and 1610 cubic centimeters, in general exceeds that of modern man both in range and on the average.

13. Our final prehistoric type, *Cro-Magnon*, is the equivalent of living man in every respect. It takes its name from the rock shelter at the village of Les Eyzies, in southern France where, in 1868, the original discovery of this form was made. There was never any question that it was an early manifestation of *homo sapiens*, whose career on earth is now regarded as antedating this form since the discovery in 1935, at Swanscombe, England, of parts of a skull, which lay in a middle Pleistocene deposit. Swanscombe man, if not *homo sapiens*, was at least closer to modern man than the Neanderthal

forms.[13] Since the original discovery of Cro-Magnon, much more skeletal material and skulls of this type have been excavated, so that we have a fully adequate idea of its physical characteristics. The males were tall, some of them reaching six feet. They were considerably taller than the female Cro-Magnons seem to have been, even when the sex differences in stature are compared to those between the sexes in modern humans. Their average cranial capacity is larger than the average for modern man. The forehead was high, the chin prominent, and the facial angle upright (orthognathous), in striking contrast to the jutting maxillae and jaws of earlier prognathous forms.

What transitions from these earlier forms gave rise to present-day races we cannot say. Some students relate Cro-Magnon to the Caucasoid (European) type, which in truth he most resembles. The Negroid race is on occasion referred to ancestral forms represented by the Grimaldi skeletons, unearthed in 1874–5 near Monaco. Certainly these, and the mixed Neanderthal-Cro-Magnon remains, excavated at Brünn and Předmost in Czechoslovakia show that even some 25,000 years ago the variations in the physical types of men then existing were pronounced. Weidenreich holds that the racial divisions of mankind reach back into middle Pleistocene periods. He speaks of a "continuous line leading from *Pithecanthropus* through *Homo soloensis* and fossil Australian forms to certain modern primitive Australian races. Rhodesian man seems to be linked, through types like the Florisbad Man, to certain South African races of today." [14] The implications of such an argument for the importance of racial differences are far reaching, but these conclusions are still conjectural. Thus Dobzhansky,[15] on the basis of these findings, argues that all races of living men belong to a single species, while Ruggles Gates,[16] using the same data, holds that present-day races represent distinct species.

In truth, the matter is so obscure that we can agree with McGregor, who says, "It is perhaps no exaggeration to say that less is known about the immediate origin of *Homo sapiens* than of *Homo neanderthalensis*." [17] It is as though we stood before a tree and beheld the lower trunk, the lower branches, and the top, but with our view of the intermediate portion blocked by some obstacle. A solution of the complex problem of the origin of present races is one of the most important tasks facing the paleoanthropologists.

5

CERTAIN conclusions from this brief discussion may be pointed out before we proceed to consider the development of culture in prehistoric times. We may,

---

[13] G. M. Morant, et al., 1938.
[14] F. Weidenreich, 1943, p. 276.
[15] 1944, *passim*.
[16] 1944, *passim*.
[17] 1938, p. 76.

first of all, reaffirm the proposition of the complexity of the process of human development, that makes for many difficulties when we seek to establish more than its broadest outlines. It is clear, however, that this developmental process is one from more to less anthropoid-like forms. On the basis of the study of his hominid ancestry, no less than from the comparative analysis of present-day anthropoid and human forms, man is seen to be a full-fledged member of the biological series.

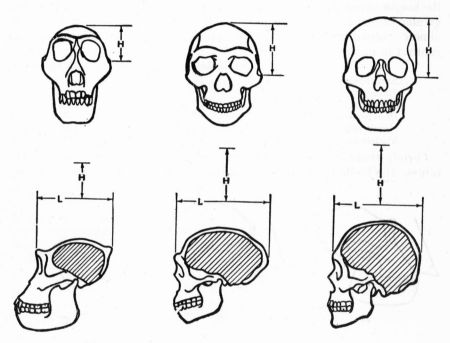

Fig. 4   *Skulls of gorilla,* sinanthropus *and* homo sapiens (*Chinese*), *showing differences in height and length of skull (adapted from Weidenreich, 1946, figs. 9 and 32).*

How evident this is, is perceived when comparative figures for such an important index of humanness as cranial capacity is considered. It will be remembered that the development of a larger brain, indicated by the size of the brain-case, is one of the most significant traits that mark man as different from other forms. It is especially useful for comparative purposes, since the calvarium, the top part of the skull, has been found more frequently and in a better state of preservation, than those other more fragile bones that make up the skeleton of the face, or elements of the skeletal structure of the body and the extremities. We may again turn to Weidenreich's authoritative study for a useful compilation of the cranial capacity of various hominid and human types.

	Minimum-Maximum Values (cc.)	Average (cc.)
Anthropoids	300–585	415
Pithecanthropus	775–900	860
Sinanthropus	915–1225	1043
Homo soloensis	1035–1255	1100
Neanderthals	1220–1610	1400
Modern man	1225–1540	1300 [18]

Or, as another example of this consistency of change, the index between the height of the skull (at the vertex) and its length may be cited. Here the greater height of the head is indicated by the larger figure; the low skull, almost without any forehead, being characteristic of the anthropoids in contrast to man:

	Minimum-Maximum Values	Average
Anthropoids	50.6–56.2	54.0
Pithecanthropus II	———	64.2
Sinanthropus	67.7–71.6	69.4
Homo soloensis	65.5–74.6	69.0
Neanderthals	64.4–92.0	77.7
Modern man	84.3–98.4	91.0 [19]

Certain traits manifest the characteristics of modern man earlier than others. The teeth, for example, become humanoid long before the jaw. Yet

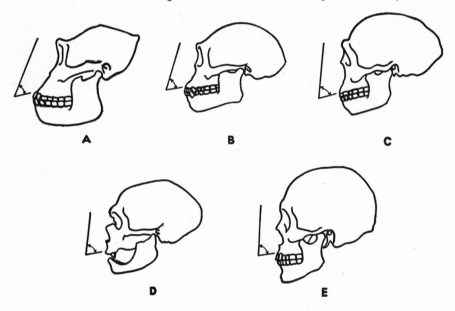

A   **B**   **C**

D   **E**

Fig. 5 *Increase of facial angle from anthropoids through hominids to* homo; **(A)** *female gorilla,* **(B)** pithecanthropus erectus, **(C)** sinanthropus pekinensis, **(D)** *Neanderthal* (*La Chapelle aux Saints*), **(E)** homo sapiens (*modern Chinese*).

---

[18] F. Weidenreich, 1943, p. 120.
[19] *Ibid.*, p. 121.

The Evolution of Mankind

for still other traits, such as the facial angle, or the prominence of brow-ridges, or the increasingly U-shaped form of the dental arch (as against the V-form of the lower primates), or a more and more erect posture as indicated by the leg-bones, the later specimens are successively closer to modern man than the older ones.

We must take care, however, not to think of this developmental process in terms of "lower" to "higher," or use any analogous series of evaluative concepts. It will be recalled that in our discussion even the use of such a word as "primitive," a valid term when employed to denote earlier biological forms in comparison with later ones, has been avoided. Above all, this long and fascinating tale of human evolution is not to be correlated with the successive changes in culture that we shall consider in the following chapter.

Only when we approach this relationship in the broadest terms is even an approximation of such a correlation to be found, and it is questionable whether it exists even then. This is what Movius implies when he lays stress on the fact that "the field of archaeology, though it utilizes and synthesizes the conclusions of the natural sciences, is directly related to the social sciences." [20] Even such an early form as *Pithecanthropus* developed a technique of making stone implements, while *Sinanthropus* knew the use of fire. In Europe, while graphic art shows a steady development during the upper Palaeolithic, it disappears at the onset of the Neolithic age, to be replaced by the crudest kind of aesthetic expression. So independent of each other were physical and cultural changes, indeed, that some students stress the fact that culture, as expressed in stone artifacts, remained relatively stable in contrast to the many different hominid forms that made these implements; but that in the comparatively brief period when *homo sapiens* has existed, culture has so proliferated that present ways of life may lie beyond the powers of human control.

Without going into the merits of either position, it can be stated that the story of man's development affords but few materials for those who would correlate physical type and culture. We recognize that man had need of the brains, the tongue, the hands to create and manipulate culture. Once begun, however, the process of culture-building continued on the basis of learning and not of instinct. And this, as we have seen, means that, at any given moment, the cultures even of the early forms comprised bodies of accepted modes of behavior which, developing out of their own traditional bases, equipped the human groups who lived in accordance with them to meet the demands of the natural and psychological setting in which they moved.

---

[20] H. L. Movius, Jr., 1944, p. 8.

CHAPTER 8

The Prehistoric Development
of Culture

IN RECONSTRUCTING the physical development of man, the logic of structure and the regularity of the evolutionary process can be called on to help the student in his difficult task. No such aid is at hand when the prehistoric development of culture is studied. When a flaked flint point is found in the earth, it can mean no more than that a human being had been present either to make it or use it. But what it was used for, or how, can merely be conjectured. It might have been hafted to a long thin stick and employed as an arrow, or it might have been thrown by hand, or used to make fire, or it might even have been an object of ceremonial usage. How different this is from the tale told by, let us say, a human or hominid leg-bone, need scarcely be suggested.

This range of variation in the employment of man-made objects, or *artifacts*, as they are termed in archaeology, is only a beginning of the problems faced by the prehistorian in his quest for an understanding of the origin and development of culture. This is why it is imperative, if we would grasp the nature of this process clearly, to understand when conclusions are based on fact, and when they are but hypotheses based on inference from the facts.

An example will make the difference clear. Deep in the cave of *Trois Frères*, in the Dordogne region of southern France, is a famous wall painting of the Magdalenian period, perhaps twenty thousand years old. In the reproduction given here, it is to be seen that this figure stands erect on human feet, for all its stag's antlers, head and body. The remoteness of the gallery where it was made, the fact that it is high on the wall, that people did not live in this gallery, has caused archaeologists to speculate whether it was not a symbol to control supernatural forces. So reasonable does this seem, that the figure has become known as a worker of magic, and has been named *Le Sorcier de Trois Frères*.

What are the facts? The painting exists, and its remoteness is a fact. That the cave was not used for human occupancy is a reliable deduction from fact, since evidence of occupancy in the gallery, such as the remains of fire or gnawed bones are absent. The rest is inference, based on the customs of present-day living "primitive" peoples. Yet we read in popularized versions ot prehistory that the Magdalenian folk who occupied the cave of *Trois Frères* are known to have practised magic!

Inference is a workable and useful tool if held within its limitations. Thus in caves inhabited during the Mousterian epoch, remains of fire are found to a great depth. In some of these caves human skeletons are present. On

FIG. 6   *The "Sorcerer" of the cave of Trois Frères, Ariège, France (after MacCurdy, 1924, fig. 151, from photograph by Count Begouin).*

some of the bones are flecks of red ochre, while the thigh-bone of a horse, and a beautifully worked flint implement, were also recovered in association with one such skeleton. The depth of the ash could only mean that the cave was consistently inhabited over a very long period of time. The further inference is irresistible, that the inhabitants, in order to leave remains of fire to this depth, formed a social group that also existed continuously over a very long period. The position of the skeleton indicates that it was buried at the place it was found. The ochre, obviously, must have settled on the bones after the flesh had disintegrated. This means that the body was decorated before it was buried. The horse's thigh and the stone implement were also obviously buried with it. We may assume, then, that, as with many living peoples, the purpose of these objects was to provide food and protection for the dead. Since the cult of the dead figures as an integral part of religion over most of the world, and can consequently be assumed to have had a long existence, we may infer that some form of belief concerning life after death, and thus some type of religious concepts, existed at this early date.

However, it must be stressed that, in assuming a social group living in our cave over many generations, no claim has been made concerning the nature of their social institutions. Whether a man had one wife, or a number of them; whether a woman had one husband or several; whether there was any family life at all, or the entire group lived promiscuously, are questions that can never be answered. Such a matter as the position in this society of the individual whose burial we have noted we likewise can never know; we cannot even speculate with profit on whether he was a secular chief or a religious leader. Nor can we make assumptions concerning the nature of the beliefs these people may have had. There are only the cave, the ashes, the bones, the artifact. They argue a social life and formal disposal of the body of at least the individual whose remains were found. But no further details can be vouchsafed us.

In essence, then, we perceive that, except by inference, prehistoric archaeology can tell us no more than the story of the development of man's physical type and of certain aspects of his *material* culture. The intangibles that are so large a proportion of human civilization can never be recovered. The ideas of early man about the tools that are dug up, or how he used them, must remain a secret, like his social and political institutions, his concept of the universe, the songs he sang, the dances he danced, the speech-forms he employed. Even in the realm of material objects, our knowledge for earlier periods is restricted to things fashioned of inorganic matter. Primaeval man often inhabited caves, but he also lived in open country. Did he have skin tents? Did he use skins at all? Did he make utensils of wood? Until a chance find of some fossilized implement made of wood or other organic material provides an answer to such questions, we can do no more than speculate about them.

All the more remarkable, then, that the archaeologists have been able, with such fragmentary data, to give us in so short a time a picture of the development of man and his culture. That blank spaces exist in the picture, especially where the development of culture in specific areas is in question, does not detract from this achievement. Enough is known of the story of man's prehistoric past to warrant all confidence that, in its principal outlines, no serious revision of the tale, as thus far written, will have to be made. That early prehistoric sites have been investigated more extensively in Europe than in other parts of the world is only a reflection of the fact that archaeologists, whose studies are but a part of the broader stream of Euroamerican scientific thought, found it easier to work at home than abroad. This is why so much of the archaeological data from Palaeolithic times comes from France, for it was here that scientific prehistory developed, and where, among the rich sites available for study, research has been most intensively cultivated. By the same token, and for the same reasons, the archaeology of the Americas is incomparably better known than that of Africa.

2

IT HAS not been found possible to devise a single series of classifications to cover all prehistoric cultures. As in all studies of prehistoric phenomena, the timetable on which reliance must be placed to order our data is phrased in terms of geological epochs. In Europe, the various glaciations left deposits that afford a convenient chronology. But such a time-table does not exist for many other parts of the world, notably the tropics. Furthermore, as we have seen in discussing the unfolding tale of human physical development, additional discoveries make for added complexities. As a result, periods which were at first set up on the basis of European prehistory, and were long held to be applicable everywhere, were found not to hold for Africa or Asia, to say nothing of the New World where, as we shall see, human occupancy has been relatively recent.

One of the best statements of the difficulty of establishing world-wide sequences has been given by Movius, on the basis of his study of the Pleistocene, the geological epoch which encompasses most of man's existence on earth, in the Far East. In summarizing his data, he says, "The material brought to light during the last ten years in Asia has opened up a new approach to the problem of Palaeolithic archaeology. . . . Since the classic Western European sequence is absent in the Far East, it is clear that, at the dawn of the Lower Palaeolithic, we have to deal with independent groups of . . . cultures that have followed different patterns of growth. In each, the basic rate of change, as judged by the technique of manufacture and form of the stone tools used over a span of perhaps five hundred thousand years, varies enormously." [1] As a consequence, in the Lower Palaeolithic, he differentiates East and West in terms of what he has called the "hand-ax cultures" of the West and the "chopping-tool cultures" of the East, deriving his classification from the imperishable implements that alone have been preserved out of the total cultural equipment of the early peoples of these two great areas.

The accepted classification of prehistoric cultures for many years was drawn in terms of Palaeolithic (Old Stone), Mesolithic (Transitional), Neolithic (New Stone) Ages, and the Bronze and Iron Ages. The Palaeolithic was in turn divided into Lower, Middle, and Upper. Movius' remarks, like those of others who might be cited, phrase a protest against too general an application of this or any other single scheme. Work from 1925 onward has tended to show that even for Europe such a classification, employed in the customary sense, is not valid. Garrod, who has perhaps most carefully considered the need for reorientation in the light of newer data, may be quoted in this connection. "In the old system," she says, "the palaeolithic cultures

---

[1] H. L. Movius, Jr., 1944, pp. 104–5.

appeared as a straightforward succession with clear-cut horizontal divisions as in a diagrammatic geological section. For the pioneers of prehistory these cultures developed logically one from the other in an orderly upward movement, and it was assumed that they represented world-wide stages in the history of human progress. Today, prehistory has suffered the fate of so many of the component parts of the orderly universe of the nineteenth century. New knowledge has given a twist to the kaleidoscope, and the pieces are still falling about before our bewildered eyes. The main outline of the new pattern is, however, already beginning to appear. We can distinguish in the Old Stone Age three cultural elements of primary importance. These are manifested in the so-called hand-axe industries, flake industries, and blade industries, and we know that the first two, at any rate, run side by side as far back as we can see, and we are beginning to realize that the origins of the third may have to be sought much farther back than we had suspected. Only a moment of reflection is needed to see that we have here the old divisions of Lower, Middle, and Upper Palaeolithic, but with a new axis; we must be careful, however, not to make these divisions too rigid. In fact, these culture-streams do not run parallel and independent; such a view of human history would be absurdly artificial. They are perpetually meeting and influencing each other, and sometimes they come together to produce a new facies." [2]

We may thus consider the prehistoric development of human culture in western Europe as one instance of the process by means of which man reached the condition of life in which he is discovered as the curtain of history rises. For thousands of generations he lived without domesticated animals, or the wheel, or agriculture, or pottery, to say nothing of metal tools. It took hundreds upon hundreds of generations for man to learn to put a decent edge to a flint knife. Millennia went by before his aesthetic impulses had even the crudest means of expression in enduring form.

The table of prehistoric correlations given on p. 120 should be continuously consulted during our discussion. It includes both the older terminology and the revisions of this that later research has introduced. The names given the periods that succeed each other, whether in the older or the newer schemes, are derived from the localities in which type specimens were found and are thus entirely unfamiliar, without association, and difficult for those who are first confronted with them. As will be apparent from our table, the most drastic revisions of terminology have come in designating the periods of the Palaeolithic. This is not only, as the citation from Garrod indicates, because, as in all scientific research, the consistent pursuit of the answer to a problem reveals new facets of that problem and causes earlier answers to be recognized as insufficient in the light of more abundant data. In addition, a more specific factor has been operative in the case of European prehistory, the growing realization that the prehistorian does not study *cultures*, but *industries*. This was forced by the nature of the data; the fact

---

[2] Dorothy A. E. Garrod, 1938, p. 1.

that, as has been suggested, the intangibles in the early life of man cannot be recovered, so that only the things made in imperishable materials are available for study.

The primary kinds of tools found in Palaeolithic sites fall into three categories. For the earlier and longer part of the epoch, *core* and *flake* types are present. The characteristic implement of the later portion is the *blade*. It

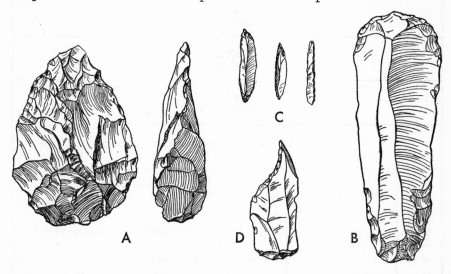

FIG. 7 *Core, flake and blade tools*: (A) *Acheulean hand-axe*, (B) *Aurignacian end-scraper*, (C) *Aurignacian backed blades*, (D) *graver (after Burkitt, 1933, and Leakey, 1934)*.

is on the basis of the predominance of one or the other of these types—for none is exclusively present in any period—that the newer nomenclature has been worked out. By this means, an overall series of designations for prehistoric data has been reached within which local variants, named after specific sites, can be discerned or, in the future, can be designated in accordance with later finds.

Childe has given one of the clearest short descriptions of the techniques of flint working that produced these basic forms. "Core tools," he says, "were made by knocking bits off a large lump or *core* until this was reduced to one of four or five standard forms. The products can all be classified as *core* tools and are currently designated hand-axes." Of *flake-tools*, he says, "Their makers do not seem to have cared much what shape was ultimately assumed by the parent lump or core; they were primarily interested in the flakes detached and trimmed these up to form implements less rigorously standardized than hand-axes." With the passage of time, skills increased, and the nodule off which pieces were struck was preworked so as to yield implements of greater precision and efficiency. During the Upper Palaeolithic man "had learned to prepare a lump of flint or obsidian so that a whole series of long narrow flakes, termed blades, could be struck off a single core once the long preliminaries had been executed." Typical of these periods, too, was the

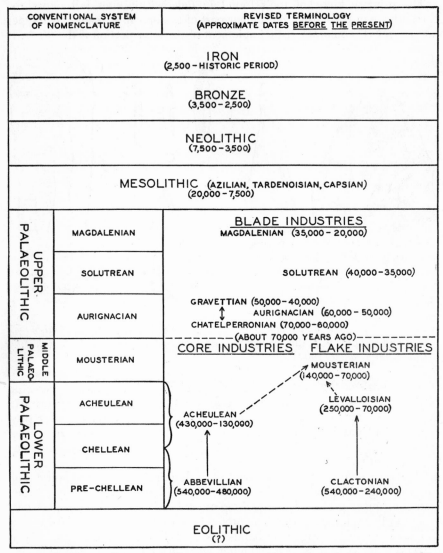

CONVENTIONAL SYSTEM OF NOMENCLATURE		REVISED TERMINOLOGY (APPROXIMATE DATES BEFORE THE PRESENT)
		IRON (2,500 – HISTORIC PERIOD)
		BRONZE (3,500 – 2,500)
		NEOLITHIC (7,500 – 3,500)
		MESOLITHIC (AZILIAN, TARDENOISIAN, CAPSIAN) (20,000 – 7,500)
UPPER PALAEOLITHIC	MAGDALENIAN	**BLADE INDUSTRIES** MAGDALENIAN (35,000 – 20,000)
	SOLUTREAN	SOLUTREAN (40,000 – 35,000)
	AURIGNACIAN	GRAVETTIAN (50,000 – 40,000) ↕ AURIGNACIAN (60,000 – 50,000) CHATELPERRONIAN (70,000 – 60,000) ————————(ABOUT 70,000 YEARS AGO)—————
MIDDLE PALAEO- LITHIC	MOUSTERIAN	**CORE INDUSTRIES FLAKE INDUSTRIES** MOUSTERIAN (140,000 – 70,000)
LOWER PALAEOLITHIC	ACHEULEAN	ACHEULEAN (430,000 – 130,000) LEVALLOISIAN (250,000 – 70,000)
	CHELLEAN	
	PRE-CHELLEAN	ABBEVILLIAN (540,000 – 480,000) CLACTONIAN (540,000 – 240,000)
		EOLITHIC (?)

FIG. 8 *The prehistory of Western Europe (after Garrod, Zeuner, Braidwood, et al)*.

burin or graver, "a blade pointed by removing a facet along one edge in such a way that it can be repeatedly repointed by simply removing another facet." [3]

---

[3] C. G. Childe, 1946, p. 24, pp. 29–30.

The Prehistoric Development of Culture

3

THE beginnings of human culture are matters of great controversy. The eoliths, or "dawn-stones," found on the continent of Europe and in England, and named in the 1880's, have never received the same acceptance as tools made and used by early man that is granted the artifacts of later prehistoric cultures. The question turns on whether the objects so named were actually made and used by man, or were merely shaped by the elements into what seemed to be the forms of crude tools. The discussion is reminiscent of the questions raised concerning the validity of the Piltdown find, which was found in association with some of these purported tools. Neither question has been resolved, and both must await the discovery of further data.

The eolith question is complicated further by the fact that it conceals two problems. The first is whether man made these crude implements; the second whether he used them, even if he came upon them ready to hand. It is possible that the use of those implements may have an affirmative answer, while their human fashioning is given a negative one. Presumed eoliths are found in the Tertiary and early Quaternary, geological horizons that far antedate the known appearance of man.

Equally possible, however, is that remains of hominids will be found in earlier strata than heretofore. Or, if eoliths are tools made by natural causes but used by men, then such stones would be expected in epochs that antedate man. Today we do not live in a Stone Age at all. Yet we use "hammerstones" when, on a walk, it is necessary to pound down a loose nail in a shoe. The stone, once we use it, is a tool. We did not fashion it, we only picked it up and utilized it. We ask, then, why could earliest man not have done the same? It is a fair question, though unanswerable.

There is no question, however, that human beings manufactured the tools found in later archaeological horizons. The earliest artifacts are crude, indeed, and one wonders how they could have been used effectively. Some of these hand-axes and flakes, as a matter of fact, might easily escape the attention of the novice, so like naturally fractured stones are they. Hand-axes are large and unwieldy; their edges and points exist more by definition than functionally. As time proceeds and we move into later stages of the Lower Palaeolithic, however, the motor habits of the makers are brought under more and more effective control. Hand-axes become smaller and better balanced; they fit the hand, and they have an edge and a point that make them recognizably useful for incising and cutting. Early flaking-tools also have a crudity that is quite comparable to the crudeness of the earliest core-tools. It is obvious that flakes must come from stone nodules, but it is by no means certain that the first flakes were by-products of a core industry. Clactonian tools are primarily flakes, as Abbevillian tools are primarily cores. But the Clactonian flakers were apparently little interested in the cores from which the flakes came. As time goes on, the flakes, like the cores, reflect the growing skill in preparation and execution of the requisite techniques, as one generation trained the next.

The Materials of Culture

The stages that for Europe have variously been termed pre-Chellean and Chellean or Abbevillian, the Acheulean, and the Clactonian and Levalloisian, lasted for periods variously estimated at from a half-million to a quarter-million years. What life was like in those times, with their alternations of cold and warm climates as the glaciers advanced and retreated, is not known. That the early beings that made these implements had the ability to learn can be seen by inspecting in any museum a sequence of artifacts of the Lower Palaeolithic. The more effective forms that appear with the passage of time reflect growing competence on the part of their makers. But of the broad repertory of culture as we know it, we cannot hint even as to the basic forms of economic life, except sparsely, and in negative terms.

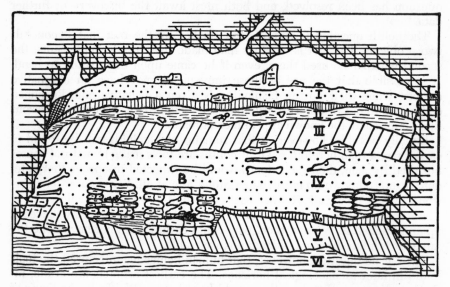

Fig. 9 *Cave at Drachenloch. (A) Hearth with charcoal, (B) "altar" with cave-bear skulls, (C) flat stones. The various strata indicated by Roman numerals presumably bear the remains of different periods of occupation. I and VI have no artifacts (after MacCurdy and Bächler).*

That is, we can say with confidence that the early European Lower Palaeolithic beings did not have fire, or the remains of ash would have been present where they lived. They had no domesticated animals or plants—these were not to come until the Neolithic—for the faunal remains are those of wild forms only. They were, then, in all probability, hunters and gatherers of fruits, nuts, roots, and berries, like all those who lived later during the Palaeolithic. As for the remainder of their mode of life, the data that have been recovered do not provide even the basis for an intelligent guess.

The *Mousterian,* which was also conventionally called the *Middle Palaeolithic,* is now known to include a number of differentiated industries, with the detail of which we need not be concerned here. The "typical" Mousterian takes its name from the rock shelters in the Dordogne region of southern

France, from which, as we have said, so much important material bearing on the prehistory of Europe has been recovered. It will be remembered that the Mousterian, as earlier conceived, was the culture of Neanderthal man, who is so closely associated with this form that the name "Mousterian man" has been suggested for him. The use of the striking platform on the prepared nodules made possible the production of the smaller, more finely shaped hand-axes that mark the ultimate form they took before they gave way entirely to different tools, some of which were made out of different materials.

The number of sites, the length of time many of these sites were occupied, the remains of fauna, and the disposition of skeletal materials permit us to infer much about other aspects of life at this time. It is plain that the people were hunters, and that, having the use of fire, their livelihood was more assured than it would have been without fire. We have mentioned how it is possible, from the position and location of certain skeletal and cultural remains of the period that have been found in association, to infer a belief in life in an afterworld. Of similar significance would seem to be the remains of cave-bear skulls, arranged somewhat like an altar, in the cavern of Drachenloch, high above the present snow-line in the Swiss Alps. It is in this cavern, too, that we come on some of the earliest European bone tools. Cave-bear fibulae seem to have been favored. They were broken in two, the broken surface polished, and the joint used as a handle. Still other bones, marked by use, could have served as vessels for holding liquids and are found in quantity, while bone splinters were employed as points.

4

As WE move to the *Upper Palaeolithic*, the stone technique becomes refined through the utilization of blades and the virtual disappearance of core-tools. The production of blades becomes more and more precise, until toward the end we find tiny pieces of flint, some less than half an inch long, an eighth of an inch or less wide, retouched by subsidiary flaking to give a fine edge and a sharp point—a far cry from the crudities of the Lower Palaeolithic. Bone and ivory were used for such specialized implements as harpoons, while it is not unreasonable to assume that some of the small flint points may have been set in wooden or bone clubs or staves to make composite weapons or implements.

So striking is the difference between the Lower and Middle Palaeolithic, on the one hand, and the Upper Palaeolithic and Mesolithic, on the other, that various students of prehistory have preferred to follow the Austrian scholar, Menghin, and class the former as Protolithic, the latter as Miolithic.[4] It is impossible here, however, to consider the arguments for this and several suggested revisions of the earlier system of nomenclature. It can only be stated that, as in other aspects of science, terminology is a means to understanding rather than an end in itself. The terminology that best describes the facts, and is most easily understood, is thus the most acceptable. "Core"

---

[4] O. Menghin, 1931, pp. 17–21.

and "flake" industries are more precise instruments of description than "old stone age," "middle stone age," and the like. The task of prehistory is, as Daniel remarks, "to describe cultures and chronology." [5] Any clearly defined terminology that furthers this task is a needed element in the prehistorian's repertory.

Whether early Miolithic or Upper Palaeolithic, then, the period represents a broadening and deepening of human resources that go beyond the use of stone and the introduction of bone and ivory tools. The environment in which the Cro-Magnon men of the period lived was cruel. This was the height of the final glaciation, and these people had to cope with such animals as the mammoth, the wooly rhinoceros, the cave-bear, cave-lion, cave-hyena, wild boar, and other great and predatory beasts. Implements that look like the spear-throwers of some modern nonliterate peoples have been found. They were probably used to propel barbed harpoons. Certainly deep deposits of debris and ash in the inhabited caves show that these afforded protection against both weather and predatory animals. The people probably clothed themselves with the skins of the beasts they killed, and their clothing may even have been sewed rather than have been of the robe-type. Buttons and toggles have been recovered from Magdalenian sites, while awls and bone needles are also present. Not all these are found throughout the Upper Palaeolithic, of course. Each of its periods, moreover, is marked by different features in its lithic industry. Among "Aurignacian" tools (Chatelperronian and Gravettian), end and side scrapers predominate; the Solutrian produced the beautiful, delicate "laurel-leaf" flints, with overall flaking on both sides; the many specialized implements of the Magdalenian, and its bone and ivory work, are noteworthy.

The greatest achievement of the Upper Palaeolithic in Europe, however, was its art. Before this time no embellishment of artifact is to be found, no attempt to depict any object on walls of caves, no scratching of lines to make a crude design. How the superb accomplishments of the Upper Palaeolithic artists began, and where they had their origin, is unknown. The three-dimensional figurines of the Aurignacian, which are among the earliest specimens, represent a sureness in the handling of form and the organization of mass that few modern sculptors surpass. These figurines disappear with the epoch, and no developmental sequence has been established for them. Pictorial art, on the other hand, shows a gradual development from crude outline drawings or more skilled sketches to the impressive realistic cave paintings, in color, of bison, reindeer, and mammoth.

The Aurignacian "Venuses," as they are termed, are interesting figures, as can be seen in the specimens illustrated in Chapter 23. Always representing the female form, the secondary sexual characteristics accentuated, the long curled hair occasionally represented, the face never modelled realistically—it is not strange that they have given rise to much speculation. Their exaggerations have been equated with the female Hottentot figure of today, but Martin has demonstrated that the form is essentially that of the mature

---

[5] G. E. Daniel, 1943, p. 54.

Caucasoid woman of the present time.[6] For what purpose were these statu-
ettes made? Among many living peoples, and those of historic antiquity, the
cult of fertility offers a possible analogy. Since we cannot be sure of our
hypotheses when we enter the realm of belief as motivating the behavior that
only survives in the mute remains of palaeolithic life, we can but wonder at
the appearance of these art objects at so early a time, without known precursor and without further expression in later periods.

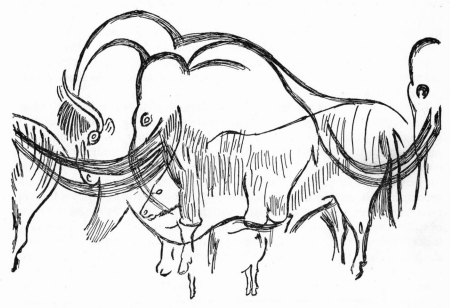

FIG. 10   *Line drawing showing superimposition of cave paintings of the
Magdalenian period. To be seen in this figure are bison, mammoth, horse,
and reindeer (after MacCurdy, 1924, fig. 130).*

Drawing and painting show a longer development, and a more orderly
one. Yet they, too, are cut off at their zenith. For when the Magdalenian is
ended, its art disappears, to give way to the scratchings and crude daubs of
the Mesolithic.[7] We see, when we follow through this art, how the earliest
attempts tried, with but little success, to master the problem of perspective.[8]
The polychrome paintings of the Magdalenian, despite the fact that like
the drawings they are at times superimposed on one another, in contrast
have the faithfulness of portraiture. Incised representations on reindeer bone
show the animal with its head turned backwards—a difficult design element
to master—while on certain wands we find a full face, head-on engraving of
various animals. An impressionistic technique was also employed to repre-

---

[6] R. Martin, 1928, vol. I, pp. 239–41.
[7] Further aspects of the development of this art, and some of the problems in art theory
it poses, are considered in Chap. 23.
[8] See Plate 11 and Figures 32–40, 42–46 below.

sent whole herds of reindeer or wild horses. Whether by accident or by intent we shall never know, but the prehistoric artist allowed the observer to fill in for himself details that are merely suggested by the lines of a drawing or a painting.

Why this art was produced is a problem that has baffled many who have considered it. As pointed out, most of the cave paintings are deep inside the grottos, and "the best works are on the walls of dark, narrow subterranean corridors." [9] This has led to hypotheses about their sacred character, since they are never found where people lived. Yet though, as MacCurdy says, in the cave of Font-de-Gaume, "the stillness and blackness. . . . have combined to preserve the figures in their original freshness," he also remarks that, "We shall never know how much of Quaternary mural art has been destroyed by being placed too near the cavern entrances or in shallow caves and open rock shelters."

Because the subject matter of the paintings is almost exclusively animal, these representations have been explained by referring to the concepts of sympathetic magic that are today found among many living peoples. The paintings are thus thought of as having been endowed, under terms of the concept of "like to like," with the "essence" of the beasts they depicted. Magic rites performed in their presence, this theory runs, would ensure success later in the hunt. It is a good theory, but has little to support it except reference to customs practised many hundreds of generations and thousands of miles removed from where the paintings were made. The theories of art for art's sake, or of a prohibition on depicting animals that drove these artists deep into the caverns to work in secret, offer alternatives that are perhaps less acceptable. Such alternatives, however, are supported by exactly the same amount of objective evidence—that is, none at all—as the explanation in terms of magic.

The *Mesolithic*, or late phase of the Miolithic, as Menghin calls it, has been regarded as a transitional period between the Palaeolithic when, in the terms used by the early archaeologists, stone was chipped, and the Neolithic, when stone was polished. This latter classification was one of the first to break down, however, for Magdalenian deposits yield polished implements, while perhaps the finest overall flaked artifacts ever made were manufactured during the Neolithic in Scandinavia. Moreover, the Mesolithic is distinguished neither for its polished nor chipped implements, though both are present. Its outstanding form is the tiny microlithic flake, retouched, and set in bone or perhaps wooden spears as darts, or used for other purposes. The bone industry continues, though it declines in importance, and ivory disappears with its source, the great mammoths that inhabited Europe during the Ice ages. For the glaciers were receding, and like the reindeer, these great beasts followed them, the reindeer to continue in Northern Europe and Asia, the mammoth to wander northeast to extinction.

In this "transitional" period, also, as we have noted, art-forms degenerate and disappear. Painting is reduced to a few geometric figures, and to designs

---

[9] G. G. MacCurdy, 1924, vol. I, p. 233.

on pebbles that some have said foreshadowed the alphabet, others have again referred to religion—divining—and still others have held to have been some game of chance. The Mesolithic, represented by the Azilian in Southern France, the Tardenoisian in Central France, the Maglemosean on the island of Zealand in Denmark, may perhaps some day come to be thought of as a series of local developments that represent an extension of the Upper Palaeolithic. As Movius puts it, "In a positive sense the Mesolithic

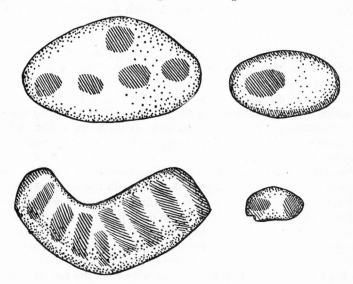

Fig. 11 *Painted pebbles of the Azilian (Mesolithic) period (drawn from specimens in the Chicago Natural History Museum).*

defines a stage in cultural development basically founded on the economy of the Upper Palaeolithic, but profoundly modified by the changes in environment induced by the recession of the ice at the close of the Glacial Period. . . . With the coming-in of the new food-producing Neolithic civilization, bringing its associated elements—pottery, domestication of animals, agriculture and polished stone—there is a break in the sequence. Certain elements from the earlier phase, however, continued in use, as no new forms displaced them, but these cannot be regarded as evolutionary. Instead, they represent the survival of types of implements for which there was still a need and in place of which no innovations were introduced by the new culture." [10]

With the *Neolithic*, the richness of the archaeological record makes it possible to reconstruct a fuller picture of material culture, and to infer much more about the non-material aspects of life than for earlier periods. Neolithic culture, indeed, would not be too strange to many persons living in Europe today; and it has even been said that the peasant of Eastern and

[10] H. L. Movius, Jr., 1942, p. xxiii.

Central Europe would find himself more at home in a Neolithic settlement than in a modern industrial city. The plants raised for food, and even the manner of raising them, would be familiar to him. The animals he used on his farm would all be about, available for similar purposes. Spinning and weaving, the construction of houses and pottery would be going on. The flint-working technique would be unknown to him, but he would find certain of the metal tools he is accustomed to using, in stone or bone—knives, axes, chisels, sickle blades, and weapons such as daggers and spears. He would find the mining industry devoted to producing flint, with miners working in underground tunnels, using picks of antler-horn to detach nodules to be worked later. He would be able to utilize well-established trade-routes. For example, Pressigny, where a kind of "beeswax" flint was mined, was a trading center which sent this distinctive type of flint over all of what is now France, and eastward as far as Switzerland. He might encounter strange forms of religious worship, though the cult of the dead would offer familiar associations. The great megalithic monuments, called dolmens or menhirs, such as are found at Stonehenge in England or Carnac in France, could not but impress him.

As we reach the *Bronze* and *Iron Ages*, the complexity of cultural development becomes ever more clear. As is the case with the introduction of writing, which opens the historic period, we find the use of metal appears at different times in various parts of Europe and the Near East. The discovery of the use of metal was one of the major developments of human history. With the continuing mastery of this technique, man diminished the degree of his dependence upon his natural setting and thus achieved new adaptations to his environment. But the productivity that the use of metals permitted did more than release human societies from the immediate pressure of their habitat. With other techniques, such as irrigation, it made possible an increase in the goods produced beyond anything previously possessed, and thus opened the way to the production of what we shall later, in our discussion of economic life, term an "economic surplus." In this manner, the basis was laid for the differences in the control of wealth that underlie class structures wherever found. It was the Bronze and Iron Ages, in short, that set the stage for the cultures we encounter as the curtain of history rises.

5

WE HAVE devoted the preceding sections to tracing the development of the prehistoric cultures of Western Europe because the consistent program of intensive research which has been carried on here makes available for study the longest series of successive industries and the cultures associated with them. It must again, be stressed, however, that this series, whether as relating to the data that have been recovered or the nomenclature employed to differentiate the various periods, must not be given a world-wide application. As Movius has said, "Since prehistoric archaeology is . . . by itself utterly incapable of establishing a reliable system of Pleistocene chronology on the

The Prehistoric Development of Culture

basis of a classification of the types of implements found in a given series of deposits, the more exacting disciplines of the natural sciences cannot be applied to it. . . . Far from being constant, human culture is an extremely variable factor; man was repeatedly faced with new situations and he was continually experimenting with new methods of adapting his way of life to the environmental factors which confronted him." [11]

How pertinent these qualifications are is to be seen when we shift our attention from the European scene to other continents. We have indicated how, in the Far East, the category of core (chopping) and flake tools has been employed. Both the sequences in which the tools are found, and the local terms applied to these sequences, however, call for fresh mastery by the specialist in European archaeology. The series of "three stages" of Stone, Bronze, and Iron Ages is interrupted in Negro Africa by a transition to metal working which, except for Egypt, entirely omits any period when bronze was used. Again, the pictographic art of Africa, which falls quite outside the problem of succession of industries, offers many difficulties. Similarities of treatment of modern Bushman rock paintings to those of some of the caves in Spain and France have often been noted. A chain of pictographs disclosing many common features, stretches the length of the African continent. Since paintings of this type found in Europe are Upper Palaeolithic, are the cultures of modern African Bushmen to be classified as belonging to this epoch? Or, to turn elsewhere, are the contemporary "stone age" cultures of Australia and New Guinea to be classed with European counterparts that existed a thousand generations earlier, on the basis of the forms of stone implements these people make? One archaeologist, W. J. Sollas, has seriously proposed such affinities, and, on similar grounds, has also equated the Eskimo with the Magdalenian peoples.

The archaeology of the Americas offers perhaps the best example of how different areas pose different problems, and demand different nomenclatures. When Europeans first came into contact with the aboriginal Indians, they were a full stone-age people. Some could be classified as Palaeolithic, as, for example, the Paiute; some, like the Iroquois, as Neolithic. These terms are occasionally encountered in the older literature. Yet most Indian tribes, whether their stone-work was crude or finished, had domesticated plants, and thus knew agriculture, which in Europe is a Neolithic trait. On the other hand, except for the dog, the turkey, the llama, and the vicuña, the Indians had no domesticated animals, despite the fact that in Europe, the domestication of plants and animals occurred at about the same time.

During the thousands of years that the prehistoric physical types and cultures of the Old World were developing, the New World remained uninhabited by man and his forebears, or by any primates except certain monkeys. Some human remains that have been found in association with extinct Pleistocene animal forms have forced the reconsideration of the date earlier accepted for the coming of man to the Americas. This was originally placed at about 10,000 years ago. It is now argued, however, that the migration may

---

[11] Op. cit., pp. 106–7.

have occurred during the last glaciation, in late Pleistocene times, perhaps 15,000–20,000 years ago. But none of the forms that reach to this earlier epoch is pre-human; as a matter of fact, none is markedly different from the Indian of today.

It is generally agreed that the ancestors of the American Indians reached their new habitat over the Bering Straits and the Aleutian Islands, though there are those who press the claim of some migration across the Pacific. Pacific island contributions to the peopling of the Americas must have been small and relatively late, however, and must have occurred after the migrants from Asia had established their physical types and cultures. Should man have come during the last glaciation, there was a corridor east of the Rocky Mountains that would have permitted migrants from the Asiatic continent to move southward despite the ice. It would have been this Pleistocene migration that left the skeletal remains that have been found in Gypsum Cave, Nevada, or in Browns Valley, Minnesota; or such artifacts as the famous Folsom points, the finding of which reopened the entire question of the antiquity of man in the Americas.

In any event, basic discoveries such as the making of flint implements, or the use of fire, were made long before the ancestors of the Indians began their journey down the length of two continents. These migrants came equipped with such techniques, and they also brought the dog with them. It has been established that their dogs are related to no New World canine form, but are of the same species as the dogs of Europe, Asia, and Africa. The new inhabitants were essentially hunters, and so effectively did they hunt that it is believed their coming brought extinction to many Pleistocene fauna that may have persisted into the Recent and might have lived till today had the migrants not disturbed the ecological balance so severely as to render impossible the survival of these animals.

The problems in New World archaeology are very different from those of Old World prehistory. The Indians, whose existence in the Western Hemisphere covers scarce a tenth or even a twentieth of the time man and his hominid forerunners have lived on earth, nonetheless developed cultures which, for variety in form, differences in the complexity of different aspects, and types of adjustment to habitat compare with the cultures of any other large region anywhere. In this period, they domesticated the enormous variety of plants they were found to have by the European explorers who had first contact with them. They had, in Central and South America, developed the technique of pottery-making to a degree unsurpassed elsewhere. From what is now New Mexico, southward to Peru, great aggregates of population formed political units, and had a standard of living that impressed all the early Europeans.

So specialized are the problems of New World archaeology that new techniques of study have had to be devised to investigate them—techniques that are difficult, if not impossible, to employ over the great stretches of time that confront the Old World archaeologist. Naturally the basic methods of excavation, whereby the geological setting is fully taken into account, the careful recording of stratification is noted, and the classification of finds

CHAPTER 9

Physical Type and Culture

WHAT is a race? Science answers the question in this way: *A race is a principal division of mankind, marked by physical characteristics which breed true.* In this sense, the word race is a biological term, and is restricted to the bodily characteristics that distinguish one group of human beings from another. This, in turn, sets off the concept as one of emphasis on the inborn as against the learned aspects of human behavior.

Even in strict biological terms, the use of the word "race" is subject to certain reservations. Not all anthropologists are agreed on the size of the groups to which it should be applied. The races of man, in the conventional sense, are three or four—the Caucasoid, the Mongoloid, the Negroid and, for some, the Australoid. Yet subdivisions in each of these must be recognized, such as the Alpine, Nordic, Mediterranean and Dinaric subdivisions of the Caucasoid race. These are often called "races," too, though it would seem better to call them "sub-racial types," or "sub-races." Krogman has pointed out that if the three or four principal groups of mankind are called "stocks," then such sub-groupings may validly be called "races." [1] Common usage dies hard, however, and the word race has been employed for so long a time to designate the larger groupings that it would be confusing to change it here. Therefore, in our discussion we shall, in the conventional manner, call the principal types of mankind races and use the term sub-race to designate the subordinate aggregates.

The traits which differentiate human groups are, theoretically, as numerous as there are measurements and observations to be taken on the human body. Relatively few of these characteristics are actually measured. Certain ones, that cannot be accurately measured or measured at all, have come to hold great importance because they are so prominently before the observer. One such trait is pigmentation, which has played a preponderant role in racial designation, since for many years it alone was employed for this purpose. The fivefold racial color scheme of the White, Black, Yellow, Brown, and Red races is widely known. Yet no one has ever seen a human being who is really white, or black, or red. "White" people are actually pink, "black" ones are brown, and so are "red" ones. The so-called yellow, brown, and red "races" are all Mongoloid, and should never have been separated.

---

[1] W. M. Krogman, 1945, pp. 48–9.

The Materials of Culture

More important, however, is the principle that no one trait can be relied upon to establish a racial category. If skin color is taken as an example, one will find Caucasoids, from Northern India, quite as dark or darker than many persons who belong to the Negroid race. Australoids will also be well within the Negroid range of pigmentation. Another example of the same sort of error is the oft-used trait of head-form, long held to be the prime racial criterion, as when the "long-headed Nordic" is the subject of description. Yet if head-form is taken as the determining trait of racial differences, not only would Nordics and Mediterranean sub-groups of the Caucasoid race have to be classed together, but most Negroids as well, since, except for some populations that inhabit the Congo basin, most of the Negro race who live in Africa are also long-headed!

In reality, no single group of human beings has a monopoly of any single trait, or cluster of traits. Every large aggregate of men runs a scale from short to tall, from broad to narrow, from light to dark. This is why, with the years, it has become increasingly evident that the outstanding factor in the study of physical types is *variability*. No two human beings are exactly alike, nor two families, nor two local populations, to say nothing of two races. To differentiate races, therefore, by defining them in terms of their physical traits, is thus a statistical problem. It brings into play those methods that have been devised for describing and delimiting any variable quantities; and consequently, how members of a given group vary must figure fully when we set off that group from another.

It follows, therefore, that the phenomenon of *overlapping* bulks large in the study of racial differences. For it must never be forgotten that *homo sapiens* represents, by overwhelming consensus of competent opinion, a single species. This means that the differences between sub-specific groups —that is to say, races—are differences of detail that play upon the basic form we recognize as man. We see this illustrated in the fact, that though there are specialized groups such as pygmies whose stature is so short that it sets them off from most other human forms, they are the exception and not the rule. Even here a tall pygmy will reach a stature that is within the range of non-pygmy groups. But were we to attempt to differentiate other populations on this basis of stature, let us say, with the degree of overlapping as great as it is, we would need to make full use of such concepts as the average and the variations about it in making our comparisons.

Let us see how this works out. It is a commonplace that the noses of Europeans are narrow, those of Africans broad; this, indeed, is one of the pronounced differences between Caucasoids and Negroids. Among the broadest-nosed Negroes are the Kajji of the Niger Delta region of West Africa; among the Caucasoids with narrowest nostrils are the Swedes. If we set down the average values of this measurement for these two populations, a striking difference between them is to be seen:

55 Kajji	45.5 mm.[2]
260 Swedes	30.2 mm.[3]

[2] A. J. N. Tremearne, 1912, p. 145.
[3] H. Lundborg and F. J. Linders, 1926, p. 102.

Physical Type and Culture

Yet when we take into account the variability of these two populations in this trait we see that even such a marked difference in nose-form does not prevent *some* Swedes from having broader nostrils than *some* Negroes, and

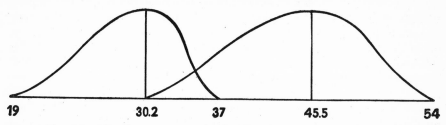

| 19 | 30.2 | 37 | 45.5 | 54 |

FIG. 12 *Distribution curves (stylized) of Swedish and Kajji noses.*

some Negroes having narrower nostrils than *some* Swedes. For Kajji noses vary between about 30 and 54 mm., while Swedish noses range from about 19 to 37 mm. Therefore, if one were to draw any line between 30 and 37 mm.

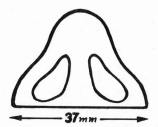

FIG. 13 *Nose, 37 mm. wide.*

long, and present it to an expert, asking him to designate whether this line represented the nose-width of a Negro or a Swede, he could not tell from which group it had been taken. This would be true in spite of the fact that we are dealing here with populations that represent extreme forms taken by their respective races in the characteristic being measured.

This demonstration could be continued for trait after trait, and only in a few of them would we find an absence of overlapping between groups. Such groups would be discovered to be those wherein the most emphatic manifestation of a given aspect was found. Differences in average values will always be apparent, as when we say that Americans are taller than Filipinos. Yet in this trait, as in the one just discussed, we will find that some Filipinos are taller than some Americans, since each group varies from shortness to tallness, and the number of either group who are taller or shorter than any individual member of the other is small indeed. As a result, we may state it as a general principle that *greater differences exist in the range of physical traits that characterize any single race of mankind, than between races taken in their entirety.*

Does this mean, as is sometimes said, that there is no such thing as a race? A statement of this sort can hold only by definition. Common sense

135

The Materials of Culture

experience tells us that different types of human beings are marked off from each other by a range of perceptibly different manifestations of the same traits. A Chinese, an African, an Englishmen will exhibit physical differences that will distinguish each from the other, and it would merely be a denial of objective reality to ignore the existence of these differences. Yet races, nonetheless, must be recognized for what they are—categories based on outer appearance as reflected in scientific measurements or observations that permit us to make convenient classifications of human materials. As we shall see later, this is an important initial step in assessing the biological nature of man and the relationship this aspect holds to his culture-building tendencies; but it is scarcely an end in itself. Failure to recognize that in setting up these classifications we have but sorted our data as a means to studying other problems has done much to bring about the widespread misunderstanding which confronts us of the nature of race.

2

THE MAJOR groupings of mankind most frequently named by anthropologists as races are the Caucasoid, the Mongoloid and the Negroid. Their distributions can be indicated in broadest lines as centering in Europe, Asia and the Americas, and Africa, respectively. This does not tell the whole tale, however, as we may also think of them as being distributed about various bodies of water. The Caucasoid race which is found not only in Europe but along the northern belt of Africa and eastwards through Palestine, Asia Minor, and Iran to Baluchistan and northern India, can in these terms be said to be distributed about the Mediterranean Sea. The Mongoloid race, which includes the peoples of all areas of Asia not inhabited by Caucasoids and, it will be recalled, all aboriginal inhabitants of the Americas, can be thought of as clustering about the Pacific. The Indian Ocean bears this same relationship to the Negroid race, which includes not only all Africans living south of the Sahara desert, but the pygmy groups of Indonesia and the inhabitants of the great region of New Guinea and Melanesia, habitat of the Papuan type, the so-called Melanesian Negroids. A word may also be said here about the Australoids, though there is less agreement concerning their identity as a race than of the others we have just considered. If we accept the designation "Australoid," for which a good case can be made, then this race will include all the aboriginal inhabitants of Australia, and the autochthonous Dravidian folk of southern India as well.

The physical characteristics of the three principal races and their sub-races have often been described. A. C. Haddon's scheme[4] is perhaps the most elaborate that has been drawn and can be consulted with profit. For our purpose, however, the table given by Krogman[5] will enable us more effectively to envisage the manner in which we may, in broadest terms, distin-

---

[4] 1925, pp. 15–36.
[5] W. M. Krogman, 1945, p. 50.

guish the several races from one another. With a slight change in terminology to accord with our usage here, this table is as follows:

Trait	Caucasoid	Mongoloid	Negroid
Skin color	Pale reddish white to olive brown	Saffron to yellow brown; some reddish-brown	Brown to brown-black; some yellow-brown
Stature	Medium to tall	Medium tall to medium short	Tall to very short
Head form	Long to broad and short; medium high to very high	Predominantly broad; height medium	Predominantly long; height low to medium
Face	Narrow to medium broad; tends to high, no prognathism	Medium broad to very broad; malars "high" and flat; tends to medium high	Medium broad to narrow; tends to medium high; strong prognathism
Hair	Head hair: color, light blonde to dark brown; texture, fine to medium; form, straight to wavy. Body hair: moderate to profuse	Head hair: color, brown to brown-black; texture, coarse; form, straight. Body hair: sparse	Head hair: color, brownblack; texture, coarse; form, light curl to woolly or frizzly. Body hair: slight
Eye	Color light blue to dark brown; lateral eye-fold occasional	Color brown to dark brown; medial epicanthic fold very common	Color brown to brownblack; vertical eye-fold common
Nose	Bridge usually high; form narrow to medium broad	Bridge usually low to medium; form medium broad	Bridge usually low; form medium broad to very broad
Body build	Linear to lateral; slender to rugged	Tends to be lateral; some linearity evident	Tends to lateral and muscular, but some linearity evident

Each of these races comprehends a number of sub-races, a fact that emphasizes the range of differences within each of them that, as has been stressed, is so important an aspect of such groupings. The Caucasoid—the -oid ending means -like, and is used to underscore the inclusiveness of such classifications—is most generally held to be composed of four sub-races, the northern European, or Nordic, the central European, or Alpine, the southern European and north African Mediterranean sub-race, and eastwardly the Dinaric. The Mongoloid sub-races have been less well defined than the others, but the Malayan groups of Indonesia are recognized as one, the southern Chinese as another, the northern Chinese and Mongolians as a third, the Siberians as a fourth; and in the Americas, the American Indians as one sub-race, the Eskimo another. The African Negroids are divided into the inhabitants of the Sahara, of mixed Negroid-Caucasoid descent, the "true Negroes" of the Guinea Coast, the heterogeneous Bantu-speaking populations of the Congo basin and East Africa, the Khoisan peoples of South Africa, (a term which includes both the Hottentots and Bushmen), the Nilotics of the Lakes region of East Africa, and the Hamites of the Ethiopian peninsula and the region southwest of it. In addition, this race includes all pygmies (Congo forest, Andamanese, Veddas of Ceylon, Negritoes of the Philippines, Aeta of Sumatra, and the like) and, as a final sub-race, the Melanesian Negroids we have already mentioned.

The Materials of Culture

Even so general a scheme of differentiating human types as we have presented omits certain groupings about which there is no agreement. The inhabitants of the islands of the Pacific Ocean, the Polynesians, are an example of this. Where did they come from? What is their descent? These are questions that cannot be answered at the present state of our knowledge. Perhaps they represent the spent force of an eastward migration from the Old World land-mass that made of them an amalgam of all the principal races. Some students, because of the Caucasoid appearance of these Polynesians, have assigned them to that category. The Ainu of the island of Sakhalin, north of Japan, are another such group. "The hairy Ainu," they are called, from the heavy deposition of body-hair of the males. Because of this, and of other traits, they have at times been classed as Caucasoid. Yet when we consider the distance between them and the Eurasiatic area where the Caucasoid race is located, the problem of how they came to their present habitat without leaving traces of their migration appears an unsurmountable barrier to any assumption of a genetic relationship between them and the other members of the race to which they are sometimes assigned.

In truth, problems such as these are historical. They cannot be satisfactorily solved on the basis of observed similarities or differences between living populations. This is another way of saying that racial classification tells us nothing except what types exist, and where. In these two last instances resemblances may validly give rise to hypotheses concerning biological relationships. But these hypotheses can never be more than hypotheses until archaeological evidence, for instance, shows a path of migration, or the genetic processes by which such groups made their appearance and were maintained down the generations to the present, in the setting in which they are found, are described. The reality of differences in human physical types must not be dismissed, but all care must be had that this reality is not given disproportionate weighting. Groups that exist by definition only are as much a departure from reality as is any claim of the nonexistence of those physical characteristics that differentiate groups of men, and mark them as members of one race or another.

3

OUR NEXT step in understanding the nature of the differences in physical type between human groups is to consider these differences in terms of the final phrase of our definition. This phrase, it will be remembered, stated that the traits which mark off one race from another *breed true*. The implication of this statement is that these characteristics are hereditarily stable. It follows, then, that the very essence of the study of race, once classification has been achieved, lies in the field of human genetics. In truth, it is only from this point of view that we can analyze the dynamic processes of human biology that lie at the crux of our problem. It is these processes that explain such matters as the purity of racial or population types, how new types have developed or may develop, and, above all, the manner in which cultural sanctions and the behavior that is their expression can influence the physical form of the populations.

Speciation is a dynamic process, and mere classification can never explain how different forms have come to differ. To hold that man comprises a single species, therefore, entails at once the assumption that crossing between the subspecific forms—races—is possible. It is needless to stress that this assumption can be proved valid merely by looking about, no matter where on the earth the casual observer happens to be. This leads us at once to the question whether or not pure races are found among man. Ideally, these could exist, despite the degree of observable mixture that is to be remarked in human beings. Actually, a pure *race*, that is, one of these major groups which includes no members whose ancestry was drawn from other races, is not to be found. But if we look at *populations* rather than races, and think in terms of the geneticist's concept of "pure strain" rather than pure races, then it is possible to state that inbreeding, whether due to geographical or sociological isolation, has induced differing degrees of homogeneity and heterogeneity in different populations.

All human groups are mutually fertile. This is a fact of the greatest importance, which has made possible the interbreeding between populations that has marked the existence of man from his earliest days on earth, and has produced the types which, when we think in racial terms, we speak of as race mixtures. Crossing under contact has been so widespread, indeed, that one of the few axioms about the human animal we can accept is that *no two human groups meet but that they produce mixed offspring*. It seems to make little difference how strict may be the rules against contact. Penalties may be assessed in this world or in eternity; they may involve ostracism, or even death. Yet love, so to speak, will find a way. This is one reason why the range of variation in human groups is so great. In short, this is why we can say that there are no pure races, why man is probably as mongrelized an animal as is to be encountered in the biological world.

From the genetic point of view, then, a race is to be viewed not as an aggregate of individuals whose physical characteristics are similar, but as a series of *family lines*. These produce offspring who, when they are adults, resemble each other to the degree that they are the product of similar genetic strains. This, in turn, will depend on the amount of inbreeding that has occurred in the population they comprise. As a consequence, it is the *population*, rather than the *race*, on which we must fix our attention.

Here the matter of relative variation is extremely important. It is conceivable that two populations could be identical in the average measurements they yield for a given trait, and yet be genetically quite different. A diagram, given on the following page, will illustrate this. Both these populations are seen to have the same average value. The distribution about the average of A, however, is broad; and this population is a heterogeneous one. B, on the other hand, with its high, narrow curve indicates an inbred group whose ancestry is homogeneous.

There is, in all probability, little difference in the variability of the major

The Materials of Culture

races in those traits that are susceptible of measurement, but there is a vast difference in the variation that any single population may manifest. The Eskimos, for example, are understandably inbred; local differences are to be found, but all the members of any single Eskimo group are closely related and, therefore, appreciably resemble one another. Let us see how such a result was achieved. The natural environment of the Eskimo holds each group to a population of fixed size, to which there are few accessions from the outside. This results in a *loss of ancestry*. Sooner or later—in this case sooner rather than later—persons mate who are related and who in

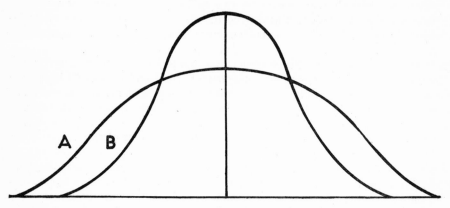

Fig. 14   *Distribution curves from homogeneous and heterogeneous populations.*

greater or lesser degree share ancestors. In certain Kentucky mountaineer communities, marriage records show that every person is at least the third cousin of every other, while many persons are more closely related. The number of ancestors theoretically required is thus reduced for their descendants. This principle can be clarified by an example. Brother-sister mating is rare among humans, but if a brother and a sister should have a child, that child would have two rather than four grand-parents, since the parents of his father and his mother would be the same individuals.

Thus two forces are constantly at work in determining the character of population mixture between groups of different types; mixture is predominant when there is contact, inbreeding occurs when there is isolation. The first makes for *heterogeneity*—at least after an initial cross—the second for *homogeneity*. The racial history of man, in a very real sense, is the result of the interplay of these two forces.

One of the significant contributions to the study of human physical types was the development, by F. Boas, of a technique for the mathematical expression and the statistical analysis of these mechanisms. Because of its importance, we may outline the reasoning he followed in determining, through the consideration of the relative homogeneity or heterogeneity of populations, the story of how their particular physical types were developed.

We begin with the fact that, as observed at any given moment, a popu-

140

lation is made up of individuals of both sexes and all ages, no two of whom are exactly alike. The physical anthropologist, ordinarily, when faced with the need to describe a group, measures adult males or females, or both—since sex differences must always be taken into account—in sufficient numbers to give him an adequate sampling. He then computes his averages and variabilities for the traits he has elected to study, and sets down his results as those which describe this people. These statistical constants, as they are called, permit him to assign the people he has studied to one or another racial or sub-racial category. What he has done, however, is to measure individuals, who, though they may be representative of the entire population, are the end-result of the processes of heredity and growth, and have been subject to the influence of their environment and of their culture since their birth.

Yet this population, like any other, is more than an aggregate of individuals. The variation they manifest is only expressed as a gross figure that does not distinguish any of the dynamic factors that have made of them what they are. To achieve this, our population must be analyzed rather as a series of families—the living representatives of the family lines that, as we have already mentioned, are the essential genetic components of any human group, racial or otherwise. To attack the problem of analyzing our population from this point of view, however, it is essential that our anthropologist measure not only adults, but entire families, children as well as grown members. He will then have data that approximate the actual composition of his population, for he will have men and women, boys and girls, of all ages and of various degrees of relationship.

For the purpose of this discussion we need not be concerned with the involved statistical treatment to which the data must be subjected before the measurements of different sex and age components are reduced to a common value, or the weighting to be accorded families having different numbers of children. The end result, which is our concern, is to resolve the gross, or total variability of the population into two terms. One represents the differences *between* families. The other indicates the differences, on the average, that exist *within* families. The first of these is called family variation, the second fraternal variation. The proposition at which we arrive is that *the variability of a population in a given trait is composed of the family variability, plus the fraternal variation in that trait.*

This approach yields two very important facts about the biological history of a given population. The lower the family variability of a given group, the more inbreeding it has experienced; the lower the fraternal variation, the more homogeneous the stock from which it is descended. Thus free mating in a population of mixed origin such as a modern American city where class lines are not institutionalized—at least among the white component—produces high family and fraternal variability. An inbred population, such as lives in an isolated mountain valley, will show low values in both. Let us look at a table of such figures for head-form, the trait that has been most utilized in analyses of this sort:

The Materials of Culture

Population	Variability of family lines	Variability within families
Potenza, Italy	2.41	2.52
Central Italians	2.39	2.72
Bohemians	2.37	2.61
Worcester, Mass.	2.36	2.36
East European Jews	2.29	2.52
Scottish	2.17	2.66
New York mixed Negroes	1.85	2.93
Blue Ridge mountaineers	1.85	2.09
Chippewa Indians	1.77	3.32
Bastaards (S. Africa)	1.26	2.52[6]

For the moment, we shall consider only the first two of these sets of figures. Potenza is in southern Italy, where the long-headed Mediterranean type prevails. In central Italy, however, Rome has attracted folk from all parts of the peninsula—from the long-headed southern populations, and from the north, where the short-headed, Alpine sub-racial type predominates. Italy is an old country, so that the populations in all these areas are relatively stable. The figures in the first column of our table indicate that free mating and inbreeding have occurred to about the same extent in both central and southern Italy, and these results are substantiated by the historical records. But if the figures for family variability be considered, it is apparent that in Potenza the breeding between persons who were all long-headed gives a lower value in this trait than we find for central Italy, where groups originally long- and short-headed mingled. We consequently see how this bio-historical analysis explains the homogeneity of the southern Italian peoples in head-form, as against the heterogeneity of the people of central Italy.

4

WE MAY here summarize the points that have thus far emerged from our discussion. They are:
1. Man comprises a single species, *homo sapiens;*
2. Human beings manifest differences in certain physical traits that breed true and thus permit the differentiation of various races and subraces;
3. Since man represents one species, and hence all members are mutually fertile without regard to race, lines of delimitation are blurred;
4. Race being a matter of classification, descriptions of racial types tell us nothing of the processes that have made races what they are;
5. These processes are of a genetic character;
6. The analysis of human genetics can be profitably approached through the study of family lines in various local groupings;
7. This leads to the study of homogeneity or heterogeneity within and between family lines, as indices of inbreeding or mixture.

---

[6] F. Boas, 1916b, p. 9. The figures for the New York Negroes (M. J. Herskovits, 1924b) and the Blue Ridge Mountaineers (I. G. Carter, 1928) have been added to the original table since they are the result of researches that occurred after the publication of Boas' original paper.

Physical Type and Culture

All these, it is evident, have to do with problems of human existence that are of a biological character. We must look to continuing investigations that are in accord with an approach implied by such statements for far more definite answers than we can now give to such fundamental questions as the incidence and effect of mutations, chromosomal change, permutation and combination of gene frequencies, in establishing, maintaining, and changing the types of human beings found on the earth. Yet even when the answers to vexing questions such as these have been found, we shall have resolved but one part of the total problem. We must of course understand the full significance of the fact that man, as a member of the biological series, resembles the other animals in his physico-chemical reactions and in the genetic and physiological mechanisms which make of him the kind of being he is. But we must also assess the implications of the further fact that he, alone of all the animals, has the capacity to develop and maintain the cultures which influence his behavior so profoundly that, as we have seen, they constitute for some students a force outside himself.

The problem of the relationship between physical type and culture—or race and culture, as it is more commonly phrased—most often turns on the question of the degree to which race influences culture. This is an important question, and the wrong answer given it can have tragic consequences, as the history of the period between the two World Wars demonstrates. Because it is so vital a problem, we must consider it carefully, and we shall do this in the final section of this chapter. First, however, we must treat of the other aspect of the relationship, the influence of culture on physical type. For the answers to the "why?" of race cannot be encompassed in biological terms alone. If this were not so, there would be little need for human biologists who, as we have seen in our first chapter, differ from other biologists as specialists in the method of dealing with their particular subjects. The answers are to be had only when the biological factors are studied as they interact with the cultural ones, influencing and being influenced by them in the life of the single entity we term man.

Let us again turn to the table of family and fraternal variabilities with this point in mind. We can see how inbreeding makes for low variability in a population; that each family will have about the same ancestry and thus be like each other; that within each family brothers and sisters will resemble one another, on the average, more or less according to whether their ancestry incorporates similar or divergent strains. But why should Potenza attract relatively few outsiders, thus making its population homogeneous, and Rome attract many, with resulting heterogeneity? This, it is clear, is due to what we call the importance of Rome—an historical, cultural fact that, from a biological point of view, is quite fortuitous. Why should there be non-selective, "free" mating, to take another point of considerable biological importance, in one population, and assortative mating—along class lines, let us say—in another? This also is a matter of tradition, not of biology; but it sets the lines within which the genetic strains of a population are formed and continued. It thus introduces a factor that may, as in England, for example, or in Sweden, result in the formation within the same population, according

The Materials of Culture

to class, of two strains that are distinct enough so that in many instances one need but glance at a man to tell of which group he is a member.

Another set of figures from our table can profitably be analyzed with this point in mind. That the Negro population of New York City manifests the same degree of family variability as the Blue Ridge Mountaineers is striking. How heterogeneous is the ancestry of these Negroes becomes apparent when it is pointed out that their forebears included not only Africans and Europeans, but American Indians as well. This means that they represent in their genetic composition all the three principal human races. This is made evident by the degree of their fraternal variability, one of the highest listed. In this, however, they stand sharply in contrast to the Mountaineers, whose ancestry is exclusively Scotch-Irish, and who have the lowest figure in the second column.

The answer to the question "why" here lies in the different factors in the situations of these two populations, that have caused inbreeding. In the Blue Ridge Mountains, geographical isolation was reinforced by a convention of suspicion of strangers, and a tradition of not leaving the valley where one was born. In the case of the Negroes, the isolation has been social; the feeling that mating across the color-line is undesirable has here been paramount. The strength of this force may be understood when it is made clear that the wall of tradition erected against cross-mating is a double one. Negroes are quite as reluctant to marry whites as whites are to marry Negroes, and the sanctions imposed on those who violate this prescript are of the same kind, and exacted where possible to about the same degree by the Negroes as they are by the Whites. A similar explanation may be given for the figures of the South African Bastaards. These people are the result of crossing, many generations back, between Hottentots and Boers. Here not only has convention frowned on acceptance of the mixed-bloods by the whites, but a certain degree of geographical isolation has reinforced the social segregation which these persons experience.

Facts such as these show with stark clarity how important an influence ideas can have in setting the stage for the operation of the biological processes in man. So powerful are ideas, indeed, that we have the phenomenon of whole groups which exist by definition only. Thus the word "Negro," as employed in the United States, has no biological meaning. This is why its use is so baffling to Europeans, or South Americans, who give the word its correct biological sense by applying it only to unmixed members of the Negroid race. In the United States, however, any degree of African ancestry makes one a "Negro." As a result, the phenomenon of the "white" Negro appears—a contradiction in terms, but used with naive unconsciousness of this fact, because a social definition takes precedence over the biological reality.

Such definitions as that of the word "Negro," however, can deeply influence the biological composition of a population. Where "Negro" takes its proper biological significance, mixed-bloods are designated as such, and in Latin countries, are classed with the majority group of predominant non-Negroid ancestry. As a result, this group becomes racially heterogeneous, while those called Negroes remain without much crossing. In the United States, in contrast, the majority population has remained relatively, though by no means entirely, free of Negro ancestry. Racial heterogeneity, however, is accentuated among the Negroes, who because of social conventions receive in their number all the mixed-bloods.

How far-reaching the influence of culture on physical type can be emerges as we consider the extreme variability that marks man when he is contrasted with other animal species. We refer here to the hypothesis that man is to be considered as a domesticated form, and that *domestication* and the *social selection* that has resulted from it, have afforded the mechanisms whereby the multiplicity of local and sub-racial human types, if not the major races themselves, have been molded into the many forms we find at the present time.

We can say that man is a domesticated animal not only because he shares the physical traits peculiar to domestication with the other domesticated forms, but also because his mode of life fulfils the objective criteria of domestication. What are the physical traits in which domesticated species differ most from related wild ones? They are, first of all, an extreme range of color differences. Blondness, especially, is restricted to them; there are no true wild blonds. Such a form as the polar bear, whose white pelt represents an adaptation to arctic conditions, has brown eyes, unlike light-colored dogs or cats, or horses. Coloring of pelt ranges from white to black, with greys and browns and tans and other shades in profusion. Spotted animals appear, also, but unlike wild forms such as giraffes and leopards, the spotted condition is inherited by strain and does not mark off a domesticated species as a whole. Hair form of wild types is usually wiry and short. Among domesticated forms it ranges from tightly curled to straight. Body build and size likewise vary greatly—contrast the Pekinese with the Great Dane or the St. Bernard. The same is true of facial features and form of the head, for noses will be long or short, ears of bewilderingly different sizes, eyes set in the head in many different ways.

It is hardly necessary to point out that the traits in which domesticated animals vary are the very ones in which men likewise vary most—the very ones, indeed, that most often mark off races and sub-races from each other. The blond, blue-eyed Nordic or Alpine Caucasoid thus has his counterpart among dogs and cats, horses and cows, pigs and chickens, both in the blueness of his eyes and in the lightness of his hair. The hair forms of the principal races of man can be duplicated in such a domesticated animal as the dog—the wavy, soft hair of the setter is like Caucasoid hair, the short, wiry hair of the airedale resembles the Mongoloid type, the kinky hair of the poodle is the counterpart of Negroid hair. The difference between the Shetland pony and the Norman draught-horse parallels the difference between the Negroid pygmy and the Caucasoid Scot—and in both horses and men, all intermediate sizes are to be found. The nose of the Russian wolf-hound is no more extreme for dogs than is that of the Nordic for men; the pug-dog, in contrast, is scarcely more removed from its long canine counterpart than is the extremely broad Negroid nasal form. It is unnecessary to labor the point—it should be clear that, on the basis of mere observation, striking parallels exist between man and the domesticated forms, not only in the distinctive physical traits that mark them off as such, but in the variation found in each of these traits.

There are four criteria of domestication:

1. restricted habitat;
2. regular supply of special foods;
3. protection against weather and predatory animals;
4. controlled breeding.

It must be pointed out that, as in all phenomena of the natural world, there are differences in the degree of domestication under which an animal may live. This depends on whether controls sit lightly or are drawn tight. If we contrast the life of the mustang of the western American plains with that of the blooded racehorse, the difference between *loose* and *close* domestication becomes clear. But both kinds of horses are domesticated varieties.

The controls imposed on the domesticated lower animals are exercised by man who, as far as we know, has brought practically all the creatures able to be domesticated under the conditions that have placed them in association with him. It is man who builds fences, or cages, or makes other devices to keep them from roaming. He raises and provides them with food, often as far different from what their wild ancestors ate or that the present day wild forms related to them eat, as is the dog biscuit from the kill of the wolf pack. He makes barns and other kinds of shelters that protect them from the weather, and watches to see that wild beasts do not prey on them. Finally, especially where domestication is close, he also watches to see that casual mating does not prevent the continuance of the pure lines he has developed, often at the expense of any survival value the animal may originally have had. This is especially significant. If there is any one word which summarizes the criteria of domestication and the conditions under which domesticated animals live, it is *protection*. And protection alone makes possible the substitution of artificial for natural selection.

In human groups, under the protective devices man commands through his cultures, *social selection* has made it possible for the many different human types found over the earth to be perpetuated once they appeared. Through his cultural proclivities, man has been able to do for himself, albeit without realizing the fact, what he has done in breeding the animals he has domesticated.

The initial domesticating factor for man was, in all probability, a knowledge which we know from archaeological remains to go back to the time of *sinanthropus Pekinensis*. Fire established the hearth which, in conjunction with the fear of unknown predatory beings—human, animal, and supernatural—must have served as a powerful force in creating a frame of mind and habit of life that came to be symbolized by the concept "home." Fire, of a certainty, made possible the preservation of foods that would otherwise have spoiled, and allowed man to devise cooking techniques that yielded end-products vastly different from antecedent forms of foodstuffs. Fire, too, afforded protection against the weather, and in a measure, against wild

Physical Type and Culture

animals. Fire, and the use of tools—the basis of material culture, and with language, of human economic, social, intellectual and aesthetic life every-where—thus made social life possible.

Selection in mating is an aspect of social life. Custom generally rules that marriage within a group is more desirable than marriage outside it. Elaborations are devised on this theme so that all kinds of restrictions of an economic, social, religious, magical, and aesthetic variety become operative. One marries or not in accordance with his resources, selects a mate because he or she belongs to a given class in society, accepts or rejects an individual as the gods are favorable or not, or in accordance with some physical trait held to be associated with some supernatural power, falls in love, all unconsciously, because of reactions to culturally sanctioned ideals of beauty. We must stress again how fortuitous these reasons are, yet how powerful their effect in influencing the physical type of a given population. They are just as fortuitous as the decision of a breeder of animals that he will elect to breed for a long-haired rather than short-haired variety of dog, or horse, or cow.

An example that bears on this point is the selection in marriage on the basis of color differences found among American mixed Negroes, one of the few examples of social selection that has been studied as such.[7] The facts given in the following table are of the comparative color of mates, first of parents as judged by their children, second through objective study of pigmentation by the use of the color-top:

	Estimate of parents by children	Color-top findings
Husband lighter	30.3%	29.0%
About the same color	13.2%	14.5%
Mother lighter	56.5%	56.5%

The reasons for the selection in mating shown here are historical, psychological, and cultural. Historically, mixed Negroes were often manumitted by their white fathers during the period of slavery and sent North to establish themselves in some trade or to find some other gainful occupation. Their light color was associated with the favorable economic position this group attained with the years, and with the resulting advantageous social position they came to occupy within the Negro community. Psychologically, there has been a transfer of the values set by the Caucasoid majority of the American population, whose white color is associated in the minds of the Negroes with freedom from the disabilities under which they live. Culturally, the American tradition that the woman marries a man who can care for her, while the man seeks a woman who can enhance his self-esteem among his fellows, is here translated into terms of color difference.

What is the biological consequence of the play of all these non-biological forces? Selectivity has reduced the number of full-bloods in the community, and increased its racial heterogeneity. But because of the barriers to crossing with the whites, a type of inbreeding exists that, as we have seen, has caused

---

[7] M. J. Herskovits, 1928, pp. 51–66.

147

the American Negro population to achieve its own homogeneity. This permits it to be described as a distinctive type that lies about half-way in its physical traits between the characteristics that differentiate its Caucasoid and Negroid ancestry.

5

THROUGH the protection afforded man by technology and social institutions, the perpetuation of mutants that might otherwise not have survived has been encouraged. Their descendants form not only the present-day local types and sub-races of *homo sapiens*, but perhaps even the major human races that are to be distinguished. What, however, of the other aspect of our problem? What is the influence of physical type or, as it is more often expressed, what is the influence of race on culture?

The scientific truth of the matter is that *culture influences physical type far more than physical type influences culture*. Full recognition of this is all the more cogent since so much of the discussion concerning the relationship between race and culture sees the problem as the determination of the degree to which race is instrumental in shaping the culture of a people and does not consider at all the influence of culture on physical type. Thus we meet with the second of the several determinisms of which we take account in studying culture.

Racial determinism, as the position which holds that physical type determines culture is called, easily slips into the political field, where this approach is called *racism*. In its most extreme form, it is exemplified by the racial doctrines of Nazism, which maintained the existence of a so-called "Aryan race," a kind of mystic grouping superior to all others, and, for political reasons, another presumed "racial" entity, the Jews, who were singled out for special indignities.

Neither the word Aryan nor the term Jew has scientific validity as a racial designation. Aryan is the name of the language from which most European tongues have been derived. Warning against its use as the name for a presumed racial entity was never more deeply nor more bitterly expressed than by F. Müller himself, the philologist who first used it, when he said, "There is no more an Aryan race than there is a dolichocephalic (long-headed) dictionary." As for the term Jew, its meaning, except when it is applied as a name-symbol for a group called Jews, who possess in common a certain historic continuity, is extremely tenuous. No traits that characterize the Jews as such everywhere they are found, have been distinguished. A rich store of evidence, on the other hand, demonstrates that the Jews of a given region resemble the general population of the region they inhabit.[8] The difference between the Jews of Germany and France, for example, is about that between the other elements in these two countries.

The operation of a psychological mechanism called the stereotype makes

---

[8] This has been made apparent for central Europe in Morant's discussion (1939, pp. 72–4, 80–7).

Physical Type and Culture

plausible a belief in the existence of fixed racial differences in physical type that is the basis for the assumption that so-called "racial" groups differ in aptitudes and ability. For example, Frenchmen are commonly visualized as dark, short, brown-eyed, vivacious people who gesticulate as they talk. That there are, in northern France, Norman French who are tall, blond, and blue-eyed, or in the east the stocky, blond Alpine French, is overlooked. When such persons are recognized as Frenchmen at all, they are dismissed as exceptions. On the other hand, every person who answers the preconceived description reinforces the conception of what a Frenchman should look like. Such stereotyped concepts are misleading in that they are highly selective. More than that, they are also fallacious in that they confuse cultural traits—in this instance vivacity and the use of the hands in speaking—with such biological characteristics as stature and eye-color.

Race, nationality, language, and culture are in actuality independent variables. They meet only in the persons of given individuals who belong to a particular race, are citizens of a specific nation, speak a certain language, and live in accordance with the traditions of their society. The word "French" can mean any of these. Only the phrase "French race" is inacceptable. Northern Frenchmen are Nordics, eastern French Alpines, southern and central French Mediterranean. All are Caucasoids—if they come of stock originating in France itself. But a Negro from Senegal may have French citizenship, an Arab from Tunis may speak French, an Annamite from Indo-China, who grew up among Frenchmen in Paris, will behave and think in ways indistinguishable from those of Caucasoid Parisians.

A negative position is difficult of proof, so that it is too dogmatic to state flatly, as is sometimes done in controversy, that there is no influence of any kind exerted by physical form on cultural behavior. Yet all the evidence in hand seems to indicate that any normal human being, *if given the necessary opportunity*, can learn the way of life of any people existing on the earth today. Everyday experience in the United States richly corroborates this. Second generation Japanese, called Nisei, dress, talk, and otherwise behave as do their fellow-Americans. Their thought-processes, value systems, and goals are those of the country in which they live. The same is true of those Negroes whose disadvantages have not been so serious as to deny them the same avenues of self-realization as are enjoyed by others among whom they live. The evidence, in short, demonstrates that every large human group, even of the order of a sub-race, runs very close to the gamut of human capability, whether in intellectual capacity, or in those particular abilities that are represented by special sensitivity to sound-waves (musical aptitude) or to light-waves (artistic ability) or some other aspect of behavior in which individuals surpass their fellows in excellence of perception or performance.

How a given group uses its human endowment is a matter of history, not biology. Language, for example, as we have seen, is learned, like any other aspect of culture. On occasion, such linguistic terms as Aryan, Semitic, Bantu, are applied to what are called racial groups. When used in a manner of speaking, or for convenience, the fault is merely one of bad logic. Too often, however, the idea becomes fixed that the two phenomena, really found only in association, are causally related. Then a given physical type comes to be identified with a specific language, and the conclusion is drawn that the members of a given race are especially and innately endowed to use the language which they, as a race, are presumed to speak. Yet nothing could be farther from the truth. As in other aspects of culture, any normal human being, no matter what his race, can speak any language, provided he begins to learn it early enough in life and has full opportunity to master it. Neither the thin lips of the Nordic nor the thick lips of the Negro of themselves condition the manner of speech of an individual of either group who, for all we know, may learn to speak an excellent Chinese!

Certainly when we come to the problem of racial superiority we are outside the limits of scientific concern, for here the question is one of evaluation. In essence, it is the same problem as that of cultural evaluation and partakes of all the difficulties that inhere in attempts to implement preconceived judgement with fact. Every people feels it enjoys superiorities over others. Such a point of view, as we have seen, when it expresses gratification at the positive qualities of one's own group, serves as an important integrating factor for the individual, and makes for adjustment and cooperation in intergroup relations. Only when this conviction takes on pathological emphasis and festers into theories of biological superiority, that find expression in aggressive desires to impose an inferior status on others, does it become dangerous. Then this essentially healthy and constructive pride turns into destructive motivations and behavior, and we find *racism* rampant. It is this racism which, upheld by arguments that distort science and supported by sanctions of force, seeks to impose the dictum of a self-styled "superior" race on all who fall outside its arbitrarily fixed limits.

Histories of racism name as the earliest expressions of racist philosophy the *Essay on the Inequality of the Human Races* by the Frenchman, Count Arthur de Gobineau, and the work entitled *Foundations of the Nineteenth Century* by Houston Stewart Chamberlain, the German-English son-in-law of Richard Wagner. The writings of these men, and the host of others who have followed them, have without doubt had wide influence in shaping racist doctrines. But New World chattel slavery gave an added impetus to racism by providing some of the earliest studies of race, made with the objective of justifying slavery, and consequently emphasized the importance and inevitability of racial differences. The vigorous arguments of abolitionists were countered by apologists for slavery on both sides of the Atlantic, in France as well as England. In the United States, the abolitionist campaign brought counter-arguments that took the form of the rationalizations of early American racism.

A certain relationship between Old and New World currents of racism can be traced. During the middle of the nineteenth century, two societies existed in England for the study of man. One was pro-slavery, one anti-slavery. The former was the Anthropological Society of London, headed by Dr. James Hunt, a distinguished scholar. His paper "On the Negro's Place in

Physical Type and Culture

Nature" in the *Memoirs* of the Society for 1863–64 asserted that "we may safely say that there is in the Negro that assemblage of evidence which would, *ipso facto,* induce an unbiased observer to make the European and Negro two distinct types of man." It went on to argue that "it is not alone the man of science who has discerned the Negro's unfitness for civilization as we understand it." Now these are sentiments quite familiar to those who know opinions current during the period and who have followed racist writings of later years; opinions that have persisted despite their lack of scientific validity. What is often overlooked in discussions of this and other racist writings is the number of American citations employed by Dr. Hunt to document his case.

The paper in this same volume which follows that of Dr. Hunt underscores this point. In it, William Bollaert makes "Some Observations on the Past and Present Populations of the New World." In the fashion of latter-day racist thought, he holds that the races of man represent different species, and lays much stress on the evils of race mixture. In his paper, we find him commenting on the work of the Americans who plead that Negro and white are creatures of a different order. "I cannot help the expression of surprise," he writes, "that we do not hear our anthropologists and ethnologists refer oftener to Knox on the *Races of Mankind,* Nott and Gliddon's *Types of Mankind,* and their *Indigenous Races.* The first work is thoughtful and original; the second, elementary; but the *Indigenous Races* is one of the most valuable anthropological contributions we have as yet in our language . . ." It is not without interest, even now, to take down this last volume, published in Philadelphia in 1857, scan its drawings of crania and living racial types and read its controversial upholdings of the polygenist position against the monogenists who held that mankind was one. But most interesting of all is to turn to its "Alphabetical List of Subscribers" at the back of the book and to note in it the name, "Le Comte A. de Gobineau."

Nott, Gliddon, Knox, van Evrie are only a few names of those who were first in the United States to give racism the forms of science. Their work fell into deserved oblivion as the frontier claimed the attention of Americans, but the seed they had propagated by no means died, though it was not until the end of the first World War that systematic expression of it appeared once more. The names of Madison Grant and Lothrop Stoddard are outstanding in this connection, Grant's *The Passing of the Great Race* and Stoddard's *Rising Tide of Color* being two of the most widely read works of the period that sought to phrase racial prejudice in scientific terms in order to achieve political ends. These men are often cited by European proponents of racism, and it is worth noting that in a work by such an outstanding exponent of German "race science" as Hans F. K. Günther, translated as *The Racial Element of European History,* tribute is paid to their racist writings.

The results of psychological testing in the American army during the first World War also influenced world racist thought. "Intelligence" tests, they were called, and though we know better today, they have been used again and again to "prove" the presumed superiority of the north European types that stood highest in them. They constituted one of the most effective arguments of the racists; so that this unhappy contribution of scholars, who were responding to a tradition whose existence they perhaps did not even suspect, became a mainstay for those who have called upon science to serve ends that are anything but scientific.

CHAPTER 10

13

Habitat and Culture

Whether we study man or any other living creature, the dimension of space is no more to be disregarded than that of time. Recognition of this has given rise to the discipline of ecology, which studies the relationship between animals and their habitat. In the case of man, where culture, as Forde puts it, intervenes as "a middle term . . . between the physical environment and human activity," [1] the problem becomes essentially one of assessing the interaction between the natural environment in which a people live and their culture. Human ecology has thus come to signify the study of this relationship rather than the investigation of how man, the biological organism, has adapted himself to his geographical setting.

Before proceeding to an analysis of the relationship between habitat and culture, let us examine the terms to be used. It is particularly relevant to weigh the use of the word "environment," in its customary and specialized meanings. In an earlier chapter, culture was defined as "the man-made part of the environment." We often hear that a child is delinquent because he has grown up in a "bad environment"; that he has been exposed to aspects of our culture that our society regards as undesirable; and that this has induced habits that are in conflict with our sanctioned ways of behavior.

No one who discusses the case of this child, whose "environment" has been responsible for his delinquency, believes or implies that he has been exposed to different degrees or kinds of sunlight and rainfall, temperature and humidity, barometric pressures and chemical components of soil and water than have other children who have not transgressed the rules of proper behavior. What is meant is that the people of the neighborhood in which he lived and the condition of his home life were not such as to encourage approved conduct in him; or that his diet, or his educational opportunities, were deficient. In short, the expression signifies that his *social* environment denied him the privileges shared by children born into more favored families.

The word "environment," in its specialized usage, refers to the natural setting and is so used by geographers whose primary interest is in this aspect of the physical world. This is the meaning it holds in the phrase "environmental determinism," wherein the position is taken that the natural environment of a culture not only sets the cultural stage but determines the

[1] C. Daryll Forde, 1934, p. 463.

153

The Materials of Culture

action that takes place on this stage. Interestingly enough, though "environment" is interpreted as meaning the natural much more than the social setting of life, those students who have been concerned with the social setting have only recently fixed their attention on the problems that arise out of the interaction between ways of life of a people and the scene in which these ways are brought into being and are continued from generation to generation.

It is essential, therefore, that these two components in the total life of the individual, and of groups of men, be clearly differentiated in our thinking. Otherwise our discussion of the relationship between culture and environment would be pointless, for we should be considering, under the same term, now one, now another aspect of human existence.

We can best achieve clarification, then, by recognizing at this point that the *natural* and *cultural* elements in man's total setting are to be differentiated in terminology, as they are in fact. To this end, we shall define the following terms:

Habitat designates the *natural* setting of human existence—the physical features of the region inhabited by a group of people; its natural resources, actually or potentially available to them; its climate, altitude, and other geographical features to which they have adapted themselves.

Culture, as used in this book, refers to that part of the total setting which includes the material objects of human manufacture, techniques, social orientations, points of view, and sanctioned ends that are the immediate conditioning factors underlying behavior.

Environment, then, is given its full etymological, dictionary significance: "the aggregate of all the external conditions and influences affecting the life and development of an organism"—in this case, man in his natural and cultural setting.

With these definitions in mind, we may now turn to a discussion of the problems of interest to us—how does man react to habitat? To what degree is man's individual life and his culture shaped by it, or how do the individual and his culture employ habitat in achieving their own ends? And finally, what are the mechanisms whereby these adjustments are reached?

2

MAN cannot exist unless he meets the challenge of his habitat. When cultures of relatively simple technologies and limited economic resources are considered from the point of view of their relationship to their habitat, this challenge seems so powerful and the influence of the natural setting so pervasive that the conclusion appears almost inescapable that habitat exercises a decisive influence in shaping ways of life. This holds especially when we take as our example peoples whose habitat is harsh, those who live in the Arctic or in desert regions. No one can fail to be impressed with the struggle to sustain life in such surroundings. Descriptions of the cultures of such groups, of necessity, place considerable stress on the means by which they achieve their adaptation.

The aboriginal Australians offer an excellent example of such a people. Little seems to be passed over by them in the way of edible foodstuffs. In northwest central Queensland they find seeds, roots, fruits and vegetables, flowers and honey, insects and crustaceans, frogs, lizards, fish and crocodiles (where there are streams), turkey-bustards, pigeons, emus, bandicoots, opossums, and kangaroos. They have no hoes, do no agriculture; their weapons are rudimentary. Their hunting techniques show great resourcefulness. When a kangaroo is sighted, the native sets out after it on the run. Though the animal easily outdistances him, he keeps after it all day. At night, both he and his prey settle down to sleep where they find themselves. But the next morning, the muscles of the kangaroo are so stiff from the unaccustomed steady pace he has been forced to keep that the hunter soon catches up with him. It is then a question of closing in for the kill with the club that is the weapon the native uses in hunting this animal—a feat calling for bravery—and then waiting for the rest of the group, who have been following the trail left by hunter and hunted, to come up for the feast.

The technique of coping with a difficult habitat used by a people having but the crudest equipment is also illustrated by the pygmy Bushman of South Africa. With his small bow and arrows in hand, the Bushman hunter conceals himself by placing over his crouched body the skin of an ostrich. Moving cautiously toward the herd, he imitates the movements of these great birds so cleverly that they do not suspect his presence until one of them falls under his arrow. The need of this people for water is paramount, since the Kalahari desert they inhabit is one of the most severe desert habitats in the world. They fill ostrich-egg shells during the short season the water-holes are not dry or use their intimate knowledge of the country to find the roots, bulbs and melon-like fruits that contain moisture or store up liquids and thus help quench their thirst. Not even the most stagnant pool daunts them, for in such cases they place grass filters at the bottom of the hollow reeds they use in sucking up water.

Nowhere in the world, it can be said, is a finer adaptation of culture to habitat revealed than that of the Eskimos, which has deservedly become classic for anthropologists. Their dome-shaped snow houses, called igloos, are models of the exercise of effective engineering techniques on the materials that are at hand. This is evidenced by the ease with which an igloo can be constructed, its durability, and the manner in which it fulfils its function of providing shelter and comfort in the savage cold of the Arctic winter. The use of walrus-ivory for sled-runners, or for eye-shields to protect against the driving blizzards, or against the glare of the sun on the snow, are other instances of this adaptation. The detachable heads of the spears used in hunting walrus or whale allow the precious wooden handles to float away unharmed once a strike has been made, to be recovered by the hunter later. Or we may cite the blown-up walrus bladders that are attached to a spear-head to irritate a struck whale when it dives, and thus, always weaker

155

from loss of blood, force it to the surface for the kill. Even such an implement as the snow-beater has been thought of to ensure that fur clothing will be free of snow so as not to deteriorate from moisture when taken into the warm igloo.

3

THE systematic study of human geography, or *anthropogeography*, as it is sometimes called, dates from the time of Friederich Ratzel. This German scholar was impressed by the influence of the natural setting on the ways of life of peoples, and his great work, in its English translation called *The History of Mankind*, which assembled what was known at the time of its writing about peoples over all the earth, was for years one of the standard compendiums of knowledge about nonliterate groups. Ratzel's position, however, which held that the habitat of a people could not be neglected in assessing those influences that play on the formation and functioning of culture, was destined to be changed to a more rigid formulation by some of his followers. These students transmuted his earlier and quite acceptable position into one which held that the habitat of a people—of all peoples— is the *determining* factor in shaping their way of life.

This, in brief, is the position called *environmental determinism*, the next of the determinisms that must be examined in our search for an understanding of what culture is and how it works. An uncompromising expression of this point of view is to be found in the opening pages of a standard work on the geography of North America, wherein the hypothesis of environmental determinism is stated as the guiding framework for the discussion that follows it. "To understand what man has wrought we must study the place, the environment, in which he has wrought," [2] states this author. Then, after rejecting such aspects of culture as government, economics, social ideals, and race as causal factors in explaining the achievements of a society—in this case, the people of the United States—we are told that ". . . natural resources, climate and accessibility are the stuff of which industry, trade, religion, national policy and to some extent civilization, are made . . ." [3]

An even more uncompromising appeal to the determining force of the habitat, especially of climate, on culture, has been set forth by E. Huntington, who combines geographical with biological determinism. Much of his discussion turns on the problem of evaluating civilizations in terms of physical types, a correlation that we have seen is scientifically inadmissible. He also appeals to the power of selection through migration in making for a people of high quality, a point that has come to be rejected by students of man as incapable of proof when all the data, such as those instances of forced migration in which human beings are but passive factors, are taken fully into account. The preponderant role of the environment as one of the de-

---

[2] J. Russell Smith, 1925, p. 3.
[3] Ibid., p. 10.

termining elements of culture is continuously urged in Huntington's work. ". . . The fact that cultural activities loom so large," he states, "must not make us forget that they are dependent upon inheritance and environment." [4]

Students of culture have reacted strongly against environmental determinism, though it should be pointed out that their arguments have not been cast in the form of cultural determinism. Those who hold that the development of culture is based on its own past have perhaps been too occupied in establishing and defending their conception of culture as an autonomous entity to enquire deeply into its relationship to the natural setting. The reaction has rather come from those who have taken the eclectic position that since many forces—geographical, biological, psychological, historical—play on culture, no one of them should be overemphasized, but that the role of each should be investigated and weighed. In practice, however, this has led to an emphasis on the negative objective of showing that the habitat does not play the all-important part in shaping culture that environmental determinism claims for it.

It is not difficult to frame a refutation of environmental or any other form of *determinism,* if only because of the vulnerability of a deterministic position in terms of its logic. That is, once a determinism is set up, if the determining force is to be *deterministic,* the operation of other forces is inadmissible. Consequently, in the case of environmental determinism, if it can be shown that two cultures found in the same habitat differ, or that the same kind of culture exists in two different kinds of setting, some other force than that assumed as the determinant must have exerted a measure of influence. With this established, habitat becomes only one of a number of forces that shape culture.

Let us recall some well-known instances that illustrate this point. Most striking are the data yielded by cultures in the circumpolar region, the rigorous Arctic habitat. We have already commented on the effectiveness of the adaptation made by the Eskimo, especially the eastern Eskimo, to their habitat. It has been pointed out with what efficiency they use the materials at hand, building igloos out of snow blocks, using walrus ivory for eye-shields, preserving the precious wooden handles of their harpoons by devising haftings that permit the handle to be recovered when the prey has been struck. The efficient use they make of their dogs, their only domesticated animal, in pulling their sleds, the waterproof boats called *kayaks* in which they can turn over completely and still survive, and other skills of adaptation that have for years intrigued students might also have been mentioned. It is accepted as a truism that anyone who would live in this harsh habitat must follow the ways of life of the Eskimo, adapting himself to the Arctic winter as they do if he would survive.

Yet when we turn to the Siberian arctic, inhabited by such tribes as the Chuckchi and Koryak and Yukaghir, though the rigors of the climate are the same as in northernmost North America, we find quite a different type of

---

[4] Ellsworth Huntington, 1945, p. 9.

culture. The igloo is unknown, and shelters are made of skins that are attached to a framework of wood, even though wood is as scarce here as elsewhere above the Arctic circle. The Siberians are herders rather than hunters, their economic mainstay being reindeer rather than the walrus, and this, again, despite the fact that many of them are not too far removed from the sea coast to be hunters like the Eskimo.

The picture that is drawn of how, early in a wintry Arctic day, when the reindeer have exhausted the tundra on which they feed, the encampment must be changed, is impressive in teaching how varied are the ways in which man adapts himself to his habitat, how tenaciously he follows the dictates of his tradition, struggling against conditions that render this difficult. With the thermometer thirty degrees or more below zero, the men drive off the herd to its new feeding-ground, leaving behind the women and children. It is the women's task to break camp. They get to work at once, dismantling the tents and loading skins, tent-poles, utensils and the young children on the pack-reindeer that must transport them. The men and the herd reach the new feeding-ground long before the women. They do not put up a snow shelter as the Eskimo would, however, and they have no wood to make a fire to warm themselves. So they sit about in the cold, waiting until the pack animals arrive and the skin tents can be erected by the women, for the men would demean themselves by doing this kind of work.

Here, in the difficult circumpolar habitat, then, we have two quite different ways of life, one based on hunting, the other on herding. The adaptation of both peoples is equally successful, inasmuch as the only test of success in adaptation is survival, and Siberians no less than the Eskimo have managed to cope with their Arctic setting for untold generations. The efficiency of Eskimo adaptation over that of the Siberians *strikes us* as greater, but this does not mean that the Siberians would concur in this evaluation. It is clear, therefore, that factors other than habitat enter in this varied adaptation. Once we perceive this, the all-powerful influence of the environment in shaping culture, as is required by the hypothesis of environmental determinism, is to be seen as calling for qualification.

Certain facts from southeastern Africa may be cited to make the same point. The wide distribution of the elephant and the zebra throughout a greater part of tropical Africa and of the eland throughout Southeast Africa, is well established. The belief that the African elephant cannot be employed by man has been disproved in recent years when it has been shown that, like his Indian cousin, he can be tamed and utilized for labor. Cultural rather than natural or geographical reasons must therefore be looked to to explain why this powerful beast is used in one country and not in another. Similarly we ask why, among the people of this area, known for their fondness of colorful possessions, the zebra has not been domesticated, but, as with the lion, has been a choice meat; while in certain other places it has been used for light travel much as is the donkey among other Bantu tribesmen whose residence is in the center of areas in which the zebra abounds. Finally, for people fond of cattle, who need beasts to draw their loads and to aid in agriculture, it is puzzling to note that the Southeastern Bantu failed to use the eland in spite of the fact that it is an easily tamed and trained beast of burden, often more powerful than their oxen.

In this same region, the BaTswa, the BaTsonga, and the BaRonga tribes have every reason to know and to use the bark of the special tree from which the neighboring BaChopi make their useful bark cloth; but none of them do. The raw materials out of which the Chopi make marimbas are found everywhere, and all these tribes like to hear, and many people like to play the instrument. However, they obtain them by purchase or trade with the Ba-Chopi. The *makwakwe* fruit is accessible to all, with its strychnine-laden meat; the Chopi and a few BaTsonga eat its sweet food and are immunized against its poison, but the others pass it by. The ocean is free for all who live near the coast; yet only the BaTonga fish and ply the waters with boats. In the same territory it is the Hlengwe group of the Batwa tribes that weave *milala*, found everywhere, into baskets and mats which people of other tribes, to whom the raw materials are equally accessible, buy or obtain by trade; while it is a Moccodoene group which make and sell or trade earthenware pots to others in the same country for corn, peanuts, or other foodstuffs, following a definite ritual in their trade practices.

Another instance, taken from the American southwest, has frequently been used to call into question formulations of environmental determinism. Here the life of the Pueblo Indians is contrasted to that of their neighbors, the Navaho. The Pueblo folk are communal village dwellers, their economic life is based on agriculture. The Navaho live in individual huts and are preoccupied with their sheep-herds. Or finally another case, from the Pacific, might be considered. The Polynesians are all island-dwellers, and, being expert navigators and sailors in their outrigger canoes, have been able to make of the sea a highway rather than a barrier. The striking unity of Polynesian culture over the vast sweep of the central Pacific indicates that this contact between the peoples living there has exerted a comparable influence over all the area in which they live. Yet the differences between the habitat afforded by such localities as the Hawaiian Islands, the Tuomotos, and New Zealand is very great. In this instance culture tends to be the constant, while the environment varies. This again implies something less than a one-to-one relationship between the two.

4

THE position of those who qualify the extreme environmentalist point of view has been that *the habitat of a people acts as a limiting rather than a determining factor in influencing culture*. In this, they express an approach that brings them much closer to the facts.

This point of view is not restricted to anthropologists alone. On the contrary, it is much closer to the position of the majority of geographers than is the deterministic concept. The reason we have considered the deterministic approach at length, indeed, is that the minority of geographers who hold to it have been more insistent on advancing their thesis than their less extreme colleagues. More important still, the writings of the extremists have had an appeal out of proportion to their bulk. This appeal is attributable largely to the fact that their thesis is at once simple, appears convincing—until analyzed in the light of all the facts—and is dramatic. Living in a complex world, we welcome simple explanations. It is appealing, for example, to be told that skyscrapers are found in Manhattan because Manhattan, an over-populated island, had to reach toward the heavens to accommodate its activities, and that this was made possible because of its rocky sub-structure. We tend to forget the bridges and tunnels and ferryboats that connect Manhattan to the mainland and to Long Island, where so large a proportion of Manhattan's daytime millions live; or that in Chicago, where the substratum is clay, skyscrapers are erected on piles driven deep into the ground. It is easy to overlook how, in the plains of central United States, where there is neither lack of space nor pressure of local population, skyscrapers still are built and are looked upon with pride by the people. It is equally lost sight of that in Rio de Janeiro not only the desire of many persons to enjoy the magnificent bay and ocean front, but also the belief that skyscrapers symbolize "civilization," have equally caused this architectural form to dominate the skyline of that city.

It is far less exciting to follow the painstaking analysis by geographers of how, in less striking situations, man adapts himself to his habitat, than to accept the simplicity and finality of the deterministic hypothesis. But so important is the fact that man must make this adaptation, that the position taken in reaction to environmental determinism, that the habitat is a limiting factor in the development of a culture, though an improvement on environmental determinism, is still too broad to be more than a blunted tool in the hands of the student of culture. Let us see, therefore, whether it is possible to sharpen our tool so as to reach a more satisfactory understanding of the relationship between culture and habitat, one that will coincide with the known facts.

It may have been noted that, in discussing the life of people whose cultures are attuned to difficult habitats, their technologies and economic activities were given most attention. Yet when we wish to analyze the relation of culture, considered as a whole, to habitat, we must range the entire gamut of custom, taking its nonmaterial aspects into account as well as those aspects that are concerned with getting a living. What, for example, is the relationship between decorative design and the habitat of the artist? What interaction is there between political structures of a society and its natural setting?

Phrased in this manner, the complexities of what seems at first glance a matter of simple statement are seen to emerge. Non-representational decorative designs afford a good instance of this. These designs do not portray any objects and most commonly are found to consist merely of a series of lines, curved or angular, which embellish some object to make it more pleasing to the eye than if it were unornamented. What interpretations these lines will be given, if they are given any at all, depend on the tradition of the people among whom this art is found. Thus, among the Indians of the Plains in

the United States such a series of lines as has been variously
interpreted as a tent with people standing in front of it, as a cloud with
rain falling from it, or as a mountain with streams running down its side. In
West Africa, a design such as ∿∿∿ is held to be the
rainbow, a path through the bush, or a snake. The only conclusion we can
draw regarding the effect of the habitat on such designs is that where interpretations are given, the explanations are couched in terms of the experience
of those who make or look at them. In this experience, the natural setting, as
it figures in the life of the people, always enters. But whether or not an explanation of design is referred to the natural setting is a matter of pure
chance. Of one thing we can be certain—those who have never seen or heard
of a mountain will never interpret any design by such a symbol. But this
merely restates the principle that interpretation does not go outside experience, and helps us but little in the process of analyzing relationships.

The influence of habitat on political structures, though somewhat less
removed from the influence of the natural setting than decorative art, is to
be discerned only after several intermediate steps have been traced. Complex political structures exist in large aggregates of population, small ones
understandably having little need for them. Concentrations of populations,
however, are found where the basic economy of the people is agriculture
rather than hunting or herding. But basic economies are tied in more closely
with the habitat than any other aspect of culture. Consequently in general
terms, the development of self-conscious political institutions, that can be
made explicit in description because they are personified in rulers, or are
typified in well-recognized systems of law, tends to be found in those areas
where sedentary populations produce enough goods to support these specialists in the direction of group concern.

An analysis of the statements set down in the preceding paragraphs indicates that the flexibility permitted cultural institutions by any habitat is a
crucial point in our consideration. Turning again to the principle of the
limiting role of the habitat, we perceive that even such a formulation is too
simple to provide a conclusive answer to the problem of the relationship
between culture and habitat. On the central plains of the United States,
hunting Indian bands once followed a nomadic existence and lived under
systems of government which were so little institutionalized that, as we
shall later see when we discuss this aspect of culture, mechanisms of control
must be sought in relationships rarely classified as governmental. Three
hundred years later, by the historic circumstance of a change in basic culture brought in by European migrants, this same area presents an entirely
different picture. Agriculture has replaced hunting, and even herding; cities
dot the region. The political structures of those who live in this region are
similarly different from that of the aboriginal Indians. Today, city, county,
and state governments, courts and law-enforcement officers, and numerous

agencies of control operate as units of the larger political entity called the United States. But the natural setting has changed not at all in the past three hundred years, except as it has been changed by the hand of man.

To assign to habitat merely a *limiting* role is thus not enough for our purpose. This explanation, it is patent, has outlived its usefulness, since it essentially expresses a negative point of view that can be called on only to refute positive claims that exceed the facts. As a negative approach, it cannot guide analysis of the problem of the habitat-culture equation that will lead to positive findings. We must, therefore, first of all recognize that as the total range of human activities is not equally affected by habitat, any analysis of the relationship must be concerned with the differing *responsiveness of the various aspects of culture* to their natural setting, rather than with attempts to erect generalizations affecting total cultures.

We may, therefore, summarize here the degree of relationship of several aspects of culture to the habitat. It is evident that the technological and economic elements in the life of a people are far more responsive to the habitat than the form of the dance, or religious rituals, or decorative art. Social and political structures, insofar as they maintain or encourage economic or technological functions, or are dependent upon them, also show some measure of response. This was seen in the examples of political structures in the American plains at two different periods. Yet many elements, even in these aspects of culture, cannot be correlated with habitat at all. Types of kinship systems, or the presence of secret societies, for instance, seem to bear little or no relation to the natural setting. Even less does the form of religion, despite the fact that everywhere its effective functioning lies in adjusting man to the universe. The universe to which it adjusts him, however, is one of his own devising, for which the actual habitat provides a background. The portrayals in the literature of the beliefs that rule the lives of such West African folk as live in the Niger Delta or Cross River jungles are a case in point. Their beliefs in magic stressed in the literature, and their stark fear of the supernatural powers reflect the hardships and dangers of life in these dark forests. A more sophisticated scientific technique of study, however, shows that the constant fear these people have been said to live under because of their habitat, is more a construct of the observer than a fact in their lives. The dangers, to be sure, are real enough, but they are no greater than the dangers of living in a world where electricity and automobiles and other mechanical devices every year injure or kill thousands. Though the comparative psychological effect of living amid these hazards is still to be studied, it is not too rash to conjecture that both the Niger Delta groups and ourselves achieve a parallel measure of integration to life as they and we live it.

5

THE fact that the total environment provides men with the raw stuff of experience and that habitat is an integral and constant element in this environment, must thus never be lost sight of. We must also, however, understand that the degree of latitude in possible variation is greater in art or religion or story-telling than in agriculture or herding. The symbolism of decorative art *may* draw on the habitat; the gods are customarily related in some way to the forces of nature; stories about animals rarely refer to creatures found outside the habitat of the tellers. Yet in the play of the imagination, the permitted variation is undeniably greater in such cultural phenomena than where the seasons dictate the agricultural cycle, or the habitat restricts the crops that may be planted, or a limited supply of grass makes it necessary for a herding people to be constantly on the move. Habitat, then, is a limiting factor, but it *selectively* limits behavior.

This principle must be still further refined, however, for the matter is even now not as simple as our amended statement of the limiting role of the habitat would imply. For it becomes clear, as we study the relationship between culture and habitat, that man not only adapts himself to his natural setting, but as his adaptation becomes more effective, he is freed from the demands of his habitat, making it possible for him at times to challenge or even defy its limitations.

Rice cultivation in the Far East affords an excellent instance of how this operates. Though there are types of rice that grow where the ground is dry, the species of rice used in this part of the world is grown in irrigated paddies. It would seem obvious that flat land is essential for this sort of cultivation, for where else could the necessary pools of shallow water be maintained? In all probability, the growing of irrigated rice began in such a habitat. Yet as the tradition of "wet" rice-growing and the taste for rice spread, either through borrowing or migration, or both, to regions where the land is rugged, a choice of adaptation or renunciation was forced.

Rice cultivation as carried on by the Ifugao of the Philippines shows how the knowledge of terracing, a technological development, permitted the growing of irrigated rice in a terrain that, on the face of it, would seem absolutely to forbid this. Rice grows to an altitude of 5,000 feet, and the terraces that have been built up the mountainsides to reach this limit sometimes soar three thousand feet from the floor of the narrow valleys that lie between the mountains. With these terraces, the only requirement for growing "wet" rice is that the water commence its flow at a point higher than the highest terrace. Then the stream can be directed as needed from its source to the highest terrace, then to the next, and so on until all the "fields" have the water they need. And the water, having finally dropped its silt in the calm pools through which it has been directed, joins the river in the valley bottom. The labor that goes into building these terraces and in maintaining them is gruelling. On steep slopes, stone retaining walls have to be built. Each rock used in these walls must be carried up the mountainside from the valley floor. Sometimes terrace walls have to be twenty feet high to permit the utilization of land about eleven feet wide. Elsewhere in the Philippines, where the mountains are steeper, the terraces rise fifty feet to allow this much space for cultivation.[5]

---

[5] R. F. Barton, 1922.

The Materials of Culture

Even more striking is the example of Pukapuka, an atoll of three coral islets in the Central Pacific about four hundred miles northeast of Samoa. Coral cannot be used for agriculture any more than any other rocky substance, so that the only earth in which the taro that supplies the staple food of the inhabitants can grow is that which they have literally made. A few coconut trees found root on these islands before they were inhabited, but their nuts could not support even a small population. The earliest native settlers dug large pits, placed coconut and other leaves in them, and allowed them to rot in the water that seeped through from the sea until a thick mud was formed in which the taro grew well. As more settlers came, the pits were enlarged, until at the present time there are enormous excavations which provide the soil essential to grow the taro that feeds the people who make up the several villages now found in these specks in the ocean.[6]

The manner in which the technological equipment of Euroamerican culture allows a far greater latitude in ways of living in the tropics than could ever be dreamed of without them, may also be mentioned as a case in point. Electrical refrigeration, for example, or air-conditioning, to cite only two of the more striking developments, permit a wide variety of foodstuffs to be utilized, and escape from high temperatures, to a degree that a tropical habitat of itself could not yield. Technological achievements such as vaccines and inoculations have similarly freed inhabitants of tropical areas from endemic diseases, and have thus directly contravened what had become limitations set by the habitat.

Culture, especially in its technological aspects, can moreover be thought of as influencing habitat in a manner analogous to the way in which we have seen it influence physical type. The analogy holds especially; for just as we rarely think of culture as influencing race, so we rarely conceive of culture as altering the natural setting. Yet it needs but a little reflection to see that this is a commonplace in human history. All groups who have built irrigation systems have changed the physical structure of their habitat in thus extending its potentialities. We need but recall the example of how the Ifugao and many other Far Eastern rice-growing folk have changed the physical features of the mountainous country they inhabit, for corroboration of the point. From these manipulations of the habitat to such engineering feats as the Suez and Panama canals, that have severed whole continental land masses, or the great dams that create man-made lakes covering hundreds of square miles, is but to traverse a series of steps that reflect an increasing technological competence.

We have thus far seen that, though the habitat limits man's culture, it influences cultures not as wholes but to different degrees in different cultures, and variously in their several aspects. It should be emphasized that though technology and economics respond most readily to the demands of the natural setting, this does not mean that habitat does not affect non-material as well as material elements. On the whole, it can be said, as a refinement of earlier phrasings of the relationship between habitat and cul-

---

[6] G. MacGregor, 1935, p. 13.

ture, that *the more adequate the technology of a people, the less direct will be the demands made by the habitat on them.* We are here expressing a principle analogous to the one advanced in our discussion of the relationship between race and culture. The fact that culture acts as a buffer between man and his habitat is a phenomenon of the same order as that which permitted us to state, on the biological level, that man, as a culture-building animal, had in large measure replaced natural selection with social selection. What we perceive is that the relationship of culture to either of these facets of human existence is a *reciprocal* one. Culture, that is, can in no wise be thought of as a passive element, to be molded by the impact of race or habitat. We need, therefore, to examine further certain of the implications that the reality of culture, as we have seen, is psychological, as this fact bears on yet another problem concerning the nature of man's environment.

6

THE environment, under the definitions given at the outset of this chapter, is the total setting of human life, encompassing both culture, or what is learned, and habitat, or the natural setting. In their interplay, the two components react selectively on each other. That is, just as differing aspects of culture are influenced to different degrees by the habitat, so within the limits imposed by its habitat in terms of its technological competence, a culture defines the effective elements of the natural environment that enter into its total setting, and indicates to what extent it must continuously be taken into account by the individual in living his daily life. This is what has been termed the behavioral world of the individual. It is this psychological environment that provides him with his defined concept of reality.

But is it possible, one may ask, to tamper with such immutable elements in experience as time and space and direction? The sun and moon, the stars, the planets—are they not fixed, unchangeable realities in the life of a man? Can these, and the rivers and mountains and forests exist only by definition? It is to be seen that such an approach, as suggested even when questions of this order are posed, strikes so deep into our thinking that the very questions seem inadmissible as subjects of discussion.

We here return to the principle of cultural relativism. It will be remembered how, in our analysis of this principle, the view of Indians of the Southwest who add zenith and nadir, up and down, to our north, east, south and west, was mentioned. How in our own case, a convention of map-reading can invade the reality of direction, as we culturally define it, is to be seen, for instance, in our difficulty in thinking of the *upper* Nile as *south* and the *lower* Nile as *north.* The spectrum can be objectively verified, but the perception of its colors is culturally conditioned. In West Africa, among the Yoruba—to cite only one example out of the many that might be mentioned —any blue as dark or darker than indigo is identified as black. Colors, on the spectrum, merge from one to another imperceptibly; it is culture that interprets these data of experience by drawing the distinguishing lines.

The Materials of Culture

Mountains may exist as barriers, as suppliers of raw materials, as elements in the landscape, as factors in influencing climate, or more; and so with rivers and other aspects of the habitat. Nor must we, for a moment, in sketching the environment of man, neglect those unseen beings that people the habitat. Myth carries quite as much conviction to those who count it as a part of their heritage as the rocks they come upon in preparing a field—rocks which, in their concept of reality, may have been placed in the way of the gardener by the creatures whose existence the myth explains. It is a commonplace that in any culture where belief is strong, one can actually encounter those who have seen supernatural beings. In our mechanistic universe, multitudes still people graveyards with ghosts whose presence, even for those who do not acknowledge them, is sufficiently a part of that particular detail of their habitat as to make them reluctant to visit such a spot late at night, or in the small hours of the morning.

In the final analysis, the problem in studying the relation between culture and habitat is to determine the degree of integration of experience achieved by a people as they adapt themselves to the conditions under which they live—how, as Gayton has phrased it, the culture is "enmeshed with its natural surroundings."[7] After describing the "fundamental culture-environment relationship" of the California Indian Yokuts and Western Mono tribes, this student points out that here "the cultural concern with natural surroundings was not limited to utilitarian concern." Rather, "a culture-environment form of integration of more than a merely mechanical sort" is to be discovered, so that "features of the environment which are not essential to basic subsistence are caught up into the ceremonial, social and religious superstructure." From this, various modes of attack on the question appear. "Does this mean," we are asked, "that a culture which carries more environmental references is less subject to change—is more stable—than one which has less?"[8] The study of the dynamics of culture-habitat interaction is indicated; as is the study of how the natural setting is integrated in the behavioral world of the members of a given society, and how the reaction to habitat differs among peoples who live in a single natural setting but whose cultures differ.

Researches directed along these lines, it may be anticipated, will do much to resolve the questions with which we have been concerned in this chapter. For the moment, we may permit the matter to rest. It need only be stated at this point that, in accepting the role of the habitat as a factor in shaping culture, as something to which culture must respond, however selectively, we must also recognize that the total environment of man, drawing on both the traditional heritage of his culture and the habitat in which he lives, is made up of no more than can be comprehended in the definition of reality that he and his fellows draw out of their experience and the experience of those from whom they have descended.

---

[7] A. Gayton, 1946, p. 254.
[8] Ibid., p. 264.

PART IV

THE STRUCTURE OF CULTURE

CHAPTER 11

Culture-Trait and Culture-Complex

THE structure of culture has been usefully phrased in terms of trait, complex, area, and pattern. This is a logical progression. The trait, the smallest unit that can be identified, combines with other traits to form a complex. Complexes are oriented so as to give to a culture distinctive forms that are termed its patterns. The distribution of similarly patterned ways of life in a given region constitutes a culture-area.

The concepts of the culture-trait and culture-complex are related to an approach that analyzes all aspects of man and his world into components which, in their permutations and combinations, form the larger wholes to be distinguished as separate cultures. The concept of pattern, however, is in line with a point of view that stresses integration and an understanding of the interrelation between elements, rather than their place as semi-independent units in a greater whole. The area concept represents still another intellectual current, in that it is an attempt to order data in terms of spatial distribution, rather than in accordance with classifications derived from form or function.

These concepts, which arose from the mass of ethnographic field reports collected prior to 1917 which were crystallized in a volume by Wissler entitled *Man and Culture,* did much to stimulate research and further the understanding of culture. Many of the studies to which we shall refer in this section were made during the period the concepts to be examined in these chapters were being formulated. Out of these studies have derived many principles that today tend to be taken for granted. The words "trait," "complex," "pattern," "area," have come to be a part of the working vocabulary of anthropology. They stand for ideas so completely accepted, indeed, that the need to investigate the assumptions raised by them rarely is questioned. In part, this acceptance arose out of the fact that these concepts, once stated, had a self-evident validity that needed little documentation. Students with experience in the study of custom, whether among literate or nonliterate peoples, found them useful in organizing and presenting data and in abstracting leads for further study. Again, shortly after these concepts were enunciated, the interest of students shifted, because of the emphasis that came to be laid on three other problems. The first of these was concerned with the functioning of culture as manifested by the integration of its various aspects. The second focused interest on the individual in relation to his behavioral world. The third centered about the phenomenon of cultural dynamics, which in a sense encompasses both the above.

With the passage of time, the concepts and terms bearing on the structure of culture have been sharpened, after the manner of scientific method, which requires the continuous refinement of all acceptable research tools. There are not many students who would still agree with Wissler's statement of 1923 that "a culture is not to be comprehended until the list of its traits approaches completeness."[1] The greater skills in field research that have come with wider experience in making studies of this type have demonstrated that no list of traits, *as such*, no matter how complete, can give us a comprehension of any culture. No listing of traits, that is, can include the motivations that underlie the drives to behavior, or give an idea of how apparently unrelated cultural elements are integrated in the thought of a people, and help make them the kind of personalities they are found to be. Why, for instance, do we consider a triangular shaped flag the suitable form for the banner of an educational institution, while a rectangular one is used for a nation? As concerns the concept of pattern, the view that a whole culture can be designated in terms of a single over-all pattern has been modified by the recognition that every society, even the smallest, devises many different patterns. Today the concept represents a very complicated series of different behavior types existing simultaneously in the same society.

2

THE idea of the culture-trait, as the smallest identifiable unit in a given culture, seems at first acquaintance to be relatively simple. But it has treacherous implications that will trap the student in the morass of definition if caution is not observed in using it. For culture, in its totality or in any phase of it, is so well integrated, its parts so inextricably intertwined, that it is extremely difficult to know when a "smallest identifiable unit" is to be regarded as such because of its objective form, or because, in accordance with the ideas of a people, it is thought of as an indivisible part of a larger whole. In brief, the question turns on another aspect of that relativism we have already seen to be so important where any kind of definition is involved.

An example, taken from our everyday life, will show how this difficulty arises, and how it is to be met. In our pattern of living, we can regard the family dwelling quarters as having both material and nonmaterial aspects. Among the material elements are the rooms into which the house or apartment is subdivided, the stairs and elevators, various kinds of furnishings and appliances used for the preparation of food, cleansing the body, cleaning the dwelling place. The nonmaterial traits include the attitudes of the individuals comprising the household toward themselves, each other, and the world outside; the skills that enable them to employ the material devices that perform such functions as we have just described; the forms of behavior

---

[1] C. Wissler, 1923, p. 51.

that every family devises as their own intimate means of communication or amusement.

Now out of this aggregate, let us take one element, the table and six chairs that comprise the dining-room set. These are a unit, just as the dining-room is a unit in the house or apartment. That is, each is a trait of a larger complex, and validly to be regarded as such in terms of its relationship to the whole of which it is a part. The very fact that this table and its satellite chairs are to be designated by a single phrase—"Our dining-room set is in the center of the dining-room"—is significant in this context. In drawing up a list of traits of our culture which, in Wissler's phrasing, would attempt to "approach completion," would we set down the dining-room as a part of the dwelling-complex, or the dining-room set as a part of the dining-room complex?

Objections to either of these possibilities at once present themselves. We recall that in the case of the table-and-chair grouping, though it is a unit when thought of as a set, the fact that it includes a table and six chairs means that it is by no means the smallest identifiable one in this context. The table is not only to be physically separated from the chairs, but any element on occasion can be psychologically abstracted from the table-plus-chairs unity, as when there are too many guests to be accommodated on the living-room chairs and those from the dining-room are used for the purpose.

Let us for the moment give the table a unity of its own. Here, at least, is a physical whole that can be identified as such. But, says the literal-minded logician, though the table is a unit, is it not itself a gathering of sub-units? We may disregard those elements that are removable, such as the boards to be inserted when the table is extended so as to provide more seating space. Reduced to its physical unity as a table, it still consists of pieces of wood that were separately shaped, and assembled with nails and cleats and glue, and covered with some type of veneer. Is not one of these nails, or a cleat, or the mechanism that permits the halves of the table to slide apart, a trait in its own right?

We need continue this exercise in frustration no farther to see that the concept "trait" cannot be delimited in absolute terms. If it were, we would finally be considering atoms, while at the same time reducing our concept in cultural context to complete uselessness. But with a reasonable degree of conceptual flexibility there is no need to spin out our idea until its utility is destroyed, by insisting that it achieve results never intended for it.

This initial problem has been faced, placed in perspective, and discussed by all who have used the concept of the culture-trait. Thus, Driver and Kroeber, after stating that "we believe that culture traits are in the main if not in absolutely all cases independent," add this note: "Within the limits of ordinary logic or common sense. Essential parts of a trait cannot of course be counted as separate traits: the stern of a canoe, the string of a bow, etc. Even the bow and arrow is a single trait until there is question of an arrowless bow. Then we have two traits, the pellet bow and arrow bow. Similarly, while the sinew backing of a bow cannot occur by itself, we legitimately distinguish self-bows and sinew-backed bows; and so, single-curved and recurved bows, radically and tangentially feathered arrows, canoes with blunt, round or sharp sterns, etc." [2] Or as Kroeber puts it in a later discussion, a trait is to be thought of as a "minimal definable element of culture." [3]

When a trait is to be regarded as constituting such a minimum, involves evaluation of two kinds. The decision in a given instance must be the result of considered study of the problem by the expert, that yet takes into account the unconsidered view of the individuals who live by the conventions of the culture being studied. Moreover, this is to be done with the realization that even such an ascribed unity may shift in terms of the larger whole of which it is a part. The chair is a unit of the set, the set a unit in the dining-room, the dining-room a unit in the house, and so on. Where the lines are drawn thus depends on the end sought in a given instance. They will have an objective validity, but there is little need to repeat, at this stage of our discussion, the precept that objective validity can take many forms. *The form a trait assumes at a given time will thus be determined by its context, rather than by any quality inherent in it.*

It can readily be shown how a list of traits can grow as, with experience, more and more details of a culture or series of cultures are taken into account. For this purpose, let us consider an extensive research program based on the trait-concept, the California culture-element study. In the first California trait list, published in 1935, Klimek included four hundred and thirty items. Under the heading "hunting and fishing," he lists twenty-four elements, under "death and mourning" seventeen.[4] Two years later, Gifford and Kroeber published a trait list for the Pomo and two neighboring tribes, wherein they recorded the presence or absence of 1,094 traits. In their list the "fishing" category, which is presented separately, includes forty-five elements, the "hunting" traits number fifty-seven. In this study, under the classification "death," forty-eight items are noted.[5] The last published trait-list from California appeared five years later. Working with four tribal groups in Round Valley, some of whose cultures had been previously analyzed, Essene recorded 2,174 elements. "Fishing" traits number seventy-two items, "hunting," one hundred and thirty. Under "death" he distinguishes one hundred and ten elements.[6] A tabulation of these figures will make their significance clearer:

	Total	Hunting and Fishing	Death
Klimek (1935)	430	24	17
Gifford & Kroeber (1937)	1,094	102	48
Essene (1942)	2,174	202	110

In other parts of California, or in other areas, studies produced lists that grew apace. Stewart [7] notes 4,662 elements for the Ute and Southern Paiute

[2] H. E. Driver and A. L. Kroeber, 1932, pp. 212–13.
[3] A. L. Kroeber, 1936, p. 101.
[4] S. Klimek, 1935, pp. 23–9.
[5] E. W. Gifford and A. L. Kroeber, 1937, pp. 127–64.
[6] F. Essene, 1942.
[7] O. C. Stewart, 1942.

bands to the east; E. Voegelin [8] has a list of 5,263 for tribes of northeast California; while Ray,[9] working in the region north and northeast of the California tribes, increased the number to 7,633.

The contrast between these earlier and later studies is no greater in the numbers of traits recorded than in the changes in method and objectives to be discerned as the research program developed. Klimek's data were all taken from published ethnographic accounts. Gifford and Kroeber's study was "the first attempt" to collect data "from natives by means of a trait question list." The success of their efforts caused all later studies to employ this method, but it has been stressed that researches of this kind call special skills into play. As Ray phrases it: "I spoke above of the importance of a trained investigator, and by this I mean not only one trained in field work but also experienced in the area in which he is to work. Failing this the technique . . . would be impossible of realization. It demands that both informant and ethnographer be intimately acquainted with the culture, and that both thoroughly understand the technique being employed. The recording of element lists is the most difficult field-work I have ever done. It is equally trying for the informant. The tempo of the work brings phase after phase of culture into review in rapid succession. . . . In my own work, . . . every ounce of previously gained experience was necessarily utilized. I cannot conceive having carried through the task without such experience." [10]

Klimek's study was made with the object of obtaining quantitative data to be analyzed statistically in order to reconstruct the historical relationships between the tribes studied. Kroeber, as we shall see in the next chapter, has used culture elements in describing and analyzing the relationship between culture and habitat in terms of cultural areas, and so as to delimit these areas more accurately than other methods permit. Ray, who "never shared Dr. Klimek's interest in statistical interpretation of the facts," set as his aim "simply the recording of useful ethnographic data." [11]

It was as a result of the increasing skill and the precise objectives of this research that the trait list grew as it did. Though the culture-trait concept was used before these studies were undertaken, no one had attempted to draw up a listing of traits to find out how many items of culture could be discovered through field investigation carried on with native informants. The idea remained on the conceptual level, without the support of systematic analysis. How fruitful was the concept when taken into the field, permitting those who employed it to go farther and farther in their task of indexing the cultures they studied, is to be seen if we consider the treatment of such a single cultural element as the house. The findings of Gifford and Kroeber for the Pomo may be compared with that of Essene, made some years later. The former trait-list sets up these categories:

> Assembly or dance house (14 elements)
> Dwelling house (11 elements)
> Sweat house (20 elements)

---

[8] E. W. Voegelin, 1942.
[9] V. Ray, 1942.
[10] *Ibid.* p. 101.
[11] *Ibid.*, p. 100.

The Structure of Culture

Essene divides the topic in this way:

> Structural Features
> Frame (12 elements)
> Covering (6 elements)
> Entrances, exits (17 elements)
> Fireplace (3 elements)
> Sweat House (32 elements)
> Dwellings (9 elements)

Thus not only growth, but refinement and penetration have come with experience. The process has also been well described by Ray, whose comments on field methods we have just quoted. Before his first field trip, adaptations of the California trait-list were made to fit it for use in the cultures he proposed to study. These revisions were tested in the field, and again worked over so as "to make a more logical sequence," and to fit additions to it. The new list was then held to be ready for use. Once more, however, "the list grew constantly, in spite of its previous expansion. It was frequently necessary to remove pages or whole sections and recopy them in order that interpolated elements might be put in more logical order." [12] Ray estimates that less than four or five percent of the entries in the first list taken into the field are to be found in the culture-element assemblage published in his final report.

3

IN THE main, the concept of the culture-trait has been used far more as a conceptual tool than as an aid in field research. In earlier periods, too, it was used with but little concern for its theoretical implications. It is difficult to see how this concept, or some equivalent one, could be omitted from the study of culture. Whether approached from the point of view of outer frame or inner meaning, culture as a subject for study must be considered as a phenomenon that has form. The analysis of the forms taken by cultures, in turn, requires the assumption that these forms are structured. This assumption, again, makes it necessary to observe the component elements in the structures when we study human behavior in a given society, or compare differing forms of behavior manifested in groups having different cultures. Thus, it is not too much to state that the entire field of archaeology is devoted to studying the incidence and development of culture-traits whose functional relationship to one another can only be guessed.

Some of these earlier instances where culture-traits were studied, even though they were not so designated, may be mentioned. Tylor analyzed different cultures from this point of view when he applied the principle of correlation between cultural elements in seeking to understand how institutions developed. [13] F. Boas' investigation into the problem of how the myth-

---

[12] *Op. cit.*, p. 100.
[13] E. B. Tylor, 1889.

174

Culture-Trait and Culture-Complex

ology of a people reflects their mode of life, documented by materials from the Tsimshian Indians of British Columbia, could not have been carried on had he not first broken down the stories into parts, prior to rearranging these items so as to give an ordered, systematic description of the culture. This is apparent from the following passage, which only differs in its manner of presentation from the kind of analysis of traits centering about the house that might be given in a culture-element survey: "*Houses.*— . . . The house is carved on the outside, and has carved timbers inside. . . . The doorway is covered by a skin flap. . . . The floors of many houses must have been simply smooth and leveled ground. . . . Platforms were arranged in the framework of the house, and some of these served as bedrooms for the children. . . . In the houses were kept stores of winter provisions, such as salmon and halibut . . . preserved in boxes." [14] About the same time as the Boas study was published, English students extended Tylor's researches by correlating certain traits such as slavery, or chieftainship, with other traits in cultures of varied degrees of economic complexity to discover the relationship between them. [15]

The comparative ethnographic studies of Nordenskiöld, Lindblom and others of the Swedish school also accept as a basic postulate the idea that cultures are composed of elements that can be treated separately. We cannot consider here the problem Nordenskiöld raises concerning the relation between the ability of a given trait to travel and whether or not it is adapted for use in the environment in which it is found. For our purpose, it is sufficient to recognize that he treats "cultural elements," as he terms them, as separate units in the cultures of the Choroti and Ashluslay tribes of the Gran Chaco of South America, in his investigation of how they combine and recombine with other elements in other cultures. In his initial volume, he maps the separate distributions of such items as wooden spades, bow-cords made from animal material, the "bird arrow," the sling, the clay-pellet bow—to name but five of the forty-four traits considered. [16] For Africa, Lindblom and his associates have similarly made separate analyses of the distribution of many distinct cultural elements—slings, stilts, fighting bracelets, spiked wheel-traps, hammocks, and string figures, to name but a few. [17]

Studies of culture-traits are not restricted to the analysis of the problems we have mentioned. They can be effectively called on to correct false notions of the presumed "simplicity" of nonliterate cultures. We may recall the listing of more than seven thousand distinguishable items in the cultures of California, Plateau, and Great Basin Indian tribes. But all the tribes named in these studies are known for the smallness of their numbers, the "sparseness" of their material equipment, the uncomplicated nature of their economic and political systems—in short, they are what is customarily regarded as "simple" cultures. What figures would emerge from a tabulation of this type carried on among the peoples of Central America, or West Africa, or

---

[14] F. Boas, 1916a, p. 395.
[15] L. T. Hobhouse, G. C. Wheeler, and M. Ginsberg, 1915.
[16] E. Nordenskiöld, 1919.
[17] K. G. Lindblom, ed., 1926—.

Indonesia can only be conjectured. But what material we have demonstrates better than almost any other available data that the "simplest" cultures are to be seen as complex, even when no more than the raw inventories of their cultural resources are taken into account. It need hardly be pointed out that any attempt to assess the ways in which these items are interrelated would add immeasurably to the complexity of the picture.

Still other uses of the culture-trait are in the delimitation of culture-areas, in the reconstruction of unwritten history of contact between peoples by weighing the significance of trait distributions, and in distribution studies which seek to understand how a given cultural element, as it travels from tribe to tribe, is combined and recombined with other elements. In later pages, as we take up problems of this order, we shall be dealing either with individual units or with groupings of them. We shall see that the use of the trait is often implicit, as, for example, in psychological studies when considering the problem of symbolic meaning, analyzing how different meanings are assigned to the same object or institution or expression of value in different cultures, or how different cultural elements can hold similar meaning for different peoples.

Nonetheless, we must recognize that however useful a tool the concept of the culture-trait may be, and however much it may enter profitably into various types of studies, methodologically, its use as an end in itself is applicable only to the investigation of specialized problems. Frequently, not the single trait, but a grouping of traits found to exist in close relationship within a given culture must be the object of study. It is these groupings of traits that comprise the describable outlines of the way of living of a people. As aggregates, they form what are called culture-complexes, the second element in the structure of culture which we now proceed to examine.

4

THE nature of the culture-complex can best be illustrated by an example, for which we turn to the discussion of ritual in the authoritative and exhaustive analysis of Pueblo Indian religion made by E. C. Parsons.

"Pueblo ritual," Parsons writes, "is kaleidoscopic. There are many ritual patterns or rites, and . . . they combine in many ways. . . . Mobilized into a comparatively constant combination, a group of rites may form a ceremony, sometimes with, sometimes without, a dramatic idea." "Each rite or ritual element," we are told, must be seen "as a separable element or unit, in an order partly logical, partly suggested by the extent the rite is used." [18] The elements she distinguishes are classed under the headings of offerings, such as prayers and prayer-sticks, meal, pollen, beads, food, and the like; "fetishes," which include stones, masks, images, scalps; altars, orientation, and favored numerals; mimetic rites, including smoking, aspersing, pouring of water; the use of musical instruments; and other items such as dancing,

---

[18] Elsie Clews Parsons, 1939, vol. I, p. 268.

running, singing, continence, and fasting. The list ends with a group of ten purificatory rituals.

The details of how each element in this catalog is made, sanctified, and used take many pages to set down. The answer to the question, "How do rites from this list of more than fifty-five ritual elements combine into a ceremony?" is given in terms of how each item fits into the total. This makes it apparent that each trait contributes to the larger unity which those groupings of elements we term culture-complexes always manifest within the context of a given culture. "And so," we are told, "rites combine and recombine, the rite itself fixed or conventional but the combination less rigid; indeed the elasticity of Pueblo ritual is ever marvellous. And yet ritual rarely appears loose-ended, probably because it is so well integrated with social life at large, expressing or directing it." [19]

This characteristic integration of the culture-complex cannot better be seen than in the way individual traits, in different cultures, make up unified wholes in each culture where they are present. Almost any folk-tale forms such a complex. The several characters, the settings and the incidents are independent variables which, though having the same combinations in no two versions, make of each version a unified whole. Most persons in the Euroamerican area are familiar with the Cinderella tale, of which some three hundred and fifty variants were published in one early study.[20] If we take but a single incident, the crucial one where Cinderella loses her slipper, we find that this sometimes occurs at midnight after a ball, sometimes at noon when Cinderella must flee a church service attended by the Prince. The complex represented by the tale as a whole is everywhere recognizable. It is only of incidental significance for the plot whether the feet of Cinderella's step-sisters simply fail to fit the slipper recovered after her flight, or fraud is employed when the step-mother slashes a piece from each of her daughters' heels to make the slipper fit, or whether Cinderella's residence is visited by the king's guards who must fit the slipper, or all the young women of the kingdom go to the palace to try it on. The ill-treated little girl is always identified as the owner, and her future is secure.

This kaleidoscopic aspect of the culture-complex is our best justification for arguing the validity of distinguishing it conceptually from the culture-traits which are its parts. It is possible to follow the manifestation of a given complex from tribe to tribe over a wide area, just as it is possible to study trait distribution. One such example is the study of Benedict on the complex of ritual and belief that centers about the idea of the guardian spirit in North America.[21] Among all the many peoples where this complex forms a part of the culture, no two manifestations are the same, yet each shows a grouping of traits about the central concept that gives it recognizable form and inner unity in tribe after tribe, and in area after area.

This central idea of the guardian spirit concept is implemented by differing rituals, and validated by the different functions it fulfils in different

---

[19] *Ibid.*, pp. 476–8.
[20] M. R. Cox, 1892.
[21] R. Benedict, 1923. The passages quoted here are from pp. 9–16.

regions. Among the Thompson River Indians all young men of the tribe, by fasting and isolation in the mountains, strove to achieve "supernatural communication, and the acquisition of the name and power and song of the guardian spirit in a vision." Yet this quest was not an exclusive preoccupation of the period of seclusion, for the element of what might be termed training entered, and the boys in their rites, like the girls who had no concern at all with the guardian spirits, spent their time "in activities of sympathetic magic" to strengthen them later in meeting the exigencies of everyday life. Thus the boys "who desired to become hunters practised hunting and shooting in a ceremonial way; those who desired to become warriors performed mimic battles."

For the Kwakiutl Indians of the Northwest Coast, the guardian spirit "was an hereditary caste mark." This tutelary being, sought by the Thompson Indians in the seclusion of their mountains, was acquired by the Kwakiutl in accordance with rights established through inheritance, or marriage, or by killing the former owner. "One might not see a tutelary in his vision until his family had arranged to 'pay for his ecstasy'; a marriage must have been arranged with a woman having the hereditary right to pass on the 'crest'; in addition, the elders of the group assembled in council must have given their consent." With this difference in the character of the guardian spirit quest went a reduction in the numbers of tutelary spirits. The "limitless guardians of the Thompson" are among the Kwakiutl a restricted group, who are "individualized with very definite gifts which they bestow upon those within their protection."

Traits of possession by the spirit and the manner of its acquisition take on still different forms in the guardian-spirit complex of certain California Indian and Plains Indian groups. Among the Shasta these spirits were the prerogative of the healers, the shamans, men or women whose predisposition toward this calling "manifested itself in stereotyped dreams." The Crow of the Plains, on the other hand, laid no restriction of position, sex, or age on who might seek a vision that would reveal a guardian. Most often, "isolation, fasting, and self-torture" were involved, though a spirit did on occasion manifest itself to a fortunate possessor who thus did not have to torture himself. Having a vision indicated the road to success, and the suppliant would cut off a finger as an offering to the spirit. Yet, among the Crow, "the seeking of visions is . . . a much more general institution than that of procuring a guardian spirit." Visions of other kinds are sought, on all occasions. The beings who appear in most visions give a song, endow one with specific powers, and indicate a token for the person to find and keep about him later, just as does the guardian spirit. In short, the kind of vision quest that figures in the Crow guardian-spirit complex is by no means confined to that complex, but is found in association with many other aspects of daily life, often nonreligious ones.

The trading complex in Melanesia affords another example of how a dominating drive, in society after society, can be the nucleus of an aggregate of traits of which no two are identical. The forms of trade in this area are countless. It can be carried on by individuals or small groups meeting to barter specific articles, as for example, in Buka, where taro, the staple food of the region, is exchanged by the women of one tribe for the carrying baskets made by the women of another tribe. A common medium of exchange may, on the other hand, introduce into the trading complex the stated market, where buying and selling goes on more in the manner of the exchange of goods in societies having a money economy. Deferred payments are known, and this introduces the factor of interest, computed either in goods or in tokens of common value.

The association of ceremonialism with the trading complex is widely spread in Melanesia, where the relationship transcends economic considerations, and the supernatural is invoked to assure the traders success. Rank similarly figures in the total picture of Melanesian trading, for those of position will have more trading partners than commoners, and the goods they exchange will consist of items of greater value than those traded by persons of lesser rank. Often the trade is carried on at two levels, one of a semi-ritual character, wherein prestige tokens are exchanged before the goods of economic importance such as foodstuffs, tools, pottery, nets, or carved wooden objects are bargained for. So deep does this trading complex strike in Melanesia, and so characteristic are its basic forms, despite the diversity of the accompanying traits, that it can be said to characterize Melanesian economy, and may eventually even be seen as important in differentiating Melanesian culture as a whole.[22]

5

Let us consider the integrative factor that gives to a cultural complex its unity, no matter what fortuitous traits seemingly comprise it. The student, who is seeking a purely rational explanation of why certain elements found together should have been combined, is at times baffled by the apparent absence of logic in their inclusion. Why, we ask, should the guardian spirit be in one tribe for the healer alone, in another validated by rank, in a third acquired by privation and self-discipline? How can we explain the fact that in Melanesia the idea of the exchange of goods has in one region a sanction of magic, in another is associated with prestige, in a third, is restricted to certain humble objects?

In Dahomey, West Africa, the men's cooperative work-group is an important economic institution. It is called the *dokpwe,* and can be regarded as a culture-complex which is susceptible of being analyzed into many component traits. The pride with which men think of themselves as members of these groups, their organization, which includes a chief and several assistant chiefs, the work they do in hoeing fields and thatching houses are all such items. The feast that is the payment for their work, the types of songs sung while the work is being done, the competitive units set up within the

---

[22] For an intensive study of this trading complex among a single people, see B. Malinowski, London, 1922. A comprehensive study of Melanesian trade is to be found in Laura T. Tueting, 1935.

cooperative group, are others. Still others are the tradition that the fields of a member in ill health are hoed by this group without compensatory feast; or that a man of position, with many wives, fulfils his obligations to his several parents-in-law to perform a yearly agricultural task for each wife's father, and to see to the thatching of the roof of each wife's mother, by calling on the cooperative labor of the *dokpwe*. In the material realm, not only the hoes used in tilling the land, but the drums, gongs, and rattles that set the beat for the strokes of these hoes, as well as for the songs that accompany the work, must be taken into account.

The logic that underlies the *dokpwe* complex and most of its component traits is evident when its economic functions are considered. In a tropical country, where the transition between dry and rainy seasons is rapid, the necessary work of preparing the earth for planting can be completed in the proper time only by group effort. When, as in the case of the head of a polygynous household, a number of fields must be hoed, or where a man has large gardens, the problem would be insurmountable without an adequate labor supply to call on. That compensation is only given in the form of a feast seems to take us outside the logic of economic demands until we recall that every man, as a member of a *dokpwe,* sooner or later completes a comparable task for those who had worked for him. The songs and drumbeats are explained by the fact that the Dahomeans hold the rhythmic accompaniment stimulates greater exertion and produces less fatigue in communal labor.

Yet the *dokpwe* complex functions not only in the economic scene, but also as an integral part of Dahomean mortuary rites. The *dokpwe* members perform many of the most important dances that honor the dead at funerals. Some of these dances require great dexterity, and much prestige accrues to those whose performance is outstanding. In one of these, six young men, three on a side, face each other with hands interlocked, the corpse resting on the outstretched arms. Holding their arms rigid, they rhythmically throw their bodies forward so the knotted ends of the cloths they wear, that are fastened at the back, are hurled upward to strike against their ears in perfect time. Each member of the *dokpwe* clamors to participate, as he does later to carry the corpse when it is taken by the *dokpwe* through the village, to visit in farewell the places the living had frequented, before the dead is taken to the grave. Again, they aid in filling the grave after the body has been interred.

The head of the local *dokpwe* presides at all funerals. In the tortuous process by means of which the dead is despatched to the after-world, during the two ceremonies, held weeks—sometimes many months—apart, that mark the "partial" and the "definitive" burials, no step is taken without his ritual permission. And he gives no consent without being ritually paid—in cloths, in cowries, in rum. Indeed, this is the widest difference between the economic and ritual aspects of the *dokpwe* complex. Of the traits that cluster about its economic phase, none is more important than the underlying idea of cooperativeness. In contrast, nothing is more striking about its ritual functions than how payment is exacted for every service. Not only the head of the *dokpwe* but the members of his group acquire substantial sums at funerals. Thus, when the corpse is taken about the village, the mourners follow it, beseeching the bearers to return the body to them. Others who hear the outcry throw gifts of money at those who carry it, and this, plus what the mourners donate, is gathered for later distribution by the one who acts as *dokpwe* treasurer. "Now is when a young man gets money," said one Dahomean in speaking of this rite, but he might have been commenting on the rewards of the funeral in general.[23]

That the *dokpwe* is at the same time associated with the production cycle and with the rituals of death, that it combines labor with song and dance, involves no contradiction in the minds of the Dahomeans. To them, this seems natural and understandable. It is an ancient sanction of the right to "disturb the earth." Somewhat farther to the west, among the Ashanti of the Gold Coast, the *asafoche*, also a men's communal organization, is devoted to warfare and has politically important prerogatives. This is equally logical to the Ashanti. In any culture-complex, little objective relationship between traits, either on the basis of logic, or need, or desirability, is to be discerned by the outsider. As Benedict has stated for the guardian-spirit complex, "The miscellaneous traits that enter in different centers into its make-up are none of them either the inevitable forerunner, the inevitable corollary, or the inevitable accompaniment of the concept, but have each an individual existence and a wider distribution outside this complex." [24]

6

ONE of the most significant aspects of culture is this fact that disparate elements, whose distribution can be individually traced, are combined and recombined into such differing expressions of a given basic concept; each complex or aggregate forming an integrated whole whose every part is not only accepted, but held as symbolically essential by the people in whose particular culture it is found.

Herein perhaps lies the principal difference between the culture-trait and the culture-complex. Both are useful devices in furthering the objective, scientific study of culture. But insofar as culture has meaning, and meaning gives to culture its reality, the trait is far more an abstraction drawn by the student than is the complex. Except as objects, or ideas, or values, or goals, that are part of a larger psychological cluster, the traits of a culture rarely rise to the level of consciousness. A tent is a tent, but those who think of tents do not consider the number of poles, or the quality and nature of the skin that covers it, or the decoration on it. The trait-complex "tent" is a unit in their thinking, and as such has the oneness of any total image. If, however, the tent forms a trait in the family complex as a living-place, then its separate psychological existence is modified, and it is merged with the other traits that go to make up the complex of which *it* now forms but a part.

---

[23] M. J. Herskovits, 1938, vol. I, ch. IV, XX, XXI, *passim*.
[24] *Op. cit.*, p. 84.

The Structure of Culture

We may approach this problem from another point of view by comparing the trait-lists that have been drawn up for tribal cultures as wholes, and trait-lists that are made within the framework of a given complex. The logic of the tribal trait-list is that of the student's conception of the organization of culture. Trait follows trait in catalog fashion. The relationship of one trait to another is here similar to the relationship of one card in a library index to the next, where alphabetical order, and not subject-matter is the guide. Such a heading in a culture-element list as "spoons," under which one finds these utensils entered as "pine, cedar, cottonwood . . . other woods, long handle, short handle, perforated, ornamented, inlaid," differs from an alphabetical order merely in the frame in which it is cast. Both are to be contrasted to the listing of traits in a complex where, disparate though they may seem, each contributes to the unity of the whole in terms of the central idea which gives the aggregate meaning to those in whose culture it is found.

|1

Culture-Areas: the Spatial Dimension

As WE move from one part of a continent to another, we find that while the cultures of no two peoples are identical, the customs of those who live close to one another tend to have greater similarities than do those groups who live farther apart. Some traits of culture, it is true, will be more widespread than others and may even have a continental distribution. Yet even in these instances, the setting of such cultural items in the total complexes of which they form parts will differ in different regions.

This simple fact derives from the fundamental principle that since culture is learned, any element in it can be taken over by any individuals or any groups of individuals exposed to ways of doing and thinking that differ from their own. By the same token, however, it follows that peoples who live close together have greater opportunities to borrow from each other than from folk who are at a distance. There will thus be a greater degree of mutual interchange between them than can ever occur between peoples far removed. This is why, when cultures are viewed objectively, they are seen to form clusters, so to speak, that are sufficiently homogeneous so that the regions in which they occur can be delimited on a map. *The area in which similar cultures are found is called a culture area.*

Kroeber [1] has discussed the development of the culture-area idea, showing how it "had its most active development among Americanists" as a result of the need to devise a technique for differentiating and describing the range of tribal customs, carried on by peoples whose lack of writing made it impossible to achieve historic depth in their study. It is interesting to note that an important early use of the culture-area was to facilitate the presentation of ethnographic specimens in museums, especially so that these could be displayed to give an idea of how the peoples who produced the objects being exhibited live. This approach, which now seems self-evident, came only at the turn of the century. It is of some importance to consider why it came to be used, since this not only illustrates the empirical character of the culture-area concept but also throws light on certain assump-

---

[1] A. L. Kroeber, 1931, pp. 248–50.

183

The Structure of Culture

tions about it that must be understood. This method of museum installation, that attempts to set forth the ways of life of peoples, is to be contrasted with the one under which objects of a given type are placed in a single hall, regardless of where they came from. This latter form of display permits the visitor to compare, for example, the different kinds of bows and arrows, spears, house-types, canoes, or clothing used by peoples all over the earth. Comparative displays of this type still predominate in certain European museums. They have their value, as is recognized by the fact that in some museums both comparative and descriptive types of installations are found.

The presentation of full collections showing the life of every tribe, especially of peoples whose cultures are similar, was never seriously entertained. For reasons of space and of available resources alone, such proposals would be as undesirable as they are impossible of realization. It is possible, however, to gather together in a single hall the specimens on hand from tribes having similar cultures. Then an assemblage of pieces can be exhibited that go harmoniously with each other, and give as complete a picture of the lives of the peoples inhabiting the region where this cluster of peoples is found, as material objects can afford. If, after the displays are arranged, the individual tribes are indicated on a map, and a line drawn to include them, the area in which these cultures are found, or the culture area is then represented.

In the instance of the rich store of materials from the American Indian, it was found that specimens from all the tribal units of a given region, such as the North Pacific coast, could be placed in one hall, those from the Great Plains of the heart of the North American continent in another, those from the wooded region of northeastern United States and southeastern Canada in a third, and so on. Though local differences still had to be taken into account, nonetheless the cedar house of the whole Northwestern area could be contrasted to the skin tent, or tipi of the entire Plains region, or the bark-covered shelter, or wigwam found over most of the east. Similarly, the striking, symbolic wood-carvings of the Northwest, best known in the totem-pole, were found to represent a unified artistic style when contrasted to the geometric designs in colored beads or dyed porcupine-quills of the Plains Indians, or the highly symmetrical, curvilinear, tendril-like motifs that dominated the art of the East.

Though E. Sapir and others were using the culture-area in theoretical discussions and museum work prior to any extended examination of its implications,[2] the culture-area, as such, was first systematically treated by Wissler, when he employed it to orient his work on American Indian cultures. His definition, though it has been since sharpened, is still useful and can profitably be repeated here. If, Wissler says, "the natives of the New World could be grouped according to culture traits," this would give us "food areas, textile areas, ceramic areas, etc., . . . If, however, we take all traits into simultaneous consideration and shift our point of view to the social, or tribal units, we are able to form fairly definite groups. This will

---

[2] E. Sapir, 1916, p. 44.

Culture-Areas: The Spatial Dimension

give us culture areas, or a classification of social groups according to their culture traits."[3]

To classify whole cultures in this or any other way is, however, by no means as simple as it seems at first glance. The individual traits into which a culture can be broken down for purposes of objective analysis may or may not have the same distributions. Boas has cautioned that since culture areas are commonly mapped on the basis of material culture traits, "The student interested in religion, social organization, or some other aspect of culture would soon discover that the culture areas based on material culture do not coincide with those that would naturally result from his studies."[4]

The relevance of this observation becomes apparent if, for instance, we consider the distribution of certain elements in African culture. East Africa is to be delimited as a culture-area largely on the basis of the place of cattle in the lives of the people there; the Congo because of its agricultural, political, and artistic characteristics. Yet in both these areas, a wife is acquired only after the passage of wealth to ensure, among other things, that a woman will be adequately cared for by her husband; while descent is counted on one side of the family rather than on both sides. The religions of Africa are customarily divided into two categories, one in which emphasis is laid on the ancestors, the other where nature-deities bulk largest. Here we differentiate East Africa from the Congo, but not the Congo from the Guinea Coast, or the Western Sudan. Or again, the languages of Africa are to be grouped into three great classifications, the Sudanic, the Bantu, and the Hamitic. In the Congo area, only Bantu is spoken; but East Africa is divided almost at the center by the line between the Bantu and the Hamitic tongues.

Nonetheless, such facts do not negate experience that the cultures of an area, considered as wholes, do "hang together." It is to be noted that Boas himself, in classifying North American Indian folktales, allocates the several types of myths and the dominant characters to areas which do roughly correspond to the conventional culture-area scheme for the continent.[5] In the case of the "human tale," indeed, we are told that "in all probability future study will show that its principal characteristics may well be defined by the cultural areas of the continent."[6] Roberts, too, when studying the distribution of musical forms of aboriginal North America, found that the musical areas, both instrumental and vocal, "coincide with those based on other cultural traits."[7]

The areas that have been mapped correspond, in a rough way, to ecological areas, and thus reflect a basic relationship between material culture and habitat. There can be no fishing-nets in the equipment of a desert people; those who inhabit the open plains are not likely to be wood-carvers. This is true even where we go outside the elements of material culture, susceptible of presentation in the museum. Cattle thrive in the open high plateaus of

---

[3] C. Wissler, 1922, p. 218.
[4] F. Boas, 1938, p. 671.
[5] F. Boas, 1914, pp. 387–400. (1940, pp. 465–79).
[6] Ibid., p. 399 (1940, p. 478).
[7] H. H. Roberts, 1936, p. 39.

185

East Africa, while the Congo forests, infested with tsetse flies, render it impossible for these animals to be counted among the possessions of the people who live in the forests.

2

CULTURE-AREAS have been formally mapped in the continents of North and South America, and in Africa. The manner in which these areas have been mapped, and the successive changes over the years in the maps that have been published, document how, in mapping culture-areas, the very idea of which was the result of "a gradual, empirical, almost unconscious growth," students have continuously reworked and realigned area classifications as new data became available.

The original map of American culture-areas, as given by Wissler, listed the following:

North America	South America
1. Plains	11. Chibcha
2. Plateau	12. Inca
3. California	13. Guanaco
4. North Pacific Coast	14. Amazon
5. Eskimo	
6. Mackenzie	*Caribbean*
7. Eastern Woodland	15. Antilles [8]
a. Iroquoian	
b. Central Algonkin	
c. Eastern Algonkin	
8. Southeast	
9. Southwest	
10. Nahua	

In this first mapping, the culture areas were designed essentially to differentiate concentrations of culture, or culture-centers. This was the reason why "more definite curved contours" were not used. "These boundaries," Wissler wrote, "in fact, are merely diagrammatic, serving to indicate the loci of the points where culture stands half way between that of the contiguous centers."

Kroeber, seven years later, did not fear these more "definite curved contours," as a glance at the culture-area map of the Americas on the next page will show. His revisions, first of all, altered the boundaries of Wissler's Mackenzie, Plateau, and California areas. "The culture of the Mackenzie region is so deficient and colorless that some students have hesitated to set it up as a separate unit. The Plateau culture is also vague as to positive traits. A plausible argument could be advanced apportioning it between the adjacent Northwest, Plains, California and Southwest cultures. In fact, usage has here been departed from in reckoning the Great Basin, that part of the

---

[8] C. Wissler, *op. cit.*, pp. 217–57.

FIG. 15 *Culture-areas of North and South America (after Kroeber, 1923, p. 337).*

187

The Structure of Culture

Plateau which is without ocean drainage, with California instead of the Plateau." In arranging his areas, to which he also applied a new series of names, he did not alter the number of divisions that Wissler gave. Kroeber's revised list comprises the following:

1. Arctic or Eskimo: coastal
2. Northwest or North Pacific Coast: also a coastal strip
3. California or California–Great Basin
4. Plateau: the northern inter-mountain region
5. Mackenzie-Yukon: the northern interior forest and tundra tract
6. Plains: the level or rolling prairies of the interior
7. Northeast or Northern Woodland: forested
8. Southeast or Southern Woodland: also timbered
9. Southwest: the southern plateau, sub-arid
10. Mexico: from the tropic to Nicaragua

The South American areas of Wissler are left unchanged, except they are called Colombia or Chibcha, Andean or Peruvian, Patagonia, Tropical Forest, and Antillean respectively.[9]

In a still later revision of the culture areas of North America only, Kroeber attempted a more specific correlation of culture and ecology than had hitherto been tried. He also produced a much more complex array of distinct units, at the same time achieving an overall simplicity that was greater than in his earlier mapping, or in Wissler's original one. He succinctly outlined his method as follows:

1) Specific attention is given to geographical and ecological factors.
2) The cultures are treated as historical nonequivalents.
3) Centers or climaxes of cultures are defined as sharply as possible.
4) Relations of subordination between and within cultures being sought and expressed, the number of basic areas is fewer, and of specific ones greater, than it has been customary to recognize.

As a result, he mapped eighty-four units termed areas and sub-areas, which made up the seven following "grand areas."

A. Arctic Coast
B. Northwest Coast
C. Southwest Area
D. Intermediate and Intermountain
E. Eastern Areas
F. Northern Areas
G. Mexican and Central American Areas.[10]

Because of the complexity that follows on the introduction of the time factor, only the "grand areas" are named here. For the purpose of classifying North American native cultures, however, these divisions are too general, while the eighty-four sub-units are too numerous to be of utility in classification. Kroeber's revision of Wissler's original map, reproduced on page 187,

---

[9] A. L. Kroeber, 1923, pp. 335–9.
[10] A. L. Kroeber, 1939, p. 20 and map 6. In his text he speaks of "six groups" of areas, placing the Eastern and Northern areas of the map together.

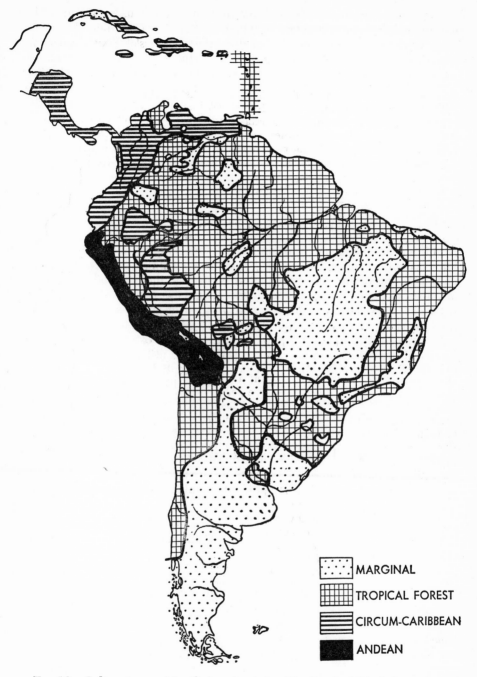

Legend:

- MARGINAL
- TROPICAL FOREST
- CIRCUM-CARIBBEAN
- ANDEAN

Fig. 16 *Culture types of South America* (*after* Handbook of South American Indians).

189

will thus be found most satisfactory in terms of the uses to which the culture-area has most often been put.

A further revision of the culture-area classification of South American Indian cultures resulted from the intensive studies and fresh information gathered in preparing the *Handbook of South American Indians*. The five areas of the Wissler-Kroeber formulation are reduced to four, while the smoothness of the boundary-lines and contiguity of regions that marked the earlier mapping is given over for a more refined system of classifying cultures lying in distant parts of the continent, on the basis of criteria empirically derived from the data. The map shows four main types which, in their distribution, are to be regarded as the equivalent of culture-areas. They are:

1. Marginal (stippled)
2. Tropical forest (cross-hatched)
3. Circum-Caribbean (broad bands)
4. Andean (black)

In this order they move from simpler to more complex, and primarily take into account ecological base as well as cultural manifestation. They betoken once again how, with more adequate information, the essentially empirical character of the culture-area encourages continuous revision and makes it a more effective instrument for the classification of cultures. Steward[11] has used the categories employed in drawing this map to relate similar types of cultures in North and South America as a step in reconstructing the culture-history of the Americas. This points a way toward utilizing the culture-area to orient data in studies where time-depth is essential.

The culture-areas of Africa were mapped in 1924.[12] Earlier, Ratzel and Dowd had recognized the differences between the cultures of certain regions of the continent, though the former merely distinguished cattle-keeping from agricultural peoples, and the latter indicated the distributions of cultures based on different basic food economies. The German students, Ankermann and Frobenius, also described what was essentially a culture-area, though their purpose in doing their studies was not description, but historical reconstruction. In the 1923 mapping, these nine areas were distinguished:

1. Hottentot
2. Bushman
3. East African Cattle Area
4. Congo
5. East Horn
6. Eastern Sudan
7. Western Sudan
8. Desert Area
9. Egypt

The first attempt followed an investigation of the East African data, and was in the nature of a test of the applicability of Wissler's procedure to the

---

[11] J. H. Steward, 1947.
[12] M. J. Herskovits, 1924a.

culture of another continent. Despite the paucity of scientific studies of African groups at the time, it was concluded that, "by a judicious utilization of such sources as are available, one can . . . obtain a fairly clear account of the cultural conditions in any given region." It was pointed out that "by . . .

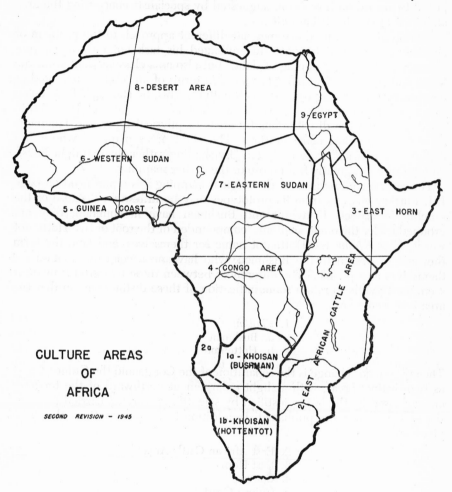

FIG. 17   *Culture-areas of Africa (after Herskovits, 1945c).*

dividing the continent . . . into the nine areas sketched . . . it will be found that the chaos a study of Africa ordinarily presents is greatly reduced." [13]

A revision of this mapping was made a few years later, so that "certain changes in accordance with the suggestions and criticisms of the earlier attempt" could be incorporated. In this revision of 1930, an "East African sub-

___

[13] *Ibid.*, p. 63.

area" was introduced to include the cattle-keeping peoples of Angola in the same general category as the East Africans, from whom they are separated territorially but not, in the opinion of students, historically; and the Guinea Coast was marked off as a sub-area of the Congo.[14] Lines were also readjusted to accord with revisions suggested by specialists concerning the area affiliation of specific tribal units.

Hambly, in 1937, used a somewhat different approach to the problem of classifying African cultures.[15] He envisaged his task not only as "a preliminary sifting and grouping of data," but also as a classification "from the social and psychological point of view," in terms of an "ethos" envisaged as the dynamic or driving force of each culture. This, he stated, if fully taken into account, would allow "all subsidiary factors" to fall in line. Included in his discussion were distributions by areas of physical types and language, as well as historical considerations. The eight areas mapped, whose "indefinite boundaries" were indicated "by shading rather than straight lines," do not differ too greatly from those of the earlier mapping.

The most recent revision of the original mapping[16] is reproduced on page 191. Further changes from its prototypes may be indicated. Because of the number of aspects Hottentot and Bushmen have in common, they are grouped under the name Khoisan, "compounded of the root of two Hottentot words, *Khoi-Khoin*, the Hottentot name for themselves, and *San*, the term they use to designate the Bushmen, who have no special designation for themselves as a people." The differences between these two groups made it seem worthwhile to retain some indication of these distinctions, so that the area is presented as

    1. *Khoisan*
      a. Bushman
      b. Hottentot

The other major change is the separation of the Congo and the Guinea Coast as two distinct areas, with a slight enlargement northward of the territory encompassed by the latter, justified by scientific researches carried on since the earlier maps were published. In addition to the above, then, the areas given are:

    2. East African Cattle Area
    3. East Horn
    4. Congo
    5. Guinea Coast
    6. Western Sudan
    7. Eastern Sudan
    8. Desert Area
    9. Egypt

As in the earlier mappings, the North African coastal strip is excluded because of its close cultural affinity to Europe.

---

[14] M. J. Herskovits, 1930.
[15] W. D. Hambly, 1937. His culture area map is opposite p. 324, Part I.
[16] M. J. Herskovits, 1945c, p. 9.

Culture-Areas: The Spatial Dimension

Asia has been divided into six culture-areas, though no mapping of this continent has been attempted. The six are:

1. Siberian (Palaeo-Siberian)
2. Southwest (the sedentary cultures of southwestern Asia)
3. Steppe (the pastoral nomadic cultures of central and southern Asia)
4. China (the Chinese sedentary)
5. Southeast Asian-Indonesian (which appears to have originated in south China and to be related to the Chinese)
6. Primitive nomadic (found in isolated regions of southeast Asia) [17]

In addition to the above areas, "four major areas of culture-blend" are recognized, where "distinct cultures have evolved following a fusion of two or more separate cultures." These are the Korean, Japanese, Indian and Tibetan.[18]

The culture-area concept has been successfully applied to Madagascar, whose culture, which had long been assumed to be "uniform throughout the island," was found on closer study to have "three fairly well marked culture areas . . . with the usual marginal tribes of mixed culture." These areas, which "agree in a general way with the main geographic and climatic divisions of the island," are named as the East Coast, the interior Plateau, and the West Coast and Extreme South.[19] Aboriginal New Zealand has also been mapped, eight areas having been distinguished in the culture of the Maori, these being "strongly marked" in material culture traits.[20]

It is interesting to consider how ocean regions, where the sea has been a highway rather than a barrier, lend themselves to division into culture-areas. The great regions of the Pacific, Australia and Tasmania, Polynesia, Micronesia, Melanesia and Indonesia, may be regarded as groupings in the nature of culture areas, as Hoijer's summary suggests.[21] Systematic analysis, as he points out, would undoubtedly show the need for more precise categories than these, especially in the case of Melanesia and Indonesia. The sub-continent of New Guinea, too, would require separate treatment.

3

DESCRIPTIONS of the cultures found in the areas that have been mapped is neither possible nor advisable here. An idea of them can best be gained by reading some of the detailed descriptions of specific cultures in the various regions that are readily available, and are named in the list of works given at the end of this book. Compressed presentations such as must necessarily be used to characterize culture-areas are deceptive unless read with proper background, since in them the complexities that mark every culture are inevitably lost sight of. Our concern is with the structure of culture, and in

---

[17] This listing of areas is a composite taken from E. Bacon and A. E. Hudson (1945) and E. Bacon (1946).
[18] E. Bacon, 1946, p. 121.
[19] R. Linton, 1928, p. 363.
[20] H. D. Skinner, 1921.
[21] H. Hoijer, 1944, p. 32, pp. 40ff.

The Structure of Culture

these terms the culture-area is important because it demonstrates how, in the dimension of space as in its inner organization, the unities of human civilization, and the inner variables that go to make up these unities, are maintained.

Let us turn to other aspects of the culture-area that will aid us in understanding its nature, and thus its significance for the study of culture in general. We have seen how areas were mapped only after the facts about the range of cultures over an entire region to be mapped were known, and how this indicates the empirical derivation of culture-areas. It will be helpful for us to probe this further. Ideally, the student considers the distribution of trait after trait in a region studied, discovering those cultures in which the greatest number of manifestations of these traits is found. It is these concentrations that then most clearly differentiate the culture-types. They represent, for the student, the peaks in the cultural landscape, and are the points about which his areas cluster.

Wissler's procedure makes this clear. Beginning his discussion of aboriginal American cultures with a delimitation of food areas, he then considers the distribution of individual cultural traits in the manner that has been described. He takes these up under such headings as the methods of transportation, textile and ceramic types, decorative designs, architecture, stone and metal work, the fine arts, social institutions and ritual, and mythology. He then considers where the most dense clustering of the greatest number of similar traits occurs, and these become the centers of his areas. Traits, he points out, may be negative or positive. The absence of traits that characterize one area, and the positive manifestations of traits of another are equally significant. These two categories are balanced even when the kind of culture that marks an area is being described. More importantly, however, negative as well as positive traits must be taken into account when we leave the center and search for the limits of the area.

Here are the positive and negative criteria Wissler used in establishing the Plains area: dependence upon the buffalo or bison (+) and the very limited use of roots (− +) and berries (− +); absence of fishing (−); lack of agriculture (−); the tipi as a movable dwelling (+); transportation by land only, with the dog and the travois (in historic times with the horse) (+); want of basketry and pottery (−); no true weaving (−); clothing of buffalo and deerskins (+); a special bead technique (+); high development of work in skins (+); special rawhide work (+); use of a circular shield (+); weak development of work in wood, stone, and bone (− +); art strongly geometric, (+), but as a whole not symbolic (−); social organization tending to the simple band (+); a camp circle organization (+); a series of societies for men (+); sun dance ceremony (+); sweat house observances (+), scalp dances (+), etc.[22]

In the Plains area Wissler counted thirty-one tribal groups. Of these he considered eleven as "manifesting the typical culture of the area." These eleven tribes are the Assiniboin, Arapaho, Blackfoot, Cheyenne, Comanche,

---

[22] C. Wissler, op. cit., pp. 219–20

Crow, Gros Ventre, Kiowa, Kiowa-Apache, Sarsi, and Teton-Dakota. They form a line that is roughly central on the north-south axis of the Plains area as delimited. To the eastward of them were "some fourteen tribes having most of the positive traits enumerated above and, in addition, some of the negative ones, such as a limited use of pottery and basketry; some spinning and weaving of bags; rather extensive agriculture; alternating the tipi with larger and more permanent houses covered with grass, bark, or earth; some attempts at water transportation; tending not to observe the sun dance, but to substitute maize festivals, shamanistic performances, and the *midéwin* of the Great Lakes tribes." On the west of the axis are other tribes "lacking pottery, but producing a rather high type of basketry; depending far less on the buffalo but more on deer and small game; making large use of wild grass seeds, or grain; alternating tipis with brush and mat-covered shelters; and not as a whole inclined to the sun dance and other ceremonial practices of their eastern neighbors." [23]

These three groups of tribes, then, have cultures that, despite their dissimilarities, do resemble each other. The variations from the type of culture that marks the central axis, however, are in the main manifest in "traits of the adjoining areas." This is why they are named marginal cultures—cultures, that, while sufficiently like those of the peoples whose ways of life are taken as typical, or central, differ from them to increasing degrees as their habitat is removed from the habitat of the central tribes. This is a reflection of the fact, noted in the opening pages of this chapter, that propinquity makes for more intensive borrowing than when peoples live at a distance.

It is not always necessary to analyze trait-distributions and to find the points of greatest coincidence of "typical" traits, in establishing and characterizing areas. It sometimes occurs that the life of the tribes inhabiting a given region is so strikingly oriented that the incidence of this focussing of interest is sufficient by itself to mark off an area. The area where cultures of this kind exist can be described in terms of this principal orientation, and mapped accordingly. In such cases, it is not the concurrence of traits that distinguishes the cultures of the area; it is the preponderant role of a complex that, *for the people who live in the area,* gives point and reason to their ways of life, and is a dominating, integrating force in their existence.

Such a dominating element in a culture-area is found in the cattle complex of East Africa. The importance of these animals has been remarked by every writer who has been concerned with tribal customs of the region. In 1913, a political officer among the Akamba told how all-important cattle are to the people of this tribe; "Even a wife is a second consideration to these, for after all she is only valued as a portion of the herd." Such an episode as this is also revealing; "I shall never forget the horror displayed by a native who complained that he was starving, when I suggested that he should slaughter a cow; such a thing is inconceivable to the Mkamba; . . . . neither will he ever think of selling a cow, even if he is on the verge of starvation." [24]

Cattle determine a man's rank, as where, among the Bahima, chiefs were

[23] *Ibid.*, pp. 218–20.
[24] C. Dundas, 1913, p. 501.

appointed to rule over a given number of cattle instead of a given region; or among the Zulu, where it is established by the derivation of the cattle that passed on the occasion of one's mother's marriage. Among the Ba-Ila, a man has an ox that he treats like a pet, that sleeps in his hut and is called by name. When this man dies, the skin of the ox is his shroud; its flesh supplies his funeral feast.

The languages of the area yield significant illustrations of the importance of cattle. Evans-Pritchard, for example, cites forty different words, each of which applies to the color of a particular kind of cow or ox.[25] The imagery in the poetry of the peoples living in this region is replete with references to their cattle. Here is a Didinga warrior song, a part of the ritual of propitiating the full moon on the eve of battle, as translated by J. H. Driberg:

> White cow of heaven, you have fed in rich pastures
> and you who were small have grown great.
> White cow of heaven, your horns have curved full
> circle and are joined as one.
> White cow of heaven, we throw at you the dust which
> your feet have trampled in our kraals.
> White cow of heaven, give your blessing on the kraals
> which you have overseen that the udders of
> our cows may be heavy and that our women
> may rejoice.[26]

The importance of cattle does not imply that the consensus of traits that mark off any culture area from any other is absent here. Many traits that lie quite outside the influence of the cattle complex can be analyzed much as Wissler listed the positive and negative traits that characterized the Plains Indian cultures of North America. Communities in the area are relatively small (+), trade is little known (− +), and markets like those that flourish in the Congo are absent (−). Few specialists are found (− +), except for the iron-workers who make hoes and spears and other implements (+). Plural marriage everywhere exists (+), though only men of means can have multiple households (+). Descent is counted on the father's side (+), and those so related share clan membership and may not marry (+). Age-groups comprising all the males born at about the same time exist everywhere (+) and play an important part in economic and political life (+), and in warfare (+). Political power is in the hands of the elders (+), usually headed by an hereditary chief or king (+). Religion seems to center about the family (+), few nature deities seem to be worshipped (− +). Ceremonial life, consisting principally of family and clan rituals, never assumes a very elaborate form (−). Music, the dance, myth, and tale are the outstanding forms of aesthetic expression (+). The graphic and plastic arts, the first so notable among the Bushmen, the latter of such great importance in the Congo, Guinea Coast, and Western Sudan areas, are rudimentary (−).

Here the conceptual apparatus of positive and negative traits has been fully employed, so that if their coincidence in a given region is held to be

---

[25] E. E. Evans-Pritchard, 1940, pp. 41–5.
[26] J. H. Driberg, 1930, p. 44.

Culture-Areas: The Spatial Dimension

the touchstone of the validity of considering it a culture-area, this East African region is indubitably one. Moreover, it is possible to isolate tribes where these traits, plus the overshadowing cattle complex, are found in the intensity required for a culture-center. It so happens that the long narrow East African area is divided midway by a strip of heavily forested territory. This harbors the tsetse fly, makes the presence of cattle impossible, and necessitates classifying the cultures found there as less representative than others north and south of this strip. But along a central axis such tribes as Nuer, Lango, Bunyoro, Ankole, Nandi, Masai, and Suk form a northern series of "typical" cattle cultures, while to the south the Ila, Mashona, Basuto, Zulu, among others, form another culture-center.

Toward the coastline of the Indian Ocean, the East African culture becomes "marginal." To the north, the traits of the East African area merge so imperceptibly with those of the East Horn and Eastern Sudan that it is difficult to justify any particular boundary. This is unlike the case westward, where the Congo forests and the southern deserts impose sharp limitations on the spread of this culture based on cattle, and thus permit a clearly defined boundary to be indicated.

Hence we have an area delimited geographically, and defined as to cultural content in a way that satisfies all the demands of the definition. In addition, however, the significance of cattle to the people here makes for a complex that lies uppermost in their thinking. This complex can thus be utilized to classify the cultures of the area as effectively as the conventional assemblage of traits that, however consistent as distributions, are not associated in the minds of the people whose cultures are being studied, as we shall now see.[27]

4

CERTAIN cautions must be entered concerning the culture-area, since an uncritical employment of this useful tool can result in serious misconceptions. It is most important, first of all, to understand that the culture-area is essentially a device that arises out of the need of the student to organize his data and depict, on a broad canvas, the range of cultures over a continent or an island region. This implies that the area, as such, exists in the mind of the student and has but little meaning to those who inhabit it.

It must be realized that the people of a given society are so close to their own traditions that they are far more impressed with differences between them and their neighbors, than they are with similarities. Now these differences, from the point of view of the student who has a continent-wide perspective, are minor. He sees overall resemblances that mark off an entire group of cultures from another entire group. The Bush-Negroes of Dutch Guiana number three tribes. Their cultures, derived from the same African sources, and carried on in the same environmental setting, seem to the outsider almost identical. Yet to a Bush-Negro it would scarcely make sense to group them all together as against the Negroes of the Guiana Coastal area.

[27] For a full treatment of these data, see M. J. Herskovits, 1926, passim.

197

Such a person would, for instance, point out how the three tribes differ in their art-styles—neglecting the fact that all of them carve the same objects, using the same techniques, and with the same fundamental motifs. It is these differences, and not the similarities, that, to him, would be important. *He* is an Awka, and thus to himself is quite different from all other groups, whether Bush-Negro or inhabitant of the coastal plain.

The culture area, then, is not an "incipient nationality," as it has been called. It is not a self-conscious grouping at all. Rather it is a construct that those to whom it is applied would usually be the first to reject. It calls for an overview that no people can have of the wider setting in which their ways of living lodge. It necessitates fixing the eye on the broad lines of similarities and differences between cultures, not on the details seen by those who are too close to a culture. It has the sweep of the mural, not the delicacy of the miniature. Where attention is centered on minutiae, the area vanishes into a mass of specific items. Area gives way to sub-area, sub-area to local culture, local culture to tribal custom, tribal custom to clan convention, clan convention to family tradition, family tradition to individual idiosyncrasies. For the student, then, the culture-area is a useful device, empirically derived from the ethnographic data. But for the people who inhabit the area where a given type of custom prevails, it has no existence at all.

A second caution has to do with the nature of the concepts "cultural center" and "marginal culture." These are constructs in the same way the culture-area itself is a construct. Like it, they have the same ethnographic validity, the same lack of psychological reality. It is this negative point that gives rise to the need for a full understanding of the limitations of these two ideas. It must be emphasized that the culture-center is the place where a cluster of traits is found, not where the richest life is lived by the people of an area. Conversely, a marginal culture is one where traits from a neighboring area are to be discerned.

All this would seem obvious, were it not for the fact that the culture-area and its subsidiary mechanisms have come to be invested by some students with a degree of psychological validity that, as we have seen, they do not possess. It is not difficult to think of a culture at the center of an area as actually having more substance than a marginal one. The semantic shift from analysis to evaluation that comes from employing words like "central" and "marginal" is, indeed, difficult to resist. In some cases, cultures central to an area where many elements are to be found, may be *quantitatively* richer than those at the periphery of the area. Thus in Mexico, it would be strange if, in pre-Spanish times, the greater numbers of people in the area about what is now Mexico City, and the concentration of power and wealth there did not offer the inhabitants greater resources than, let us say, were available to the Tarahumara of what is today the northern state of Chihuahua. The same would be true in the Guinea Coast area of Africa, where the richness of cultural materials among the numerous and powerfully orgazined Ashanti is palpably greater than among the Guro or Gagu tribes of the Ivory Coast, where small local entities provide fewer cultural resources. Our discussion of the principles of cultural relativism need only be recalled to remind us how difficult it is to justify qualitative evaluations of culture on quantitative grounds. The enculturative process, the basis of learning that channels all experience, makes it certain that no matter how sparse a culture may seem to the observer, it carries its satisfactions to those who live in terms of it. Qualitatively it does what we have seen every culture achieve —it affords the individual a life that for him is meaningful in its organization and the ends it sets up as desirable. It is thus hazardous to maintain that, in these psychological terms, the individual Aztec lived a richer existence than the individual Tarahumara. The same can be said of the Ashanti when contrasted to the Guro or Gagu.

Some difficulty has been experienced in applying the idea of culture-areas to Euroamerican groupings, when attempts have been made to extend it to literate societies on the basis of its successful application to nonliterate ones. Experience has shown, however, that it is not adapted to use where the distribution of geographical differences between peoples is overridden by class stratification resulting from the high degree of specialization that, as we shall see, characterizes larger population aggregates. As Benedict has well said, "When traits group themselves geographically, they must be handled geographically. When they do not, it is idle to make a principle out of what is at best a loose empirical category." [28] Area, that is, is only one of a number of criteria that can be usefully employed to distinguish cultures, and, more particularly, sub-cultures. Industrial centers do differ from agricultural regions. All of them, however, in the United States, for instance, have such preponderant cultural similarities that it obscures rather than brings out the significance of the differences between them to consider these differences as of the order of culture-areas. The typical behavior of social class or occupational group is important here. Categories derived from distinctions drawn empirically on the basis of local differences are obviously inapplicable to such cases, and should be replaced by those that are functionally relevant.

A final point where caution is essential has to do with the use of the culture-area as a dynamic device. In its original use, it was purely descriptive, employed to classify the cultures found at a given period in time, in accordance with similarity of content over a geographical region. That period was, roughly speaking, the time when native cultures first came into contact with historic, usually European peoples, or as soon thereafter as valid descriptions of them were available. This lack of time depth was stressed, and materially strengthened the usefulness of the concept. Otherwise the important variable of time that needs to be taken into account in making comparisons could not have been held constant.

In this, the culture-area is to be contrasted to the "culture-circle" of the culture-historical school of ethnological thought. Here we can but mention the culture-circle concept, and indicate briefly how it differs from the culture-area; since an extended discussion of the tenets of this school must await our consideration of the mechanisms of diffusion. At this point we need to bear in mind only that the culture-circle differs from the culture-area in

[28] R. Benedict, 1934, p. 230.

The Structure of Culture

that it not only envisages geographical distributions of the "culture-complex" its students set up and analyze, but also strives to dissect the history of cultural development in various areas by studying a presumed stratification of these elements.[29]

Though he works on a more limited scale and with far more precise control of his data, Kroeber has also attempted to introduce the dimension of time in studying the culture-area. There can be no differing with his contention that the mere description which has been the objective of the culture-area concept is no end in itself; that process must be analyzed, if we are to understand the nature and functioning of culture. Yet he feels that to limit the culture-area to a descriptive function gives it "only incidental utility," and "therefore defeats really historic understanding." Because of this, he advances the argument, "that space and time factors are sufficiently interrelated in culture history to make the culture area a valuable mechanism, rather than a distraction, in the penetration of the time perspective of the growth of cultures so relatively undocumented as are those of native America." [30]

In achieving his end, he adds the concepts of cultural intensity and climax to that of area. "Intensity" is reflected in the way in which cultures and areas achieve what is termed their "level." "A more intensive as compared with a less intensive culture normally contains not only more material—more elements or traits—but also more material peculiar to itself, as well as more precisely and articulately established interrelations between the materials. An accurate time reckoning, a religious hierarchy, a set of social classes, a detailed property law, are illustrations of this." [31] "Climax" is to be thought of as the dynamic equivalent of the descriptive term culture-center. It is the part of the area where the tribes have "a larger content of culture; and a more developed or specialized organization of the content of the culture—in other words, more numerous elements and more sharply expressed and interrelated patterns." [32] The "above-average developments" he regards as centers from which cultural stimuli have flowed, decreasing in intensity as the marginal regions are reached and the emanations from the next center encountered.

That the idea of climax, which in quantitative terms expresses elements to be recorded for different tribes of an area, can be useful in solving that most vexing problem of the culture-area, the setting of boundaries, is evident. Whether "intensity" can be used to express in objective form the values of a people, and balance these values against one another, is quite another matter. So is the question whether the usefulness of the culture-area concept can be extended to an analysis of historic relationships, for at this writing the case for its utilization in the study of such problems cannot be considered as established. With these reservations, however, "climax" and "intensity" may be regarded as valuable refinements of earlier concepts of the spatial dimension of culture.

---

[29] For a discussion of the theories of the culture-historical school, see below, Chap. 30.
[30] A. L. Kroeber, 1939, pp. 1–2.   [31] Ibid., p. 222.   [32] A. L. Kroeber, 1936, p. 114.

CHAPTER 13

12

The Pattern Phenomenon

IN CONSIDERING the pattern phenomenon, we are confronted with two differing aspects of it that, though they have given rise to much controversy, are in actuality, when fully explored, complementary rather than contradictory. The first meaning is that of pattern as the form which the institutions of a culture characteristically take, as when we say that it is a pattern of our culture that church windows are of stained glass rather than of clear glass. The second meaning is a psychological one, as when we say that the pattern of behavior in churches calls for subdued speech. It is this dual significance of the pattern concept that allows us to employ it so as to move back and forth from the examination of the objective, structural aspects of culture to the study of its psychological values.

We must at this point repeat our caution that a culture is more than any individual member of the society whose life is lived within its framework, though at the same time culture is never separate from the individuals who share it. Conceptually, then, patterning acts so as to reduce to a minimum the confusion of finding one's way in the sufficiently complicated business of living, throwing into focus the outlines, or contours, or designs of related units of experience. To illustrate: even though we may never generalize from our experiences, the fact that so elementary a thing as the technique of conveying food to the mouth is regularized, sets for us a model of sanctioned behavior to which we adapt ourselves and which, in following, we in turn set for those who come after us. Having adjusted our behavior to this model —this pattern—we are then competent in this item of our culture. We behave, that is, in accordance with the patterns of etiquette followed by our group insofar as eating habits are concerned. We achieve this result by means of the lifelong conditioning of the enculturative process, which gives each of us a set of individual behavior-patterns that resemble, to a greater or lesser degree, those of every other member of our society.

In this instance, it is plain that we have moved from the objective to the psychological side of our problem. This follows from the fact that it is impossible to treat of culture patterns without taking into account individual behavior patterns. Everything we have stated concerning the psychological reality of culture implies this, no matter in what descriptive, objective terms we draw the outlines of patterned conduct sanctioned in a given society.

The Structure of Culture

What we have stated, however, does not preclude the possibility of describing those modes of sanctioned behavior which, in their observable and structured forms, represent the consenses of conduct that make men and women truly members of their group.

We must, then, draw our definition of pattern so as to reflect these two aspects of our problem. Patterned structure, regularized form, we recognize, can be described as can any structure, since all structure has form and every form has describable limits. But we also recognize that patterned behavior and sanctioned responses, learned so well as to provoke automatic reactions to the approved cultural stimuli on the part of each member of a society, are the raw stuff out of which the structured forms are made. We take both these aspects into account, then, when we think of cultural patterns as *the designs taken by the elements of a culture which, as consenses of the individual behavior patterns manifest by the members of a society, give to this way of life coherence, continuity, and distinctive form.*

No small part of the discussion about the character of the pattern phenomenon arises from undue emphasis on one or the other of these two aspects. This, too, is the source of many of the questions raised regarding the significance of the pattern concept for the understanding of culture. One can stress the designs into which the elements fall, or give attention primarily to the patterned modes of behavior that are cast in accordance with these designs. In reality, however, the scientist abstracts the designs from the behavior of people who are under observation, describing patterns of conduct which, in their institutionalized forms, mold behavior and shape attitudes, beliefs and points of view. Any person, in any society, performs essentially this same operation when a stranger asks him a question about the ways of his group. "We do it this way," he says. That is, he abstracts the patterns of his culture from the experiences of his own everyday existence, and from the behavior of his fellows as he observes it.

It is far simpler to describe consenses of behavior than to delimit the variations that mark off individual modes of conduct. The problem is, in a sense, a statistical one. Granting that we may consider accepted cultural behavior as the norm, how can we indicate the deviations from it that we know exist? It is a pattern of Euroamerican behavior, for example, that a man bare his head in the presence of a woman acquaintance. But by no means all men in this culture do take off their hats whenever they meet women they know. Many men, for one thing, go hatless, so this gesture, interpreted as a sign of respect, cannot be made at all. Some men are careless of their "manners," some are too carefree to be troubled about etiquette, some refuse to conform in protest against conformity, some because their vision is poor and they do not recognize acquaintances at a distance. In the United States, there are sanctioned exceptions to the head-uncovering pattern. When a man and a woman enter an elevator, the man removes his hat *unless* it is in a business building. It is apparent that to catalog and interpret all the individual deviations from the accepted pattern, in addition to such standard departures from it, would require a technique that as yet does not exist. Even to set down the recognized exceptions to this head-uncovering pattern would require a considerable amount of space. Nevertheless, we *can* say that a pattern exists whereby men show respect for women in certain ways, and that one element in this pattern is the convention under which a man removes his hat as a token of this respect.

The patterns that order behavior and in turn arise out of behavior are thus not fixed. They are flexible, permissive, even challenging. They are to be envisaged rather as a series of limits within which accepted behavior may vary; limits that allow the play of individual bent and talent and yet prevent the cultural apparatus from running wild.

2

How definitely the consenses of behavior that characterize culture can be described will become apparent if we briefly sketch the patterns which, in two societies, regulate and sanction behavior in a specific phase of one broad aspect of culture, marriage. We shall of necessity disregard deviants, except where they figure so prominently that they themselves constitute a sub-pattern. In short, we shall do what any ethnographer, concerned with institutions rather than with individual behavior, does as he describes the accepted conventions of a culture he has studied in the field.

What is the pattern of mating, we may ask first of all, in that particular segment of Euroamerican society that exists in the United States? On a broad, comparative base, certain principles, both positive and negative, are to be discerned. In the first place, marriage, on the whole, is the affair of two contracting parties, who are usually adults. Marriage here, that is, is not an arrangement between family groups. It is, again, a matter in which personal choice plays an important role, and financial considerations have no overt recognition. Limitations on the choice of a mate imposed by kinship or age or class lines are relatively few. One can marry up to the degree of first cousin, while marriages even between those standing in this relationship are only exceptionally penalized. Eyebrows may rise when there is disparity in age between the two parties, but it is "their own business," and no taboos forbid such a marriage. And while it is quite true that marriages occur most often between those whose social position, economic status, and education are similar, this is because persons of similar background are more likely to meet and to find interests in common than because conventions dictate class endogamy. The number of matings that cut across all kinds of lines show that restrictions of this nature are informal and individual rather than patterned.

Other elements in the marriage pattern may be described with equal sharpness. Marriage is preceded by a formal announcement of intent, an "engagement," marked by the gift of a valuable ring to the young woman from the young man. The "engagement" is a kind of interim period during which it is recognized that the two persons enjoy mutual priority on each other's leisure. Association, except in groups or officially, with others of the opposite sex, is not sanctioned. Also unsanctioned, however, is the indulgence in sexual relations between the engaged couple, an item in the moral code that differs from the practices of other societies, where the "engagement," so to speak, permits full participation in the experiment of living together.

This engagement period is typically of greater importance to the woman than to the man, and is marked by certain social-ritual gatherings, called "showers," whereby gifts are given the bride-to-be by her friends or the friends of her mother. These "showers" are held at the homes of her friends, or the friends of her mother, and are designated by special names in accordance with the type of gifts the guests are directed to bring, such as "linen shower," "kitchen shower." It is a mark of prestige to have several of these proffered to honor the engaged young woman, and to her material benefit. Announcement of an engagement is not always made, though it is customary to make it known at a social gathering, and through news items in the special columns of the local press where matters of this kind are given particular attention. During the engagement, the principals assume reciprocal duties toward the families of their prospective spouses, particularly the parents. Visits are exchanged, birthdays and feast days calling for gifts or notes of greetings are not overlooked.

Invitations to the wedding reception that follows the actual marriage rite require that a gift be sent the couple by the recipient; marriage announcements sent after the ceremony do not call for such gifts. The marriage is predominantly a religious ceremony, though it need not be so. Secular marriage rites, however, are carried on with less ritual than religious ones, and are regarded as deviants from the pattern. The controls of the state are satisfied by obtaining a license to wed; the ritual is pronounced by the proper official of a religious group, who is customarily feed by the bridegroom, though other expenses of the ceremony are borne by the father of the bride. The clothing worn by the bride at the ceremony is more important that that of the groom. The symbolism of the veil and bouquet of flowers she carries, and of the color white (in the case of a first marriage) assumes great importance. The rite is followed by a feast, the most important feature of which is the cake which must be ceremonially cut by bride and groom together. Certain mild forms of hazing follow the ceremony, such as throwing rice and other objects at the newly married pair as they depart for a period of seclusion and release from customary routine. This period is termed a "honeymoon" and concludes this series of events.

The major aspects of this pattern would hold for the entire Euroamerican area, though class, denominational, national, and even local variants strike one immediately. The custom of announcing an engagement among upper-class English families by advertising the event in certain newspapers with the formula, "a marriage has been arranged" is one such difference. The French *dot*, or payment of dowry by the father of the bride to the bridegroom, presumably to give the young couple adequate resources for their marital adventure, is another. On the whole, parental consent figures more in the European pattern than in the American, though the process of diffusion seems to be breaking this down. In many European countries, a dual ceremony is the rule, the first at the registry office, the second at the church. Yet despite these differences, in the main, and in broad outline, the pattern of getting a mate and obtaining social sanction for the mating, sketched for the United States, does obtain in Euroamerican culture as a whole.

Let us contrast this pattern of mating with another that is equally susceptible of being described in the same institutional terms. We may select one that is operative in the Solomon Islands, among a Melanesian people inhabiting the region about Buka Passage, a strait to the north of Bougainville.[1] As in any small society, the range of variation in behavior is less than in larger groupings. Hence a picture can be given that need not allow for as much deviation from the sanctioned norms of conduct as is to be found in the great aggregate we have just been treating. Deviations do occur, of course—a fact that must never be forgotten, even though the society appears to be most homogeneous. Here, too, we may disregard most of the deviations as we disregarded all but those most often encountered in our earlier example. We are at this moment interested in patterned norms and not in variants.

In Kurtatchi, a community in the Buka region, marriage is a matter primarily of family concern, and betrothal occurs when the parties to a match are young indeed—the girl an infant, the boy when he is less than seven or eight years of age. The boy's father opens preliminary negotiations with the mother of the girl, without the knowledge of his son, who is not informed of his betrothal until later. Betrothal, like later marriage, essentially involves the passage of valuable goods from the family of the groom to that of the bride, a transaction that is obviously of no concern to a pre-adolescent youth and that, in any event, would be far beyond his competence.

Here is a table of the events that lead up to marriage. It clearly shows how the arrangements that have to be made, and their sanctions, beginning with the betrothal, and following through to marriage, conform to a definite scheme. The importance of the ritual exchanges at each step, which give meaning to this series of ceremonies, are to be especially noted:

Occasion	*Transactions*
1. Betrothal, when both are children, the girl often quite a baby.	Father of boy presents spear hung with one string of *beroan* (ceremonial currency made of shell disks) to mother of girl. Betel-mixture chewed.
2. First visit of mother of boy to mother of girl. Soon after 1.	Aromatic plants brought by mother of boy to decorate girl. Betel-mixture chewed.
3. Visit of boy's mother to take back girl for her first visit. When girl is about 7 or 8 years old.	Paint for head of girl brought by boy's mother. Betel-mixture chewed.
4. Visit of girl's mother to see her daughter in mother-in-law's hut, 3 or 4 days after 3 above. Girl remains with mother-in-law for	Food and areca-nut provided by boy's mother for girl's mother and accompanying women. No pig given at this stage.

[1] B. Blackwood, 1935, Ch. III, pp. 82–131.

a month or more.

If she runs away, her mother must make *menak* (ceremonial pudding of taro and coconut) for the boy's mother and must bring her back.

5. Request for handing over of ceremonial currency. At discretion of girl's mother, but usually at first signs of breast development.

Girl's mother sends food, including pigmeat, to boy's mother, the pig being a hint that it is time to produce the currency.

6. Boy's mother collects ceremonial currency from her brother and other male relatives.

Boy's mother sends pieces of pig to relatives who are expected to help provide the currency.

7. Visit of boy's people to girl's people to hand over currency, and to bring back girl for long visit. As soon as enough currency has been collected.

Agreed amount of ceremonial currency handed over for division among the girl's relatives. One string given as personal gift, secretly, by boy's mother to girl's mother. One string given by girl's mother to boy's relatives "to pay for the boy."

8. During the next few years girl spends much time with her mother-in-law, returning to her mother only for occasional visits.

9. Special visit of girl and her relatives to boy's mother to pay for *tagoan* (the front end of the house with its verandah, usually reserved for men, and occupied by women only on certain special ceremonial occasions, such as rites connected with marriage).

Girl's mother and relatives bring *menak* and a live pig to boy's relatives, and small amount of ceremonial currency.

10. Marriage ceremony. Usually not until boy has taken off *upi* (special headgear worn by boys during adolescence) and girl has been through her first menstruation ceremony.

Exchange of ceremonial baskets of taro. Much food given by bride's mother to bridegroom's relatives.[2]

It would be pointless, even if space permitted, to detail the elements in the final culminating ritual of the marriage pattern, though this could be outlined in much the same manner as has the long progression of events that mark finding a mate for a boy or girl and bringing them to the status of married persons. Certain general aspects of this pattern should, however, be taken into account. Plural marriage, though not the rule, is permitted. These societies know certain class distinctions, so that, "it is usual for the father of a boy who is *tsunaun* [a member of the most important lineage in a village] to choose for his son's first wife a girl who is his equal in rank, but there appears to be no hard and fast rule on the subject. A *tsunaun* girl may be betrothed to a commoner if her mother agrees." The reason for this

[2] *Ibid.*, pp. 95-7.

emphasizes another aspect of the pattern, since "it involves the handing over, at a later stage in the negotiations, of a larger amount of ceremonial currency than a commoner is likely to have at his disposal."[3] In this society, the virginity of a girl at marriage is taken for granted, since her betrothal occurs when she is very young. For their part, the boys are surrounded by an elaborate series of taboos and restrictions until they reach the age of marriage, restrictions that effectively prevent them from having access to the girls. Thus, even though a girl visits her prospective parents-in-law for long periods, the boy to whom she is engaged is kept from her because of these restrictions. Similarly, she is denied all opportunity for sex experimentation with older men.

We have considered two systems whereby socially sanctioned mating is achieved—two patterns of conduct that accomplish one of the ends every society must provide for, if it is to be perpetuated. In these two societies, however, the means employed to achieve the common end are so different as to coincide only in aim and accomplishment. Choice of mate is free in one, almost entirely controlled in the other. Choice is exercised by individuals in one, dictated by families in the other. In one, there is a wide range of ages at which marriage is consummated, in the other the age of the principals is relatively fixed. In one society, the passage of valuable goods during betrothal and at marriage is secondary and informal; in the other, essential and highly regularized. Yet in each, the "proper" way is explicitly recognized; and what is more, the members of each society can describe this "proper" way, if questioned.

This is the kind of patterning of institutions which we find in all cultures, in all their many different phases. Gist has demonstrated how sharply the lines that describe the institution of the American secret society can be drawn. Even in such a culture as that of the United States, where so broad a range of choice exists for those who differ in aptitude and interest, Gist finds the principle, "there is a desire to be different, *but not too different*," fully applies.[4] Patterning, however, is not a strait-jacket; it is not even a high wall that bars wandering in adjacent cultural fields. It is, as we have noted, a model. It constitutes a pattern in the technical sense of the term, but with its outlines and contours flexible and alterable, permitting experience to fall into meaningful forms despite the changes that continuously mark its expression.

3

LET us return again for a moment to the individual in society. From his enculturative experience, he has learned a set of socially sanctioned behavior patterns which, while permitting the play of variables—minor or pronounced as in idiosyncratic behavior—yet keep his acts within the matrix of his culture. A society is thus composed of individuals whose behavior is to a very great extent alike in the day to day situations they face. Yet, as we have seen,

[3] *Ibid.*, p. 83.
[4] N. Gist, 1940, p. 19.

The Structure of Culture

no society is entirely homogeneous. It is composed, for one thing, of men and women, a fact that makes for a line of division so fundamental that there is no phase of conduct not affected by it. Age differences likewise order different types of behavior, and so do those of a social, economic, or occupational nature, to name but a few of the factors that make for variation in the sanctioned forms of behavior within a given society.

It is because of these differences that some students seek to deny the validity of considering cultural patterns as consenses of individual behavior patterns. The occupations of men and women—to say nothing of their patterned preoccupations—differ to such an extent that it is inadvisable, they hold, to speak of a pattern that includes both. Similarly, the ruler and the ruled, the canoe-maker and the potter, the adolescent boy and the elder, behave differently enough that, they argue, it is not possible to abstract a valid least common denominator from the behavior of all. If persisted in, they add, such an attempt will distort rather than clarify, for its effect will be speciously to present as a smooth surface what is really a very roughened terrain.

Let us examine this point of view and weigh the argument it presents. As before, we will do well to look at what we know from first-hand experience before venturing into foreign fields and strange cultures. Let us consider first of all the matter of differences in behavior, manifested by men and women.

The conditioning to different patterns, not only of outward behavior but of interests, goals, and meanings begins very early in life. Clothing types are differentiated when boys and girls emerge from infancy, and this extends to hair-styles as well. What else was the source of the patterned misery of the small boy who was forced to wear curls, except the reluctance of his mother to permit his father to take him to the barber shop? To him, and to his father, these curls were no adornments at all. The boy was but the victim of the invasion of a female pattern of response into the male sphere. Patterned differences in the life of girls and boys are present in many other phases of their existence. Little girls are encouraged to play with dolls, little boys with weapons or mechanical devices. Little girls play at keeping house, little boys organize themselves into firemen or hunters or even business men. Little girls skip rope or play jacks; little boys play football or do the high jump. And while there will always be little boys who enjoy girls' games and girls who would like to play football, it is rare to find a boy who can skip rope as well as the girls or a girl who continues to remain absorbed in ball playing. The skill that comes from continuous practice, carried on because it has full social approval—or at least does not incur disapproval—is just not there.

In later life, further standardized differences in characteristic activities appear. There is no reason why women should not be as good mechanics as men and, given the opportunity, many women do show themselves highly competent in the mechanical arts. But again, this is the exception; and when, as in a war emergency, women do the work of mechanics, they seem not loathe to give up the trade they have learned when "the boys come home" and "normal" conditions reassert themselves. Except during adolescent

208

and post-adolescent years, when other influences enter, a group of persons together for an evening's recreation tends to break into two. The men discuss those matters that are of concern to them, the women talk over women's affairs. On occasion they may come together for a while, as when certain matters of common concern, such as some civic enterprise, are under discussion. But men, though they are fathers, will not long be held by debate over problems of infant feeding or children's clothing or the ingredients that make a child's favorite dish, while questions of tax policy, sports, details of a recent hunting trip, or fishing excursion will prove equally uninteresting to the woman who finds herself ensnared by a conversation of this sort.

We may continue with instances drawn from differences in the behavior of other groupings in Euroamerican society. The boy or girl finds little to discuss with the friend of his father and mother, and the elder is equally at a loss when he is left alone with his friend's child. This difficulty in communication only underscores the lack of common interests it implies. We have already remarked how change is a fundamental aspect of culture, and we shall later assess the far-reaching consequences of this fact. Here we merely note that one type of cultural change takes place when the new generation shifts the pattern of procedure from that which its predecessor followed. Generation lines congeal, with mutual misunderstanding giving rise to mutual irritation, especially where moral values are involved, or the new forms of behavior are associated with such deep-seated complexes as center about matters of sex.

Even where there is no such emotional association, the changing patterns of belief, of interest, of taste can make for strain between the generations. Music offers numerous instances. The devotion of a young man or woman to jazz and swing and boogie-woogie will cause excessive irritation to a parent enculturated to other kinds of "popular" musical expression. On a somewhat different level, "atonal" progressions that come easily to the young musician and to whose values the younger listener reacts with deep emotion, will present enormous difficulties for his elder who wishes to play it, and will tax his patience as listener.

Occupational or class lines similarly dictate different patternings of individual habit and interest. In many European countries, speech is an index of position, and one with a "lower-class accent" will see to it that his manner of speaking is corrected if he has ambitions to rise in the social scale. Economic differences are invariably reflected by typical differences in reaction to different situations. The eating habits of the ditch-digger and of the banker, of the janitor and of the lawyer whose office he cleans are as different as the work they do, the remuneration they receive, the clothing they wear while working or even when they are not at work. It is not unlikely that there will be patterned differences in their behavior toward their wives and the techniques they use in correcting their children; certainly, there will be differences in the kind of furnishings they have in their homes, the kind of pictures they have on their walls, in the use of their leisure time, in the lodges or clubs to which they belong.

The same kind of differentiation that marks the behavior of sub-groups in our society exists in all human aggregates. The degree to which there is this differentiation of patterns depends on the size of the group, which in turn largely influences the degree of specialization it manifests. The Eskimos, the Australians, the Bushmen, the people of Tierra del Fuego, or of the Great Basin region of North America, whose numbers are few, whose technologies are simple or whose environments are rugged have no class or occupational patterns, since their societies have no class structure and there is no specialization in production. Their sub-groupings are those of sex and age—that is, along lines that are found in every society, without exception. In other societies, where increased resources make stratification possible, specialized patterns, restricted to those who are members of a given class, or follow a given occupation, are to be found. The very fact we distinguish them as such implies that we recognize constant differences in their ways that serve to set off one group from another in a given society.

Thus men and women in the West African culture of Dahomey have assigned to them clearly differentiated manual skills, economic pursuits, codes of etiquette, degrees of participation in family and political councils. The categories of male and female tasks and behavioral sanctions are quite as sharply, if not more sharply marked off than in our own society. For example, under the patterns of economic division of labor, men do iron-working, and the weaving and sewing of cloth; they are the hunters and wood-carvers; they do the heavy agricultural work of breaking the ground, and along the sea-coast they are the fishermen. The women care for the children, tend the growing crops, prepare food, sell in the markets, make the pottery. And these differences are reflected in the conversation, the concerns, the interests of men and women.

Or, to take an example from another aspect of this culture: ask an elderly man for an animal tale—a fable that in its moral teaches a lesson—and he will reply that such stories are told by children; that he has long ago forgotten those he knew. Actually he does remember them, but he would not tell them except to his grandchildren. For an adult to ask him to recount these is an affront to his age. The patterns of behavior of his age-group in this, as in all other aspects of living, differ from those of the younger generation. The tales he tells are of the heroes who lived in the olden times, or of the gods. If, at a funeral, he recounts a story that has animals as its protagonists, it is a ribald tale or one whose broad humor is fully savoured by those present. It would be no fable. "We do not moralize to the dead"—one rather amuses the spirits of those who are about to leave this world for the next so that, in high good humor, they may be well disposed toward the living.

Class distinctions in Dahomean society produce similar differences in patterned behavior. The inferior prostrates himself before the superior; the superior alone may wear sandals, walk in the shade of an umbrella, smoke the long pipe that is an evidence of his rank. The upper-class Dahomean is reserved, circumspect in speech, deliberate in his gestures, showing proud bearing in the way he wears his great toga-like cloth or in the handling of his wand of office. He does not dance to the fast compelling rhythms of the commoner. It is a saying in Dahomey that as a man advances in the social scale, his dancing becomes more restrained, keyed to slower rhythms. The steps of the chief's dance are deliberate and move steadily forward with controlled pauses. Few side-steps, and none of the pirouettes, leaps, or sharp turns that mark the dancing of those who hold inferior rank, are seen in his performance.

Let us, then, return to the larger problem of the patterns of a culture as consenses of the differing individual behavior patterns of those who live in accordance with its ways. Understandably, it is a fallacy to postulate a single pattern as marking off any one culture, as has been done in some studies. Such a construct disappears in the welter of differing forms of behavior dictated by considerations of sex, age, class, occupation and other distinctions. Yet, when these are closely observed, least common denominators in behavior do emerge. The men who are interested in football at one end of the room, their wives discussing the feeding-formula of the infant at the other, are all using the same language. They have similar food preferences, they live in the same kinds of houses, read the same newspapers—the concurrences in their lives, in actuality, far outweigh the divergences. In the same way, the Dahomean chief and commoner also employ a common language; they enjoy the same musical forms, recognize and respect the same forces that rule the universe, live within the framework of a single economy.

Sapir, who was one of the first to recognize the psychological base of the phenomenon of cultural pattern, after asserting that "all cultural behavior is patterned," goes on to express the importance of the unifying element of comprehension. "It is impossible to say what an individual is doing," he points out, "unless we have tacitly accepted the arbitrary modes of interpretation that social tradition is constantly suggesting to us from the very moment of our birth. Let anyone who doubts this try the experiment of making a painstaking report of the actions of a group of natives engaged in some form of activity . . . to which he has not the cultural key. If he is a skilful writer, he may succeed in giving a picturesque account of what he sees and hears, or thinks he sees and hears, but the chances of his being able to give a relation of what happened in terms that would be intelligible and acceptable to the natives themselves are practically nil." [5]

Instances of this kind of misinterpretation are innumerable. The obeisance of the Dahomean inferior before his superior has been considered a sign of degradation. But the Dahomean sees it as an acknowledgement of the regard an elder brother is held in by his younger, or a chief by those whose respect he commands. Nor must it be overlooked that the one who prostrates himself also receives this same patterned token of respect from those inferior to him in the social scale. The treatment of religious spirit possession, by writers who do not have the "cultural key"—that is, who are not cognizant of the patterns of behavior that govern the phenomenon—offers many masterpieces of misunderstanding.

One thinks, again, of the pleasure with which the early explorers among

---

[5] E. Sapir, 1927, p. 119.

the Kikuyu of East Africa recorded their reception in the villages of the tribe—how, in recognition of their superior position, the warriors turned out in full panoply to escort them to the place where the chief awaited them. Of the fact that this was a military measure, a sign of hostility, they were quite unaware. That is, friendly intercourse among these people takes entirely different forms. A visitor's entrance to a village is greeted with studied indifference. He sits quietly and silently by a friend, who finishes whatever he is doing, until at last he addresses to him a few casual phrases of greeting. Now not all the inhabitants of a given Kikuyu village participated in the military display that greeted the early Europeans. Neither women, nor children, nor elderly men took part in it. But the act was to them decidedly a part of the patterns of their culture and as such, it was understandable, significant, predictable.

What is of signal importance is to perceive that in every society all know, recognize and can cope with sub-patterns of their culture other than their own. A man may not be concerned with bottle formulae of infants, but he can feed the baby if he has to; he may not be interested in cooking, but he can do enough of it to provide for himself when he must. His wife may not be enough interested in football to center her conversation about it, but she may enjoy seeing a game; she may not be concerned with business matters, but she is fully cognizant of their importance and, on occasion may step in and manage affairs with entire competence. The Dahomean elder may not care to tell fables, but he recognizes their role as an educational device for the young; the chief will not dance violently, but he will enjoy the dancing of the commoners and he will reward those whose performance is outstanding.

The conception of culture-pattern as the consensus of individual behavior-patterns presents no difficulty if two things are held in mind. The first is that the concept confuses rather than clarifies unless the term "culture-pattern" is used and thought of in multiple terms when the institutionalized modes of existence of any people are being examined. The second point to remember is that the phrase "behavior-patterns" means more than overt behavior. It comprehends not only acts but the clues to action, the values that provide the motivation for action, the meaning conferred by the act. In this broad sense, then, we can conceive of a culture as composed of a series of patterns that reflect the habitual individual responses—motor, verbal, or ideational—of all those who make up the society where these responses are dominant. We can then without difficulty think of the pattern phenomenon in culture as a reflection of the common elements in the individual behavior of those who live in the culture into which they have been born.

4

In accepting the dictum that "all cultural behavior is patterned," it follows that the patterns of a culture direct the behavior of the members of a society into broad channels whose courses are known to all. The pattern phenomenon thus makes it possible for the student to orient his analysis of the traits and complexes he observes in coherent terms. It likewise permits him, as it does the members of every society, to predict the behavior of all those whose lives are lived in terms of a given pattern system.

Turn once again, briefly, to the patterns that govern selection of a mate and marriage, and consider this brief summary of the methods that prevail among the Sangara group of New Guinea Keraki Papuans: "The rule that marriage should be negotiated by exchange is observed almost without exception. . . . In the ideal instance two men give one another their true younger sisters; . . . but when a man has no true sister to dispose of he will be furnished with a classificatory sister from among his kin; and failing this he will procure a woman of the same moiety from another locality, not as a wife but as a 'sister' to exchange for a wife." [6] Even so concise a statement makes it possible for the reader to translate it into behavioristic terms. He envisages a young man seeking out another who, like himself, has a sister to exchange, or failing to have a sister, arranges with his clan-mates to provide him with a young woman—a "classificatory sister" who will serve the purpose—and then establishing his household.

In truth, it is not too much to state that without these cultural patterns, these consenses of individual habituation, social life would actually be impossible. In even the smallest tribes with the rudest technologies, this factor of being able to count on someone else behaving in a way that can be foreseen is essential, in enabling each member of the group almost literally to survive. In the great aggregates of modern Euroamerican culture, this is overwhelmingly the case. We know—that is, we reliably predict—that the driver of the automobile will respond to the stimulus of the red stop-light and permit us to walk across the street unharmed; that the chef who prepares food for us in a public dining-place will use the ingredients sanctioned by customary usage and thus neither outrage our sensibilities nor poison us; that an open outstretched hand will bring us a handshake and not a blow in the face.

Insofar as science is prediction, then, we are all effective scientists in our everyday life. We employ the technique of anticipating the results of a given set of circumstances as easily, and as unwittingly, as M. Jourdain found he could write prose. By the same token, it becomes evident that for the scientific study of culture, there is no single concept that can serve better as a tool for the analysis and understanding of its structure and its dynamic processes than can the concept of cultural pattern.

---

[6] F. E. Williams, 1936, pp. 134-5.

CHAPTER 14

The Integration of Culture

THE structure of culture, as described in the preceding chapters, exists only for the student. Even when men and women generalize about the customary behavior of their own group, or give the reasons that justify the institutions of their culture, they but enlarge the field of their own experience to include the similar behavior they observe among their fellows. They no more comprehend the structural framework which supports their manner of living than they are conscious of the rules of the grammar that give their language describable form, or the system of scales, modes, and rhythms that governs their singing.

The linguist, however, for all his dissection of a language into its component parts, does not lose sight of the unity of the language he is studying —a unity that permits it to function as a means of communication. The musicologist, for all his preoccupation with intervals, accidentals, and rhythms, does not forget that the song he is studying is the essential unit he must take into account. In the same way, the ethnologist, however he may divide and subdivide his materials in order to dissect a particular culture or analyze culture as a whole, must always remember that, in the end, the reality with which he is dealing is the unity that results from observations of the behavior of different individuals. The underlying forms and broad principles that he delves beneath the surface of everyday life to bring to light, are essential to his understanding. But they function implicitly, without verbalization; as far as the experience of men is concerned, they are only another construct of science.

Because the life of every group is unified for those who live it, it is essential that we fully comprehend both the need to study how a culture is synthesized, and the usefulness of breaking down this unity into its component parts. In considering any individual way of life, we must see it in compass of the integration of the whole, a whole that is more than the sum of its parts. It is such a unity that the research worker, insofar as he observes life as it is lived, faces as he studies any people in the field. When we analyze human social behavior, we can isolate form from meaning, action from sanction. We can describe in minute detail the structure of a building, tell how it is made, by whom, and of what materials; and we will have an assemblage of traits whose distribution can be traced without the slightest reference to

The Integration of Culture

their functioning. Or, we can study the different uses to which structures are put by a people, indicating that some are lived in, some are used as storage bins, some are places of worship, and some centers of government, with equal disregard of their formal elements. We could then say, perhaps, that the range of variation in the functions of houses are here broad, there narrow, and draw our conclusions. But the human beings out of whose behavior these structures stem would have no place in our study.

It follows, then, that it is unnecessary to lay down any principle in this matter, except the principle that different problems call for different materials, and that the best procedure is to utilize that attack that holds greatest promise for the solution of a given problem. The analysis of culture into components represented a step of the first importance over earlier, less oriented modes of study. The emphasis on the functional interrelationship that followed was a further step that forcefully brought to the attention of ethnologists the need to take the unities of a culture, as well as its disparate elements, into full account. This, in turn, has led to the question whether or not the patterns that are perhaps the best expression of the diversity existing within the unity of each differing way of life are not to be comprehended under still broader, psychological formulations, called configurations, or themes, or affirmations. These are thought of as least common denominators of whole cultures, or of great segments of a culture, that yield clues to some of the most deeply recessed springs of behavior among a people. Whether or not they represent the master-clues to all the institutions, value-systems and goals of a people is a matter on which there is as yet no agreement. Later in this chapter, we shall review the arguments advanced for the usefulness and validity of such an approach.

For the moment, we need to bear in mind that, as in other aspects of the study of culture, the problem of cultural integration presents two faces. One, the *functional* view, attempts to study the interrelation between the various elements, small and large, in a culture. Its object is essentially to achieve some expression of the unities in culture by indicating how trait and complex and pattern, however separable they may be, intermesh, as the gears of some machine, to constitute a smoothly running, effectively functioning whole. Its emphasis, that is, is on the forms, the institutions, of culture.

The *configurational*, or *thematic* attack, one aspect of which we have considered earlier,[1] represents the psychological approach to cultural integration. As we saw, there the unity of the formal aspects of culture is taken as established fact, to be accepted without the need for further analysis. The problem, then, aside from the matter of the determination of personality structures that prevail, is to discover the threads of aim, of objective, of satisfactions that give to the institutional unity the particular quality, the special "feel" that everyone senses when he compares one culture with another, and attempts to phrase the differences between them in objective terms. We have already considered this point of view in our discussion of the individual in society. In this chapter we shall analyze it further, this

---

[1] See Chap. 4, above.

time from the point of view of the emphasis it lays on cultural integration, rather than as it treats of the problem of individual behavior in terms of these overall patterned drives that are held to characterize cultures.

It is apparent that in discussing the problem of cultural integration, we must consider both structural and psychological aspects. We shall, therefore, first see how elements of a culture, seemingly quite unconnected, are, in fact, integrally related. We shall then follow through by considering whether this integration of cultural forms is to be thought of as the manifestation of certain deeper psychological drives that give ultimate significance to the formal elements of cultural structures, and thus permit a way of life to achieve its final unity.

2

THE functionalist point of view, as described in an early exposition of its tenets by B. Malinowski, with whose name this method is most closely identified, "aims at the explanation of anthropological facts at all levels of development by their function, by the part which they play within the integral system of culture, by the manner in which they are related to each other within the system, and by the manner in which this system is related to the physical surroundings." In terms of the functional method, "the real identities of culture appear to lie in the organic connection of its parts, in the function which a detail fulfils within its scheme, in the relation between the scheme, the environment and the human needs. Meaningless details disappear, shape becomes alive with meaning and with function, and a testimony of irrelevant form falls away as worthless." [2] The method is applied both in field-research that aims at comprehending a single culture, and in understanding relationships which, generalized from specific instances, are to be applied in the study of culture as a whole.

From this latter point of view, the functionalist contribution yielded its most fruitful results. This was especially true of its critiques of earlier *a priori* theories that had developed out of a neglect to take into account the associations between seemingly disparate elements in culture. Thus, in this same discussion, Malinowski speaks of the family as "a link between instinctive endowment and the acquisition of cultural inheritance." He stresses its function as an educational institution, an aspect that was and still tends to be overlooked in the attention paid to the role of the family in regulating mating and providing for the continuation of a social group. The legal, economic, and ritual functions of wider kinship structures, such as the clan, appear as important aspects of these groupings we now take as commonplace, but which were formerly by no means always recognized. The wide ramifications of economic and political structures come to the surface when studied in terms of their functioning, or the working of the supernatural sanctions "for social integration, technical and economic efficiency, for culture as a whole —indirectly therefore for the biological and mental welfare of each indi-

[2] B. Malinowski, 1926, pp. 132, 139.

vidual member." The nature of magic, the role of myth and tale likewise have become clarified through the inductions derived from field research. Students have followed their integration with other aspects of culture and have ferreted out their roles in the lives of the people who use them.

Various elements in functionalist theory have been vigorously debated. For instance, Malinowski's system derives the principal subdivisions or aspects of culture from biological necessity, and envisages the ultimate function of culture as the task of satisfying these needs. This is a point we shall have to consider in our next chapter, where the division of culture into these universals will be treated. Functionalism has also laid stress on the study of culture on a single time-plane, and has argued against attempting to reconstruct unwritten history. This, too, we must take up later, since it is of importance in any discussion of the dynamic aspects of culture. But there can be no question of the need to determine how each element of a culture influences and is influenced by those other elements with which it is associated. We have indicated, in brief, how fertile this approach is for the understanding of certain broad theoretical problems, many of which we shall take up in some detail in the chapters of the next section. Let us here see how the interrelation of cultural forms is manifest in a specific instance, where their integration into the entire "cultural scheme" of which they are a part can be readily documented.

The comparatively simple culture of the Bush Negroes of Dutch Guiana, South America, affords us pertinent materials for a presentation of this kind.[3] Their numbers are small, their villages compact, their economy direct, with an absence of middlemen to intervene between the functions of production and consumption. Their social structures form an ascending hierarchy of immediate family, extended family and sib, on the latter of which governmental institutions are predicated. The universe is for them ruled by a series of nature-deities, worshipped with song and dance. To these the forces of magic and of the dead are to be added as powerful supernatural agents. Their art, expressed primarily in the carving of highly ornamented wooden implements, is of great excellence. In the oral arts, they have a full complement of myths and tales, while their musical resources in the form of singing and drumming show range, versatility, and an extensive repertory. The culture is a going concern, little influenced either by the Europeans of the coastal belt or the Indians of the interior. We consider it here, in the functional manner, in order to lay emphasis on its integrations, and without regard for its historical background of African origin, or such borrowings as it has effectuated from these other two cultures with which the Bush-Negroes have had contact.

We can take such a simple element of the culture as the dwelling-place as our starting point. We could, with equal facility, take any other cultural element—a carved stool, a religious ceremony, a song, a meeting of elders to decide a dispute, a story, the birth of twins, a sudden death. But since the house is a material trait, immediately in sight as one enters the village, it will do us nicely.

[3] M. J. and F. S. Herskovits, 1934, *passim*.

The Structure of Culture

The Bush-Negro house, in its physical appearance, is a rectangular, gabled structure, entered by a low door—so low that it requires a stooped posture to pass through it. The sides are woven of palm-fronds in a pleasing basket-weave design. The house has a thatched roof, so well made that it lasts for many years; it is windowless, and has no chimney. Air enters through the interstices of the woven sides, while smoke from the fire that burns in the center of the hard earthen floor escapes through the thatch. Here, already, we envisage purposeful functioning, in this case in terms of adaptation to the habitat. The windowless, woven sides permit enough light to enter to see what one is doing, yet leave the house cool and darkened, making it a grateful refuge from the tropical sun. The smoke of the fire is an effective fumigant against the insects that would otherwise infest the thatch, and it keeps off the mosquitoes that swarm in this tropical forest.

Inside the house is an inventory of many of the material possessions of the household, particularly those of the woman. In the corner lie the woven hammocks which are slung at night and in which those who live in the house sleep. Low carved stools, with round or rectangular tops provide seats and can conveniently be taken outdoors where a group may gather. The interstices of the wall hold carved combs, food-stirring paddles, and other small objects, such as wooden and woven fire fans. At the base of the walls rest decorated calabashes, in which other possessions such as cloths, are kept, and rice, or cassava meal, or maize is stored for immediate use. In the corners are carved canoe-paddles, while from the cross-poles beneath the roof still other gourds containing articles not in everyday use, are suspended. The door itself is carved in low relief, and is fastened by an ingenious lock made entirely of wood. Door-posts, too, are carved; those of a village elder with the symbol of his clan, or with other symbolic designs.

The house is a part of a complex of dwellings and accessory structures; several such complexes form the village. Certain of these structures merit special attention for a moment. One is the *gudu-woso*—the house where a man keeps his wealth. It is made differently from the dwelling-house, especially if its owner is a man of means, when the sides will be of lattice-work, so that people can peer through and wonder at the city-bought objects, the carved drums, bush-knives, and other possessions that make of the owner a person of substance and standing in the community. The floor will be of wood, raised on piles, above the ground, the door protected by a charm, a *kandu*, that would be violated by no one who valued his health, his sanity, or his life. By no one, that is, except a relative in the male line—a point whose significance we shall return to shortly. This type of structure, forbidden to the women, permits a man to conceal his belongings as well as to reveal them; and, in commenting on the fact, the native does not fail to phrase the advantages of both. For the wealthy man thus guards himself against wives who are importunate; the man whose *gudu-wosu* tells no tales of what he may or may not have, is guarded against his nagging or fault-finding wives.

Still another structure that marks the village is the *krutu-wosu*, the place of assemblage which, when death strikes, becomes the center of long and elaborate funeral rites. This is but a frame, roofed, and open on all four

The Integration of Culture

sides. Here men and women sit during the day to discuss matters of interest, and to gossip; here the village council assembles when affairs of common concern are to be debated and decided. This house is at the center of the village, and before it is a broad clearing, the sand meticulously swept each day. When a death occurs, the corpse is brought to lie for a day or two on a broken canoe until a coffin can be constructed; and later, for the remainder of the week, in its coffin. It is from this house that the grave-diggers leave each day, and here they return to "carry the corpse," balancing the coffin atop their heads as the spirit of the dead is questioned about the cause of his death, or is required to clear itself of charges that the dead person had been guilty of practising evil magic. Here, too, the old men sit with the dead the day long, playing interminably the game of *adji-boto* with its permutations and combinations of seeds as they are dropped successively in the holes of the board they use; and here the village gathers each night the dead lies there, to dance in his honor, or to tell the tales of Anansi, the trickster, that delight his spirit.

We have moved far from the simple element in Bush-Negro culture with which we began. We have touched on art, on the economic base of prestige, on one aspect of the relation between the sexes, on the political system, on the rites of death, on games and dancing and folktales. The phrase "touched on" is to be emphasized here, for we have had but fleeting glimpses of the functioning culture in our exposition. Nor is it our purpose to be exhaustive. We are concerned here with integration—with how things "hang together." We have but made a beginning; and though we cannot follow through, since this would require a volume in itself, we can pursue the interrelationships further.

We return, then, to the dwelling, and consider its human occupants. In some houses we will find a man and a wife and their children; in others, however, we find only a wife and her children, with a man residing there periodically, and then moving for a time to another house inhabited by another woman and her children. Thus we soon learn that the family structure is in some cases polygynous. If we pursue this clue further, we find that here, as elsewhere, the men who have plural wives are those whose means permit, since marriage is always a matter that requires resources, and as in most polygynous societies, it is only those who command wealth who can afford to maintain more than a single household. This signifies that the heads of such households are either elderly men, or men of rank—though the two categories are not by any means exclusive.

As we observe these groupings, we find that many well-defined patterns of division of labor, of personal relationships, of kinship designations, and of wider affiliations ramify from this center of our concern. We observe the women going off to the field to tend the growing crops, their infants slung on their backs, tools in baskets atop their heads, to remain at the provision-ground for several days before they return, laden with produce, which they will later prepare and cook. The man of the household will have broken the ground for the planting; but for the rest he is busy with his wood-carving, or canoe-making, or engaged in cooperative timbering enterprises. Some

219

The Structure of Culture

households we will find for the time being are without men. The absentees will be away down the river, taking timber and balata to the coast where they will exchange the proceeds for iron pots and machetes, and cloth for the women to sew, or brass tacks with which to ornament their carvings, or gunpowder for their ancient flint-lock guns. Some men will be gone for longer periods than others, working as canoemen on another river, "on the French side." When they return, their canoes will be heavily laden indeed, their earnings converted into goods for their relations and themselves.

The personal relationships that exist between the members of the household and their wider kinship groups define Bush-Negro social structure. Generally, we will find that a woman lives in her husband's village, though there are exceptions; but we will also find that the husband's village is not that of his father, but of his mother. As we observe the behavior of the inhabitants of our house, we find that a father will ask permission of his wife's oldest brother before taking his own son on a journey down the river. For the child belongs to the family of the mother. Yet we observe a relationship of deep affection between father and child, and one of great freedom between children and their grandparents. We observe a son or brother of the father going into a house, or opening a box protected by a charm, and we discover that though relationship is traced through the mother's side, the soul one inherits is the father's, and only he who shares the same type of soul may tamper with a *kandu*, or spiritual "lock" set by another. We notice, too, that while children are deferential toward those of their parents' generation, including their parents, they joke broadly with their grandparents.

Our excursion into the supernatural deepens. Before the house is a crudely-carved whitened image, with a low thatched roof over it; nearby a three-pronged pole inserted into the ground, with a whitened calabash set in the prongs, open to the sky. The first is a shrine to the spirit that protects the village, the second to the all-powerful god of the sky. Over the doorway, unobtrusively placed, is an *obia*, a charm to protect those who live in the house; another is about the neck of a baby lying in front of the door, another about the wrist of a young girl watching the infant, another worn like a necklace by a boy who comes up from the river, paddle in hand; even the hunting-dog wears one as a collar. Out of the door steps the woman of the household, her body streaked with white. It is the day sacred to her god, and this evening she and others of the village who worship this god will dance for him, to rhythms struck from the drums by the hands of her husband.

It is unnecessary to continue this account further, to make plain how each element in this culture impinges on every other to make a satisfying, integrated way of life. None of the major divisions of culture, as these are set down by ethnologists and which, as we shall see, form logical subdivisions for study, is not represented in this account. The traits of this culture we have named do stand out, both alone and in the complexes with which they are associated; as do the socialized behavior patterns that dictate division of labor, or attitudes toward grandparents, or give to the stylized carvings their significance as symbols of a fertility cult.

Yet life, as we observe it from the vantage point of our village, flows as a single current. The generalization "culture" we abstract from our observations, is not haphazard, or disjointed. The little group we have studied comprehends in its day-to-day activities all aspects of the culture in the society to which it appertains; the lines cross and recross, but they rarely become entangled. All behavior is meaningful, each act performs some function, every object has its place and its usefulness.

This same demonstration could be given for any other culture we might select for analysis. Malinowski's pioneer study of the Kula ring of the Trobriand Islands,[4] the first in which a given phase of a single culture was traced through all its ramifications in disregard of conventional modes of approach, has been the model for many that followed it. His study did much to explode the theory that primitive man was no more than an economically burdened creature whose sole preoccupation was subsistence. Assessing the economy of this island folk, he followed their patterns of production, distribution, and exchange out of the subsistence range, into the realm of their prestige economy, into the area where magic reigns, into the reaches whereby specialization in production makes for exchanges wherein the utilitarian goods are secondary, and arm-bands and necklaces become primary objectives of the elaborate Kula expeditions. Such relationships as those revealed by Audrey Richards among the Bemba between the natural setting, the dietary, the kinship structure, the political system, and other elements in the culture of this folk give us another demonstration of cultural integration.[5] These, and others that could be named, teach us that, when the structure of culture is under scrutiny, the unity of a way of life must never be lost sight of, no matter how concentrated the attention on one or several of its elements.

3

IT IS far easier to sense the underlying psychological unities of cultures than it is to subject these unities to scientific analysis; far simpler to trace relationships between the elements of a culture as evidenced in behavior than to ferret out the unspoken, usually implicit sanctions that are firmly fixed in the cultural matrix. So tenuous are such materials that in attempting to phrase our attack, we must be on guard against giving expression to any form of cultural mysticism.

Benedict, who has given the most considered analysis of the configurationist point of view, states, "The cultural pattern of any civilization makes use of a certain segment of the great arc of potential human purposes and motivations, just as . . . any culture makes use of certain selected material techniques or cultural traits. The great arc along which all the possible human behaviours are distributed is far too immense and too full of contradictions for any one culture to utilize even any considerable portion of it. Selection is the first requirement. Without selection, no culture could even achieve intelligibility, and the intentions it selects and makes its own are a

[4] B. Malinowski, 1922.
[5] A. I. Richards, 1929.

much more important matter than the particular detail of technology or the marriage formality that it also selects in similar fashion." [6] It is thus clear how, in the thinking of this student, the selectivity of cultures, which causes them to shape "their thousand items of behaviour to a balanced and rhythmic pattern" [7] is crucial. Integration results from the conformity that follows when all items are selected and molded in terms of an overall principle.

Benedict makes it clear that there are differing degrees of integration, just as there are different principles on the basis of which various societies develop the configurations that characterize their cultures. One reason for this is a tendency to borrow cultural elements from societies having different configurations—"exposure to contradictory influences," such as is to be found "on the borders of well-defined culture areas." Or a migrating tribe, that "breaks off from its fellows and takes up its position in an area of different civilization," can experience a similar disorientation of fundamental drives.

Let us now examine the configurational approach. That in some cultures the deep-seated guiding principles that govern the lives of men are more consistent than in others is a proposition that is of the greatest importance in dealing with the problem of cultural configuration. It is the more important because it has been almost lost sight of in the controversies aroused by the dramatic examples of configuration Benedict has employed, and by the terminology she used to designate the cultural "types" into which she holds cultural configurations to fall.

Her use of the phrase "the cultural pattern" stands in striking contrast to the manner in which other anthropologists have interpreted it, as illustrated in our preceding chapter. Various suggestions have been made to differentiate these differing concepts by different names. One such term, that has proved useful in these pages, is *sanction.* The underlying drives, motivations, "unconscious system of meanings" that govern the reactions of a people can be thought of as the sanctions of their culture, in the fullest sense of the term. Sanctions, viewed from another point of view, are those validations of custom that people tend to rationalize, when they express them at all. They are the underlying forces that give an inner logic to the behavior of a people, which, in patterned expression, make possible that prediction of behavior whose importance for the study of human social life we have already discussed. It is these sanctions, in short, that in the unity of the unexpressed ends they promote give a culture its integrations, whether in the outer forms taken by its institutions, the professed ends of living that make existence meaningful to people, or the generalized personality types of a given society.

Other terms have been brought forward which, despite their different shades of meaning, are pertinent. Kluckhohn has suggested the division of cultural phenomena into "overt" and "covert" aspects. The overt forms are those institutions and other manifest elements to which, he says, "the technical term *pattern* be rigorously restricted." The covert culture includes the

---

[6] R. Benedict, 1934, p. 237.
[7] *Ibid.*, p. 223.

The Integration of Culture

sanctions that lie on the unconscious levels of thought. To these he would apply the term "configurations." "A pattern," he states, "is a generalization of what people do or should do; a configuration is in a sense a generalization of 'why' they do or should do certain things." The "broadest type of configuration," he suggests, might be referred to as "integration." "Even though we recognize that 'integration' is a polar concept which is seldom if ever fully realized in any culture it is a useful conception just as 'health' is useful, although few higher organisms are completely normal." [8]

Opler, on the other hand, feels that "to borrow terms and concepts from art, psychology, and philosophy may add flexibility and sparkle to the social scientist's descriptive offerings, but it has its limitations for serious analytical work." He therefore prefers to employ the term "themes." The precise meaning of this concept is best expressed in his own words. It is his thesis, he states, "that a limited number of dynamic affirmations, . . . *themes*, can be identified in every culture and that the key to the character, structure, and direction of the specific culture is to be sought in the nature, expression and relationship of these themes . . . The term 'theme' is used here in a technical sense to denote a postulate or position, declared or implied, and usually controlling behavior or stimulating activity, which is tacitly approved or openly promoted in a society." Themes, translated into conduct or belief, give rise to "expressions"—"formalized" when "conventionalized and ordered," or "unformalized" when their "precise character, time, or place are not carefully defined by the culture." They may, in their direct expression, be "primary," but when given oblique or implied expression are "symbolic"; they may likewise be "material" or "nonmaterial." [9]

These discussions reflect the ferment that has followed a desire by anthropologists to revise terminology and approach so as to account for the fact that there is more to culture than its expressions in behavior or the reification of behavior into institutions. They have especially followed on the realization of the widespread use, in ordinary speech, of expressions of cultural mysticism evidenced in such common phrases as "the genius of a culture," or its "spirit," or its "feel," which brought into relief the need for the systematic examination of cultural differences and the factors that lend themselves to such formulations. That there are various expressions for this phenomenon—"pattern," "covert culture," "theme," "sanction"—should not confuse us; it should rather stimulate thought and research into the real problem, to be attacked on many fronts, of why cultures *do* differ. The terms that have been suggested are, of course, more than mere designations. They are handles to the conceptual tools for our research, on which alone their validity must rest. This being the case, let us see how they have been, or can be employed.

We may first consider a configurational study, by Ackerknecht, in which a single aspect of culture, in this instance medicine, is analyzed. This student uses data from an American Indian, a Melanesian, and an African culture, studying the medicine in each, not as a separate compartment of the culture,

---

[8] C. Kluckhohn, 1941, pp. 124–8.
[9] M. E. Opler, 1945, pp. 198–200.

223

The Structure of Culture

but as part of its broader configuration. In each case, he shows how the pattern of medical beliefs and practices—the curing of the sick, that is—conforms to the broader underlying sanctions of the culture. Thus among the Cheyenne the cause of disease primarily consists of the "invisible arrows shot by the spirits of wells, the mule-deer and other spirits," and treatment is in terms of the "small ceremonial," whereby the expulsion of the intruded object from the patient is believed to be accomplished. In Dobu, witchcraft or sorcery is held to be the cause of illness. This Melanesian people, in conformance with their pattern, envisage no supernatural being as bringing on illness, but shape their cures to meet the supernatural dangers that are reported to be so important a manifestation of the basic drives in their culture. The Thonga of South Africa, on the other hand, are reported as envisaging disease largely as "the outcome of . . . a taboo-situation," the transgression of a rule laid down by the ancestors. On the basis of these differing configurations, Ackerknecht sets forth the principle that "the differences between primitive medicines are much less differences in 'elements' . . . than differences in the medical 'pattern' which they build up and which is conditioned fundamentally by their cultural pattern. . . . Disease may be regarded in its narrowest physiological limits . . . or may become a symbol for dangers menacing society through nature or through its own members. It may seem a mere incident or reach the rank of a goddess. Society unconsciously gives these different places to disease in the course of history." [10]

Kluckhohn illustrates the meaning of the term "covert culture" by an example from his field-work among the Navaho Indians. He tells how, during the early days of his research, he approached eleven persons, independently, with a request for information about witchcraft. In seven instances, the response was "Who said I knew anything about witchcraft?" Later, in testing the patterned character of this "overt" response, he repeated the question to twenty-five informants. Sixteen of these responses took this same form. Having established the existence of this pattern, he then juxtaposes it with still other, seemingly unrelated, types of response to typical situations in the culture. One is the care the Navaho take to hide their faeces and prevent others from obtaining anything else that comes from their bodies, such as hair, nails, or sputum. Another is their secretiveness about personal names. All these, when put together, form a configuration phrased by Kluckhohn as "fear of the malevolent intentions of other persons." Only rarely, we are told, does it rise into consciousness enough to permit a Navaho to state that, "These are all ways of showing our anxiety about the activities of others." Another covert configuration of the Navaho is their "distrust of extremes" that, for instance, brings accusations of witchcraft against persons who are very rich or very poor. These data, Kluckhohn concludes, show how such principles "order all sorts of concrete Navaho behaviors." Although *covert*, he says, "they are as much a part of Navaho culture as the overt pattern of verbal symbols." [11]

Opler turns to the Chiricahua Apache to document his concept of themes.

[10] Erwin H. Ackerknecht, 1942.
[11] C. Kluckhohn, op. cit., pp. 124–5.

224

The Integration of Culture

One theme of this culture, he tells us, is that men are physically, mentally, and morally superior to women, "a concept that is far from being exclusive to Chiricahua Apache society," but is nonetheless a significant one for these people. Thus if a fetus has "lots of life," it is assumed it will be a boy. Women are believed to be less stable than men, and more likely to cause domestic strife. They are held to be more easily "tempted," whether sexually or where witchcraft is involved. Tribal councils are for males, tribal leaders are men. Men precede women on the path; at feasts men have special places, while women eat where they can. A menstruating woman is believed dangerous to men's health and the well-being of male horses; women are not allowed to use sweat lodges or impersonate important supernatural beings. Another theme is the importance of old age, as evidenced in rituals such as the girl's puberty rites, the deference paid the old, the anxieties aroused by the belief that evil beings seek to shorten life, and the like. Yet the influence of such themes, it is pointed out, is not so great that they give society an imbalance that renders its functioning difficult. The influence of the theme of old age is held in check by the value set on performance as against wisdom and experience—a theme Opler terms "validation by participation"; male predominance is checked by the "limiting factors" that arise out of the human situations inherent in the day-to-day relations between the sexes.[12]

Later, writing of the Lipan Apache, Opler further developed his concept by noting twenty themes which give this culture its particular quality. They range widely over the content of culture, as can be seen by naming some of them. Thus, for the Lipan, "The elements of the universe are actually or potentially animate and personified," "Security and harmony are attained largely through the conquest of fear and danger and through self-discipline," while "Socially approved contacts with the supernatural must occur within the limits of a recognized ritual frame." Again, "The Lipan are culturally distinct from and are morally superior to all other groups of people," "Women play an important part in the social, economic, and religious life of the tribe," and "Childhood is a period of preparation for adulthood rather than an important phase of life itself," where "Industry, generosity, and bravery are the cardinal moral-social virtues." [13] It is apparent that a series of propositions of this sort will materially supplement the descriptions of institutions found in the conventional monograph, and add reality to the analysis of the structural aspects of the cultural life of a people.

An example of what we have called "sanction," but might be equally describable by any of the other terms just cited, is to be drawn from responses of West African and New World Negroes to many different kinds of situations. These reactions may be considered manifestations of a principle of indirection. Quite contrary to what would be anticipated in view of the too readily accepted stereotype of the "extraverted" Negro, this sanction dominates their behavior and dictates the circumspectness with which their life is characteristically lived. Indirection takes innumerable forms. The oblique use of imagery, as exemplified particularly in the constant employment of

[12] M. E. Opler, op. cit., passim.
[13] M. E. Opler, 1946, passim.

225

proverbs—in ordinary conversation, or in arguing a case before a court, or in teaching proper behavior to the young—is one example. "Behind the mountain is another mountain," says the Haitian, when he expresses skepticism about motives. "It is not for nothing the worm crawls from side to side," comments a Bush Negro when he expresses his suspicions of another, or "He who has no fingers cannot make a fist," he says to caution an impulsive person. In West Africa, quarrels are often carried on by the use of songs which, never mentioning an adversary by name, convey their message of insult and disdain by metaphor and allusion. Again, one does not ask a direct question. One waits and observes, until assertion based on some command of fact can open the way to further information. The taxation system of the native kings of Dahomey is the best instance of this sanction manifest in institutionalized form. Here no one was asked directly what he possessed, or how numerous was his family, or how much maize he had grown the previous year. Devious enquiry, however, elicited all the requisite information to the royal bureaucracy charged with gathering revenue, and no sources of income for the royal treasury were overlooked.[14] Only in Guiana has this reserve, that gives form to the sanction of indirection, been phrased in nonsymbolic terms. "I cannot say more," said one man after he had for a time discussed a commonplace element in his culture. "Long ago the ancestors taught us not to tell more than half of what we know. I have said more than enough."

4

WHETHER we analyze the objective manifestations of a culture, or approach it along the broader avenues of its fundamental sanctions and intent; whatever the terminology we may apply to clarify our data and set them in a significant conceptual context; the fact of cultural unity, of cultural integration is established. Its outer forms frame inner meanings; sanctions mold conduct; and life as a whole goes on, permitting human beings to seek and find fulfilment.

As a scientist, the student of culture must divide his data into categories, just as the student of living organisms dissects his specimen. Culture is not an organism, so that the analogy must not be pressed too far. It is enough that the ethnologist, like the biologist in his laboratory, recognize that the subject as he studies it in its several parts is not the living totality. He takes his scientific liberties so that, when he turns again to the functioning whole, he can at least know what these parts are, how they are related to each other, how they combine to make the whole. It is in this sense that he must study structure and distribution. And it is in this spirit that, in another dimension, he again divides culture into the formal aspects, the kinds of institutions to be discerned in all cultures as we move over the earth, comparing one way of achieving a given end with another, assessing the varied means mankind uses to reach the same goals.

---

[14] M. J. Herskovits, 1938b, vol. I, pp. 107–34.

PART V

THE ASPECTS OF CULTURE

CHAPTER 15

The Universals in Human Civilization

ALL cultures are made up of *institutions* that represent formalized and sanctioned responses to the demands of living. The institutionalized ways of behavior in which these responses are manifest, appertain to the various *aspects* of culture. These are like great blocks of experience which the student carves out of a functioning body of custom in order the better to achieve a workable description of it. Aspects are, so to speak, a kind of table of contents of culture; the framework about which, however unrealized, a people organize their life.

It is worthwhile to see how these large blocks of culture have been envisaged by different students who have given the problem of cultural universals their attention. E. B. Tylor, in a general work written in 1881, after treating of man's place in the biological world, takes up the following topics: language; the "arts of life"—the food quest, implements, dwellings, clothing, fire-making, cooking, and those topics that today would be termed economics, such as barter, money, and commerce; the "arts of pleasure"—poetry, drama, dance, the graphic and plastic arts; "science"—counting, weighing, and other methods of reasoning about the physical world, and magic; the spirit-world, or religion in its various forms; history and mythology; and "society" or social institutions.[1] Here the more systematized schemes of dividing culture that came later are definitely foreshadowed. Here also we encounter a terminology with expressions such as "the arts of life" that, though somewhat strange to present-day usage, employ an imagery that might well have been retained in later discussions of the principal divisions of culture.

Wissler's "universal pattern" is based on the additional anthropological experience of the four decades that separated the publication of his book and that of Tylor. Except for the order in which the topics are presented and for the items of language and war, his "culture scheme," as he terms it, follows section and chapter headings of many conventional monographs of the period when it was written. It is here reproduced in its original form:

---

[1] E. B. Tylor, 1881, *passim*.

The Aspects of Culture

1. Speech
   Languages, writing systems, etc.
2. Material traits
   a. Food habits
   b. Shelter
   c. Transportation and travel
   d. Dress
   e. Utensils, tools, etc.
   f. Weapons
   g. Occupations and industries
3. Art. Carving, painting, drawing, music, etc.
4. Mythology and Scientific Knowledge
5. Religious Practices
   a. Ritualistic forms
   b. Treatment of the sick
   c. Treatment of the dead
6. Family and Social Systems
   a. The forms of marriage
   b. Methods of reckoning relationship
   c. Inheritance
   d. Social control
   e. Sports and games
7. Property
   a. Real and personal
   b. Standards of value and exchange
   c. Trade
8. Government
   a. Political forms
   b. Judicial and legal procedures
9. War [2]

Let us glance at some of the subjects not included in this list which later students of culture have felt necessary to consider. The economic phases of man's existence are treated by Wissler in a manner that now appears fragmentary and disjointed. "Occupations and industries," or the production system, are grouped with the material things employed in meeting the exigencies of the habitat. Ownership, termed "property," however, is set up as a main head, with a series of subdivisions that include canons of value, and such aspects of the distributive system as trade. Again, except for "mythology," such arts as music and dance are ignored, and so are the other literary forms—poetry, tale, proverb. The heading "religion" fails to specify the systems of belief, the theological concepts that underlie all rituals (unless this is comprehended in the category "mythology"), while Wissler's listing of "treatment of the sick" and of the dead fails to take cognizance of such an aspect of religion as the widespread belief in impersonal forces that govern the universe, or systems of divination, or of magic. He has no place for birth and puberty, nor child-care and education, except insofar as this last might be included under the sub-heading "social control."

---

[2] C. Wissler, 1923, p. 74.

The Universals in Human Civilization

We may contrast Wissler's cultural scheme with another, presented two decades later, to obtain a measure of "how numerous and diverse are the elements common to all known cultures," as Murdock, the author of this "partial list of items" terms it. The listing introduces an alphabetical order, in contrast to the customary systematic treatment of cultural topics, "to emphasize their variety," since they are stated to occur "in every culture known to history or ethnography." The number of elements is impressive: "age-grading, athletic sports, bodily adornment, calendar, cleanliness training, community organization, cooking, cooperative labor, cosmology, courtship" and so on to "religious ritual, residence rules, sexual restrictions, soul concepts, status differentiation, surgery, tool-making, trade, visiting, weaving, and weather control." [3]

Such a catalog, as Murdock points out, by no means represents the extent to which this process of fragmentation of universals can go. Many of the items included are themselves to be subdivided into still smaller units, which are likewise universals. "Not only does every culture have a language, but all languages are resolvable into identical kinds of components, such as phonemes or conventional sound units, words or meaningful combinations of phonemes, grammar or standard rules for combining words into sentences. Similarly, funeral rites always include expressions of grief, a means of disposing of the corpse, rituals designed to protect the participants from supernatural harm, and the like." The analysis of many individual cultures from this point of view, as found in such an attack as the cross-cultural survey, instituted by this student, documents the fact that the "resemblances between all cultures are . . . exceedingly numerous."

Obviously, an alphabetical listing such as that just cited needs to be brought together under a series of logical categories if it is to be of use in analyzing cultural unities and assessing the differences between cultures. The cross-cultural survey, out of which Murdock's list has been drawn, has developed such a series of systematic headings which we will consider shortly. This survey—perhaps aside from *Notes and Queries*—is the most elaborate catalog of culture that has as yet been devised. It was first set up in tentative draft in 1937. This draft was then revised, and published the following year. It was designed, as the foreword to this first edition states, "primarily for the organization of the available information on a large and representative sample of known cultures with the object of testing cross-cultural generalizations, revealing deficiencies in the descriptive literature, and directing corrective field work." [4] Inevitably, also, it became a kind of guide for those going into the field, a frame of reference for all-round descriptions of culture, and it was so represented in the title of its Spanish translation.[5]

The organization of cultural materials, as given in the second revision of this scheme (1945) comprehends forty-six categories, numbered from 10 to 55, with subdivisions and elaborate cross-references also numbered some-

---

[3] G. P. Murdock, 1945, p. 124.
[4] G. P. Murdock et al., 1945.
[5] *Guía para la investigación etnológica.*

The Aspects of Culture

what after the manner of library reference guides. That is, 16 is "technology," 162 is "textile industries," 1621 is "cordage." Certain items merit our attention as departures from earlier usage, and will be discussed in turn, as we follow the progression of the major headings.

The first division is entitled *10. Basic Data.* It includes the location of a people studied, its name or names, the works already available concerning it, its habitat, physical and psychological characteristics of the people, and such population data as are available. Next comes *11. History and Culture Contact,* wherein such historical documentation as exists is called for, as well as information about the past as it is reflected in archaeological data and traditional history. The setting of a tribe among its neighbors, and the cultural contacts it is known to have had in early or more recent times are also to be analyzed under this heading in terms of the borrowing apparent in its various traits. In the third section, *12. Total Culture,* topics are included which will give "a background against which to project specific instances"— general orientation and principal interests ("ethos"), degree of integration, the complexities that cut across the various parts of the culture, the participation of the individual in it, and the extent to which this total configuration has been affected by changes from within or without. With *13. Language,* and *14. Communication,* what may be thought of as the sections dealing with the background of a culture end, and give way to the aspects of the culture as these are more narrowly construed.

The first group of these aspects—though they are not so brought together in this culture-scheme—come under the conventional headings of technology and economics. Beginning with *15. Exploitative Activities,* those activities having to do with the extraction of raw materials, it continues with *16. Technology,* the "processing of raw materials," and *17. Capital,* the goods that are the finished products of these processes. It then moves to *18. Housing, 19. Food, 20. Drink and Indulgence,* and *21. Dress and Adornment.* Following this come those aspects of the daily round entitled *22. Routine of Living,* after which more strictly economic phases of the culture are considered; *23. Labor, 24. Specialization, 25. Exchange, 26. Finance* and *27. Transportation.* A series of categories follows which is difficult to class under a single rubric, since it includes items that are treated in various sections of most ethnographic studies, when they are treated at all. They include *28. Travel, 29. Recreation, 30. Art*—which deals with all aspects of the aesthetic culture —*31. Numbers and Measures, 32. Lore and Learning* and, as a transition to the next broad grouping, *33. Reaction to Nature.*

The next set of categories comprehends the phenomena ordinarily classed as religious. Here it is divided into two parts, *34. Religion* which includes theology, ceremonialism, "religious personnel," and magic, and *35. Ethics.* From this the outline moves to the aspect of culture usually classified as social organization—*36. Property and Contract, 37. Social Stratification, 38. Family, 39. Kinship, 40. Kin and Local Groups*—and proceeds logically to the political structure—*41. Government, 42. Law and Social Control.* It then makes a place for two phases of social life to which but little attention has been given, *43. Ingroup Conflict,* and *44. War and Peace.*

The Universals in Human Civilization

The remaining topics deal with what is generally called the life cycle. *45. Human Organism*, *46. Sex* and *47. Reproduction* serve as a kind of introduction to these topics. Ideas a people have about the body and how its functioning is influenced by their conceptions, for instance, of fatigue, or pain, come under the first of these headings; the other two are more or less self-explanatory. Of life-cycle topics, properly speaking, there are *48. Infancy, 49. Childhood, 50. Youth, 51. Marriage, 52. Adulthood, 53. Old Age, 54. Sickness*, and *55. Death.*

Not every culture comprehends or needs to include all the items listed under each of these headings. The more specific an item, the less chance there is of its being a universal in culture. Some of them, indeed, are contradictory in the sense that they present alternative possibilities, such as exist under plural marriage, where plural spouses may either be men or women; and hence give rise to the categories of polyandry and polygyny, which never occur together in the same society. The listing, however, in its broader categories, is one of universals. As such, we gain from it a sense of how complex even the simplest culture can be, and yet, despite unities, how varied the ways in which human groups go about solving their common problems.

2

ONE of the earliest postulates of anthropological science was that the ends achieved by all human cultures are basically similar. This universality in the general outlines of cultures supported the theory of the "psychic unity of mankind," which held that the resemblances between the institutions of different cultures are to be accounted for by the similar capacities of all men. This theory was at the basis of Herbert Spencer's elaborate scheme for the study of comparative sociology, as without an assumption of cultural equivalence, whether expressed or implicit, no such attempt at drawing comparisons could have been undertaken. This was also implied in the work of E. B. Tylor. The concept of equivalence was likewise implicit in the writings of such an early anthropologist as Lewis H. Morgan. He studied the evolution of culture by means of comparative data on the kinship structure, the economic and the political systems of many differing peoples, using this material to document his theoretical deductions.

In accepting the concept of cultural similarities, the question as to the reason why they are found remains to be answered. Our problem here parallels the one we faced when it was seen that all cultures have the same kind of structures—that all are built up out of elements that comprise larger units; that this process is not haphazard but results in a patterned form of living; that these parts have specific distributions over a continent or an ocean area that can be delimited and described; and that they exhibit unified cultural affinities defined by region. The resemblances in structure between one culture and another are an expression of the conformities of individual behavior transferred to the level of the social group. As for the subsidiary traits and complexes, we saw how their similarities in form had resulted from contact

The Aspects of Culture

between peoples, the resultant selective borrowing, and the integration of the new ways into pre-existing patterns.

Wissler, who was one of the first to direct attention to the specific problem, inclines toward a biological interpretation of cultural universals. "It seems reasonable to suppose that what all men have in common is inherited," he states at one point. He also holds that men "have a type of behavior as inevitably fixed as that of any social insect." That is, "man builds cultures because he cannot help it; there is a _drive_ in his protoplasm that carries him forward even against his will." [6] This drive is then shaped by the conditioning process, that causes an infant to manifest the behavior of his group through the process of learning that we have called enculturation. Tool-using and ritual-forming drives, he assumes, are given at birth. With these, he states, "the universal pattern for culture is . . . largely determined by the number and kind of these inborn responses the baby possesses." The variants in cultural behavior, it follows, become "largely variants in the conditioning of inborn responses." The "content of culture" is thus to be differentiated from the universal pattern. "The former is, in the main, acquired behavior, the latter is an expression of inborn behavior." [7]

We can agree that certain cultural uniformities do arise out of the similarities in the situations with which all human beings must cope, such as some kind of family to care for the young, or even some system of belief with which to achieve a sense of security in an otherwise overpowering universe. But this is far from postulating inherent drives to account for the phenomenon that everywhere, all of culture can be subsumed under such a listing as Wissler's "universal pattern." A genetic basis for culture implies a genetic mechanism; and this has never been discovered. Man is a "tool-using animal" as Tylor called him, because his physical type makes it possible to devise the extensions of his anterior extremities we call tools. He is a "speaking animal" because he has the anatomical and neurological structures that make speech possible.

The most elaborate attempt to account for the universality of certain aspects of culture appears in a posthumous work of B. Malinowski. Here, in its broadest terms, is set forth the function which each of the cultural responses incorporated in these aspects is held to fulfil in satisfying what are termed the basic needs of men. His scheme is as follows:

(A) Basic Needs	(B) Cultural Responses
1. Metabolism	1. Commissariat
2. Reproduction	2. Kinship
3. Bodily Comforts	3. Shelter
4. Safety	4. Protection
5. Movement	5. Activities
6. Growth	6. Training
7. Health	7. Hygiene [8]

[6] C. Wissler, op. cit., pp. 260, 265.
[7] Ibid., pp. 267–9.
[8] B. Malinowski, 1944, p. 92.

The Universals in Human Civilization

This list, its author holds, "has to be read with each pair of horizontal entries regarded as linked up inseparably. The real understanding of our concept of need implies its direct correlation with the response which it receives from culture. . . . The needs for food, drink, and oxygen are never isolated, impelling forces which send the individual organism or a group as a whole into a blind search for food or water or oxygen, nor do people carry about their needs for bodily comfort, for movement, or for safety. Human beings under their conditions of culture wake up with their morning appetite ready, and also with a breakfast waiting for them or else ready to be prepared. . . . It is clear that the organism becomes adjusted, so that within the domain of each need specific habits are developed; and, in the organization of cultural responses, these routine habits are met by an organized routine of satisfactions." [9]

These basic needs, manifest in the cultural activities of men, in turn set up a series of "derived needs." This concept, says Malinowski, means that "culture supplies man with derived potentialities, abilities, and powers." In addition, it "also means that the enormous extension in the range of human action, over and above innate abilities of the naked organism, imposes on man a number of limitations." [10] These derived needs set up a series of "cultural imperatives," which in turn give form to the institutions of a culture that go to make up its broadest divisions, that we here term aspects. Malinowski indicates how these are built up in the following tabular expression:

Imperatives	Responses
1. The cultural apparatus of implements and consumer's goods must be produced, used, maintained, and replaced by new production.	1. Economics
2. Human behavior, as regards its technical, customary, legal or moral prescription must be codified, regulated in action and sanction.	2. Social control
3. The human material by which every institution is maintained must be renewed, formed, drilled and provided with full knowledge of tribal tradition.	3. Education
4. Authority within each institution must be defined, equipped with powers, and endowed with means of forceful execution of its orders.	4. Political organization [11]

In scrutinizing these two tables, we are struck with the omission of any reference to religion or the aesthetic elements of culture. Is the universality of these aspects less securely established than are the domains of economics or social organization?

Malinowski, in a later essay on functionalism in this same volume, does include these facets of custom. He there defines culture as "essentially an instrumental apparatus by which man is put in a position the better to cope with the concrete specific problems that face him in his environment in the course of the satisfaction of his needs." Then, he continues, its "activities,

---

[9] *Ibid.*, pp. 93–4.
[10] *Ibid.*, p. 119.
[11] *Ibid.*, p. 125.

attitudes and objects are organized around important and vital tasks into institutions such as the family, the clan, the local community, the tribe, and organized teams of economic cooperation, political, legal and educational activity." Finally, he states that "from the dynamic point of view, that is, as regards the type of activity, culture can be analyzed into a number of aspects such as education, social control, economics, systems of knowledge, belief and morality, and also modes of creative and artistic expression." [12] But what needs are satisfied by these "systems of belief" or "modes of creative and artistic expression" we are not told.

Murdock posits that "only a small proportion of men's actions in any society spring directly from any of the demonstrable basic drives," citing as illustration how acquired appetites channel hunger reactions toward certain foods, or taboos stand in the way of satisfying hunger drives. He then sets forth a second reason for "rejecting the impulse factor." This arises out of the fact that "most social institutions or culture complexes actually give satisfaction to several basic impulses as well as to a variety of derived drives"—as when marriage becomes as important for the prestige it confers as for the sexual satisfactions it affords. He therefore refers cultural behavior to two mechanisms. The first is instinct, defined as "a precise organization of behavior developed through natural selection and transmitted through heredity," which man shares with all other organisms. The second is habit formation, which man shares with the higher forms. These operate "to mediate between two types of situations in which organisms find themselves, namely, those in which impulses are aroused and impulses are satisfied." The satisfaction of an impulse results in the reduction of the drives which stimulated the activity.

Culture lends itself to this end, both through directly satisfying basic needs, and by means of secondary, or "instrumental responses." Finally, culture comprehends "a third and very large category of cultural habits . . . in which behavior is followed by rewards that bear no relation, or only an incidental one, to the impulses prompting the behavior." Such a one is when a rain-making spell evokes a storm, or a magic charm "works." The establishment of these patterns is referred to a kind of selective process, whereby the institutions best fitted to achieve their ends survive at the expense of those less fitted.[13]

This is a reasoned analysis of the persistence of one manifestation of a given aspect of culture as against another, or even one culture as against another. It explains, why, for instance, belief in a given type of magic may have persisted in one culture to the exclusion of other types, or why one group practises plural marriage and another does not. Nonetheless, it is difficult to see how, in attempting to explain why magic beliefs are so widespread in human culture, or why all societies have the institution of the family, it carries us much farther than the other explanations we have discussed. It is scarcely necessary to restate here the importance our concept of the nature and mechanisms of culture places on the learning-conditioning process, that

---

[12] Ibid., p. 150.
[13] G. P. Murdock, 1945, pp. 128–33.

PLATE 4a *Terraced valley, showing method of cultivating rice in the Philippines.*
PLATE 4b *Close-up of rice terraces. See page 163.* [*Photographs by R. F. Barton, cour-tesy F. Eggan*]

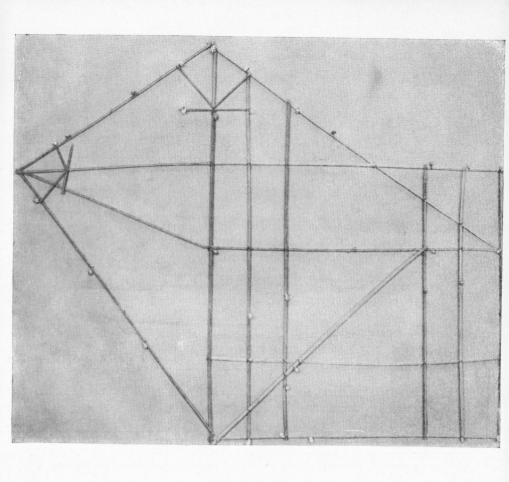

PLATE 5   *Sailing chart used by Marshall Islanders. See page 246. [Photograph courtesy Chicago Natural History Museum]*

we have termed enculturation, and which Murdock stresses in terms of habit formation as a result of the reduction of innate or acquired drives.

In referring cultural *universals* to such processes, however, the problem is merely moved to a different plane. That is to say, if we envisage our universals as satisfying basic needs, out of which the acquired drives arise, then we find ourselves exactly where these other hypotheses have taken us. If, on the other hand, we stress the secondary responses, and refer the broad aspects of human culture to them, we must treat universals as historic phenomena. This means that we are assuming for them an origin so early in man's life on earth as to have caused them to be passed on from one generation to the next, to be preserved everywhere mankind travelled as the earth became populated.

In truth, the question in the comprehensive study of culture with which we are concerned here, apparently so elementary, is a most difficult one. It involves the weighing of fundamental points concerning the origin and development of culture on which we have no information, and as far as we can tell at present are unlikely to have. Each of the theories we have considered is persuasive until we study it closely and become aware of its incompleteness. Incontrovertibly, there are biological bases for the behavior of individuals that fashion culture, and requirements of the habitat that must be met. This fact has been pointed out many times in our earlier chapters and will enter again in later pages. Our discussion of the materials of culture was oriented toward demonstrating how man's status as a member of the biological series, and the fact that he must meet the demands of his habitat, influence his cultural proclivities. The story of his development in prehistoric times was seen in large measure to be the story of how these phases of man's existence were reconciled in the development of his culture. But "life is not lived by bread alone," and to account for "the arts of life" tends to lead us into rationalizations rather than explanations that are today scientifically verifiable.

Most of the students whose hypotheses have just been discussed do in fact recognize that the institutions in which these broad adjustments are manifest in given societies are by no means to be explained in simple terms. Does not culture often seem to defeat its ends, as when food-taboos interpose a cultural restraint that entails deprivation, rather than the satisfaction of hunger? Wissler phrases this distortion by tradition in terms of the conditioning process, Malinowski speaks of the resulting psychological drives as derived needs. All this is aside from our problem of the moment, the question why the content of all cultures can be referred to what Boas speaks of as, "a cultural morphology . . . founded on comparative studies of similar forms in different parts of the world." [14]

We may here leave the question of why there are universal aspects in culture, and accept the insights each position affords us, without fully accepting any of them. There can be no doubt that, viewed in the large, culture does fulfil the needs of man, psychic no less than biological; that it solves for him problems whose solution is demanded both by the character of his bio-psy-

---

[14] F. Boas, 1938, p. 675.

chological make-up and the need to meet the demands of his habitat. He does this by setting up institutions which, for each society, exact conformities from the individuals who compose it, in the interest of adjustment and survival. That they vary so widely from one society to another only means that multiple solutions stemming from an underlying universal base characterize human culture.

3

It is impossible for any study of a culture, no matter how comprehensive it may be, to describe more than a portion of the aspects of the life of a single people. Even those whose aim is to give the most rounded portrayal possible find certain limits which, for technical reasons of time, space and competence they cannot exceed. In practice, language is left to the specialist, and so is music. If any attempt is made to include expressions of the literary arts, this material must commonly be reserved for separate treatment because of its bulk. Some aspects of culture are rarely studied as such; forms of dramatic expression, for instance, since in nonliterate societies drama is customarily a part of ritual. The dance, also, has too rarely been analyzed, because of the technical difficulties it presents in the way of valid recording.

It is worth while noting how a rounded study of a culture has been organized in terms of its principal aspects. For this purpose, we may turn to the study of a Mexican village community, Cherán, a Tarascan group in the state of Michoacán, west of Mexico City.[15] The discussion opens with a description of the natural setting of this village, its size and its physical organization, which is documented with detailed maps illustrating house-types and political subdivisions. The culture itself is treated under five principal headings, entitled technology, economics, the community, religion and ceremonial, and the individual and his culture.

The first heading considers how the natural resources are utilized—minerals, forests, water supply; how agriculture is carried on, and the crops that are raised; the use of domesticated animals, and various manufacturing processes—ceramics, textiles, woodworking—and the preparation and use of foods. Under economics, we learn of the organization of production, in terms of the use of land, labor, and capital; the costs of production and the income yielded by those who work at the various specialties whose technical aspects were discussed earlier; the mechanisms of distribution; and such matters as consumption as reflected in family budgets, or the values and prices of various goods and services, and how wealth is distributed and regarded. The community is described both as to its social structure and the governmental instrumentalities it comprehends, while the section on religion and ceremonial treats of the place of the Catholic Church in the lives of the people, and the particular forms which its rites take in this Mexican Indian community. Here, too, the secular dances are described, and witchcraft and other beliefs outside the purview of the Church are discussed. The life of the individual

---

[15] Ralph L. Beals, 1946.

The Universals in Human Civilization

follows the principal events in the life-cycle, and the analysis ends with a discussion of certain problems in the study of culture raised by this body of materials.

The assumptions that underlie the progression of topics in such a presentation is that of most descriptive studies. They derive from a logic that proceeds from the consideration of those aspects that supply the physical wants of man, to those that order social relations, and finally to the aspects which, in giving meaning to the universe, sanction everyday living, and in their aesthetic manifestations afford men some of the deepest satisfactions they experience.

Such a progression will be followed in the chapters that ensue, where the universal aspects of culture are individually considered. We may summarize this progression as follows:

Material Culture and its Sanctions
>Technology
>Economics

Social Institutions
>Social organization
>Education
>Political structures

Man and the Universe
>Belief systems
>The control of power

Aesthetics
>Graphic and plastic arts
>Folklore
>Music, drama and the dance

Language

It must be stressed that in dividing cultures in this way, we are but utilizing another of those scientific devices whose justification is their utility in throwing light on the problems that are the subject of study. Ideally, as we have seen, cultures should be considered as wholes, but it has also been pointed out that as entities they are too complex and present too many interrelations to permit such a comprehensive attack. With this in mind, for example, it is clear we will not be deceived into regarding material culture as distinct from the nonmaterial aspects of civilization. We will recognize that no single object, no matter how tangible it may seem, but has a *cultural* existence by definition. A cartwheel that serves as a chandelier is no longer a cartwheel but a lighting device. The batik cloth that is an article of clothing in Java becomes translated, in another culture, into a wall hanging. Even the hardest-bitten engineer includes "know-how" as part of the technical equipment of his profession. But "know-how" is the nonmaterial aspect of technology.

The Aspects of Culture

Graphic and plastic arts offer another instance of how data cast even in the broadest categories can refuse to stay within the scholar's bounds. Painting or sculpture do not exist apart from their expression, and this expression can only be given in some tangible form—the painting on a cave wall, the decoration on a pottery jar or on a woven basket, the figurine carved of wood, or the statue hewn out of stone. It is for this reason that in many cultural schemes, art follows material culture and technology. But we find that in monographs dealing with specific tribal cultures, art rarely stands in this relation to the description of the tangible objects used in everyday life. The ethnographer disregards the fact that art is manifested in material objects. His approach strikes through to the cultural reality that the essence of art, that which gives the tangible object its appeal and its meaning, to say nothing of the impulse to create it, cannot be touched. These constitute what we call the aesthetic conventions of a people that, in the last analysis, find realization in the genius of the individuals who decorate the pot, or paint the wall, or carve the statuette.

What, then, of our categories of culture? Does this mean that they, too, vanish on examination; that to be concerned with them is to waste time in the analysis of unreality? All experience with the study of culture indicates that this is not the case. A position which held for the fruitlessness of such an approach would disregard the basis on which the various scholarly and scientific disciplines have been erected. It would be a hardy advocate of the study of whole cultures indeed, who would insist that the economic aspects of life failed to present problems that could not be studied, in disregard of the fact that at some few points the economic system might be involved in matters of religious, or aesthetic, or even sociological import. Problems of composition, color, and mass are problems of art and do not impinge on questions about government.

CHAPTER 16

Technology and the Utilization
of Natural Resources

MEN wrest from their habitat by means of their *technology* the food-stuffs, the shelter, the clothing, and the implements they must have if they are to survive. The objects they make and use for these purposes are generally classified under the heading of *material culture.*[1]

The study of technology is essential for an understanding of culture, just as a comprehension of the material basis of social life is indispensable to those concerned with human group behavior. More than this, we have seen that the technological equipment of a people figures more than any other aspect of their culture when current judgments of advancement or retardation are drawn. There are various reasons why such judgments are made, but in essence they may be referred to the fact that technology is the only aspect of culture susceptible of objective evaluation. These evaluations follow a pattern that, with the rise of the scientific tradition and of a system of production based on the power machine, has become exceedingly congenial to our culture.

We need not again consider the validity of evaluating culture on these or other grounds. We may content ourselves with the observation that often even the technique that has the appearance of marked simplicity proves on analysis to be far from simple when the skills it calls forth are taken into account; and that, moreover, in their techniques, nonliterate peoples employ a very large proportion of the fundamental principles of engineering. The fact remains, however, that not only does Euroamerican culture, based on a machine technology, differ strikingly from the non-machine cultures in wealth of objects, a vast array of power-machinery used to make them, and a resultant standard of life, but this has affected many other aspects of living as well. It is seen, as in no other culture, in the pecuniary economy of our society, especially as this is reflected in the fluctuations of the business cycle and the resulting accentuation of extremes of poverty and wealth.

The "labor market," as we know it, is also unique to the machine society. In nonliterate cultures, as in pre-machine-age Europe, the craftsman is predominantly the owner of the means of production he employs. He is thus the master of his own economic destiny, and the phenomenon of the man or

---

[1] M. J. Herskovits, 1940, *passim.*

woman who sells time for subsistence is unknown. This technological system also induces a degree of specialization never found in non-machine societies. The mechanistic habit of thought is likewise absent where power machinery is not the dominant element in shaping material culture, thereby exerting its influence on the culture as a whole.

The machine, however, is by no means unknown to nonliterate peoples. As Digby points out, the essential problem of the machine is "to convert and

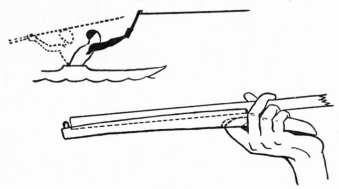

Fig. 18   *Eskimo spear thrower, showing manner of holding and mode of employment.*

guide the movements of four prime movers into channels whereby they would perform useful work." Most of this work, he shows, is done by the use of stationary man-power as the prime mover, and in this the hands are used far more often than the feet. Also found as movers are human or animal power combined with the force of gravity or used tractively, water-power, and windpower—though the last is employed so rarely that it need not be taken into account, except in the use of sails.

The methods of application are two, the first of which is found in by far the greater numbers of instances: a reciprocating or uni-directional motion "as a result of constant repetition and less need for muscular control," and the second, rotary motion. Instances of the rotary method of applying the force of man-power are not numerous. They include the Tibetan prayer-wheel, the Eskimo string-maker, and the New Guinea drill. Direct motion is employed in the fire-plow, the pestle and mortar, and bellows and looms, to name but some of the instances cited by Digby. Wedges are used for lifting weights, levers in deadfalls, and with the auxiliary power of gravity, as in the cassava-squeezers of the South American Indians. Rollers are employed in spinning, while nonliterate folk utilize the principle of the axle and bearing, converting power by a means of a cord or crank, as in such devices as the Eskimo bow-drill or the Samoan rope-twister.[2]

Even peoples whose equipment is of the simplest, who have no machines such as these, employ mechanical principles that are quite complex. The boomerang of the Australian, the heavy knobkerry of the African Kaffir, or

---

[2] A. Digby, 1938, p. 73.

the spear-thrower all show a shrewd utilization of forces that give to the individual far more flexibility and power in using his physical capacities than would be possible without this aid. The use of the principle of the spring in

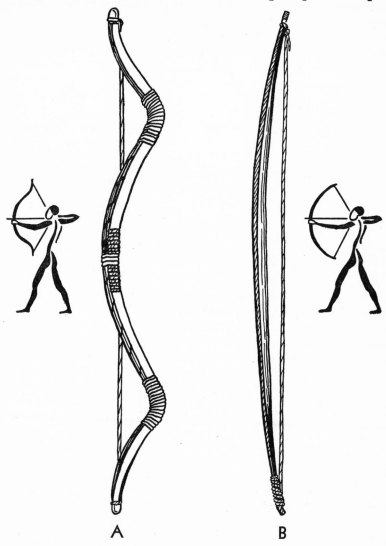

A   B

Fig. 19   (A) *Eskimo compound bow,* (B) *Sauk and Fox simple bow.*

the manufacture of the compound bow is another instance of this. Even the simpler type of bow, made of one piece of wood, recognizes and allows for the elasticity of wood, while the bow-string compounds the same principle, and the feathered arrow insures greater accuracy of aim.

How many widely used implements we owe to the basic inventions made

The Aspects of Culture

when stone was the material most employed in the manufacture of tools, is demonstrated in the following table, given by Nelson. In it, he lists the primary stone tools, indicating their original functions and "the specialized implements made, mostly in metal, to serve these functions at the present time." The second column of this table names many implements of contemporary nonliterate societies that are made out of the materials available to the peoples who do not have a metal-working technique.[3]

Generic Form	Functions	Specializations
Hammerstone	Throwing	Slingstone, bole, bullet
	Clubbing	Club, nightstick, blackjack, bat
	Pounding	Hammer, maul, piledriver
	Crushing	Blacksmith's sledge, steam hammer
	Shattering	Flintknapper's hammer, rockbreaker's hammer
	Abrading	Stonecutter's hammer
	Grinding	Pestle
Perforator	Stabbing	Dagger, lancet, spear, arrow, rapier, bayonet
	Digging	Digging stick, planting stick, spade, shovel
	Punching	Brad awl, punch
	Sewing	Awl, bodkin, needle, stiletto
	Boring	Drill, auger, gimlet, bit, reamer
	Fastening	Pin, nail, screw, hook, buckle
Chopper	Cutting	Chopper, cleaver, axe, adze, gouge
	Hoeing	Hoe, pick, mattock
	Splitting	Wedge
Knife	Cutting	Knife, scalpel, scissors, razor, burin, sickle, scythe, reaper
	Shaving	Drawknife, spokeshave
	Sawing	Saws of various kinds
Scraper	Smoothing	Sidescraper, ordinary scraper
	Planing	Endscraper, chisel, burin, plane
	Shaving	Drawknife, spokeshave
Rubbingstone	Grinding	Upper mealing stone, mano, upper millstone
	Sharpening	Grindstone, whetstone, hone, steel
	Abrading	Rasp, file, lapidary grinder
	Smoothing	Sandpaper, sharkshide rasp
	Polishing	Ceramic polisher, lapidary polisher, burnisher
Anvil stone	Supporting	Anvil, mortar, lower mealing stone, metate, lower millstone

---

[3] N. C. Nelson, 1932, pp. 116–17.

Technology and the Utilization of Natural Resources

It should be noted that the products of the technological equipment of a people are the only man-made elements in culture that have a physical existence of their own. It is because of this that they form the greater part of ethnographic museum collections. But this fact of their physical autonomy has theoretical implications as well, in that the physical autonomy of material culture must be taken into account, even where culture is treated in purely psychological terms. Though Osgood, for example, in his comprehensive study of the material culture of the Ingalik Athapascan Indians of the upper Yukon, defines culture in psychological terms when he describes it as "all ideas concerning human beings which have been communicated to one's mind and of which one is conscious," he nonetheless allows for the physical autonomy of material culture when he delimits it as "ideas about objects external to the mind directly resulting from human behavior as well as ideas about human behavior required to manufacture these objects"—that is, material culture and technology.[4]

Quite aside from the question whether the category "material culture" should include all material elements in a culture or only those used in getting a living, it is a fact that most of the material equipment of a people is employed toward the latter end. Osgood's classification of Ingalik material culture, especially when the number of items included under each class is taken into account, documents this point well:

Primary tools	40
Lines	15
Containers	41
Miscellaneous manufactures	60
Weapons	11
Fishing implements	23
Snares, deadfalls and other traps	12
Clothing, cradles and personal ornaments	46
Shelters, caches and racks	29
Travel implements	25
Dyes and paints	13
Tags and games	22
Puberty paraphernalia	8
Funerary objects	14
Religious and ceremonial objects	41

Of the 400 elements included, only those of the final four or perhaps five classes are outside the category of those objects used in getting a living. It must be pointed out, however, that an implement in Osgood's first category, a primary tool such as an awl or a barkscraper, is equally useful in making a food-container or in manufacturing some object of a puberty rite.[5]

Not all elements in material culture, nor all the elements of technological equipment found among nonliterate peoples are equally distributed over the world. Some are ubiquitous—techniques of obtaining food, for example, are of necessity a part of the equipment of all societies. Such a technique as the

---

[4] C. Osgood, 1940, pp. 25–6.
[5] Op. cit., passim.

making and use of fire, which is not essential to survival, is, with the exception of one or two instances such as the inhabitants of the Andaman Islands in the Bay of Bengal, present in all human cultures. The building of shelters is widespread, but by no means universal, and the same is true of clothing, though there are few peoples who do not cover some portion of the body on certain occasions. Other technical processes, for a variety of reasons, have still more restricted distributions. In some instances, the habitat lays its prohibition, as it does for basketry or wood-carving in the arctic. Sometimes considerations of utility enter, as is evidenced by the almost complete absence of pottery vessels among nomadic peoples. Skin containers, or baskets, are light in weight and reduce the hazards of breakage to a minimum. On occasion historical reasons explain why the distribution of a given technique is restricted, as in the instance of iron-working, which was developed in the Old World but was never worked out in the Western Hemisphere.

Irrespective of their material equipment and technological knowledge, certain principles of universal applicability may be abstracted from the data gathered widely and from many peoples. First, every society has worked out a material culture and techniques of exploiting the natural resources of its habitat that provide the basis for those other nonmaterial aspects of the culture that lie predominantly outside this realm. Second, in exploiting the resources of their habitat, every group evinces a hard-headed approach to the problem this presents. They so act in accordance with the physical principles involved that it becomes evident that their techniques are based on processes of inference from cause to effect, that these techniques demonstrate ingenuity and inventiveness, and that the people are quite able to profit from the method of trial and error.

We have commented earlier on the soundness of the reasoning with which "primitive" man approaches his practical problems, and how in this he manifests no special type of mentality that inhibits his powers of reasoning objectively where questions of utility, to say nothing of survival, are at issue. For example, skills such as are involved in making a boomerang or a compound bow are displayed by peoples whose "level of culture," as this is phrased, is low indeed. Or, we scarcely expect to find the pygmies of the Congo forests constructing suspension bridges, but they do. Without a knowledge of swimming and lacking any form of river-craft, they negotiate passage across a stream by utilizing a ropelike vine to swing one of their number across, who carries the first cord that will later be reinforced so as to permit the structure to be completed. Again, some of the more complex achievements of science have their parallels among nonliterate peoples. Examples often cited are the precision of the Maya calendar or the architectural skills of the pre-Spanish Peruvian structures. Not so well known is the indigenous practice among certain African tribes of smallpox vaccination; or that the Polynesians, who navigated their small craft over great distances, employed charts made of rattan which indicated prevailing winds and currents and thus incorporated full sailing directions.

The picture of nonliterate man we draw from studying his technology and material culture is of a hard-working individual who effectively calls on the

Technology and the Utilization of Natural Resources

skills which he draws from his enculturative experience, skills that are adequate to gain him the living he desires. Understandably, few members of any group, literate or nonliterate, are creative enough perceptibly to change its way of life. But nonliterate man, like men who live in literate societies, is neither automaton nor infantile. He is practical, seeing an advantage when it is presented to him—provided it not be too far removed from the technological patterns of his culture—and using it if he is convinced that it will accomplish the results that he desires.

2

Foodstuffs are of two kinds, animal and plant. These are used either in their wild state, or in a state of domestication. The fourfold classification that results from these alternatives is so important that it was for a long time used as the basis for distinguishing the different economic systems of nonliterate peoples, in this manner:

Economy	Foods
food-gathering	plant—wild
hunting	animal—wild
herding	animal—domesticated
agriculture (*cultivation*)	plant—domesticated

The order in which these are given was believed to be that sequence in which the economies of human societies evolved. We must defer a discussion of this aspect of the problem until later pages; here it will be sufficient to quote Forde's caution, that "People do not live at economic stages. They possess economies; and again we do not find single and exclusive economies but combinations of them." The classification he substitutes for the systems conventionally named are collecting, hunting, fishing, cultivation, and stock-raising.[6] His stress on the fact that none of these is exclusive in any society is most important.

This follows from the nature of dietary requirements. A diet restricted to meat would be monotonous indeed. Even the Eskimo, forced by the circumstance of their habitat to eat nothing else during the long winter, in summer become food-gatherers, and institutionalize the change by tabooing the eating of the sea-mammals whose flesh comprises their food-resources most of the year. It is difficult to think of any people, even with a well advanced agricultural system, who do not supplement their garden produce by hunting; while, conversely, the hunting Plains Indians raised some maize, and the herders of East Africa have imposed their use of cattle on an agricultural subsistence economy. As in all aspects of culture, we find that clear-cut classifications are difficult, if not impossible to achieve. Man draws on the food resources at hand, and employs the techniques that are known to him. He is rarely committed to any one way of doing anything.

[6] D. Forde, 1934, p. 461.

The Aspects of Culture

There can be little question that in the history of mankind, gathering, hunting, and fishing existed long before herding or cultivation. This is well established by the archaeological evidence, which, as we have seen, dates the domestication of plants and animals at about the beginning of the Neolithic. Before that time, life was lived on the basis of finding and utilizing the foods offered by the habitat, with no way to control the supply except insofar as there was knowledge of the location of roots, nuts, and berries, or of the habits of game animals. There are many peoples who, to the present, have food economies based on one or the other of these techniques—that is, who have neither domesticated plants nor domesticated food animals. Among those who are primarily gatherers are the Indians of the California and Great Basin areas, the peoples having "marginal" cultures in the eastern and southern open country of South America, the pygmies of Central Africa and elsewhere, the aboriginal inhabitants of the Andaman Islands. Hunting peoples include the Eskimo, most of the Canadian Indians and Plains Indians, the South African Bushmen and the Australian aborigines—though these last two are as much food-gatherers as they are hunters.

Food-gathering and hunting economies require technical competence, despite their simplicity. To find and gather wild roots, nuts, seeds, and berries, to hunt or trap the food animals, takes knowledge not only of the terrain but of the most favorable times, and the best conditions under which to obtain these foods, to say nothing of preserving them for future use. The life of the wild rice gatherers of the Upper Great Lakes strikingly demonstrates this. Out of the study of these people, furthermore, has come the principle that the food of gatherers and hunters "varies with the season of the year and the section of the country in which they are," so that "they frequently live on one staple at a time." [7] During March, April, and May these Indians lived principally on the maple sugar they made, then they ate early berries, and later green corn. In the autumn and later, the wild rice that was stored for early winter use was consumed. During the spring and summer they supplemented their diet with the wild fowl to be found in the rice fields; in the late winter they subsisted on the meat of the animals they hunted, and pemmican, a compound of dried meat and berries.

Peoples who live on what their habitat yields must command more than a knowledge of the location of edible plants or the habits of wild animals. They must have containers for what they gather; they need traps, snares, spears, bows and arrows, nets, and other paraphernalia for hunting and fishing. The list of material objects we have already quoted from Osgood provides us with one example of how many things such an economy requires. It will be recalled that this hunting-gathering-fishing Athapascan people make fifteen different kinds of lines, forty-one types of containers, twenty-three fishing implements, twelve types of snares, deadfalls and other traps; while of the twenty-nine types of structures described, eleven are designed for smoking fish and storing foodstuffs for later use.

The number of animals that has been domesticated is relatively few, and

---

[7] A. E. Jenks, 1900, pp. 1095–7.

most herding economies are based primarily on the predominance of a single one of these forms. The principal domesticated animals are the horse, ox, reindeer, camel, and sheep, and like all the domesticated types except the llama, vicuña, and turkey, were domesticated in the Old World, to which their aboriginal distribution was confined. Reindeer form the basis of the economies of most Old World peoples living in the circumpolar zone, from Lapland to eastern Siberia, while on the Asiatic steppes to the south, horses, and in East Africa, cattle predominate. In the Sahara and Arabian deserts, the camel and the horse are the principal animals. Most herding folk have sheep, and other smaller forms, which furnish them with food to supplement the yield from the larger animals. The camel and the horse, however, are rarely if ever sources of meat.

In contrast to the limited number of animals that have been domesticated, the number of domesticated plants is legion. In every region where cultivation is practised, certain cereals form the basis of the food economy. Students speak of three principal agricultural areas. The first includes Europe, northern Africa, and the Near East, where wheat, oats, and barley are the most important crops. The second, where rice predominates, comprehends Asia, Malaysia, and Indonesia. The third, or maize area, is the New World. Africa is more eclectic, with maize and millet and yams and cassava today all having important places in the food economy of various parts of the continent. In Polynesia, taro, yams, bread-fruit, and sugar cane predominate, no cereals being cultivated.

The rich contribution of the New World to the inventory of domesticated plants differs markedly, it should be noted, from the few domesticated animals the Indians developed. Maize, cacao, various kinds of beans, manioc, peanuts, pineapples, potatoes, pumpkins, squash, sweet potatoes, tobacco, and tomatoes are only the best known from a list of more than thirty such plant contributions.

The techniques of cultivation are numerous. The simplest agricultural implement is the digging stick, a pointed branch hardened by fire. In Australia its use represents a transition between gathering and cultivation. The women loosen the earth about the roots of the wild tubers to facilitate the growth of the plants. Elsewhere, however, in Africa, the Americas, and the South Seas, the digging stick breaks the earth preparatory to planting and is thus a kind of hoe. In some instances, as among the Maori of New Zealand, or the Zuñi, a cross-piece is attached to the digging stick, or a crotch provides a foot-rest so that the implement can be employed as a crude spade.

Hoes represent a vast improvement. They are essentially an Old World tool. The African broad-bladed, short-handled iron hoe contrasts with the European long-handled, narrow-bladed implement. When placed in the competent hands of an experienced user, it is almost as effective for breaking the ground as a plow, particularly because of the force with which it strikes the earth, and the volume of dirt turned with each stroke. The plow, which puts the domesticated animal to work, is a Euro-Asiatic implement and is not found elsewhere.

Many nonliterate cultivators fully recognize that continuous use of a plot of ground exhausts the soil. Where land is plentiful, this presents no problem, since new gardens can be prepared from virgin soil. Where land is not plentiful, however, a technique used especially in tropical countries is to burn off

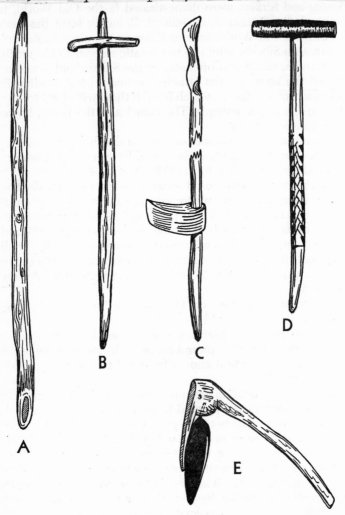

Fig. 20   *Agricultural implements.* (A) *Australian digging-stick (length 3¾ ft.)*; (B) *Cowichan hafted digging-stick (length 3 ft.)*; (C) *Maori dibble with foot-rest (length 5 ft.)*; (D) *Thompson Indian dibble (length 2½ ft.)*; (E) *African (Nigerian) broad-bladed hoe (length of handle 20 in.).*

the growth of the preceding year to supply ash as fertilizer for the next crop. The Indians of eastern United States who planted their maize in hills, put a fish in each hill as fertilizer. These Indians also practised multiple planting. In each hill squash and bean seeds were placed, so that the bean plants might climb the corn stalks and the squash vines run along the ground. The same principle is operative in West Africa, where gourds take the place of squashes. The native theory that governs this practice indicates how inductively native peoples reason about such matters. They hold that a plant that grows erect, one that climbs, and one that hugs the earth each takes different foods from the ground—a deduction not too far at variance with the principles of soil chemistry. Notable techniques in growing crops are irrigation and terracing. An outstanding example of irrigation is found in the American Southwest, where it has been practised since early pre-Spanish times. The terracing of the nonliterate peoples of the Philippines has been discussed in an earlier chapter. Another group who produced remarkable examples of terracing as an aid to agriculture are the inhabitants of the Andean highlands.

Whether plants or animals were domesticated first is a question that has aroused much controversy. Its theoretical importance comes from its bearing on the hypothesis of stages in the development of food economies for, obviously, if the sequence gathering-hunting-herding-agriculture is valid, the domestication of animals must have preceded that of plants. Various researches, however, seem to indicate that the domestication of animals succeeded the beginnings of agriculture. Another unresolved question is how plants and animals came to be domesticated. It is reasonable to assume that the domestication of plants may well have followed upon the astute observation of some unknown culture-hero—or, more likely, heroine—of how dropped seed reproduce themselves. As for the domestication of animals, the answers range between two extremes—that the earliest animals to be domesticated freely associated themselves with man, or that man conceived the idea of domestication and experimented until he achieved the desired result. It is quite possible that both of these processes were involved. What we know is that practically all the domesticated animals were brought to the service of man in a very short period of time. Once this was accomplished, few others susceptible of living under domestication, and complying with its conditions, have since been discovered.

One result of the domestication of animals seems to have been to bring men prominently into the field of agricultural activities. The invention of the plow appears to have involved a far-reaching reorientation in deepseated patterns of sex division of labor. For if it is not uniformly true that cultivators everywhere assign the work of growing crops to women, it is a fact that nowhere is plow culture carried on except by men. To understand this relationship it is necessary to consider the presumed patterns of sex division of labor antedating the period of domestication. Hunting was clearly the work of men rather than of women, while, conversely, food-gathering, that permitted the women to remain nearer home, was probably more in consonance with the requirements of their childbearing and child-rearing functions.

With the development of domestication of plants and animals, women seem to have extended their gathering activities so as to perform the work of caring for the crops, while men assumed care of the larger animals as an extension of their earlier preoccupation with these forms in the wild. Whether

251

men in those early days also took over the hard labor of breaking the ground and preparing it for planting cannot be said. Most societies today assign this work to men. The discovery of the plow that called for a domesticated animal to pull it, posed the problem either of the transfer of the beast, whose care was in the male sphere of the economy, to the economic sphere of women, or of agricultural work, heretofore the concern of women, to that of men. The latter is what did occur. The world over, in plow-cultures, women have a minor role in agriculture, whereas in cultures where the plow is not used, their role is a dominant one.

3

THOUGH a food supply is indispensable, it is quite possible to get along without *shelter*. Not many peoples, it is true, omit this item from their cultural equipment, but it always surprises the novice in the study of culture to what a minimum it can successfully be reduced. There is ample documentation of the position that shelter is primarily a means of adapting existence to the demands of habitat, if contradictory data are not scrutinized too closely, and if the principle of the limiting role played by the habitat, that was advanced in our discussion of the relationship between culture and its natural setting, is not borne in mind.

That a rough correlation does exist between habitat and shelter must be readily granted. Where extremes of temperature exist, the limits of human endurance make imperative demands on the peoples who inhabit such climates. The Siberian Chukchee and the Eskimo can function under conditions of extreme cold that not only astound the visitor from warmer regions, but would be beyond his endurance if he tried to imitate them. Bogoras tells of Chukchee women sitting out of doors sewing without gloves when the temperature was at its winter's arctic lowest. That the hands should be so exposed is sufficient cause for remark; but it must not be overlooked that the rest of the body was warmly clothed, and that a skin tent stood nearby to provide shelter when it was felt this was needed. Similarly in the tropics, there is frequent comment on the imperviousness of the inhabitants to the rays of the sun. Again, habituation to a tropical milieu does undoubtedly make the indigenous dweller better able to resist the sun than those who come from more temperate zones. Nonetheless, the student will soon observe that little work is done at midday, and that natives then seek the shade of a tree, or the dark coolness of a thatched hut, until the period of the most severe heat has passed. In actuality, we find that the minimum of shelter necessary to preserve life is much less than casual consideration would indicate. Conversely, the maximum degree of shelter attained by most societies is so much greater than necessary for survival that we must seek other reasons to account for it.

Absence of constructed shelters marks the life of those peoples whose cultures are the poorest technologically, and who inhabit areas where the materials are lacking out of which shelters can readily be constructed. Cer-

Technology and the Utilization of Natural Resources

tain South African Bushmen tribes inhabit caves, or live in rock-shelters. The Australian aborigines use fire-screens to give them some shelter. This is a shield of skin attached to two sticks that are placed upright in the ground, so as to shield from the wind those who huddle between the skin and the fire. Both these folk inhabit desert areas, but let no one imagine that a desert environment cannot be cold. Such habitats are rather marked by wide fluctuations in their temperature, so that one can be as uncomfortable in the cold of the night as in the heat of the day. Rain, when it does come, is not too much of a problem, even though it can cause discomfort, for those not burdened with clothing are less troubled by rain than persons in wet, clinging clothes.

The saving grace of all these situations, as where shelters of pitiful adequacy are erected by pygmy folk of Africa and elsewhere, or by societies of North and South America, is a knowledge of the use of *fire*. This aspect of the technology, which we have noted to be a well-nigh universal possession of mankind, is as important in affording protection against the elements as it is in making possible the preparation and preservation of foodstuffs. Its revolutionary role in the life of man is widely recognized. A vast number of myths recount the bringing of fire by a culture-hero. Many peoples assign ritual significance to the hearth-stone, and a rich imagery accompanies the symbolism of an undying fire. The use of matches, and even of flint, have so improved technical competence in fire-making that no one who has not attempted to use the methods of most nonliterate peoples can guess how difficult it is to make fire without them. Those who use these methods do not underestimate the task, however, as witness the fact that many peoples carry coals with them on a journey, and take the greatest pains to insure that once a fire has been started, it will not be allowed to die out.

Two basic methods are employed to make fire. Harrison classifies these as the wood-friction method, which predominates, and the percussion method. The former is of three types, "boring or *drilling* one piece of wood into another, . . . rubbing or *ploughing* along the grain, and . . . *sawing* across the grain." The first is the most often encountered. Harrison describes it in the following terms: "The essential feature of all fire-drills is that one piece of wood, cylindrical or flattened in form, which is usually spoken of as the *hearth*, is held horizontally on the ground, whilst another piece, always circular in section, which may be called the *drill-stick*, is twirled rapidly with its lower end pressed into a shallow pit previously made in the hearth. The wood-dust produced by the friction is ignited, after a period varying in length according to the nature and condition of the wood used, and the method and skill of the operator. . . . In most cases, drill-stick and hearth are made of different kinds of wood, one being harder than the other; both parts of the apparatus must be very dry, and sometimes the parts where the friction occurs are intentionally charred beforehand, though when the pits have been previously used some charring will have already occurred. The drill is often thicker towards the bottom, than at the top, so that greater downward pressure may be applied during the twirling." Harrison adds a comment whose validity can be attested by all who have tried to use fire-

The Aspects of Culture

sticks: "A great deal of the skill in fire-making by this means lies in bringing the hands back to the top of the stick so rapidly that the drill scarcely comes to rest before the twirling begins again, no time being allowed for the bearing to get cool."[8]

A variant of the drilling method is the bow-drill, where a bow-cord is wound about the drilling stick, while pressure is applied by means of a socket into which the top of this stick fits, held by the hand, or in the mouth, as

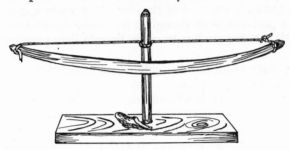

FIG. 21   Bow-drill.

among the Eskimo. The fire-plow is identified with Polynesia, the fire-saw with Malaysia, though both have wider distributions. Percussion usually employs flint and tinder, though Harrison reports the use of bamboo in southeast Asia, two pieces of which are struck together to obtain a spark, or a fragment of china and a length of bamboo are used.

Let us return now to the contribution fire-making has made to the increased effectiveness of shelter. Though the Australian fire-screen shields a person from the wind, it is the fire on his other side that protects him from the cold. Mountford[9] recounts how the aborigines, when travelling through the night, carry "blazing fire sticks" to help them support the bitter low temperatures they encounter. In the forests of tropical South America, where the nights can be chilly indeed, especially in the rainy season, the natives sling their hammocks inside their shelters over a bed of coals or a low fire. The snugness of the Eskimo igloo is enhanced by its blubber-lamp, the smoke of the fire in the African's thatched house keeps the insects away. Without fire, indeed, the effectiveness of housing would be immeasurably reduced. Structures would do no more than give protection from the elements where, in warm and temperate zones, people could huddle, miserable from the cold, while areas with extremely cold climates would be forbidden to them.

As we have indicated, the simplest shelters are the cave, the wind-break, the hut. More complex types are to be differentiated as to materials, design, and permanence. They vary between the simple skin tent of the American Indian or the wooden lean-to erected in many parts of the world, and the truly architectural structures of Peru and Mexico, West Africa and Indonesia. In North America are found the wigwam and tipi, tents covered with birch-bark and skins respectively, the multi-family dwellings of the southwestern

[8] H. S. Harrison, 1925, pp. 32–4.
[9] C. P. Mountford, 1946, p. 99.

Technology and the Utilization of Natural Resources

Pueblos, the dug-out, or half-underground sod-covered dwelling used by the Mandan of the Upper Missouri and other tribes, the plank house of the Northwest coast, the Iroquois long house. In South and Central America, structures humbler than the monumental achievements of the Peruvian and Mexican builders are the lean-to and the beehive hut of the south; the thatched dwelling of the Guianas; the communal structure of the Amazonian tribes, made with timbered framework and covering space up to 10,000 square feet; and the simple rectangular dwelling of the mountainous areas. The thatched rectangular or round house characterizes Polynesia, but in Melanesia a great variety of types exists, from the lean-to to the great gable-roofed men's house, with the front peak of its roof sometimes rising to a height of more than a hundred feet. Africa runs the gamut from the simple beehive type shelter of the Hottentots, consisting of poles bent over to intersect at the top as a framework for a covering of skins, through the thatched round houses of East Africa and the rectangular ones of the western part of the continent, to the architectural structures of such Sudanese cities as Kano and Timbuctoo, where the arch and the dome were known and liberally incorporated in buildings made of sun-dried, plastered brick.

It is customary to think and write of most nonliterate folk as though their cultures were characterized each by a single house-type. This again simplifies what is, if not a complex matter, at least one which offers alternatives. In many tribes, the kind of housing depends on the season, or the function a given kind of dwelling is to fulfil. The Mandan half-underground house, like the Eskimo igloo, gives way to the skin tent for summer use. Men and women may inhabit quite different kinds of houses, especially where men have a communal dwelling, while women live with their children in individual shelters. Nor is the term dwelling by any means synonymous with shelter, or building. We speak of the magnificence of Central American structures, or those of the "lost" civilizations of Malaysia. Yet these were not dwellings at all. They symbolized the power of the ruler, the splendor with which the gods were worshipped. It will be remembered that the point was made, in introducing our discussion of housing, that men build for less tangible reasons than mere protection against the elements. Reasons of prestige enter here, and aesthetic motivations, as shown by the decorations that are so frequently lavished on all kinds of structures. More than this, and not to be overlooked, are the emotional ties that bind men and women to their places of residence and cause them to regard their dwellings as havens of security and often sources of beauty, because of the symbolic significance that results from life-long attachment.

4

Clothing can be either sewed and fitted to the contours of the body, in which case it is tailored; or it may consist of materials loosely draped or thrown over the human frame, in the form of ponchos, togas, great-cloths, or other coverings. As we have stated, there is no essential correlation between the amount of clothing worn by a people and the nature of their habitat. In the main, however, it is possible to generalize that tailored—that is, fitted—clothing is found among aboriginal peoples who live in colder areas, while draped cloths are used by peoples who inhabit warmer regions.

Clothing requires materials that are pliant and reasonably soft. It is also desirable to make clothing out of stuffs that lend themselves readily to stitching or painting, or to which decorative objects can be attached. The available materials seem to be quite few—or, at least, man has employed only a limited variety of goods for his clothing. These are woven fabrics, skins, and barkcloth. Exceptions are especially found in the materials of ritual garb, or of garments that are marks of status, as, for example, feather-capes, or capes made of finely-woven matting, or the metal armour of the mediaeval knight, or armour made of thick spiked fish skin, such as is worn by the warriors of the New Britain archipelago.

With a few exceptions, as where leaves and grasses are employed, we find that none of the materials that clothe mankind can be used in its natural state, so that various processes must be employed to fit them for use as clothing. The most complex of these are the processes whereby cloth is manufactured. Cloth is woven from threads, which in turn must be spun from fibres of some kind, either animal or vegetable. Sheep and goats in the Old World, llamas and vicuñas in South America, are the principal sources of animal fibres. Cotton and flax are those most widely employed of vegetable derivation. Dirt and other extraneous material, and the seeds of the cotton, are first removed, after which the mass is "carded" by means of a kind of combing process that causes the fibres to be approximately parallel to each other.

The fibres must now be spun into yarn. This is done in various ways, but the essential technique is one whereby the fibres are twined together so that they make a continuous cord. This twisting process gives strength to the resultant yarn. The simplest method, widely distributed among nonliterate peoples, is to roll the fibres on the thigh. The cord is gathered on a spindle, which supplies the tension needed to make thread of varying degrees of fineness. Spindles are twirled by twisting with the hand, and are usually weighted with clay or a piece of heavy wood, or a shell or bone or stone disk, to provide continuous motion and even tension.

Yarn is made into cloth by the process of weaving, a process also employed in mat-making and basketry. Essentially the difference between matting and cloth is that the latter is manufactured from fibres that have been spun, while the former consists of intertwined materials of a flat, strip-like nature. Though some delicately woven Polynesian mats become soft and pliant after laundering, in the main mats have a coarser texture than cloth. The distinction between them cannot always be drawn in absolute terms, since such a material as the pile-cloth made of grass by the Bushongo tribe in the Congo takes on all the characteristics of materials woven of yarn.

The loom is the prime implement in cloth-making. It consists of a frame across which parallel strands of yarn—the warp—are stretched. The weft threads are then inserted at right angles between these strands, once over and once under, or in any combination of strands over and under. Warp-

256

Technology and the Utilization of Natural Resources

strands customarily are placed vertically or, if the loom is parallel to the ground, stretch away from the weaver. In the simplest looms the warp-strands are free, but it apparently did not take long for weavers to discover that they could save much time by attaching half—or any required number—of warp threads to an arrangement whereby they could be raised by one motion, leaving a clear space through which the yarn could be passed. In still more complex looms, this is accomplished by attaching the rod by which the strands are elevated or depressed to a foot-pedal, or treadle. A sword,

Fig. 22 *Simple loom used with twilling stick* (*Cowichan tribe of Pacific Northwest, North America*).

or beater, is often passed through the space thus made. By turning it on its side, it enlarges the opening through which the weft strand passes, its edge is used to press down each cross-strand on the preceding ones, so as to give the finished cloth a firmer texture. In many looms of nonliterate folk, too, a shuttle is employed to carry the weft-strand across the warp. Sometimes this is no more than a stick to which the weft is attached—in which case it is used like a large needle—or about which it is wound. Sometimes, however, it encloses a spool that permits the weft-yarn to be payed out as the shuttle is passed across the loom.

Skins must be dressed before they can be used for any purpose that re-quires a pliant material. In many instances, skins are pegged on the ground, so that the hair may be shaved or cut off. Accretions of meat and fat, and the inner layers of the skin itself, that if left would render the resultant material too unwieldy, are also removed, sometimes by an adze-like process of chip-ping that leaves only the outermost layer. Sometimes the skin is soaked in materials containing wood-ash, that supply a natural alkali. More often the tanning process is carried out by rubbing the skin with brain tissue, and working it either with the hands, or with the use of an instrument such as an iron or wooden beater, or even chewing it until the fibres are loosened and it is quite soft. The skin of almost any animal can be treated in this manner, considerations of size being most important where clothing is concerned, as

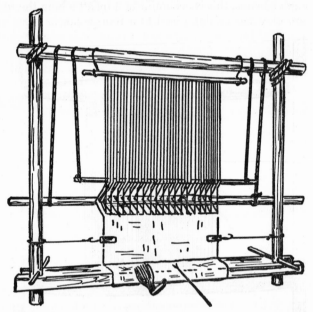

FIG. 23　*Loom with treadle (Arabs of North Africa).*

it is desirable to make as much of a garment from a single skin as possible, in view of the difficulty of sewing leather.

Bark-cloth, best known in the tapa-cloth made by the Polynesians, is derived from the inner bark of certain trees whose fibres cross each other at right angles, as do the warp and weft of true cloth. It is found only in the South Seas, central Africa, and tropical South America, where the requisite trees grow. The manufacture of bark-cloth is relatively simple. The bark is first soaked in water. It is then beaten to loosen the fibres, and in some instances to separate it into layers, since its texture is such that it can produce a cloth of lacy fineness. Beating also spreads out the bark, thinning it at the same time it gains a firmer texture. Beaters either take the form of clubs, as in the South Seas, or hammers, as in Africa. Their macerating effect is increased by the grooves that are cut at right angles across the working surfaces; the cloth is usually beaten on a smoothed hard log rather than on stone. The resulting material is soft, and becomes softer with washing. It lends itself readily to decoration, as is evidenced by the painted and block-printed designs on South Seas tapa-cloth displayed in most ethnographic museum collections.

Technology and the Utilization of Natural Resources

Though there are few cultures where more than one of these materials is not used for clothing, it is rare to find a culture where one or the other of them is not predominant. Textiles are woven in Africa, in Mexico, Central America, and the Andean highlands, and in Eurasia except in the arctic and steppe areas, where skin clothing is found. Skins also predominate in the southern parts of Africa, among the Hottentot and Ovambo and Ovaherrero. In the American arctic and sub-arctic, and in the Plains area, skin clothing is tailored, while in the wooded region east and southeast of this, and in southeastern South America, skin robes prevail. Elsewhere, clothing is not worn at all, or is rudimentary, consisting of a loin-cloth, or other brief covering of the genital organs or other portions of the body which custom

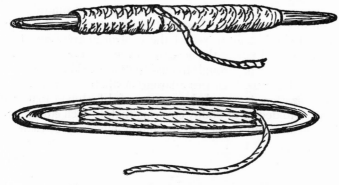

Fig. 24 *Simple shuttle; spool shuttle.*

requires be concealed. Where temperatures are high, clothing may be held to a minimum while a person is at work. This does not militate against his wearing a substantial amount of clothing at other times, or when his rank requires it, as in parts of West Africa, where the man's cloth, made of native cotton or of silk and worn like a toga, is seven or eight feet long and four or five feet wide and has an appreciable weight.

The problem of why clothing is worn cannot be answered by any simple formula. We have but to consider the canons of taste, of conduct, of occasion that rule the use of clothing in our own society to make this clear. As with housing, there is, of course, a rough correlation with the nature of the habitat. Yet convention on occasion seems to defy requirements of this sort, as is clear when we consider the long skin mantle of the tribes of Tierra del Fuego, and contemplate the pitifully inadequate protection it affords against the penetrating cold of this region. Or one need not stray far from home to see how inappropriate, from this point of view, is the clothing of women in our culture, worn on formal occasions on the coldest nights, or conversely, the formal dress of men on hot summer evenings.

Of equal—perhaps even of greater—importance than the function of clothing in facilitating the adaptation of man to his habitat, is its association with sex. Here it plays a dual role, providing as in the obverse and reverse of the same shield, those mechanisms that channel the mating drive, and take the form of *modesty* and *coquetry*. As with all cultural phenomena, the variation in their expression is endless. But wherever clothing is worn, the sexes are distinguished by their garments. These garments—or the ornamentation of the human body by such means as scarification, or tattooing, or hair-dressing —are everywhere held to enhance the physical attractiveness of the individual, by giving to the body a means of concealment, or of heightened aesthetic appeal that stimulates this powerful inherent drive.

There are also a number of other reasons why clothing is worn. Where class differences exist, clothing marks off the individual who commands position and means from those of inferior status. This prestige factor can be expressed in various ways. Clothing of those in positions of power and rank may be more lavishly decorated than that of others, as with the feather-capes of the Hawaiian nobles; or may be of a different type from others, as in all armies, where the uniforms of officers differ from those of the common soldier; or may, in subtlest form, reflect the control of resources by extreme simplicity and restraint where the accepted means of display are within the reach of all. By extension, through the association of clothing both with the sex drive and with status, it carries a strong aesthetic appeal that, however much a rationalization, is nonetheless a powerful factor in maintaining the patterned form and degree of bodily covering that, in each culture, influences the reactions of men and women to the fellow-members of their society.

5

OTHER than weaving, the crafts most often found in the nonliterate world are basketry, and pottery-making. Neither of these techniques, with the possible exception of basketry, has anything like the universality of those which implement the needs for food and shelter, or even of clothing. It must not be assumed, however, that this exhausts the list of the technological resources of nonliterate man. He works stone, wood, metal, and leather; he has developed medical skills that extend to surgery, and he practises the arts of navigation.

Baskets and pots can be put to many uses. It is plausible that before either technique was devised, man had recourse to natural objects, such as skins, gourds, shells, and similar containers for his belongings. Peoples like the Australians or the Bushmen, who today do not make either pottery or basketry, employ such objects as their habitat affords them for these purposes. The most striking instance of this is the use of ostrich-egg shells by the Bushmen to store water.

Basketry is made by three processes, called weaving, twining or twilling, and coiling. If the material used in weaving a basket is broad and flat, the product may have a checker-board design, since there is little that can be done in weaving such strands except to pass them alternately over and under. The ordinary American fruit-basket or market-basket is of this type, and is the lineal descendant of the baskets made by the Indians of the Northeastern part of the United States. When narrow strands are used,

Technology and the Utilization of Natural Resources

however, the weaving may be very complex indeed, as is to be seen in the patterns introduced by Amazonian and Guiana Indians into the tray-like cassava-meal sifters they manufacture. Twilled or twined baskets are made by weaving pliant strands about a framework of twigs or other rigid materials. Twining can be done so finely and tightly that baskets can be made by this process to hold water. In such cases, it should be noted, the basket may pass out of the container category and become a cooking vessel, since water can be boiled in such baskets by the simple device of dropping heated stones in the water. Wissler notes that in North America most of the tribes who use the twining and coiling techniques in making their baskets are "stone boilers."

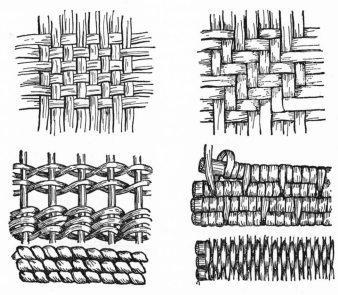

Fig. 25   *Details of basketry-making techniques: weaving; twining; coiling.*

Coiled baskets are sometimes termed sewn basketry, because of the technique of making them. This is made clear in the description given by Mason of how they are manufactured by California Indians: "The elements are a stiff root or rod for the fundamental coil, and a soft splint or strip of the same material for the sewing. In making her basket, the woman starts in the centre of the bottom, coiling the rod and wrapping it as she proceeds with the split root or rattan, so as to bind it to the preceding turn, drawing her splint between the spirals. When the rod comes to an end, she neatly splices the end to that of a new one and proceeds as before, carefully concealing the joint. When the splint is exhausted, the end is tucked in behind the spiral and another one started in the same manner, but so carefully joined as to defy detection." [10] Sometimes the "rod," as Mason terms the foundation, is a bundle of twigs or grasses, about which the wrapping material is passed in

[10] O. T. Mason, 1895, p. 235.

such a way that each turn takes a stitch through some of the preceding coil, thus anchoring the whole firmly together. In the New World the California Indians are notable for the quality of their sewn baskets; this form predominates in Africa, where outstanding examples are also found. This type of basketry has great flexibility. There are, for example, limitations on the size of woven or twined baskets, but coiled basketry is produced that ranges from miniature specimens to such forms as the Pima storage-basket, which is large enough to hold a man.

It is not difficult to envisage how early man, by intertwining grasses and twigs, came to the discovery of basketry. To discover pottery, however, was quite another matter, for as with iron-working, the finished product can only result after several operations, whose relationship to each other and to the resulting utensil is by no means obvious. The first step in making a pot is to find clay which contains sand or some other siliceous material, but no stones. This is then kneaded to give it the proper consistency, after which it is shaped to form the desired vessel. This step presents no problem, nor the next, in which it is allowed to dry. It can now be handled, but is still useless, since the dry clay will shred at the touch like the dried mud of a river-bed in summertime, or will disintegrate if exposed to water. It must, therefore, be fired—baked in a fire to fuse the siliceous sand or other materials used as a binder with the clay to make the final porous, water and heat resistant utensil. The firing is a critical test of the potter's skill, since too much heat will crack a pot, while too little will leave it soft and brittle.

Once this step has been achieved, the clay has been transformed into a material that is durable, despite the ease with which the objects made out of it can be broken. Broken pottery produces only potsherds, that never return to clay, but remain without further alteration for an indefinite time. This is why pottery is so important for the archaeologist. Given a pottery-making people, the shards they leave behind them tell much about the nature and contacts of their culture. Pottery remains, for example, allowed Reisner, in his excavations at Karma, on the Upper Nile, to reconstruct the history of the contacts this outpost of Egypt had with the Nubians, and to tell the story of how these contacts influenced the technique of both Egyptians and Nubians, bringing into existence new pottery forms.[11] Similarly, the study of pottery has permitted the New World archaeologists to tell the tale of the successive civilizations of the Andean and South American West Coast regions, that culminated in the ceramic and other achievements of the Inca Empire; or of the development of Pueblo culture in the southwestern part of the United States.[12]

The distribution of pottery is restricted by various factors we have already mentioned. It is not found at all in Polynesia, for coral islands provide no materials from which it can be made. If the South Sea Islanders had knowledge of it at one time, it must soon have died out in the new habitat. As far as is known, few peoples with simple technologies possess pottery. It was probably never known in Australia and Tasmania, and is lacking in

[11] G. A. Reisner, 1923, Ch. XXXII.
[12] P. S. Martin, G. I. Quimby and D. Collier, 1947, Part IV.

most pygmy groups and in the simpler North and South American cultures. Its quality, where it is made, varies from extremely crude, soft products, as in certain parts of New Guinea, to the technically perfect pottery made in the Andes, Central America, Mexico, and the southwestern part of the United States. Indeed, the pottery of these regions, which include such technical tours-de-force as the polychrome portrait jars of pre-Spanish Peru, rank among some of the finest ceramic achievements of any culture.

Hand-made pottery is fashioned in three ways, by molding, by modelling, and by coiling. Molded pottery, the least frequently encountered, is made by spreading the clay over a basket or an old pot in order to give it the desired shape. Potsherds which show the indentations of basketry molds, recovered in pueblos of pre-Spanish occupancy, demonstrate that this was long practised in the New World; and the use of pots as molds is reported from Africa. Modelling is far more widely distributed. An example of this technique can be taken from an early report of the process as observed among the Hottentots: "The clay was obtained from termite heaps, cleared of sand and gravel, and kneaded together with the ants' eggs mixed in it. A lump was placed on a smooth flat stone and modelled into the shape required. Next it was carefully smoothed inside and outside by hand, and exposed to the sun for a couple of days. When perfectly dry, it was finally put in a hole in the ground and burned by a fire around and inside it, till it was baked through and hard." [13]

Coiled pottery is made by a process first of pinching a rope-like length of clay on to a base, and then by continuing the process so as to build up the vessel until it has the desired shape and size. The Southwest has provided many examples of this. A very small coil, pinched on with consistent force and at regular intervals can result in a design that is not unpleasant. Generally, however, the pinching is smoothed over with the hand or by the use of some wooden or other kind of spatula, and no sign of the process remains in the finished pot.

One of the remarkable facts about the pottery that is the product of nonliterate cultures is the sureness with which the potters shape their vessels. Not only do they achieve a perfect circular form without the use of any measuring device, but their vessels are so shaped as to be objects quite as much of aesthetic as of utilitarian value. This quality of aesthetic form arises only after training that betokens careful observation and effective use of resources, and which yields motor skills that permit the play of such creative ability as the potter may have. Here, however, we move out of the field of technology and into that of art. We may, therefore, defer any discussion of this phase of pottery-making—or basketry, or weaving, or other elements in material culture that serve as vehicles for artistic expression—until the art of nonliterate man is examined.

The two broadest categories of pottery-making are those which distinguish pottery made by hand and by the use of the potter's wheel. The potter's wheel, however, is restricted in distribution to the literate cultures of Europe

[13] I. Schapera, 1930, pp. 313-4.

and Asia, and is not found at all in the nonliterate world. Almost everywhere that pottery is produced with the aid of a potter's wheel, men make it, but where it is made by hand, it is woman's work. Here we meet another of those irrationalities in culture that so often confront the student. They are of historical derivation, and document a concept in the study of culture known as *adhesion*—the fact that two apparently unrelated aspects of culture become associated and take on a functional relationship.

To understand this particular instance, we return to the division of labor in early human society, when men hunted the larger game animals while women, remaining nearer home, were occupied with gathering activities. It will be remembered that this association is believed to be the historical and logical antecedent of the fact that while cultivation with hoe or digging-stick is customarily woman's work, plowing is invariably allotted to man's sphere of activity. In the case of pottery, it is not known whether this was initially the work of men or women, but everything points to the conclusion that it was woman's responsibility. The discovery of the wheel occurred during the Neolithic, and seems to have been made in connection with transport. With the wheel, it was possible to utilize domesticated animals to pull carts; and since, as we have seen, the care of the larger domesticated forms is the concern of men, it is understandable how the manufacture and use of wheeled vehicles likewise became their province.

When the utility of the wheel for pottery-making—and for spinning, as well—became apparent, the same choice had to be made as was presented by the discovery of the plow. Either agriculture could remain woman's work, which would bring the domesticated animal that drew the plow into her sphere, or the growing of crops could become man's work. In the case of agriculture, the latter choice was made, and in pottery also. But where the wheel was employed as a device for spinning, the adhesion of this cultural trait, among many peoples, was different. Women retained the spinning and weaving functions, and continued to hold them until the advent of the power loom. But men are potters in the plow-cultures of Eurasia; elsewhere women make the pottery. The logic of this is the logic of history, and its implications present some of the more difficult problems with which the student of culture must cope.

Of such techniques as metal-working and wood-carving we need only make mention. Metal-working for other than aesthetic and prestige ends was a rarity among the nonliterate peoples of the New World, despite the skills in fashioning silver and gold that gave to the empires of Mexico and Peru their fabled quality and in the end aroused the cupidity of the invading Europeans and brought on their downfall. New World metal-work as a distinctive element in technology is thus significant for its aesthetic rather than its utilitarian values.

Old World metal-working began in prehistoric times, with what was long termed the Age of Bronze. Iron-working soon appeared, and is outstanding today in the cultures of most of Africa, and of the nonliterate folk of southern and eastern Asia. So prevalent is the smelting of iron ore among African peoples, and the use of indigenously manufactured iron implements, that it was held for many years that the original discovery of the processes of smelting and forging iron must have been made by the people of that continent. More recent evidence, however, seems to indicate Asia Minor as the region where this occurred. Nonetheless, the distribution of iron-making in Africa is impressive, especially in view of the varied and distinct processes through which particular kinds of ore-bearing rock must be put before they can be transformed into quite different material, which in turn must be heated to allow its being shaped into knives and hoes and spear-heads and pins and many other durable and efficient tools. Small wonder that this knowledge is so frequently kept in the hands of family guilds, whose power is believed to come from the supernatural controls they exercise, quite as much as from their technological knowledge.

CHAPTER 17

Economics and the Fulfilment of Wants

EVERY people have wants that exceed their technological competence. Where technologies are simple and the demands of the habitat rigorous, most of these wants lie in the realm of subsistence. They concern the satisfaction of primary needs such as food and water and protection from wild animals. In societies where the technological base is broader and the habitat presses less closely, needs exist that are outside the survival category. Here psycho-cultural wants develop, that are beyond the range of biological necessities, such as those that arise out of prestige patterns. For the individuals who respond to the urge to satisfy needs of this kind, however, they have all the immediacy of the primary satisfactions that in simpler economies lie on the surface of life.

The problem of maximizing satisfactions through the utilization of "scarce means"—the need to economize in the broadest sense of the term—derives from the basic fact of the existence of wants in excess of the capacity to produce. In societies where a machine technology pours out an abundance of goods, and where an economic system based on the use of money imposes many steps between the producer of goods and the ultimate consumer, the processes are complex indeed. That these complex processes, in machine societies, should have become the principal, if not the exclusive preoccupation of the discipline of economics, is quite understandable. For the student of culture, however, the economic systems of the peoples who live by the machine constitute only one out of the many different ways that man has devised of utilizing scarce means. It is, so to speak, an extreme case, resting at one pole of a series that stretches in an order of diminishing complexity to the societies whose economies are so immediate, so simple, that the problem of survival is paramount.

In broad outline, the economic principles that have been worked out by the economists for our economy hold everywhere. There is no society but has its methods of production, of distribution, of consumption, and some form of exchange; though this may be rudimentary, and take the form of exchange of services rather than of goods. There is no group without some expression of value, even though these concepts may not be formulated in

266

Economics and the Fulfilment of Wants

terms of some commonly accepted monetary symbol. In every society, the maximization of resources is at least implicit in the desires of a people. Some specialization in effort is manifest, some concept of reward for labor is found.

What marks off our economic system from all others is the special relation found between a machine technology and a pecuniary orientation. This relationship has given rise to certain institutions found in no other culture. A unique focussing of economic effort on production for profit rather than for use has had repercussions on all other aspects of life. Technological unemployment is one such result, the business cycle is another; both are intimately related to a system that requires scarcity, artificially produced if necessary, for its functioning. This, in turn, makes it difficult for many persons, without regard to their ability or willingness to perform a required task, to obtain the fundamental necessities of life. In almost all non-machine societies, and in all nonliterate ones, this is unknown. Resources may be meager, and subsistence difficult to obtain, but where there is not enough to go around, all go hungry, as all participate when seasons of plenty provide abundance. "No one ever went hungry," among the Baganda of East Africa, "because everyone was welcome to go and sit down and share a meal with his equals," is a good expression of the tradition, universal among nonliterate folk, that none must be allowed to want in the face of plenty.[1]

The specialization that is a commonplace in our own culture is not found among nonliterate groups, nor are capital goods often controlled by those who do not use them. The former trait represents a difference of degree rather than of kind. Some specialization is found in every culture, if only along the lines of sex division of labor. Experts in some craft or other are to be encountered in all societies, except where the economies are on the level of subsistence, where only enough is produced to provide for basic physiological needs. The control of capital goods by those who profit from them without using them, however, represents a difference of kind. Capital goods, it is true, are concentrated to unequal degrees in the hands of different individuals in nonliterate communities. The economic basis of differences in status is known wherever the technology permits production to rise above subsistence requirements. Thus slavery is found in many nonliterate societies —though this entails considerations of a special kind—and in this case almost always involves personal control of the slave by the master who benefits from his toil. But such an institution as the labor-market, where those without tools or raw materials sell their time and energy to those who control resources and implements, is not found even in cultures where individuals occasionally work for others for pay, using tools not their own. Such work, in nonliterate groups, supplements income; it is not the primary source of income, essential to the existence of the worker.

Other differences between our own economy and the economies of small groups which command simple technological resources may also be mentioned. Money, as we have said, is widely used outside Euroamerican culture, but nowhere does it have so exclusive a function in expressing value.

---

[1] J. Roscoe, 1911, p. 12.

The Aspects of Culture

If to the factors of population mass and specialization of labor we add that of money as a medium of exchange, we arrive at the complexities of the market, with its paraphernalia of credit mechanisms, the interposition of middlemen between producer and consumer, the vastness of the apparatus which channels goods to buyer and reward to producer, and the like. All this, which comes under the head of business enterprise, represents an elaboration of economic phenomena developed to a degree not found elsewhere.

The role of the pecuniary symbol in setting the molds whereby prestige is established has similarly been carried to a point far beyond anything found in any other culture. The importance of the money-symbol has invaded all aspects of our life, and, in consequence, has greatly complicated the task of the economists. Whereas in many societies subsistence and prestige economic systems are distinguished from each other by the use of different symbols of value, or in the differing means of exchange used by the two, or in the ends to which they are put, this does not hold for our culture. Money is the symbol of prestige, as well as the means of acquiring commodities. The prestige dollar or pound sterling or milreis or franc that buys oil paintings or pays for a debut are no different from the tokens with which the humblest citizen buys groceries.

2

INASMUCH as the technological aspects of production have been considered in the preceding chapter, we shall here be concerned with the economic phases of the process—*who* makes *what*, and *why*, rather than *how* things are made. These economic phases tended to be overlooked by earlier anthropologists in favor of descriptions of technical processes, on which we have a wealth of accurately treated and detailed information for tribes living in many parts of the world. Why there was such emphasis on technical processes, to the exclusion of others, is not entirely clear. In part, the reason was the undoubted accessibility of material culture to objective analysis, which rendered it attractive to the field-worker. On the negative side, the almost complete concern of economic science with economic systems of the historic cultures gave the anthropologists no conceptual frame of reference that might give their research direction and their findings meaning. With the passage of time, however, this blind spot in the study of cultural data has come to be corrected, and the need is now fully recognized that economic, as well as technological data, are to be comprehensively collected and analyzed.

Among the stereotypes most widely held about "primitive" man is the belief that he works as little as possible, and that, where natural conditions permit, he works almost not at all. The facts are quite otherwise. Even in the most idyllic settings, men have not rested content with what nature has provided. In most cases, moreover, the setting is by no means idyllic. The knotty problems nonliterate peoples must solve in coping with desert or arctic habitats are obvious, and it is not difficult to see how even the tem-

PLATE 6a   Inca masonry; wall of fortress above Cuzco, Peru.
PLATE 6b   Inca masonry; pre-Spanish walls still used as house-walls in Cuzco. See page
246. [Photograph courtesy Wendell Bennett]

PLATE 7   *Pueblo pot, showing design resulting from even pinching of clay on preceding coil. See page 382. [Photograph by Mary Modglin, Chicago]*

Economics and the Fulfilment of Wants

perate zone, with its changing seasons, presents special problems that call for sustained effort and planning. The tropics, which seem to offer a life of ease, do, in point of fact, provide a harsh, not a benign setting. The dweller in the Amazon forests, the Congo basin, or New Guinea, is beset by many vexations. When he prepares a field, he must clear dense forest growth; as his plants mature, he must protect them against rapidly growing parasitic vines that thrive on tender vegetation; his crops must be guarded from voracious insects, the depredations of wild animals and birds.

The study by Provinse, of the Siang Dyak of Borneo, where the activities of several individuals were studied, provides a good instance of the degree of individual application.[2] His materials are given in several different forms, but the aggregate time spent over a period of twenty-seven days by three men and twenty-eight days by three others, is best shown in the following tabulation:

Activity		Number of Days
Work in rice fields		$60\frac{1}{2}$
working for self	$36\frac{1}{2}$	
working for others	24	
Work in jungle		20
hunting	19	
gathering firewood	1	
Work as medicine-man		$8\frac{1}{2}$
Work at home		18
Total productive time		107
At home, resting		32
At home, sick		18
Travelling		8
Total non-productive time		58
Total		165

The individual records on which this tabulation is based show considerable variation in the amount of work performed by any one person. They also indicate the range of individual differences in the disposal of available time within the limit set by the needs of subsistence. The table given here shows that almost one-third of the total amount of time was spent in tending the principal crop, rice. If to this is added the time spent for hunting, almost one-half of the working hours were devoted to the food-quest, which suggests how much attention must be paid by a people with a relatively simple technological equipment to this basic aspect of their economy. The idea that native peoples are lazy could not better be refuted than by the fact that even if we allot the time spent in travel to non-productive effort, only one-third of the hours recorded were devoted to activities not of economic significance.

Another study that shows how a nonliterate people work comes from the island of Wogeo, off the north coast of New Guinea near the mouth of the

---

[2] J. H. Provinse, 1937, pp. 77–102.

The Aspects of Culture

Sepik River. Hogbin's discussion of this economy [3] includes two schedules of gardening. That given here concerns a clearing made by a man named Waru. This garden "was a level area of 1,300 square yards which when planted eventually contained nearly 3,000 taro, 65 bananas, and a few tobacco plants, yams, sweet potatoes, herbs and greens." The time consumed in making and planting this plot was as follows:

Day 1. Waru left home accompanied by Gris at 7:30 a.m. Arrived at the garden site at 7:50 a.m. Both worked till 12:10 p.m. cutting down trees. Gris returned to the village, but Waru rested till 2:15 p.m. Worked cutting down trees till 5:04 p.m. During the afternoon he had two rests totalling twenty-five minutes.

Day 2. Waru left home accompanied by Gris at 7:26 a.m. Arrived at garden site at 7:45 a.m. Both worked till 11:56 a.m. cutting down trees. Gris returned to the village but Waru rested till 2:17 p.m. Worked at cutting down trees till the whole area cleared at 4:31 p.m.

Days 3–12. Timber left to dry.

Day 13. Waru and Mujewa arrived at garden at 8:02 a.m. Picked over timber together till noon, with a rest for twelve minutes at 10:56 a.m. Rested till 1:58 p.m. Picked over timber till 2:38 p.m., when work was abandoned on account of rain.

Day 14. Raining

Day 15. Waru fencing 8:01 a.m. to 12:03 p.m. and 1:50 p.m. to 4:16 p.m. Mujewa burning rubbish and clearing ground 8:01 a.m. to 12:03 p.m. and 1:50 p.m. to 3:04 p.m. Both rested for twenty-two minutes.

Day 16. Waru fencing 7:56 a.m. to 11:59 a.m. and 2:01 p.m. to 4:21 p.m. Mujewa clearing ground 7:56 a.m. to 12:04 p.m. and 2 p.m. to 2:40 p.m.

Day 17. Waru finished fencing and divided the area into allotments 7:40 a.m. to 11:58 a.m.

Day 18. Waru and two youths cleared away stones 8:30 a.m. to 10:20 a.m.; 11:04 a.m. to 12:16 p.m.; and 3:01 p.m. to 4:02 p.m. Long pauses due to rain.

Day 19. Waru brought banana suckers and Mujewa taro shoots.

Day 20. Raining

Day 21. Waru planted banana suckers 8:00 a.m. to 12:10 p.m. and 2:02 p.m. to 4:05 p.m. Several pauses, totalling thirty-five minutes, to chat to passers by. Mujewa planted taro shoots 8:05 a.m. to 12:05 p.m. and 2:01 p.m. to 3:29 p.m.

Day 22. Both Waru and Mujewa occupied elsewhere.

Day 23. Mujewa planted taro shoots 8:02 a.m. to 12:20 p.m. Waru planted yams 8:02 a.m. to 8:50 a.m.

Day 24. Mujewa finished planting taro shoots, greens, etc., 8:14 a.m. to 2:17 p.m.

Waru's family group was small. He had one wife, Mujewa, an infant, and Gris, an orphan boy seventeen years old who lived with him. To make this garden Waru gave forty-two hours of labor over eight working days, Mujewa thirty hours, over six days; there were eight hours from Gris, and four from each of the two youths who helped in the work. This was only one of six garden plots Waru made. These provided his small family with the very substantial amount of 7,000 taro and approximately 70 bunches of bananas,

---

[3] H. I. Hogbin, 1938–9, pp. 286–96.

Economics and the Fulfilment of Wants

or about 4,200 of this fruit, in addition to sugar cane, vegetables, and tobacco.

Hogbin compares the work on this garden with that on another belonging to Jaua, the head of a polygynous household, a site twice as large as that belonging to Waru. This latter one required a total of 79 hours' work from the men and 60 from the women, as against 58 and 30, respectively, on that of Waru. These data would seem to testify to the efficiency of cooperative group as against individual labor, a theory that is widely held. In this case, it is given expression by the natives themselves in these terms:

A man who toils by himself goes along as he pleases: he works slowly and pauses every time he feels like having a smoke. But when two men work together, each tries to do the most. One man thinks to himself, "My back aches and I feel like resting, but my friend there is going on: I must go on too, or I shall feel ashamed." The other man thinks to himself, "My arms are tired and my back is breaking, but I must not be the first to pause." Each man strives to do the most, and the garden is finished quickly.[4]

There is no agreement, however, that cooperative work is equally efficient in all societies, or as economical as work done individually for remuneration. Foster has published some figures, gathered among the Popoluca Indians of the state of Vera Cruz, Mexico, bearing on this point. Friends aided a man to daub his house, the framework of which had already been built. Later paid labor was called in to help finish the task. The labor costs were calculated at the going rate per person as follows:

	Communal Work	Hired Help
Man hours available	120	54
Square feet completed	96	150
Time in minutes per square foot	75	20
Total labor costs in pesos	30.00	8.00
Cost per square foot in pesos	.32	.05

In this case, cooperative labor, a "social" event, was seen to be more costly. The use of cooperative labor in this culture is therefore properly to be referred to prestige motives, of the kind later to be considered.[5] Where there is no precedent for paid daily labor, or where the seasonal factor demands concerted effort for which no casual labor market exists, or where cooperative groups work as competing teams, however, the use of cooperative labor seems to have worth-while efficiency.

One element in the effort of those not living in machine cultures is what Richards, in her study of the Bemba of Northern Rhodesia has called "the rhythm of work." She points out that this African people are dependent on seasonal change of "light, dark and temperature" to a degree unknown in machine cultures, and that the "work-time interval which dominates our ac-

---

[4] Ibid., p. 296.
[5] G. M. Foster, 1942, pp. 29–34.

The Aspects of Culture

tivities and calculations" does not exist for them. "We, after all," she continues, "can hardly conceive of time except in terms of energy expenditure and, to many of us, a fixed money value as well. But the Bemba, in his unspecialized society does different tasks daily and a different amount of work each day. . . . The working hours also change in what seems to us a most erratic manner. In fact I do not think the people ever conceive of such periods as the month, week or day in relation to regular work at all. The major agricultural tasks have to coincide with certain seasons and moons, and that is all. A man says he has to cut trees between such-and-such climatic changes, but not that he has so many hours of work to get through, and daily work, which has become from habit almost a physiological necessity to many Europeans, only occurs at certain times of the year. The whole bodily rhythm of the Bemba differs completely from that of a peasant in Western Europe, let alone an industrial worker. For instance at Kasaka, in a slack season, the old men worked 14 days out of 20 and the young men 7; while at Kampamba in a busier season, the men of all ages worked on an average 8 out of 9 working days. The average working day in the first instance was 2¾ hours for men and 2 hours gardening plus 4 hours domestic work for the women, but the figures varied from 0 to 6 hours a day. In the second case the average was 4 hours for the men and 6 for the women, and the figures showed the same daily variation." [6]

The amount of work done in nonliterate societies can also be gauged by productivity. The yield of the New Guinea gardens has been mentioned. Wild rice gatherers in the Great Lakes region of North America are reported as harvesting substantial amounts of this crop. In 1864 three Chippewa groups having a total population of 3,966 individuals gathered 5,000 bushels, while in addition they obtained, by hunting, a large quantity of valuable furs, and produced 150,000 pounds of maple sugar besides growing potatoes and maize.[7] The members of one kin-group in Umor, a settlement of the Yakö of Eastern Nigeria, composed of 97 "adult able-bodied men" and their families, planted gardens whose estimated average size was 1½ acres, each having about 2,440 yam-hills, with a mean yield of 2,545 yams, the harvest ranging from 235 to 11,410 tubers. In addition, coco-yams, corn, pumpkins, okra, three varieties of beans, sugar-cane, gourds, cassava, and peanuts are grown.[8]

The problems of division of labor and specialization, because of their importance in the cycle of production, merit further examination. We must, first of all, make clear the distinctions to be drawn between the phenomenon as it is found in nonliterate societies and in machine cultures. In the former, such division of labor as exists is by whole industries, and rarely, if ever, represents the kind of intra-industrial specialization that this latter term signifies when used by the economists for our own society. In all nonliterate groups, as we have seen, certain work is done by men and other work by women. One may, therefore, speak of the universality of sex division of labor. Within this category, many societies exist whose technologies call for a division of

[6] A. I. Richards, 1939, pp. 392–4.
[7] A. E. Jenks, op. cit., pp. 1074–5, 1078.
[8] C. D. Forde, 1937, pp. 32–4, 41.

Economics and the Fulfilment of Wants

labor by crafts. In such cultures, some men will be iron-workers or wood-carvers or canoe-builders; some women will make pottery or baskets or weave cloths. But we practically never encounter a people outside the machine cultures where, for instance, one man mines ore, another smelts it, and a third fashions it into hoes; or where one woman gathers wythes and a second strips the bark from them while a third fashions baskets out of them.

This does not mean that lines of division of labor are not well defined and perfectly distinguished in nonliterate cultures. It has already been pointed out, in a general way, how true this is of sex division of labor. In societies living near the survival level, this may be the only form this phenomenon takes. Here every man will know how to perform man's work, and every woman how to do the things that are allotted to woman's sphere. Even in more complex economies, this is the most important division, for it transcends economic lines and invades all aspects of every culture. Few descriptions of the ways of life of nonliterate peoples fail to include some tabulation to show where this line is drawn. The fact has played its role in the development of social theory. Out of it has come such an hypothesis as that of Durkheim, who attributed to it the function of promoting social solidarity; and the numerous speculations as to its biological significance. Its deep-seated character is not only to be inferred from its universality but also from the emotional reaction to the behavior of a person of one sex who may perform labor commonly done by the other.

It is quite possible too, that the forms of sex division of labor in a culture are stabilized and continued by means of obscure psychological associations between occupation and sex. "In Dutch Guiana, the Javanese who have been brought in considerable numbers to work on the plantations continue their own aboriginal modes of life. In visiting one of their houses, attention was drawn to the variety of mats that are part of the furnishings, and the excellence of the workmanship in them was admired. As each mat in turn was commented on, the Javanese host, who was also the maker, smiled his appreciation. But when admiration was expressed at his ability as displayed in an especially fine bed mat, his smile vanished, and had he not been tolerant of the ignorance of the stranger, he obviously would have shown active resentment of the implications of the comment. For this particular type of mat, it soon was made patent, is woman's work, and to credit a man with its making is to bring into play associations that are anything but acceptable." [9]

Craft specialization, as found in nonliterate societies, seldom involves engaging exclusively in one particular kind of work. It is rather that only those who are "specialists" in this sense carry on a given craft. Craftsmen do other things—in particular, they provide for their subsistence, at least in part, by working in the fields, producing crops that they and their families will consume. Craft specialization in these societies does not provide a living in the sense that the much narrower intra-industrial specialization of machine cultures does. But in those societies where there is enough subsistence goods produced to release some members from a portion of the task of producing for their own primary needs, craft specialization is widespread.

[9] M. J. Herskovits, 1940, pp. 110–11.

Specialization of this kind can be based on hereditary calling, as with the California Indian basket-makers, or African iron-workers, or South Sea Island canoe-builders. The presence of these specialists makes for a greater variety of goods, and goods of better workmanship than would otherwise be available. On occasion, as in Melanesia, a type of regional or tribal specialization is found. That is, an entire group may manufacture pots, and exchange them for the fishing nets another people make, and so on. This is but another way in which the same ends are met; in this case, the benefits of the technical proficiency that comes with specialization accrue to societies so small in number that, of themselves, they could not support specialists of any kind.

A question that inevitably arises when the productive cycle is being investigated, is why men work. Men work, of course, because they must. But this simple answer by no means suffices. "I began this paper," says Hogbin in the discussion we have earlier cited, "by stating that these natives depend for their subsistence on tillage and collection. Though this remains true, they have many additional motives for the practice of agriculture and gathering of the fruits of the forest: food has become associated with personal prestige, status and vanity; with the desire for immortality; and even with aesthetics. In Jaua's words, it is the most important thing in Wogeo." [10]

No discussion of the motivations that underlie the drive to work may omit the satisfactions that come when a craftsman can point to an object and say, with pride, "I made it." Herein lies one of the most difficult problems of an industrialized society, where the means of production are no longer in the hands of the worker, and where specialization of labor has been carried so far that this identification with the finished product is not possible. It is only under such circumstances that labor becomes distasteful, and where release from work is envisaged as the requisite to desirable living. We become aware with astonishment that the concept "vacation" is unique to our society, until we reflect how, in other cultures, the rhythm of labor is set by sanctions accepted by all, where the ends of labor are the possessions of the one who makes the goods, to dispose of as he desires; where he can identify himself with what he has wrought with his skill and his strength. We tend to overlook the fact that a vacation is no release from the expenditure of effort, but that it rather affords an opportunity to expend energy without outside intervention. This, and this alone, is what makes it desirable.

3

IN MANY nonliterate societies, the distribution of goods presents no economic problem. Often no more is involved than allocating the available goods and services within the households of the producers, since these are also the functioning units through which consumption is achieved. Even where there is some degree of specialization, and exchanges are effected, these are personal, direct, and specific. It is only where population density is appreciable, and some degree of specialization is present, that we find the mechanism of the

---

[10] Op. cit., p. 325.

Economics and the Fulfilment of Wants

market as a formal element in the economy. Since among nonliterate peoples these conditions are relatively rare, market operations usually facilitate the exchange of goods between members of different communities rather than within a given society.

It is unlikely that the origin of the tradition of exchange of goods or services will ever be established. Mauss has derived it from the psychology of gift-giving.[11] That is, a present, however freely given, entails an obligation of reciprocal return. Countless instances of this are to be found all over the world. In our own culture, the obligation to return a dinner invitation or a wedding present come to mind at once. The ritualized gift-giving of the Kwakiutl, Haida and other tribes of the Northwest Coast of North America, classical in the literature of anthropology, affords an outstanding instance. So do the ceremonial exchanges of Melanesia, or the funerary gifts of West Africa, or the passing of presents in northern Australia, which serve notice that a future return is expected.

The sociological significance of *gift exchange,* as such forms are called, or *covert exchange,* as Firth terms it,[12] will be considered later when we discuss the topic of prestige economics. Here we are concerned with it as a mechanism whereby the circulation of goods is facilitated. Its importance in this respect is patent if one but traces the flow of valuables from their source most often and most strikingly through the channel of the ritual exchange, to their destination, and back again. Buck states that "reciprocal feasts and presents form the standard pattern of Polynesian weddings."[13] In Mangaia, social position was determined by the quantity and quality of the gifts proffered by the family of a bride on the occasion of a marriage, and the elaborateness of the bridal feast. For the family of the bridegroom not to reciprocate with a feast that surpassed the original in the amount of food provided and the quantity of gifts presented was to admit inferior status. In Tonga, when marriage gifts were exchanged between the families of the principals, the father of the bridegroom remembered what each relative had contributed, and undertook to return twice this amount. He would strip his house of all its possessions to do this, lest the social position of his family suffer, and his remaining children, as well as their offspring, be unable to make desirable marriages.

To what extent these ceremonial exchanges of goods and services figure in the total distributive systems of nonliterate economies—or those of literate peoples—cannot be said. Most studies of them have been focussed on their ritual and sociological characteristics rather than on their economic function. Such figures as are available for them—500 mats given at the marriage of a Polynesian woman of royal rank, 15,000 blankets presented at a Kwakiutl potlatch, taro puddings four feet square as an Ontong Java ritual food gift, eight hundred cattle in a Kaffir dowry—indicate that they constitute an important mechanism for the circulation of goods among the many peoples where this type of exchange prevails.

Trade, properly speaking, consists in the direct exchange of values, either

[11] M. Mauss, 1923–24.
[12] Raymond Firth, 1939, p. 310.
[13] P. H. Buck (Te Rangi Hiroa), 1934, p. 91.

The Aspects of Culture

designated in terms of one another or of a least common denominator, such as money. In the societies with which we are concerned, where institutions are not sharply differentiated, gift-giving shades imperceptibly into trade. The logical categories drawn to designate the different forms taken by exchanges of various sorts are, therefore, at times extremely difficult to distinguish in a given instance. They are, besides gift and ritual exchange, barter, money barter, and exchanges based on the use of money.

Barter is the direct exchange of goods for goods. A special form is the "silent trade." The silent trade has been known for many hundreds of years. It is mentioned by Herodotus as the way the Carthaginians traded with Africans who lived beyond the Pillars of Hercules—that is, on the west coast of Africa. Ibn Batuta, the Arabian traveller, tells how it was the means of carrying on trade for furs in the far northern "Land of Darkness." Modern instances have been cited between the Chukchee of Siberia and the Alaskans, between the Congo pygmies and their Bantu neighbors, in California, Malaysia, New Guinea, and elsewhere. Essentially the procedure is as follows: one party to a transaction leaves goods at a stated place, either going away or withdrawing to a vantage point, to watch unobserved. The other party then comes, inspects what he finds, and if satisfied leaves a comparable amount of another commodity. How this system developed, and why—whether due to inequality of size or of weapons, or because of language difficulties—is not known. It has, however, been reported among enough peoples to demonstrate that, with continuous good faith, it is a workable means of effectuating simple exchanges.

Face-to-face trading of goods for goods is the most prevalent form of exchange in nonliterate societies. Bargaining may or may not be present. Barter seems to be carried on between different tribes more than within a society, and this is reflected in the literature, wherein many more instances of intertribal barter are given than intra-tribal exchanges. North and South America knew numerous instances of this form of intertribal exchange; such as when the Tewa of the Southwest trafficked corn, corn meal, and wheat bread for the buffalo hides of the Comanche, or the Choroti of the Chaco bartered dried fish for maize, red paint, and necklaces. Melanesia is replete with instances. Even in Africa, intertribal exchanges take on more importance than intratribal ones. Schapera, however, has given one instance among the South African Tswana of intra-tribal barter, together with examples of intertribal transactions carried out by this method.[14]

In order to trade, a person must want something he does not himself have, but that another individual does. The measures taken to effect an exchange involve arriving at some agreement about the relative value of these goods. Hence the problem of how value is expressed, and how values shift as goods move from one hand to the next is critical in this connection. One of the reasons why the study of economies that are self-sufficient, or where exchange is based on barter, requires special methods is because there is no way in which values can be expressed except by detailing each instance where a good was

[14] I. Schapera, 1938, pp. 241–4.

Economics and the Fulfilment of Wants

produced, or exchanged, or consumed. Values may be quite capricious, as among the Arawak in South America, where the value of each object bartered is dictated by the strength of its appeal at the moment it is offered. Sometimes values of one commodity are expressed in terms of another, as in Buka, in the Solomons, where a bundle of 6 or 7 carrying baskets is traded for a basket full of taro. Here the implication of shifting value is interesting, since a basket-maker who trades with a strong woman who can carry a heavy load will obtain more taro than if she did business with a smaller, weaker woman. In this case, however, there seems to be no seeking out larger trading partners, and no disputing over equivalence. The latter device, called haggling, is widely spread, both in barter and where there is a standard expression of value.

Money-barter occurs when some consumption good is used as a least common denominator of value. One of the best examples of this has come from the Ifugao of the Philippines, where in addition to transactions on the level of pure barter, rice acts as money. Barton provides a table of 1922 values, with their equivalence in Philippine dollars:

Unit	Number of bundles of rice	Unit	Value during harvest and spading (pesos)	Value in season of growing rice (pesos)
1 botek	1		.02½	.05
5 botek	5	1 hongal	.12½	.25
4 hongal	20	1 dalan	.50	1.00
5 dalan	100	1 bongale	2.50	5.00
10 dalan	200	1 upu	5.00	10.00
4 upu	800	1 lotak	20.00	40.00
2 lotak	1,600	1 gukud	40.00	80.00
10 upu	2,000	1 ⎰nabukene ⎱pigil	50.00	100.00

Here we see how the introduction of a token of common value brings order into calculations. We also see how a commodity of this sort, used as money, can reflect its different values as a commodity in terms of its function as money. Rice is, of course, more plentiful at harvest-time than during the growing season. Not only is this apparent when translated into terms of money, strictly speaking (the Philippine peso), but as reflected in the prices of the commodities it buys. A fowl that in growing season brings 1 *hongal* of rice, will at harvest-time, when rice is plentiful, bring 2 *hongal,* and so on.[15] Many other examples of societies where money-barter figures in the exchange of goods have been reported. Iron objects such as rods, hoes, axes, double gongs, and other commodities were used for this purpose in the Congo, salt in West Africa, tobacco in Siberia, cacao in pre-Spanish Mexico.

To so great an extent do commodities used as money act like money, properly speaking, that it is difficult to distinguish them in their functioning from those objects whose worth as a commodity, if they have any, has been lost sight of in their specialized use as tokens of value. *Money,* properly speaking, has the characteristics of homogeneity, portability, divisibility, and durabil-

[15] R. F. Barton, 1922, pp. 427–31.

The Aspects of Culture

ity. In this it differs from the good used in money-barter, or from "valuables" that are symbols of wealth, like the great stone wheels that are repositories of "congealed values" on the island of Yap, or the cattle of East Africa we have considered in a previous chapter. In nonliterate societies, where the lines between different kinds of cultural phenomena are blurred, distinctions such as those between the use of money in trade and of the commodity tokens of a money-barter system are very difficult to draw. This need not trouble us greatly, however, since either type of value-expression performs the functions of money as readily and as effectively as the other. Hence except for purposes of classification, the distinction between the kinds of tokens of value used is of minor importance.

The distribution of those nonliterate peoples in whose economy money, properly speaking, functions is relatively restricted. The use of money was found in the aboriginal cultures of West Africa and the Congo, Melanesia, and western North America. The cowry-shell was current in Africa before European occupation. Like any currency, it could be translated into terms of another system, as was done in 1793 by Dalzel for the cowry in early Dahomey:

Unit		Number	Value sh.	d.	Weight lb.	oz.	tenths
40 cowries	1 tockey, or string	40	0	1⅛	0	1	7
5 tockeys	1 galhina	200	0	6	0	8	4
5 galhinas	1 ackey	1,000	2	6	2	10	0
4 ackeys	1 cabess	4,000	10	0	10	8	0
4 cabess	1 ounce, *trade*	16,000	40	0	42	0	0[16]

In recent times, the cowry has given further testimony that it is actually money. In 1883, the value of the cowry in French West Africa was about 500 to the franc, which was then worth 20¢. Later it fell to 800 to the franc, where it remained until 1918. After 1918, however, when the franc depreciated, the cowry increased in value, until by 1930 it had stabilized to the figure of 600 for a 5-franc note, or 120 cowries to the franc.[17] Among the Yurok of California dentalium shells were employed as money, and farther south clamshell disks. In Melanesia the media of exchange are so numerous as almost to defy enumeration. In some instances they are true money, as in the case of dog's teeth in the Admiralty Islands, where they not only express the values of other commodities, but like any medium of exchange, are subject to manipulation in the money market.

These business activities—for so they may be termed—have characteristics that relate them to business dealings everywhere. Markets and middlemen are found, and mechanisms of credit are widespread in nonliterate cultures. One of the clearest statements of this mechanism has been given by Boas. Of the Indians of British Columbia, he says, "This economic system has developed to such an extent that the capital possessed by all the individuals of the tribe combined exceeds many times the actual amount of cash that exists;

---

[16] A. Dalzel, 1793, p. 135.
[17] Cf. M. J. Herskovits, 1940, pp. 218–21, for a fuller discussion of this point.

278

that is to say, the conditions are quite analogous to those prevailing in our community: if we want to call in all our outstanding debts, it is found that there is not by any means money enough in existence to pay them, and the result of an attempt of all the creditors to call in their loans results in disastrous panic, from which it takes the community a long time to recover." [18] Credit, as in Euroamerican culture, is usually extended for a consideration, and interest rates, in many cultures, are very high. Pawning of children was a recognized means of obtaining money in West Africa, and palm-groves are still pledged where a man is hard-pressed for funds.

Money is a repository of value as well as a medium of exchange. In nonliterate societies, the two economic systems reflected by this dual function of money are often made explicit. The subsistence economy may be carried out on a barter basis, for instance, while the prestige system operates with the aid of money. Du Bois first made this distinction explicit in studying the Tolowa and Tututni Indians of California. Here, while the dentalium shell and other "treasures" were employed "in the purchase of social protection and prestige, in sex, and in maintaining familial status, . . ." they "entered hardly at all into the subsistence equation." [19] The blanket of the Northwest Coast Indians was a token in the prestige economic system, and figured but little in exchanges of subsistence goods.[20] In Melanesia, such symbols of value as the arm-bands and necklaces of the Kula ring of the Trobriands are restricted to the prestige system.

There are no hard and fast differences between these two systems. Thus on Rossel Island, the prestige currency also figures in regular trading operations. The essential thing is that their existence, however expressed, should not be overlooked. As has been remarked, the fact that our economy employs only one unit of value masks the dual nature of our economic system. The purchase of a consignment of wheat and of a precious jewel are both effectuated by means of money. But the wheat is to be used for food, while the jewel is a repository of value, designed to bring to its owner the prestige that goes with owning it. It is striking that in so highly specialized a society as our own these two phases of the economic system, functionally so distinct, should be blurred. The fact that we have but one set of value-tokens, however, has made it extremely difficult for us to distinguish between them, either in the forms in which they manifest themselves, or in their dynamic aspects of gift-exchange as against the buying and selling of more ordinary, workaday commodities.

4

THE technological capacity of any people is directed toward making consumption goods, production goods (or what has been termed auxiliary capital), and depositories of value. Like all our other categories, these must be considered as flexible. Their interpretation must be in accordance with the

---

[18] F. Boas, 1898, p. 54–5.
[19] C. Du Bois, 1936, p. 51.
[20] F. Boas, 1897, pp. 341ff.

The Aspects of Culture

actual functioning of a given element in the economy of a given culture. The first of these categories has to do principally with the economics of consumption, the second with the processes whereby capital goods are acquired and used, the third with the broad category loosely termed property or wealth. The first two have been little studied among nonliterate peoples, but anthropologists have devoted much attention to the third, principally because of its function of maintaining kinship structures.

Food and clothing are the primary *consumption goods*. In most nonliterate societies the economic processes by which they are distributed are relatively simple. Here the real problem largely lies outside the economic sphere. We have seen how, even among peoples living on the subsistence level, they do not utilize all available food-stuffs, either because of patterned concepts of what is fit for human consumption, or of special taboos of a religious or sociological character. The same kind of selectivity is found in clothing, as among groups where the productive capacity permits class differentiation and clothing becomes a mark of rank. To what degree such non-economic, especially prestige factors, are significant in channelling the consumption of goods in nonliterate societies is to be seen in the following list, given by Firth, of the amounts of foodstuffs consumed at certain specific Maori feasts in New Zealand, as reported over two decades by various witnesses:

Date	Quantity of Food Consumed
1829	462 baskets of potatoes counted
1831	More than 1,000 bushels of potatoes, in addition to joints of beef, and shark-meat
1831	3,000 bushels of *kumara* as presents, 2,000 more to be consumed; 290 pigs killed
1836	About 2,000 bushels of *kumara;* 50 or 60 pigs
1837	6 large albatrosses, 19 calabashes of shark oil, several tons of fish, 20,000 dried eels, many pigs, and more baskets of potatoes than could be counted
1844	11,000 baskets potatoes; 100 large pigs, 9,000 sharks, much flour, sugar, rice, tobacco
1846	Several pigs, 6 canoes full of flour and sugar, besides potatoes and *kumara*
1846	Several tons potatoes and *kumara;* 500 pigs, quantity of eels, 16 casks tobacco
1849	Potatoes, cooked pigs, dried shark, pumpkins, *kumara,* in number difficult to ascertain. At one stage 200 pigs arrived. About 2,000 baskets of potatoes (40 tons) collected by then, and supplies continued to arrive.[21]

One aspect of the economics of food in nonliterate societies is the relation of the consumption of food to the immediate needs of the people. Studies of this kind are few, but they already have thrown light on certain aspects of the consumption economy of nonliterate folk that had not previously been understood. Thus the production of the Tallensi of the Gold Coast, when balanced against seasonal needs, yields the following conclusion: "It will be seen

---

[21] Raymond Firth, 1929, pp. 318–20.

Economics and the Fulfilment of Wants

that domestic food-supplies are at the lowest at the time—recognized as such by the natives—of the most strenuous output of physical labour, i.e., in May-June, and highest when there is least agricultural work. In other words, it would seem that food consumption is inversely correlated with food requirements, if we may assume that more food is needed to sustain the arduous agricultural labour of the rainy season than the leisure months of the dry season." Yet it is precisely in the dry season that feasting occurs. Despite the recognized need of the period when hard work will require more food, and the fact that this people know how to store foodstuffs and have the concepts of frugality and thrift, customary habits take precedence in an ordered and regular manner over physiological needs.[22]

Among the Bemba, "The most pronounced feature of this dietary is its alternation between hunger and plenty, a characteristic common to African peoples in areas where the distribution of rain allows only one season of cultivation a year, and where one staple crop is relied upon. In this territory the existence of a definite scarcity is noticed at once by the most casual observer. The Bemba constantly talk about 'hunger months' as distingushed from the food months. . . . When the scarcity becomes marked the whole appearance of village life is changed. For adults meals are reduced from two to one a day, and beer is rarely if ever brewed. Children who seem to munch extras all day long in the plentiful season (April to October) are reduced to a single dish late in the day. . . . Most adult natives can remember occasions when they went two days without food, and 'sat in the hut and drank water and took snuff.' "[23]

It must be remembered that this, like the former instance, has to do with a particular situation, differing from those in other cultures having different technological bases and economic orientations. This seems to be the case among the Malayan fishermen of Kelautan, who even "during the difficult period of the monsoon" live above the subsistence level. "It seems probable," we are informed, "that the fisherman's family enjoys a diet which at most times of the year is sufficient for the energy needs of the people, not too unvaried, and, prima facie, not badly balanced." Adequate subsistence during the year is also reported by Wagley for the Guatemalan Chimalteco, though here the intervention of a full money economy and the availability of goods for purchase must be taken into account.[24] Seasonal variations may cause differences in diet at different periods of the year, rather than a cycle of plenty and want. This is what is found among peoples as different as the Mexican Cherán, the Minnesota wild rice gatherers, and the Eskimo.

Another phase of consumer economics in nonliterate societies concerns the budgeting of family resources. Most of the works just referred to include materials of this order, and others not available elsewhere have been summarized.[25] Here we may cite one budget from the series of detailed accounts collected by Harris among the Nigerian Ibo who inhabit the village of Ozuitem.

---

[22] M. and S. L. Fortes, 1936, p. 260–1.
[23] A. I. Richards, 1939, pp. 35–6.
[24] Rosemary Firth, 1943, p. 136; C. Wagley, 1941, pp. 51–5.
[25] M. J. Herskovits, 1940, pp. 255–8.

These budgets vary in detail; we reproduce the first one reported. This budget was given by an elder, the head of a large relationship group; a member of two secret societies; a widower, with two sons, a daughter, and his eldest son's young "wife" living in the household. The eldest son was a trader and laborer, the younger a worthless young man who refused to work. The daughter, about 13 years old, was going through the year's "fattening" period that follows first menstruation and precedes marriage. The family head was not well, so "most of the work is done by the nine-year-old 'wife' of the elder son."

Income	£	s.	d.
1. Share of bride-price of various girls of kindred		3	0
2. Sale of yams	3	0	0
3. Sale of coconuts, oranges and kola		5	0
4. Fees from rental of land		5	0
5. Interest on loans		10	0
6. Rec'd from elder son		10	0
Total cash income	£4	13	0

Expenditures	£	s.	d.
1. One-fourth of son's government tax		1	0
2. School tax			6
3. Contribution for purchase of cows eaten at Bende Division Union meeting			2½
4. Contribution for sacrifice to the deity Kamálu			2
5. Contribution for annual sacrifice to Earth Deity			2
6. Food for household	1	0	0
7. Clothes for self		4	6
8. Meat, palm wine, and kola to greet visitors		5	0
9. Contributions to burials of those in his kindred, his mother's kindred, and affinal relatives		5	0
10. Stockfish, meat, and			

Expenditures (continued)	£	s.	d.
money to women who gave him food during "famine" period		1	6
11. Soap		1	0
12. Blood sucked when ill		2	0
13. Sacrifices for well-being, medicines and purgatives		3	0
14. Calendric ceremonial sacrifices to ancestors, deities, and other supernatural agencies		4	9
15. Kerosene		3	0
16. Tobacco, potash, and snuff		2	6
17. Hired workers to clear bush and plant—wages and food		7	0
18. Fine and costs of case against younger son, who ran away (fine 2 s., 10 s. bribe to court members)		12	0
19. Meat, palm wine, and food to relatives who worked for him		6	0
20. Contribution to bride-price of wife his elder son is marrying		10	0
21. Church fees for "wife" of elder son			3
Total cash expenditure	£4	9	6½

In addition to these items, the non-monetary returns from the harvesting of certain crops, food exchanges, cooperative labor, and the like, should rightly be calculated, as well as the reserves of food, clothing, and personal property owned by this man. Despite these omissions, however, "because so much of the life entails monetary transactions of one sort or another, these budgets present not only a sharp insight into the economic life of the Ibo individual but they cast into relief many other aspects of his culture." [26]

The *capitalization* of resources among nonliterate peoples is simple and, in the main, obvious. Tools of various kinds, which even tribes with rudimentary technologies have, make up the bulk of their capital goods. In all but the

[26] J. S. Harris, 1944, pp. 303–5.

poorest cultures, too, more permanent works are found. More complex economies permit the centralization of capital goods in the hands of certain members of society, so that "capital" in its specialized sense is present, as is manifest in the instances where the phenomena of credit and interest accompany the presence of money capital. In the main, however, the capital goods of nonliterate societies include those items comprised in the material culture, plus such permanent improvements as terraces, irrigation ditches, and other "public works." The essential need in the study of the capitalization of labor in these societies is not only a listing of goods of this kind, but the quantities in which they are owned, how they are distributed among the population, and the returns they yield. Such information, however, is quite lacking. Hence we may but note that the concept "capital" is in a broad sense applicable to non-machine cultures, and indicate the desirability of further study of the problems this fact poses.

As in all societies, *property* in nonliterate communities consists of land, material goods, and intangibles such as "rights." There has been much discussion of whether "primitive communism" is not manifest in the ownership of any or all of these among "primitives," but on examination we find that the problems of ownership in societies that vary so greatly cannot be encompassed under any such simple formula. Where land is plentiful, it becomes something in the nature of what the economists term a "free good," since where there is no scarcity, considerations of fixed ownership need not enter. Among hunting and herding people, the ownership of land is almost never in the hands of individuals, but in that of some group—a family hunting band, or a clan, or a tribe.

The formula for land ownership in nonliterate societies—and also for property in general—is that title rests on use. Hence it is a general rule that land under cultivation is free from trespass, while the tools, clothing, and other objects used or made by an individual are generally recognized as his, whether or not convention requires that what he owns be made available to other members of his tribe. This is particularly pointed by the way in which trees that have been planted or require cultivation, are held in various parts of the world to be private property. Coconut trees in Polynesia; mango, lemon, and other trees in Mexico; palm-trees in Africa; maple-sugar trees utilized by the Ojibwa of the Eastern Woodland area, are all owned as any property is owned, without regard to who may be cultivating the land on which they grow. In all such cases, access to the trees must be permitted the one who planted them, and who continues to own them though his fields may now be elsewhere.

Intangibles form an important category of property in all societies, as witness the economic value placed on patent rights, on good will, on copyright in our own culture. The knowledge of ironworking, retained jealously in East African families, or of curing processes restricted to members of certain societies among the American Indians, furnish analogous instances among nonliterate groups. A further example of the importance of incorporeal property includes an assortment of rights called *topati* by the Nootka of British Columbia—knowledge of family legends, a ritual for spearing fish, honorific

283

names of many kinds, the right to carve certain designs on totem-poles and grave-posts, to sing certain songs, to dance certain dances, to perform certain specific parts of certain rituals.[27] Membership in many Melanesian men's societies is another valuable good, that can only be acquired by the expenditure of considerable wealth. In the South Seas, personal names, incantations, songs, charms, and family traditions all figure as family wealth.

5

WE HAVE seen that most societies have a dual economy, one for the satisfaction of material needs, and one that is directed toward satisfying the desire for prestige. The *prestige economy* can only operate where the mechanisms of production provide more than is needed for the fulfilment of the requirements of living. This means that the existence of a prestige economic system is dependent on what is to be termed an economic surplus. We must, therefore, examine the circumstances under which such a surplus is produced, before we enquire into its nature and functioning.

Though no comprehensive study of the relationship has been made, the comparative analysis of data from different cultures seems to indicate that the production of an economic surplus is a function, first of all, of population size. The nature of the habitat and the state of technological competence also enter. The former, as we have seen, plays a passive rather than an active role, however, while technology is more developed in large than in small societies. It is apparent from the facts that have been cited earlier in this chapter that the problem of survival is most pressing in the smallest societies, living in harsh environments. Conversely, specialization that is required to produce more goods than necessary for the mere support of the population is to be found in larger groups, living in more favorable habitats. This means that the larger groups reach a *per capita* productivity that is greater than their needs, while the smaller ones do not. The excess that is produced is called the *economic surplus;* its role in giving partial release from the work of gaining subsistence is to provide *social leisure.*

The correlation that exists between population size and excess productivity can be exemplified by comparing peoples living at and near the subsistence level, whose habitats and cultures are otherwise enough alike so that some of the numerous variables that enter into the equation may be held constant. The Bushmen and Hottentot of South Africa are two such peoples. The former, in pre-European times, are estimated to have totalled about ten thousand individuals, split into minute tribal groupings. The latter, as late as 1900, were enumerated at the figure of 50,000. The Bushmen, as has been pointed out, produce little more than the necessities of life; the Hottentots are a cattle-keeping people and live on a more secure economic level. The Bushmen have no chiefs, except in a most rudimentary sense. They likewise have no priests, or any other specialists; rituals in honor of their gods or other ceremonial observances are quite simple. The Hottentots, on the other hand, were

---

[27] E. Sapir and M. Swadesh, 1939, note to p. 222.

Economics and the Fulfilment of Wants

organized into bands that recognized wider affiliations to clan and tribe, and each tribe had its chief, who was attended by his headmen. The chief was generally the wealthiest man of the group, and could levy fines, which he shared with his councillors, in criminal and civil cases. Priests or other specialists the Hottentots do not have, but their religious rites were on occasion marked by large feasts.[28] Other examples from the Americas and Melanesia could be cited which make the same point—that where there is no economic surplus, there can be no specialization. For specialization implies that the specialist who is not producing immediate subsistence goods, is supported by the excess his fellows produce over survival needs while he works at his particular craft.

The specialists who are thus supported in return for the services they render, outstandingly include two types, those who exercise administrative functions and direct the affairs of the tribe or country, and those who are expert in controlling the supernatural. That is why, in comparing the Hottentots with the Bushmen, the point was made that the former have chiefs and the latter none. Both are so close to the subsistence level that neither can afford priests. But in richer societies, these two functions are in time separated except where a priest-ruler, as chief-executive by divine right, fulfils the functions of both offices. In accounting terms, this signifies that the primary charges on income over and above the costs of subsistence are those of management and of insurance. We shall see in later chapters how all but the sparsest groups do provide for the regulation of their affairs by putting these matters in the hands of designated individuals called chiefs and rulers. And we shall further see how all groups set up systems of thought about the nature of the universe and work out sanctions for enlisting the guardianship and curbing the malevolence of the forces that rule it; so that wherever resources permit, they refer these matters to the expert guidance of specialists who can concentrate their powers on techniques to further the well-being of the group.

The cost of government is met by taxes, and taxation is found in all societies having rulers, though it may not be recognized as such at first glance. In the West African kingdoms of Ashanti [29] and Nupe [30] and Dahomey [31] specific mechanisms of taxation have been reported, and among the Bavenda [32] and Lozi [33] of southeastern Africa. Peru and Mexico have long been known for the taxes levied by the rulers in the pre-Spanish kingdoms. In the Pacific, where institutions of government are less sharply outlined, and the problem of getting a living is relatively simple, contributions to the chief may take the direct form of labor, or first-fruits and the first catch of fish may be the ruler's share. Even among the essentially democratic North American Indian tribes, certain individuals customarily received gifts from persons of lesser standing

---

[28] I. Schapera, 1930, *passim.*
[29] R. S. Rattray, 1929.
[30] S. F. Nadel, 1942.
[31] M. J. Herskovits, 1938b.
[32] M. A. Stayt, 1936.
[33] M. Gluckman, 1943, pp. 70–81.

in the group. In the southeast and northwest, where governing hierarchies were well established, the customary rule prevailed of allotting labor, or a portion of the harvest, or part of the yield from the hunt to those in office.

It is more difficult to discover the mechanisms whereby those who serve the supernatural are remunerated. The mere fact that the office of priest and ruler are often combined in cultures where there is little specialization complicates the problem. It must also be apparent that the basis on which the power of the priests rests differs from that of the ruler, and that this makes the levying of fees the primary means of return for his services. In many cases, the priest is clearly subordinate to the chief, but in almost all instances the two work in harmony. Many examples of close, and not disinterested cooperation have been recorded. Thus, among the Yokuts and Western Mono tribes of California, the shaman would cause illness to come to a man who refused to contribute to a dance ordered by the chief, from the contributions to which both benefited. Or in Dahomey, the priests, by proclaiming the anger of the gods, would ordain minute offerings for each goat a man owned. Thus they made available to the royal tax gatherers a count of goats, village by village, so that levies could later be laid with precision.

As we move from less to more complex economies, we find that those who participate in the allocation of excess resources become more numerous, and their functions become more varied. In societies as large and as productive as our own, or in India and China, the disparities in distribution are such that we find a large group whose primary occupation is the utilization of this excess productivity, while at the other end of the scale are those whose bare survival needs are scarcely met.

What use, we may ask, is made of this surplus by its beneficiaries? What are the drives underlying the economic functions of such persons? The classical study of this problem has been made by Thorstein Veblen, in his analysis of what he termed leisure-class groups. Veblen analyzed that "differentiation in consumption" which, he held, was made possible by the "specialized consumption of goods as an evidence of pecuniary strength." In many societies, it appears, this process produced experts whose specialization, in itself, caused them to become experts in consumption. They have so developed techniques of utilizing goods and services that this aspect of their socioeconomic roles becomes an art, and an end in itself. This process Veblen termed "conspicuous consumption," a phrase that, because of the penetration with which it summarizes what seems to be a universal process in human society, has come to be a part of everyday speech.

The phrase "conspicuous consumption" gives profound insight into the psychology that underlies prestige economies. The economic surplus can be distributed in two ways. There can be a spread over a whole population of the socialized leisure it represents, thus releasing all members from some part of the manual labor they would otherwise perform in growing crops, working forges, and doing other tasks of the subsistence economy. Or it can be concentrated in the hands of those members of the society who function as specialists in various non-subsistence callings. Such persons Veblen termed members of the "leisure class." These individuals maintain their preferred

Economics and the Fulfilment of Wants

position by expending, as conspicuously as possible, the surplus that is produced by others, but is theirs by special right. They do this because it is expected of them. The psychological processes of identification so function that those who do not participate in the economic surplus, even though they produce it, derive satisfaction from this conspicuous expenditure rather than resent it.[34]

Examples of the process in nonliterate societies are manifold. Veblen's exposition of its operation in historic cultures shows us how, with greater productivity, consumption becomes more conspicuous, as in the coronation of a monarch, or the debut of a millionaire's daughter. *Social Advancement in Guadalcanal* is the telling title of a paper [35] which details the elaborate expenditure of foodstuffs that mark the rise of a man from common status to that of a leader in his community. We see in this account how he works, with his wives and relatives, to amass resources to make possible increasing participation in the reciprocal feasting that is essential for the attainment of a more favorable social position. Then, when he can afford it, he proffers a feast where gifts of food are so lavish that, in the words of the natives, "We eat till we sicken and vomit." This feast, if elaborate enough when compared with other feasts, marks his arrival at the desired stage in his progression, where he remains until he is in a position to resume the continuing process of giving and receiving gifts that marks the man of recognized position.

During the Kwakiutl potlatch, literally thousands of valuable blankets were burned, several canoes broken, and a slave killed to establish a chief's prestige. At African upperclass funerals, the goods placed in the grave of a family head or of a chief, or given to participants outside the family, or destroyed, represent substantial wealth. The houses of Samoan chiefs reflect the position of their owners. The degree of elegance associated with a structure is determined by the elaborateness with which those who built it were entertained while engaged in this work. Clothing differentials that mark rank are common—the Ashanti chief ceremonially wears a silk cloth of exclusive pattern, the commoner wears one of cotton. The elaborateness of religious rites is also a part of the complex of conspicuous consumption, and represents the allocation of more surplus goods to those who control this aspect of a culture.

The prestige economy is a topsy-turvy system, where gain comes through expenditure rather than through saving, and the highest position is reserved for those who most conspicuously spend the contributions of the less privileged, for the vicarious enjoyment of the contributors. It is a commentary on the nature and functioning of culture, and, beyond this, of the human psyche, that this phenomenon should be so widely spread as to make it almost a universal in human experience. Every people, we have said, have wants in excess of their technological competence. There could be no better evidence that such "wants" are culturally established. Their expression is only remotely related to the requirements of the biological organism, or the natural setting in which they are found. Their rationale is one of convention, their sanctions wholly those of tradition.

---

[34] T. Veblen, 1915, *passim*.
[35] H. I. Hogbin, 1937-38.

287

6

ALL this has direct bearing on one much discussed problem in the comparative study of economic systems—economic determinism. Here we come to the
last of the trio of deterministic theories that have entered into the study of
culture; the first, it will be recalled, having been biological, the second environmental determinism. The problem of economic determinism has been particularly obscured by a failure to distinguish it from the concept of historical
materialism, both of which derive from the writings of Karl Marx. In a single
passage, Marx, who did not himself employ the terms, gave expression to
them. "The method of production in material life determines the general
character of the social, political and spiritual processes of life"—this is economic determinism. "It is not the consciousness of man that determines their
being," he then goes on to say, "but, on the contrary, their social being determines their consciousness." [36] This is historical materialism. It is not difficult
to see that the second is but the thesis that underlies all scientific study of
culture, while the former is the proclamation of a position that is open to the
same criticism lodged against any single, and therefore simplified explanation
of the complexities of human social life.

Innumerable instances from subsistence economies controvert any simple
statement of the economic deterministic position, even if the patterns of prestige economic systems did not of themselves do this. Thus among the tribes
of Travancore, India, it is the rigidity of the religious rites that makes the
Urali more successful farmers than their neighbors, the Paliyan and Mannan,
whose rituals are "casual and haphazard." [37] The productivity of Dahomean
iron-workers could be increased appreciably if every eighth instead of every
fourth day were reserved to the god of iron. The resources of the Navaho
Indians would be materially greater if the house and personal effects of a man
were not destroyed at his death.

This is not to deny the role that the economy and its technological base
plays in shaping the mode of life of a people. Not to recognize the very significant part it does have is a repudiation of all our evidence. This is especially true where a group is small, technology simple, resources scarce, and
the problem of survival is paramount. But, as we shall see when we consider
the mechanism of cultural focus, there are too many societies whose dominant
orientations lie in non-economic aspects of life for us to attribute to the economic phases of culture more than the functionally variable, albeit substantially significant influence they exert in providing the material base, without
which no human activity could be carried on.

[36] Cited by G. D. H. Cole, 1933, p. xvi.
[37] D. G. Mandelbaum, 1939.

CHAPTER 18

Social Organization: the Structure of Society

SOCIAL organization includes the institutions that determine the position of men and women in society, and thus channel their personal relationships. The category is customarily subdivided into two broad classes of institutions—those that grow out of kinship, and those that result from the free association of individuals. Kinship structures include the family and its extension into broader relationship groupings such as the clan. The association of individuals who are not kin gives rise to a wide range of forms that vary from blood brotherhood and institutionalized friendship to secret and non-secret "societies" of various kinds. Age-groupings, though more often than not informal in character, can play important roles in societies where they hold the formal position of age-grades.

In a still broader sense, social structures must also be thought of as including those relationships of a political character based on locale and status. The educational function of various social institutions, especially the family, is also of signal importance. Because these present particular problems, however, they merit treatment apart from the groupings customarily classified under the heading of this chapter. Nonetheless, taken together, all social institutions and functions, by organizing behavior and providing for the inculcation in the oncoming generations of the prevalent sanctions and accepted behavior patterns of the group, make possible the cohesiveness and continuity of cultures.

It is enough to enumerate some of the ways in which social institutions influence the life of any group of individuals to understand why they have been given primacy in the study of man. In dictating the relationships between the sexes, and providing for the continuation of the group, they tap some of the deepest biological springs of man's being. In assigning to the individual his place among his fellows, and affording him a ready means for achieving the prestige that, as we have seen, men everywhere crave, they call forth some of the most compelling psychological motivations known to man. In the more restricted sociological sense, as well as in their political aspects, they bring order into life. Without the social institutions that provide the mechanisms for regulating conduct, the integration of the individual into society would not be possible. Thus it is not chance that the field of social organization has been one of the aspects of culture most assiduously studied; out of this has come so great a body of data, and some of the most widely discussed hypotheses bearing on human behavior and human relationships.

In this chapter, we shall be concerned with the institutionalized ways in which human groups are organized. How men and women conventionally seek their mates, the lines along which mating is permitted, and the resultant family structures—these are fundamental to our discussion. How these primary groupings proliferate into the broader units we have already mentioned, and what the recognized sanctions of these larger structures are, must also be described. Finally, the non-relationship categories, based on age and free association will claim our attention. In these, as in all other aspects of culture, we will seek to obtain a sense of the variety of means employed to achieve common ends. But we will also bear in mind how, in reaching these ends, neither logic nor patterned coherence is sacrificed by those who, in each society, achieve integration in living in relation to the integrations of their culture.

2

THE biological and social family may be two quite distinct entities. In many societies, as a matter of fact, the sociological concept of the family represents biological fiction rather than biological fact. The biological fact is simple— two parents are required to produce offspring, and the number of ancestors doubles with each ascending generation. Some societies do institutionalize this fact of *bilateral descent*, as it is technically termed. Ours is one such society, the Eskimo is another. More often, however, descent is counted in accordance with a *unilateral* pattern, whereby a person belongs to his father's or to his mother's family. In the former case, descent is *patrilineal*, in the latter, *matrilineal*. In either instance, in counting descent, only one significant ancestor appears in each generation. It is father's father, and his father, and his father, and so on, that count in a patrilineal society; or mother's mother, and her mother, and her mother, that are regarded as ancestors by a group that is matrilineal.

This flaunting of the biological reality by the sociological convention of unilateral descent has its own logic, despite the fact that it is difficult for those who, like ourselves, think of descent in bilateral terms, to understand this. It does, however, greatly simplify the problem of counting descent, and hence of determining relationhip. When an African chief says he knows his ancestry for forty generations, he is stating a fact within the sociological conventions of his society. He need command a knowledge of only forty names, in contrast to the 1,048,576 ancestors the stickler for biological accuracy would be compelled to know.

The impossibility of counting ancestry in accordance with biological reality must be recognized even in cultures where the bilateral system prevails. Thus while Euroamerican conventions of descent are bilateral in that relationship to both mother's and father's families is fully acknowledged, as far as names

Social Organization: the Structure of Society

are concerned, the spirit of the system is patrilineal. The phenomenon of the "hyphenated name" is known, outstandingly in Spain and in upperclass usage elsewhere. But even here it persists for only a generation or two. Otherwise a calling card would have to be the size of a small book! Not much thought is required to make us realize how this unilateral aspect of our descent system operates in facilitating genealogical identification on the father's side, and tending to obscure the contributions to our ancestry made on the side of our female antecedents whose "maiden names," as we term them, were given up on marriage and not perpetuated by their offspring.

Because this patrilineal tendency makes descent on the father's side familiar to us we can most profitably draw our examples from cultures having matrilineal descent, since these will be the more striking to us and thus more impress us with the points to be examined. It is not accurate to assume that matrilineal descent-patterns predominate in nonliterate cultures. Many small societies, with limited resources, have bilateral descent—the Eskimo, the Bushmen of South Africa, the Yahgan of Tierra del Fuego in South America. Patrilineal descent is widely-spread in East and West Africa, in Melanesia, and among the North and South American Indians.

There is no doubt that different traditions of descent greatly influence the psycho-social relationship between members of families in matrilineal and patrilineal societies. One aspect of the patrilineal spirit of our family convention is the father's role. He is what has been termed the "surrogate" for society—he is the family head, the arbiter of its destiny. By convention, and in some countries by law he controls its economic resources. Most important is his function as court of last resort in the disciplining of children. Because of all this, he stands in a relationship to his offspring and collateral relatives that is quite different from that of his wife. Outside the home, it is he who customarily speaks for the group; while inside it, the wife's role, allowing for differences in forcefulness of character, especially in relation to her children, is a softer, gentler one. If this is the situation that results from a family structure that is patrilineal only in certain aspects, and is not formally recognized as such, it is readily understandable how these features can be emphasized in the families of societies where patrilineal descent is given the stamp of full social recognition.

In contrast, the organization and functioning of the matrilineal descent-group, and the relationships that exist between its members, are quite different. Though there is much variation in practice, the tendency where matriliny prevails is for the headship of the family to be lodged in the hands of mother's brother, rather than in that of the father. In some cases, the matrilineal tradition of the culture may be associated with *matrilocal* residence, under which the man, upon marriage, takes up his residence in his wife's village, though there is no necessary correlation between the two. When the wife comes to live at her husband's home, this is called *patrilocal* residence. Where matrilocal residence is associated with matriliny, the feeling about the primacy of women in the family may be so strong that the husband may be regarded as a kind of outsider in his wife's family and may, as among the Zuñi Indians, live in it on sufferance. Among these people, there is no question in anyone's

The Aspects of Culture

mind but that the home of a man, for all his life, is that of his female relatives, of his "family"—the home of his mother or, after her death, of his sisters. In what *we* would term "his own home," the dwelling of his wife and his children, he has no status at all, except the position he may enjoy as a result of long residence and the personal regard in which he may come to be held by his wife's kin.

It is obvious that relationship within the family will be deeply influenced by all this. The transfer of the functions held by the father as family head in patrilineal societies, to the mother's eldest brother, is frequent. The mother's brother controls family finances, speaks for the family, and, as far as the children are concerned, is the court of last resort, and, as they mature, is the instrumentality whereby their correction and punishment are brought about. This leaves the father the pleasant role of playmate, councillor, and friend to his children. The emotional overtones that are associated with the concept "father" in patrilineal societies, or in bilateral societies having patrilineal weighting, will thus be quite different from what is found in such matrilineal cultures. Malinowski, in some of his best-known pages, has pointed out how, in the Trobriand Islands, this relationship has been given a striking socialized rationalization that makes of it almost a classical extreme of what results when matriliny holds fullest sway. The passage cited in an earlier chapter, showing this relationship between father and child among the Bush Negroes will also be remembered in this connection.

In the Trobriand Islands, the sociological fiction of unilineal descent is reinforced by a convention that the male plays no physiological role in reproduction. A woman is held to become pregnant when certain supernatural beings enter her womb, the passage to which has been opened by the circumstance of her having had sexual intercourse. The Trobriand father is held to be unrelated to his child biologically as well as socially, a view, it should be pointed out, that is held in several other societies, not all of which have matrilineal descent systems. He fulfils the role, within the family, of nurse and playmate. The relations between him and his children are described as wholly delightful. He fondles them, amuses them, spoils them, but never corrects, never punishes them. As a consequence, it is believed children resemble their father, to whom they are not held to be related biologically, and not their mother, since, according to native theory, in fondling an infant, the father shapes him to his own likeness. It is regarded as a compliment to tell a person he resembles his father, but a distinct slight to intimate resemblance to a mother.[1]

It must be stressed that the nuclear family, the grouping of father, mother, and children, is universal. Even in the few instances, when the physiological role of the father in reproduction is not comprehended, the socio-economic institution, the immediate family grouping, is a fully functioning element in society. Furthermore, there is a vast store of data that proves beyond any doubt that, whatever unilinear convention of descent may obtain, both parents, and their families, however these may be defined, have a full place in

---

[1] B. Malinowski, 1927b.

Social Organization: the Structure of Society

the regard of all members of the family group. In Australia, where patrilineal descent is the rule, Radcliffe-Brown has shown that the ties that bind a child to its mother, no less than its father, are extended to collateral relatives as well. "Since there is a close bond between a child and its mother, and another bond between the mother and her brother the child is brought into a close personal bond with the mother's brother. The latter is not treated in any way as similar to the father or father's brother, but is treated as a sort of male 'mother.' Similarly the father's sister is treated as a sort of female 'father.' In all Australian tribes the actual mother's brother and the actual father's sister of an individual have important places in his life, and the whole system can be understood only when this is fully recognized." [2] There is no more fascinating aspect of social organization, nor none where a greater variety of practice is encountered, than in relationships of this type. We shall come on them again when we consider the larger social groupings, and the systems of kinship terminology that express the forms they take.

The immediate family can either be *monogamous* or *polygamous*. Statements of the type of family found in a given society are not, however, to be taken as indicating fixed categories, but rather sanctioned forms. There is no society where polygamy is countenanced that does not have a large proportion of monogamous families, and few societies that are denoted monogamous where what would be called in Euroamerican culture extra-legal plural matings, often of some stability, are not present. The incidence of polygamous families in a society that sanctions plural marriage is held down by biological and economic circumstances. Except where infanticide is practised, the equivalence of the sexes in numbers permits only relatively few individuals to have multiple spouses. Otherwise, a sizeable proportion of one sex would be deprived of all chances to marry; and this situation is found in no culture that has been studied.

Even where male or female infanticide is practised, the expense of marriage is such that it is difficult for most persons to meet the costs of more than one mate. This is why monogamy is the practice, even though it is not the required form of marriage, in societies which produce little economic surplus. Quotations from descriptions of the social institutions of such peoples everywhere in the world make this very clear. Of the Yahgan, Cooper states, "Monogamy was by far the most prevalent form of marriage. . . . Polygyny was permitted, but was uncommon." [3] The Bushman family "is constituted by a union between one man and one or more women. . . . The Auen at Rietfontein all have only one wife 'because of the scarcity of food.' . . . Among the Kung a second wife may be taken, if the first consents; but owing to the difficulty of providing for more than one wife . . . polygynous marriages are extremely rare." [4] Even where productivity permits differentials in economic status, this factor in controlling polygamy is clearly apparent. Among the Western Apache, Goodwin informs us, "Because a poor man, or one of average situation, would find it difficult to support more than one wife, polygyny

---

[2] A. R. Radcliffe-Brown, 1931, p. 100.
[3] J. M. Cooper, 1946, p. 92.
[4] I. Schapera, 1930, pp. 103–4.

293

was almost wholly confined to the wealthy, such as sub-chiefs and chiefs."
Plural marriage "was accepted as a rich man's prerogative and the outcome
of personal desires." [5]

Polygamous marriages are of two types, *polygynous,* where a man has
plural wives, and *polyandrous,* where a woman has more than one husband.
The former type is far more widespread than the latter, which in fully institutionalized form is restricted to the aboriginal tribes of India, and to Tibet.
One of the best known examples of polyandry is that of the Todas, who practise female infanticide and thus artificially create a differential in sex ratio.
This system has been described by Rivers. Here a woman who marries a man
becomes the wife of his brothers; if it is a child marriage, the privilege of
being her husband is reserved to any brothers yet to be born. When a wife
becomes pregnant, the eldest brother ceremonially presents the woman with a
bow and arrow, and "for all social purposes," becomes the father of the child.
Thus the offspring will belong to this man's clan if the common husbands belong to different groupings, though this is seldom the case where the husbands are not "own brothers." This one will continue to be the "father" of all
children subsequently born to the common wife until another husband performs the rite of giving the bow and arrow. Even "a dead man is regarded as
the father of a child if no other man has performed the essential ceremony."
Where common husbands are brothers, all are equally regarded as the fathers
of the child, though the most influential one will be named by a person when
asked who is his father.[6]

Polygyny exists in all parts of the world, though because of the economic
factors (that do not seem to be operative in polyandrous matings) and the
absence of significant differences in the number of men and women, the incidence of these plural marriages in different polygynous societies varies
greatly. Even though in plural marriages the problem of personal adjustment
figures prominently, friction seems less prevalent than is anticipated by those
living under monogamous patterns. In another connection, it has been
pointed out how a first wife will urge her husband to add another spouse to
the household, because it brings the family and herself prestige, and because
she wishes companionship and a lightening of domestic tasks that sharing the
work of the household will bring about.

But this reaction is not always manifest. Goodwin's insight into Apache
culture stands us in good stead in showing how complex the reactions to the
institution of polygyny may be: "The average Apache woman seems to have
resented her husband's taking another wife. . . . Accordingly, a woman,
whether past the menopause or not, did not intentionally aid in the procuring
of another wife for her husband. Sometimes the first she knew of his having
taken another wife was the woman's appearance at the camp, but usually a
man would tell his first wife, 'I want to marry that woman.' She would answer, 'Don't ask me about it. Go ahead and do what you want.' This was ordinarily not an expression of approval but one of submission. If he intended to
stay with his new wife in her parents' encampment for the first few days, as

---

[5] G. Goodwin, 1942, p. 351.
[6] W. H. R. Rivers, 1906, pp. 516–18.

was often the case, he would say to his wife, so that she would not think that she was being deserted, 'I will leave now, but all this property here is yours; all this of mine is yours. There is lots of work to be done about the camp, and the other girl will help you to do it.' " [7]

In many societies, friction is lessened by a system whereby each of the several wives has her own dwelling place, where she lives with her children. In such cases, the husband may either stay with his wives in turn, or they may alternate in visiting the separate dwelling where he lives. The human factor is constantly operative in such situations, however, and a favorite wife may receive more attention, an elderly spouse less, than strict apportionment of the common husband's time would dictate. Ordinarily, the first wife administers the affairs of the household, and her responsibilities are heavy, as in the great polygynous families of African chiefs where the wives may be numbered in scores. On the other hand, the daughter of a man of rank, married late in the life of the common husband when he has amassed the resources necessary to make a match of distinction, may take precedence over the older wives of the household. Considerations of this kind become very important where the question of inheritance is involved. This is especially true where the eldest son of the principal—as against the oldest—wife succeeds to his father's rank and property.

In every society, whatever the type of family structure, marriage involves far-reaching adjustments. Not only are new responsibilities incurred, but a new and intimate association with another personality must be established. Many societies ease this personal adjustment by permitting a period of experimentation before the marriage compact is sealed. In some instances, experimentation is sanctioned on a wide scale, as among the Masai of East Africa, where girls live with first one, then another young man in the common house of the age-grade to which these warriors belong. In some cultures, a marriage is not regarded as concluded until a child has been born to the girl —for few societies neglect the fact that the primary function of marriage is procreation.

Relations of a new kind must likewise be established with the family of a mate. Often these individuals will have had the determining voice in deciding whether the marriage could take place. The recorded customary forms of behavior between a man or woman and a father-in-law or a mother-in-law have often been employed as a vast field for pseudo-psychological speculation. The misinterpretation of the mother-in-law taboo, for example, has come from reading conventions of one culture into another. The avoidance that requires a man to turn his back when he meets his mother-in-law on the path, never to be alone in the same dwelling or converse directly with her, never to partake of food at the same meal, is usually interpreted as hostile behavior; whereas these conventions signify respect. Whether or not, in addition, unconscious motivations of hostility are sublimated in this fashion cannot be said, though a logical argument can be raised to support the position. Speculation has also centered about the meaning of the joking relationships that are

---

[7] *Op. cit.*, p. 354.

The Aspects of Culture

widely found in nonliterate groups between brothers- and sisters-in-law, especially where the *levirate* or *sororate* makes potential mates of younger sisters or brothers of a husband or wife.

Local and kinship affiliations govern the choice of a mate. Since more often than not these matters are controlled in nonliterate societies by the rules of larger kinship units, discussion of them must be deferred until the following section. Irrespective of the lines that dictate choice in marriage, however, the family in all societies is distinguished by a stability that arises out of the fact that it is based on marriage; that is to say, on *socially sanctioned mating entered into with the assumption of permanency.*

This ethnological definition is drawn with relevance to considerations of morals only insofar as they are culturally defined for a given group. From this relativistic point of view, the anxiety we hear voiced about the disappearance of the family falls into historical perspective. Human societies cannot survive without some kind of family institution. Whether the family is monogamous or polygamous depends on the tradition of a people who give sanction to its form. As long as the accepted code is understood and followed, the stability of the institution is assured. Because cultures change, changes will from time to time be effected in the form of any institution. To this the family is no exception; but whatever form it may take, it must continue to fulfil its procreative and educational functions.

3

IF UNILINEAL descent systems simplify the process of counting ancestry and indicating relationships, they also facilitate the placing of a given nuclear family group in a much wider context of kinship than is customary in bilateral aggregates. The diagram that is appended will show the ramifications of kinship under a matrilineal system, in a relationship group, carried through five generations. *Ego*, a male, traces his descent through his mother (17), his mother's mother (9) and his mother's mother's mother (4), which is as far as our genealogy takes us. He has a sister (33) and a younger brother (35); his sister's children (53 and 54) are under his control, but he is not related to his brother's children (55 and 56) at all. His mother's sister (18) and his mother's mother's sister (10), are related to him, as are their descendants in the female line—that is, the children of his mother's sister's daughters (37 and 39; 57, 58, 59, and 60) but not of this woman's son (41; 61, and 62). Similarly, collaterals descended from (10) are members of his relationship group.

Study of our chart will soon show why kinship terminology has taken on so many different forms in differing societies. Despite the seeming inevitability of a system of relationship terms that reflects biological affiliation, it would actually be most unwieldy, if not impossible, to specify all the facts of descent, marriage ties, generation, age, and the like. Every people thinks its own system, however complicated it may seem to the outsider, to be obvious, logical, and simple. We are no exception, yet numerous points in our kinship terminology might well puzzle a Crow Indian, or an Australian, or a Vandau of East Africa. A person's male parent (16) is "father," female parent (17)

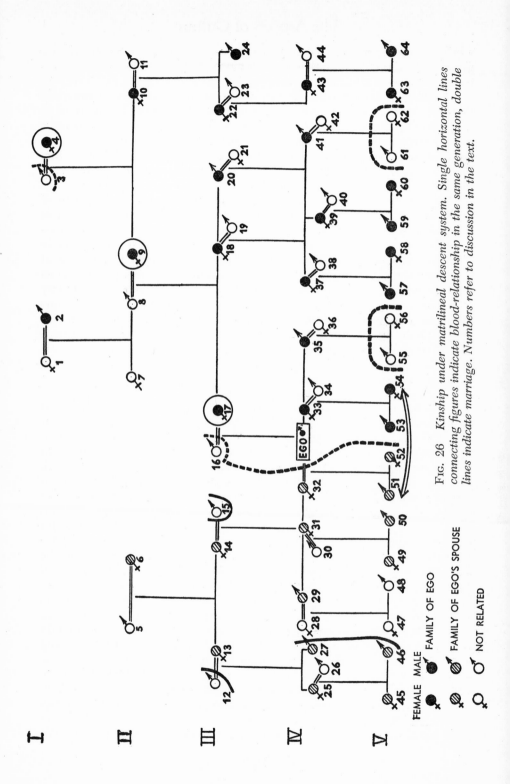

FIG. 26 *Kinship under matrilineal descent system. Single horizontal lines connecting figures indicate blood-relationship in the same generation, double lines indicate marriage. Numbers refer to discussion in the text.*

FEMALE   MALE

● ❀ FAMILY OF EGO

◑ ◈ FAMILY OF EGO'S SPOUSE

○ ♂ NOT RELATED

The Aspects of Culture

"mother." These terms are precise, and each applies only to one individual. But when we say "grandfather" do we mean "father's father" or "mother's father"? Descent line is here neglected, as age is neglected in other terms we use. "Brother" means the male child of my father and mother; we do not name age differentials by indicating whether a particular individual called "brother" was born before or after the person speaking. But many peoples hold it very important to indicate whether he is an older brother or a younger one. Our term "cousin" carries this grouping of individuals of different sex, age, and generation so far that we ourselves find it cumbersome and confusing.

Kinship terminology is studied by anthropologists for many purposes. It has figured in the reconstruction of historical contacts between peoples, in speculation as to the derivation of social institutions, in assessing the significance of various kinds of conventionalized behavior that would otherwise seem meaningless. Most important, however, is the insight into the social structure that regularizes behavior and thus underlies culture, given by such a listing of terms and an analysis of the rights and duties that are identified with the status of those called by the various terms. "It is largely the character of these kinship usages that differentiates family life among different tribes and divides its operations in primitive society from those of our own"; states Lowie, in his volume on social organization. "They involve both duties to relatives and claims on their help and property; both strict prohibitions as to intercourse and sanctions of extravagant forms of intercourse." [8]

One of the most widely spread systems of kinship terminology where unilateral descent is employed is the *classificatory* system, in which generation is paramount and degree of relationship is subordinated. In our diagram, under such a system, Ego calls his grandmother's sister (10) by the same term as he calls his grandmother (9); he calls his mother's sister (18) "mother" and also the daughter (22) of his mother's mother's sister (10). All the daughters of his "grandmothers" are his "mothers" and all the children of his "mothers" are his "sisters" and "brothers." That is, he would not only call 33 "sister," but use this term for 37, 39, and 43; he would call 41 "brother" as well as 35. Because he is a man in a matrilineal system, what he would call his younger relatives would vary, but it would probably not be "son" or "daughter." That is what 33, a woman, would call 57 and 58, 59 and 60, 63 and 64 as well as 53 and 54. Some term such as "sister's son" and "sister's daughter" would be Ego's name for these individuals, and they would probably call him "mother's brother," the term by which he would call 20 and 24.

It would be pointless to attempt to indicate even a portion of the different systems of kinship nomenclature that have been recorded. The important thing for the student of culture to recognize is how such a social framework influences the lives of those who live within it. The function of the wider relationship groupings in regulating marriage is perhaps their best-known role. The ease with which incest lines can be drawn in a unilineal system is striking. Any child of any "mother"—or of any "father" in a patrilineal system

---

[8] R. H. Lowie, 1920, p. 81.

Social Organization: the Structure of Society

—is my "brother" or "sister." To marry a brother or sister is incestuous. Therefore, when a match is under consideration, the genealogies of the principals are examined to discover if the descent line of either party contains the name of a "significant ancestor" found in the other. If this is discovered, the generation principle comes into play. They are "brother" and "sister," and therefore to mate would be incestuous.

The broadest extension of a unilinear descent group has been given various names. *Clan* is employed almost without exception in the writings of the English anthropologists. In the United States, however, anthropological usage from the time of the earliest studies has distinguished groups where descent is counted on the mother's side—that is, clans—from those counting descent on the father's side. These have been called *gens*, after the Latin word that reflected Roman custom. Lowie chose the word *sib* as a common term, making possible the differentiation of the two types into *mother-sibs* and *father-sibs*.[9] It has been widely accepted, and will be used here to denote these broad unilineal kinship aggregates.

The sib performs numerous functions, but its most common task is to regulate selection in marriage. One instance of this is to be found in systems of *preferential mating*. Preferential mating exists in many societies, usually between *cross-cousins*—that is, the children of a brother and a sister, real or classificatory. This is possible because these offspring belong to different sibs. In our diagram, 54 and 55 are cross-cousins; 54 belongs to the sib of her mother, 33, while 55, who belongs to the sib of *his* mother, 36, is not sociologically related to 54, though she is the child of the sister of 35, who is the father of 55. Technically, it can be noted, cross-cousins are the opposite of *parallel cousins*, children of two brothers or two sisters. *Ego* is the parallel cousin of 37 and 39, and it would be incestuous for him to marry either of these women. Indeed, in some societies, he would be at considerable pains to avoid social contacts with them.

The Ashanti, who practise dual *exogamy*, as marriage outside one's group is termed, afford an instance of preferential mating that has economic implications as well as sociological significance. Membership in the mother-sibs dictates social position, family affiliation, inheritance. But an individual's soul is derived from the father. One may therefore not marry a person whose relationship, however remote, can be traced in the sib line; nor an individual related on the father's side where common ancestry is not at least four generations removed. Because the soul is inherited in the male line, and belief holds that the soul regulates conduct, a father is responsible for *his* son until the boy comes to have full adult status. The sowing of wild oats is not restricted to Euroamerican society, so that it is advantageous for a father, who is legally held for the son's premarital adultery fines, to arrange for his son to marry as soon as possible. Marriage here, as elsewhere, however, entails expenses, especially where valuable goods must pass from the family of the youth to that of the girl.

The Ashanti solution of this is simple, as can be seen if our diagram is again

---

[9] *Ibid.*, pp. 111–12.

consulted: 51, let us suppose, is of an age to marry. His soul is that of *Ego*, who is his father, but his family is that of his mother, 32. Ego, as the elder brother of 33, has rights over and obligations toward the children of this woman, one of whom is a girl, 54. These cross-cousins, who are thus sociologically quite unrelated—she has her *father's* soul but is of her *mother's* sib—become potential mates under this system. The terms of address they employ when speaking to each other, and their behavior when together, reflect this relationship. They call each other "husband" and "wife" from the time they can talk, and continue to do this throughout life, whether they marry or not. Their conversation, too, and other aspects of their behavior is freer than would be countenanced between a man and a woman, though actual sexual contact is allowed them only in the event of their marriage.

The sanctions that give the sib its power are varied, but most important are the sib mythologies, the sacred tales that recount the origin and history of these groupings and explain codes regulating marriage or other conventions, such as the taboos of various sorts it enforces. Though by no means a universal aspect of the sib, the sanctions behind sib regulations are in many instances derived from a mythological being technically called a *totem*. *Totemism*, then, is the belief that a mystical relationship exists between a group of human beings who make up a kinship unit and a species of plant or animal or, less commonly, some natural phenomenon.

There are many definitions of totemism, and controversy at one time was acute as to the meaning of the term, the origin of the institution, and its sociological significance. It is as often designated a religious as a social phenomenon. The imposition of food taboos, taking the name of the totem animal as an *eponym*, the duty of the totemites to assure the propagation of the totem animal, are some of its features that have at various times been emphasized as essential to it. Best known is Sir James G. Frazer's monumental study, which tends to see all totemic practices as typified by the Australian belief in the reincarnation of the totemic spirit, associated with a given locality, in each child.[10] Goldenweiser [11] injected a needed note of induction, however, by establishing the fact that so many different manifestations of the relationship between men and animals are to be found that none of these, by itself, can be used to characterize the phenomenon in general.

Certainly, when the social institutions over the world that have been termed totemic are compared, the variation to be discerned in their sanctions is great. Most people abstain from eating the totem animal, but some do eat it. Many sibs are *eponymous*, but others do not take the name of their totem. Some groups make artistic representations of the totem, others do not. Totemism can even exist where there is no belief in descent from the totem, as in West Africa, where a relationship that has been termed "totemism of respect for services rendered" is found. Here the totemites take the name of their totem, and do not kill or eat it, because the sib myths tell how this animal befriended their ancestors in a critical period of their early history. It

---

[10] 1910, *passim*. Cf., however, vol. IV, p. 5, where Frazer speaks of "pure totemism, such as we find it among the Australian aborigines. . . ."

[11] A. A. Goldenweiser, 1910; reprinted 1933, pp. 213–332.

Social Organization: the Structure of Society

has been found that various kinds of totemism exist even in the same society, so that among the same people one group will claim descent from their totem, another will not; one sib will eat the flesh of the totem animal, another will not; one will take the name of the totem, another hold it too sacred to be revealed. It is thus apparent that while the institution of totemism is a powerful force in the lives of those who live under it, the term applies to a wide range of phenomena.

Totemism is not to be thought of as an odd quirk of the "primitive" mind. Those who live close to nature are not unique in assuming a symbolic relationship between men and animals. The eponymous feature of totemism, for example, is more prevalent in American culture than is realized. It is present when a lodge member proclaims himself a Moose or an Elk, or when a college man or woman is spoken of as a Bulldog or a Gopher or a Wildcat. Its development in more specific form during World War I in the American Expeditionary Forces, as recounted by Linton, shows that this mystical relationship could develop to a point lacking only exogamy to make it fit the totemic pattern of nonliterate societies.[12]

In concentrating on the problems of the family and the sib, students of social organization have tended to neglect other intermediate social structures. Chiefly, the reason for this is that much of the field-work of anthropologists was carried on among societies of small size, where social groupings between the immediate family and the sib play a minor role and could thus be taken for granted.

In African societies, however, where tribal populations are large, the sib is too unwieldy to stand without the support of intermediate institutions. Thus, among the Beni-Amer of the Sudan, Nadel reports that, in the upper classes, "the genealogical pattern repeats itself, with diminishing range, throughout the social structure of the tribes down to the smallest unit. Each clan is subdivided into kinship groups . . . , in turn . . . composed of a number of families, each under its family head."[13] Or, turning to West Africa, the forty-eight sibs and sub-sibs of Dahomey seem a considerable number, until it is realized that there are about a million Dahomeans. In Nigeria and the Gold Coast, towns are divided into quarters, each predominantly inhabited by the local representatives of some of the sibs spread over the total tribal area. The concept of the *extended family* was developed in Africa, therefore, to designate these local groups, composed of the members of a series of *immediate* families inhabiting the same locale. When large enough, the extended family is to be thought of as a *sub-sib*, which, through a process of growth and fission, can develop into a full-fledged sib. This is the traditional account of the origin of a number of sibs, and field research corroborates this process as continuing into the present.

The institution of the extended family has now been found to exist in many parts of the world. It would seem as though it were essential, as a matter of fact, to the functioning of society. For if the clan is too broad a grouping, the immediate family is too small to stand alone. Thus, in modern Peru, "The

[12] R. Linton, 1924, pp. 296–300.
[13] S. F. Nadel, 1945, p. 6.

301

extended family is the basic unit in Aymara society and the most important economic group." It includes a man and his brothers, their wives, sons, and unmarried daughters, and each "conjugal family" (that is, immediate family), has its own cluster of houses within the compound where the entire group live.[14] In McKern's older study of the "functional family" among the California Patwin, what he describes there as the "family social group" can readily be reinterpreted as an extended family.[15] Citing many references to the earlier literature, Drucker states that among the Indians of the North Pacific Coast, "when we come to examine the constitution of the typical local group of the area, a more striking fact appears: everywhere this social division was no more and no less than an extended family (slaves, of course, excluded) and was so considered by its members." [16] Or turning once more

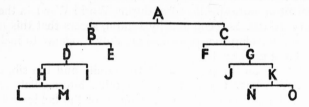

Fig. 27   *Relationships between Nuer lineages (after Evans-Pritchard, 1940).*

to Goodwin's study of the Western Apache, we find his analysis included groupings of "several households choosing to live together because of blood, clan, marital, and economic ties." These he designates as "the extended family, or 'family cluster.'" [17]

It is becoming apparent, moreover, that even a tripartite scheme of dividing kinship aggregates is by no means adequate to express all the social structures based on kinship. Lineages, as groupings of kin within a sib and without reference to size may be termed, vary considerably from one society to another in the number of sub-units they comprise. This has been demonstrated by Evans-Pritchard, who describes four orders of such groupings among the East African Nuer. "A Nuer clan," that is, a sib, "is the largest group of agnates who trace their descent from a common ancestor and between whom marriage is forbidden and sexual relations considered incestuous." It is "a highly segmented genealogical structure." The genealogical segments are the lineages. Lineages are of four degrees, *maximal, major, minor,* and *minimal.* Their relationship is shown in the diagram given above. Sib A "is segmented into maximal lineages B and C and these bifurcate into major lineages D, E, F and G. Minor lineages H, I, J, and K are segments of major lineages D and G, and L, M, N and O are minimal lineages which are segments of H and K." [18] These aggregates are recognized in native

[14] H. Tschopik, Jr., 1946, pp. 542–3.
[15] W. C. McKern, 1922, pp. 235–38.
[16] P. Drucker, 1939, p. 58.
[17] Op. cit., p. 123.
[18] E. E. Evans-Pritchard, 1940, pp. 192–3.

terminology and practice, yet each stands as a unit "only in relation to each other" and in contradistinction to another of the same degree. Thus "M is a group only in opposition to L, H is a group only in opposition to I, D is a group only in opposition to E." Conversely, "there is always fusion of collateral lineages of the same branch in relation to a collateral branch, e.g. in the diagram L and M are a single minor lineage H, in opposition to I," and so on. This means that "a man is a member of a lineage in relation to a certain group and not a member of it in relation to a different group." [19]

It is apparent from this analysis that the institutions of family and sibs are but points of reference in a continuum that may, in terms of form and function, extend beyond these points and describe a progression whose elements are far more complicated than is often realized. Where families are polygynous and wives inhabit separate houses, this seemingly minimal unit may be broken down into smaller nuclear ones, consisting each of a woman and her children, as is the case in large West African compounds. At the other end of the scale, sibs may be combined into clusters called *moieties*, as in North America and Australia.

<h1 style="text-align:center">4</h1>

IN ADDITION to the various kinds of groupings based on kinship, human societies include aggregates that derive from other criteria, such as sex, or age, or common interest. To all these the term best applied is *associations*, a word that was first consistently used by Lowie, in the same work in which he suggested the use of the term "sib" for larger kinship groups. The name "association," in his words, is to be used for "social units not based on the kinship factor." [20]

The size of associations, and the ends they seek, are even more varied than kinship structures. Earlier students emphasized groupings based on kinship and quite disregarded these others, and it was not until the turn of the century that this oversight began to be corrected. Even then, however, attention turned to the factor of sex differences, as expressed in the separation of the sexes in secret "societies," age grades, and men's houses, all of which were held to reflect the importance of the role of men in society as against that of women. Yet, though those who stressed the importance of nonrelationship groupings in human social life neglected to take into account their variety, or to sense many of the significant functions they perform, the mere fact that these associations were brought to the attention of students was of importance in placing the study of social organization in proper perspective. Earlier studies investigated the larger nonrelationship groupings, especially those that, because of their secret character, or their political or military functions, exhibit a dramatic quality and numerical weight which smaller size and less esoteric aims cannot achieve. The investigation of the more modest

---

[19] *Ibid.*, pp. 197–8.
[20] *Op. cit.*, p. 257.

types came later, when the importance of studies that probe humbler, more humdrum institutions, came to be stressed.

Institutionalized friendship, first described as such for Dahomey, offers an excellent example of this. As late as 1920, Lowie wrote of the "diminutive association" represented by "the union of two unrelated friends pledged to mutual support and lifelong comradeship" as something "of altogether peculiar character" among the Dakota Indians and related tribes. This sort of "Damon-Pythias relationship," as he termed it, resulted in the creation of an indefinite number of friendly couples, representing so many independent separate units. The significance of this fact was stated to be that, while similarity of age undoubtedly enters in forming such attachments, they do not represent the "complete cross-section of society along lines of social cleavage" demanded by the theory of associations that was then current.[21]

With the leads furnished by the African material, however, data, either gathered independently or recovered from older sources, have established the importance and indicated the functions of institutionalized friendship in the social organization of many peoples. Mandelbaum, in a paper giving details of such friendships among the Plains Cree Indians of Canada, also cites ten earlier references to various types of friendship alliance in North America. Among the Cree, attachments formed between two boys during the summer Sun Dance period are the beginning of these friendships. The two call each other by a word meaning "he with whom I go about." They address the parents of one another as father and mother, and each avoids the sisters of the other as he does his own sisters. Should one die, the other lives at the dead youth's home for a time, and thereafter regards it as his own. Their wives call each other by the "sister" terms used by wives of brothers. Women also enter into friendships. Two other variants, one involving temporary wife exchange between an older and a younger man, are likewise recorded.[22]

In Malekula, an island of the New Hebrides group in Melanesia, the ceremonial significance of friendship is stressed. In this society, currency in the ritual and prestige economy is the pig. At funerals, the rites "may be said to depend essentially upon the killing and giving of one pig." This animal, which must have belonged to the dead man, is produced, and then, "his greatest friend . . . steps forward with a spear and seizes hold of the rope to which the pig is tied, as though for the moment he were about to kill it." He does not do this, however, but hands the rope and spear to the second-best friend of the dead man. This individual repeats the performance, turning the rope and spear to the third-best friend, and so on, until they reach "a man who was not a friend of the deceased and who, therefore, is going to accept the pig." He kills the animal, and takes it and the banana and yams given him to his village, where they are eaten. This refusal to perform the duty arises out of the "very intense bond . . . something that may be described almost as love," experienced by "two men who habitually eat to-

---

[21] Op. cit., p. 320.
[22] D. Mandelbaum, 1936.

gether, sharing a common meal." Thus, "seeing a pig which had belonged to the . . . (dead man) . . . , the survivor thinks: 'If he were alive it is we, who would eat this pig together; but he is dead now, let those who are his enemies feast on it.'" Should clansmen of the dead later make gifts of food to great friends of the dead in other clans, "they would be liable to be shot at or poisoned."[23]

A form of institutionalized friendship from New Guinea has also been reported by Hogbin who tells how, in Wogeo, two men enter into a relationship termed *wasabwai*. This "bond-friendship," which becomes less strong after marriage, is one in which the two young men exchange confidences regarding their love-affairs and "walk arm in arm," something that is "the more remarkable since other persons, including spouses, shun bodily contact in public."[24] Similarly, "pairs of friends" are found in New Ireland, several cases of this kind of close association between boys, one older and one younger, having been observed in the village of Lesu.[25]

Dahomey provides an example of institutionalized friendship from West Africa, the Didinga from the other side of the continent.[26] The Dahomean has three friends, the *honton daho*, or first friend; the second, whose name is derived from the fact that at one point in the funeral ceremony, he takes his place against a wall; and the third, "the friend who stands on the threshold." Here, as in Malekula, the ritual functions of friendship at funerals take on great importance, though in Dahomey they figure on many other occasions. The relationship demands complete mutual confidence, which is the more striking in view of the great circumspectness that usually marks relationships between Dahomeans. A man withholds nothing from his first friend; to his second he tells no more than half of what he knows; while the third "stands at the threshold and hears what he can." The best friend transmits the desires of one who has died concerning the disposal of his property, and confirms the heir; he is the first after the eldest son to make funerary gifts; when an ancestor is deified, the soul of his best friend is summoned to possess one of its descendants, who makes the proper offering. The deep emotional tone that marks this relationship caused incidents like the following to occur repeatedly. When, in the days of the native kingdom, a man was sought by the king's officers and could not be found, his best friend was arrested. This was not because it was felt that torture could induce him to reveal the hiding-place, but because when news of his detention reached the fugitive, he would come forward to free his friend. As a Dahomean tale explains, "In the life of man, when the choice must be made between the father-in-law, diviner, or best friend, a man must always be closest to the best friend. The others a man may leave to one side, but the best friend of a man is first."[27]

It is apparent, from these examples, that the distribution of institutionalized friendship is very wide, though it will remain for later studies to

---

[23] A. B. Deacon, 1934, pp. 537–40.
[24] I. H. Hogbin, 1946, pp. 193–4.
[25] H. Powdermaker, 1933, pp. 87–9.
[26] J. H. Driberg, 1935.
[27] M. J. Herskovits, 1938b, vol. I, pp. 88ff., 239–42, 361ff., *passim*.

permit its full incidence to become known. Some of this information will come from fresh ethnographic research. Much, however, is to be gained from hints in the literature such as Mandelbaum found, and from citations where more striking aspects of friendship, such as blood brotherhood, have been described. There seems to be much likelihood that these are but ceremonial phases, which bring into high relief an association that, over the years, plays a constant role in the complex of personal relationships shaped by the social organization of a people.

Larger groupings are better known, and we may here indicate some of the many different kinds that exist. Among the Plains Indian tribes, in addition to the relationship of friendship we have already cited, Lowie notes associations "based on a common supernatural experience," feasting societies, dance societies, and military societies. In addition he names the Cheyenne women's crafts guilds, the Hidatsa bundle fraternities, and the Tobacco order of the Crow. Many more types are to be found if this list is extended to other parts of the world. They include groupings which have police or executive functions, societies with insurance features, or those dedicated to cooperative labor (as are found in Africa), as well as religious orders, and, especially in the eastern part of the continent, age sets. Age grades are outstanding in Melanesia. Most—though by no means all—of these groupings are restricted to men. One already mentioned is a woman's society, while still others, such as West African aggregates that pool savings for a common end or for ultimate redistribution, may include both men and women.

Functions are by no means clearly distinguished, but an association can best be classified according to its principal aim. Most African secret societies have some kind of judiciary and punitive function, but in the vast majority of cases, the power which sanctions their activities is a supernatural one. Conversely, in the same areas, the cult-groups into which devotees of the gods are initiated have many aspects of secrecy. In the interest of differentiation, we may classify the first as groupings whose validating powers derive from the dead, and where secrecy of membership and proceedings are so important, as in the "secret societies"; while the latter, for all their esoteric initiatory rites, are religious groups, the secrecy of the rites being incidental and not primary. So intimately related are the functions of ancestors and gods among the Nigerian Yoruba of Ife, however, that Bascom, on the basis of field research, raises the question "Are there any secret societies, properly speaking, in West Africa?" That is, do not the religious aspects of these associations play so important a part in all such groupings that this phase should be held paramount? [28] It is clear that a reinvestigation of the field of secret societies must be undertaken and a new definition formulated.

Associations may exist where formal organization is so slight that the term "society" can be applied only with difficulty. An instance of this is the skein of *compadre* relationships among the Yaqui Indians of Arizona, consisting primarily of a series of mutual obligations between godparents and godchildren, and co-sponsors of the same godchild. These sets of ceremonial

---

[28] W. R. Bascom, 1944, p. 73.

sponsors are enough institutionalized, however, so that they may be called "padrino groups." [29]

Nonliterate societies are no different than our own in the number, or type, or functions of associations. Nor, for all the specialization that marks our culture, do they differ from us in the absence of clear-cut objectives that permit classification that is always satisfactory. Our lodges, too, have supernatural sanctions, just as do African secret societies; the Knights Templar division of the Masonic order, for example, could easily be classed by a visiting Melanesian ethnographer as a religious grouping. Labor unions are often called lodges, with pass-words and ritual, and recreational as well as economic functions.

It would seem that we can do little more than note the fact that in all human societies men and women form attachments and set up groupings that transcend the lines of kinship. Propinquity is perhaps one reason for this, community of interests another, the possession of the same skill a third, and the establishment of status by exclusiveness a fourth. Specific hypotheses regarding their development, such as that which held secret societies to have sprung from the initiatory rites which, in many nonliterate cultures, boys and sometimes girls must undergo at puberty, are interesting but impossible to establish on the basis of adequate documentation. The multiplicity of forms and purposes that such groupings have been found to manifest do demonstrate, however, that no study of the social organization of any people can be regarded as adequate, unless they are taken fully into account.

5

THE study of institutionalized forms of social structures, described in the preceding pages, has been extended by researches that have sought to describe and analyze the dynamic personal interrelationships out of which these institutions stem. In such researches, the mechanisms that achieve the socialization of the individual have been given intensive treatment. Attention has also been given the later adjustments that mark the status of the individual as a member of his society, and the changing relationships with his fellow-members that accompany such changes in his position.

An early instance of this dynamic approach to social organization is had in the work of Bateson, who, in a study of the Iatmul people of New Guinea, subjected to intensive analysis his field materials bearing on a rite called *naven*. "I found," he says, "that I could think of each bit of culture structurally; I could see it in accordance with a consistent set of rules or formulations. Equally, I could see each bit as 'pragmatic,' either as satisfying the needs of individuals or as contributing to the integration of society. Again, I could see each bit . . . as an expression of emotion." [30] The terms of specific reference he uses need not be introduced into our consideration of Bateson's analysis. It is enough to indicate that he found he could isolate "five major

---

[29] E. H. Spicer, 1940, pp. 91–116.
[30] G. Bateson, 1936, p. 262.

307

The Aspects of Culture

points of view for the study of the behaviour of human beings in society—structural, . . . emotional, . . . economic, developmental and sociological." [31]

The sociological relationships, with which we are here primarily concerned, were found to give rise to fissions between various groupings within the tribe to which Bateson gave the term "schismogenesis." This is defined by him as "a process of differentiation in the norms of individual behaviour resulting from cumulative interaction between individuals." [32] The dynamic character of his approach is clear when, in defining anthropology as the study of "the reactions of an individual to the reactions of other individuals," he states that, "It is at once apparent that many systems of relationship, either between individuals or groups of individuals, contain a tendency toward progressive change." [33] The concept of schismogenesis, then, is to be used in helping understand the process of "shaping . . . cultural norms," such as the relationships obtaining between the sexes, or between members of sib-groups, and the like. The applicability of the concept, Bateson holds, goes farther than Iatmul culture. He suggests its utility in understanding "all intimate relations between pairs of individuals"—such as the institutionalized friendships we have discussed; in studying "the progressive maladjustment of neurotic and prepsychotic individuals"; in the study of culture-contacts; in politics. [34]

Warner, who has conducted a most extensive investigation into the social structure of a New England community, approaches his data from a point of view that is basically similar to that of Bateson. Society, for him, is "a group of mutually interacting individuals." Therefore, it follows that "if any relationship of a given social configuration is stimulated, it will influence all other parts and in turn be influenced by them." Within this configuration, the "several relations mutually determine the activities which take place at any given time in one or all of the relations." The complexity of the resulting give-and-take is such that several modes of attack on the problem of "understanding an event or a number of events" must be employed. First, the "events or activities under observation" are placed "in an immediate social relational context"; then this immediate context is articulated with a larger one; finally this latter is in turn placed in "the total situation of interrelations which compose the whole community." [35]

Chapple, who is likewise concerned with social interaction, holds essentially the same position. "Almost all an individual's life is spent in interaction with other individuals in institutions. From the time of birth, when an individual becomes a member of a family and begins his conditioning to others, through the whole course of his waking hours . . . his behavior is constantly being modified by the actions of others. If we hope to describe the behavior of individuals and from our descriptions predict the future course of events, we must analyze these institutions. This means that we have to develop

[31] *Ibid.*, p. 266.
[32] *Ibid.*, p. 175.
[33] *Ibid.*, p. 176.
[34] *Ibid.*, pp. 178–187.
[35] W. L. Warner, 1941, p. 13.

methods of describing the relations of a number of individuals in a state of mutual dependence."[36]

This approach leads to the analysis of society in terms of what Chapple envisages as a hierarchy of institutions, depending on the complexity of the interrelations involved in them. The quantitative methods he employs sets off Chapple's attack from that of Warner, who calls on a minimum of statistical analysis in working through the large amount of data handled in his study. Yet like Chapple and Bateson, Warner is much more concerned with relationships within structures than with the description and classification of social structures as such. This is to be seen in his definition of a social structure as "a system of formal and informal groupings by which the social behavior of individuals is regulated."[37] Here again, attention is directed toward dynamics; the description of forms is but a means toward understanding the functions of social institutions in regulating social behavior.

That approaches of this kind must complement and extend the significance of the earlier descriptive study of social organization is self-evident. Is is essential that we know more than *how* people are organized; we must also know what the systems of social structures *do* in ordering the lives of people who live in accordance with them. These newer approaches will understandably require the test of time to demonstrate their effectiveness. It will also be essential that their validity as instruments of cross-cultural study be investigated, since except for Bateson's work most analyses of social relationships in these dynamic terms have been made on the basis of studies of American communities.

Yet this is but a matter of detail, involving the refinement of techniques, in the light of needs, for the most effective analyses of the problem of man interacting with his fellows within the terms of reference of the social institutions of many different groups, having many different cultures. Of the importance of solving the problem itself there can be no doubt, if an understanding of the nature and functioning of human society is to be reached.

---

[36] E. D. Chapple, 1940, p. 51.
[37] W. L. Warner, *op. cit.*, p. 14.

CHAPTER 19

Education and the Sanctions
of Custom

In its widest sense, education is to be thought of as that part of the en-culturative experience that, through the learning process, equips an individual to take his place as an adult member of his society. The process, in most nonliterate communities, is carried on until the onset of puberty for girls, and slightly later for boys. In Euroamerican groups, especially at upper socio-economic levels, the period is appreciably lengthened. A much more restricted sense of the word "education" limits its use to those processes of teaching and learning carried on at specific times, in particular places outside the home, for definite periods, by persons especially prepared or trained for the task. This assigns to education the meaning of *schooling*.

Despite the fact that, in the broadest sense, education can be regarded as synonymous with the cycle of early enculturation, it is important for purposes of analysis to differentiate the conceptual significance of enculturation from that we shall assign here to the word education; and equally important to set off both these terms from the designation "schooling." All three are to be regarded as expressions of a single process, whereby an individual masters and manipulates his culture. But, as we have seen, enculturation continues throughout the entire life of an individual. It not only includes the training he receives at the hands of others, but also the assimilation of elements in his culture that he acquires without direction, through his own powers of observation and by imitation. A new dance he learns as an adult is a part of his enculturation, but hardly of his education; so is the manner in which, so to speak, he absorbs the motor and speech habits of his group. Training in etiquette, however, is education, as is instruction in some special technique such as pottery-making or gardening, or the inculcation of moral values by the tales a boy or girl is told for the purpose.

We must, therefore, be as cautious in evaluating definitions of education that are too inclusive, such as that which holds this process to be "the relationship between members of successive generations,"[1] as in accepting definitions that are drawn too narrowly. Just as enculturation is a term of wider

---

[1] O. Raum, 1940, p. 62.

Education and the Sanctions of Custom

the smallness of nonliterate groups, and the homogeneity of their cultures. Those from outside a society who wish to acquire a technique, a healing formula, a rite, or a knowledge of certain tales, must seek to learn it. Once learned, it is taken home, where it is made available for others either as a free good, with the reward for its transmission expressed in prestige, or for a price. Pressure is rarely laid on even at this point to convince fellow-tribesmen it should be accepted. Except where the new acquisition is sold for a price, those who wish to learn it, may; those who do not wish to, need not.

The urge to learn is basic in all children, and in nonliterate societies, this drive is pointed toward culturally sanctioned ends that are much broader in relation to the cultural resources available than in a highly specialized culture such as our own. Here, where because of intense specialization choices are numerous, training must be along narrower lines—whether in terms of general behavior associated with one class as against another, or for a particular occupation, or even in chosen recreational pursuits. In nonliterate societies there are few square pegs in round holes. These are essentially the product of cultures wherein there are so many alternative possibilities that no individual can range at will over the entire body of traditions of his society, knowing the totality of his culture, being competent in most of it, and attaining special skill in such of its aspects as may appeal to him. To permit a child to explore as he wishes first one, then another compartment of a machine culture of Europe or America would make of him, in much more than the occupational sense, a "Jack of all trades and master of none."

It must not be supposed that because nonliterate peoples do not ordinarily educate their children in schools, educational devices are lacking. Knowledge must be acquired by learning, and it is not sufficient to lay it before even the most eager learner without organization and direction. Therefore, though schooling is not a factor in the education of the young of nonliterate peoples, there is no lack of educational techniques to encourage, to discipline, to punish. Punishment can be harsh indeed where consistent failure in some important aspect of life is continuous or incompetence is wilful. On the other hand, methods of arousing interest through rewards for the performance of duties laid on a child, or even by dramatizing the right to learn these duties, are frequently reported. Where a culture stresses competition, the play of competitive drives will be utilized to induce learning. Where competition is not important in ordering behavior, other methods of stimulating a child to want to be competent will be found. The process of educating the young, that is, like any other aspect of culture, is patterned and institutionalized.

2

CHILDHOOD is a carefree period of life for most human beings, despite the fact that they are continuously subjected to pressures and disciplines to shape them into functioning members of their society. The techniques of education used by nonliterate peoples vary as widely as any other aspect of their

313

culture. They are expressed in overt training by elders, in emulating older children, in observation at ceremonies where only the mature are active participants, or sitting by while a parent or other elder relative goes about the daily tasks of a man or a woman, and watching what is done. They include the inculcation of moral values and proper conduct by direct instruction, the correction of an infringement of an accepted code by admonition, ridicule, or corporal punishment. Positive as well as negative measures are employed in bringing up a child. In many cultures, praise is lavished on the child who successfully performs an act, and various ways of encouraging him to attempt to do things he may be hesitant to try have been recorded, as where in West Africa bells are attached to the ankles of an infant who is learning to walk, so that he will increase his efforts.

It must be remembered that when we emphasize the primacy of the family in the education of children, we must accept this institution in a given culture in whatever form it may be defined. Within the family, education is principally carried on by the members of a household. Where family units are small, as among ourselves, this means that the father and mother, with perhaps a grandparent or uncle or aunt who is for a time a member of this grouping, discharge this obligation. In unilineal systems, where the classificatory relationship pattern prevails, the immediate contacts of the child will be far different from those of the individual brought up in a household whose members count their collaterals bilineally. Under a classificatory kinship structure, there will be several "fathers" or "mothers" to whom the upbringing of a child is of concern. All of these, by right, can admonish, encourage, punish, or reward in ways that even uncles and aunts in our own culture would rarely presume to do. Thus in a survey of the educational practices of American Indian tribes north of Mexico, Pettitt [3] names forty-three groups where the mother's brother plays a principal part in the education of the child.

In Zuñi, Li assigns this broad base of supervision an important place in the "working mechanism" of educational discipline the child is submitted to. "All the members of the family besides the parents coöperate to see that the child behaves well. In fact, any member of the community who happens to pass by will say something to correct some misbehavior of a child. Confronted with this united front of adults, so to speak, the child does not have much chance in trying to play one against the other. And if he is not unduly constrained, why should he make it unpleasant both for himself and for others? It is often observed that a very obstreperous child is easily hushed by a slight sound of any adult, in fact, by any facial expression which is seen by the child." [4] Here we have an extension of the function of correction from classificatory relatives to the other adults of the community. This, again, entails no difficulty. The homogeneity of the culture makes for a unity of teaching objectives that reflect unity of cultural aims and methods of inculcating them in the young, and thus leaves little room for conflict between the directives given by different preceptors.

---

[3] 1946, pp. 19–22.
[4] Li An-che, 1937, p. 70.

Education and the Sanctions of Custom

This conflict in directives is perhaps the source of the most serious difficulties in larger, less homogeneous societies, where the total educational process includes schooling as well as training in the home. Serious conflicts and deep-seated maladjustment may result from education received at the hands of persons whose cultural or sub-cultural frames of reference differ. The educational processes of nonliterate societies by no means make for perfect adjustment, or reflect complete cultural homogeneity. Such terms are always relative, and since culture is never static, continuous changes imply some measure of departure, everywhere, from the utter homogeneity that has mistakenly been held to characterize nonliterate societies. There are many sources of conflict and maladjustment other than imbalance in the educational system of a people, and many instances of these conflicts and maladjustments are reported in the ethnographic literature. Nonetheless, where a single agency—the family, however constituted, in most nonliterate communities—has for all practical purposes the sole responsibility for training a child, there is little opportunity to introduce the contradictions and confusions that can arise where multiple channels exist to teach the growing boy or girl.

Zuñi methods of "education for daily life," which, as Li puts it, "are in a sense more pervasive than formal school education," include three principal factors other than the one already mentioned, of supervision by a number of persons. He points out first, that though parental love is on occasion manifested in outward behavior, there is no excessive demonstrativeness. "The children are allowed a much greater independence in a free world of their own." They play in groups by themselves, so that the parents have no need to help in amusing or otherwise occupying their time. Parents are rather "taken for granted as the source of . . . wellbeing." In the next place, children are chastised if necessary. This, however, "is done deliberately and effectively. There is no fussing around on the part of the mother, nor is there endless talk among the adults so that the child is encouraged to be mischievous by giving him so much publicity and attention." Finally, as a fourth factor, religious beliefs lend appreciable weight to the educational system. Each religious group includes a functionary who, posing as one of the supernatural beings worshipped by the Zuñi, has the task of punishing children who misbehave.

Among the Chiricahua Apache Indians, says Opler, "the memory of training is synonymous with the consciousness of self." The following account by a native informant both documents this statement, and shows the injunctions one Apache remembers his elders to have given him in the process of inculcating in him the norms of sanctioned behavior:

As far back as I can remember my father and mother directed me how to act. They used to tell me, "Do not use a bad word you wouldn't like to be used to you. Do not feel that you are anyone's enemy. In playing with children remember this: do not take anything from another child. Don't take arrows away from another boy just because you are bigger than he is. Don't take his marbles away. Don't steal from your own friends. Don't be unkind to your playmates. If you are kind now, when you become a man you will love your fellow-men.

315

The Aspects of Culture

When you go to the creek and swim, don't duck anyone's children. Don't ever fight a girl when you're playing with other children. Girls are weaker than boys. If you fight them, that will cause us trouble with our neighbors.

Don't laugh at feeble old men and women. That's the worst thing you can do. Don't criticize them and make fun of them. Don't laugh at anybody or make fun of anybody.

This is your camp. What little we have here is for you to eat. Don't go to another camp with other children for a meal. Come back to your own camp when you are hungry and then go out and play again.

When you start to eat, act like a grown person. Just wait until things are served to you. Do not take bread or a drink or a piece of meat before the rest start to eat. Don't ask before the meal for things that are still cooking, as many children do. Don't try to eat more than you want. Try to be just as polite as you can; sit still while you eat. Do not step over another person, going around and reaching for something.

Don't run into another person's camp as though it was your own. Don't run around anyone's camp. When you go to another camp, don't stand at the door. Go right in and sit down like a grown person. Don't get into their drinking water. Don't go out and catch or hobble horses and ride them as if they belonged to you the way some boys do. Do not throw stones at anybody's animals.

When a visitor comes, do not go in front of him or step over him. Do not cut up while the visitor is here. If you want to play, get up quietly, go behind the visitor, and out the door.

Understandably, such a series of admonitions would not be given at one time. Yet the fact that parents were able to instil a code of proper behavior in an individual so that he could, when grown, tell it as consistently as it is given here demonstrates the effectiveness of the teaching. The Apache not only teach deportment and ethics; they point out to boys and girls the kind of work each will have to do, and see to it that they learn how to manipulate their technology: "The boys watch the men when they are making bows and arrows; the man calls them over, and they are forced to watch him. The women, on the other hand, take the girls out and show them what plants to use for baskets, what clay for pots. And at home the women weave the baskets, sew moccasins, and tan buckskin before the girls. While they are at work, they tell the students to watch closely so that when they reach womanhood nobody can say anything about their being lazy or ignorant. They teach the girls to cook and advise them about picking berries and other fruits and gathering food." [5]

Children in this culture are as a rule subjected to little corporal punishment: "We do not whip the child if we can help it." A blanket is thrown over the head of a child who persists in crying, until it stops, or a cup of cold water is poured slowly over its head. Enuresis is cured by putting a bird's nest in the bed. "Then the nest is thrown to the east, and the child won't wet the bed any more." Yet some men beat their sons. A girl who commits a breach of chastity is publicly flogged by her father, or if she is rude, may receive a "box on the ear" from her grandmother. More often children are disciplined by threats of punishment by fearsome creatures. The Gray One, a masked-

[5] M. E. Opler, 1941, pp. 27–8.

Education and the Sanctions of Custom

clown dancer, figures most often as one of these. "The clown is going to put you into a basket and carry you off somewhere. Say this to a little child and he is going to mind right away." And when, as a child grows older, scepticism renders this threat no longer impressive, this being is made to "appear." The owl, associated with the dead, and as feared by adults as by children, is sometimes called on, or a child will be frightened by telling him that an old man "who looks fierce" will take him away. In one instance, an old man was called and did actually put a little boy in his sack, whereupon a promise to obey came immediately.[6]

These varied techniques of teaching and disciplining the young make a point that controverts both of two stereotypes concerning the relationship between parents and children in "primitive society." One is that "primitive man" is savage and brutal towards children, regarding them as wealth and exploiting them to his advantage; the other is that because of his love of children, he permits them to grow up without correction, giving in to their every whim, until they metamorphose as full-fledged, responsible adult members of their group. Either view can be documented by examples from the literature, but not from the studies of those who in their field-work have been trained to record variation in custom even to the point of setting down practices that seem quite at odds. Here, in one culture, we find high-minded ethical precepts, and appeal to terror-inspiring beings. Among these Apache, a pattern of using the gentlest methods of correction and the heartiest encouragement does not preclude the use of corporal punishment when this is held to be necessary.

This wide range of educational procedures and methods of correction has been reported from every culture where careful studies of the training of children have been made. The South African Kgatla, for example, employ "exhortation and reprimand, as well as . . . chastisement, as the occasion arises. Mistakes are corrected, ignorance is dispelled, good behaviour is applauded, and insolence or disobedience are immediately followed by punishment." This is generally a scolding or whipping, but sometimes a beating is administered: "The Kgatla say that thrashing makes a child wise, and helps it to remember what it has been taught." But they also say "A growing child is like a little dog," and even though it may annoy grown-ups, it must be taught proper conduct with patience and forbearance.[7]

The children of Lesu, a Melanesian village on New Ireland in the Bismarck Archipelago, are likewise exposed to various sorts of enculturative techniques. After the nursing period, a child receives the "careful attention" of adults and older children, though without the earlier petting and fondling. "Children from three to six are rarely left alone. They are either with their parents in the village, or, if the latter are away in the gardens or fishing, they are with their older brothers and sisters, classificatory ones if there are no real ones. . . . When the parents are in the village the little children follow them about. They are present at all adult activities—dance rehearsals,

---

[6] Ibid., pp. 29–34.
[7] I. Schapera, 1940, p. 253.

rites, communal preparations of food, etc. . . . . Occasionally they carry small, light articles, such as a basket for taro, from the house to the beach for their parents." Discipline begins at this time, too, and young children are spanked when they are disobedient. However, the hurt is mitigated by the fact that "if one parent quarrels with a child, the other will take the child's part," a pattern that "applies not only to parents but to other relatives." [8]

As the child grows older in Lesu, the process of learning by emulation and direction continues. The former is doubly important: "Respect for the wishes and commands of their elders is also impressed upon the children by their observation of adult behavior. They see their own parents meeting the wishes of the grandparents, and always it is the oldest people present who are the more important." [9] Knowledge of sexual behavior is likewise gained by observation, but this includes obtaining an understanding of the prohibited degrees of relationship as well as of the techniques of the sex act. Thus in the sex play of early life, if a boy and girl of the same moiety are found together, they are scolded, beaten, and made to feel thoroughly ashamed of their acts. "The adults appear to be well aware of the laws of habit formation, and they take no chances on letting the children transgress an incest taboo even in play." [10] Girls, on the whole, are given more work than boys, but both sexes lead a relatively care-free pre-adolescent life. Formal teaching is at a minimum, being confined to the definite instruction provided by the telling of folk-tales, wherein, during a period of three or four weeks, the elders nightly recount the tales which explain the canons of proper behavior. On these occasions the code of etiquette and the accepted taboos are inculcated, and the punishment meted out to those who transgress them is made clear.

In a study of educational processes employed by the Kwoma, a New Guinea people of the Sepik River area, Whiting gives numerous instances to show that these people put to use all the customary teaching techniques. They motivate by punishing, scolding, threatening, warning, and inciting; they guide by leading, instructing, and demonstrating; they reward by giving gifts, helping and praising. These differing devices are not systematically used, but are rather to be abstracted from the day-to-day incidents observed in the field. A blow of a stick, the use of a word having associations of disgust or danger, will punish or scold. Showing a younger boy how to light a fire in a strong wind is instructing. Giving presents to young boys who participate in cooperative labor is training by rewarding them for meritorious behavior. [11]

We again see how in this region, as in the other parts of the nonliterate world, the education of the young is accomplished by the use of no single device. Rather each society calls on the resources of persuasion and compulsion to develop its young into the kind of individuals it holds desirable. In some cultures, it has been seen, more emphasis is laid on one method, or a particular group of methods, than on others; while still other devices, for all practical purposes, are excluded from the training repertory. They may be

[8] H. Powdermaker, 1933, pp. 81–2.
[9] Ibid., p. 84.
[10] Ibid., p. 85.
[11] J. W. M. Whiting, 1941, pp. 18off.

Education and the Sanctions of Custom

seldom employed, or may even be regarded with distaste, as in the case of corporal punishment among many American Indian tribes. But in no culture is education haphazard. Children nowhere "just grow," like Topsy. The elders watch, guide, supervise, correct. That all of them can perform this function is one of the reasons why, in nonliterate societies, education is so integral a part of day-to-day life that students could for many years have overlooked its existence as a ubiquitous aspect of culture.

3

THOUGH the things any group may teach its young are limited only by the scope of its culture, education lays different emphases in different cultures. This must be so. No two cultures have similar orientations, and the transmission of cultural identity requires the continuation of the orientations that are the expressions of the differing interests people have in different aspects of their cultures. A complete catalog of what is taught a child would thus in the fullest sense constitute an ethnographic description of his culture. The order in which he is taught what he must learn reveals the maturation patterns of his group and indicates what they hold important in their culture.

Certain aspects of education are universal. Every people conditions the infant to control his bodily functions. This is a phase of the educational process whose far-reaching effects on the personality structure of the adult are only beginning to be comprehended. All encourage linguistic communication, and see to it that the semantic values of the phonetic combinations in a language are properly used and understood. All instruct the young how to interpret the behavior of their fellows, and teach them how to act in specific situations and toward persons to whom they stand in particular kinds of relationships. There is none that does not teach ways of getting a living, and inculcate a sense of the economic values accepted by the group. Moral codes are everywhere emphasized, and those methods whereby an individual not only gets on with his fellows, but comes to be esteemed by them. Etiquette, in the widest sense of the term, is given continuous attention. As an extension of this, the meaning of the rituals of all kinds, and a knowledge of how to conduct such of them as will fall to a given individual are taught, as well as the causes and cures of sickness, and the facts of birth and death.

In general, the practice of marking off literate from nonliterate societies as great categories is indefensible because of the variation in custom among "civilized" no less than "primitive" peoples. Nonetheless, certain widespread emphases are placed in the education of the young in a great many nonliterate cultures that, for historical reasons, are touched on with relative lightness by literate peoples, certainly in those societies that lie in the Euroamerican cultural stream. Two of these can be considered here. One is the importance of learning proper attitudes and behavior-patterns toward relatives; the other has to do with education for accepted sexual behavior.

When we read of the complex order of kinship terminology that exists in most nonliterate cultures, we must remember that the intricate system re-

The Aspects of Culture

flects certain sanctioned forms of polite conduct, certain emotionally toned affects, certain duties and obligations between individuals that have to be learned. "At every moment of the life of a member of an Australian tribe," writes Radcliffe-Brown, "his dealings with other individuals are regulated by the relationship in which he stands to them. His relatives, near and distant, are classified into certain large groups, and this classification is carried out by means of the terminology, and could apparently not be achieved in any other way. Thus in any part of the continent when a stranger comes to a camp the first thing to be done, before he can be admitted within the camp, is to determine his relationship to every man and woman in it, *i.e.*, to determine what is the proper term of relationship for him to apply to each of them. As soon as he knows his relation to a given individual he knows how to behave towards him, what his duties are and what his rights." [12] These things, obviously, are not just absorbed. An Australian aborigine has to be taught the complicated kinship structure of his people, without which he would literally be unable to function as a member of his society. No sharper contrast could be cited to the way in which a man or woman in Euroamerican society may, without affecting his life, take only the closest relatives into account.

Kinship and sex may be intimately connected in the social structure of a people where institutionalized relationships of avoidance or preferential mating are found. The care with which the Trobriand child is taught to guard conduct where his *luguta*, his classificatory brother or sister is involved, is to the point here, for "the prohibition of any erotic or even of any tender dealings between brother and sister" is the "supreme taboo" of the Trobriander. "Round the word *luguta* a new order of ideas and moral rules begins to grow up at an early stage of the individual's life history. The child, accustomed to little or no interference with most of its whims or wishes, receives a real shock when suddenly it is roughly handled, seriously reprimanded, and punished whenever it makes any friendly, affectionate, or even playful advances to the other small being constantly about in the same household. Above all, the child experiences an emotional shock when it becomes aware of the expression of horror and anguish on the faces of its elders when they correct it." [13]

The Chaga child, in East Africa, must first of all learn the difference between the use of his parents' personal names and the terms of address he must use in speaking to them. This is much the convention of our society, where the child is taught that though his mother addresses his father as "John," he must call him "father" or "daddy" or by some other appellation. The Chaga child, as he grows, must learn that terms are used in the singular for reference, and in the plural for address when speaking to those of the parental and grandparental generation to whom reverence must be shown. "From birth," we are told, "the child is taught the proper terms for addressing his relatives. He is told about paternal and maternal grandparents, uncles, and aunts before he understands one word of his language. It is the mother

---

[12] 1931, p. 95.
[13] B. Malinowski, 1929, vol. II, pp. 519–20.

Education and the Sanctions of Custom

and nurse who teach the child to use the terms in appropriate situations. . . .
Father, mother, elder siblings and nurse admonish the impolite child and
advise it. . . . It is not to be wondered at that children are masters of kinship
etiquette when they are six years old and that at fourteen they know most
of the terminological subtleties." [14]

Similarly, "The Navaho child learns early that he can expect certain relatives to follow a prescribed way of behaving toward him. He finds that his
mother's brothers will scold him severely or punish him, but that he can get
away with playing tricks upon them or making broad jokes about their sex
life or disparaging their ability as hunters. He is taught, as he grows older,
that toward all the persons whom he calls 'my sister' he must be respectful
and practise certain avoidances. . . . He likewise notes that his elders preserve the same type of respect-avoidance relationship with their relatives
by marriage and again follow different linguistic usages from those they
employ with their blood relatives." But the manner in which he learns this,
and the intensity of the experience, depends on many things—the size of the
extended family to which he belongs, the number of playmates he has, the
isolation of his immediate family. Whatever his situation, however, by the
time he is grown, he has mastered the system of usage and behavior and
functions effortlessly in it. [15]

In nonliterate societies, as we have seen, the knowledge and practice of
sex is not left to chance. Some of the mechanisms that are employed demonstrate deep insight into the working of the human psyche. One instance of
this is the practice in West Africa of requiring a newly circumcised youth
to have sexual relations with an elderly woman, one who has passed the
menopause, "to take off the burn of the knife." By her experience she not
only aids him to perfect the technique of sex, but also helps to overcome any
traumatic shock that may have resulted from the operation. The pre-marital
experimentation that many nonliterate cultures sanction has a very definite
role in inculcating skill and finesse in sex behavior. Those who enter on marriage are thus not exposed to the psychological hazards, manifest in the frequency of frigidity in women and impotence in men found by modern
psychopathology in our own society, where matters of sex must be spoken
of secretively, are often considered as partially evil, and for which the young
person is prepared in a haphazard manner. Euroamerican culture, however,
has no monopoly on puritanical attitudes toward sex. There are nonliterate
groups where the conspiracy of silence is as strong where matters of sex are
involved as was ever the case in Europe or America in mid-Victorian times.
Yet these are in the minority. Most peoples, in numbering the facts of life,
do not draw the line this side of the problems of reproduction.

Training in sexual habits can be formalized, or informally given, or both
methods may be utilized even in the same culture. Much of the formal schooling given nonliterate boys and girls in the various "initiation" rites they
undergo at puberty is concerned with preparation for marriage. A mother,
or more often a grandmother, may inform the nubile girl about the conduct

---

[14] O. F. Raum, *op. cit.*, pp. 169–75.
[15] D. Leighton and C. Kluckhohn, 1947, pp. 44–5.

of sexual relations, and the behavior expected of her as a married woman, just as later she will attend her on the first night of her marriage, and officiate at the birth of her child, and teach her how to care for it. The men of the family will teach the boy how to behave toward his female companions. In many societies, the maternal uncle is especially charged with imparting this information to his sister's sons. The attitude toward instruction in sex is generally marked by consciousness of a serious duty on the part of the older people, rarely by lasciviousness. Lasciviousness, like obscenity, is found among all people. Both the occasions permitting their expression, and the forms this may take are often institutionalized and channeled. Their universality documents the psychological release they afford, and their stimulus to sexual play. But situations where sex instruction is given differ in setting and tone from the lighter moods of the young folk as they go about the business of satisfying their sexual desires, before they eventually enter into an arrangement whereby they establish families and in turn take up the parental role.

4

EDUCATION carried on by means of schooling in the hands of specialists cannot be overlooked in considering the training of the young among nonliterate peoples, even though this is only a minor aspect of their educational systems. In the aggregate, the variety and number of these forms is greater than earlier studies have recorded. They vary from rather temporary groupings, meeting informally, as when a Plains warrior takes some boys with him to learn how to hunt, to the long periods of seclusion and intensive courses of instruction of some of the African "schools." In these schools, boys and girls who have attained puberty are initiated into the status of young men and women, stoically sustaining the ordeal of circumcision or excision of the clitoris, and thus demonstrating their right to be full-fledged members of their society, warriors, and mothers. Peristiany describes the purpose of these rites as practised by the East African Kipsigis as follows: "To sharpen the endurance of the initiate, to make good warriors out of men, and to teach women to love and care for their husband's cattle. To teach men that they are part of a complicated organization, family, clan, *puriet* [warrior group], and age-set, to each of which they must show obedience." [16]

Africa and Polynesia provide most instances of schooling, properly speaking, in nonliterate cultures. The East African example can be matched with similar institutionalized modes of instruction from all parts of the continent. They vary considerably in the period of seclusion, and in the rites they practise. But they differ little in their objectives, since all mark the transition from the status of child to that of adult, and demand the proofs of competence and endurance that set off the social life of the adult from that of the child. Junod's description of the formal educational processes among the Bathonga of Portuguese East Africa [17] has deservedly become classic, though

---

[16] J. G. Peristiany, 1939, p. 26.
[17] 1927, vol. I, pp. 71–94.

Education and the Sanctions of Custom

this has been superseded by Stayt's more detailed study of the *thondo,* as the boys' school is called among the Venda. These schools are attended by every boy of the eighteen districts where they are located. Attendance begins when the lad is but eight or nine years old, and continues until after he has attained puberty, when he completes his initiation and his age-set is recognized. The boys live at the *thondo,* undergoing the discipline that will make of them a military unit. Instruction is given in such techniques of warfare as ambush and night attack, and in spying. Such tasks as mat-making that are assigned them must be finished on time. The rules of tribal etiquette must be carefully observed, otherwise punishment, consisting of a severe beating with a stick, is inflicted. The youths also practise dancing while in school. They emerge from their training "hardened and disciplined, ready to shoulder the responsibilities as well as to share the privileges of a fighting man of the tribe."

The Venda girls' schooling is brief. It lasts only six days and nights. The *vhusha,* as the rite is called, marks the passage of girls from childhood to adolescence, and occurs shortly after initial menstruation. Tribal rules of etiquette and obedience, dancing instruction, and sexual behavior are the principal subjects taught. Still another occasion for formal instruction is in a mixed school called *domba,* described as "general preparation for marriage." Its intricate ceremonial, "by means of symbols and metaphors," teaches boys and girls "to understand the true significance of marriage and childbirth," and warns them "of the pitfalls and dangers that they are likely to encounter during the course of their lives." [18]

From the western part of Africa many examples of schools have been reported. We may cite Watkins' analysis of the *poro* and *sande* schools of Liberia and Sierra Leone. The first of these schools is for boys, the second for girls. As with the Venda, the boys' school involves protracted training; periods varying from eighteen months to eight years are mentioned for different tribes. How important these schools are is to be seen from the fact that despite growing European influence, they still function over periods varying from eighteen months among the Vai to three years among the Gola. Here circumcision precedes entry into the school, which is under the general supervision of a leader whose position in the community reflects the importance of his office.

The training the boys receive is outstanding in the nonliterate world. "The boys are divided into groups according to their ages and aptitudes," states this report, "and receive instruction . . . in all the arts, crafts and lore of native life. . . . It is by this means that the character is molded and a youth is prepared to take his place among the generation of adults. . . . The first instruction involves a series of tests in order to determine individual differences, interests, and ambitions. . . . A youth who shows special aptitude for weaving, for example, is trained to become a master of the craft; while those who show distinctive skill and interest in carving, leatherwork, dancing, "medicine," folklore, etc., are developed along these specialized lines. This

---

[18] H. A. Stayt, 1931, pp. 101ff.

early training also includes work in the erection of the structures which are used while the session lasts. . . . All the laws and traditions of the tribe are taught, as well as duty to the tribal chief, tribe and elders, and the proper relations to women. Training is given in the recognition and use of various medicinal herbs, their curative powers, and various antidotes. Also, the secrets of wild animals are taught—how they live, how to recognize their spoor, and how to attack them." Finally, "all this training is tested out in the laboratory of 'bush'-school life," as when warfare is simulated, and the boys are called on to utilize, in planning and executing a campaign, what they have learned. The *sande* school, for girls, parallels in the organization of its staff, and other characteristics the *poro* training for boys. Its curriculum is directed toward training girls in their duties as grown women—wives and mothers—and thus with different content fulfils the same educational ends.[19]

In Polynesia, schools trained the young for the priesthood, and as specialists in entertainment. Luomala, in her useful summary of Polynesian literature, points out that, "New Zealand and the Society Islands had famous houses of learning, really primitive universities, at which the ancestral lore, genealogies, traditions, religion, magic, navigation, agriculture, literary composition, and all the arts and crafts were taught by learned priests." Schools in New Zealand were open for five months of the year, and the work was intensive, the pupils studying from sunrise until midnight in the special building dedicated to the holding of classes. Two branches of learning, the "Upper Jaw, having to do with the gods and cosmology, and the Lower Jaw, having to do with terrestrial matters," were taught. Emphasis was placed on repetition of religious formulae and lay precepts, rather than on investigation; but "changes . . . to suit the current winds of political and religious schisms" were made when the occasion demanded.

Formal courses of higher learning have also been reported from other parts of Polynesia, such as the Hawaiian college of heraldry. In general, we are told, "the hallmark of any well-born and well-trained chief was his ability to give orations with an abundance of religious and historical allusions, metaphors, similes, and proverbs"—which obviously required special training; and such training was also required if a person was to qualify as a member of the companies of dancers, or as an entertainer, of the kind found in Hawaii. For the most part, those who received training "in composition, narration and chanting were usually of noble birth. . . ." though they "did not form a special, intellectual class except in Mangareva, Marquesas and Easter Island." On the other hand, Polynesians of all ranks and both sexes might cultivate the art of oral literature, and some became specialists in reciting the long and complicated narratives about "a single favorite character." Furthermore, "daily life in Polynesia . . . required knowledge of many incantations, chants, traditions, proverbs, and fables. Every craft and occupation had its magical formulae, religious history, myths, and traditions. Besides their practical value in gaining the assistance of the gods, these gave dignity, prestige,

---

[19] M. H. Watkins, 1943, pp. 670–1; 673–4.

Education and the Sanctions of Custom

and background to the worker and to those who used the results of his work." [20] These motivations would seem largely to explain why, here, the tradition of specialized training that marked the area developed and maintained itself as an important part of the culture.

Elsewhere, though initiation of boys and girls at puberty into the tribe is common, and is almost invariably employed as an instrument to point earlier instruction and extend its scope, the teaching function is somewhat more submerged in the ritualistic aspect of the "school," though these ritualistic elements are everywhere prominent, even in Africa and Polynesia. The initiation of young Australians into manhood has long been famous in anthropological literature. It lasts for several months, and is marked by both circumcision and subincision. The lad is beaten frequently, and is ceremonially tossed in the air by the older men. The educational aspect of these transition rites consists of imparting certain secret information concerning the supernatural beings who are held to rule the universe. Eventually they reveal to the youth his *churinga*, the object which symbolizes his totemic affiliation and is the place where the double of that portion of the ancestral soul believed to animate him is held to reside.[21] None of the teaching of practical matters of daily life, especially of sex, that is so important a part of the African curriculum, is found here, however.

This Australian example brings into relief one further trait of education in nonliterate cultures that must be mentioned. It has been said that in nonliterate societies education continues until adolescence, or shortly after, but that the process is somewhat longer among literate peoples. Concerning the "everyday business of life" this is true. Yet when we touch the supernatural we come on a phase of the transmission of knowledge that is substantially confined to adults. The importance of religion as a force in the daily life of nonliterate peoples will become fully apparent when we discuss this aspect of culture. The control of the powers of the universe is conceived as an essential to the successful solution of most of their problems. But children, whose physical power is slight, are rarely conceded any greater amount of spiritual power. The religious training of children, therefore, is of a passive and very general nature. Not until they become older are they taught the theological concepts, the ritual practices of their tribe. For the most complete account of any religion we go to the elders, who, even though they are not specialists, are the ones versed in the supernatural sanctions of their society, and the accepted means of propitiation and expiation.

The education of nonliterate peoples, then, must not be thought of as reaching its completion with the assumption of adult status. Not even formal teaching ends then. But in the sense of education as *the process whereby the knowledge of a people is passed from one generation to the next*, a definition that refines the too inclusive one of Raum, a man or woman is fitted to carry on in his culture at an earlier age, and without the prolonged institutionalized

---

[20] K. Luomala, 1946, pp. 772–5.
[21] Cf. B. Spencer and F. J. Gillen, 1904, pp. 328–73.

training that exists where writing and the machine technology condition modes of living. In affairs of the spirit, however, this is but a beginning point. Those who are charged with the direction of affairs continue to be taught by their elders, as long as there are those older than themselves. From them they eventually learn the means whereby they themselves, and those for whose existence they are responsible, may live in harmony with the forces of their world, supernatural no less than human.

CHAPTER 20

Political Systems: the Ordering of Human Relations

THE universality of mechanisms for the regulation of affairs that concern the group as a whole has made the inclusion of political organization mandatory in any listing of the aspects of culture. These mechanisms range from governments having the whole apparatus of rulers and their administrative subordinates, recognized forms of legal machinery, police, and armies, to institutions so generalized, so informal, so amorphous that some students refuse to call them governments even when they recognize their political character.

This is not only apparent when we consider the nonliterate world as a whole. Most continents, and even some culture-areas, show this variation. South American political institutions ranged from the centralized autocracy of the Incas to the almost complete absence of institutionalized political forms of the Ona, where respect for age and integrity were the basis on which the leader of a local grouping maintained established custom. In the Congo culture-area, we contrast the simple controls of the pygmy bands with the well-defined, complex political mechanisms of the Lunda and Shongo and Luba kingdoms.

The reason for this variation would seem to be that while governmental *patterns* behave much like other elements in culture, the *forms* in which these patterned elements are expressed represent responses to the demographic and economic aspects of the life of each individual group. It has long been accepted that migratory folk exhibit a greater degree of individualism than sedentary peoples. This principle applies in many cases when it is phrased somewhat differently—that is, that the most sharply defined, complex political structures are to be found in sedentary societies, where population mass is large and economic productivity high.

To understand this we must refer to the concept of the economic surplus. It will be remembered that this surplus permits the release, to varying degree, of certain members of the community from subsistence activities, to allow them to specialize in some other occupation. One of the most ubiquitous forms of specialization in human cultures was seen to be that of administering the affairs of the group as a whole. This fact leads us to a more precise formulation of the setting in which political institutions of differing complexity develop. We assume, to begin with, that *no people is without ways and means of controlling conduct and directing the affairs of the group.* This being the case, it can be further stated that *governmental institutions are more complex where population mass is great and where the technological base permits the production of an economic surplus sufficient to support those who must exercise the functions of supervision, control, and direction, than where the population is small and the technological base is less adequate.*

2

THERE was a time when scholars held that early man lived in a kind of beneficent anarchy, where each person was granted his rights by others and in turn conceded them to his fellows, and there was no governing or being governed. It is an old fantasy, psychologically based on the nostalgia many persons feel for "the good old days"; an escape from problems that, incapable of being adequately resolved, nonetheless press for solution. Various early writers looked back to this Golden Age, but the point of view that man was originally a "child of nature" is best known to us in the writings of Rousseau and Locke and Hobbes. These men developed the concept of the "social contract" that, when entered into, put an end to the "state of nature" in which earliest man is supposed to have lived. This concept deeply influenced the Jeffersonian modification—that all men, having been created free and equal, were endowed by nature with the inalienable rights that must be recognized by the state if they were not to be asserted by force.

Lewis H. Morgan and Sir Henry Maine were among the first to attempt the comparative study of political institutions on the basis of facts established through systematic investigation of ways of life existing outside their own immediate culture. Morgan worked primarily with materials from primitive societies, Maine with historical data from Ireland and India and early England, and with materials garnered from his profound knowledge of the classical writers of Greece and Rome. Their findings were in essential agreement. Both held that kinship was the bond that brought earliest men together, and that only the more advanced aggregates formed States, properly speaking, which were based on territory. "From the moment when a tribal community settles down finally upon a definite space of land," wrote Maine, "the Land begins to be the basis of society in place of the Kinship. . . . For all groups of men larger than the Family, the Land on which they live tends to become the bond of union between them, at the expense of Kinship, ever more and more vaguely conceived." He puts his point, pithily, in these words: "England was once the country which Englishmen inhabited. Englishmen are now the people who inhabit England."[1]

This point of view dominated political theory for many years. Students of politics, particularly in England and on the continent of Europe, tended to

---

[1] H. S. Maine, 1888, pp. 72–74.

ignore the fresh materials made available to them as the result of the development of scientific ethnography. In the United States, currents of thought characterized by pragmatism held to a minimum interest in such essentially philosophical problems as the nature of the State. Here political scientists did give a place in their writings to anthropological materials bearing on the political institutions of "primitive" societies. This place, however, was one in which stress was almost exclusively laid on the problem of the origins of political phenomena, and only by implication was any concern shown for the range of variation of these phenomena in human societies.[2] On occasion, reference is even made to the prehistoric development of government.[3] This approach is marred by two methodological faults. As has been stressed, the origins of intangibles such as political institutions can only be inferred, and never scientifically established on the basis of factual data. Furthermore, such attempts to reconstruct the prehistory of political development, in which living "primitive" man is equated with his prehistoric forerunners, violate a basic principle of anthropological method, which holds that present-day nonliterate peoples are not our "contemporary ancestors."

Very few, if any, students of politics have made comparative studies of political institutions that move outside the literate world. Theories of government are thus framed in terms of the political forms of the historic societies of Europe and America. As a result, anthropologists concerned with the study of political institutions in nonliterate cultures have had to collect and analyze their data on the basis of rough and ready judgments of what are to be classed as political phenomena. This, however, was not entirely unprofitable. It forced ethnographers to describe instruments of political control in the societies they studied without preconception, as a part of the total range of social institutions. Particularly important was the fact that political institutions were described without prejudice as to whether the unifying principle of a given system was kinship or common interest or age or language or territory.

Nevertheless, where anthropologists have devoted themselves to the problem of the state, the hand of the past has rested heavily on them. The necessity of bringing modern data to bear on older theories, the constant examination of accepted hypotheses in the light of new facts that is the primary obligation of the scientist, has inevitably claimed their attention. As late as 1927 Lowie, in writing a treatise on the subject, could define his specific problem in these terms: "to determine whether 'savage' society recognizes the territorial tie or whether political order is maintained solely on the basis of personal relations as Maine and Morgan contended."[4] Realization of the hold that theories of Maine and Morgan have had on students of government is also why Radcliffe-Brown, more than a decade later, felt it necessary to register his disagreement with them: "To try to distinguish, as Maine and Morgan did, between societies based on kinship (or, more strictly, on lineage) and societies based on occupation of a common territory or

---

[2] Cf. E. M. Sait, 1938, pp. 99–136.
[3] Cf. for example, C. G. and B. M. Haines, 1926, pp. 1–8, 58–9.
[4] R. H. Lowie, 1927, p. 113.

locality, and to regard the former as more 'primitive' than the latter, leads only to confusion." [5]

The scope of political mechanisms, and thus the function of governments, has been indicated in the following terms by this same student: "In studying political organization, we have to deal with the maintenance or establishment of social order, within a territorial framework, by the organized exercise of coercive authority, through the use, or the possibility of use, of physical force. In well-organized states, the police and the army are the instruments by which coercion is exercised. Within the state, the social order, whatever it may be, is maintained by the punishment of those who offend against the laws and by the armed suppression of revolt. Externally the state stands ready to use armed force against other states, either to maintain the existing order or to create a new one. In dealing with political systems, therefore, we are dealing with law, on the one hand, and with war, on the other." [6]

But law and war are two of the most highly institutionalized, most closely regulated aspects of our own way of life. This is why their less formal manifestations have proved difficult for those whose experience is restricted to the formalized governmental structures of Euroamerican and other historic cultures—the kings and presidents, assemblies and parliaments, the apparatus of police and other instrumentalities of the law, the rigidly structured armies, with specific tasks that call them into action only in particular situations. To restrict the concept of government in general, or warfare, or any other manifestation of the political order by employing such criteria is to disregard an important lesson of scientific ethnography. This is that the form of any institution in any single culture should not be taken as a criterion to define the institutions employed to effect similar ends in other societies.

It thus follows that the institutions by which the affairs of any society are directed, and the conduct of its members is regulated, must be regarded as governmental institutions, however informal they may seem. Llewellyn and Hoebel preface their analysis of Cheyenne law with this statement by High Forehead, one of their informants, which might well serve as a definition of police function anywhere: "The Indian on the prairie, before there was the White Man to put him in the guardhouse, had to have something to keep him from doing wrong." [7] Of warfare, it has well been stated, "War is war. Its outward forms change, just as the outward forms of peace change. But from the stylus to the typewriter is just as far as from the club to the machine-gun—a weapon also known affectionately or otherwise as a 'typewriter.' And the development of tactics is neither more nor less remarkable than the development of office methods. Strip any military operation of external, identifying details, and one will find it hard to put a place and date to the story." [8] Nadel, discussing the organization of the small Nuba tribe inhabiting the Kadero hills of Kordofan, in northeastern Africa, says that "primitive

[5] A. R. Radcliffe-Brown, 1940, p. xiv.
[6] Ibid., loc. cit.
[7] K. N. Llewellyn and E. A. Hoebel, 1945, p. 2.
[8] H. H. Turney-High, 1942, p. 16. Quoted from O. L. Spaulding, H. Nickerson and J. W. Wright, Warfare (New York, 1925).

Political Systems: the Ordering of Human Relations

political organization is essentially an organization for war and peace—war without, and peace within. Attacks on human life outside the political unit are conceived of as legitimate warfare and entail no sanction—save the diffuse, voluntary sanction of the revenge which chances of war might offer. Within the political unit, such attacks are branded as crime: the society imposes penalties upon the perpetrator, or lays down compulsory acts of retaliation (in the form of blood feud) or expiatory rites, which will restore the peace that had been broken." [9] Radcliffe-Brown's designation of the political organization of society as "that aspect of the total organization which is concerned with the control and regulation of the use of physical force," despite the narrowness with which it is drawn, does give a frame of reference within which many different forms of this aspect of society may be treated.

Certain other questions of terminology which inevitably arise in the study of government, or any phase of it, will of necessity require careful consideration. A long tradition in the study of law and politics, that still persists in the writings of some students, makes definition "of the essence," and discussions of nomenclature take on great importance to those whose tradition is to take a "legalistic point of view." Perhaps, by definition, it can be said that groups with rudimentary political organization, who manage their lives in terms of common consent, "lack government." Even with the sharpest definition, however, one would be hard put to it to draw the line between intermediate cases. There would be agreement, in all probability, that the Papuan Keraki, as described by Williams, are without government, despite the fact that each group does have a local headman, who, though "he does not issue orders to be obeyed, . . . is none the less definitely the leader of the group." [10] But what of the South American Chaco tribes considered by Métraux? These people have chiefs of considerable power, responsible for the welfare of the community, with "vague judiciary powers" that may force a thief to return stolen goods. In external affairs, these chiefs represent their people in dealings with groups outside the tribe. Yet they dare not give orders that are contrary to the will of the people, and a chief will readily lose his followers if his regime is not successful.[11] The classification of the political organization of these people as government, or pre-government, or as rule by custom—to use various terms that have been employed—would require far sharper delimitation of terms than has yet been attempted, granting this sharpness can ever be achieved.

When is the political structure of a people to be designated as a state? Is the state something different from a tribe? If so, then when, we might ask, does a tribe become a nation? One possible answer to questions of this sort has been given by Fortes and Evans-Pritchard in their consideration of African native political systems, some of which have "centralized authority, administrative machinery, and judicial institutions, . . . and in which cleavages of wealth, privilege, and status correspond to the distribution of power and authority," while others do not. "Those who consider that a state should

[9] S. F. Nadel, 1942b, p. 59.
[10] F. E. Williams, 1936, p. 113.
[11] A. Métraux, 1946a, p. 303.

be defined by the presence of governmental institutions will regard the first group as primitive states and the second group as stateless societies." [12] Yet even these students speak of the first group as having governments, and the second as lacking them, thus once more throwing the question open to debate!

We shall return later to some of the problems of classification. It is enough, for our purpose at the moment, however, to note that all human groups regulate behavior within their society, and contacts between it and other groupings. Order may be maintained by police as in Africa, or by moral suasion, as in Papua. Sanctions may be enforced by kings, as in Polynesia, or by blood revenge, as in Melanesia. The questions we must explore are: What is the role of all these ways of achieving order in the lives of the people? What variation is to be seen in the forms they take? With what degree of effectiveness do they function?

3

OF THE areas inhabited by nonliterate peoples, Africa exhibits the greatest incidence of complex governmental structures. Both from the point of view of organization and administration, the political acumen of these institutions in tribe after tribe equals, where it does not surpass, anything known in the nonliterate world. Not even the kingdoms of Peru and Mexico could mobilize resources and concentrate power more effectively than could some of these African monarchies, which are more to be compared to Europe of the middle ages than referred to the common conception of the "primitive" state. Not all of the political structures of the continent were so complex. The variation in this aspect of culture found in any single part of the world has already been stressed, and the fact indicated that Africa is no exception to this rule. It is rather that the weighting of the scale on the side of complex entities, being greater here than elsewhere, gives the impression that Africa is actually the continent of kingdoms it is sometimes said to be.

It is interesting to speculate what the effect would have been on the development of political philosophy if, during the late seventeenth and early eighteenth centuries, the writings on Africa had received the attention that was given the accounts of travellers in North America, the West Indies, and the South Seas. Why the works of Dapper and Barbot and Bosman and others were not used is a problem for the historian of the intellectual currents that flowed in Europe during the period. The charge cannot be laid against these men that they made "such poor use of their eyes and ears," as did early travellers in many other parts of the world. Their works could not have led writers so inevitably to the conclusion that "not merely . . . a pre-social state had once existed, but that some barbarous peoples had not yet emerged from it," [13] as Myres summarizes the misconceptions of the period that arose

---

[12] M. Fortes and E. E. Evans-Pritchard, 1940, p. 5.
[13] Sir John L. Myres, 1916, p. 51.

Political Systems: the Ordering of Human Relations

out of preoccupation with the "noble savage" as personified in the Iroquois, the Huron, the Carib, the Pacific Islander.

One of these African kingdoms that has been longest known, has also received the most careful analysis by means of modern field study. The Gold Coast was a center of the slave trade, and the traders wrote a number of descriptions of the Ashanti and Fanti nations with whom they trafficked for their human goods, and whose customs it was to their advantage to know. That these kingdoms, like those of Dahomey, the Yoruba, and Benin to the east had stability and permanence is apparent from the historic record, that reaches back more than three hundred years. So vital are the political mechanisms of these kingdoms as, indeed, are those in other parts of the African continent, that even their extinction as autonomously functioning institutions has not been able to eradicate certain of their aspects. The clarity with which they can be detailed by even young persons who have never known anything but foreign control also attests this vitality.

The Ashanti form of government, its "Constitution," as Rattray designates it, is summarized by him as their attempt "to correlate nature's laws with the human laws and regulations to which they are subject." [14] The Ashanti had a full complement of governing officials, from family and sib heads to territorial rulers and their entourages, and the King with his court. Outwardly an aristocratic government, this, like most African political structures, actually had a large measure of democracy. Rattray lays down three basic principles of Ashanti government, that the Ashanti were governed "patriarchally rather than aristocratically," that a man named to any office "succeeded to obligations rather than to rights," and that every "lesser loyalty" was fostered as a means to achieving a greater.[15] The "little democracy" of the household was the core of the broader controls exercised by the people. Grouped into larger entities, each social unit was represented by its head in the councils of the group immediately superior to it. Every "concentric circle of loyalty" had its own tradition, its own genealogical record, its own officers.

Emphasis on local authority was thus the rule. Only in times of danger, when resources had to be mobilized efficiently and unity of action had to be based on decisions quickly forced by the circumstance of the moment, did the seeming autocracy of the political hierarchy function as such. Otherwise, a chief who acted without the full consent of the members of his council, men who in turn only gave an opinion after consultation with their subordinates, and so on down the line to the individual family member, was liable to be deposed. This was made explicit when the chief assumed power, in the series of injunctions publicly recited to him on that occasion. This does not mean that the Ashanti state was utopian. Rulers had power, and knew how to exercise it to maintain the preferred economic and social status they had in whatever segment of the total structure each headed. Yet this power always had to be exercised within the limits of the conventions set for it, and with an eye to the obligations it entailed toward those of lesser place in the hier-

[14] R. S. Rattray, 1929, p. 398.
[15] Ibid., pp. 401–403.

archy. In the final analysis, the structure was such that every Ashanti male sensed and exercised his right to participation in government.

Originally, the Ashanti were divided into small groups, by villages and clans, each autonomous. The organization of the kingdom was a process of amalgamation, whereby larger and larger entities were forged. The final step in this process was when the chief of one of the territorial groupings, Kumasi, attained primacy, and became *Asante Hene*, or king of Ashanti. Rattray, who has traced this process, has indicated many similarities in it to the rise of feudalism, especially with regard to control over the land, of which the king became the superior owner, the top of a series of graded inferior ownerships that reached from him to the holder of family land. The surface resemblance of these West African kingdoms to the feudal states of Europe has often been noticed; data such as these indicate that the resemblance was no less in the processes of their formation.

In the Ashanti political structure as it existed at the time of its fall, and as in many respects it still exists under British rule, each of the five territorial divisions was headed by a Paramount Chief. He was guided in the administration of his stool—the Ashanti synonym for our word throne—by a group of Elders analogous to the senior members of a kinship unit who act as advisers to its head. The honorific titles borne by these men reflected their position in the military organization headed by their Paramount, since each territorial unit had its own army, in which every adult male had his place. Under the Paramount were the chiefs of divisional units and sub-units, each with its own court, attendants, and war organization, which stood in the same relation to the Paramount Chief as he stood in relation to the King. The office-holders in a territorial division may be listed as follows:

1. The Chief (*Ohene* or *Omanhene*) who, like all other officers, was selected by the elders from possible candidates in the matrilineal line. By virtue of his position, he had a certain sacred quality that lasted, however, only as long as he held office, since on destoolment he again became an ordinary individual and liable to be called severely to account for his misdeeds.

2. The Queen Mother, a powerful personage, described tellingly by Rattray as " 'the whisper' behind the Stool." She was consulted by the Chief on all important occasions, and her voice carried weight far beyond the modesty of her outward bearing.

3. The *Ko'ntire* and *Akwamu* Chiefs, the deputy commander of the army and his second. They figured importantly in the native tribunals, and took a prominent place in the enstoolment of the Chief.

4. The Clan Chief, who looked after the interests of members of the kinship group to which the Chief belonged. He himself might or might not have been a member of this group. He took from the Chief the necessity of passing on cases involving those who were of the royal sib, and thus freed his superior from charges of nepotism.

5. The Military Officials, which included the leaders of the right and left wing of the army. The leader of the advance-guard, the commander of the main body, the head of the Chief's personal body-guard, and the commander of the rear-guard were next in rank.

6. The *Gyase Hene*, chief of those who made up the "palace" organization,

334

Political Systems: the Ordering of Human Relations

the heads of particular departments of the Chief's household. These are named to show clearly how large and complex a ceremonial organization he headed:

Spokesmen	Hammock-carriers
Stool-carriers	Floor-polishers
Drummers and horn-blowers	Treasurers and sub-treasurers
Umbrella carriers	Eunuchs
Caretakers of the Royal Mausoleum	Heralds
Bathroom attendants	Sword-bearers
Chief's "soul-washers"	Gun-bearers
Elephant-tail switchers	Shield-bearers
Fan-bearers	Minstrels
Cooks	Executioners [16]

The functions of officials named *Birempon* and *Adamfo* must be understood to grasp the lines of authority along which the kingdom of the Ashanti was administered, and on which the hierarchy of local divisions still rests. The *Birempon* is an official who is Chief of a smaller unit in respect to his immediate superior. These men are not members of their superior's Council, but have their own. The *Adamfo* is the patron of a given *Birempon* at court, since etiquette demands that an inferior present himself to his superior only with due ceremony, and through the intercession of an intermediary. The *Adamfo* is therefore that member of a Chief's Council who sponsors a given lesser chief, a *Birempon*, in his dealings with the superior.[17]

Rattray's diagram [18] which presents in graphic form the organization of a territorial division, and permits the lines of authority and the relationship of groups composing it to be traced, will be useful. "The outer circle, A, represents a Territorial Division under a Head-Chief . . . and a Queen Mother, who are represented by the centre of this circle. Inside the circle A, and concentric with it is another lesser circle, B, with figures 1, 2, 3, and 4 marked on its circumference. These are supposed to stand for four of the Head-Chief's Elders, who [with others] surround him and form the royal *entourage*. Just outside circle B, but not concentric with it, lie four smaller circles, D, E, F, and G. These circles represent smaller outlying villages which owe direct allegiance to the Head-Chief. Circle C surrounds all, and within it lies the hub, as it were, of the Territorial Division. Outside this circle C, but eccentric from it, lie four slightly smaller circles, marked A¹, A², A³, and A⁴, which represent four subdivisions of four *Birempon*, each of whom owes allegiance to the Head-Chief. Within these lesser circles A¹ to A⁴ lies an organization exactly similar, if on a somewhat smaller scale, to that which is embraced in the great circle, A. Each has its own local head-chief, councillors, villages under these councillors, and finally there are towns outside the circles C¹, C², &c., which are represented by the circles A⁵ to A⁸ and are under Chiefs of lesser importance than the *Birempon;* these are subject to him directly, and thus subject indirectly to the Head-Chief.

---

[16] *Op. cit.*, pp. 81–91.
[17] *Op. cit.*, pp. 93ff.
[18] *Op. cit.*, p. 97.

The Aspects of Culture

With respect to the *Birempon* of circle A², the lesser Chiefs of A⁵ to A⁸ are in the nature of miniature *Birempon*."

It will be noticed that all lines lead eventually to the Head-Chief, the center of circle A. The chain of communication that brings a lesser official to the Head-Chief is traced by the dotted line in the diagram. "It commences from the centre of the circle A⁶ and represents a Chief of a town directly under the *Birempon* of Division A². Commencing from the centre of A⁶, the

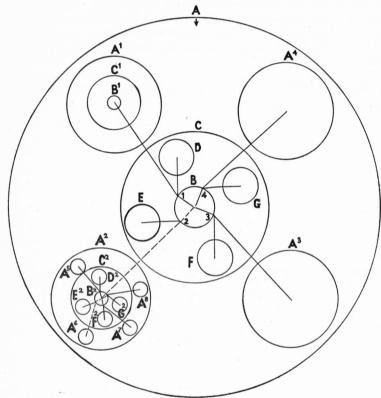

Fɪɢ. 28   *Ashanti political organization (after Rattray, 1929).*

line goes directly to a point on the circumference of the circle B², which is its first point of contact. This point represents one of the Elders of the Chief of the Division represented by the circle A² . . . the *Adamfo* of the Chief who rules over A⁶. Thence the line passes straight to the centre of the circle A², i.e. to the *Birempon* of the Head-Chief. From here it leads to a point marked '2' on the circumference of circle B. This point stands for one of the Elders of the Head-Chief, who is the *Adamfo* of the *Birempon* of circle A². Thence the line connects directly with the centre of circle A, i.e., with the Head-Chief of the whole Territorial Division."

A further point made by Rattray is revealing. "It should be observed that the only line of communication between the centre of a circle and that of

336

any other circle lies by the way of the centre of the circle A. Remove this central point of common contact, and all that remains is a series of greater or smaller disconnected circles." This principle held for the entire kingdom, which was but a more complicated extension of the diagram given for a division. Any attempt to pass over any of the contact points where an official of one jurisdiction, for instance, had a dispute with another, "would be deeply resented by all the persons concerned, and systematic attempts to ignore any of the intermediaries would lead to such dissatisfaction as eventually to throw out of gear the smooth working of the Administrative machine." This is why, as Rattray puts it, "To understand this diagram . . . is . . . to possess the key to an understanding of the decentralized Constitution of Ashanti." [19]

The Ashanti Kingdom had most of the appurtenances of a modern state—a well-defined system of collecting revenue, a system of finance, courts to administer the laws of the realm and adjudicate disputes, and an army. To do more than sketch any of these requires pages, but they can be outlined briefly. Revenues were derived from a complicated system of death-duties, from certain kinds of temporary trade monopolies that gave the rulers an advantage in the disposal of seasonal goods, taxes (or rather, toll-charges) on imports, court fines, and fees, and a percentage of all gold mined. Special levies might also be laid to cover the expenses of a chief's funeral, a proportion of the spoils of war, a war tax, treasure-trove, fees assessed on the enstoolment of a chief, and levies of food-stuffs, game, and fish. Revenues were distributed among officials in accordance with an established series of proportions, while the remainder was employed for buying arms and powder, to pay for regalia, and for entertaining. This last constituted a heavy charge on the income of any official, since all who came to a chief's palace must be provided with food and drink. This meant that every chief, in effect, had to hold continuous open house for the many who took advantage of his hospitality. A record of income and expenditures was kept by this nonliterate people through the ingenuous use of cowry-shells. This process was aided by the prodigious memories of those charged with taking care of the exchequer.

Something of the organization of the army has been indicated in naming certain of the chiefs attached to a stool. It was undoubtedly due to the care given it that the Ashanti owed their success in warfare, a success that made them among the best known and most feared peoples of all West Africa. Court cases were heard by a chief and his elders, and appeal through the chain of higher authority could be taken. Offenses brought before these tribunals were murder, suicide (that is, the dead was tried for offenses it was believed he must have committed), certain sexual offenses, such as incest, certain kinds of abuse, insult, or stealing, the invoking of a curse on a chief, treason and cowardice, the practice of evil magic, and the violation of tribal taboos or of an oath. Cases involving land tenure and alienation—a complicated matter—were also brought before the courts for judgment, as

---

[19] Op. cit., pp. 96–101.

well as cases involving pawning, loaning, and the recovery of debts. Punishment was severe. Execution, mutilation, and flogging were some of the penal· ties assessed, while in earlier times a culprit could be sold into slavery. Court procedures included the taking of testimony and submission to the ordeal.

What did this apparatus of government mean to the individual Ashanti? It is apparent that he was assured that he could go about his affairs with the knowledge that if he followed the rules of procedure set down by custom, he would not be molested. He was assured, furthermore, that not only would he be protected against any evil intent of his fellows, but that the demands of the supernatural powers would be cared for, and he would not be liable to indiscriminate manifestations of their ill-will. If he were unjustly charged with crime, or if a dispute with one of his fellows arose, he could have recourse to the orderly processes of law. His family was protected against foreign enemies; as an Ashanti, he had a sense of participation in the affairs of his tribe that, though exercised remotely, gave him some say in the determination of his fate. It must be emphasized again that this state was no more perfect than any other political system that has been devised by human beings. The ordinary man was exploited, sometimes brutally, by his superiors. Courts on occasion failed to function, and the Elders were not always scrupulous in rendering justice. To overlook these defects would be to erect a fiction of the kind that led to the concept of the carefree life of the untrammeled savage. Yet within its human limits, the Ashanti state—for it would be difficult for any not to accord it that term—functioned well, and efficiently performed its task of regulating the behavior and assuring the peace of its many citizens.

4

THE Ashanti represent an extreme degree of complexity in governmental institutions among nonliterate societies. Variation moves from cultures such as this to the point where, in small societies with simple technologies, political structures exist only by definition, and law and custom are almost impossible to differentiate.

It has been indicated how, in Africa itself, out of eight sketches of tribal political systems, three were so loose as not to be held worthy of the designation "government" at all. Among the Bushmen, some of the larger bands have a chief, but in most of them the "common affairs," such as migration and hunting, are under the direction of men whose skill alone earns them the respect and obedience of their fellows. Where chiefs are found, they seem only to direct the group as it moves from one locality to another, to see to the burning-over of the hunting territory, and to lead in combat. This "official" is thus a leader, with authority only as he demonstrates his ability to use it. He does not judge his fellows, and does not even control the grown members of his own family. There is no code of law except the customary habits and beliefs of the group. Adultery, theft, and homicide are punished by blood vengeance; as for other offences, the supernatural powers whose taboos have been broken can be expected to exact their own punishment Each band is a unit conscious of its own identity, with a hunting territory whose boundaries are recognized and within which it confines its activities. The relations between them that result from the circumstances of marriage, trade, and common need suggest that their contacts do not go entirely unregulated, though the evidence on this point is slight. Feuding can occur between bands when an individual of one band commits an offense against a member of another.[20]

Is this government? Can we speak of such a small, loosely organized group as a state? Is their adherence to customary sanction to be termed law? Can their feuds be called warfare? These questions become more pointed when we compare these rudimentary forms of political mechanism with the robust institutions of the Ashanti. And such questions, together with those that have been raised in earlier pages, become more puzzling as we turn to still another African people, the Nuer. They number some 200,000 individuals, and are divided into several tribes. According to Evans-Pritchard, they live in an "ordered anarchy" that makes of their political system an "acephalous kinship state" lacking legal institutions or developed leadership.[21]

Tribes are split into segments, segments into lineages, and identification of an individual with any component of his tribe depends on the situation of the moment, particularly on whether a group to which he potentially belongs happens to be in opposition to another corresponding one. We have seen how Nuer segmentation operates in its social structures; in the political aspect of tribal life it gives rise to "the principle of contradiction in political structure." Again, a diagram will aid in clarifying the point. "When Z^1 fights Z^2, no other section is involved. When Z^1 fights Y^1, Z^1, and Z^2 unite as Y^2. When Y^1 fights X^1, Y^1 and Y^2 unite, and so do X^1 and X^2. When X^1 fights A, X^1, X^2, Y^1, and Y^2 all unite as B. When A raids the Dinka A and B may unite." In

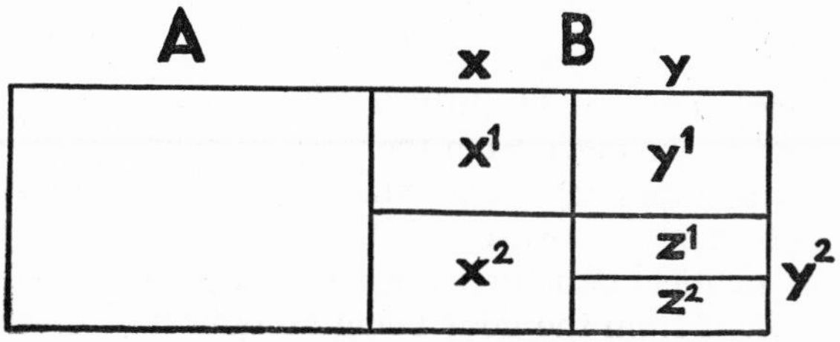

FIG. 29   Nuer political segmentation (after Evans-Pritchard, 1940).

the political structure of the tribe, "a member of Z^2 tertiary section of tribe B sees himself as a member of Z^2 in relation to Z^1. . . . But he regards himself as a member of Y^2 and not of Z^2 in relation to Y^1 and is so regarded by members of Y^1. Likewise he regards himself as a member of Y and not of Y^2 in relation to X, and as a member of the tribe B, and not of its primary section Y, in relation to tribe A. . . . Political values are relative and . . . the political system is an equilibrium between opposed tendencies toward fission

[20] I. Schapera, 1930, pp. 149–59.
[21] E. E. Evans-Pritchard, 1940, p. 181.

and fusion, between the tendency of all groups to segment, and the tendency of all groups to combine with segments of the same order." [21a]

This is a fighting people, a group of arrant individualists. No authority exists to whom a man can appeal when he has suffered a wrong, so a duel is the only way out, and this may develop into a feud. Yet when one man has slain another, he can seek sanctuary with a personage known as a leopard-skin chief until negotiations can be completed looking toward compounding the offense. The larger the group involved—that is, the wider the groupings that set off one party from another—the more difficult his task. Yet he is usually successful, if the groups are not too large. Other disputes involving damage to property, adultery, loss of limb, are settled by compensations, the amounts of which are fixed by common usage. Except for the good offices of the leopard-skin chief as mediator, however, there is no legal source such as a court, to which a man can look for redress. Nuer law, then, exists as "a moral obligation to settle disputes by conventional methods, and not in the sense of legal procedure or of legal institutions."

We turn once again to our questions. On the African continent alone, a vast number of tribal regulatory systems run the scale between explicit and tightly-knit integration to little more than sanctions enforced by the personality of a leader and the accepted traditions of the people. Despite their differences, all these systems are means whereby a people, whose affiliation transcends kinship groupings, and which identifies itself with an area it inhabits or dominates, is enabled to regulate the conduct of its members and direct its affairs when it must treat with another autonomous group. More than this, however, we cannot say, and still comprehend the diversity of form found in the functioning units that achieve these ends which we term political.

5

THIS same principle of flexibility in definition must guide the study of political phenomena as we move from the African continent to consider their forms among nonliterate peoples elsewhere, since on no continent does any single formula describe the institutions that are present. In Polynesia it can be said that the political structures are almost theocratic in their base, the descent of the chiefs from the gods being an outstanding sanction of their position. They emphasize rank more than power, and the taboos that go with rank, plus the display that validates position, are dominant factors in establishing and maintaining them. In Melanesia and New Guinea, political institutions are weak. Williams tells us that in Papua, the tribe is defined by "(1) a common territory, (2) certain idiosyncrasies of custom, (3) a distinct dialect, and (4) its common enmities," and that "Orokaiva chieftainship is of the most elementary kind." [22] Where men's societies exist, an important member of a high grade or "degree" in the men's society is looked to for decisions affecting the group. In the islands of eastern Melanesia true and

---

[21a] *Ibid.*, pp. 143–4, 147.
[22] F. E. Williams, 1930, pp. 156, 325.

Political Systems: the Ordering of Human Relations

explicit chieftainship appears, but the mechanisms for directing affairs are rather simple, and ruling is a personal matter, as is possible in small communities. In Indonesia, on the other hand, population mass necessitates more complicated controls.

The democratic nature of government in aboriginal North and South America has long been recognized. The exceptions are notable, however, for as has been pointed out, some of the most complex systems of political organization known to nonliterate man were found in the New World. Even outside the Inca empire of Peru, Ecuador, and Colombia, and the Maya, Toltec, and Aztec kingdoms of Mexico, non-democratic peoples existed, having well-institutionalized governing structures administered by persons who had this right because of inherited status. The stratification of Northwest Coast society has long been an anthropological by-word, though Lowie has pointed out that "the strictly political powers of a chief were disproportionately small when compared with his social eminence." [23] The Natchez of the Southeast had a government that was farthest removed from the prevalent democratic patterns of North American Indian tribes. Here the equalitarian principle seems to have disappeared completely. The reservation must be made to such a statement, however, that we are entirely dependent on the early French travellers for descriptions of this system, which vanished as a functioning government long before the advent of scientific anthropology. Yet the facts as set down, discounting any tendency to interpret them in the light of seventeenth and eighteenth century European absolutism, were striking enough. An absolute sovereign, held sacred by the subjects over whom he exercised absolute power of life and death, administered the controls that enabled him to command blind obedience.

The federation known as "The Five Nations," the League of the Iroquois, represented a governmental form more common in eastern North America. The five tribes that originally formed the league were the Mohawk, Oneida, Onondaga, Cayuga, and Seneca. Each was autonomous in local affairs, but in matters involving relations between tribes, or with groups outside the federation, a Council of fifty representatives acted for all. The tribes were not represented equally on this body, the number of representatives ranging from eight to fourteen. This disparity was due to pre-confederacy conditions in the constituent tribes. Since unanimous decisions were required, the difference did not involve any surrender of tribal rights. The council could bar any of its members for cause. It was highly responsive to public opinion, since anyone could argue before it concerning any matter it was considering. It was charged, in the main, with keeping the peace, making treaties, and deciding all disputes between tribes, with the war-path as a final resort. It must be noted, however, that each tribe had its own internal organization, with a council composed of its League delegates plus appointed war-chiefs. The sib-groups that composed each tribe were represented in the tribal council, and the fact that sibs cut across tribal lines gave firmness to the confederation by providing a weft of kin affiliation to bind together the separate tribal political strands that made up the political warp.

[23] R. H. Lowie, 1920, p. 383.

341

The Aspects of Culture

Particular interest attaches to this confederation because of the role of the women in it. So important were the "matriarchs," as they have been called, that it has often been cited as an instance of female government. This, however, is something of a distortion of the facts; the women were more in the nature of the power behind the throne than the active administering agencies. Thus the members of the tribal councils were men, but they were named by the matriarchs of their families and could be removed for cause by the appointing power. Women also appointed the sib-chiefs who became the tribal representatives in the League. But the actual decisions were reached and effectuated by these men.

Generally, government in the Americas was informal. Ridicule by cross-cousins, for example, was an effective mechanism in regulating conduct in the Plains, where, during communal buffalo hunts or tribal gatherings, war societies or other organizations that fulfilled police functions were more formal instruments to impose order. Crow chiefs were men who had outstanding military achievements to their credit, and the principal chief held his office because of his preeminence in this. His functions were fairly simple —essentially, he decided where a new camp should be located, and assigned places for the tents of his group; he also indicated which of the men's societies should police the camp during a given season. But his office was not hereditary. He had no judicial functions, and he was subject to removal as soon as he incurred the displeasure of his people.

These amorphous institutions could take on form and stability, as among the Cheyenne, with its Council of Forty-Four, and its military societies. This Council was "a self-perpetuating body of tribal trustees," and the term of office was ten years, when a rite of "renewing" the chiefs took place. Five of the group were head chiefs, whose functions were religious as well as political. They were responsive to public opinion, and were expected to be exemplary in conduct and models for other members of the tribe. The officers of the military societies were the war chiefs, who held their offices nominally for life. In practice, however, they turned their posts over to younger men as they advanced in age. Their authority could be coercive in times of emergency, and they were known to impose penalties, such as whipping, on erring followers. Yet their power was in some measure held in check by the force of opinion.

In considering the total range of political structures, another problem of terminology confronts us. Plains Indian institutions were democratic, runs the formula. And, as labels go, it is not a bad designation. In economic and social, no less than in political aspects of life, class stratification was at a minimum, and opportunity to enjoy the rewards the culture held important was limited only by ability. But when the African monarchies are labelled autocratic, as they most often are, we must pause. We have seen how, beneath the seeming power of the Ashanti King lay the broad base of considered popular consent to his decrees. Moreover, in African societies with rudimentary political institutions such as the Bushmen and Nuer, the same absence of class stratification and special privilege are found that distinguish American Indian cultures.

Political Systems: the Ordering of Human Relations

The designation "socialistic," often applied to the Inca empire, must be given particular scrutiny. This great organization, headed by its absolute ruler, did see to it that every man, woman, and child was cared for, and that he labored according to the capacities with which his age, strength and training endowed him. Yet when we investigate more closely the mechanisms by which this almost perfectly functioning instrument attained its ends, we find it marked by features that no student of political theory would ever term socialistic. Class lines were strictly drawn, neither economic nor political democracy existed. Punishment for refusal to obey orders was severe.

It is significant that the custom of designating this Peruvian government as "socialistic" grew up at the turn of the century. Thirty years later it would have been called "authoritarian"—a better term. In it man lived for the State, which controlled his every move by means that were striking counterparts of twentieth century dictatorships, complete with secret police and youth movements. In it, communication never moved across the levels of the governing hierarchy, but reports passed up the line of control to the central authority, and orders were handed down. Consultation among equals was unknown; there were, in this sense, no equals, but only those who stood at identical levels on steps of different stairways.

The lesson to be taught by such facts is again one of caution in applying a term, established to describe a particular kind of phenomenon or system of ideas and institutions, to something analogous to it. The need for concepts cannot be denied, nor need we stress the importance of classifying data so as to enable us to compare, analyze, and thus comprehend their nature and functioning. Labels ready made, however, tend to obstruct rather than further the attainment of these ends. It cannot be too often emphasized that to apply terms cross-culturally, without thorough regard for correspondences in other than outer appearances, is as inadvised and hazardous as it is to interpret the values of one culture in terms of another, or to draw judgments regarding the morals of peoples in different cultural settings.

6

POLITICAL systems order the relations between groups by means of diplomacy and warfare. They control conduct within the group by the exercise of law. We may briefly consider these important phases of the political concerns of nonliterate folk before we turn to the other aspects of culture of which we shall treat.

Diplomacy is the peaceful resolution of disputes between autonomous groups. That nonliterate peoples, in their dealings with each other, had and still have techniques of settling differences is known. But no element in their cultures has been less studied, so that precise description of how various peoples went about accomplishing these ends can not be given. We read of ambassadors being sent other tribes by such aggregates as the League of the Iroquois or certain African kingdoms. It is difficult to assume that such states

343

or confederations could have carried on their affairs without certain channels of communication with their neighbors. But such matters as the immunity enjoyed by their envoys, or the ceremonial with which a case was debated, or how compromises were arrived at, elude us. Whether the loss of autonomous rule by most nonliterate peoples still permits the systematic investigation of the ways they settled disputes without the use of force can only be known when field research on this particular topic has been carried out.

War was waged by nonliterate peoples on a level of simplicity that, according to Turney-High, scarcely permits it to be called by that name. Most students tell something, in a general way, of how fighting was carried on, and weapons have been described much more meticulously than the uses to which they have been put in combat. Perhaps, as Turney-High says, this is "a civilian failing," the counterpart of the ethnographer's earlier tendency to describe technological culture but give little attention to the economic processes that governed the production and distribution of goods. Turney-High's criteria for the conditions that divide war from "sub-military combat" can be given to differentiate these two levels of operations. War, he says, is marked by tactical operations; by definite command and control; by the ability to conduct a campaign for the reduction of enemy resistance if a first battle fails; by clarity of motivation, which must move a group rather than be a matter of individual or family differences; and by adequate supply of forces in the field.[24]

These criteria differentiate warfare from feuds and raids, and other operations of short duration which have as their end the attainment of very limited objectives. They make it clear why warfare, thus narrowly defined, was as rare among nonliterate peoples as are legislative bodies constituted like those of Euroamerican states. Demographic considerations alone forbid a small people to have an army. There is no man-power to enable them to do more than raid an enemy, or on a longer term basis to carry on more than feuding operations. Simple economies cannot provide supplies for campaigns, and warriors cannot always be sure of their ability to live off the land.

The Zulu armies, or those of Ashanti and Dahomey, or, in the New World, of Peru and Mexico were armies in every sense, and carried on war. We would apply the term "soldiers" to the men who composed them, the word we use for the troops of literate societies, as against "warriors," which, significantly enough, we use for those who carry on most combats of nonliterate peoples. Here, too, is an area for systematic analysis. This would, first of all, contrast the fighting practices of small nonliterate aggregates with the warfare waged by larger, more prosperous groupings. It would, however, also analyze the relationships of these practices to the total socio-economic setting and technological equipment of the peoples who used these various forms of the final appeal to force.

The study of *law* in nonliterate societies was for many years made difficult by the tendency to draw distinctions between codified and customary law. In this field, where definition, as we have observed, is of the highest impor-

---

[24] H. H. Turney-High, *op. cit.*, pp. 21-2.

tance, the rigidity with which unwritten codes of conduct could be enforced by recognized modes of procedure went unrealized. Difficulties in the study of "primitive" law were imposed, also, by the fact that the rules and regulations of a people, literate or nonliterate, by no means conform to their customary behavior as it is to be observed. "To seek a definition of law is like the quest of the Holy Grail," says Hoebel, in discussing the relationship between law and anthropology. He lays the "remissness of anthropologists" in attacking the study of law among nonliterate peoples to two causes: "(1) a misconception (or non-conception) of the nature of law; and (2) a failure to set realistic and genuine problems for their attack in the field of jurisprudence." On the other hand, we encounter another familiar strain when we read his further criticism that "too much parochialism among the men of law" is also to be held responsible for "the anthropologist's failure to understand the nature of law"—a parochialism "which sets up a conception of law in terms of the specialized characteristics of law in western civilization." [25]

Where, then, does custom end and law begin? This same student has given us a useful ethnological definition of law. "A social norm is legal," he states, "if its neglect or infraction is met by the application, in threat or in fact, of the absolute coercive force by a social unit possessing the socially recognized privilege of so acting." [26] Here the essential element is authority. "The legal has teeth," say Hoebel and Llewellyn. "What it protects is *protected;* if its prohibitions be disregarded, somebody can *do* something about it." And while a custom that prevails need not be legal, it becomes so if it comes to appertain to what these students term "part of the going order" of the group. [27]

No precision in the study of unwritten law could be attained until the case method was applied. Otherwise, only a kind of ethnographic statement of ideal or normative procedures could be arrived at. Such an early study as that of Dundas on the Kikuyu is replete with statements that report a consensus of behavior, much in the manner of any student of culture laying down the patterns of conduct in a society he is studying. These studies had, and still have, their value. No one can read Barton's report on Ifugao law and maintain that "primitive" people live only by the rule of force, or that they have no concepts of justice and means of enforcing just resolutions of disputes and the punishment of crimes. These studies, too, have had the result of sharpening perceptions of how varied are the offenses for which a society may exact punishment, and how arbitrary the categories of various classes of offenses recognized in different communities.

The variety of ways in which justice can be administered also gives impressive testimony of how differently the same ends can be achieved in different societies. The use of religious sanctions, such as the ordeal or the oath, or of secular ones, such as citing proverbs or weighing testimony as to the facts, all enter into the determination of justice as practised over the world. Courts with presiding officials who render judgment, advisers who act as a kind of jury, and even special pleaders who perform the functions of the lawyer are

[25] E. A. Hoebel, 1946, p. 839, 836.
[26] E. A. Hoebel, 1940, p. 47.
[27] K. N. Llewellyn and E. A. Hoebel, 1941, pp. 283–4.

by no means unknown in nonliterate cultures. But generally, in nonliterate societies, the lack of specialization makes procedures more direct and participation more general than in these instances. In this, as in all other phases of political structures, lines we draw sharply are blurred. Hence, as in the study of the law, the need to enlarge categories and make flexibility the outstanding characteristic of definition is particularly important.

CHAPTER 21

Religion: the Problem of Man
and the Universe

RELIGION and the arts, to which we now turn, form the third broad grouping of cultural aspects, the other two of which stem directly from the requirements of the organism, and from the nature of social life. Through technology and economics the basic physiological wants of man are satisfied. Social organization and education provide for the perpetuation of the group and its way of life, while political structures assure that this life will be led by each member of society with stated regard for the rights of others. Religion and the arts complete the adjustment of man to his universe by providing security against forces more powerful than himself and creating channels for the positive expression of his aesthetic drive.

We have seen that the presence of beliefs in an existence beyond death must be inferred from remains that date to the middle Palaeolithic in Europe, and how the graphic and plastic arts of early man appear shortly afterward. Man thus developed some conception of the nature of life and death and the universe in which he lived, and contrived to surmount the requirements of daily life and achieve aesthetic gratification long before he was agriculturalist or herder, or knew how to make pots or weave cloth.

When we ask why these least utilitarian aspects of culture developed so early in the experience of man, and why they are universals, we find ourselves with many hypotheses but few data to support them. The simplest answer holds that since they are found everywhere, and strike so deep into the past, they must represent some inborn response to necessity. Though this is unassailable from the point of view of logic, the fact remains that students of man as a physical organism have found no mechanism to account for these particular aspects, any more than they have found a mechanism that would permit us to assume a genetic basis for man's culture building ability taken as a whole. Explanations of a more mystical nature need not concern us here. They are legion, but they are also, on inspection, found to be essentially rationalizations based on the historical experience of peoples who lived in given periods and had given cultures. They must, in any event, be thought of as parts of the religious and aesthetic facets of the cultures that have produced them, rather than as explanations of religious and artistic phenomena in general.

347

The Aspects of Culture

Our difficulty in reaching a satisfactory explanation of why religious and artistic phenomena are universal has its counterpart in the difficulty we experience in defining them. This difficulty may be said, in large measure, to be the result of unconscious ethnocentrism, which has full play because the conventions of religion and art are in the nature of the case arbitrary. An additional factor arises out of the specialization that so marks Euroamerican culture. We specialize not alone in the technological and economic sphere. The practice of religion and the arts have likewise become the province of experts. In a compartmentalized culture such as ours, they tend, consequently, to become removed from life, a fact whose implications will be explored later in this and in following chapters, when we search for least common denominators to permit definitions of these phenomena.

2

In 1871, E. B. Tylor offered as a "minimum definition of Religion, the belief in Spiritual Beings." To this "deep-lying doctrine," he applied the term animism. For him, animism was important because, in his view, it "characterizes tribes very low in the scale of humanity, and thence ascends deeply modified in its transmission, but from first to last preserving an unbroken continuity, into the midst of high modern culture." We need not be concerned here with Tylor's preoccupation with sequence—since this will be discussed when the doctrine of cultural evolution is taken up—but with the phenomenon as he conceived it. This is best expressed in the following passage: "It is habitually found that the theory of Animism divides into two great dogmas, forming part of one consistent doctrine; first, concerning souls of individual creatures, capable of continued existence after the death or destruction of the body; second, concerning other spirits, upward to the rank of powerful deities. . . . Thus Animism, in its full development, includes the belief in souls and in a future state, in controlling deities and subordinate spirits, these doctrines practically resulting in some kind of active worship." [1]

Many criticisms have been lodged against this hypothesis, especially against the position that animism is the basis of all religion. The most telling of these criticisms has pointed to the purely intellectual processes that Tylor assumed to have produced the basic animistic concept of "soul." Enough is known about the psychology of culture to refute assumptions that man calculatingly answers the problems of the universe. In religion, as in any other aspect of tradition, the power of conditioned emotional drives is so strong that rational thought tends usually, if not invariably, to be rationalizing rather than exploring. It is thus apparent why such statements as the following became especially vulnerable: "In spite of endless diversity of detail, the general principles of this investigation seem comparatively easy of access to the enquirer, if he will use . . . two keys . . . first, that spiritual beings are modelled by man on his primary conception of his own human soul, and sec-

---

[1] E. B. Tylor, 1874, vol. I. pp. 424–7.

ond, that their purpose is to explain nature on the primitive childlike theory that it is truly and throughout 'Animated Nature.'"[2]

The question was also raised whether beliefs of a broader, more undifferentiated character must not have preceded any religious system based on animistic thought. The answer to this question was believed to have been found when Bishop Codrington described the belief of the Melanesians in the impersonal force called *mana*, and McGee discovered the Siouan Indian *wakanda*. For Marett, who pressed the enquiry most strongly, and for whom the material for good and bad religion, as well as for white and black magic lay in the idea of "the supernatural," the twin concepts of *mana* and its counterpart, *tabu*, represented the most generalized, and hence, the basic force of religious belief. This he held to be especially true when mana was compared to animism with its intellectualistic component, lacking "the emotions of awe, wonder, and the like." To the sense "of the attribution of life and animation which many peoples have toward inanimate objects," Marett gave the name "animatism." Thus he distinguishes this belief from the narrower category of the *animae*, the spirits which actuate men and beasts and objects of nature and which, for Tylor, constituted animism.[3]

We do not hold the service these scholars have performed in shaping concepts as any the less valuable, because we reject those of their findings that appear untenable in the light of subsequent knowledge. We can agree with Marett who, in advancing the hypothesis that animatism is antecedent to animism, disclaimed any intent of depreciating the contribution of Tylor: "I am no irreconcilable foe who has a rival theory to put forward concerning the origin of religion."[4] The search for origins of culture has become more hazardous with the years. Neither animism nor animatism are now regarded as earlier, or original, or universal forms of religion. No more valid from this point of view is the conception of Durkheim, derived from his analysis of the data from Australia and elsewhere, that religion has grown out of the social experience of men;[5] or the theory of Andrew Lang, that religion was first manifest in the belief in High Gods;[6] or Father Schmidt's extension of this concept by adding the corollary that present beliefs of nonliterate peoples represent a degeneration from this purer form.[7]

Each of these scholars has provided more than enough evidence, on the face of it, to document his theory and to satisfy any who will read what he has written. Enough, that is, until the evidence for some other theory is studied, a cup equally filled to the brim and running over, and equally convincing. The contribution of these scholars, however, lies not in their having solved the riddle of how religion originated, or the steps by which it developed, or its social or psychological roots; but rather in the different phenomena of religion each emphasized and, by so doing, imprinted indelibly on all

---

[2] *Ibid.*, vol. II, p. 168.
[3] R. R. Marett, 1929, pp. 119–22.
[4] *Ibid.*, p. xi.
[5] E. Durkheim, 1915, p. 10 and *passim*.
[6] A. Lang, 1887, vol. I, pp. 327ff.
[7] W. Schmidt, 1931, pp. 283ff.

future discussions of the subject. They have in this way provided conceptual tools that have enabled students in the field to probe new avenues of native belief and thought and to interpret these beliefs and thoughts in clearer cultural perspective. The controversies over the nature and origin of religion have produced, almost as a by-product, an awareness of the range of religious beliefs and practices, and of their role in the lives of the people that have stimulated field-workers to look for all these forms, and to investigate all the ways in which they influence a culture as a whole.

We shall put them to an analogous purpose here. Whatever their developmental order, it is essential that we consider each of these established categories of religious experience in classifying and organizing our materials. Animistic and animatistic beliefs, the concepts of spirits and ghosts, polytheism and monotheism, and magic—all characterize types of religious phenomena that must be understood, whether in a given culture they stand alone or in combination, or are entirely lacking. The order in which they are considered is a matter of no importance, since we are taking them as no more than different forms of belief concerning the universe that, in part or in their entirety, may be found in any specific culture at a definite period of its existence.

3

BELIEFS that not only human beings, but animals and inanimate objects are actuated by spirits that give them volition and purpose—that is, the beliefs we call animistic—have come easy to men in all kinds of societies. They are no monopoly of "primitive" man, or of children. Even in a machine culture, where physical causation is well understood, the owner of an automobile will berate it for the stalled engine, the punctured tire that interrupts his journey, as he would a companion who had failed him, or a balky animal. We refer to a locomotive or a steamship as "she," and those charged with their operation anthropomorphize these great masses of inert matter as though they did not move and have their being only at the will of those who operate them. The responses of children to objects that cause them harm have been used repeatedly as examples of animistic thought. But to correlate a "civilized" child with an adult "savage," as has often been done in this connection, is not admissible. The child who says, "Bad rock!" when he stubs his toe, or beats the chair against which he bumped himself, is the precursor of the man who berates his stalled car. He is in no way to be equated with the nonliterate man who stands in awe before a magnificent waterfall, or a great tree or a rock of striking formation.

If we could reach into prehistoric times for information about the beliefs of earliest, or at least early man, many tantalizing problems could be solved. Only then could we test hypotheses of how the concept of spirit developed, and, with access to the requisite data, determine the validity of Tylor's persuasive explanations. There are few peoples living today who do not have the concept of soul or spirit. Everywhere we encounter the postulate of an incorporeal thing—a quality, an essence—that gives man his being, makes of him the individual he is, and persists after his death. We may conjecture how primeval man must have been filled with consternation and awe to have a person, apparently dead, arise and tell of his epileptic visions. To observe a man's body at rest, sleeping, and yet have the sleeper awaken and recount how he talked to a father long dead, or how he visited with a friend in the next village, or met a monstrous creature must have elicited some kind of an explanation of the dream experience. Since the teller had not left the habitation, must there not have been some part of him that wandered away, some part that could not be seen, that was able to detach itself at will?

There has long been evidence that explanations for experiences of this order are verbalized by peoples all over the world. Many resolve the mystery of the shadow by attributing to it a spiritual quality, often making of it a second or complementary soul. The fact that a person who looks into a still pool of water sees an image of himself and of any companion who may bend over it at the same time has undoubtedly given rise to what has been termed the concept of the mirror-soul. Personality differences that distinguish one individual from the next have not gone unnoticed. These differences are often attributed to different qualities of inherent endowment, to different kinds of soul-stuff, or to differing guardian spirits. The mere fact of the existence of elaborate burial rites among all but a very small proportion of human societies is evidence of how important it is to give proper care to that part of the individual that continues to exist, unseen, after it has completed its stay among the living.

A few examples will document the widespread belief in a soul. "In the religious system of the Montagnais-Naskapi the soul of the individual is the focal center of attention. Whatever we mean by the term 'soul' its lexical equivalent in the language of these nomads . . . designates one's shadow. Another native term embracing the same word element . . . is met in the term for 'mirror' . . . 'see-soul-metal.' It is interesting to observe that over much of the territory in America where Algonkian languages are spoken, the same stem and even most of the linked concepts are found. . . . Another term . . . in frequent use . . . means 'spirit' in the sense of 'intellect, comprehension'; hence, 'mind.' " In addition, we are informed, the Naskapi use a proper name "which is more descriptive of the soul's function." "Great Man" is the name given the "soul in its active state." This provides "guidance through life and . . . the means of overcoming the spirits of animals in the life-long search for food." The customary and significant usage is to employ the word for "my friend" when speaking of the soul, so that when a hunter has performed some act that gives him satisfaction, he will declare, "I wish to content myself," which, literally translated, means "I wish to make my friend (my soul) feel good." [8]

The Keraki of New Guinea distinguish the soul from the ghost, "the spiritual part of a living man and the spiritual substitute for him which survives his death," and may plague those who are left behind.[9] In Malekula, while

---

[8] F. G. Speck, 1935, pp. 41–2.
[9] F. E. Williams, 1936, p. 361.

every person has one soul that exists after death and can return to the land of the living, certain sacred plants that play an important ceremonial and economic role also are believed to have souls. A pig with a well-developed tusk-curvature, the index of its value, has much spiritual power. If a small boy eats of its flesh, the spirit of the child is held to be in danger of being devoured by this more powerful spirit and the lad will die.[10]

Soul concepts of African peoples are highly elaborated, as in Dahomey, where all persons have at least three souls, and adult males have four. One is inherited from an ancestor, and is the "guardian spirit" of the individual. Before this spirit assumes his role of guardian, however, it finds the clay out of which the body it is to guard is to be made. The second is the personal soul, while the third is the small bit of the Creator that "lives in every person's body." The first, in terms of Euroamerican thought, is to be conceived as the biological aspect of a man, the second his personality, and the third his intellect and intuition. The fourth soul of adult males is associated with the concept of Destiny. This soul occupies itself not alone with the affairs of the individual who has established its formal worship, but also with the collective destiny of his household, since, "the Dahomean reasons that when a man reaches maturity, his own life cannot know fulfillment apart from the lives of those who share that life with him." [11]

Beliefs of this order can flourish to a degree that not only human beings but a great many objects in nature as well, are thought of as endowed with spirits. To the Aymara of the Peruvian highlands, Tchopik says, "the world is so densely populated with supernatural beings that it is literally impossible to enumerate them. They exist almost everywhere in nature and vary from vaguely defined 'powers' to clearly personified supernatural beings." All unusual natural phenomena are held to be inhabited by good or evil spirits, though the word applied to such phenomena is also used for twins, as well as for persons with a harelip and other abnormal individuals. Plants and animals, being "owned" by supernatural beings of a higher order, are not believed to have spirits of their own. The spirits that are associated with places such as mountains and rivers are of great importance, since they can do much harm or much good to people. They are conceived as old folk, principally men, who live under the earth. They may punish evil-doing, and can cause people to fall ill for reasons of their own. There is a class of evil beings who inhabit ruins and caves. House-spirits guard property left in the house.[12] Among these people, the concepts of soul and ghost are confused. Ghosts are greatly feared, however, since it is believed the spirits of the dead can return to earth to reward or punish their living relatives.[13]

Except when used in the loosest possible fashion, the total system of belief of no people can be labelled "animistic." To characterize a religion in such terms is so broad as to be meaningless. Christianity is animistic in that the belief in the human soul is an integral part of it, but Christians do not offi-

[10] A. B. Deacon, 1934, pp. 547–8.
[11] M. J. Herskovits, 1938b, vol. II, p. 238.
[12] H. Tschopik, Jr., 1946, pp. 558–9.
[13] Ibid., p. 552.

cially believe automobiles have spirits. On the other hand, a belief that a waterfall or a rock or a bear or moose has a spirit does not necessarily exclude belief in a pantheon of gods who direct the larger concerns of the universe, or in quite impersonal supernatural forces. Both these, in turn, can and in most instances do coexist, as part of the same system, with ghosts and other manifestations of the spirits of the dead, perhaps formalized as an ancestral cult.

Wherever students have investigated the interrelationships of these co-existing beliefs, they have found all such forms to be integrated into a unified world-view—a world-view which, moreover, is not to be taken as evidence of a deficient or particular kind of mentality, but as the expression of a system of logic that moves with sureness from the accepted premises concerning the nature of the world and man. It is not difficult to see how a people who believe in a human spirit can attribute a comparable endowment to animals, and even to inanimate objects. Just as an obdurate person may be regarded as having a "strong spirit," or a compliant one is thought to have a weak soul, so with animals and objects. They, too, can be obstinate or compliant, friendly or hostile. The dog will refuse to track the animal being hunted, or the prey will defy the best efforts of the hunter. The knife that for years has performed its task, will of a sudden turn on its user and cut him. How explain these happenings? Out of the many possible ways to account for them man, everywhere, has attributed to the animal or inanimate object the same wilfulness to action he has observed in human beings. In turn, animals and inanimate objects are assumed to be energized by the same kind of power—though of lesser quality or intensity—a soul or spirit, that is, of the kind believed to be the prime mover in human behavior.

The high gods of nonliterate cultures may be few or many. They may be immanent or removed from men. They may personify the forces of nature or be abstractions. But their concern is with the affairs of the universe and all things living and inert it contains; to the end that friction may be done away with, and harmony achieved. This is not to say that a belief in gods who reward proper behavior and punish offenses necessarily implies that religion must have an ethical content, for there is good evidence that such a criterion is by no means universally applicable. There are societies, for example, where reward and punishment are cared for quite satisfactorily by human agencies, without the aid of supernatural sanctions.

Conversely, there is no justification for holding that only the "higher" religions have ethical content. The gods of too many peoples are marshalled for the support of sanctioned behavior and the suppression of evil, to permit a distinction to be drawn between systems of belief on these grounds. In a majority of nonliterate cultures, it is true, the gods have many preoccupations, in addition to the support of an ethical system. They must see to it that the crops grow, that children thrive, that their worshipers prosper, that wars are won, that trade flourishes. The suppression of evil is but one of their duties, and it lies on the level of these others.

Tylor's thesis that the concept of deity is derived from the belief in souls has much logic, and is documented by materials from many living peoples.

Again, it may be asked, what is more natural than that in a world where everything is endowed with a spirit, and man is the dominant creature, the spirit of man, or his soul, should be the most powerful of all? And that, given the concept of different kinds of souls, the spirits of those who exert the most power while on earth should continue to manifest their power in the world of the dead, finally attaining to such command as to dominate, as gods, the very universe? That "the conception of the human soul is the very 'fons et origo' of the conceptions of spirit and deity in general," Tylor believed was proved, "by the fact of human souls being held to pass into the characters of good and evil demons, and ascent to the rank of deities." Even the mightiest deities, we are told, "are modelled on human souls, that in great measure their feeling and sympathy, their character and habit, their will and action, even their material and form display throughout their adaptations, exaggerations and distortions, characteristics shaped upon those of the human spirit." [14]

Yet there are gods that are removed from men. Among the peoples with the simplest technologies—those whose cultures are held by some to be the living examples of primeval man's way of life—these gods are much more important than the animistic beliefs that should have preceded them. Father Schmidt has been the most emphatic proponent of the view that the development of religion has not been along lines such as Tylor suggested, but that the earliest, the primeval systems, must essentially have been the worship of the high gods. Spirits and ghosts, and the souls of animals and plants and inert objects are thus to Father Schmidt but manifestations of the degenerative tendency in speculative thought that has brought man from the high level of his presumed aboriginal monotheistic world-view to belief in the multitudinous variety of forms he worships today. The fact that some peoples did worship beings who were not to be regarded as extensions and magnifications of the human soul, as Andrew Lang earlier showed, undoubtedly supplied a much-needed corrective to the animistic doctrine that, because of its massive documentation, had come to have too uncritical an acceptance. Yet, as Marett has argued, from what could the concept of the high gods have developed? Either there had been a forerunner to the idea of deities, or we must assume that the differing gods revealed themselves in the early days of man on earth. But were this the case, how account for religions where deities are but minor expressions of the power phenomenon that, impersonal as the rain, permits all controls to function?

Once again we must stress the futility of the search for the absolute origin of any nonmaterial element in culture, or of seeking simple explanations for the complexities of custom. Animism is an important part of the world-view of so many peoples, that to regard it as the irreducible minimum of belief is persuasive until we look at all the facts. The high gods and their complementary beings are found in cultures simple and complex, but many other kinds of beliefs are found in association with them. The categories of animatism, animism, polytheism, and monotheism are important as classifications of religious phenomena, but not as a developmental progression.

---

[14] *Op. cit.*, vol. II, 247–8.

Religion: the Problem of Man and the Universe

4

THE supernatural force that gives power to gods and ghosts, and makes it possible for inanimate objects to become entities motivated by good or ill will, is a humanly controllable essence. Sometimes benefiting from the prompting of the spirit-gods, and sometimes by his own discovery or intuition—also the voice of these spirits—man has learned how to influence the decisions of even the highest, most remote spiritual beings. Man's approach has been through supplication, propitiation, expiation. For does not even the most austere, the most remote god have much in him that is human? *Mana, wakanda, orenda, manitou,* are, however, not anthropomorphized at all. They represent what is best termed blind power, and there is little point in petitioning them.

Mana, the name most commonly given this phenomenon, is found in Melanesia, but the ideas it expresses are by no means restricted to that area. Together with other religious beliefs, it exists in many cultures, under many guises. We ourselves are no more without it than we lack animistic conceptions; in our culture, it is called "luck." For what is luck if not an uncontrollable force, that comes and goes as it wills, without regard to the wishes of those whom it may at one moment favor, at another abandon? Some people, our idiom goes, are just "lucky." Those whose reputation for consistent good luck is known are often "touched" by others to allow of some transfer of power. Some are "just unlucky," or unfortunate, and are to be avoided. Try as we will, however, luck cannot be induced to come to us. Those who have played cards know how desperately the loser—at poker, let us say—will walk about his chair, blow on the cards, turn three times before taking his seat, so as to "change his luck." To no avail; luck will not be petitioned, or coerced. The mathematician can tell us about probability, but we know better. The luck either was there, or it wasn't.

That this is not a farfetched analogy is patent when we turn to Codrington's classical description of mana. The Melanesian mind, he says, "is entirely possessed by the belief in a supernatural power or influence, called almost universally *mana.* This is what works to effect everything which is beyond the ordinary power of men, outside the common processes of nature; it is present in the atmosphere of life, attaches itself to persons and to things, and is manifested by results which can only be ascribed to its operation. When one has got it he can use it and direct it, but its force may break forth at some new point; the presence of it is ascertained by proof." A stone of uncommon shape may have mana if, when it is buried in a garden, the yield is bountiful; and its power can be transferred to other stones. Songs can have mana, also. "This power, though itself impersonal, is always connected with some person who directs it; all spirits have it, ghosts generally, some men. If a stone is found to have a supernatural power, it is because a spirit has associated itself with it; a dead man's bone has with it *mana,* because the ghost is with the bone; a man may have so close a connexion with a spirit or ghost that he has *mana* in himself also, and can so direct it as to effect what he desires; a charm is powerful because the name of a spirit or ghost expressed in the form of words brings into it the power which the ghost or spirit exercises through it. Thus all conspicuous success is a proof that a man has *mana;* his influence depends on the impression made on the people's mind that he has it; he becomes a chief by virtue of it." [15]

This passage has been quoted at length not only because it gives a clear picture of the concept that has so considerably influenced thinking about the nature of religion, but also because it shows how no single formula can encompass the beliefs of a single people. In the quotation, we find the power that is mana lodged not only in stone, but it is also to be found in a bone because the bone of a dead person has associated with it the ghost of the dead. Furthermore, Codrington names a second category of beliefs in spirits found among these same people, "beings personal, intelligent, full of *mana,* with a certain bodily form which is visible but not fleshly like the bodies of men." [16] Such spirits are different from ghosts, which are the spirits of men that have left the body. In some of the islands, beings, even more difficult to describe, called *viu,* enter into the system of belief. Thus, when we speak of mana as the religion of Melanesia, the term is used as inadvisably as when we label the religion of the Plains Indians animistic.

Though mana is neither god nor spirit, its power, in the areas studied by Codrington, can be manipulated. It "attaches itself to persons and things" and can be transmitted from one individual to another. The instance of its use to maintain power in the family of a certain chief exemplifies this. This man, who was "the most conspicuous chief" in the island of Florida at the time of first European contact was a native of a different island. But while as a young man staying there he had played a prominent part in fighting the enemies of the people of Florida, and had been victorious. His reputation for mana—that he was a man of power—was thus established, and increased with the years. Like other chiefs, it was believed that he had access to a powerful ghost, a *tendalo,* so that, like them, because of his mana, he could utilize the power of this spirit for his own ends and might pass on to his successor the power that maintained him.[17]

The comparison has frequently been made between mana and electricity. Like electricity, mana is impersonal, and like electricity it can be channelled, directed, and used to achieve a desired end by one who knows how to manipulate it. In other regions, it is not so easily controlled, while in still others, its power is more specifically directed. The association of power with rank in Polynesia partakes more of this last order, since it is almost synonymous with the term "sacred." It attaches itself so strongly to a chief that certain parts of his body, or such of his possessions as he specifically names and touches become charged with his power and thus dangerous to all others. As a mechanism for the maintenance of power it is highly effective; the simile of electricity that is transmitted by contact comes even more to mind than in the classic Melanesian example.

---

[15] R. H. Codrington, 1891, pp. 118–20.
[16] *Ibid.*, p. 120.
[17] *Ibid.*, pp. 51–3.

Religion: the Problem of Man and the Universe

The mana-like power-manifestations that have been reported from the North American continent may also be considered. The impersonal nature of the Algonkian concept of *manitou*, of the Siouan *wakanda*, of the Iroquois *orenda* comes out quite clearly, as we see if we turn again to the Algonkian Montagnais-Naskapi for an analysis of their version of this power: "The background upon which rest the supernatural relationships of the Montagnais-Naskapi must be understood in the term *məntú*, variants being *manətú* (Lake St. John), *mantú* (Mistassini). The term cannot be adequately translated, since it is an abstraction having no definite compass in the genius of a vague philosophy. To the native it is not as difficult a thought to grasp as it seems to us, for we use the term 'power' to think of transcendental qualities, whereas he does not. Everything not understood is implied in it. He intends the term to have no definite application. One informant will try to illustrate the meaning of the term by comparing it to natural physical force observable in electricity, gravity, heat, steam, while another will liken it to psychic principles operating in thought, invention, memory, coordination, in animal generation and human procreation, in heredity, and especially in supernatural control. While *məntú* cannot be lexically defined, we can glean some little idea of its purport from the extensive use to which it is put in the spiritual vocabulary of the people. In the sense of 'spiritual being' or 'deity' . . . [it has been adapted] . . . to Christian theism. In the sense of 'power' we find it in common use in the translations given by thoughtful Indians in explaining the miracles of the shaman or conjuror. It often appears, moreover, in terms expressing mental states which result in producing physical effects."[18]

The power concept among American Indians is not always as completely impersonal, and as sharply definable in terms of mana as the Algonkian *manitou* and similar beliefs, as we see if we turn to the Puyallup-Nisqually of the Pacific Coast. "Every individual characteristic and every cultural complex, except those related to sexual life, was understood and was thought to operate through power. Adult life without power was inconceivable and childhood was viewed as a period of preparation . . . for the reception of power." This preparation, under the control of the trainer lasted from the age of five to six until puberty, and was essentially a process of physical hardening. At puberty, most boys went on a power-quest, though this was not the exclusive means of obtaining power; girls, who might also receive power, never went on these quests, but bathed and fasted as a part of the isolation enjoined at initial menstruation.

There were two kinds of power; those associated with some trait of personality or aptitude, and shamanistic powers. The first type was very generally distributed, and made of a person a good hunter, fortunate in economic pursuits, or a lucky gambler. The shamanistic power was of a sterner quality. It came to a person without regard for his wishes, and "failure to meet the ceremonial requirements of one's power caused a friction which resulted in the illness or ultimate death of the human who was thus stubborn in refusal." Furthermore, "Weakness of the body through fatigue or physical illness

---

[18] F. G. Speck, *op. cit.*, p. 35.

might cause the power to become detached or dislodged, a state, again, which involved illness and ultimate death if the power could not be recovered." These shamanistic powers, like other powers, were associated with animal or abstract beings. They were widely distributed, but "in the average person were overbalanced and held in check" by the possession of stronger ordinary powers.

Numerous powers are recognized by these people, though the long list of powers given is by no means complete. Thirty-five of those listed are associated with birds and animals and objects such as rocks, trees, or stumps. Chicken-hawk power, to take an example at random, makes a good gambler; grizzly bear power makes a man "apt to be mean and always brave"; snake power "is just a 'cuss.' You can't do anything with a man who has it, he just goes off and lives away from the others. People don't like him, and he doesn't like them." The more generalized powers, including the shamanistic ones and certain maleficent types that are avoided if possible, number eighteen more. One, for example, protects the home. Another is the principal wealth power, another gives a man the ability to dance, another makes a man brave. The variety of powers is confusing, but the general principle underlying them all is clear. All powers, whatever their variegated forms, represent the force in the universe that endows men and women with ability, with aptitudes, with insights that make of them the persons they are.[19]

The idea of impersonal power also seems to be present in Africa, but here the role of polytheistic worship and the ancestral cult is so important that beliefs in non-anthropomorphic forces appear in the literature only by implication. The sense of power as conveyed by impersonal, indwelling spirits, maintained by Pechuël-Loesche to characterize the use of charms among the Loango tribes, has been interpreted as analogous to the mana concept. A hint of this same feeling of power in the impersonal sense is given in the following passage from Stayt, who, "on inquiring minutely into the history of a small piece of wood, worn as a charm round the neck of a MuVenda for protection when travelling, it transpired that this wood was taken from a bough of a tree overhanging a difficult climb in a well-frequented path. This bough was grasped by every passerby in order to assist him over the difficult place. In this way the power of that particular bough was inordinately increased by helping the wayfarer, and it became the obvious source from which effective charms for the timid traveller could be obtained." This illustrates "the belief that every object, animate or inanimate, possesses a kinetic power for good or evil," that is basic to the medico-magical arts of the BaVenda.[20]

In West Africa, however, charms are empowered by deities or little people of the forest, or other creatures. Thus, while of themselves charms either function or do not in accordance with the care given them, the ultimate source of their strength is derived from some supernatural being. There is some possibility, however, that where the cult of the gods is less formalized, belief in an impersonal force behind charms coexists with that which traces the source to the power of those supernatural beings. For example, though

---

[19] M. W. Smith, 1940, pp. 56–75, 189–95.
[20] H. A. Stayt, 1931, p. 262.

among the Negroes of West African derivation who inhabit the West Indian islands *obia* is generally accepted as the term for evil magic, in Dutch Guiana it implies power of an impersonal variety that, imparted to charms, makes of them objects, called obias, that can work good or evil in accordance with the specific powers their maker has given them. Even more significant is the concept of *kunu* held by the Bush Negroes. For while *kunu* derives from the power of the ancestors, and is a force that only punishes and does not help a man, it is fully impersonal. When a serious transgression of ancestral precepts, such as murder or incest, has been committed, it kills—not the offender but his family. Less serious offenses, such as repeated theft, bring on lesser penalties. But one does not pray to it, or try to send it to anyone or in any way influence it. That would be to no purpose, since it operates as automatically as does the electricity that kills the murderer when the switch is thrown.[21]

5

OUR discussion of religion has led us through animistic beliefs to concepts of deity and of power. We now, finally, come to the idea of magic, the nature of which we may briefly consider, leaving the manifestations of magic to be treated at greater length in the next chapter. The important point to be stressed here is that magic, which for many years was held to be without relationship to religion, is actually an integral part of religion. We cannot even distinguish it fully from the worship of the gods in terms of criteria often met with—that magic is compulsive while the worship of the gods is propitiatory; or that magic is effected by formula, while the gods are moved by prayer; or that magic is always used with reference to a specific problem, while the gods are petitioned for general well being.

Magic has been differentiated from religion in other ways. Frazer has held it to be antecedent to the worship of the gods. He based his conclusions largely on data reported from the Australians; for many of the earlier students of "primitive man" they were our contemporary ancestors *par excellence,* whose practices, it was believed, were the customs of primeval humanity. With somewhat better reason, Frazer has also equated magic with science, though to call magic "primitive science" [22] will not bear too close a scrutiny. There can be no question that the element of direct causation of specific ends does characterize much of the magical practices of man, as it does the routine of the scientist. The differences between them, however, are important. The scientist works in a closed, mechanistic system, where causation is effectuated by putting in operation forces invariably of a material nature. In magical operations, however, while a given combination of factors must produce a desired result, the system is not a closed one, but departs from the natural to include and account for the play of supernatural forces.

Magic is no more the exclusive property of nonliterate peoples than is monotheism the monopoly of certain literate cultures. Goldenweiser has

---

[21] M. J. and F. S. Herskovits, 1934, pp. 62–79.
[22] Sir J. G. Frazer, 1935, vol. I, pp. 220–5.

given example after example of the utilization of magic in our culture, masked by the use of other terms. Even though, as he states, it "is no part of our institutionalized religion," yet the sacredness we attribute to holy objects, even the good that is dimly felt accrues through attendance at church and contact with its beneficent powers, is not too far removed from the psychology that places faith in the efficacy of a carved piece of wood, or a rock or a waterfall.

A word should be said about the term we use to designate the magical practices we employ without admitting we are doing so. We call them "superstitions"; and then extend the meaning of the word to include any form of belief with which we do not hold or that is not officially recognized by a particular body of religious doctrine in which we find satisfaction. Superstitions are, however, but beliefs of which there is no longer a whole-hearted acceptance. They are practices that are followed without conviction, but with an uneasy feeling that it will do no harm to carry them out, and may do a great deal of good, if by chance we thus get on the good side of powers whose existence we may at times doubt.

From this comes the rather shamefaced attitude toward magic that is familiar to us, and which has given rise to rationalizations so often encountered as to have become standard explanations of behavior that can be interpreted as belief in "superstitions." We avoid walking under a ladder, and then explain that we fear it will fall, or that a bucket of paint will come down on us. We politely fail to note audibly that our hotel, following standard practice, has no thirteenth floor. A man carries a buckeye "as a pocket-piece" rather than as a preventive for rheumatism; he surreptitiously raps three times on wood for good luck when he thinks no one is looking, or makes a game of it. This attitude toward beliefs held without conviction is by no means unique to Euroamerican culture. The same feeling about superstitions was shown by the West African who, expressing scepticism at the belief of his fellows in the power of the earth, nonetheless knelt, touched his hand to the ground and kissed his fingers as he discussed the earth-deity whose wind-storms destroyed the crops.

If we recognize that magic is an integral part of most belief-systems, we may then distinguish it from other forms of religion, so as better to understand it. Magic, for example, is actuated far more by the use of formulae than when men are dealing with the gods. But, as Lowie has put it, "both magic and religion are best regarded as extremely ancient components of the human world-view." [23] As such, they are like parts of a single mechanism that helps to assure man his place in a scheme of things so vast, and so complex, that without these varied controls he would be hard put to it to make meaning out of his life, or to achieve a sense of security in it.

---

[23] R. H. Lowie, 1924, p. 147.

CHAPTER 22

Religion: the Control of
the Universe

HOWEVER he defines the universe, man everywhere uses religion to find and maintain himself in the scheme of things. This scheme of things, as expressed in the beliefs of any people, is their *cosmology*, though the current meaning of the term *theology* is a closer designation for the systematized religious concepts of a group. Whichever term is employed, however, a whole series of instruments, whereby the forces of this universe are shaped to reach the ends desired by man, are always a part of the total religious system of a people. These instruments, called *rituals*, may be grouped under the term *ceremonialism*.

In most societies, it will be recalled, religion *does* things for people. Belief describes the ways of the powers of the universe, the range and intensity of these powers, and the particular manner in which they influence the lives of people. Ritual comprehends the methods whereby these powers may be enlisted in behalf of man, not alone as benevolent guardians, but as potent agents who may be induced or compelled to mobilize effort on behalf of sanctioned ends, often to achieve very specific results.

In other words, religion, like all other aspects of life, is a functioning element of culture. Even in cultures where a relatively high degree of specialization permits differences between "official" and "popular" religion, or where a systematized theology diverges from humbler views, religion is not removed from life. In most cultures, the validity of this statement would be self-evident. There are two ways, however, in which Euroamerican cultures are distinct in this respect. The first is found in the narrowness with which the term "religion" is defined; the second, in the manner in which the powers of the universe are approached. These two so deeply influence our conception of the nature of religion, and our attitudes toward it, that they must be clarified before we proceed further.

The narrowness with which we define religion stems directly from the intense specialization of our culture. Without prescribed training, we approach the powers of the universe with no more feeling of competence than if we were called on to operate a power-lathe, derive a formula for the manufacture of gasoline, or compose a tone poem for orchestra. Religion, for vast

361

numbers of us, has become a matter of adherence to an accepted world-view. In this we approach as near to the point of being entirely passive in our religious experience as, in all probability, the history of man has ever known. Performance is left to the experts; in proffering our faith, we lend our presence and our ears, but not a hand. The immediate relevance of belief to action, so essential a characteristic of religion in most cultures, seems, somehow, to be absent.

This is not to say that there are not men and women everywhere who take into their own hands, with concentrated intensity, the instruments whereby the power of the universe may be brought to bear, when events set up emotional tensions that seem to them capable of resolution in no other way. Mystical experiences of this kind, as we term them, are by no means infrequent in our society, despite the fact that they occur in the lives of but few individuals. When events progress without crises, we are content to leave the universe to those who are professionally concerned with it. Other cultures, however, move from this extreme to a state of affairs where every adult has some competence in dealing with the supernatural, even though specialists may be called on to aid in solving particular problems.

Codrington has described how, in Melanesia, religious specialization stands at almost the opposite pole to what is known in Euroamerican culture. "There is no priestly order," he says, "and no persons who can properly be called priests. Any man can have access to some object of worship, and most men in fact do have it, either by discovery of their own or by knowledge imparted to them by those who have before employed it. If the object of worship, as in some sacrifices, is one common to the members of a community, the man who knows how to approach that object is in a way their priest and sacrifices for them all; but it is in respect of the particular function only that he has a sacred character; and it is very much by virtue of that function that a man is a chief, and not at all because he is a chief that he performs the sacrifice." [1]

Nonliterate peoples and most literate societies alike take belief for granted. The powers that rule the universe are known, and the ways in which they are approached are part of the routine of living. To make a token offering of food to gods or ancestors before eating, to murmur a formula before the arrow leaves the bow, or to strengthen the power of a charm by sprinkling it with palm-wine, takes no more thought, and occurs as frequently as our conventional "Excuse me" or "Thank you." For a man or woman who lives in terms of a system of thought that takes a symbolic group of invisible forces into daily account, as it does the human and observable natural setting, belief will not be narrowly framed, and attitudes will be relaxed and natural. Many students have commented on the absence in other cultures of the hushed voice, the restrained movements that mark our approach to the forces of the universe. Where these forces are thought to be all about and never aloof from any part of life, there is no place for such attitudes.

The problems we dealt with in the preceding chapter are essentially philo-

---

[1] R. H. Codrington, 1891, p. 127.

sophical problems. What are the sources of power? What are the drives that actuate man? The nature of the world, the place of man in it are problems that in most societies are dealt with by religion. All peoples, in every known society, at some time in their history have called upon their creative imagination to express their views about fundamentals in ways we should call philosophical. But in most societies, the men and women who formulate their views of the universe, the "philosophers," that is—with contradictions recognized where they cannot be resolved—will be found to be priests or diviners or workers of magic.

The ways in which men seek to bring themselves into harmony with the powers of the universe are many. They may be intensely personal, or require participation by the entire group. They may be public, or private. They may involve highly keyed emotional improvisation, or demand precision of movement, set by an ancient tradition. They may call for the recitation of elaborate formulae, or may be wordless. They may utilize special objects, carefully made and of intricate form, or they may be restricted to nonmaterial expression in word or song or dance. Any of these, moreover, may be found alone or in combination with others. And any of them, or all, may be used to petition or compel action by powers whose resources transcend those of the human being who invokes them.

2

Prayer is one of the principal categories of worship. It may be defined as the use of words to bring about the favorable intervention of the powers of the universe in the affairs of men. It can vary from casual address to formalized plea, and may be specific or general in its reference. "The gods are like children; they must be told what to do," said a Dahomean. This expresses a widespread attitude toward the relationship between men and supernatural beings that can make a prayer informative (with the implication that being informed, the divine agent will feel disposed to friendly intercession), or can be an admonition, or even a compulsive prompting. Prayer is often phrased with such beauty of imagery that some of the finest poetic expressions of nonliterate peoples have been collected in the form of prayers.

Let us cite some prayers that have been recorded from various parts of the nonliterate world. On the Polynesian island of Mangareva, an annual ceremony celebrated the appearance of the first or second breadfruit crop. Like all rites in Polynesia, this involved long preliminary preparation and the participation of many persons. At sunrise of the first day, the trumpeter sounded the shell trumpet, and the high priest invoked the deity, bidding him to come to the festival and to clear the path that the breadfruit trees, awakened by the call of the trumpet, might produce their fruit:

> Behold, this is the announcement
> An announcement of much to do,
> To invoke Tu,
> Tu-of-the-outer-space, Tu-eater-of-people,
> Tu-who-floats-up-the-land . . .

The Aspects of Culture

The priest continued his recital of the ritual names of the god, and then, after the offerings were made, he went to the plantations and spoke the following lines, directing his words toward the bark cloth streamer that had been erected:

> The streamer! Streamer for us,
> Streamer for the gods,
> Streamer that protects the back,
> That protects the front.
> The interior was void,
> The interior was empty.
> Let (productivity) appear
> And spread to the foothills.
> Grant the smell of food,
> Grant the growth of food,
> A portion of fatness,
> A breeze that calls for fermentation.

Finally, the names of the ancestors were called. Here the end sought was clearly expressed. That the prayer was spoken in the elaborate setting that marked its use did not alter the spirit that motivated it.[2]

The following address to the Sun by a Crow Indian, spoken when dedicating to him an albino buffalo skin, reflects a similar motivation:

Greeting, Father's Clansman. I have just made a robe for you, now I give it to you, this is it. Give me a good way of living. May I and my people safely reach the next year. May my children increase; when my sons go to war, may they bring horses. When my son goes to war, may he return with a black face. When I move, may the wind come to my face (so game shall not scent me), may the buffalo gather toward me. This summer may the plants thrive, may the cherries be plentiful. May the winter be good, may illness not reach me, may I see the new grass of summer, may I see the full-sized leaves when they come. May I see the spring. May I with all my people safely reach it.

Shorter and less formalized prayers are also known to these Indians. When a standard-bearer of a war society had been elected to office, his emblem was handed him by a predecessor who prayed in his behalf with these words: "I had such a stick in battle and had good luck. I hope this man will do the same." Or, the sponsor of a novice in a medicine lodge prayed for him as follows: "I want him to be an old man. All you above, let him live to be an old man."[3]

An Ashanti who marries a widow addresses this prayer to the ghost of the late husband:

Asumasi, they say that when a cutlass breaks, they put a new shaft to it; today they have taken your wife and given her to me, I beg you to look well after me and her. Let these children prosper and serve me, and let me beget others to add to your own.[4]

[2] Peter H. Buck (Te Rangi Hiroa), 1938, pp. 434-5.
[3] R. H. Lowie, 1935, pp. 115, 177, 286.
[4] R. S. Rattray, 1929, p. 28.

Religion: the Control of the Universe

From the Bushmen of South Africa comes this prayer, spoken when the sacred New Moon appears:

Ho, my hand is this
I shoot a springbok with my hand
By an arrow.

I lie down
I will early kill a springbok
Tomorrow.

Ho Moon lying there,
Let me kill a springbok
Tomorrow,
Let me eat a springbok;
With this arrow
Let me shoot a springbok
With this arrow;
Let me eat a springbok,
Let me eat filling my body
In the night which is here,
Let me fill my body.

Ho Moon lying there,
I dig out ants' food
Tomorrow,
Let me eat it.

Ho Moon lying there,
I kill an ostrich tomorrow
With this arrow.

Ho Moon lying there,
Thou must look at this arrow,
That I may shoot a springbok with it tomorrow.[5]

Here the directness of the appeal bespeaks a sense of close relationship between the Bushman and the being he worships. The urgency of the food quest causes the petitions of this people to be phrased in terms of the basic necessity, food, the need for which is made patent in this poetic invocation.

Exhortations such as these are the means whereby man prevails upon the supernatural beings about him to favor his needs and his desires. But that prayer is universal has not been established. It seems plausible to assume that where power concepts dominate belief, recourse to prayer is at a minimum, and the materials in hand seem to bear this out. In Melanesia, where the idea of *mana* predominates, prayers are addressed to the *tindalo,* or ghosts of dead men who had had power, but not to the power itself. Among the Puyallup-Nisqually, "power demonstrations" are recorded, where the power is called on at a public ceremony to show its strength, though we are not told whether the power was directly addressed or not. But there is no doubt as to the impersonality of the *məntú* of the Naskapi. "In none of the bands," says Speck,

---

[5] D. F. Bleek, 1929, p. 306.

"have prayers or ceremonies been found to indicate that any more benefit may be derived from these sources than those so graciously and constantly bestowed by the spirit-forces without insistence or recompense from the tongue of men. Acts of minor sacrifice, respect, and submission seem to be sufficient to avert malevolence." [6]

3

THE techniques of *magic* stand in contrast, though by no means in opposition, to prayer. The relationship is analogous to the way in which magic, broadly conceived, is to be differentiated from those forms of worship that are directed toward influencing the gods or achieving rapport with impersonal powers of the universe. But just as magic and prayer are in many cultures intimately related, so in their manifestations they move so evenly from one category to the other that the lines between them can be drawn only by following native distinctions. That is, it is reasonably safe to conclude that magical and religious practices are to be differentiated if, for example, distinguishing words are used for prayer and for the magic spell, or to designate the powers of a deity as against the power of a magic charm, or to name those who serve the gods as apart from those who work with charms.

The application of this technique is well demonstrated in Evans-Pritchard's analysis of magic among the Azande, who live just north of the Congo basin, west of the East African area. In studying their methods of controlling the supernatural world, this student has been "mainly concerned with following Zande thought." "I have classed under a single heading," he says, "what Azande call by a single word, and I have distinguished between types of behaviour that they consider different." These people have a well-developed system of witchcraft, by means of which injury can be caused to the person or belongings of an individual. Divination is employed by witch-doctors, who use various techniques, called oracles, to discover who has set evil against a man. Magic is used as the principal means of combatting witchcraft.

All these concepts have native designations. *Mangu* stands for the "witchcraft-substance" found in the bodies of the dead and discovered by oracles in the living; for "witchcraft," the psychic emanation from the substance that causes injury; and "witchcraft-phlegm," believed to be found in the bodies of witch-doctors. *Boro* (*ira*) *mangu* is one who practises witchcraft. *Soroka* are the oracles that operate in four ways, each with its name—by poison administered to fowls, by use of a rubbing-board, by utilizing termites, and by employing three small sticks. It is different than *Pa ngua*, called divination, where, by experiment and logic, a human being, inspired by ghosts and medicines, or both, is used.

Magic is called *ngua*, and so are medicines and what Evans-Pritchard calls "leechcraft"; the term is also applied to certain groupings that practise magical rites. Magic is defined as "a technique that is supposed to achieve its purpose by the use of medicines. The operation of these medicines is a magic rite

---

[6] F. G. Speck, 1935, p. 62.

Religion: the Control of the Universe

and is usually accompanied by a spell." Medicines are designated as "any object in which mystical power is supposed to reside and which is used in magic rites." Leechcraft is healing—"the treatment of pathological conditions, whether by empirical or magical means, through physic or surgery." In opening his discussion of magic, Evans-Pritchard states that "witchcraft, oracles, and magic are like three sides to a triangle." It testifies to the complexity of the phenomenon that even in a discussion restricted to the practices of a single people, and drawn strictly in terms of their concepts, we learn that "in Zande opinion some magic is to be classed, from the legal and moral standpoint, with witchcraft." [7]

Two kinds of magic are often distinguished by students. First named by Frazer, they are "imitative" ("homeopathic") and "contagious." Both are held to operate in accordance with a principle of "like to like," also called a "principle of sympathy." There is not much doubt that this principle operates in a very large proportion of magical usages. "Contagious" magic is exemplified when a hunter drinks the blood of his kill to acquire its craftiness or its strength. "Imitative" magic would, let us say, be found in the performance of a dance in which the simulated killing of an animal to be hunted the following day was enacted so as to assure the success of the enterprise. These categories, however, while quite valid as far as they go, neither constitute the entire field, nor are they absent from certain practices to which the term "religious" is also customarily given.

The charm and the spell are widely-spread devices employed in the use of magic. A specific power that is held to reside in a specific object is set in operation by the pronouncement of a formula that of itself can wield power. Here, once more, especially as regards the spell, we intrude on what has been held to be the domain of religion; except that the magic spell is held to exercise a compulsion over whatever power it summons, while its religious counterpart, the prayer, is a supplication that may or may not be granted at the will of the being addressed. This, however, does not always follow. "Name magic" is as often directed toward the gods as it is used to control human beings, or to invoke the power of a charm. This is why, in many cultures, the "real" name of a person, or a god, or even an object, is held secret. The name is a compelling symbol. We do not believe in magic, we say; yet to hear our name accompanied by an ugly imprecation brings a prompt emotional response, just as it would if we were to see a picture of ourselves thrown to the ground and stamped upon.

The name is an integral part of what William James called "the Me." By extension, then, a god summoned by name responds as does a human being. In many cultures, therefore, the "real" name of the god may only be known by those with the power to cope with him when he comes. "Thou shalt not take the name of the Lord thy God in vain," is an injunction known far more widely than among the ancient Hebrews and those who have continued their beliefs or taken over elements of them. The Biblical command was held to so closely that the pronunciation of the Hebrew character we transliterate as

---

[7] E. E. Evans-Pritchard, 1937, pp. 9–11, 387.

Jahveh (Jehovah) is today unknown. The secret name was used only once a year, on its most sacred day, to summon the Deity to the most sacred spot known to the early Jews. Analogously, the Suriname Bush-Negro on the river does not pronounce the name of a rapid until his canoe is well beyond it, lest he summon unnecessarily the indwelling spirit of this stretch of agitated water. Supernatural beings, summoned without reason, react with irritation. It is, therefore, well to call them only when they are needed. For once summoned, they will come, because they must.

On a humbler level, this is the psychological essence of the spell, whether used by itself or with a charm or "medicine." The way the Tarascan Indians who live in Cherán induce suppurating sores on the genitals of an enemy clearly shows this:

> Buy oil for lamps and let it burn several days before a holy image. Take what is left and mix it with a bit of earth recently stepped on by the person it is desired to injure, or put in the oil something of the victim, such as hair, fingernails, or some piece of used clothing, and burn the oil, saying "So and so, you must have sores on such and such a part of the body." In addition, if the person is a man, he must be given a glass of *aguardiente* in which an herb from the hot country has infused a number of days; and if the person is a woman, a *gorda* made from maize dough or nixtamol in which the same hash is mixed.[8]

The magic charm takes innumerable forms. It most often includes some part of the object or individual over which its power is to be exerted; or some element that, because of outer resemblance or inner character, habitually achieves the result the charm is supposed to bring about. One word that has been applied to charms is *fetish,* and no term has proved more troublesome than this and its companion, *fetichism.* The derivation is from the Portuguese *feitiço,* "something made," and was used by the early Portuguese to denote the charms and images of African peoples. These terms are mentioned here because they are encountered so often in the literature, as when it is said that "fetichism is the religion of Africa." When used at all, they should be employed in the sense of "charm" and "magic"; but they are far better omitted from any discussion of the means whereby man controls the supernatural.

The impression has been given that the use of magic charms, being a highly individual matter, is diffuse and lacking in known principles as compared with the regularity of those group procedures whereby the worship of the gods is carried on. If, however, accounts of magic are carefully read, it becomes evident that there is nothing haphazard about the way it is conceived or executed. The "internal organization . . . in the seeming chaos of magical practices" of Dahomey is apparent not only in the clear-cut theories of these people as to how magic originated and what forces have endowed man with given charms, but also in the ways in which charms themselves, called *gbo,* are classified as to materials and function.

Classification of the forms of *gbo* and their ingredients are as follows:

1. *amasi* (literally, leaves and water), "medicine"; this group is most frequently used for washing rather than for internal use.

---

[8] R. L. Beals, 1946, p. 160.

Religion: the Control of the Universe

2. *ati*—powdered ingredients, used internally as well as externally.

3. *kã*—ingredients wrapped and tied inside with black or white cotton and worn about the arms, legs, waist, or neck.

4. *sa*—bits of smooth wood, wrapped in red, blue, white, or green cotton.

5. *defife*—substance reduced to powder, wrapped in cloth and tied with cotton.

6. *alogã*—rings of iron or brass, a type that usually includes preventives against danger.

The principal functional categories into which *gbo* are separated are these:

1. *gboglo*—preventive against all magic sent by another.
2. *golo*—protects the house and possessions of its owner.
3. *nudonome*—protects the fields.
4. *holõhõlõgbo*—gives power to its owner, i.e., strengthens his self-confidence in his dealings with people, as well as his physical powers.
5. *afiyõhwedji*—causes black magic to recoil upon the sender, and prevents evil to the recipient.
6. *supikpa*—holds danger for another.
7. *djido*—insures longevity.
8. *gbodudõ*—sends evil that kills.
9. *wayinume*—creates feelings of good-will, affection, and love toward the owner.
10. *yivo*—helps the owner realize his desires.
11. *hweglõ*—makes the owner secure in the courts.
12. *azõgbwlenu*—cures physical illness.
13. *kasiso*—(or *kandudo*)—preserves the hunter in the bush.
14. *vigbo*—protects infants and pregnant women.
15. *hwelili*—guards the house; is also the name of the *gbo* imbedded in the walls of a house when built.
16. *azomaso*—guards owner against illness.
17. *dokoglo*—prevents accidents.
18. *kugbo*—determines whether or not a person who is ill will die.[9]

Magic is often divided into the categories "black" and "white," the first being of evil intent, the second beneficent. In the literature, emphasis tends to be laid most heavily on the first category. The reason for this is twofold. There is, for one thing, the challenge to the investigator to uncover what his informants are least willing to divulge. More than this, though, is the nature of the appeal "black" magic holds in the imagination of the people themselves. It is dramatic, fraught with climaxes as recorded in the past or anticipated in the future. Once a willingness to talk about it is established, informants will dwell on the subject with full relish and exuberant detail, leaving "white" magic in the background of cultural elements taken for granted and not worthy of exposition.

Nonetheless, it is evident from the list given above, and from the innumerable instances of magic reported from other parts of the world, that the practice of "black" magic by no means predominates. The category of "white" magical devices, indeed, must be extended to include much of native medicine; just as "black" magic includes the use of devices, such as poison, that we

---

[9] M. J. Herskovits, 1938b, vol. II, pp. 263–4.

would term anything but supernatural. The categories of good and evil magic, as a matter of fact, in large measure arise out of the patterns of Euroamerican thought, whereby the reality of shading is distorted, and extremes are emphasized. There is, in truth, so little in the actual experience of any human being that is absolutely "good" or absolutely "bad" that the concepts hinder clarity of thought rather than aid analysis.

Nonliterate peoples are more realistic than we. They recognize neither black nor white, but a series of greys of varying shades. The magic I set to prevent my house from being robbed will harm the robber; his thieving magic will benefit him and does hurt to me. From this one moves to the extremes. The magic rites of fertility that are to assure bountiful crops, or charms that are designed to safeguard the pregnant woman and ensure her a safe delivery, are good. Magic that kills is bad, and the worker of such malevolent devices is everywhere feared, and in most cultures regarded as a criminal and punished as such when apprehended. And at this point, we come again the full circle to the gods, who in many instances themselves empower magic and punish its misuse to attain evil ends.

4

THE need to ascertain and interpret the will of the gods and to negate the factors of time and distance is felt by many peoples. Various techniques have been devised to accomplish these ends. *Divination,* the general term for them, must be considered as another way in which the control of the supernatural is attained. The phenomenon takes two forms. One is by the use of devices that are independent of the diviner, and whose operation is determined by the fall of lots, or by some other technique where chance is the principal element. The second is by contact with a divine spirit, which displaces the personality of a priest or medium and speaks through him. Both are of wide distribution in the Old World; in the New World, the second type predominates.

Our own history makes both types familiar to us. Divination by reading the entrails of slain beasts was regular practice among the Romans, while the Greek oracles revealed the will of the gods through possession of those dedicated to their service. At the present time, too, though the fortune-teller and spiritualistic medium do not have the position they hold in non-mechanistic cultures, their revelations are accepted without scepticism by many persons in literate Europe and America. They represent an attempt to solve the eternal riddle that challenges man—how to foretell the future. For if the future were known, then, by preparing for the events to come, a man's destiny would be in his own hands. He could compound whatever the future held of good, and take steps to avoid the ills in store for him. It is, indeed, the riddle of riddles, and man would be less than human were he not to seize on attempts to solve it.

Techniques of divination are many. One, that we have mentioned, the scrutiny of the entrails of animals killed for the purpose, is found everywhere in the Old World. Often an autopsy is performed on the human dead to the same end. Another method is the inspection of scapulae. These bones are placed in the fire until they crack, whereupon the diviner inspects the lines and makes his interpretation. Perhaps as complex a series of systems of divination by mechanical means as is found anywhere exists in Africa, where divining techniques have proliferated to a degree unknown elsewhere among nonliterate or even literate peoples. In one small region of the Cameroons, for example, palm-leaf cards with special markings are thrown, other kinds of cards are placed at the hole of a trained tarantula so he may scatter them, cowry-shells are cast to attain combinations of open and closed sides, human and animal entrails are inspected, states of possession are induced to permit the gods to speak. Each of these techniques, however, could be duplicated in many other areas of the continent.[10]

New World divining practices, which also extend to Siberia, are generally of the shamanistic variety, and are essentially concerned with healing and the quest for power. The shaman is an individual endowed with supernatural power to heal, or one who by calling his spirit can find out what is beyond time and space. Among the Saulteaux, a small conjuring lodge is built, into which the "specialist in invocation," as Hallowell calls him, enters and summons his "spiritual helpers." When each comes it sings a song and gives its name, and further manifests itself by the movements of the lodge. "With the aid of his spiritual tutelaries, a conjurer is able to secure news about people who are hundreds of miles away, or learn of events that are taking place in another part of the country. He can discover what is going to happen in the future and he can find out a great deal about the past lives of his fellows. As occasion demands he may recover lost or stolen articles for their owners or discover the hidden cause of some puzzling malady. On the other hand, with malevolent ends in view, he can abduct the souls of human beings, causing sickness, mental disorder or even death, if this vital animating agency is not returned to them." Conjuring of this sort is of the "non-inspired type" wherein the spirits speak *to* or *in the presence* of the shaman, rather than enter his body and speak *through* him.[11] "Inspirational shamanism" is predominant in Siberia, but is found to a lesser degree among American Indians.

Possession, however, is more than merely a mode of ascertaining the will and the intent of supernatural beings that direct the universe. It has, indeed, been held by some students to be the supreme religious experience. It is an awesome performance, and presents many baffling psychological problems. Its interpretation as a psychopathological phenomenon has been considered in earlier pages,[12] and rejected in the light of the principles of cultural relativism. It is an experience framed by the conventions of worship of the individual to whom it comes, and in these terms is never haphazard, but patterned to a degree often unrealized by students. It may come in the solitude of a remote haunt to which a man or woman has gone to receive his god, or may occur during a public ceremony to which a supernatural being has been called. Under states of possession, devotees experience a change in their cus-

---

[10] From an unpublished study by Paul Gebauer.
[11] A. I. Hallowell, 1942, pp. 9–13.
[12] See pp. 66–68 above.

tomary behavior, even the timbre and pitch of their voices may alter. They may speak "in tongues" or remain silent, prophesy and cure, be acquiescent or recalcitrant. As the spirit, the human being possessed may walk on burning coals, or chew glass, or lash himself with thorny bushes, or otherwise castigate himself without apparent harm. Many such cases have been recorded by competent observers.

Rapport with the supernatural not attainable by ordinary persons is vouchsafed to the worshiper who experiences possession. Whether a guardian spirit, a ghost, or a deity comes to him, he has a sense of personal security and assurance of power; while in many cultures preferred social position is his because the being by which he is possessed has chosen him as his vehicle. His visions enable his fellows the more confidently to face the forces of the universe; the pronouncements of the god, spirit, or ghost who speaks through him may indicate the way to fortune, to good health, and to those other ends men strive for. Of all the means by which the individual achieves oneness with the supernatural, none is more striking, more convincing to those who believe, and apparently more satisfying, than possession.

Ceremonialism, more than any other aspect of religious experience, calls on the pageantry of ritual to reinforce belief by dramatizing the deeds of the gods and their place in the universe. Not all ceremonialism is religious; for every culture has secular rites of various sorts as well. Religious ceremonies, however, provide the widest opportunity for group worship. In societies that can afford specialists to mobilize the power of the supernatural forces to aid the group as a whole, religious ceremony is the agency through which devotees are guided and directed in formalized expressions of worship. Here, too, are to be found the elaborate costumes, the decorated wands, the masks, and other paraphernalia that impress and give enjoyment to participants and spectators alike, and yield aesthetic as well as religious satisfaction.

More than this, ceremonialism is a powerful agent in uniting a people. Whether they are active participants in the worship, themselves experiencing the emotional force of a rite, or whether they are spectators, the bonds that bind them to their fellows are strengthened by ceremonialism. Therefore, though the hypothesis advanced by Durkheim—that the origin of all religion is to be sought in ceremonial—must be seriously modified, it is by no means to be completely dismissed. On the other hand, we cannot define the sacred as strictly as Durkheim does when he describes religion as activity exercised in institutions analogous to churches. The fact that he derived his materials from existing accounts of Australian aboriginal religious practices, and that he himself, as a social philosopher, never had first-hand contact with any cultures other than his own, perhaps explains why his conclusions have been subject to severe and telling attack. It requires but little experience in the field to discover that among the vast majority of nonliterate peoples, the line between religious and non-religious rites, between the sacred and the secular, is as blurred as are such divisions in all cultures even where a high degree of specialization is present.

The ceremonial aspects of religion are the first to strike the outsider; and most descriptions of the religion of nonliterate peoples, given by people with-

PLATE 8a   *Yoruba masked dancer, showing manner of wearing mask.*
PLATE 8b   *Closer view of same masked dancer. [Photographs 8a and 8b courtesy W. Bascom]*
PLATE 8c   *Yoruba mask in position customarily exhibited. See page 382. [Collection of W. Bascom; photograph by Mary Modglin, Chicago]*

PLATE 9a *Bush-Negro tray used for winnowing rice. See page 383.*

Religion: the Control of the Universe

out anthropological training, are in actuality no more than descriptions of ceremonies. As almost nowhere else in the range of culture, it is here essential to call into constant play the "Why?" that is the primary tool of the field worker. Rituals, whether simple or complex, whether group or individual, are but the implementation of belief. This means that not only must the rite itself be detailed with as much care as any observable fact, but that the sanctions for it must also be probed. In other words, the theological foundations of ritual must be fully explored if the rite is not to rest, unliving, in the pages of the notebook. Why does one dancer wear red beads, another white? What does it mean that all the participants in a ceremony have a vertical streak painted in the center of the forehead? For what reason does the action move in a clockwise direction? The observed fact, of itself, tells us nothing; it is not until we learn the reasons for the observed behavior that we begin to comprehend the ritual we record.

Usually the "Why?" of the ethnographer leads to mythology. The symbolism of a rite, often to its most minute detail, tends to derive from some instruction that a supernatural being is said to have handed down concerning his proper worship; or incorporates the pantomime of the creation as recounted in the myths; or strengthens, in ways only to be explained on the basis of mythological statement, the very power of the gods themselves. Mythology is the charter of belief, and gives point and meaning to the ritualistic behavior that derives from its sanctions. Very often the myth will itself take on a sacred quality; this quality can render the task of the ethnographer a most difficult one. The story, conceived as partaking of the power of the characters of which it treats, then becomes not only sacred but secret, and is not to be imparted to the outsider—not because he is an outsider, perhaps, but because like the younger members of the tribe, he does not have the strength to render its spiritual impact harmless to himself.

The point becomes clear when attitudes in Euroamerican culture toward the Bible are considered from this point of view. That the Bible is written and not transmitted orally is aside from the point, except insofar as its sacred character is emphasized by the feeling that alterations in the text are not to be tolerated. Something of this attitude is found in Polynesia, where texts, recorded in the Tuomotu Islands from grandfather and grandson, of specialists in reciting the myths, were found to have been memorized practically letter-perfect. But in nonliterate societies this is the exception rather than the rule. Just as Bible-stories told to children tend to disregard the text for the substance of the tales, so in nonliterate cultures it is the substance rather than the details of the myth that are remembered and transmitted from one generation to the next so that power will not be lost and the gods will be served according to tradition.

If mythology gives belief its charter, ritual is the instrument by which conviction is renewed and strengthened. For initiate and non-initiate, and even for those who in many societies are forbidden to witness certain rites, the mere knowledge that the proper ceremonies have been performed gives assurance that the powers of the universe have been won to favor the well-being of the people and to avert malevolent happenings. Thus added to the

373

sociological significance of ritual as a binding force for the group as a whole is its psychological importance as the mechanism that validates belief.

The economic implications of religion are also most clearly to be seen in the ceremonialism of a people. It will be recalled that, in the discussion of nonliterate economies, the role of the economic surplus in maintaining specialists to mediate with the powers of the supernatural world, and those who specialize in governing, was pointed out. Support of priests, diviners, and their attendants takes an appreciable proportion of the economic surplus devoted to the maintenance of amicable relations with the supernatural powers. But just as with those who govern, the outer emblems of power are such as to mark off and give distinction to those who rule, so it is with the religious experts. Thus a considerable portion of the surplus that is made available to these specialists is used to stage the rituals wherein the work of the gods is dramatized and their worship is conducted.

Those who set the stage for the rites that validate belief, for the most part are quite sincere in discharging their obligations to those for whom they intercede. In the literature, claims of sincerity contend with assertions that these persons are mountebanks, exploiters of the believers who turn to them for aid and guidance. Especially has this charge been levelled against diviners, shamans, workers of magic, and other healers. But we have too many authenticated acounts of such specialists turning to their colleagues when they themselves were in need of aid, to permit a general charge of fraud against them to go unchallenged.

On the other hand, one need not be naive and defend them all, as a group, against such accusations. The men who advise, who prescribe, who predict, after a time come to have the practical skills of the lawyer, the doctor, the minister, in handling human situations. Much of the setting of the shaman's lodge, the dim interior of the magician's hut, is to be equated with the special atmosphere of the lawyer's office, the psychoanalyst's couch, the doctor's bedside manner, the pastoral visit. In their own way, all these, like the paraphernalia of the nonliterate practitioners, involve minor rituals. Their psychological value is recognized in bringing the petitioner into rapport with the one whose efficiency in wielding the power and skill he controls is heightened by his own belief in their essential soundness.

5

IT IS far easier to say what religion is not, than to frame a definition of it in positive terms. We have seen that Tylor's "minimum definition" as the belief in spirits was by no means minimal; rather it comprehended only a segment of beliefs and practices we term religious. Moreover, to define religion in terms of any particular system of belief or dogma restricts our view out of all reason, since in such terms religion can only exist by definition. Some have sought to find the basis of religion in fear; others have stressed ethical content as its essential element; and we have commented on the hypothesis that it developed out of ritual.

Religion: the Control of the Universe

All these, we must recognize, are but partial answers. The mere fact that powers greater than man are conceived in the universe, means that some element of fear enters, especially when there exists a complementary belief that some act of human omission or commission may provoke retaliatory acts of hostility. The ethical role of the so-called "great" religions has received much emphasis and has been advanced as the primary differentiating factor that sets them off from the religions of nonliterate peoples. But concepts of right and wrong, of acceptable and inacceptable behavior, can be found among all groups. As has been stated, one of the principal tasks of the supernatural beings that inhabit the universe is to punish violations of the traditionally sanctioned code, even where positive rewards are not held to follow proper behavior.

It follows, therefore, that though all these elements enter into the religious experience, none of them is a universal aspect of religion; none constitutes a least common denominator to be extracted from every religion known to us, and we must seek other attempts to define the phenomenon.

Marett and Goldenweiser, approaching the problem of the nature of religion from somewhat different points of view, have agreed in holding that supernaturalism is the essence of all religious phenomena. "Magic and religion . . . belong to the same departments of human experience—one of the two great departments, the two worlds, one might almost call them, into which human experience, throughout its whole history, has been divided. Together they belong to the supernormal world, the x-region of experience, the region of mental twilight." [13] Goldenweiser divides beliefs in the supernatural into the tenet of *animistic faith* and the tenet of *magical faith,* underlying both of which is "the third and most important tenet of supernaturalism," the *faith in power.* But all these are given reality through the experience of the *religious thrill,* which is "the concrete living participation of the individual in this world of supernaturalism." [14]

Important in these formulations is the stress laid on the psychological satisfactions derived from participation in the exercise of religion. In this we approach the least common denominator of the many forms of the religious experience we seek, the unity that can be abstracted from them.

Here, however, we must enter still another qualification. For though, as Goldenweiser says, the "thrill" is the essence of religious participation, this thrill, which is the exceptional rather than the common religious experience, stands out as a mountain peak seen from the plain of everyday religious practice. But the less spectacular phases of everyday religion, which are certainly of no lesser importance, are, in point of fact, the ones that pervade religious behavior. All men, at all times, have sensed frustration and fear when faced with problems that their own human resources could not solve. Such frustrations and fears come not alone with dramatic displays of nature, with thunder and lightning and hail, with blizzards, and insect pests, and drought. They also arise, in everyday life, in the give and take of human

---

[13] R. R. Marett, 1912, p. 209.
[14] A. A. Goldenweiser, 1922, pp. 231–3.

relations, in encounters with fellow humans who deny, forbid, dominate, challenge, or inflict pain. The Freudian explanation of religion, in terms of the unconscious desire for the security of childhood, where a parent, as surrogate for society, solved problems and made decisions as well as directed conduct, is too simple to be fully acceptable; but it does give us an important insight into probable motivations that lead to religious expression.

The propensity for intense mystical experiences is no more universal among men than is the length of their noses. Some human beings reach an accord with the Powers that is denied to their more stolid fellows. The Dahomeans recognize these differences in the reaction of individuals to mystical religious experiences. "Skeptics among the Dahomeans themselves state that many of the cult-initiates derive nothing deeper from their experiences in the cult-house than the enjoyment of freedom from routine and, after emergence, the pleasure of appearing before their acquaintances in the fineries of a cult-member. It is also said that particularly in the case of women is it advantageous to have gone through the initiatory rites of the cult-house, because this gives a woman certain advantages in her relation to the other members of her family, and a certain favorable position with her husband. It is said, further, that some go through the initiatory experience merely to satisfy curiosity. Yet even skeptics admit that there are some who experience the real 'mystery,' that is the *vodū*. Such persons feel an exaltation, a sense of awe and of unity with the god that, though held in check between ceremonies, wells forth at once if the proper songs or drum rhythms are heard. On such occasions, as the cult-initiates stand ready to dance, a figure taller than any human stands before them, the left hand outstretched to touch their heads. This is the *vodū* (the god). And when the hand touches them they feel a great strength. As they dance, they are no longer themselves, and they remember nothing of what happened when the *vodū* leaves them. But, when they regain consciousness of the world outside and are themselves once more, they feel as though something heavy had left them." [15]

This statement, the summary of how a native skeptic described the experiences of cult-initiates under possession, illustrates clearly a point made by Radin [16] covering the varying degrees of religiousness found among men and women in every society. This is why, in defining religion in terms of crises or of the religious thrill, we must remember that crises are by no means always severe; that the thrill is only manifested at intervals, and not to every member of a society. Our definition, therefore, must allow for the less dramatic, quieter, everyday forms of religious belief and practice that tend to be overlooked when religious phenomena are delimited in terms of more spectacular manifestations. We must, also, in drawing our definition consider the emphasis on supernaturalism that plays so prominent a part in most discussions of religion.

Among most peoples, literate or nonliterate, belief in supernatural, or super-normal, or mystical forces of the universe does undoubtedly comprise the core of religious belief. Yet if we approach the phenomena of religion

[15] M. J. Herskovits, 1938b, vol. II, pp. 199–200.
[16] P. Radin, 1937, pp. 9–10.

Religion: the Control of the Universe

from the point of view of their essentially emotional character, we recognize that many reactions that have no basis in supernaturalism must be thought of as religious.

In our mechanistic culture, where there is progressively less place for supernaturalism as a functioning element comparable to the manner in which it is operative in an Indian tribe, the emotional drive, the deep faith in the transcendental importance of what is undertaken, the dedication to the experimental tradition that marks the scientist in his laboratory, is essentially religious in its psychological orientation. The thrill that comes when the formula is discovered to be correct, when the last stroke of the adding machine proves the validity of the mathematical calculation, is no different from that experienced by the nonliterate man when he comes face to face with his spirit.

The crusading spirit of the convinced atheist, or the intransigent selflessness of the political revolutionary must, in psychological terms, be thought of as falling in the same category, if only we consider the phenomenon from the point of view of its motivating drives and not in terms of the forms in which it manifests itself. Wissler, in 1923, perceived this modern religious phenomenon in another perspective when he characterized our "real" religion as belief in the efficacy of education and in the use of the ballot. One .of the reasons it is so difficult for those in the stream of Euroamerican culture, especially for intellectuals, to grasp the essential homely, everyday nature of religion is that we think of religion as supernaturalism, while our religious emotions are lavished on aspects of our experience we label as secular.

We must, then, recognize that, however frequent a concomitant of religion supernaturalism may be, any definition drawn in terms of it lacks a requisite comprehensiveness. If, in addition, we recognize further that an adequate definition must take into account the everyday functioning of religion in terms of its more placid manifestations as well as its more dramatic elements, then, in these terms, we may think of religion as *belief in, and identification with a greater force or power.* The belief may so pervade attitude and action as rarely to enter the stream of conscious thought, except in moments of crisis when it is called upon to steady a world that seems to be falling about one's head; or, under more commonplace circumstances, when tradition and conviction assure success in some undertaking; or in effecting a cure, or insuring a good crop by the performance of established rites. The greater force or power that stands for order and protection in the life of the individual may be a supernatural being or beings, an impersonal force, a concept such as society, or science. It is enough that man have faith in its unfailing potentialities, that he feel that it is to be called on when needed, that it will not fail him when his own resources are insufficient.

Above all, religion implies the emotional response to the power that rules the universe, however it may be conceived. Though the supreme religious experience, the "thrill," is felt by relatively few persons, and by them but sporadically, yet the raw material of emotion is ever present, and on a less intense scale is experienced by all those whose emotional susceptibilities are keyed to a religious response.

377

CHAPTER 23

The Aesthetic Drive: Graphic and Plastic Arts

PHILOSOPHY, from its earliest recorded days, has struggled with the problem of whether the impulse to create and appreciate beauty is inherent in man's nature; whether beauty, in itself, arises out of a conception of what is held to be beautiful or transcends the ways in which beauty is manifested. The universality of the drive to embellish useful objects, often so elaborately that the utility of an implement is lessened in the process, has posed questions that seriously embarrass those who have interpreted human experience in strict rationalistic terms.

It will be enough for us to recognize that the search for beauty is a universal in human experience. The innumerably varied forms that express beauty, that have sprung from the play of the creative imagination, afford some of the deepest satisfactions known to man. Toward the comparative study of art, a strictly relativistic point of view must be taken. Otherwise the number of differing conceptions of beauty will so confuse us as to stand in the way of our understanding of those general principles of the form and the functioning of art that emerge from a comparative approach to the arts of many societies. As one philosopher has put it, . . . "To a superlative degree the arts express the qualities which an age prizes, the human actions which it cherishes, and the ideals which it ennobles. . . . In the aesthetic attitude a culture can be captured and held, not as a set of bare facts to be statistically tabulated, but as the fruition of the travail of human minds."[1]

To understand how closely integrated with all of life, and how expressive of a way of living art can be, is again not easy for us who live in the highly specialized societies of Euroamerican culture. As with every other aspect of culture we have discussed, we are here confronted with the effect of compartmentalization on the cultural reality implicit in the phenomenon before us. By drawing definitions too finely, we tend to shut out many significant manifestations of a phenomenon because we find no room for them inside a narrow concept. We have observed this in the case of religion, of politics, of education—to cite but three examples. In the analysis of art, when

[1] B. Morris, 1943, p. 6.

The Aesthetic Drive: Graphic and Plastic Arts

we differentiate "pure" from "applied" art, we similarly restrict the play of our aesthetic appreciation. Furthermore, we set up invidious distinctions between the "artist" who produces this "pure" art and the "craftsman" whose art, if it is admitted that he has one, is held to be of a different category, of a quality which we call "applied."

It is worth our while to consider the implications of this point of view which derives so characteristically from the specialization of our society. It has pervaded all the arts; it has bearing on their appreciation no less than on the creation of the forms that are differentially evaluated. The distinction has been drawn between those who "know" an art form, as the result of special study, and those who, on a more popular level, are content with a less trained aesthetic evaluation. In the graphic arts, just as we differentiate the painter and the industrial designer, so we distinguish sharply between the quality of aesthetic sensitivity of the one who grasps the mastery of a Rembrandt etching and the person who accepts as beautiful the winter's scene printed on a commercial calendar. We speak of "classical" and "popular" music, of "poetry" and "folk verse." An architectural masterpiece is evaluated in terms of structure—line, mass, design—not its functional qualities.

The arts, in the conventions of Euroamerican culture, have been dissociated from the principal stream of life. Artistic creation is the function of the specialist; while the appreciation of what these specialists create is the privilege of those who at least command the leisure to pursue their avocation. The painting hangs on the wall, often of a museum; the sculpture is on its pedestal. The symphonic theme is somehow deemed vulgarized, violated, when it is transmuted into a popular dance tune. We speak of "significant form"; yet the aerodynamic streamlining of the high-speed train or aeroplane, or other utilitarian forms of this type are largely held to be "applied art" in disregard of the creative mastery with which the significant form of these useful instruments has been realized. The highest expression of the aesthetic experience is held to reside in objects that are not "profaned" by use, but are there to be looked at; or which, in music, are heard as "pure" forms. Considerations of utility, or associations with everyday living renders the object, the melody, the poem, something less than a work of art.

It can safely be said that there are no nonliterate societies where distinctions of this order prevail. Art is a part of life, not separated from it. This by no means implies that no specialization exists in such cultures; for wherever the creative drive comes into play, individuals are found to excel, or to be inept, in their performance. Even in a small group, for example, a visitor will be directed to some one person who is an outstanding wood-carver. The other men do carve, though less well, and some perhaps not at all. All the men, however, and the women, who may be forbidden by tradition to work in wood, will be able to appreciate and make informed judgments about any carved piece. All will know stories, but a particular old woman will be pointed out as the best story-teller in the village. Even where, as among the Navaho Indians, only certain individuals know the sacred designs of a given sand-painting, all the men present at a session where one is being made know how to control the colored sand that flows through their fingers to

379

describe an even line and will participate, under the direction of the priest, in the making of this intricate and beautiful composition.

In the widest sense, then, art is to be thought of as *any embellishment of ordinary living that is achieved with competence and has describable form.* Competence can become virtuosity, which is the supreme control over technique that gives every society its finest aesthetic products and, as we shall see, is a significant factor in the creative process itself. Even where no question of virtuosity arises, however, competence must be present if the artist is to realize any effective measure of the expression of his art. Form, function, design—all these are similarly necessary to the execution of any art form. Within these limits, however, any manifestation of the impulse to make more beautiful and thus to heighten the pleasure of any phase of living that is so recognized by a people, must be accepted by the student of culture as aesthetically valid, and is, in consequence, to be given the designation "art."

It is in these terms that we shall first discuss the widely varying forms of this drive in the fields of the graphic and plastic arts, and some of the questions that this raises. We shall then turn to less tangible aesthetic expressions—the literary, musical, and dramatic arts. This analysis should yield some perspective on the values these phenomena hold for the scientific student of culture, and permit us to abstract some general principles concerning the role of the arts in the life of man.

2

DRAWING, engraving, and painting are the most representative of the graphic arts. The plastic arts are those that involve the manipulation of materials to yield three-dimensional forms—that is to say, carving and modelling in high and low relief and in the round. Since we know that in all nonliterate societies these forms have a close relationship to the rest of culture, we need not search for criteria that separate art expression into "pure" and decorative art categories. Moreover, since our concern with the arts of all peoples surveys a broader horizon than the description of art-provinces, or the evaluation of comparative art-forms, we must be prepared on these grounds to admit as valid art much that might be overlooked under more conventional and specialized aesthetic formulations. This means that we must be prepared to widen our conception of art; to admit what may seem like rough attempts of peoples with poor technological equipment to beautify their simple tools, or huts, or to peck out crude designs on rocks, as falling into the category of the aesthetic aspect of culture.

When our lines are thus drawn, we find that there is actually very little art in any society that is not associated with some object having utility. This is especially true if we recognize the use to which even the art derived in association with religion is put—such as the carved representations of deities, the headdresses worn by officiants in religious rituals, the wall paintings in temples, objects carried by participants in sacred rites. But even leaving such objects to one side, most art will still be outside what we term "pure" forms. In cultures where technological achievement produces specialization of function, there may be art forms that, as among ourselves, are the possessions of those who can afford them, and whose function takes on a subtle duality, the satisfaction of aesthetic impulses and the enhancement of prestige as a concomitant of such ownership. However, except for such forms as the gold and silver replicas of flower gardens found in the palaces of the Incas of Peru, or Dahomean appliquéd cloths and brass figures decoratively displayed in the houses of the chiefs, the art of nonliterate and many literate peoples is predominantly represented by such designs as they make on their pottery, or by carvings on their canoes, or by paintings on their shields, and the like.

Because, as we have seen, there is no art without design, the interpretation of experience by the artist, in no matter what medium he may work, is the quintessence of artistic expression. This fact, that art involves the interpretation of experience, at once brings us to one of the most controversial and most discussed matters in the field of art study—the problem of realism as against conventionalization, of representation as against symbolism in art. The problem has two facets, which must be clearly differentiated. The first is how the tradition of a people, in defining the framework within which reality is perceived and in supplying the materials with which the artist works, influences the nature of design or the alignment of masses, and the interpretation of that which is carved, woven, painted, or modelled. The second has to do with the play of the individual artist's creative impulse and his technical skill as these find expression through the stylistic patterns and accepted media of his culture, and exert an influence in changing these patterns by introducing new elements into what he creates. We shall consider both of these in later pages; first, however, we must clarify our understanding of the terms "realism" and "conventionalization" and indicate how they are manifested.

It is not too much to say that no work of art achieves complete realism. If realism were the end of artistic striving, then the most perfect example of it would be a stereoscopic, colored, talking motion picture. More than one ethnographer has reported the experience of showing a clear photograph of a house, a person, a familiar landscape to people living in a culture innocent of any knowledge of photography, and to have had the picture held at all possible angles, or turned over for an inspection of its blank back, as the native tried to interpret this meaningless arrangement of varying shades of grey on a piece of paper. For even the clearest photograph is only an *interpretation* of what the camera sees. We are too accustomed to looking at pictures to be conscious of the fact that they interpret a three dimensional world in two dimensional terms, or that they change a setting of color into a composition in black and white. Because a photograph is an interpretation, the person who looks at it must have a clue to the arrangement of forms and shadings if he is to grasp the meaning of what it reproduces. That this is easier, once the clues are grasped, merely means that the photograph is more realistic than other forms whose interpretation is more arbitrary.

We must not think that we are dealing with alternatives, then, when we consider the problem of realism in art as against conventionalization. We are once more rather concerned with a continuum that moves from complete abstraction, from designs that are wholly non-descriptive, through various degrees of conventionalization, to compositions where the translation of experience in the most precise terms possible is attempted.

Design is often the result of technical competence that translates a sustained rhythm in time into space rhythms. Pre-Spanish Pueblo pottery is an excellent example of this. These pots are made by the coiling process, whereby each round of clay is joined to the preceding one by pressure of the fingers. With the skill that comes with virtuosity, the potter, exerting the same pressure each time she pinched on the clay, left thumb-prints of the same size and depth, and at regular intervals. A pleasing design emerged as a result of a process that may well have begun without conscious intent to decorate the vessel. Many instances of this phenomenon, such as results from the virtuosity of the Neolithic flint-chipper, could be given. Other examples of decorative, non-representational art are chevron designs, and geometric arrangements that have no reference at all to objects in the world of everyday experience.

Realism is best defined as an attempt to *approach* reality in art. But this attempt is, as we know, always made in terms of cultural definitions, so that a cross-cultural interpretation of the intent of the artist is very apt to be overlaid with misinterpretation. An outstanding example of this is furnished by certain conventions of African wood-carving. The type of Yoruba dance-mask reproduced in Plate 8 is invariably discussed by Euroamerican art critics as a conventionalization of the human face, wherein the skillful manipulation of masses is achieved through a reworking of the proportions of face and head. Invariably, too, the discussion is based on study of the mask as it is fixed in a perpendicular position, a perspective that does, indeed, bring out the distortions that give rise to the elaborate analyses of much art criticism. It happens, though, that this mask is actually a realistic reproduction of the Negro face when looked at in the horizontal position in which it is intended to be used. For it is a "mask" only in the sense that it is worn by a person whose identity it aids in concealing. It is worn atop the head, and concealment is achieved by long fibre strands that descend from it to cover the whole body of the wearer. The second photograph of it shows how the Yoruba see it, and how the artist intended it to be seen. Here the "distortion" turns out to be skilful foreshortening, and makes of the presumed stylized presentation an artistic, realistic portrayal. The now current interpretation thus becomes a well-intentioned misstatement.

Examples of forms that are meaningful only by cultural definition, and that lie far toward the more abstract role of the scale from realism to conventionalization are to be found without end. In some instances, a single motif may be given different interpretations by different artists, or by different members of the same society who are presented with a design and requested to explain it. Thus, among the Yurok and Karok Indians of California, O'Neale obtained differing explanations for various individual motifs used to decorate their basketry. In the accompanying figure, *a* is called "flint"

The Aesthetic Drive: Graphic and Plastic Arts

or "flint-like"; *b* is a snake or a long worm; *c* is "spread finger" or "frog hand"; *d* is variously interpreted as "sharp tooth" or "points."

Extreme conventionalization in design is found in the art of regions where an attempt is only exceptionally made to achieve realistic portrayal. A striking example of this is found in the wood-carvings of the Bush-Negroes of Dutch Guiana, where conventionalization is carried to such a degree that, though not difficult to interpret when clues have been provided, the motifs are impossible to understand until the natives themselves can be induced to reveal the significance of the designs traced in low relief or cut through the wood.

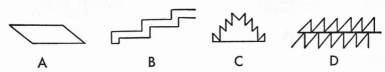

A   **B**   **C**   **D**

Fig. 30   *Yurok-Karok basketry design elements (after O'Neale, 1932, fig. 13).*

This art tradition is expressed in symbols that, for the most part, are concerned with fertility. The carvings are made by men, and most forms are for presentation to their wives or sweethearts. The tray used for winnowing rice, (shown on Plate 9a) affords a good example of this type of conventionalization. When first seen by one who is not familiar with the conventions of this art, the tray suggests nothing. The design is notable not alone for the beauty of the individual motifs, but for the mastery with which the circular space is utilized. To ascribe the meaning given by the Bush-Negroes to the total composition, however, or to any of the elements in it, defies the most agile imagination.

Yet any Bush-Negro can independently interpret this carving in realistic terms. The two large figures on either side of the central line are women. The outer units of these figures are their arms, the inner corresponding elements are their legs. Of the rest of the body, only the vulva is represented, while the small triangular figure represents the male principle, the sexual organ. The opposed series of alternating squares cut into the border outside the figures is the hair of the woman, the tacks inserted in the incised design are the cicatrized cuts that are made on the body of men and women for purposes of beautification. The two small figures represent the twins it is hoped will be born to these women, for twins are prized in this culture as the bearers of good fortune. The twins, however, are of different sex. The male is the figure at the top of the illustration, that has the fine line traced about it; the female has no line. Here is an instance of how purely arbitrary conventionalization can be.

The lace designs made by Paraguayan Indian women—*ñanduti,* as they are called—described by the Brazilian anthropologist Roquette-Pinto, afford another instance of extreme conventionalization. Diffused into the country as a result of European contact, these circles are worked into patterns to which native names are given in consonance with the meaning ascribed to each. Thus of the patterns depicted here, the following interpretations are given:

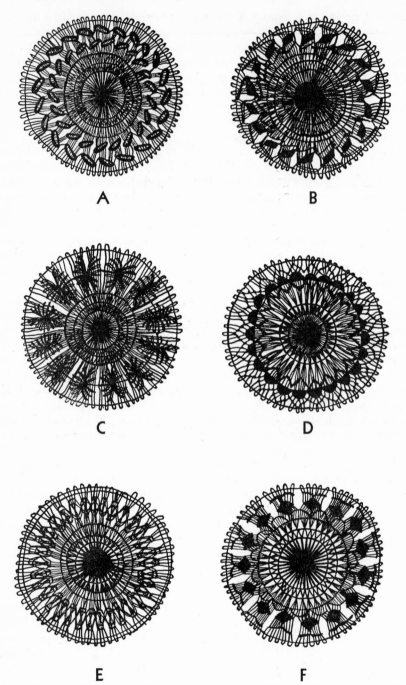

Fig. 31   *Lace figures (ñanduti) from Paraguay:* (A) *rice,* (B) *scorpion,* (C) *spider,* (D) *oven,* (E) *dew,* (F) *pregnancy (after Roquette-Pinto, 1925).*

The Aesthetic Drive: Graphic and Plastic Arts

1. Rice 2. Scorpion 3. Spider 4. Oven 5. Dew 6. Pregnancy. In some cases, the association between the design and its interpretation is recognizable, so that the manner in which "the imagination of the Paraguayans evolved and perfected, with the ideas suggested by things about them in their charming country, the delicate designs and the accomplished symbolism" [2] can readily be grasped. The spiders and scorpions can be traced with the eye once the clue to their meaning is had from the names used to designate them. But even with this clue, the "oven" and the "dew" designs tax the imagination to discern any semblance of realism.

At the other end of our scale, we find that realism in the art of nonliterate societies is by no means absent. It tends to be manifest more in three-dimensional figures than in graphic forms, though the realistic portrayals of Eskimo engravings caution against too sweeping a generalization in this regard. Often realism and conventionalization are combined by those who work in the same medium, even in the same piece. The metal-work of West Africa illustrates this, as can be seen in the Dahomean brass figures shown in Plate 9b. The man hoeing is a realistic presentation; the elephant is conventionalized, and so is the human figure he holds in his trunk, though the agony of the victim is convincingly depicted.

That nonliterate art can, in effect, be portraiture, is shown by the Ife bronze heads that were recovered from the West African Yoruban town of Ife in 1938.[3] Of lifelike dimensions, they have frequently been compared, in the quality of their execution, to Greek sculpture of the classic period. The striations on the face represent the markings that, though no longer made in this form by the Yoruba, are today found among various tribes in northern Nigeria. The male head has a series of holes that mark the line of head-hair, moustache, and beard, and it is possible that the realism of the figure was enhanced by inserting hair in these apertures much as is done today with masks carved out of wood. The meaning of the diadem atop the woman's head at the front can only be conjectured. It might be a head ornament, a decoration of ritual significance, a mark of rank. That it represents some adornment can be acceptably concluded in the light of the degree of realism that characterizes the heads in all other aspects of their treatment—a treatment that demonstrates how nonliterate art, no less than the art of literate peoples, stretches the full gamut from extreme conventionalization to the most faithful realism.

3

THE question of realism and conventionalization has prominently entered into discussions of the development of art forms. The realism of the Palaeolithic cave paintings, which followed earlier strivings toward representational portrayal of animals, has been stressed as an argument for the beginnings of art, in realism. On the other hand, the importance of conventionalization in

---

[2] E. Roquette-Pinto, 1924, pp. 103–12.
[3] W. R. Bascom, 1939. These are reproduced in Plate 10.

The Aspects of Culture

the art of nonliterate peoples has been urged in support of the opposite position. The problem posed is well worth investigating.

FIG. 32   *Mural engravings of elk, Middle Aurignacian, France (after Mac-
Curdy, 1924, fig. 114).*

If we look closely at a series of drawings and paintings from the Palaeolithic period in France, we see how, beginning with the early Aurignacian
and proceeding through the Magdalenian, a continuously greater skill in
realistically depicting the animals with which upper Palaeolithic man was in
contact, is to be observed. Thus the earliest engravings and drawings on the
walls of French and Spanish caves show how realism was limited only by
technical inability to suggest depth. The treatment of figures in profile par-

FIG. 33   *Aurignacian drawings of horses from cavern of Altamira, Spain
(after MacCurdy, 1924, fig. 115).*

ticularly—as with the elk in the first series, and the mammoth—as well as the as yet unsolved problem posed by the need to draw all four of the animal's

FIG. 34 *Aurignacian drawing of elephant on cave wall, Santander, Spain (after MacCurdy, 1924, fig. 116).*

legs, disclose the absence of any command of skill rather than an absence of desire to achieve realistic portrayals.

The wall engraving and drawing next shown of a mammoth and a woolly rhinoceros, indicate more flexibility in the direction of realism. All four legs of each animal are either depicted or suggested, while hair is also indicated

FIG. 35 *Mammoth, from cave wall in the Dordogne, France; Aurignacian (after MacCurdy, 1924, fig. 117).*

and posture is more adequately shown. The end of the mammoth's trunk is especially well done. Yet in both animals the eye is schematized, and in the case of the mammoth the problem of drawing the trunk so as to conceal the tusk behind it, while in turn being concealed by the tusk in front, was too much for this artist. The treatment of the hind legs also merits scrutiny. The one farthest away from the observer is seen, as it were, through the leg closest to him. This is to be contrasted to the fidelity with which the hind legs of the rhinoceros are shown.

FIG. 36 *Wooly rhinocerous, Font-de-Gaume, Dordogne, France; Aurignacian (after MacCurdy, 1924, fig. 119).*

Later, when Palaeolithic art afforded us masterpieces such as the polychrome paintings of bison, reindeer, and other creatures, variation in skill, or in the artist's conception of how a design is to be executed, makes for marked differences in the degree to which realistic portrayal is achieved. Thus the Magdalenian mammoth of Fig. 38 may be contrasted with our Aurignacian example. The ear and eye, the treatment of the hair, and the outline of the body, indicate a sure hand. Yet the trunk shows through the tusk in front of it, the end of the trunk is not depicted at all, one of the forelegs is barely suggested, and one of the hindlegs is so spindly as to give us a feeling almost of discomfort. Nonetheless, this mammoth was drawn during the same period when the techniques in use permitted one prehistoric artist to engrave on horn, a stag looking backward, or to demonstrate a greater command of perspective by engraving a moose as viewed from the front (Figs. 39 and 40).

The hypothesis of A. C. Haddon, that art styles change from realistic portrayal to symbolic form, is perhaps the best known of those theories that draw on materials from nonliterate peoples for illustrative data. Asserting that "we may recognize three stages of artistic development—origin, evolution, and decay," Haddon develops his conception of the process in the following terms: "The vast bulk of artistic expression owes its birth to realism; the representations were meant to be life-like, or to suggest real objects; that they may not have been so was owing to the apathy or incapacity of the artist or to the unsuitability of his materials. Once born, the design was acted upon by constraining and restraining forces which gave it, so to speak, an in-

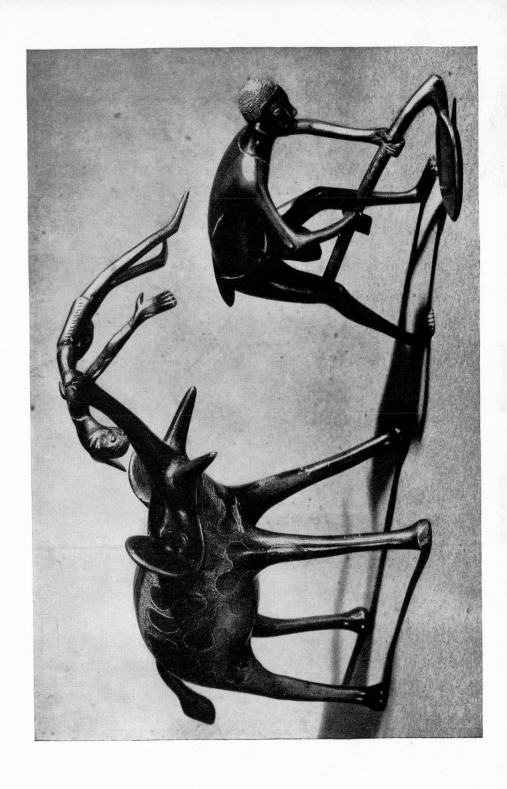

PLATE 9b   *Dahomean brass figures. Man in grasp of elephant (height, 6 in.) and man hoeing (height, 3¾ in.). See page 385. [Photograph by Mary Modglin, Chicago]*

PLATE 10   *Bronze heads from Ife, Western Nigeria, collected by W. R. Bascom. Female head (height, 9¾ in.) and male head (height, 12½ in.). See page 385. [Photograph by Mary Modglin, Chicago]*

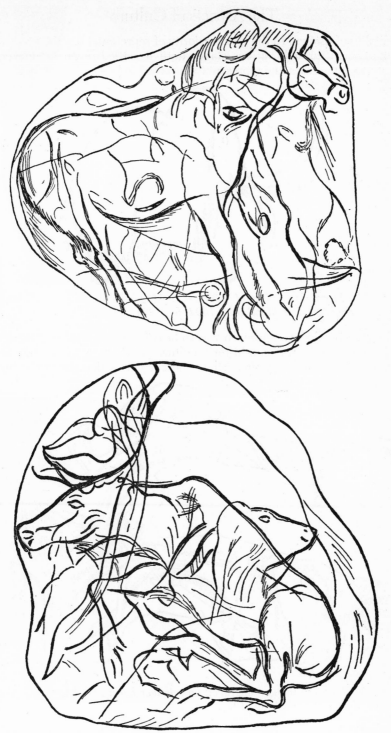

Fig. 37   *Magdalenian engravings on stone (natural size), showing superim-position of figures (after Breuil, 1936).*

The Aspects of Culture

dividuality of its own. In the great majority of representations the life-history ran its course through various stages until it settled down to uneventful senility; in some cases, the representation ceased to be—in fact, it died." [4]

Fɪɢ. 38 *Mural engraving of mammoth. Magdalenian, cave of Font-de-Gaume, France (after MacCurdy, 1924, fig. 122).*

This quasi-biological approach was so heavily documented with materials from both historic and non-historic cultures that its wide acceptance by students of art is scarcely surprising. The current of thought at the time it

Fɪɢ. 39 *Stag and salmon, engraved on reindeer horn; Magdalenian, France (after MacCurdy, 1924, fig. 127).*

[4] A. C. Haddon, 1914, p. 7.

was enunciated was especially hospitable to this view, as evidenced by such earlier studies as those of Holmes on American pottery,[5] or Balfour's analysis of decorative art in general.[6] Best-known of Haddon's illustrative data are the arrows from the Torres Straits area, decorated with carvings representative of the crocodile. The series given in Fig. 41 shows how such arrows

FIG. 40 Moose, engraved on reindeer horn. Magdalenian, France (after MacCurdy, 1924, fig. 136).

can be arranged to demonstrate change from realism to conventionalization. In the first of these, marked "A" in Haddon's sketch reproduced there, the long snout can be discerned, though the nostrils projecting above the smooth line that delineates the top of the head are placed one after the other. Behind the head, at the thickest part of the arrow, are the forelimbs, shown as an acute angle, with cross lines at the bottom indicating the claws. Then come the body, represented by vertical lines between which are short horizontal ones; the hind legs, given as an angular line that balances, and is opposed to the forelegs; and finally the tail, indicated by cross lines or protuberances.

Every part of this design can be followed through from "A" to "F," each showing a greater degree of conventionalization. In "F," indeed, it would be impossible for the most assiduous seeker after realistic interpretations to discover any clue to its meaning. As Haddon phrases it, "the front part of the mouth has disappeared; . . . the forelimbs and body are absent. The hindlimbs are narrow, but retain their characteristic forward bend; the dorsal

---

[5] W. H. Holmes, 1886, pp. 445ff.
[6] H. Balfour, 1895.

The Aspects of Culture

caudal scutes are replaced by numerous parallel transverse lines."[7]

Does not a series of this sort, then, demonstrate how variations in a design that attempts to represent some element in the experience of a people indicate the way in which conventionalization must have developed out of realism? Is this case not made the stronger by the fact that the materials

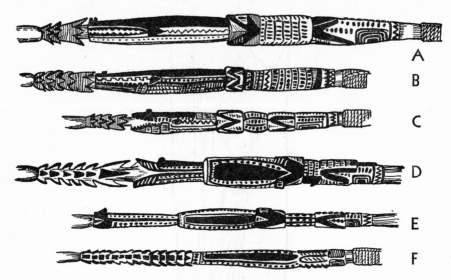

FIG. 41 *Torres Straits "crocodile-arrows and derivatives," as arranged in a presumed developmental series (after Haddon, 1894, fig. 19).*

from prehistoric sites, such as the forms we have reproduced, show that the development of art in these early times represented a striving toward ever greater command of techniques which would perfect an ability to portray in realistic terms the creatures that shared man's habitat with him?

Like all other attempts to devise developmental formulae of universal applicability, this one fails both because of its faulty method, and a failure to take all the facts into account. Haddon's arrows, or Holmes' pots were arranged in accordance with a scheme that existed *in the mind of the student*. The postulated development has validity only *ex hypothesi*—in terms of the hypothesis. All the objects belong to the same epoch and do not represent a developmental series in the sense that one item can be shown to have preceded the other. It could be argued, with equal plausibility, that a meaningless form, once produced, had meaning read into it, and that there then ensued a growing competence in the realistic portrayal of the form suggested by the lines of a meaningless design.

The development of European Palaeolithic art is itself not nearly as clear as would seem from an analysis of the cave paintings alone. Representations of the human figure executed in the round, for example, not only fail to exhibit a parallel developmental sequence, but are restricted to a single period,

[7] A. C. Haddon, 1894, p. 57.

The Aesthetic Drive: Graphic and Plastic Arts

the Aurignacian. The Aurignacian "Venuses" that date from this epoch are varying conventionalizations, in bas-relief or full sculpture, which always stress the secondary sexual characteristics of the female torso and sometimes emphasize them out of all semblance to reality. The head is treated in summary fashion, as are the arms and legs; at most, the hair of the head is indicated by a series of lines. Most famous is the so-called "Venus of Wil-

FIG. 42   *The "Venus" of Willendorf, Austria. Aurignacian epoch.*

lendorf." This statuette is intermediate, as regards its degree of realism, to the bas-relief from the Dordogne, France, wherein the female figure is treated in a way that approaches normal proportions—in contrast to the treatment of the head—and the extreme stylization of the figurine in ivory, wherein the remarkable handling of masses and proportion that give it its great distinction, entail so wide a departure from reality that its character as a human form must be read into it (see Figs. 43 and 44).

A similar range is to be found in the graphic arts of the upper Palaeolithic. The developing realism of the several epochs, that culminated in the polychrome paintings of the Magdalenian, take an impressionistic turn in engraving on stone, bone, and horn. The herd of reindeer depicted by a Magdalenian artist on the wing-bone of an eagle (Fig. 45) is justly famous. Except for the three front animals shown in this composition, and the one at the rear, a realistic portrayal is not even attempted. That this engraving is a well-marked aspect of the art of the period is apparent when its distribution in other French sites is recognized. The similar treatment of a herd of horses (Fig. 46), engraved on stone, from a different locality than that in which the

FIG. 43 *Aurignacian "Venus" carved in low relief, from Laussel, Dordogne (after MacCurdy, 1924, fig. 162).*

other composition was found, is evidence that it was more than a local development or the idiosyncracy of an individual artist.

Boas has thrown considerable light on our problem. His study of Alaskan Eskimo needle-cases has demonstrated how "the various parts of the flanged

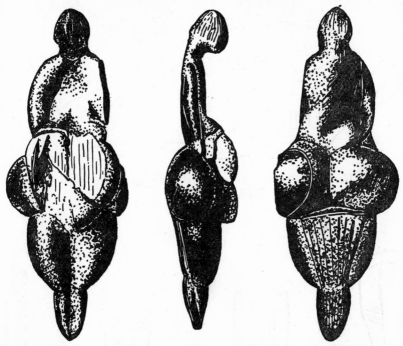

FIG. 44 *Aurignacian figurine in ivory, known as the "Venus" of Lespugue (Haute-Garonne, France); front, side and rear views (after MacCurdy, 1924, fig. 159).*

FIG. 45 *Engraving of reindeer herd on wing-bone of an eagle. Upper Magdalenian, France (after MacCurdy, 1924, fig. 131).*

needle-case excite the imagination of the artist"; and how "a geometrical element here or there is developed by him, in accordance with the general tendencies of Eskimo art, into the representation of whole animals or parts of animals."[8] (Fig. 47.)

---

[8] F. Boas, 1908, p. 337; 1940, pp. 587–8.

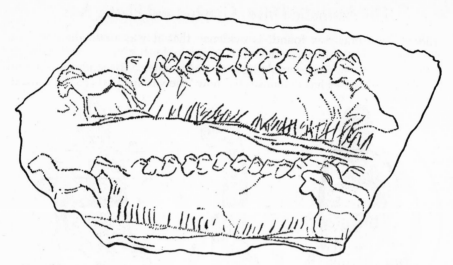

Fig. 46 *Herd of horses, engraved on stone. Upper Magdalenian, Vienne, France (after MacCurdy, 1924, fig. 132).*

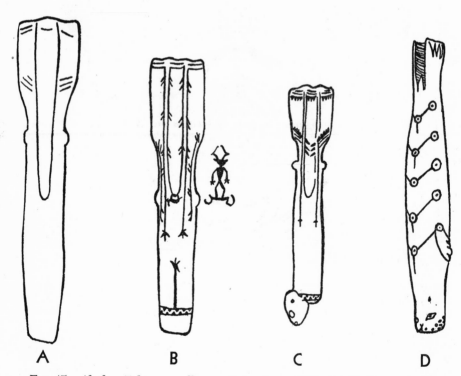

A   B   C   D

Fig. 47   *Alaskan Eskimo needlecases [after Boas, 1908; (A) Pl. 23, no. 1; (B) Pl. 24, no. 2; (C) Pl. 26, no. 5; (D) Pl. 30, no. 4].*

Boas has also shown how, in Mexico, "factory production and . . . slovenly execution" have operated to effect a cycle from realism, through meaningless form, to realistic execution in the decoration of certain types of wooden and calabash dishes. These dishes are painted orange, and then overlaid with designs in green. Older specimens, made of wood, wherein

Fig. 48   *Transformation of designs painted on calabash dishes, Oaxaca, Mexico (after Boas, 1927, fig. 122).*

the motifs consist of animal forms or fish, are excellently executed. Later workmanship, however, is far inferior, and shows a decided change in the original design. In some cases, there seems to be a reinterpretation, though whether through misunderstanding or the process of "the substitution of new subject matter for old, in which process the new subject was rightly controlled by the old, stereotyped form" [9] cannot be stated. The series Boas has reproduced, like the designs on pottery Boas also figures in his work, demon-

[9] F. Boas, 1927, p. 131.

strate how changes of this order can occur. In the instance of these plates, the fish that in the earlier forms were painted lying horizontally within a circular frame, broke down into an almost meaningless design. This design then seems to have been reinterpreted as an equal number of leaves, placed about the outer edge of the circle, this time enclosing an inner circle within which a new, flower-like unit has been introduced.

It is apparent from our discussion that no developmental principle of universal applicability concerning any tendency to move toward conventionalization from realism, or toward realism from abstract design, can be established. Rather the principle of consistent change in either direction, or both, is the rule. Hasty manufacture, ineptitude in the use of the medium, calculated "abbreviations" of various kinds may, as we have seen, cause a form realistically conceived to break down into conventionalized, symbolic variants. On the other hand, a combination of lines, the protuberances on a rock, or any other kind of fortuitous form may have significance read into it by the imaginative mind, and gradually come to be accepted as meaningful by all members of a society, who thereupon may move toward realism in its portrayal. In this, as probably in all other instances of change in art convention, the considerations of an established style and the customary media prevail. We, therefore, turn next to a discussion of art-style, since this is one of the central problems in the study of any art.

4

IT IS essentially in its style that the art of one people, one epoch, one artist, even, is marked off from another. Under situations that might be considered conducive to change, an art style can often show great tenaciousness. Yet its resistance to change does not preclude continuous developments that may eventuate in a given style becoming markedly different, over a relatively short period of time. In the art of Euroamerican societies we are accustomed to trace the "periods" in the work of certain individual artists, as for example when we describe the art of such a painter as Picasso, or Braque, or the early and later Renoir. Even in cultures where a greater degree of stability exists than in that of Europe and America of the twentieth century, changes in artistic style are everywhere discernible, as in the decorations on the pottery of the Indians of Southwestern United States.

The analysis of style, it must be clear, can be carried on quite without reference to the significance of art forms to the people of a given culture where they are produced. We have, in this particular instance, a parallel to our dual approach to the study of culture as a whole—the psychological and the institutional. In the first of these approaches, as in the study of symbolism in art, meaning is indispensable to comprehension. In the second, we are concerned with the forms institutions take—forms that, like elements in style, can be analyzed without reference to their meaning for the people who live in terms of them.

A study of the stylistic conventions of Melanesian art, carried out by

The Aesthetic Drive: Graphic and Plastic Arts

Reichard, offers an excellent illustration of how the graphic and plastic arts can be analyzed from this objective point of view. Admiralty Island natives carve wooden bowls, which on inspection can be divided into three types, in accordance with their form, which is their outstanding artistic aspect. The first of these types (shown below) are round bowls, resting on feet or stands of different kinds (Fig. 50). The unity of style these bowls show in their outline can be seen in the diagram given here, as well as the variation

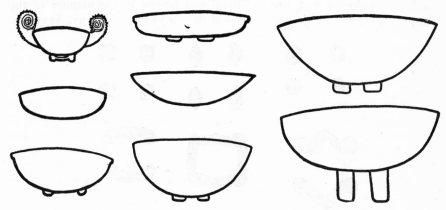

Fig. 49 *Analysis of forms of Admiralty Island wooden bowls (after Reichard, 1933, vol. I, fig. 1).*

found within the limits of this style, and the variety of their feet and stands. Bowls of the second type have realistic handles carved from the same piece of wood as the bowl, and thicker rims. A third type has carvings of birds, crocodiles and other animals, executed in realistic enough fashion to make possible their identification. These bowls, in their outline as well as their decoration, follow a style that is distinct from the style of similar bowls from the small island of Tami (Cretin) off eastern New Guinea shown in Fig. 51. Here the form of the bowls is rounded; they rest on no legs and have no handles. The outlined forms show their contrast with the Admiralty Islands types.

The style of an art is what permits the expert, with a degree of precision that mystifies the layman, to tell where a given piece was made, or from what period of a given culture it derives, or even the name of the individual artist who produced it or the "school" to which he belonged. It is possible, on the basis of style, to set off art provinces in terms of the distribution of forms similar to each other. This broad view of style is especially useful where the differentiation of specimens of unknown provenience is involved. A Southwest pot among a collection of Guiana Indian pottery stands out in unmistakable contrast; but one who knows the pottery of the Southwest can do more than recognize it as coming from that area. He can identify the pueblo from which it derived, and perhaps even the period when it was made.

In one early work on African art, its author included four illustrations of

The Aspects of Culture

carved pieces that, to one familiar with the various styles of carving done by nonliterate peoples, were obviously not from the continent of Africa but rather from the Marquesan Islands.[9a] Certainly, the proportions of head and body, and the treatment of arms, legs, and torso in pieces of the type illustrated in that work (reproduced in Fig. 52), bear enough surface resemblances to trick the unwary. No sooner, however, do we inspect certain outstanding details of the carvings than critical differences appear. The African wood carver does not stylize the hand and fingers in the manner of the Marquesan carver, nor does he represent the ear in the same way. As can be

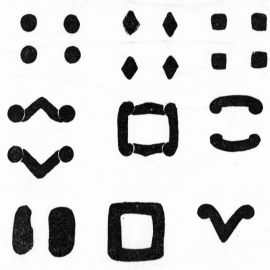

Fig. 50   *Analysis of rests of Admiralty Island wooden bowls (after Reichard, 1933, vol. I, fig. 2).*

seen in Figure 52, the Marquesan patterns in these respects are quite distinct from the African, and no one who has handled any appreciable number of carvings can mistake the art of one area in this medium for that of the other.

How tenacious stylistic elements may be is apparent when art-forms from one culture are treated by artists of another. The style of wood-carving of the New Zealand Maori is characterized by the application of intricate patterns, derived from tattooing, to the object that is to be decorated. A piece from the Chicago Natural History Museum, which shows a bone carving, and a wooden figure, now in the Copenhagen Ethnographic Museum, illustrate the basic pattern. Reichard figures a crocodile on a carving from a coffin, which shows how this creature, realistically conceived, is also carved in terms dictated by the patterns of Maori style. But more striking is the New Zealand carver's conception of the Madonna and child, which she also figures, borrowed from Christian missionaries, but executed in full accord

---

[9a] C. Einstein, 1920, pp. 42 and 43, 79 and 86.

The Aesthetic Drive: Graphic and Plastic Arts

with the prevalent treatment of the human form, and with the overall pattern of decoration, characteristic of Maori art.[10]

Another example is from Benin, in West Africa, a culture whose bronzes and ivory carvings are famous in the world of art. Benin was first visited by Europeans in the fifteenth century. Such was the mastery of their medium by these Negro workers in bronze, and their disciplined perceptiveness of significant detail, that they have left realistic portrayals of the Portuguese

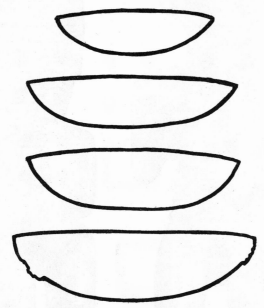

Fig. 51 *Analysis of shapes of wooden bowls from Tami Island (after Reichard, 1933, vol. I, fig. 13).*

arquebusquiers of the period—helmet, breast-plate, short pleated tunic, and weapons. In the treatment of the face in representations of Europeans in those bronzes, the long, narrow nose is accurately portrayed, but the nostrils flare after the African conventions of this art.

A Benin container is shown in Fig. 53 and Pl. 13; the top has been lost, but holes for its attachment remain. The central figure is Christ on the cross. The head is carved with representations of the type of moustache, beard, and hair style of the sixteenth century; the body proportions are those of European art of the period. Two doves, representing the Holy Ghost, are found in the squares above the upper arms of the cross, stylized in a manner more African than European. Below them, on the left, is Mary, in an attitude of prayer; to the right, St. John with his chalice. The bonnet of the female figure, the ruff of the male, are recognizable as the European dress of the time. From left to right, the four other figures that fill the rest of the space represent saints, each being marked by his appropriate symbol—St. Paul,

[10] G. A. Reichard, 1933, vol. II, pl. cxlix, figs. 634 and 635.

FIG. 52 *Marquesan carved figure (right) included in a work on African art, and an African figure (left) from same work (after Einstein, 1920, plates 79 and 86).*

with a sword; St. John (a second time), with his chalice; St. Andrew, with the particular type of cross associated with him; and St. Peter, with the key. All this is mainly European. The total composition, however, is conceived in a manner quite African, while the decorations that frame the figures and outline the cross, and particularly the intercrossed curving lines at the bottom, can be seen in many Benin pieces.

FIG. 53   *Designs on Benin container.*

The directives laid down by any traditional style govern the artist even as he introduces change into its art-forms. In every society the artist is the experimenter, the innovator, the rebel. But he is an innovator only within bounds. For in his experimentation, he is influenced by factors that all unwittingly guide him in his creative experience, as they guide the behavior of all human beings in every aspect of their lives. In other words, the creative life does not lie outside the influence of the enculturative experience. Indeed, it is just because the artist, the supreme technician, in playing with his technique does inevitably experiment as a result of his virtuosity, that he so effectively reveals to the student of culture the force of cultural conditioning. In art, as in all culture, experimentation produces constant and continuous change. As in all culture, so in art pre-existing patterns are the governor-bearings that prevent change from being haphazard; that enable the student, looking back over a long period of time, to trace the continuities that characterize changes to be perceived as generation succeeds generation.

It is important to stress this function of the artist in inducing change, especially where the art of nonliterate peoples is under discussion, inasmuch as stability, rather than change, is generally emphasized when these art-forms are being considered. It has even been seriously contended that the nonliterate carver, potter, or painter is not a creative artist at all, but rather a copyist, who slavishly follows the designs laid down for him by some gifted ancestor. Nothing, however, could be farther from the truth, as any field investigator can attest.

For an example of change in a specific form, we may take the appliqué cloths of Dahomey. These cloths are made as wall hangings for chiefs, with motifs drawn from the life of the people. The sewing is done by men who belong to a cloth-sewer's hereditary guild. The guild has in its possession the patterns of a large series of motifs. When a cloth is being designed, and the subject matter and its thematic sequence is decided upon, the requisite motifs are grouped and regrouped on the ground, until a satisfying composition is realized. Reproduced in Pl. 14 are four cloths that show how a given subject has been successively altered in its treatment by men of four generations. The theme is a lion-hunt. The first of the series was made by the grandfather of the contemporary chief of the guild for the Dahomean king who reigned from 1858–1889. The son of the originator criticized the earlier conception on the ground that it paid insufficient honor to this feline, associated as it is with royalty, to have it attacked by men armed only with clubs. He, therefore, placed bows and arrows in their hands, and also omitted the prey held in the mouth of the animal in the original.

The chief from whom the series was acquired, in his turn, felt that the cloth made by his father lacked dramatic quality, and he radically altered the composition to show one of the hunters caught by the beast. He also emphasized its power and heightened the struggle between hunters and hunted by equipping the hunters with guns and machetes; and he portrayed the lion with greater realism. The final revision was made by the son of this man, his potential successor as chief of the guild. Among other changes, the young man added a third human figure to the attacking group and improved the treatment of the lion by outlining it with a strip of cloth so as to separate the black of the lion's body from the gold of the background.

The problem of the artist as experimenter within the limits set by the conventions of the art of his society has been exhaustively studied among the Pueblo Indians by Bunzel. Writing of the Zuñi, she says, "Although the women do not recognize any very definite proprietorship in designs, every potter claims that she can distinguish readily between the work of her fellow artists. 'I can always tell by looking at a jar who made it.' One Zuñi woman was more explicit: 'If I painted my bowls like every one else, I might lose my bowl when I took dinner to the dancers in the plaza. I am the only person who makes a checkerboard design around the rim, so I can always tell my bowl by looking at the edge.' " [11]

A Hopi Indian potter described the sources of her design in this way: "I am always thinking about designs, even when I am doing other things, and whenever I close my eyes, I see designs in front of me. I often dream of designs, and whenever I am ready to paint, I close my eyes and then the designs just come to me. I paint them as I see them." An Acoma artist re-

---

[11] R. Bunzel, 1929, pp. 64–5.

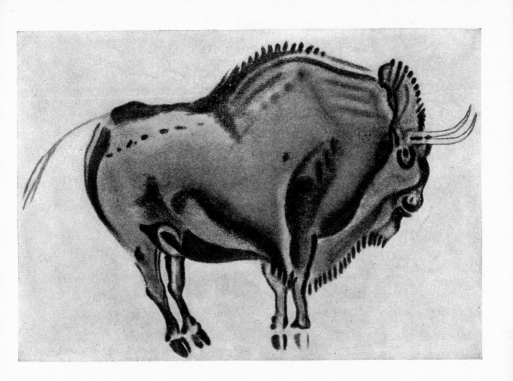

PLATE 11a   *Bison painted in polychrome on the cave ceiling of Altamira, Santandar, Spain.* [*After Cartailhac, Breuil, and MacCurdy*]

PLATE 11b   *Wild boar, from the cavern at Altamira, Santandar, Spain. See page 388.* [*After Abbé H. Breuil*]

A

B

C

PLATE 12a   *Admiralty Island bowl. See page 399.*
PLATE 12b   *Maori bone carving. See page 400.* [*Photographs 12a and 12b courtesy Chicago Natural History Museum*]
PLATE 12c   *Maori carving, showing tattooing designs. See page 400.* [*Photograph courtesy Royal Ethnographic Museum, Copenhagen*]

marked: "I like all kinds of designs. My jars are all different. I don't make the same design twice. Sometimes I make two or three alike, but not often. I don't like to do that." [12] Statements of this kind must be taken in conjunction with the criticisms levelled against designs that lie outside the range of the accepted pattern, as recorded from these Indians and from other societies. They thus further clarify how, whatever the talents of an artist, his creativeness will express itself along lines laid down by the established art-style of his culture, within the limits of which he must work.

5

THE elements that go to make up a style are termed the formal aspects of art. They include all manifestations of form that can be expressed graphically or plastically—rhythm, symmetry, the use of color. The ways in which the totality of a design is built up out of units that can be found, in most decorative arts, variously associated, are an expression of this. Designs may be conceived as horizontal or vertical—though this is less often found. They may be adapted to a circular form, as in a pot or a basket; in such instances their movement may be clockwise or counterclockwise. The medium is itself a determinant of form. This is apparent when attempts are made to reproduce figures realistically in such media as basketry or weaving. The instance of the representations of human and animal forms woven by the Cayapa Indians of Ecuador (Fig. 54) offers a case in point. Here conventionalization is imposed by the difficulties inherent in weaving a curved line. This control over expression is to be contrasted with the relative freedom of the artist to depict figures realistically—always in terms of the stylistic patterns of his art—when he paints designs on pottery or wood or some other background or in carving.

The supreme mastery of technique of the outstanding artist of any culture permits him to mold the formal elements recognized by the conventions of the art of his society as he wills; to experiment, to "play" with his technique as a virtuoso in the manner we have already discussed. Without this command of technique, this virtuosity in the use of the materials at the artist's command, there could be no great art in any idiom. Much of the appeal of art arises out of this fact. What attracts the person who sees specimens of an art unfamiliar to him is the skill with which they have been executed—the juxtaposition of color values, the manipulation of elements of form that comes from the long acquaintance of the creator of a given piece with the materials he employs.

One point to be stressed, however, is that virtuosity in one medium or one art-style does not by any means imply command of another. This is particularly true where the new medium is strange to the artist, and derives from the conventions of a different culture. When an artist in a nonliterate culture,

---

[12] *Ibid.*, pp. 51–2.

therefore, is given pencil and paper and asked to sketch a scene, he produces a series of crude outlines. Such drawings have too often been cited to bolster the specious identification of "primitive art" with the productions of our children, or of psychoneurotics. Yet the "primitive" man's crudities are no more crude than the drawings of artistically untutored "civilized" men and women. This has been demonstrated by Cameron,[13] who asked "scientifically

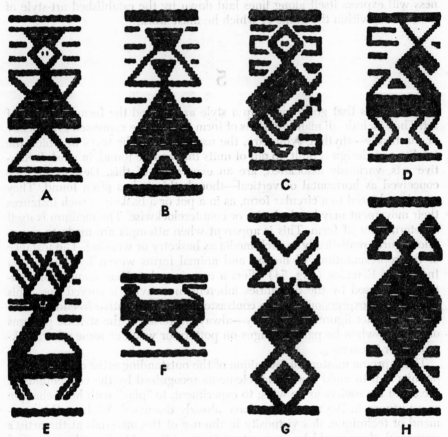

FIG. 54 *Stylizations of human and animal forms woven by Cayapa Indians of Ecuador. (A) and (B) human beings, (C) monkey, (D) horse, (E) deer, (F) dog, (G) spider, (H) toad (after Barrett, 1925, Pl. 123).*

trained adults," in this case staff physicians of the Johns Hopkins Hospital, to draw "certain objects from memory" when each was alone and at leisure. These drawings were to be of "a girl pushing a baby-carriage" and of "a man on horseback." These scientifically but not artistically trained men, when presented with this novel request, did what the nonliterate artist who is unaccustomed to pencil and paper does—they produced drawings that, as can

[13] N. Cameron, 1938, passim.

be seen from the reproductions of them given here, are essentially childlike in character. However skilled the artist may be in his own medium, virtuosity counts for nothing in one foreign to him. He is a novice in this new form, and draws like one.

FIG. 55   *"Girl Pushing a Baby Carriage." Drawing by a scientifically trained adult (after Cameron, 1938, fig. 1).*

FIG. 56   *"Girl Pushing a Baby Carriage." Drawing by a scientifically trained adult (after Cameron, 1938, fig. 6).*

Boas has recounted how an Eskimo was asked to draw an igloo and a dog-team with human figures on paper with pencil. He struggled with these strange modes of expression for a time; then, taking up his engraving tools and seizing a piece of ivory, he quickly and surely etched for the visiting ethnographer the scene comparable to the one illustrated in **Pl. 16a.**

The skill of the artist will not be called on vainly if enough opportunity is given to him to master the new medium. There is substantial evidence in hand from various cultures to illustrate this. For example, the Indians of the Southwest, through contact with the whites, have come to

FIG. 57 *Two drawings, "Man on Horseback," by scientifically trained adults. The one on the right is by an experienced horseman (after Cameron, 1938, figs. 4 and 5).*

know the use of water-colors and have learned to be at ease in this medium. They paint the masked figures of their sacred rites, the *kachinas*, singly or in groups, and paint them so well that these representations have become collectors' items.

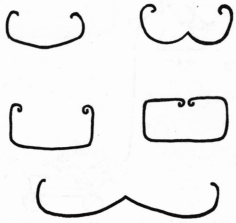

FIG. 58 *Basic double-curve motifs in Northeastern Algonkian art (after Speck, 1914, fig. 1).*

In other words, proficiency in a medium is built on experience, and a long tradition in its use frees the artist to achieve mastery and to express himself creatively. Some media taken over cross-culturally will lend themselves to ready adaptation by artists working in a culture that is hospitable to playing with new techniques; some will be rejected or will be used crudely. But regardless of the degree of responsiveness to a foreign medium, or art style, the criterion of success or failure in taking over something new involves neither a problem of inherent competence nor of maturity.

FIG. 59   *Elaboration of two basic double-curve Northeastern Algonkian motifs (after Speck, 1914, Pl. 1, 2, 4, and 17).*

Within a culture, the way elements of form are built up into a composition that is in consonance with the patterns of a particular style is to be seen in the intricate designs that mark the decorative art of the Northeastern Algonkian Indians. The basic motif is a "double-curve" unit, "consisting of two opposed incurves as a foundation element, with embellishments more or less elaborate modifying the enclosed space, and with variations in the shape and proportions of the whole." Some of the varieties of the "primary foundation element" are given in Fig. 58. This simple beginning, we are told, is "capable of being subjected to such a variety of augments, not infrequently distortive, as to become scarcely recognizable at first or second sight." [14] This, in a very real sense, represents the playing of the virtuoso with the thematic materials of the style in which he works. It can be seen further if series of double-curve designs are graded in accordance with their complexity, as in Fig. 59. How far the process can go is shown by the modifications introduced in this decoration of a Penobscot Cradle board:

FIG. 60 *Elaboration of Northeastern Algonkian double-curve motif as found on Penobscot cradle-board (after Speck, 1914, fig. 3).*

A discussion of art forms brings up the question of the relationship between form and function in art, or, as it is sometimes phrased, between the forms of a given art and the media in which it is expressed. "Primitive" art, it is sometimes maintained, does not stray outside the requirements of the media in which the artist works—the wood-carver emphasizes mass and does not attempt delicate traceries. The fact of the matter, however, is that such an assumption is no more valid than any generalization about nonliterate cultures considered as a whole, and in opposition to the historic cultures.

No carving could be less characterized by solidity than the ceremonial wooden statues of New Ireland (Pl. 15), which quite refute statements that "primitives" in some mystical way "feel" certain qualities of the medium in which they work. In a similar manner, ceremonial objects such as the jade adze in Pl. 16b, useless except for its token significance, show how the desire to beautify can triumph over any considerations of utility. This is to be found even where ceremonial considerations do not enter. Of the three Bush-Negro pieces in Pl. 17, the two at the top, a pounder used in washing clothes, and a comb, are functional in the sense that they are fitted to do the things

[14] F. G. Speck, 1914, p. 1.

they were made to do, despite the embellishments they bear. But the piece at bottom is a tray for carrying produce and to winnow rice. Its cut-through designs, therefore, completely rule out the winnowing function, for it very evidently cannot hold any grain. From the standpoint of the villagers, how-

FIG. 61   *Design on Sauk and Fox Indian rawhide box before folding (after Boas, 1927, fig. 13).*

ever, it was one of the most beautiful examples of their art, both because of the excellence they recognized in its design and the artistry of its execution.

If the concept of art for art's sake is unique to our culture, in practice all cultures produce examples of art forms where utilitarian needs are disregarded, or where the aesthetic impulse refuses to be bound by the distortions of design in an object destined for use. Two instances cited by Boas afford illustrations of this. The first has to do with the rawhide boxes made by the

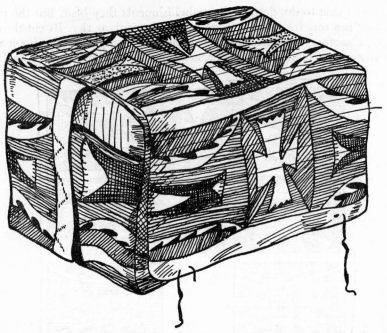

FIG. 62   *Sauk and Fox Indian rawhide box, folded (after Boas, 1927, fig. 12).*

Sauk and Fox Indians, which are decorated with symmetrical units that make a pleasing design on the hide as it lies flat. However, once these hides are folded to make the box, only a portion of the design is visible. The units that are then seen stand in no artistic relationship to each other, since the totality of the composition is quite lost.

The second instance concerns the bead-work decorations on the fringe along the outer seam of leggings of a Thompson River Indian. "These strips are decorated in rhythmic order, a string decorated by one glass bead and two bone beads in alternating order is followed by a plain string, next by one alternating glass and bone beads, then a plain one and finally one like the first. When we indicate the plain and decorated strips by letters, we find the arrangement . . . /ABCBA/ABCBA/ . . . repeated over and over again. The important point to be noted is, that when in use, the fringe hangs down without order along the outer side of the leg so that the elaborate rhythmic pattern cannot be seen. The only way in which the maker can get any satisfaction from her work is while making it or when exhibiting it to her friends. When it is in use, there is no aesthetic effect." [15] A further example that bears on the artistic drive to achieve decorative effects, irrespective of display value, is in the elaborately woven cassava-trays made by Indians of the Amazon basin. Here the intricate designs can only be seen when the light strikes the tray at a particular angle, and they cannot be seen at all when

---

[15] F. Boas, *op. cit.*, p. 29.

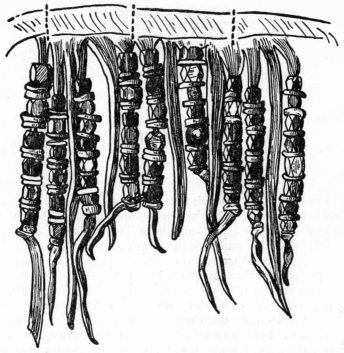

Fig. 63   *Fringe from legging, Thompson Indians, British Columbia (after Boas, 1927, fig. 16).*

the tray is in use, since the damp meal covers the basketry-work, effectively concealing the weaving.

We may say, then, that in all societies the aesthetic impulse finds expression in terms of the standards of beauty laid down in the traditions of the people. Where art is close to life, as it is in all nonliterate cultures and in many strata of literate societies, the technical virtuosity of the artists will be lavished on objects of everyday use, far more than may be the case with the forms we classify as "pure" art. But whatever forms art may take, however it is manifested, it will be present. No art, that is, is haphazard or inchoate. It is the expression of the desire for beauty that finds fulfilment in the application of technical skill through sanctioned form, in terms of the patterned perceptions and imaginative resources of the artistically endowed members of every society.

CHAPTER 24

Folklore

THE folklore of nonliterate peoples consists of their myths, tales, proverbs, riddles, and verse, together with their music; and comprises the least tangible expression of the aesthetic aspects of culture. To varying degrees, these forms combine with each other and with the graphic and plastic arts, to make up the rituals, dances, and other means of group expression we term drama.

Folklore performs varied functions. Myths explain the universe and, as has been demonstrated in an earlier chapter, provide a basis for ritual and belief. Tales, which are customarily distinguished from myths because of their secular character, are often regarded as an unwritten record of tribal history. They act not only as a valuable educational device, but are equally valuable in maintaining a sense of group unity and group worth. Proverbs, which with riddles have essentially Old World distributions, garnish conversation with pointed allusion, help clarify an obscure reference to one deficient in worldliness, and moralize. They may even, as in Africa, be cited in courts of justice in the pleading of a case, just as legal precedents are introduced in our courts of law. Riddles divert by serving as a test of wits; they give prestige to the one who can "pull" them with sureness and ease. With the insight of the artist, Anatole France has summarized the principal role of folklore. "Nations live on mythology," he has said. "From legends they draw all the ideas necessary to their existence. They do not need many, and a few simple fables will suffice to guild millions of lives."

The separation of stories into such general categories as myth and tale cannot be done validly for folklore as a whole. Only the stories of certain cultures may lend themselves to such classification; others may not. For example, a tale told only for amusement by one group, may, as it travels, take on another quite different function than it had in its original habitat. Thus the type of Negro stories known to Euroamerica as the Uncle Remus tales, derived from Africa, and retained in almost unchanged form, are told chiefly for recreation in the New World. In Africa, many of them fall into the category of myth, where they are called on to explain some of the most important phenomena of the universe. Animal stories like them are widely distributed throughout the Old World. One instance is the mediaeval European cycle of Reynard the Fox. Other examples are Aesop's fables and the elaborate Panchatantra cycle of tales from India, both of which groups show many similarities to the African animal stories and the European Reynard tales. However, whereas the Reynard cycle was aimed at providing enjoyment, the Aesop fables and Panchatantra tales were told to educate the young. The same type of animal stories reappear as we continue eastward to China, but here the Jataka tales become the sacred myths of the Buddhist sects.

Many other examples of how a specific tale may shift from one category to another in transmission come to mind as we consider what has happened to European stories that have been taken over by native folk. The tale of the ant and the grasshopper, made familiar by La Fontaine is, as we know, a moralizing fable. Its moral is conveyed, and its climax reached, when the hard-working ant says to the carefree grasshopper, "He who sings in summer will not eat in winter." A tale told by the Shuswap Indians of western North America is obviously derived from this story. Like other American Indians, the Shuswap only rarely moralize in their tales. The La Fontaine fable here becomes an explanatory myth. As the Shuswap tell it, a grasshopper-man refuses to help his tribe catch salmon for the winter—he prefers to dance and to eat grass. When winter comes, and the grass is covered with snow, he goes everywhere begging for food, but he is told to go and eat grass. Half dead of hunger, he transforms himself into the creature that bears his name. And it is ordained that ". . . since you are lazy, you shall eat only grass and you will pass your existence jumping here and there as you make your noise."[1]

Another instance of change, in this case showing how a tale can lose its sacred character and become explanatory, is found in the Zuñi Indian version of the Biblical account of the Flight into Egypt and the birth of Jesus. In a culture where stress is laid on fertility, Jesus is translated into twins. Where the original recounts the persecution of Herod, Mary, who becomes a Mexican girl, is pursued by "soldiers"—volunteers who, in Zuñi ritual practice, guard the saints. The tale is as follows:

In the West, there lived a Mexican girl who never went out. She staid all the time in her own house. She would sit where the sun shone in. The sun . . . "gave her a child." At this time, the soldiers were guarding her. One of the soldiers saw her, and said to the others, "The one we are guarding is pregnant. If she does such things, what is the use of guarding her? Let us kill her!" The next day in the morning she was to die. That evening the Sun by his knowledge came into her room, and said, "Tomorrow you are to die."—"Well, if it is to be, I must die," she said. He said, "No, I won't let you die, I will get you out." The next morning early by his knowledge he lifted her up out of the window. "Now go to where you are to live." So she went on till she came to a *sipaloa* planting. She said, "What are you planting?" He said, "Round stones." Because he did not answer right, she did something to the seed, and his corn did not come up. She went on a little ways, and she came to another one planting. She asked him what he was planting. He said, "I am planting corn and wheat." Because he answered her right, she did nothing to his seed, and they all came up. Then the soldiers found she was gone, and they came on after her. They asked the first man if he had seen a girl com-

---

[1] This tale is recounted by A. Van Gennep, 1920, p. 74.

ing. He said, "Yes, she has just gone over the hill." They said, "Well, we must be nearly up with her, we will hurry on." So they went on over the hill, and they saw no one. They came to another little hill, and they could not see her. They came to a river, and it was very deep. They cut some poles, and they said, "We'll see how deep it is." They stuck the poles down, and they said, "It is too deep. There is no use in hunting any more for her." So they turned back. But the girl had crossed the river, and went on until she came to Kluwela, and there she lay in. She had twins. The pigs and dogs kissed her. That is why the pigs and the dogs have children. The mules would not kiss her. That is why the mules have no children. . . .[2]

A tale collected from the Negroes of Haiti, which also explains the sterility of the mule, similarly indicates how diverse materials from the sacred mythology of one culture can be rewoven into a new fabric and made to serve a new purpose. In this case, it is told how Jesus was riding a mule when, at a crossroad, a snake suddenly appeared. Frightened, the mule reared up, throwing Jesus to the ground. In his anger, Jesus decreed that the mule should bear no offspring. But in this tale, another element of Biblical derivation is introduced, for Jesus also cursed the snake, and decreed that henceforth it should get about only by crawling on its belly.

All stories are composed of three elements—character, incident, and plot. These elements are independently variable, and can move in new groupings, and in any combination. Even in the same culture, different characters will be found performing the same sequence of acts that constitute the incidents which, in turn, make up a specific plot. Or a given character may move from tale to tale, and become involved in the most diverse kinds of situations that are combined into many plots. This is why the cataloging of *motifs* and the analysis of *variants* is so important a part of the work of the folklorist.

Tales are great travellers. One of the most fascinating and profitable tasks in the study of folklore is to see how, in their travels, they have been altered to fit a new natural setting, and a new cultural matrix. Some stories have a distribution that is almost literally world-wide. For instance, the "Magic Flight" tale is found in Europe and Asia, in aboriginal North and South America, in Africa and among New World Negroes. Basically the story concerns a girl, or two sisters, pursued by an evil being. The only protection the girls have is a comb, a glass, and one other object, such as a red cloth, that have magic power. As the pursuer, steadily gaining on the fugitive, is heard to approach, first the comb is thrown down, whereupon a forest appears through which the ogre must cut his way. As he again gains in his pursuit, the glass is thrown down, and becomes a lake he must cross. Eventually, the pursuit fails and the girl or sisters live in peace.

Another story that completely covers the Old World and has been diffused to the New World is given the general title "The Good Child and the Bad." In the Grimm Brothers collection of German tales (*märchen*), it is known as "Mother Holle." It will be remembered how, in this version, a cruel stepmother forces her step-child, who has dropped a spindle down a well, to go

---

[2] E. C. Parsons, 1918, pp. 258–9.

after it. As the child descends into the well, to her astonishment, instead of water, she finds a door at the bottom. Opening this door, she discovers a pleasant land and a beckoning path. As she passes an apple tree, it begs her to shake its boughs to relieve it of their weight of fruit, and she does; an oven beseeches her to remove its burning bread, and she complies. She finally reaches the house of Mother Holle, where she is made welcome and only asked to shake the featherbed each morning. Though she is treated well, she wishes to return to her father. As she passes through the door leading to the upper world, she is covered with gold. When she returns home, her envious step-mother sees no reason why her own daughter should not also have these riches, and sends the other child down the well. But this spoiled little girl refuses to shake the apple tree, or to take out the oven's bread, and neglects Mother Holle's simple task. Therefore, when she passes through the door, she is covered with pitch.

Where this tale originated, we do not know. Its beginnings can in all probability never be discovered, but it is undoubtedly very old. Two instances can be cited of the many versions that have been reported. The first is from the Kolyma of Eastern Siberia, who borrowed it from the Russians, transforming it to fit their arctic setting.[3] Here we find the child, who can no longer bear the punishments inflicted by her step-mother, begging her father to take her to the Unclean Idol. Yielding finally to her plea, the father hitches his dogs to the sled, provides his daughter with some coals and food to eat while awaiting the monster's arrival, and leaves her to her fate. But no sooner does she put her kettle on the fire, than it is "full to the brim of cooked meat and fat" and as she is about to eat with her horn-spoon from a birch bowl, a floor-board is lifted, and there appear "a great number of mice and toads, ermines, and all kinds of small vermin"—the children of the Unclean Idol, who, it turns out, have been without food for some days. They implore her to feed them, and she allows them to eat from her kettle. When they have finished, nothing is left for her, and she goes to bed hungry. The next morning, when the Unclean Idol returns and is about to devour the child, the vermin plead for her, telling their father how she had saved their lives. In gratitude she is given "a sable overcoat and a bagful of silver money," and she is brought home by her joyful father, who had come to gather up the heap of bones—the only remains he had expected to find of her. The rest of the tale follows the Frau Holle pattern—the step-mother's own daughter is taken to the Unclean Idol, refuses to share her food, and is eaten by the monster.

The Negroes of Paramaribo, Dutch Guiana, combine this story with the "Cinderella" tale, and with a motif known as "The Magic Whip," transmuting the setting into the tropical scene in which they live.[4] Here the *dramatis personae* do not include the father, but only the step-mother, and her three daughters, and a *kweki*, a child, not this woman's own, living with her as a maid of all work, whom she exploits unmercifully. This child is given a cow's

---

[3] W. Bogoras, 1918, pp. 83–6.
[4] M. J. and F. S. Herskovits, 1936, pp. 317–21.

belly to wash in the river, but it is lost when a fish carries it off. Desperate, she runs away into the bush. Here she meets an old woman who asks her to scratch her back, which proves to be full of broken glass. She does not refuse to scratch the old woman's back, and is given a small box. When she wishes for something, the old woman tells her, she has but to rub this box and say, "My little box, my little box, what did your mistress tell you?" The child returns home, and is soundly beaten.

The story then moves to the "Cinderella" motif, telling of a church celebration which is to be attended by the King. The mother and her daughters leave for the service and the child rubs her box, speaks the formula, and is transformed into a beautiful young woman, splendidly dressed, with a carriage at the door awaiting her pleasure. The king admires the beautiful stranger, and on his orders to discover her identity, one of her slippers is taken from her as she hurriedly reënters the carriage. She returns home and is again the browbeaten drudge. The king commands his soldiery to try the shoe on all the girls of the town, in order to discover its owner. The mother hides the *kweki* in an oven before their arrival, but the family parrot cries out to the soldiers to look in the oven for another girl. The slipper fits the *kweki*, and she again rubs her box that she may go to the King in the clothes he had seen her.

Shifting once more to the "Good Child and the Bad" theme, the story recounts how the mother then gives one of her daughters a cow's belly to wash and lose in the stream; how this daughter meets the old woman and is given a box, even though she refuses to scratch the old woman's back. But when she opened it—the tale in conclusion moves to the "Magic Whip" motif— "she did not come into fine clothes. A whip came out of the box. It began to whip them, so that they all had to run. They did not know what to do (to stop it), because she had not scratched the old woman's back for her."

2

IN THE tales that have been summarized, it can be seen how folklore reflects both its natural and cultural setting. A substantial body of folktales is more than the literary expression of a people. It is, in a very real sense, their ethnography which, if systematized by the student, gives a penetrating picture of their way of life.

This was demonstrated by Boas in his study of the myths of the Tsimshian Indians of the Pacific Northwest, a *tour de force* of folkloristic analysis that has never been equalled. From this great collection of myths are abstracted descriptions of Tsimshian material culture, economy, social structures, and religious beliefs; accounts of the life cycle of the individual, of secret societies, of the prestige-giving contests of economic waste known as the potlatch; of their ethical concepts and emotional life.[5] Thus literary expression, in whatever form it exists, draws its materials from the experience of its

---

[5] F. Boas, 1909–10.

creators. The artist who uses words as his medium, no less than the artist who works with paints or in wood or stone, acts as a creature of his culture; his responses are always relative to its formal patterns, and his values reflect its underlying values.

A folktale that incorporates details of an earlier period in the history of the people who tell it, documents that earlier life. The stories of the Pueblo Indians, where the characters go in and out of rooms by the use of ladders, describe the means of ingress and egress of a period when Pueblo structures had no doors or windows. For reasons of security, access to the communal structure was only by means of ladders which, when drawn up, made it impossible for an unwelcome outsider to get in. Many of the fairy tales we ourselves tell, of kings and queens, princes and knights, represent the living lore of an earlier period of our own culture. It is interesting to speculate, for instance, on the age of such a story as Little Red Riding Hood, which, because of its forest setting, makes us wonder whether it is perhaps not a legacy of late prehistoric times.

Certainly, we have not adapted the folk-tale to the mechanized world of modern times. John Henry, with his hammer, who worked on the railroad, perhaps approaches the theme of the individual pitted against the machine most closely; though as protagonist, he is also the descendant of a widespread type of West African being, supernaturally favored with prodigious strength. Paul Bunyan, on the other hand, is a creation of the frontier. Stories that anthropomorphize the locomotive, the aeroplane, the electric light, still appear forced. We may speculate whether this is why they have not as yet taken the popular fancy. Perhaps our mechanistic world, in its very conception, is incompatible with the kind of play of the imagination that created the folktales most peoples have produced. The unwritten lore of modern Euroamericans is very largely confined to anecdotes that involve human relations and misconduct, in a vein that is light, often risqué, sometimes bitingly ironic.

In addition to reflecting the life of a people as of the period when a given story of a living lore is told, folklore also reveals much about their aspirations, values, and goals. It has been seen how the emphasis on fertility of the Zuñi Indians is reflected in the turn these people give the Biblical nativity tale. Many other instances, drawn out of tales that are not the result of contact with a foreign people, can be given.

Striking in this connection are the myths of the inhabitants of the Pacific Islands. Here great stress is laid on rank, a consideration which dominates the lives of the people. Different forms of address are employed for chief and commoner. At ceremonies, or gatherings of any sort, the demands of protocol strictly regulate the place of each individual. Polynesian mythology treats the universe in terms congenial to this fundamental pattern. Creation is conceived as an orderly process, having a kind of evolutionary character, wherein each phenomenon appears in due time and in proper sequence, to achieve a stratified universe that begins with chaos and ends with the existing order of things. Among most North American tribes, in contrast, there is no hierarchy of beings, no chaos to be ordered into the present scene by the will of a creator. And this, it is not too much to assume, is not unrelated to the absence of ruling classes, to the democratic structures that have resulted from the classless character of most Indian societies.

The flexibility in personal relations that marks the Indian's contacts with his fellows, organized as these people are in small tribal units, is further reflected by the absence of the moralizing tale and the proverb. These forms, on the other hand, dominate African folklore. Particularly in West Africa, the mythology reveals the underlying motivations and drives that support the highly integrated social structures characteristic of the continent. Here, too, are reflected the attitudes that permit no one to take anything for granted but, with a sophisticated and perhaps cynical view of human relations, cause him to probe beneath the surface of behavior to reach the underlying motive for an act, even when it is in no way hostile. We understand this attitude better, for instance, when we hear the wide-spread myth that tells how, in creating the world, and dividing the work of administering it to lesser gods, the Creator, whose children these deities are conceived to be, gave each a separate language so as to ensure that no conspiracy might be formed to take over ultimate power. Or, again, it is revealing to learn that though the Creator is held to have endowed these lesser beings with extensive powers, especially of discipline and destruction, the power to create was never given over, lest terrible creatures might be given life, to prey on mankind.

Again, the African tendency to moralize reflects the value set on accepted behavior; a value that, though present in all groups, is rarely so explicitly stated, or so frequently emphasized as in these African cultures. The use of the proverb is part of this same complex, whereby the relation between man and man is carried out on a level of established convention. Outside the family circle, rebuke is never administered directly; but the use of a proverb, that names no names, will make the point by indirection. Even so perfunctory an act as asking that a statement be repeated so as to be more clearly understood, is achieved among the Liberian Kru by such oblique reference as is contained in the saying, "The sound of the snapping of the trap that has caught me stays in my ears." To remark, "Chicken says, 'The feet of the stranger are small,'" is an effective reply to one who boorishly injects himself into an argument that does not concern him. "To take out and put back never empties the pot," cautions the too liberal giver, while at the same time, it warns him to be on his guard against those who would take advantage of him. No better indication of the deep feeling that one should never accept at face value any declaration of intent could be imagined than in the African proverb heard among the Negroes of Suriname, "Chicken can lie about her eggs, but not about her chicks," or "All showing of the teeth isn't a laugh"; or of the realistic view of life taken by the Haitians who say, "The rock under the water doesn't know how the rock in the sun suffers."

Folklore also gives us clues to the hidden reactions to social sanctions that on the surface seem to be complied with willingly enough. In this, indeed, we find a psychoanalytic mechanism at work, wherein customary behavior is often distorted in a manner that tells us much about the desires individuals must suppress in ordering their lives so as to conform to the ways of their society. It is enough in this connection to mention how, in Indonesian and

B

A

PLATE 13 *Carved ivory container from Benin, West Africa (height, 3⅛ in.). (A) Section showing Christ on the cross, the spirit of the Holy Ghost (doves), Mary and St. John; (B) opposite side, showing St. Andrew and St. Peter. See page 401. [Photographs by Mary Modglin, Chicago]*

PLATE 14 *Dahomean appliqué cloths, showing changes (A—D) in design over four generations of cloth-sewers. See page 404.*

Melanesian groups where rigid brother-sister sexual taboos obtain, the origin-myths often tell of the beginning of mankind in the incestuous relationships of a brother and sister.

One of the earlier folklorists, Andrew Lang, was so struck by this phenomenon of ascribing to deities conduct abhorrent to mortals, that he considered at length the problem of the bestial traits of the godly characters in many of the mythologies. These he held to be survivals of a less disciplined state in which he believed early man lived. Though his hypothesis has with time come to be rejected, there is little question that the gods of many a mythology do violate the codes of behavior by which men must live. One need go no farther, for illustrations, than the philanderings of Jupiter, or in aboriginal American Indian tales, the obscenities of Coyote. As we see it today, these stories afford an impressive documentation of the hypothesis that we derive powerful satisfactions from identifying ourselves, all unconsciously, with characters who transgress the codes we ourselves may not violate.

Another manifestation of how, so to speak, folklore creates a world where vindications that the world of reality denies, are granted, is to be found in the stories wherein the weak prevail over the strong, where evil meets an avenger, or where many other of the less pleasant conditions of life are resolved in ways that are not those of the workaday world. Here, in terms of a kind of socialized fantasy, men and women are comforted for the hardships, the inequalities, the injustices of the daily round. They achieve this by identifying themselves with characters who get the best of those stronger than themselves, or who right the wrongs of the oppressed, or defeat the hard realities of time and distance and even solve the ultimate riddle of restoring life to the dead. All this is no different than the release afforded in Euroamerican culture by the novel, the theatre, the motion-picture. By transporting men and women into a realm where the problems of life are solved as they rarely are disposed of in actual living, folklore thus affords a release that provides them with courage, and shows itself as a many-faceted vehicle of self expression on both the conscious and unconscious levels.

3

When we define folklore as the literary arts of a culture, we depart somewhat from the conventional definition of this term, which, particularly in England, the continent of Europe, and Latin America has tended to hold more closely to the implications of its original statement than in the United States.

The word "folklore" was first employed in a letter signed by Ambrose Merton, published in *The Athenaeum* of London, 22 August, 1846. Its writer, who used this pseudonym for his real name, William J. Thoms, urged that accounts of "the manners, customs, observances, superstitions, ballads, proverbs, &c. of the olden time" be recorded so that later students could turn for information to these dying remnants of the unrecorded past that were termed "popular Antiquities, or Popular Literature." In Europe, where peasant populations preserved customs of an earlier period, there was a real place for the systematic, scholarly investigation of the ways of life that no longer survived among the urban people of industrialized centers. In the United States, however, the customs of peasant Europe had been given over in the westward thrust of the frontier.

When, therefore, in 1888, the American Folklore Society was founded, of the four categories of "the fast-vanishing remains of Folklore in America" that were set up as the objects of study, only one, "Relics of Old English Folk-lore (ballads, tales, superstitions, dialect, etc.)" was equivalent to the content of folklore as it was conceived in the Old World. The "Lore of Negroes in the Southern States of the Union," turned out to comprise literary forms to a predominant degree, and so, in practice, at least, were the materials collected under the heading "lore of French Canada, Mexico, etc." But the other category, "Lore of Indian Tribes of North America, (myths, tales, etc.)" made it essential to distinguish between literary and other aspects of culture. "Here," says the original statement, "the investigation has to deal with whole nations, scattered over a continent. The harvest does not consist of scattered gleanings, the relics of a crop once plentiful, but, unhappily, allowed to perish ungarnered; on the contrary, it remains to be gathered, if not in the original abundance, still in ample measure. Systems of myth, rituals, feasts, sacred customs, games, songs, tales, exist in such profusion that volumes would be required to contain the lore of each separate tribe." [6]

This conclusion came to be recognized as valid even by those students of folklore who retained the original formulation of the field, once they moved out of their own countries to those parts of the world where nonliterate peoples lived in accordance with aboriginal custom. In these instances, vestiges of ways of life no longer current could not be found, as they could for the rural dwellers of Europe. The Maypole dance, the Christmas tree, wishing on the new moon, beliefs about witches and black cats, the rituals at the laying of cornerstones—all these manifestations of earlier European belief were legitimately to be regarded as "folk-custom," and studied in terms of the frame of reference laid down by Ambrose Merton in his original letter. But in Africa and Australia and the South Seas, as among the North American Indians, the distinction between folklore and other aspects of culture— that is to say, the distinction between folklore and ethnography—had to be drawn. This, from the anthropological point of view, is the basis for the limitation of folklore to the forms indicated in the opening sentences of this chapter.

Yet these forms—myth, tale, riddle, and proverb—are not by any means to be thought of as a monopoly of nonliterate peoples. All societies have their lore. Where the presence of writing makes possible a written literature, a substantial stratum of "popular" stories and sayings exists—forms that are never reduced to writing except when some folklorist studies them, or where

---

[6] For an extended account of this development, see M. J. Herskovits, 1946. The quotations are from the same Journal, vol. i (1888), pp. 2–5.

Folklore

some theme, first presented in writing, finds popular appeal and is elaborated as it passes from mouth to mouth; as, for instance, the "Little Audrey" stories about the child who "laughed and laughed." How rich this vein can be is to be discerned in any of the several anthologies of American folklore that have been published—and significantly have achieved wide circulation. The compiler of one of the most popular of these, defined folklore incisively and with insight, when he wrote, "What makes a thing folklore is not only that you have heard it before yet want to hear it again, because it is different, but also because you want to tell it again in your own way, because it is anybody's property." [7] Such tales invade even the most "sophisticated" circles, as for example, the cycle of folk stories heard in faculty clubs about the psychiatrist who is consulted by a man obsessed by the notion that insects are endlessly crawling up his arms. As the patient gestures to brush them off, the psychiatrist exclaims, "Well, don't brush them off on me!" and begins to brush his own sleeves.

The tenacity of such tales, even where writing is prevalent and formal literary values are supreme, is impressive. Consider, for example, the "moron" stories that were popular during World War II, of which a typical instance follows:

Two morons were fishing. They pulled in lots of fish. In the evening one said, "You'd better mark this place." When they got to the pier, the first one asked, "Did you mark it?" "Yes, I put a cross on the side of the boat just over the fishing hole." "You fool. How do you know we'll get this boat tomorrow?" [8]

Almost exactly the same tale is heard in Brazil, where stories that parallel many "moron" tales are told to make sport of the Portuguese:

João and Manoel were out fishing, and found a spot where the catch was especially good. "Be sure and mark the spot, so we can come here tomorrow," said João. Manoel took a piece of chalk from his pocket, and made a large "X" on the side of the boat. As they were rowing in, João asked, "Did you mark the spot carefully?" "Yes, see the cross on the side of the boat?" "You fool, you! Don't you know we'll have a different boat tomorrow?"

Few who laugh at these stories realize their age. Yet we find this very tale in the European Till Eulenspiegel trickster-cycle, popular since the Middle Ages. In the equivalent version, Till tricks a man who thinks he hears the drums beating war, to join him in raising a false alarm in the city of Schoppenstadt. The burghers fear that the beautiful new bell in the court-house steeple, if captured, will be melted to make gun-barrels. Till advises that it be sunk in the sea:

Another of the councilmen spoke. "How will we be able to tell where we have sunk the bell, when the time comes to bring it up again?" he asked. "You need have no worries on that account," answered Till. "Come with me and I will show you how to mark the place." All the men of Schoppenstadt gathered together and in a short time they had unfastened the bell. They put it into a boat and rowed

---

[7] B. A. Botkin, 1944, pp. xxi–xxii.
[8] J. Davidson, 1943, p. 101.

423

a little way out to sea. Here they lifted the bell and lowered it over the side of the boat. "Now," said Till, "I will show you how we will mark the spot." He took a knife from his pocket and cut a notch on the side of the boat. "When you want to raise the bell, you need only to row out here again, and you will find the bell right under the notch in the side of the boat." [9]

Many other examples could be shown of how folklore in the sense of popular literature is confined neither to nonliterate cultures, nor to particular strata of literate societies, but is a universal in human civilization, and is consequently to be treated as any other aspect of culture is treated. Because in nonliterate groupings, however, it encompasses the whole range of "literary" expression rather than any single segment of it, in this discussion we have drawn primarily on the folklore of peoples where writing has no part in their cultural equipment.

4

THERE are a number of problems in the study of folklore, especially those that treat of its purely literary values, of which considerations of space forbid more than passing mention. One problem bearing on folklore as a cultural phenomenon, whose study aids significantly in the understanding of the culture of which it is a part, may be briefly mentioned. This concerns the distribution of tales and their elements. Some aspects of this problem we shall touch upon later, in our discussion of diffusion. Each tale, in itself a cluster of elements that, as we have seen, are independently variable, yields materials for the understanding of how any complex of cultural traits can vary in transmission from one people to another. Again, because of the stability and tenaciousness of folk-tales, we are appreciably aided in the task of reconstructing the contacts of nonliterate folk, by the use of methods to be discussed when the problem of historical reconstruction is considered.[10]

Out of the study of distributions we derive the concept of the principal folklore areas of the world, which can be briefly outlined here. These areas are three in number—the Old World (Africa, Europe, and Asia), North and South America, and the South Seas. The unity of the folklore in these great regions, each of which, of course, has its local sub-areas, is very striking. The distribution of recognizably similar animal trickster or moralizing tales over all of the Old World, that has already had our attention, is a case in point. Equally significant is the fact that the use of proverb and riddle mark off this region from the North and South American and South Seas areas. Another distinction of this Old World area is the prevalence, in its mythologies, of the concept of the universe as directed by pantheons of gods who stand in relation to each other as members of a family of supernatural beings, as the study of Greek, Roman, African, Norse, and Asiatic myths reveals.

The South Seas area is characterized by the presence of elaborate creation myths, as heretofore commented on. These myths are of a formal, fixed

[9] T. Yoseloff and L. Stuckey, 1944, pp. 57–9.
[10] Cf. S. Thompson, 1932–1936.

structure, and of great length, so that their narration calls upon the services of those specialists whose training for this work we have mentioned in discussing the specialized educational forms of the South Seas. It is perhaps the only area in the nonliterate world that has produced what may be regarded as epic poetry. The recital of the way in which the world evolved, and the adventures of the gods, in breadth of scope and beauty and power of imagery is comparable to the epics, strictly speaking, of literate European and Asiatic peoples. The tales are searchingly philosophical in content, as has been commented on by those who have recorded them from the earliest contact of the Polynesians with Europeans. In Melanesia, as elsewhere in the South Seas, the creation is of lesser concern, and the culture-hero is not as important as in Polynesia. Less formalized "fairy-tales" are employed for magical purposes, while cycles of stories that recount the adventures of dualistic heroes—one wise and the other foolish, one good and the other wicked—take on a place that such tales, if they exist at all in Polynesia, do not have.[11]

In the Americas, the explanatory tale plays a prominent role, while the myths everywhere show a preoccupation with celestial phenomena. Trickster tales, especially of the trickster-transformer type, abound in western North America. Extensive cycles of these tales, such as the raven stories of the northwest and California, have been collected from individual tribes. Boas, in his analysis of North American Indian folklore,[12] distinguishes the mythologies of various regions in terms of their degree of systematization, noting the loose grouping of Plateau tales concerning a single hero, or the absence of migration legends in the northern part of the continent, where the people regard themselves as always having lived in their present habitat. He also contrasts the characters—raven, mink, blue jay, coyote—who in different areas play the trickster. Tales of the same general categories—of tricksters and culture heroes, of transformation of men into animals or animals into men—also abound in South America. The number of categories is not very great. Métraux gives the most important types of South American Indian tales as: "Creation myths, in which are included the adventures of the Culture Heroes that gave the world its present physiognomy; myths about cataclysms, which may or may not be related to the Culture Hero cycle; transformation; star myths; myths purporting to explain the origin of institutions; myths validating a rite or charm; ancestor stories; ghost and spirit tales; animal stories, properly speaking." [13]

In order to comprehend and adequately assess the literary qualities that characterize the folklore of nonliterate peoples, large numbers of tales and myths from a single society must be studied with the critical apparatus, and in terms of the concepts that guide the analysis of any literary form. In these terms, the mechanisms employed by nonliterate folk to develop plot, sustain interest, and achieve adequate characterization will be found not too far

---

[11] Cf. R. B. Dixon, 1916, and K. Luomala, 1946.

[12] F. Boas, 1914 (1940, pp. 451–90); see also S. Thompson, 1929 and E. Voegelin, 1946.

[13] A. Métraux, 1946b, vol. II, p. 851.

at variance with those used by any skilled teller of tales, whether his medium be the oral folktale or the written narrative. Yet one distinction between the stylistic conventions of the written and the unwritten tale must be drawn. The fact that the folktale is recited gives it certain values that the written story can never achieve—just as certain features of the written story are necessarily absent in the tale. These nuances are such that they can only be recorded by the use of a phonograph—pauses in speech, interjections, intonation, stress; or by the motion picture—gesture, facial expression, and the like. Oral literature, that is, as the instrument of the able teller of tales, is dramatic in form. To this point we turn, then, as we consider the drama among nonliterate folk.

CHAPTER 25

Drama and Music

THE drama in nonliterate societies affirms some of the deepest sanctions of living. The myths declaimed and acted, the choreography of the dances, the rhythms of the drums, the verses sung and spoken, call forth responses from participants and onlookers that bear profoundly on the value system of the individuals who compose the group, and their adjustment within this system. They give assurance that the rains will come, that crops will be abundant, that calamity will not befall, that the group will continue. Our own reaction to a deeply moving dramatic presentation, that gives a sense of identification with a problem we feel more or less consciously is close to our own experience, yields a like response. But we respond largely as spectators, whereas the members of nonliterate societies actually take part in the figures of a dance, the telling of myths, the acting out of a dramatic sequence. In these societies, indeed, the spectator, as often as not, is participant and actor as well. "Theatre," in the sense we understand it, does not exist. The stage of nonliterate peoples has no need of the proscenium.

We shall understand this better, perhaps, if we turn to an example of the dramatic expression of nonliterate folk, and consider the cycle of *hevehe* rites, which mark the various stages in the making and destruction of the magnificent coconut-frond masks associated with the sea monsters which are believed to inhabit the coastal region of Orokolo Bay. Here, at the head of the Papuan Gulf, some three days by coastal boat west of Port Moresby, New Guinea, the Elema folk live.[1] It is hard to discover any parallel in our civilization, we are told, for this ceremony that often lasts for two decades. "There is feasting and crowding together of people; the jollity of rehearsals and initiations; brilliant spectacles and pageantry—enjoyed by the onlookers and still more by the actors; the humor of the *eharo;* and the bliss of the dancing women." But the cycle must be regarded as primarily serious. The "real dramatic interest" it holds, "contrives to renew itself up to the very end." The author's summary helps us understand why this is true: "Every episode is played out with theatrical effect. *Hevehe Karawa,* the monster rising by night from the sea; dancers and *eharo* brilliantly thronging the arena; Yellow Bark-Cloth Boys bursting out of the silent *eravo;* the ethereal form of the first *hevehe* standing at dawn on the threshold; all these and a

---

[1] F. E. Williams, 1940, *passim.*

score of others—fire-fight, procession, slaying of the leader, retreat of the spirits, conjuring of the sea-monster, casting out of Iko—constitute one long dramatic sequence. It is a drama adorned by spectacles, pageantry, and *coups de théâtre*, and abounding in comic relief, but not without its solemn passages and even its moment of tragedy." [2]

It is impossible even to sketch this intricately organized rite, for to do only this, and to give its meaning for the people requires the entire book from which these excerpts are taken. The theatrical effects obtained can, however, be grasped in the description of a single episode, the Fire-Fight:

The bathers, men, boys, and girls, were seen gathering for a moment about the bright fires by which the scene was illuminated. They seemed to be drying themselves, and as they did so they joined spontaneously in the chorus which rose to tremendous power. But they had something else in view, and this was merely an interlude. All were arming themselves with bunches of dry, inflammable coconut leaves, one in each hand, in readiness for the Fire-Fight.

Now they divided themselves into two parties according as they were associated with the east and west sides of the *eravo*, and faced each other across the fifty yards open space directly in front of it. Across this space a rough hurdle of bamboo poles had been hastily run up while the bathe was still in progress, and it now stood as a flimsy frontier between the two forces.

Suddenly on the east side all the torches seem to flare up simultaneously, and a moment later those on the west also, making perhaps 200 in all. The foremost on either side dash forward and shatter their torches on the hurdle, so that they seem to burst in a shower of sparks. Reinforcements charge in regardless. In a moment the barrier is broken down and the two sides mingle in a welter of flames and flying sparks. They pursue one another around and about with screams of laughter, striking, dodging, and clashing their weapons together, while lighted torches, flung spear-fashion from the hand, travel through the darkness in blazing arcs, like meteors. For a few minutes the battle rages in the village, and then with one consent the combatants turn on to the broader spaces of the beach and the black distance is soon alive with darting and circling points of fire. Meanwhile the village constables have been blowing their whistles in a well-meant effort to restore order, though happily they are completely disregarded and their shrill blasts only succeed in adding a frolicsome tribute to the revels. But in a few minutes more the thing is all over. The remaining torches are dashed out on the sands, and all return to the village. [3]

Though the theatrical quality of this performance is clear, it raises certain questions. Should we use the term "dramatic" to describe it? Can it be thus equated with our own theatrical performances? Does not the presence of spectators as well as participants vitiate the statement that in primitive societies this distinction is blurred to the point of negation?

Let us return to our earlier analysis of the term "primitive"—especially to the point that the difference between nonliterate societies is of the same order as the difference between any one of them and our own. It must again be stressed that except for the fact that certain peoples do not have writing, and possess economies based on handicraft rather than power machinery, the dis-

---

[2] *Ibid.*, pp. 415–16.
[3] *Ibid.*, pp. 310–11.

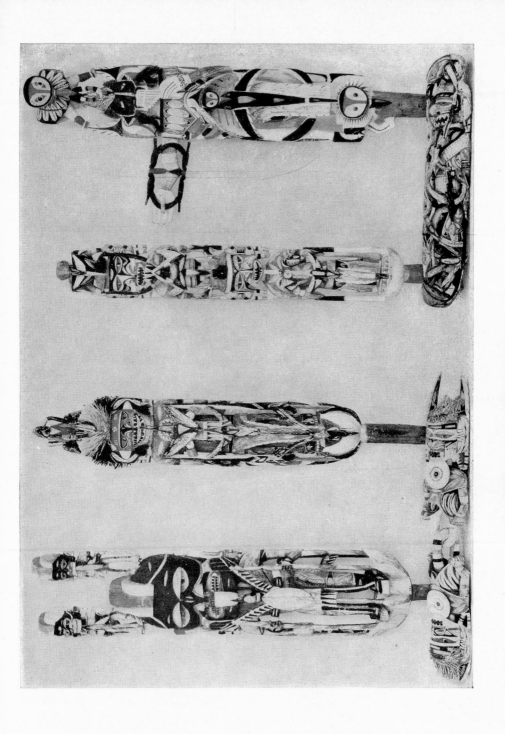

PLATE 15   *Ceremonial carved wooden statues from New Ireland. See page 410. [Photograph courtesy Chicago Natural History Museum]*

PLATE 16a   Eskimo ivory implements from Point Barrow, Alaska, showing realistic treatment of motifs. See page 407. [From J. A. Mason, 1927; photographs courtesy University Museum, Philadelphia]

PLATE 16b   Ceremonial jade adze from Hervey Island. See page 410. [From Krieger, 1932, Pl. 14] similarities between all societies are relative. Nonliterate groups are relatively small, but they vary in size from bands numbering only a few families to kingdoms of a million or more inhabitants. Their isolation, their conservatism, the complexity of their institutions are never absolute, either among themselves, or compared with ourselves. And the degree of specialization they manifest—a matter to which in the final analysis all the questions just raised refer—is also relative.

Thus participation in the dramatic representation of nonliterate societies may range from complete participation, to representations given by trained, specialized performers, before spectators whose only role is to watch and appreciate; that differ, we may say, only from those familiar to us in that they are not performed in a theatre. We may contrast the initiatory rites of the Australian aborigines, which no one except candidates and those who have already been through the initiation may witness, and wherein all have roles to play; with the elaborate dance dramas of Bali, with their highly trained, professional performers, whose entire lives are pointed toward these skills.

2

THERE is one feature that all forms of dramatic expression have in common, whether simple or complex, performed by specialists or the group as a whole, manifested in the open-air performances of nonliterate folk, or in the modern theatre. All performances have structure; all manifest the unities that distinguish any artistic production. There is a beginning and an end. There is a sequence in time, and in incident. There is a sense of progression—of climax —whether the tradition of the group orders it in terms of heightening or diminishing of effect, or conceives it in a more flexible mold. Furthermore, all such performances, however they may be integrated in nonliterate cultures with other aspects of living, are clearly differentiated from the ordinary round of life. They are something special, anticipated, often calling for the amassing of provisions and ceremonial regalia. They may at times afford the release of comedy, or may introduce the motif of tragedy. Their actual presentation is a break in the customary routine.

The nonliterate drama is similarly marked by plot, an important expression of its formal element. This element enters when one least expects it. A simple dance may, on closer study, be discovered to have the elements of complex dramatic organization. It is not chance that in West Africa, English-speaking natives use the word "play" to designate their dances, and any of the wide variety of the dances in the area may be taken as an instance of the structured drama of these performances.

One learns, let us say, when among the Ashanti, that a dance is to take place the next afternoon. The village is small and remote; the dancing space open to the glare of the hot sun, with but little shade to protect the spectators, drawn from other villages. As one arrives, the drums are sounding, and the dancers are already circling the enclosure. There are perhaps ten or twelve of them, some men, some women. All are in a state of possession, or approaching this condition. A shriek is heard—and a woman falls to the ground, rolls along it, attempts to get up. Others come to her assistance, but she signals for a stick; then, painfully rising, begins to crawl about the enclosure, barely able to use one foot. Another dances violently about the circle, arms swinging, facial muscles working, pausing before the drums to dance backward and forward, backward and forward, always facing the instruments whose tone is the compelling voice of the god. The rhythms of the percussion orchestra, the massed voices and hand-clapping of the singers, the vividly colored silk and cotton cloths of the spectators, the red of the earth and green of the forest background, the constant movement of dancers and attendants, and, over all, the brilliance of the afternoon sun—these make up the settings for the action to follow.

One man, a priest, now becomes possessed. All follow his magnificent dancing with an intentness that reveals tensions hitherto unremarked. He goes about the dancing space several times, dances to the drums, circles again, and then, with a cry, breaks out of the ring and runs into the village. Some—but only those qualified—follow him, and from them soon comes a shout echoed by the spectators as the drums take up a quickened beat, and those left behind go on with their dancing with renewed energy. The woman with the staff throws it from her, dancing as energetically as the rest. She is joined by the priest, who, returning with something in his hands, leads the others in dancing to the drums until he is escorted to the cult-house. The dance lasts well into the night, but the priest does not rejoin the dancers; the end of the dance comes when there are no more possessed by the gods.

A simple enough rite, this. Yet, if one reaches beneath outer form and touches the meaning of the performance, the dance becomes an episode in the drama of expunging the evil which threatened the village, and of attaining a peaceful way of life. For some time before this dance, misfortune dogged the group. Crops were bad, houses burned, children died. Divination revealed magic laid against the people. The dance, which brought the gods of the village to the heads of their worshipers, was to seek out and drive away the evil. When the god of the priest possessed him, he became this being, and as such revealed the hiding place of the charm that actuated the evil. This was why tensions mounted with his possession, why anxiety followed his dancing and his muttered utterances, why the shout announcing that the cause of the evil had been found was followed by the vigorous dancing of the devotees remaining behind. The situation was resolved; the plot had worked to its conclusion. But for all its simplicity of form and directness of line, the dramatic quality of the dance was of the highest, carrying performers into states of possession, and holding spectators taut with excitement and expectancy.

Plots may vary in complexity of organization. Where, as in Polynesia, rituals dramatize portions of a complicated mythological system, a performance may rival, in intricacy of organization and delineation of character, those with which we are familiar. One essential difference between such representations in nonliterate society, and our own, follows upon the presence or absence of writing. The drama of native peoples has been developed by the people; for us, a play is written out by one specialist for other specialists to stage. Much of dramatic form among nonliterate peoples consists of ceremonies which enact various myths, or recapitulate group experience of an earlier day; or comprise rituals demanded by the current system of belief to achieve ends held imperative for survival, such as insuring rainfall, or fertility, or victory in combat. Perhaps the only analogies in our culture are survivals of earlier rites, such as weddings, christenings, or funerals, wherein lay persons play their parts in what were once full ritual dramas.

An instance of group dramatization of a theme relating to their past was witnessed as an interlude in an African rite performed by a group of Negroes in Paramaribo, Dutch Guiana. This dance took place at night, the worshipers circling about within a rectangle made by the benches on which spectators were seated. As the drums finished the rhythms that saluted the last of the principal deities of the group, the drummers began to beat the "Anansi story" motif, to honor the ancestors who had worshipped these gods in their lifetime. This introduces a secular dance interval to lighten the seriousness of the principal rites of the evening. Spectators who had been sitting, joined the circle of dancers, and followed, one close behind the other, until the song leader shouted, "You'll be called early tomorrow. There's a lot of work to do!" The character was that of the overseer; the time was the slave regime. Instantly the dance slowed. The line became a succession of grotesquely bent, twisted, aged figures. Groans were heard, "crutches" appeared, and each, as he passed the "overseer," protested his illness, or his pain, or gave other reason for having to be excused. Finally the "overseer" looked at the hobbling dancers, and asked, "Today's Friday, isn't it?"

"No, Master, today's Saturday."

"Then tomorrow's Sunday?"

"Yes, Master."

"Tomorrow's Sunday. Well, then, you won't be called to work. But be sure to come for extra rations."

The change in tempo was too spontaneous to have been rehearsed, though these people must have danced this satire innumerable times. "*Tamara Sondel!*" they sang in unison, and then, to the quickened tempo of the drums, they repeated the phrase as a chorus to the recitative of the leader, "Tomorrow's Sunday! Tomorrow's Sunday! Tomorrow's Sunday!" Away flew "crutches" and sticks, bent backs straightened, limps turned to vigorous dancing. In this dance play, these Negroes were re-enacting a page from their history with a skill, a degree of verisimilitude, not to be excelled by the trained actor.

The Indians of southwestern United States offer many examples of ritual drama in highly developed form. The Navaho Night Chant, for instance, is a particularly intricate and sustained presentation, wherein the sense of the dramatic is given freest rein. A simple rite illustrating Navaho dramatic expression will serve our purpose—a curing "sing" or a private sand painting. The "sing" is an all-night affair; its setting, the inside of the dimly lit hogan. The patient sits facing the priest, who leads the singing, continuing without interruption until the climax at dawn, when the door is thrown open and the priest steps outside to perform the concluding rites alone. The sand-painting sessions similarly work to their climaxes with the destruction of the beautiful, stylized images of the gods made on the floor, by the sweeping up of the colored sand on which the one for whom the rite has been given has been placed, to obtain power from the spirits and their aid.

The Pueblo Indians have the same feeling for drama in their ritual. The snake dance of the Hopi is perhaps the most famous of these rites, though this very fame brings so many tourist spectators to witness it that much of the artistic unity of the ritual is lost to the observer. Far more impressive artistically, because it is free of intrusive strangers, is the antelope dance of the preceding day, when the beauty of the setting can be appreciated, the singing heard, the movements of the priestly dance followed.

In Zuñi, too, dances have this dramatic quality. To stand atop the high communal dwellings and watch masked figures appear in the distance, to see them advance into the pueblo and there dance until they disappear into their underground kivas, to watch the antics of the clowns and observe how attentively their every move is followed by those on the rooftops, is to share an emotion that only the superlative in our theatre can call forth. We are, in fact, witnessing a well-staged music drama. The organization that is called for to produce these dances, the amount of preparation required to achieve the performances, and the mythological sequences that furnish their plots become clear when the various published analyses of these rites and of the characters taking part in them are read.

In considering the ritual drama, the spectacles connected with religious rites, it is important not to take the point of view often encountered, that the dramatic expressions of nonliterate peoples are all ritualistic. That this hypothesis should have been accepted so widely is understandable. For one thing, ritual performances bulked large in the early stages of our own drama. Then, too, dramatic expression in nonliterate societies is, in fact, much more frequently found in association with religious than with secular rites. And finally, since cause and effect are so closely related in the drama of these societies, few students have been on the watch for secular drama, even where they have been conscious of the drama as a subject for study.

In many instances, the matter turns on how a given performance is classified. We may consider another dramatic spectacle of the Ashanti people, partially religious, partially secular—the Kwasidae rite. This is held once a month, and its purpose is to strengthen the "stool," or throne, of the ruler of a village, a province, or the Ashanti kingdom as a whole. Here the pageantry is so lavish as to beggar description—the golden ornaments and emblems; the ornate palanquin in which the chief is carried to the market-place, as his drums, sounding rhythms of praise to his ancestors, precede and follow him; the great lavishly ornamented state umbrellas, twirled by their dancing bearers; and the throngs of subjects in their colorful cloths that, excluded from the rituals inside the compound of the chief, line the route and crowd the market-place where dancing societies from many outlying villages and towns compete for the ruler's approbation. It may be argued with cogency that this rite is secular, since it is an integral part of native political life, with equal validity that it is religious, in that it figures in the ancestral cult. But it is of the essence of ancestral rites that secular dances and songs figure prominently, and improvisation is encouraged as a special prerogative of the powerful dead. The student of the drama, naturally, does not make such a problem his primary concern. Yet it is of some importance, if only because the accepted position tends to focus attention on religious rites to the exclusion of secular ones.

Secular drama, it is true, customarily takes on humbler forms than religious performances. There is less pageantry, a smaller group; yet drama it nonetheless is. Let us return to the field of folklore, and take as an instance an evening of story-telling in a West Indian village. The setting is the hut of some member of the community, in front of which the story-teller and his audience, many of them children, sit about in dim lamp light or in the brilliance of the moon. "Cric-crac!" begins the leader, and points to some member of the group who "pulls a riddle," demanding an answer from his neighbor. The session is fairly begun, and after the riddling those who do not know the answers pay their penalties in tales they must tell. One story concerns the spider-trickster Anansi, and perhaps recounts how, because of him, knowledge spread over the world; or how he got the best of a larger but duller-witted comrade; or how, as in the Tar Baby tale, he paid the penalty for his misdeeds.

As the story unfolds, the teller acts out each detail of the developing plot. His voice becomes high and whining when the trickster, in difficulty, pleads with those who can, to aid him; it is stern when the victor in a contest speaks. But the audience, whites of wide-open eyes gleaming, is more than audience. The tale is broken by exclamations, and from time to time a song sung by one of the characters enters—a song which the audience, now fully participating, carries as a chorus to the solo of the story-teller. It is an humble occasion, but it has all the elements of theatre; the story furnishes the plot, and the acting is superb. Properties only are lacking, but they are no more needed than by the *diseuse*, who holds her audience with a monologue despite the bareness of the platform on which she stands.

3

One further point is to be made concerning the drama in nonliterate societies. If the unified character of life there has made drama an integral part of the daily round, this fact has, by the same token, joined manifestations of the dramatic art the more firmly to other artistic forms. Song, dance, myth, poem —all these are integrated closely in performances of primitive peoples when they worship their gods, bury their dead, marry, or celebrate other events in their life cycle. Just as poetry exists only as the words to music, and music and words are essential parts of the dance, so all these contribute in giving to the dramatic performances of nonliterate folk their aesthetic appeal and artistic validity.

The Aspects of Culture

We have numerous instances of the poetry with which drama is embellished; two examples may be taken from the rituals of the West African Dahomeans. The first is from rites for the Earth God, the second from a funeral ceremony.[4]

> Thy need is great,
> And great our need to sing,
> For days of trouble are upon us.
> The bullock of Abomey
> Says to him of Cana,
> It is the day of trouble;
> The carrier of grain,
> Says to the bearer of salt,
> Thy load is heavy, brother,
> And this the day for carrying;
> The bearer of the dead
> Says to the carrier of ladders,
> It is the day for carrying loads,
> It is the day of trouble.
>
>   ❋   ❋
>
> *Leader*: Do not weep,
> Nothing stays Death
> Nor the day of its coming.
>
> *Chorus*: Death troubles us—o!
> Death troubles us.
>
> As the flies fret our backs,
> Returning, and returning,
>
> So Death troubles us—o!
> Death troubles us.
>
> As the pigeons alight
> On a housetop,
> And dance, and dance,
>
> So Death dances—o!
> Death dances.
>
> Ai—yo!
> Ai—yo—o!

In addition to music, poetry, and dance, moreover, we must not forget the contributions of the graphic and plastic arts to the drama of nonliterate groups—the variety of masks, of costumes in all forms and of all kinds of materials, of other paraphernalia of various sorts. All these are used in combination with other art forms, and do their part in carrying on the action and providing the setting that make drama of the total performance.

---

[4] F. S. Herskovits, 1934, p. 76 and 1935, p. 95; reprinted by permission.

Drama and Music

4

THE comparative study of the music of peoples outside the stream of Euro-american culture, on a scientific, objective basis has had to wait on the development of mechanical recording devices. The significance of this fact, however, transcends its status as an item in the history of the development of anthropological musicology or, as it is generally termed, comparative musicology. For its implications lead us to some of the most fundamental truths about the nature and functioning of culture, and suggest the importance of the contribution that investigations carried on in this special field can make to the study of culture as a whole.

The music of non-European peoples has, actually, long attracted the attention of travellers and others who have had occasion to hear it. In the eighteenth century, for example, the African explorer Mungo Park set down and published some of the songs he heard among the peoples of the Senegal River area in which he travelled. Folk-music of European groups, of American Indians and Negroes has been copied down and made available in this form to those interested in it. Yet today we know that transcriptions of non-European music are only approximations of the songs and rhythms actually heard by those who note them down. We hear, no less than we produce, music in terms of very subtle conditionings that make up our musical enculturation.

It is an interesting exercise for one who hears a melody that is from a musical tradition not his own to attempt to reproduce it. The greater his musical training, the less he will succeed; for, quite unconsciously he will translate it into his own idiom. This can easily be proved if one will listen to a recording of an African or American Indian song, playing it several times to memorize it. Then it should be sung for several days, without reference to the recording, before playing the record again. It will be found that the song as then sung, whether in tonal progression or in rhythm, has turned into something quite different from the original.

It is only the recording phonograph that can render a song as it is actually sung, or catch the rhythmic complexities of a musical style dominated by rhythm rather than melody. The standard notation of Euroamerican music in terms of the eight-note scale with a series of accidentals that allows no place, let us say, for quarter-tones, results in the need for special adaptations before it can even begin to permit the transcription of music in modes where finer intervals are the rule. Our relatively simple system of time-signatures, with fixed measures, is less than satisfactory when, for example, a piece on the xylophone must be set down that has a 4/4 beat in the left hand and a 5/4 in the right, making a "measure" that is more than we are trained to carry as a unit.

Euroamerican music, as a matter of fact, is almost unique in the stress it lays on pitch. This has resulted from the predominance of mechanically tuned instruments, such as the piano, which always plays true to pitch when properly tuned. This conditions us, whether we produce music or listen to it, to react in terms of notes that stand in a fixed relation to each other. The importance we attach to proper intonation where deviation from a fixed tone is possible, as in singing or in playing the violin, is only the most obvious aspect of this tradition. In most cultures, not only is singing in a fixed key not the rule, but deviation from true pitch causes the listeners no discomfort. That is, the intervals of a song are relatively, not absolutely, the same when different singers render it, or the same performer repeats it. On different occasions, when the song begins on a still different note, it will be transposed from key to key without difficulty.

Differences in tonal values make up only one element in musical style that renders it difficult for those trained in the music of one culture to appreciate, or comprehend that of another. Thus, our music is polyphonic in conception. An orchestra, a band, a choir, is made up of units, each of which plays or sings in such a way that at a given moment the sounds made by all will be in harmony, as we term it. These sounds will be separated from each other by intervals, culturally determined, that by definition are within the range of differences that notes heard at one time may have. From this derive the various degrees of manipulation of thematic materials—that is, of tunes—which lead to the elaborations of the developmental sections in symphonies, and outstandingly in that most sophisticated musical expression of our culture, the fugue.

These manipulations are analogous to the way a painter or a wood-carver or any other artist plays with his medium, to produce works of supreme beauty because of his supreme technical competence. Yet a listener from a culture where polyphony is unknown will not even hear the shadings of harmony; or if he does hear them, they will be but a confusing jumble of sounds that obscures the single melodic line he searches for. Even more subtle to distinguish are the ways in which a note is attacked—cleanly, as we demand, or with a slur, something which we dislike even when we are not conscious why we react as we do.

Let us return for a moment to the point of the simplicity of our rhythms. In Euroamerican music, beats are regular and phrases are short. As von Hornbostel has said, the syncope, where emphasis lies on the off-beat (one-*and*, two-*and*, etc., instead of *one*-and, *two*-and, etc. as in a march-tune), an African commonplace, is a European achievement. We count in two, three, four, six, eight, and occasionally, where beats are rapid and units of time small, in twelve, as in 12/16 time, which in essence reduces itself to 3/4. Many other possibilities remain that we do not utilize at all. Those conversant with symphonic literature will think of the difficulties of counting 5/4 time, as in one of the Tschaikowsky symphonies, and which for many resolves itself into 2/4 and 3/4 counts.

A simple test of this, too, may be made by anyone. We are all familiar with the way we divide into units—"measures"—a steady beat, like the ticking of a clock, or the click of the wheels of a train on the rails. It is interesting to try to break down this regular beat into units of five rather than three ("waltz-time") or four ("march-time"). It is difficult, but it can be done. But then, this accomplished, one should next try to hear this regular beat as though it

Drama and Music

were separated into units of *seven*. In most cases, it will soon either slip into units of six or eight, or if by resolution we hold to sevens, it will become a combination of threes and fours. The next step is even more difficult. When one has trained himself to hear units of seven, then he should make up some tune to go with this rhythm—that is, a tune that would have the time-signature of 7/4 or 7/8. This, it has been found, will, in Euroamerican culture, frustrate all but the most determined experimenter, who is willing to give much time to the reconditioning process necessary.

Yet, there are many cultures, notably those of Africa, where rhythm is the essence of the music rather than melody. Here melody can often best be thought of as accessory to the rhythmic structure rather than otherwise. Even so astute a student of non-European cultures as Boas, writing as late as 1938, could state that "the all-important element of music is tonality, the use of fixed intervals that may be transposed from one point of the tone series to another and which are always recognized as equivalent." [5] Except by definition, however, music must be thought of as including rhythm as well as tone. Music styles are found where polyrhythms are the counterpart of the polyphony of Euroamerican music, where drums are more important than singers; where voice quality is of little significance, but alertness to rhythmic details paramount; where the drummer, not the singer, is recognized as the virtuoso musician. Except in jazz, which is derived from a non-European source, and represents the reworking of an African idiom, drum solos are practically unknown in Euroamerican music. In Africa, however, they are an appreciable element in the tribal musical repertory, and hold such a place in the musical tradition that in the New World they are everywhere a part of Afroamerican music and its derivatives, such as jazz.

The importance of rhythm in nonliterate societies is reflected in the relative number of instruments that are used for percussion as against the number employed to carry melody. One may almost say that for melody to be carried by other than the voice is the exception rather than the rule. Not only this, but melody in these societies is relatively simple. It is not quite true, as some students of comparative musicology have claimed, that the music of "primitive" peoples is marked by an absence of part-singing. There are enough instances on record to demonstrate the presence of sustained singing in stated intervals, and thus to refute so sweeping an assertion. But the statement is true in so many cases that it is easy to understand how the principle was reached. Unison singing is thus the rule, rather than the exception.

To accompany song with an instrument that is played to complement the melody enunciated by the singer, as a piano does, is, however, rare in nonliterate societies. When musical instruments are played while singers sing, they either "accompany" the song by emphasizing its rhythmic qualities, or play in unison with the singer. Whether or not it is this emphasis on rhythm that has given rise to the dance cannot be said, but rhythm and dance are inseparable. The dance, however, is an art-form impossible even to discuss in a work such as this, until a systematic approach to it has been devised and ap-

---

[5] F. Boas, 1938, p. 602.

437

plied on a comparative basis. Until then, only general statements can be made such as the one we have just made, and a note recorded of the universality, variety, and complexity of the dance among nonliterate groups.

The great number of musical instruments that have been devised by non-literate peoples can only be discussed briefly here. They can be classified into the categories with which we are familiar—string, wind, and percussion, of which the first have the most restricted distribution and the fewest types, the last the greatest number of different forms and the widest spread. Stringed instruments, found aboriginally only in the Old World, may be plucked or played with a bow, and are provided with some resonating device to amplify the resulting weak sound. These devices may take the form of calabash or wooden attachments to the instrument; the chest of the player will also serve the purpose. The musical bow, a single string plucked with one hand while the other varies the length of the portion permitted to vibrate and thus pro-duce changes in pitch, is the simplest form of stringed instrument; more com-plex forms are harps and lyres.

Wind instruments include various kind of flutes, flageolets, and trumpets. They are made of different materials—wood, horn, bamboo, bone, pottery—and are capable of sounding one note, as in the case of the trumpet, or to make melody, as in the instance of the flute. Instruments of this latter cate-gory are of great use to musicologists, especially when they are made of ma-terials that permit their preservation in archaeological sites. For they indicate, as no other means could, the scale and intervals characteristic of the musical patterns of peoples long dead, and thus yield at least some clues concerning earlier aspects of this most intangible phase of culture.

Wind instruments are not always employed for musical purposes alone. The trumpet, particularly, is widely used for signalling. Where a language has semantic patterns of tone and stress, it joins the drums in transmitting messages. Forms of wind instruments such as the nose-flute of the South Seas require the use of techniques different from any method known to Euroameri-can culture. Pan-pipes, that have Old and New World distributions, likewise require special technical ability, since it is essential to blow over them, rather than in them. Here melody is achieved by using pipes of different length to obtain different tones.

Between tonal and percussion instruments are various "transitional" forms. One such is the xylophone (marimba); another the aggregates of bells hav-ing different tones. In this transition category the "African piano" or *sanza* is noteworthy. This is an instrument having strips of metal of different lengths suspended over a resonator in such a way that each, as its end is pressed and released by the thumb, gives off a different note.

Even when we consider purely percussion types, such as the drum, the ele-ment of tonality is by no means entirely lacking. African hollow-log drums, headed with skins, are tuned, and if struck different types of blows, at differ-ent places on the drum-head, as many as four distinct tones can be produced by a single drum. The wooden slit-drum of the Congo basin and, perhaps de-rivatively of the Amazon, gives various tones, also depending on where it is struck. Besides drums, rhythms are produced by rattles, by beads worn on the ankles of a dancer, by calabashes or wooden blocks with striations cut in them over which a stick is rubbed or, most simply and universally, by hand-clapping.

It is apparent that the music of nonliterate peoples is far from the simple phenomenon it was for so many years held to be. The difference between the musical culture of such peoples and that of ourselves is not as much one of difference in means or complexity of expression, as it is in the extent to which it is a subject for analysis on the part of those who compose, perform, or listen to it. In this the musical parts of our culture, like so many other parts, reflect the degree of specialization that we have seen to result from population size, economic productivity, and complexity of technological equipment. As Herzog has stated it, the musical theory of nonliterate groups comprehends "comparatively few analytical statements and a modest technical vocabulary. . . . The units distinguished by primitives are not as minute as ours. They are apt to differentiate music according to general differences in the melodic and rhythmic configuration, which in turn tend to become connected with differences in usage and social function. They are, however, very concise and definite when it comes to questions which we are at some loss to answer: the origin and ultimate meaning of music."[6]

Now that the mechanical devices necessary for the adequate recording of unwritten music have been developed, and a more effective analysis of this music has thus been rendered possible, the student of culture can use these materials as he has employed the patterns of language in his study of human behavior. Music, like language, has basic structural forms that are only re-vealed after their manifestations in the everyday life of a people are objec-tively investigated. On analysis, however, they go far in disclosing the cul-tural factors, in both pattern and process, out of which they take on their as-cribed form and meaning. This will be seen in later pages, where musical and linguistic materials will be used in considering hypotheses of cultural dy-namics. Everywhere man sings, and in singing experiences the satisfactions that go with all forms of self-expression. But in singing, too, he all unwittingly provides precious data by the use of which the student of culture, transmut-ing artistic expression into scientific analysis, can extend our knowledge and understanding of the life of man.

---

[6] G. Herzog, 1938, p. 5.

CHAPTER 26

Language, the Vehicle of Culture

THE nature and social functioning of language is indicated in the following definition: *A language is a system of arbitrary vocal symbols by which members of a social group coöperate and interact.*[1] This signifies that in its organization it is regular and not haphazard—that is, it is a system; and that as a series of symbols its meanings must be learned as must all other cultural phenomena. The definition, however, stresses the social functions of language. So that the full significance of language as an aspect of culture may be grasped, we therefore add the phrase, "... *and by means of which the learning process is effectuated and a given way of life achieves both continuity and change.*"

Without language, the accumulations of knowledge that mark off human from other animal aggregates could not have developed or have been maintained. Through language man has been able to devise, continue, and change the great variety of cultural institutions of a material and nonmaterial nature we have seen he possesses. If a phenomenon has cultural relevance, it is because it holds *meaning* in thought and in behavior. This, in turn, is because men have the linguistic equipment to grasp and express its significance. The importance of language in furthering the creative aspects of culture is obvious. There is much reason, furthermore, to believe that the very nature of reality itself, as conceived by a people, is a reflection of the categories of their thought, that stem from their linguistic usages.

It comes as a surprise to the novice in the study of speech that language is not instinctive. It should not, however, surprise those who have assimilated the point of view and facts about culture in general found in the preceding pages. Undoubtedly, many individual acts of speaking *seem* instinctive, as when we emit cries of great emotion under stress. Furthermore, are not the organs we use, in uttering the sounds by which we communicate, a part of our biological equipment? Do we not employ them *because* they are there, in the same way we react to hunger, or draw air into our lungs?

An analogy can be drawn between language and man's tool-using propensities. Upright stance and the release of the anterior extremities as grasping organs have made it possible for man to use tools. Yet we have seen that we are hardly justified, for that reason, in saying that the tools man does use de-

---

[1] E. H. Sturtevant, 1947, p. 2.

rive from a "tool-using instinct." The variety of tools he uses, and above all the fact that he must learn to use the tools put into his hands by those of his society who have preceded him, make any assumption of inherent aptitude untenable. So with language—and so, it need not be repeated, with culture as a whole.

The forms of any speech-system, it must also be emphasized, have no relation to structural peculiarities that mark off the physical characteristics of those who employ it. Any human being can make any sound, or fashion any combination of sounds, that any other person can make, no matter what his racial affiliation. He can, that is, provided he is given the opportunity to do so, and particularly if he has this opportunity at an early enough age. Linguistic reconditioning is not easy, as anyone who as an adult has to master a new tongue, can testify.

It is quite likely, indeed, that this difficulty of linguistic reconditioning has more than any other fact led to the conception of the physical basis of linguistic differences. Yet whether lips be thick or thin, noses be broad or narrow, every sound made in any language is within any individual's range of possible use. The process is no different than that of learning any other phase of a new technique that involves the use of muscles. The motor behavior employed in weaving on a new sort of loom must be re-learned just as, on an infinitely more delicate scale, the muscles of the tongue must be re-trained to make new sounds. A new concept, a new grammatical structure, likewise require reorientation. These readjustments may be difficult, but they can be, and are, made.

2

For purposes of study, every language is to be divided into three parts. The first consists of its sounds, and makes up its phonemic system. The second is the combinations of sounds into units that have distinct significance, its vocabulary. The third is the manner in which these sound-combinations are themselves combined and recombined into larger units, and is what is ordinarily meant when we speak of grammar. There is no system of speech that lacks any of these.

The complexities implied by a general statement of this sort are not easy to grasp by one who knows only his own language, or even those who have had contact with several of the various written languages of Europe and America. The range of sounds, of combinations of sounds, of structured grammatical forms is so vast that no single language represents more than a small proportion of possible modes of speech.

This is simplest to discern in the case of vocabulary, for everyone recognizes without difficulty that there are languages he cannot understand, since the words used in them differ from those he employs. He soon discovers that not only must he learn new combinations of sounds to convey meaning to those whose speech is different from his own, but that he must also accustom himself to using his speech organs in ways he had hitherto not used them, if he is to pronounce the words so they will be recognized. The nasalized -*ão* of Portuguese, the umlauted *ü* of German, the "soft" Russian *l* or the Polish voiceless *ł* are examples of this, just as is *th* of English, with which non-English speakers have so great difficulty.

The task of achieving proper grammatical expression in a new tongue is equally trying. The Brazilian must think carefully lest he say, in English, "How many years do you have?" instead of "How old are you?" And this, it must be realized, is a simple adjustment compared to what is necessary when a person even of some linguistic sophistication steps outside the historic grouping to which his own tongue belongs. Here he must master forms that not only have no counterpart in his previous linguistic experience, but differ from any forms he has ever heard of. In the new language sex gender may be absent, or the tense system may designate near and distant periods of the past or future, or a word may be split by an infix, instead of using a prefix or a suffix to indicate a change in its meaning.

Like any other aspect of culture, languages are to be studied both from the point of view of form and of function. The former type of analysis, which inquires what language *is*, has the importance the study of form holds in any other phase of culture. Its significance in this respect is heightened, however, by the fact that the forms of speech are so deeply imbedded in the habits of people that they afford especially good materials for the study of the objective manifestations of culture as a whole. Most studies of language are concerned with linguistic form, whether they be conventional analyses of written tongues, or are based on field research among peoples who do not have writing.

The second approach, which is concerned primarily with what language *does*, presents considerable difficulties of method. This approach includes what one student has termed, "the conception of speech as a mode of action, and not merely of expression. . . ." [2] It is what Sapir meant when he characterized "the fundamental ground-work of language" not only as "the development of a clear cut phonetic system," but also "the specific association of speech elements with concepts, and the delicate provision for the formal expression of all manner of relations." [3] It is to be regarded as one of the outstanding accomplishments of anthropological linguistics that emphasis has been laid by it on function, no less than on the study of forms that for so many years dominated the study of language.

Of similar import is the concept, advanced by Bloomfield, of the *speech-community*—a "group of people who interact by means of speech." [4] The speech-community, Bloomfield holds, "is the most important kind of social group," since "all the so-called higher activities of man—our specifically human activities—spring from the close adjustment among individuals which we call society, and this adjustment, in turn, is based upon language." Speech-communities vary enormously in size, and merge sometimes imperceptibly into one another, as in the case of minor dialectic differences, such

---

[2] Grace A. de Laguna, 1927, p. 21, note.
[3] E. Sapir, 1921, p. 22.
[4] L. Bloomfield, 1933, p. 42.

as mark off the speech of the South from that of the Middle West in the United States.

They can be special-interest groups, based on class or occupation, as well as represent geographic differences. It is in terms of the differing usages of speech-communities that changes in languages and the development of dialects are coming to be interpreted. These dialectic differences, in turn, form the basis for more comprehensive divergences which, with time, become the separate languages, which linguists group as *language families*. English, for example, represents a development parallel to that of Dutch, German, Swedish, and Danish, all of which stem from a common Germanic base. This earlier Germanic language, in turn, was related to the forerunners of the Slavic, Romance, and Celtic groups of tongues; and all these point to a still earlier language, known as Indo-European.

3

THE study of the sound-making devices of the human organs of speech, their functioning, and of their total range of sounds, is called *phonetics*. In the case of a given language, the significant sounds, which are combined to convey meaning, are called *phonemes*. It is apparent that this aspect of the study of language is basic, and represents a point of departure in all linguistic work. In a sense, too, analysis of the phonemic structure of a given speech-system is one of the most revealing phases of linguistic research, especially as it holds significance for the study of culture. We need only refer to the contributions the early students, who instituted the systematic analysis of related languages, made through their research into the Indo-European tongues. Through the comparative study of sound-shifts it was possible to discover historic relationships between tongues as seemingly different from each other as Russian and English. This, in turn, forced a reconsideration of the entire problem of the processes at work in the development, through contact, of the cultures of Europe and the areas which contributed to them.

To comprehend how wide is the range of possibilities in any phase of linguistic expression we must, however, broaden our perspective and move outside the literate societies. Only by doing this can we realize, here as in other aspects of culture, how man can use differing means to achieve the same ends. The fact of linguistic variability is blurred for us because, for one thing, the symbols used in writing are conventionalized approximations of phonemes rather than representations of them. In English, for example, the symbol *a* stands for sounds as different as the *a* in f*a*r, in h*a*t, in c*a*me, in *a*bove. Not only that, but the same phoneme can be represented by different letter-symbols, as, for instance, the *a* in f*a*r, which is the same phoneme as the *o* in Midwestern h*o*t. The series given by Bloomfield makes the point. "The words *oh, owe, so, sew, sow, hoe, beau, though* all end with the same phoneme, variously represented in writing; the words *though, bough, through, cough, tough, hiccough* end with different phonemes but are all written with the letters -*ough*." [5]

---

[5] L. Bloomfield, *op. cit.*, p. 85.

The Aspects of Culture

In the scientific study of language, special symbols are used so that each sound-unit has its particular sign. This permits the student, whether he is studying a new tongue or a local dialect, to approximate the sounds of speech closely enough so that a trained linguist, reading these signs, can reproduce sound combinations quite accurately in pressing his analyses or comparing the speech-habits of different groups. This is particularly important in studies of linguistic geography represented by the dialect-atlases that have been compiled of many European countries, and for certain regions in the United States.

A simple exercise will show how a certain group of the sounds we conceive as separate and distinct, the vowels, are actually no more than points on a continuous scale. First purse the lips so as to sound a *u* as in yo*u*. Then, expelling the breath and continuously activating the vocal cords, gradually open the mouth through *o* as in h*o*pe until a broad *a* as in f*a*r is reached. Continue the process, extending the corners of the mouth to attain *e* as in th*e*y until the phoneme *i*, the *ee* of f*ee*t is heard. Finally return slowly to the pursed lip position through the German *ü* until the original *u* is once more being pronounced.

These stopping-points can be indicated on a vowel chart that represents our progression:

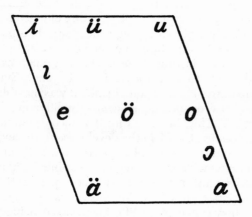

Such stopping points, however, are quite arbitrary. In the actual speech of any group, many minor variants of these points are found, most of which are ignored by those who speak a given language. Try once again to run the gamut of sounds, but stop halfway between *o* and *a*. It will be found that a sound results that we indicate by the *au* in c*au*ght but that students of language write ɔ. About half-way between the *a* and the *e* we reach *a* as in h*a*t, which phoneticians denote by the symbol *ä*. Between *e* and *i* lies ι, the sound made when the word h*i*t is pronounced. Still another progression, ignoring the full opening of *a*, produces the sequence *o→ö→e*, the middle term being one foreign to English, but heard in Scandinavian tongues. With practice, finer shadings can be pronounced, at will; and linguists have found that many of those sounds have significance—that is, have phonemic value—in

Language, the Vehicle of Culture

languages which, in turn, disregard some of the points on the progression we utilize.

Vowels are produced by permitting the air expelled from our lungs, that actuates the vocal chords, to flow through the mouth unimpeded by tongue or glottis. When the breath is obstructed, we produce the sounds classified as consonants. They, too, have a range that extends far beyond the usage of any single speech-system. They are customarily classified under one of five headings. First are the stops, made when the stream is halted for an instant. If the vocal cords are actuated, then voiced stops such as *b* or *d* result; if not, then corresponding voiceless sounds, in these cases *p* or *t* are heard. Another category is made up of the fricatives, or spirants, sounded when the breath comes through a narrow passage. Voiced sounds in this class would include *v* and *z*, whose unvoiced correspondences are *f* and *s*. Trills are exemplified by the rolled *r*, familiar in Latin tongues, usually voiced; laterals by *l*; and nasals by *m* and *n* and their variants. These may be voiced or unvoiced; in Indo-European languages, however, only voiced forms of them are significant.

Other phonemic elements exist that are not included in the above categories. Outstanding is the group comprised by the "clicks" of the Bushman and Hottentot languages of South Africa. These differ from all other phonemes of human speech in that they are made by creating a vacuum in the mouth, into which the air is introduced, making a sharp sound. When they employ the lips, a kissing-like sound results. When the middle part of the tongue is pressed against the palate and released, a sound much like the reproachful one we have in mind when we write "tut, tut" is obtained. The tip of the tongue, held against the middle palate and quickly released makes a third, while mid-tongue and mid-palate combine in the sound used to urge on a horse. How complicated the resulting phonetic combinations of this language can be becomes apparent when it is realized that these clicks join with other consonants, and vowels, voiced and unvoiced, nasalized and free from nasalization in differing pitch-registers, to form the words it uses to convey its meanings.

This by no means tells the entire story. Devices such as the glottal stop are of paramount importance in Polynesian tongues—that is, the separation of the vowels pronounced when a mother reproves her infant by exclaiming "A-a-a-a!" The name of the island Hawaii, pronounced *Hawaya* on the American mainland, is actually *Hawai'i* (the apostrophe standing for the stopped breath after the diphthong *ai*). The mainland pronunciation, *Hawaya,* indicates what happens to such a form in a speech-community where the glottal stop is not the rule; where stops only occur when two words that begin and end with the same consonant, as in the phrase *this ' song*, must be pronounced separately. Stress and duration and tone are other phonemic elements. The initial consonant *s* in the combination *sō*, in the Kru language of Liberia gives it the meaning "two"; but when the *s* is prolonged, the word *s·ō* means "to be rotten." In Ibo, another African language, the word *ákwá,* in which each vowel is pronounced with high pitch, means "cry"; when the first vowel is high and the second low (*ákwà*) it means "cloth"; first low and second high (*àkwá*) is "egg"; while both low (*àkwà*) signifies "bridge."

Thus we see how different languages use different series of sounds and accessory devices to build up the sound-clusters to which are assigned specific meanings. We also see how each series represents, in its totality, only a selection of the possibilities presented by the vocal equipment of human beings. This leads us to two salient facts about the phonemic system of every language, *consistency* and *limitation*. Boas has phrased the point in this manner: "One of the most important facts relating to the phonetics of human speech is that every single language has a definite and limited group of sounds, and that the number of those used in any particular dialect is never excessively large." [6] Both principles are essential if the function of language as a means of communication is to be served. This is why we encounter the phenomenon of standardization that enables the hearer to disregard the minor idiosyncracies of individual pronunciation, and "hear" only in terms of the limited number of sounds that, with a consistency nothing but disciplined analysis can reveal, make the exquisite pattern we call a language.

4

WHAT is a word? The question seems simple enough, until one begins to analyze it. Then it becomes apparent that the forms that may be conventionally taken as words by the speakers of a language, by no means necessarily appear so to a person ignorant of it. Take the summons "Come here," as an example. Here we have two clearly differentiated complexes of phonemes, one meaning motion toward, the other the place at which the speaker stands. Suppose, however, a foreign student of American English, who was analyzing this language only in its spoken forms, was to set this phrase down in his notebook after the manner of those who make field analyses of unwritten tongues. It would without doubt find its place in his notebook as *kumír*, in which form it looks like a word, and could be treated as one. The actual instance may be cited of the puzzled Brazilian visitor who, while in the United States, asked an American friend what the word *filidúp* meant. "I know that when I drive up to a gasolene station and use it, I get a tank-full of gasolene. But I have never been able to find it in a dictionary," he explained.

How to divide the flow of sounds is one of the very real difficulties in learning to understand a foreign language. Conversely, a person who speaks a new language marks himself as a beginner by failing to elide at the proper places. Each unit is carefully set off from the preceding and the succeeding one, so that his speech is formal, and stiff, and unpleasant to follow. Not until he is proficient can he run word into word as do its native speakers—not until then, as we say, does he become fluent in it. When he does become fluent to this extent, the problem of understanding the elisions of those with whom he talks is solved, for he separates their words just as his listeners separate his elisions into their component parts.

Various definitions of the concept "word" have been advanced. Boas has defined a word as "a phonetic group which, owing to its permanence of form,

---

[6] F. Boas, 1911, p. 16.

clearness of significance, and phonetic independence, is readily separated from the whole sentence." [7] There are many languages, however, in which we come upon combinations of phonemes that look like words but are what we would term sentences, despite the fact that in the whole complex there is no element that can stand alone any more than can the English suffix *-ed* which means "time past" (*depart, depart-ed*).

Some examples of these "word-sentences" will make the point clear. A good one has been given by Boas himself, in the very discussion that follows the definition we have cited. This is the Chinook Indian "word"—for it is so termed by Boas—*aniā'lōt*. It means "I give him to her," and is to be broken down into the following elements: *a* (tense), *n* I, *i* him, *ā* her, *l* to, *ō* (direction away), *t* to give. As he phrases it, here "the weakness of the component elements and their close phonetic association forbid us to consider them independent words; while the whole expression appears to us as a firm unit." [8] A combination in the Polynesian language spoken by the inhabitants of the Tuomotu group of islands has a similar character. Here, the complex *'i'āiai'ai'āia'i* signifies "that fish already mentioned was thoroughly cooked before it was eaten." It is to be analyzed as follows: *'i* was, *'ā* well cooked, *ia* that thing already mentioned, *i'a* fish, *i* was, *'āi* eat, *ā'* (past tense), *i* therefore.

Sapir gives an example from the language of the Paiute Indians of Utah. *Wii-to-kuchum-punku-rügani-yugwi-va-ntü-m(ü)* means "they who are going to sit up and cut up with a knife a black cow (or bull)." In the order of its elements, its literal translation is: "knife-black-buffalo-pet-cut up-sit (plur.)-future-participle-animate plur." Sapir, however, raises the question whether this really is a word in the sense we think of the term; or, by implication, whether any combination of this sort can be comprehended under such a definition as that given by Boas. "In truth," he says, "it is impossible to define the word from a functional standpoint at all, for the word may be anything from the expression of a single concept—concrete or abstract or purely relational (as in *of* or *by* or *and*)—to the expression of a complete thought (as in Latin *dico* 'I say' or, with greater elaborateness of form, in a Nootka verb form denoting 'I have been accustomed to eat twenty round objects [e.g., apples] while engaged in [doing so and so]'). In the latter case the word becomes identical with the sentence." [9]

The functional units of speech, Sapir concludes, are the "radical (or grammatical) element and sentence, . . . the former as an abstracted minimum, the latter as the esthetically satisfying embodiment of a unified thought." "We may put the whole matter in a nutshell," he goes on to say, in clarifying his approach, "by saying that the radical and grammatical elements of language, abstracted as they are from the realities of speech, correspond to the conceptual world of science, abstracted as it is from the realities of experience, and that the word, the existent unit of living speech, responds to the unit of actually apprehended experience, of history, of art. The sentence is

---

[7] *Ibid.*, p. 28.
[8] *Ibid.*, p. 29.
[9] E. Sapir, *op. cit.*, pp. 32–3.

the logical counterpart of the complete thought only if it is to be felt as made up of the radical and grammatical elements that lurk in the recesses of its words. It is the psychological counterpart of experience, of art, when it is felt, as indeed it normally is, as the finished play of word with word. As the necessity of defining thought solely and exclusively for its own sake becomes more urgent, the word becomes increasingly irrelevant as the means. We can therefore easily understand why the mathematician and the symbolic logician are driven to discard the word and to build up their thought with the help of symbols which have, each of them, a rigidly unitary value." [10]

In addition to the "word," linguists have adopted the concept of the "morpheme" in analyzing language. The morpheme, which is the unit of linguistic form, consists of one or more units of sound (phonemes) plus a unit of meaning. Two important types of morphemes are recognized, "free morphemes" which can be used alone, like words, and "bound morphemes" such as prefixes and suffixes, which "are genuine linguistic forms and convey a meaning, but . . . occur only in construction, as part of a larger form." [11] Bound morphemes are never used as sentences. Examples of them are to be found in the -ess in "countess," or the -ish in "greenish," or the -s in "hats," while in the same words "count," "green" and "hat" are free morphemes, since they can be and are used separately. The difficulties of analyzing the word-sentences cited above from Chinook, Tuomotu, Paiute, and Nootka disappear when the unit of analysis is the morpheme, which does not necessarily have the "phonetic independence" usually attributed to a word.

Following this type of analysis, it is possible to define a word as "a minimum free form," or "a free form which does not consist entirely of (two or more) lesser free forms." [12] In terms of this definition, words are to be classed as secondary and primary, each having two sub-types. Secondary words are compound or derived. Compound words, such as "hat-rack" have more than one free morpheme, since both "hat" and "rack" are susceptible of independent use. Derived secondary words are composed of one free morpheme and one or more bound morphemes, as in "boy-ish." Primary words are those that do not contain a free morpheme in combination with bound morphemes. They may be "morpheme-words," such as "man," "boy," "cat," "run," or "see," where the word is identical with the morpheme; or derived primary words which are composed of two or more bound morphemes, such as "receive" or "re-tain." [13]

Word-structure is so basic in linguistic study that it has been set up as the criterion for one of the most widely employed systems of language classification that has been devised by linguists, that counts languages as isolating, agglutinative, inflective, and polysynthetic. Chinese exemplifies the first, where independent units merely follow each other as a series of concepts are expressed. An instance of a word from a so-called isolating tongue would be namímanawὲ, from the Fõn language of the African Sudanic family, which

[10] Ibid., pp. 33–4.
[11] L. Bloomfield, op. cit., pp. 177–8.
[12] Ibid., p. 207.
[13] Ibid., p. 209.

means "wife exchange." Broken down, it is found to consist of the following components: *na* give, *mí* us, *ma* we, *na* give, *wè* you—"give-us-we-give-you." Agglutinating languages bind these separate forms together in words that follow each other, or are used with prefixes and suffixes. In inflectional languages, meanings are changed by adding such elements as prefixes or suffixes to free forms, and include most Indo-European tongues. The polysynthetic languages are those in which ideas are expressed by synthesizing to an elaborate degree. Some American Indian tongues are assigned to this category, and the examples of "word-sentences" that have been given can be taken as illustrating the type. That this classification is no more satisfactory than others that have been set up on the basis of word-forms, or grammatical structures, or any other single aspect of language, is aside from the point. That point will be considered when the problem of classification on the basis of form as against process is treated in later pages. Here we merely mention this system to indicate the importance of word-formation in the study of language.

The devices that are employed to shade meaning vary greatly from language to language, but each follows well-marked and clearly patterned usage. English, for example, is rich in prefixes and suffixes, but does not use the infix, a phonetic combination that is inserted within a form to change its meaning. In Portuguese, for example, the future, third-person, singular of the verb *diser*, to say, is *dirá*. In this tense, the pronomial form is inserted between the syllables of the future verb, resulting in *dir-lhe-á*, "he will say to him." In the language of the Bontoc Igorot, of the Philippines, where *tengao* means "to celebrate a holiday," *tumengao-ak* (*t-um-engao-ak*) means "I shall have a holiday." In Sioux the verb *cheti* "to build a fire" gives *chewati* "I build a fire," in which the infix *-wa-* means "I."

Reduplication, though uncommon in English usage, is found in such forms as "so-so," or "boom-boom." It is more prevalent in the speech of English-speaking children who are not linguistically enculturated, as when "far, far" is used to indicate considerable distance. In the language of the Kwakiutl Indians reduplication regularly expresses the idea of occasional repetition of an action: *mēxa* "to sleep," *mēxmēxa* "to sleep now and then"; *hanꞭa* "to shoot," *hanꞭ-hanꞭa* "to shoot now and then." In the speech of the Saramacca Bush-Negroes, reduplication transforms a verb into a noun: *hesi* "to go fast," *hesihesi* "speed"; *nyam* "to eat," *nanyam* or *nyamnyam* "food."

Internal vowel changes are frequently used to alter meaning, such as "man—men" or "sing—sang" found in English. Consonantal change occurs much less often, but is occasionally employed in various tongues as where, in English, we pronounce "rise" with a *z* (*riz*) when it is used as a verb, and with a terminal *s* (*ris*) when we speak of "the rise of a statesman to power," employing the word as a noun.

"Significant tone," that involves the pronunciation of the same phonetic complex at different registers, is much more widely employed than is ordinarily thought. It may have both semantic and grammatical use, changing the meaning of a word or affording the basis for paradigm-systems. Chinese is the language most often thought of when tone is mentioned, but many American Indian tongues have significant tone, and most African languages are marked by pitch variation that gives them their "musical" character. In the language of the Shona of southern Africa, for example, *rudzí* (rising tone) is a "bark rope" while *rudzì* (falling tone) means "tribe"; *edzá* is "to try"; *edza* (even tones) signifies "fish." Other examples are *rambá* "to be sterile," *rambà* "refuse"; *chúro* "orphan," *churò* "have." In Zulu, a neighboring tongue, *ńyaga* means "moon," *nyàgà* "doctor."

5

ONLY when we are dealing with pure lexical changes are we concerned with words and nothing else. When we consider the differences between "man" and "men," however, we introduce the concept of number, which has to do with language-structure as well as change in meaning. The study of word-forms and of grammar, that is, differs from the analysis of the sounds of a language in that the sounds, by themselves, are meaningless, while words and combinations of words always convey meaning. Linguists have therefore come to distinguish the study of phonemics, on the one hand, from grammar. Grammar, in turn, is divided into *morphology*, which has to do with word-structure, and *syntax*, that is concerned with the manner in which words are combined into the larger groupings of phrases and sentences.

As with other aspects of culture, the syntactic constructions of a language seem to its speaker utterly obvious, logical, exclusive, and irrevocable. One's own language seems to offer the only possible series of valid categories by which experience can be interpreted and transmitted from person to person. Let us consider, however, the forms that the verb "to cut" can take in Kru, the Liberian tongue we have already mentioned. We can do this without reference to the native words, since we are here concerned with the categories, which can be given by the translations alone:

Present:
I cut now
I am through cutting just now
I am continuing to cut now
Recent Past:
I did cut a little while ago
I cut several times a little while ago
I kept on cutting a little while ago
I had the purpose in mind of cutting a little while ago, but didn't
Distant Past:
I did cut a long time ago
I cut several times a long time ago
I kept on cutting a long time ago
I had the purpose in mind of cutting a long time ago, but didn't
Near Future:
I will cut pretty soon
I will cut again and again pretty soon
I will keep on cutting pretty soon

Language, the Vehicle of Culture

Indefinite Future:
  I will cut in an indefinite time in the future
  I will cut again and again at an indefinite time in the future
  I will keep on cutting at an indefinite time in the future
Present Reflexive:
  I cut myself
  I am through cutting myself
  I am keeping on cutting myself
Recent Past Reflexive:
  I did cut myself a little while ago
  I cut myself several times a little while ago
  I kept on cutting myself a little while ago

It is apparent that the way action is conceived in this series of tenses and modes is quite different from English. Not only do we here encounter the past, present, and future familiar to us, but distance in time is also taken into account. Furthermore, it is specified whether action is continuing or intermittent, whether it is to take place at a given moment in the future or at an indefinite period; while, in one mode, intent is indicated. It is interesting to note that the reflexive of our verb is not represented by future forms. All attempts to obtain such forms failed, though they can, of course, be constructed by following the pattern for forming future tenses in other verbs. But the particular verb used as an example carries a connotation. It means "to cut," it is true, but intent is implied in it. Therefore, to the Kru, for a person to declare "I will cut myself intentionally"—the future reflexive— makes no sense, and is apparently not employed.

As another example of categories quite different from those to which we are accustomed, that function regularly, and with entire effectiveness, we may take certain verb-forms in the grammar of the Tübatulabal Indians of south-central California. Here every verb-stem has two forms. One, called the *telic*, "is used for an action (e.g., *to take a bite*) or condition (e.g., *it got green*) performed or arrived at in an instant, . . . and for this reason the action or condition is generally, though not necessarily, felt to be completed at the time of talking." The *telic* is usually a reduplicated form of the *atelic*, which is found only with suffixes or an auxiliary verb. The atelic "is sometimes used when an action requires some duration for its performance (*to eat*), but frequently the atelic is quite vague as to aspectual meaning." It is pointed out that "since the telic and atelic are the only basic forms of the verb, verbal notions regarding these aspects must be first of all squeezed into one category or another (telic or atelic) before the meaning of the verb is further defined by the optional categories of tense, mode, or even other aspects, such as the habituative, distributive, or iterative."

Of these complexities, let us consider the three aspects that have last been mentioned. Thus the verb "to dig" is *wac-* (atelic), *awac* (telic). *awaʹcini·ʹ- iniʹm* means "he dug first here, then there." *anañ-* (atelic), *nañ* (telic) means "to cry." *aʹnañi·ʹniʹnimu̧ʹt* signifies "he is crying wherever he goes," while *nañi·ʹniniʹm* has the significance "he cried out first here, then there." The habituative "bears a meaning of continued action of considerable extensity,

451

repeated in an habitual way." But it is circumscribed in its use, since it is only employed for past action, and to indicate a continuing past action "no longer performed habitually at the time of speaking." For example, *yo'-* (atelic) means "to be lame," so with the addition of the past habituative suffix -(*i*)*ukañ*, it becomes *yo·'"iuka'ñ*, "he used to be lame." Iteration is most often expressed by reduplicating the stem of the verb, or some portion of it. Thus *pic-* (atelic) is the verb "to go out"; *pica·'bica·'a't* means "he is going out repeatedly," *nu·l-* (atelic) signifies "to push"; *nu·ula't* is the form for "he is pushing him." *nu·'la'a't*, which reduplicates the -*a*- element in the verbal suffix, thus comes to mean "he is pushing him repeatedly." [14]

These verb-forms have been used to illustrate how differently ideas can be expressed. Similar ranges of difference, however, are to be found in all other forms of speech. Consider, for example, the demonstrative pronoun, which in English is found only as "this" and "that" (with their plurals). These really indicate "position-near" and "position-away." In the Bantu languages of the Congo, which we shall have occasion to mention later, there are three positions indicated. Thus *mo-nkanda mumu* in the speech of the Ngala tribe, means "this book (near to me, here)"; *mo-nkanda muna* indicates "that book (near you, there)"; while *mo-nkanda munowo* is "that book (there, yonder, previously mentioned)"—that is, in no special relation either to the speaker or the one addressed, except as to its distance from them. Further refinements of this are possible. In Tlingit, a language of the Northwest Coast of North America, *he* indicates an object very near and always present; *ya* one very near and present, but a little farther away; *yu* something still farther away, almost in the indefinite sense such as the English article "the chair," "a horse"; while *we* is used for something very remote and quite invisible.

Gender offers another example of variation in categories that seem fixed by experience which, to speakers of English, dictates distinctions drawn on the basis of sex. This is by no means the only type of gender-classification that can be made. The Sudanic languages of Africa have no words to express difference in sex, such as our pronouns "he," "she," "it." Sex must be specifically distinguished, in particular instances, by the use of different words, such as "father" or "mother," or by adding words for "male" or "female." How confusing the differentiation of sex in Indo-European tongues can be to one whose linguistic enculturation is to such a mode of speech is to be seen when a West African, speaking English, will say, "My sister, he is going to the market." But these same languages have forms that set the categories of "big" and "small," or distinguish between living and non-living beings, or between persons and things. This is like Fox, an American Indian language of Algonkian affiliation, where the rigid classification of experience into things animate and inanimate dominates all forms. Verb forms such as *pyä'w*a "he comes," *pyä'miga'tw*i "it comes" are familiar to us, and also the pronouns *in*ᵃ "he (an.)," *ïn'* "it (inan.)." But in this language *i'nig'* is "they (an.)" while *i'nin'* is "they (inan.)." The word for "dog" is *a'nemō'·ᵃ*. "My dog" is *ne't*ʌnemōhe'*m*ᵃ. "Rock" in this language is *a'sen'*; "my rock" becomes

[14] C. F. Voegelin, 1935, pp. 94–110.

netʌ'seni'm'. The final vowel, that is, is -a with animate possessed nouns, -i with inanimate.

Still another grammatical device, used by the many millions who inhabit the heart of the African continent and speak the Bantu languages, is its elaborate pattern of prefixing, which gives rise to the principles of *classification* and *concordance*. The prefixes indicate the place of a word in the classificatory system that includes all phenomena, drawn up in accordance with some descriptive criterion. Some of these classes include "human beings (males); trees and plants, wooden things and long objects; round, bulky objects, stones, and abstract nouns; leaves and fibres, with objects made from them, and flat, thin objects in general; boughs of trees; forked branches; human and animal extremities." [15] The word *bantu* itself illustrates the principle of classification; *ntu* means "a living thing," *mu-ntu* "a man," *ba-ntu* "people."

The operation of this principle of classification gives rise to the phenomenon of concordance. One of the first grammars written about the Bantu languages spoken in the Congo gives the following example:

> *Ma-kemba ma-na ma-tanu ma-lau ma-kwe*
> Plantain those five fine fell
> "Those five fine plantains fell down"

From the language spoken by the Baganda who inhabit Uganda (observe the principle of classification again at work in these names), Werner gives the following example:

Kikompe	*kyange*	*ki-menyese;*	*omu-ntu*	*ono*	*a-ki-menye*
Cup	my	it-is-broken;	man	this	he it has broken
"My large cup is broken;			this man has broken it."		

Under the principle of concordance, that is, every word in a phrase is related to the noun to which it refers by the prefix that precedes it.

Various numbers of prefixes have been recorded for various Bantu tongues, but it is safe to put the quantity for any given dialect at between fifteen and twenty. Their utility is increased, and their use made easier, by the fact that the normal Bantu word-stem is of two syllables, to which prefixes, suffixes, and on occasion infixes can be added to give subject-pronoun, tense, and object-pronoun. How much flexibility the use of suffixes gives can be seen from the following forms, which are derived from the verb *kang-a* "to tie": *kangema* "to be tied," *kangela* "to tie for, by," *kangana* "to tie each other," *kangia* "to cause to tie," *kangola* "to untie," *kangomela* "to be tied for," *kangenela* "to tie each other with," *kangolela* "to untie for" or "with," etc.

These are only a few of the many different ways in which languages, with precision, convey meaning, and thus ensure communication. Principles such as word order, or stress, which Sapir hypothetically advanced as "the primary methods for the expression of all syntactic relations," and out of which "the present relational values of specific words and elements" become "but a secondary condition due to a transfer of values" [16] may lead to a deeper

---

[15] Alice Werner, 1930, pp. 39–40.
[16] E. Sapir, *op. cit.*, p. 119.

comprehension of the nature of language than we now have. Yet this is not as yet achieved. For the student of culture, the fact of variation in linguistic phenomena, regarded in world perspective, and the regularity of the particular structure assumed by each tongue as a manifestation of the broad category of culture we term language, are the paramount attributes of the grammatical, no less than the phonemic and lexical parts of speech.

6

THE importance of studying language as an aspect of culture becomes apparent when we recall that the use of language is one of the two criteria by which man is differentiated from other creatures, as when we say that man is the only speaking, tool-using animal. This does not mean that man is the only creature that can communicate with his fellows, or even communicate so as to convey to others different shades of meaning. A dog, for example, conveys quite effectively his caution when he growls, while a bark can be playful, or friendly, or hostile. Animals have quite elaborate systems of signalling by the use of sounds that are, in effect, ways of communicating with each other.

But while man is like many other forms in that he can communicate, his mode of communication differs fundamentally from theirs. Being non-instinctive, the symbols he employs are, as we have seen, arbitrary in their selection though systematic in their combination. Animal sounds, on the other hand, are fixed, instinctive, and exhibit only the most limited range. Language, in a very real sense, is to communication what human social institutions are to the social structures of infrahuman beings. Like all other aspects of culture, language not only varies greatly but, since it is learned, is capable of the same sort of accumulation over periods of time that is manifested by culture as a whole.

This factor of accumulation presents a problem that, in general, is no different from the one faced by the student of change in any other aspect of culture. In the chapters which follow, where the dynamics of culture will be treated, linguistic data will be called on to document hypotheses of cultural changes in the same way as other kinds of cultural facts. There is, however, one point that we can consider here, since it is primarily, though by no means exclusively, a problem of linguistic usage. That is the question of the effect the presence of writing has on linguistic change.

That writing is important for culture as a whole has been made apparent in our discussion of the basis for the distinction between "primitive" and "literate" societies, long drawn by students of culture. There is no question that command of writing does make it possible to store up knowledge, so to speak, in a way that is much more effective than when other mnemonic devices, or memory alone, are used. Yet the extension of memory afforded by writing has apparently little to do with whether or not, in a literate society, change is retarded or hastened. We tend to pride ourselves on our reasoned susceptibility to what is new. Literacy is consciously employed as a factor in the reenculturative process we term educating people to accept new inventions, for example. Yet if we go back but a relatively short time in our history, we find that though our culture has been literate for many centuries, change has not always been rapid.

What of language itself? The invention of writing dates to a period about five thousand years ago, when, in the Near East, the translation of ideas and sounds into graphic forms was achieved; or more recently when, in Central America, the Maya devised a system whereby they were able to record dates and other items in their experience. The development of the many different written languages found today is a demonstration of the fact that change in them does occur. Conversely, however, the consistency of unwritten tongues also implies a high degree of stability. Their regularity refutes the idea, held by many persons unacquainted with them, that since they are unwritten, they must be cast in molds that are less durable than when speech is channeled into the forms set by written expression.

Obviously, one cannot investigate the problem of change in unwritten languages with the same resources that the study of change in written modes of speech can be made. Because it is unwritten, we must, on the one hand, rely on such fragments of data as are found in words or phrases (often very poorly transcribed), as set down by early explorers; or, on the other hand, make more reliable reconstructions of the past of present-day languages. But, where written languages are concerned, we can investigate the problem from fuller records as well as by reconstructions. One or two bits of evidence, taken from English, will be useful. Thus we can compare meanings of words used in Elizabethan times and today. Such a word as "fist," for example, then meant no more than we mean by "hand," so that the poet could write a sonnet to "my lady's dainty fist."

A striking example of change in the meaning of a written English word, and the conservatism of a society without writing which has retained its earlier significance, can be given. "Wench," in modern English, conveys the sense of a young woman whose ways are not in accord with the patterned sanctions of society, especially as regards her sexual behavior. In earlier times "wench" meant simply a young woman, particularly a serving-woman. The modern meaning is that given by the Negro-English speakers of Paramaribo, in Dutch Guiana, to the word *wenki*, its counterpart. In the deep interior, however, the Bush-Negroes, who escaped from slavery in the seventeenth century and had little subsequent contact with Europeans, have retained the earlier, more innocent significance. To witness a literate coastal young woman fly into a rage as a nonliterate Bush Negro chief summons her with the request "Come here, wench!" is to experience how a twentieth-century reaction to a written word, spoken by a nonliterate who has retained its seventeenth-century meaning, can create a profound emotional disturbance in the person addressed!

Slang is perhaps the most striking example of how new meaning can be read into old words of a written language, while the anguish of old-fashioned grammarians over their inability to stem the tide of such usages as "It's me," offers further illustrations of the process. Trade tongues, the languages of various "speech-communities," such as those of the theatre or of musical circles devoted to jazz—"jive"—offer further documentation of the change in written language.

In London, the Smithfield and Billingsgate markets have taken English words and assigned to them meanings quite different from their customary ones. "I've got a linseed on my bushel," makes no sense without the clue to the changed significance of the key words, which are determined by a simple rhyming scheme. "Linseed oil—boil," gives the meaning of the first word; "bushel and peck—neck" provides our clue to the second. The word pronounced rhymes with the unused term of a pair of words commonly coupled; the unrhyming term is then substituted for the one whose common meaning —"I've got a boil on my neck"—is to be conveyed.

Linguistic change, it would seem, is thus influenced relatively little by the circumstance of writing, even though to those who are literate, writing and language are often regarded as synonyms. Yet beyond the written forms are the spoken ones; and language, expressed in speech, constantly changes. Individual differences in pronunciation, or in the use of words, tend to be taken over by others, and thus variants occur that may develop into different dialects and even into those mutually unintelligible modes of speech we call languages. Writing, though it must be recognized as one of the great achievements of mankind, follows rather than determines changes in the speaking habits of peoples who employ it.

The problem of *meaning* is fundamental, as we seek to comprehend the function of language as a basic, even a determining element in culture. For it is through the emission and consequent comprehension of meaningful complexes of sound that men express their desires, give voice to their hopes, transmit their knowledge and inculcate the values by which they live. In essence, however, the sound-complexes that symbolize all experience and the projections of experience, are so arbitrary that we can do little more than wonder at the causes that have permitted men to identify the most abstract concepts with a given group of sounds, and have permitted them to transmit ideas through the manipulation of words.

How words come to hold the meanings they convey is only the beginning of the problem. Many hypotheses have been advanced concerning this. Some of them raise assumptions as to the origin of human speech itself. It is not difficult to see how the symbolism of language, where words are immediately relevant to objects, has developed. But the symbols that express attitudes, or ideals, and that take us into the most abstract concepts dealing with relationships and causal sequences, are something of quite a different order.

Reichard, for example, has shown how the imagery of an Indian vocabulary, that of the Cour d'Alène of northern Idaho, derives from the assumptions these people make about the properties of various parts of the body. When the Cour d'Alène says he is lonesome, he speaks of himself as "involuntarily abandoned in the heart"; one who is anxious has "become bitter in the heart." [17] Or again, how revealing is it when we find that the English-

---

[17] G. A. Reichard, 1943, p. 100.

Language, the Vehicle of Culture

speaking mother admonishes her child "Be good," the French mother says, *Sois sage*—that is, "Be wise,"—while the Brazilian parent tells a child *Não seja feio*—"Don't be disagreeable." In still another case, an analysis of word-lists from the Fulani of French West Africa showed that "the moral vocabulary" of these people "is as complete as the completest subject (in so far as such things are commensurable), and is far more complete than most all the other categories." [18]

To the student of culture, language, it must now be apparent, offers rich resources for his investigations. Not only are its manifold and complex forms subject to analysis in terms of their structures and modes of change, like the forms of any other aspect of culture. In addition, the symbolic values of language lead to a comprehension of the least tangible elements in any body of custom—the values, the goals, the ideals that direct conduct and order convention—while at the same time they reveal some of the deepest roots of culture itself. It is, in truth, symbolisms of this order that justify us in regarding language as "an index to culture," as it has been termed; in thinking of it, in the widest sense, as the vehicle of custom.

---

[18] F. Fligelman, 1932, p. 215.

PART VI

CULTURAL DYNAMICS

A

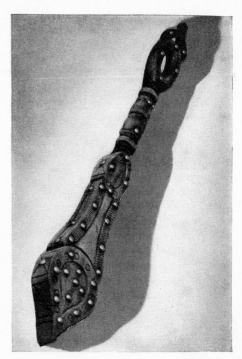

B

Ç

PLATE 17   (A) *Bush-Negro comb,* (B) *clothes-beater,* (C) *tray. See pp. 410 and 411.*

PLATE 18 Indians of Papory River, Colombia, doing basketry-work. Note design on the tray resulting from the type of weaving. See page 412. [Photograph courtesy Chicago Natural History Museum]

CHAPTER 27

Cultural Origins and Cultural Evolution

THE problems in the study of culture that will occupy us in this section may, in the broadest sense, be termed historical, and they bring us to some of the most controversial issues that have marked the growth of anthropological science. Thus, though an outstanding scholar could write shortly after the turn of the century, "By and by anthropology will have the choice between being history and being nothing," [1] the development of the psychological and integrational approaches to the study of culture brought the historical point of view under severe attack.

The functionalists, who stressed the integration of culture, claimed that to attempt to unravel the development of an unrecorded past was to accept a mandate based on a contradiction in terms. It was a waste of time, they said, and they would have none of it. Those interested in the psychology of culture, on the other hand, did not so much deny the value of studying cultural development; their concerns rather lay in the present, with the relationship between culture and the individual, as this could be observed here and now. Most of them recognized the importance of understanding the historic processes of the cultures with which they had to deal, but they tended to leave the prosecution of this aspect of the study of culture to others.

A science of culture, however, must have full regard for all approaches. The study of cultural forms is basic, and the analysis of cultural integration and the psychology of culture indispensable. Without the full appreciation of the meaning of process, however—that is, of *cultural dynamics*—these approaches produce only a truncated structure of investigation and understanding. It is more than a mere aphorism to say that change is one of the few constants in human existence. But the changes that come with the passage of time give meaning to the word "historic." It follows, therefore, that any discipline concerned with man that fails to take the historic factor into full account, restricts its competence to the degree that it neglects a fundamental element of experience.

As we move to consider the various approaches to the dynamics of culture

[1] F. W. Maitland, 1911, p. 295.

461

that have been so vigorously debated, we must underscore the fact that it is not necessary to choose between these differing positions. It is only their more vigorous proponents, indeed, who have viewed them as mutually exclusive. It is not a question of history *versus* integration, for example, or the study of cultural structures *versus* the investigation of the psychology of culture. How the elements of culture fit into one another, or how the individual enculturated to a given body of custom adapts himself to his society are phases of our problem that complement, but in no wise supplant the study of how such relationships change within a given culture or in a given region over a given period of time. Similarly, the question of origins, either in human culture in general, or in specific cultures at given moments in their existence, must be answered as fully as possible.

In the development of anthropological thought, these various approaches form a fairly well-defined sequence, which may be regarded as reflecting the more general currents of scientific, and sometimes popular, thought of the period in which they are found. Each represents the concerns of scholars who, even though they emphasized the errors of their predecessors, nevertheless built on the findings of those who had gone before them. The conception of nonliterate peoples as the living representatives of "natural" man, that we considered briefly in discussing the political institutions of nonliterate groups, was based on the theory that human society had regressed from an original, almost idyllic, state. The evolutionists, with their fundamental postulate of human progress expressed through a succession of socio-cultural stages of development, followed. Then came the diffusionists, stressing the need to reconstruct the history of mankind, with postulates of world-wide migration of culture, or the more restricted view that the processes governing the spread of culture must be studied within a circumscribed region.

The reaction to diffusion was two-fold. One current took the form of denying the validity of any attempts to reconstruct culture-history. It insisted on the study of cultural integration as the primary aim of logical analysis. This brought to the fore the study of the relationship of social institutions to each other, and the analysis of how the individuals who compose a society become adjusted to their fellows and to the way of life of their group. This was called the functional approach. The other current extended the study of the dynamic problems which had occupied the diffusionists. It centered its attention, however, on culture change as this could be observed, rather than on hypothetical reconstructions of culture history. This approach is that comprehended under the term acculturation. As has been stated, none of these points of view is all-important, except in the negative sense that *any one of them comes to be of outstanding significance when it is left out of account.*

It is in the spirit of this principle that we turn to an analysis of the historic factors that characterize and govern the dynamic processes of culture. In this we will roughly follow the developments that marked the growth of anthropological theory itself. That is, we will first of all consider the hypothesis of cultural evolution, and indicate the arguments and counter-arguments that have marked its past and have characterized its resuscitation. We will then, in later chapters, discuss the differing situations that facilitate or retard change, the mechanisms that effectuate it, and the ways in which changes have been found to manifest themselves. We shall, finally, inquire into the problem of direction in change, since this is critical if the aim of scientific investigation in general, the establishment of principles whereby prediction is to be achieved, is to be realized by the science of cultural anthropology.

2

When, in 1877, Lewis H. Morgan wrote his study of the development of human institutions, *Ancient Society,* he phrased a position that, with its English and continental parallels, was to become known as social or cultural evolution. This position, because of its underlying philosophy, disputed earlier controversies concerning the origin and destiny of man, and initiated protracted debate in terms of new conceptions of man and his past.

"The great antiquity of mankind on earth has been conclusively established," reads the opening sentence of Morgan's preface. "Mankind are now known to have existed in Europe in the glacial period," he continues, "and even back of its commencement, with every probability of their origination in a prior geological age." He then states what may be regarded as the essence of his hypothesis. "This knowledge changes materially the views which have prevailed respecting the relations of savages to barbarians, and of barbarians to civilized men. It can now be asserted upon convincing evidence that savagery preceded barbarism in all the tribes of mankind, as barbarism is known to have preceded civilization. The history of the human race is one in source, one in experience, one in progress." [2]

This quotation can advantageously be coupled with another that indicates a point of view which Morgan, and those who took a similar position, had to combat in establishing the hypothesis that man had moved through lower to higher stages of development in obtaining his present estate. "The views herein presented contravene, as I am aware," he says, "an assumption which has for centuries been generally accepted. It is the hypothesis of human degradation to explain the existence of barbarians and savages, who were found, physically and mentally, too far below the conceived standard of a supposed original man. It was never a scientific proposition supported by facts." The "Aryan and Semitic tribes" who "represent the main streams of human progress," do so "because they have carried it to the highest point yet obtained." But before these peoples were their ancestors, who, "there are good reasons to suppose . . . formed a part of the indistinguishable mass of barbarians." Therefore, "as these tribes themselves sprang more remotely from barbarous, and still more remotely from savage ancestors, the distinction of normal and abnormal races falls to the ground." [3]

Quotations of this kind clearly express the principal considerations, posi-

---

[2] *Op. cit.,* pp. v–vi.
[3] *Ibid.,* pp. 513–14.

463

tive and negative, that channeled the thinking of the great scholars who, in various disciplines, grounded the concept of evolution so firmly in Euro-american thought. These same considerations, expressed in different form, influenced the work of Lyell in geology, of Darwin and Huxley in biology, as they influenced Morgan and Tylor and others in anthropology. Their hypotheses represented a positive affirmation of the aspirations of Victorian times embodied in the word progress, and in the same measure, formulated a reaction against the religious dogmas of degeneration and of revealed and absolute truth that, buttressed by the sanctions of long-established belief, were used as an argument for the *status quo*.[4]

It is essential for an understanding of cultural evolutionism that it be regarded as more than just a reflex of the biological theory of evolution, where it is customarily held to have been derived. Teggart, the student of intellectual history, has pointed out how Darwin's work, *The Origin of Species*, that appeared in 1859, was "just too late to have an effect upon the remarkable development of ethnological study in the second half of the nineteenth century." The works which initiated this development, such as the contributions of the Germans Waitz, Bastian, and Bachhofen, or the English scholars Maine, McLennan, and Tylor, appeared between 1859 and 1865. This means that they were being planned and written about the same time Darwin was carrying out his researches and organizing and writing down his conclusions. Teggart, moreover, shows that cultural and biological evolutionism differed in certain important theoretical respects. He points out that "Tylor, in 1873, and McLennan, in 1876," were "disclaiming dependence upon Darwin, and maintaining their allegiance to an earlier tradition of development or evolution. The concept of 'evolution' in ethnology is, in fact, distinct from the type of evolutionary study represented in Darwin's writings."[5]

This dissociation of Tylor from Darwin is made very plain in the preface to the second edition (1870) of the work, first published in 1865, from which we have already quoted. "It may have struck some readers as an omission," he says, "that in a work on civilization insisting so strenuously on a theory of development or evolution, mention should scarcely have been made of Mr. Darwin and Mr. Herbert Spencer, whose influence on the whole course of modern thought on such subjects should not be left without formal recognition. This absence of particular reference is accounted for by the present work, arranged on its own lines, coming scarcely into contact of detail with the previous works of these eminent philosophers."[6] Teggart summarizes this distinction succinctly as he continues the passage from which we have quoted: "In the pre-Darwinism tradition, the term 'evolution' is synonymous with 'development,' and is intimately associated with the doctrine of the fixity of species. Ethnology has followed Comte in regarding the study of

---

[4] For an extended discussion of the position of those who held for the "progression-theory of civilization" as against those who held for the "degradation-theory," see E. B. Tylor, 1874, Vol. I, pp. 35–68.

[5] F. J. Teggart, 1941, pp. 110–11.

[6] E. B. Tylor, *loc. cit.*, p. vii.

'evolution' as concerned with tracing the course of development of mankind, and with the construction of 'ideal series.'"

This brings us to another point of importance that is also customarily overlooked in the discussion of cultural evolutionism. Most of the students of man who took part in the exciting search for the ladder by which man had climbed from his earlier savage condition—and would continue to climb to an ever-better world—were eminently men of good will. They thus permitted no assumption that a people on a lower rung, retarded in their cultural achievements, were of inherent inferior capacity. Briefly stated, and in the terminology of this work, their position was that *cultural differences do not imply innate racial differences.* Tylor, writing in 1871, said, "Surveyed in a broad view, the character and habit of mankind at once display that similarity and consistency of phenomena which led the Italian proverb-maker to declare that 'all the world is one country,' 'tutto il mondo è paese.'" Later in this same paragraph, he makes the point even more explicitly: "If we choose . . . things which have altered little in a long course of centuries, we may draw a picture where there shall be scarce a hand's breadth difference between an English ploughman and a negro of Central Africa. These pages will be so crowded with evidences of such correspondence among mankind, that there is no need to dwell upon its details here, but it may be used at once to override a problem which would complicate the argument, namely, the question of race. For the present purpose it appears both possible and desirable to eliminate considerations of hereditary varieties or races of man, and to treat mankind as homogeneous in nature, though placed in different grades of civilization. The details of the enquiry will, I think, prove that stages of culture may be compared without taking into account how far tribes who use the same implement, follow the same custom, or believe the same myth, may differ in their bodily configuration and the colour of their skin and hair." [7]

But, we ask, was it not illogical to assume cultural inferiority and superiority and specifically to deny the racial basis of such differences? This is the case only if the unity of physical type and culture is postulated. These early students, like those who have followed them, however, realized that there was a fundamental difference between learned traits of behavior and innate physical characteristics, even if they did not have the concepts at hand to phrase these principles in this way. In some instances, as in the system of Spencer, where the presumed evolutionary line moved from inorganic through organic to superorganic (cultural) phenomena, the distinction between race and culture is not made. But when Morgan says, "With one principle of intelligence and one human form, in virtue of a common origin, the results of human experience have been substantially the same in all times and areas in the same ethnical status," [8] he uses "human form" in the sense we employ "physical type" or "race," and his phrase "ethnical status" is what we should term "cultural position."

---

[7] E. B. Tylor, *loc. cit.*, pp. 6–7.
[8] L. H. Morgan, *op. cit.*, p. 562.

3

LIKE any theory of moment, that of social or cultural evolution was the work of many minds, and took on many forms. Some, the best known of its proponents, worked on broad canvases and attempted to describe and account for the development of human civilization in its totality. Others restricted their efforts to specific aspects of culture, taking up the evolution of art, or of the state, or of religion.

Some of these we have encountered in previous chapters. It will be recalled how Haddon and others postulated evolution in art forms from realism to conventionalization; how Maine stressed the evolution of the state from organization based on kinship to one based on territory; how Tylor, who worked on all aspects of culture, assumed a sequence in the field of religion whereby the original concept of spirit developed through belief in ghosts and in the soul to polytheistic and finally monotheistic systems.

Many other names, famous in anthropological theory, could be cited from the roster of evolutionists—Pitt-Rivers, Lubbock, and McLennan in England, Bachhofen in Switzerland, Bastian and Wundt in Germany, Comte in France are names that recur again and again in the history of intellectual development when social evolution is under consideration. After them came others, who refined their concepts and stood off the attacks that were directed against the basic postulates of evolutionism. Frazer, Balfour, Marett, and Radcliffe-Brown would be included here; also the Finnish scholars Westermarck and Landtmann, and the Swedish student, Stolpe.

Not only did these scholars study different aspects of culture, but they also differed in the interpretations they laid on the facts they employed to establish their positions. This was inevitable, for no theory of the evolution of human society or of culture could be other than hypothetical, except insofar as the history of certain elements in man's material culture is read from archaeological remains. It will be recalled how it was pointed out, in our discussion of prehistory, that the facts concerning the earliest manifestations of non-material culture are irrevocably lost to us. Language, the form of the family, political structure, religious beliefs, value systems, music, and folklore are intangibles whose precise forms cannot be recovered when a given body of unwritten tradition gives way to another.

This is why the phrase "social origins," that once had such currency, has come to be rarely heard; why anthropology is no longer a discipline whose mandate is primarily to reconstruct the history of human institutions. Where we can recover the remains of civilizations long gone, we utilize these data to the full to document the course of human prehistory. Through the comparison of the customs of different peoples, we seek to establish their contacts, and what they gave each other of their cultures. But, in the main, the earlier concern with reconstruction has been replaced by interest in problems having to do with the forms and processes of custom, studied on the basis of first-hand observation.

Cultural Origins and Cultural Evolution

The social and cultural evolutionists, then, were unable to maintain their classical position because their fundamental postulates were invalidated by the use of more refined techniques and the accumulation of more adequate data. Let us see what these postulates of theory and method were. We may best consider them in their broadest outline, disregarding the special points of view about social evolution that gave rise to internecine warfare, a logical result of the hypothetical nature of the assumptions on which evolutionism was based. We can distinguish three outstanding elements, always present in the studies that hold to the cultural evolutionist position:

1. The postulate that the history of mankind represents a *unilinear sequence* of institutions and beliefs, the similarities between which, as discerned at the present time, reflect the principle of the *psychic unity of man.*

2. The *comparative method,* whereby the evolutionary sequence of human institutions and beliefs is to be established by comparing their manifestations among existing peoples, who are assumed to be the living exponents of earlier *stages of culture* through which the more advanced societies are held to have passed.

3. The concept of the survival of customs among peoples regarded as more advanced in their development; these *survivals* to be taken as evidence that such societies have passed through earlier stages whose customs, in vestigial form, appear in their present ways of life.

1. Every exponent of cultural evolution provided an hypothetical blueprint of the progression he conceived as having marked the development of mankind, so that many examples of *unilinear sequences* have been recorded. Some of these progressions were restricted to a single aspect of culture, as has been indicated. Not all students, moreover, were equally insistent on the inevitability of the developmental stages they sketched. As we move away from the heyday of the evolutionary hypothesis, we encounter a greater degree of tentativeness and flexibility. Yet some sequence is always described in these latter works, whatever exceptions to them may be noted.

Of the evolutionary sequences that were formulated in the classical works of this school, none is more specific than that given in Morgan's *Ancient Society.* Three principal periods in human socio-cultural development were distinguished by Morgan—savagery, barbarism, and civilization. The first two of these were each held to have been divided into older, middle, and later periods, marked by conditions of society to which were applied the designations lower, middle, and upper status of savagery or barbarism. Morgan phrased his criteria cautiously, as befits a scientist, recognizing the obstacles in the way of classification. "It is difficult, if not impossible," he wrote, "to find such tests of progress to mark the commencement of these several periods as will be found absolute in their application, and without exceptions upon all the continents. Neither is it necessary, for the purpose in hand, that exceptions should not exist. It will be sufficient if the principal tribes of mankind can be classified, according to the degree of their relative progress, into conditions which can be recognized as distinct." [9]

[9] *Op. cit.*, p. 9.

Cultural Dynamics

The "recapitulation" he gives of his series may be reproduced here:

Periods	Conditions
I. Older Period of Savagery,	I. Lower Status of Savagery, From the Infancy of the Human Race to the commencement of the next Period.
II. Middle Period of Savagery,	II. Middle Status of Savagery, From the acquisition of a fish subsistence and a knowledge of the use of fire, to the
III. Later Period of Savagery,	III. Upper Status of Savagery, From the Invention of the Bow and Arrow, to the
IV. Older Period of Barbarism,	IV. Lower Status of Barbarism, From the Invention of the Art of Pottery, to the
V. Middle Period of Barbarism,	V. Middle Status of Barbarism, From the Domestication of animals on the Eastern hemisphere, and in the Western from the cultivation of maize and plants by Irrigation, with the use of adobe-brick and stone, to the
VI. Later Period of Barbarism,	VI. Upper Status of Barbarism, From the Invention of the process of Smelting Iron Ore, with the use of iron tools, to the
	VII. Status of Civilization, From the Invention of a Phonetic Alphabet, with the use of writing, to the present time.[10]

Despite the exceptions that Morgan recognized, this system was justified for him by the readiness with which he could classify cultures in different parts of the world as falling under one or the other of these categories; excepting only the Lower Status of Savagery, which admittedly was hypothetical in the sense that no living peoples were to be found who could be regarded as coming under this heading. The comparability of tribes in the other categories, however, was held to form "a part of the accumulating evidence tending to show that the principal institutions of mankind have been developed from a few primary germs of thought; and that the course and manner of their development was predestined, as well as restricted within the narrow limits of divergence, by the natural logic of the human mind and the necessary limitations of its powers." [11] We could scarcely ask for a clearer expression of the first principle of cultural evolutionism, the assumption of fixed stages of development resulting from the psychic unity of mankind, than is to be found in this quotation.

---

[10] Op. cit., p. 12.
[11] Op. cit., p. 18.

Cultural Origins and Cultural Evolution

Tylor expressed his point of view concerning the stages through which human culture is supposed to have evolved much more tentatively than Morgan. Despite all his reservations, however, he says, "The thesis which I venture to sustain, within limits, is simply this, that the savage state in some measure represents an early condition of mankind, out of which the higher culture has gradually developed or evolved, by processes still in regular operation as of old, the result showing that, on the whole, progress has far prevailed over relapse." [12] The cautions Tylor enters are nonetheless impressive. Everywhere in Tylor's argument we encounter the qualifying phrase, the recognition of the tentativeness of a conclusion: "Even those students who hold most strongly that the general course of civilization, as measured along the scale of races from savages to ourselves, is progress towards the benefit of mankind, must admit many and manifold exceptions," he says. "Industrial and intellectual culture by no means advances uniformly in all its branches, and in fact excellence in various of its details is often obtained under conditions which keep back culture as a whole. . . . Even in comparing mental and artistic culture among several peoples, the balance of good and ill is not quite easy to strike." [13]

Spencer's approach, less specific in naming stages, but also far less flexible in its employment of the evolutionary hypothesis, yields us our final examples. "That seeming chaos of puerile assumptions and monstrous inferences, making up the vast mass of superstitious beliefs everywhere existing," he says, with the determined ethnocentrism that marked his thinking, "thus falls into order when, instead of looking back upon it from our advanced stand-point, we look forward upon it from the stand-point of the primitive man." After summarizing the "superstitions" discussed at length in his earlier pages, he states, "How orderly is the genesis of these beliefs, will be seen on now observing that the Law of Evolution is as clearly exemplified by it as by every other natural process. I do not mean merely that a system of superstitions arises by continuous growth, each stage of which leads to the next; but I mean that the general formula of Evolution is conformed to by the change gone through." Thus integration of belief accompanies increase in mass and coherence, from the indefinite to the definite, so that, "Undeniably, . . . a system of superstitions evolves after the same manner as all other things." [14]

2. The *comparative method,* the second element in the system of the evolutionists, held that living nonliterate peoples bear witness to the early condition of man. It is from the consistent use of this method that, as has been pointed out in earlier pages, we have come to regard "primitive" man as our contemporary ancestor. For the evolutionists, it should always be remembered, "primitive" man was "primeval." His arrested cultural development was thus held to make it possible for students to draw on accounts of the customs of "savage" peoples to provide examples of the early life of mankind as a whole.

---

[12] *Loc. cit.,* p. 32.
[13] *Loc. cit.,* pp. 27–8.
[14] H. Spencer, 1896, vol. VII, pp. 423, 432–4.

Cultural Dynamics

Morgan states this postulate as follows: "So essentially identical are the arts, institutions and modes of life in the same status upon all the continents, that the archaic form of the principal domestic institutions of the Greeks and Romans must even now be sought in the corresponding institutions of the American aborigines. . . ." [15] Tylor also is clear about why he uses the comparative method: "To general likeness in human nature on the one hand, and to the general likeness in the circumstance of life on the other, . . . similarity and consistency [in cultural manifestations] may no doubt be traced, and they may be studied with especial fitness in comparing races near the same grade of civilization. Little respect need be had in such comparisons for date in history or for place on the map; the ancient Swiss lake-dweller may be set beside the mediaeval Aztec, and the Ojibwa of North America beside the Zulu of South Africa." [16]

Tylor has described in detail the procedures for utilizing the comparative method. "A first step in the study of civilization," we are told, "is to dissect it into details, and to classify these in their proper groups. Thus, in examining weapons, they are to be classed under spear, club, sling, bow and arrow, and so forth; among textile arts are to be ranged matting, webbing and several grades of making and weaving threads; myths are divided under such headings as myths of sunrise and sunset, eclipse-myths, earthquake-myths, local myths which account for the names of places by some fanciful tale, eponymic myths which account for the parentage of a tribe by turning its name into the name of an imaginary ancestor. . . . Such are a few miscellaneous examples from a list of hundreds, and the ethnographer's business is to classify such details with a view to making out their distribution in geography and history, and the relations which exist among them." [17]

These quotations make it clear why the term "comparative method" is employed to designate the analysis of their materials by the evolutionists. It is also plain why this method is to be contrasted to the later point of view that cultures are integrated ways of life, not aggregates of discrete parts to be studied out of cultural context. One can, indeed, classify bows; and by arranging all bows, for example, in a single room of a museum, in the order of their complexity, exhibit them as an instance of the development of the bow, and as an example of the evolution of one phase of culture. One can also keep collections from a given people together, and use the bow to illustrate its contribution to the life of the tribe, regardless of the similarity or difference its form exhibits when compared with the bows other peoples use. That the method of studying forms rather than processes left the evolutionists particularly vulnerable will become apparent when later in this chapter we discuss the criticisms lodged against their hypotheses.

3. Tylor says, in the introductory chapter of his *Primitive Culture*: "Among evidence aiding us to trace the course which the civilization of the world has actually followed, is the great class of facts to denote which I have

[15] Op. cit., p. 17.
[16] Loc. cit., p. 6.
[17] Loc. cit., pp. 6–8.

found it convenient to introduce the term 'survivals.' There are processes, customs, opinions and so forth, which have been carried on by force of habit into a new state of society different from that in which they had their original home, and they thus remain as proofs and examples of an older condition of culture out of which a newer had been evolved." So effective was this method held by Tylor to be "for tracing the course of the historical development through which alone it is possible to understand their meaning," that for him it was "a vital point in ethnographic research. . . ." [18]

This concept of the *survival* was much more a feature of European evolutionism than of American. Tylor, his interest centering on religion, folklore, and other nonmaterial aspects of culture, found it a tool that fitted well in his hand. It was most elaborately developed by Frazer, who was to be its last great exponent. In the United States, however, the concept of survival could have little more appeal in ethnology than it had in folklore where, we saw, if not rejected, it was never employed to any extent. This was in the nature of the case. For Tylor or Frazer or their colleagues, the living representatives of presumed earlier cultural stages inhabited distant lands. Their customs, gathered for study from the works of those who had visited these savage peoples, recalled customs of the English countryside. To Tylor, such customs were thus in England and on the continent of Europe nonfunctioning vestiges of a past given over by the intellectual circles which, in his system, represented the flowering of that way of life he meant when he used the word "civilization." For Morgan, on the other hand, and for his American contemporaries, "primitive" man was no distant being, but an inhabitant of their own country. A belief in earlier stages did not have to be documented by them in terms of "the ordeal of the Key and Bible, . . . the Midsummer Bonfire, . . . the Breton peasants' All Souls' supper for the spirits of the dead." [19]

Morgan lived in Rochester, New York. The Iroquois Indians, who for him represented an earlier stage in human development, were, so to speak, at his doorstep. He was himself an adopted member of this Indian tribe. Their customs, for him, were not survivals, but full-blown functioning elements of their culture. The "earlier" conditions of "savage" life postulated by Tylor and the European folklorists and others who were concerned with primeval man could have nothing of the living reality that American Indian ways of life held for students in the New World. In the New World, moreover, the future was important, not the past. The demands of frontier life destroyed many of the earlier customs and beliefs the pioneers brought from Europe, so that the concept of survival seemed uncongenial if only because it was so patently inapplicable. That is perhaps one reason why, as a student of this concept has put it, "when survivals came to be frugally employed [by Morgan] . . . they were discovered, not as by Tylor, among the practices and ideas of civilized men for the purpose of restoring primitive man to a place in the developmental series. On the contrary, they were found exclu-

---

[18] *Loc. cit.*, pp. 16–17.
[19] E. B. Tylor, *loc. cit.*, p. 16.

sively in the culture of one primitive people, the Hawaiian . . . and were used to establish the existence of a condition still more archaic." [20]

The doctrine of survivals took on many forms and has had a hardy career. McLennan, whose study of "primitive paternity" antedated Tylor's work, used the concept, though with a different phrasing. Long before that time, as we have seen, the originator of the word "folklore" had the same idea in mind when he appealed for the preservation of "popular antiquities." The concept of survivals moved from the camp of the evolutionists to that of the anti-evolutionists. W. H. R. Rivers, one of the most distinguished followers of Elliot Smith, the English diffusionist, whose ideas we shall later consider, invoked the "survival" of kinship terminology among primitive folk as a means of reconstructing their unwritten history, so that it forms the justification for his monumental and controversial work, *The History of Melanesian Society*. In 1913, in a paper discussing and defending the idea of survival, he shows that he specifically accepted it in its technical sense, defining it as "the persistence of the useless." He points out that it is not exclusively a concomitant of an evolutionary process, and attempts to explain away the attack, couched in psychological terms, that held the concept of survival, as the carry-over of "meaningless" elements in culture, to be secondary if not pointless in a study of historical processes. [21]

In analogous fashion, Father W. Schmidt, the German diffusionist, who has likewise attacked cultural evolutionism in its classical form, uses the concept of survival to dissect, in nonliterate societies themselves, the "origins" of religion. Thus he accepts as evidence for a presumed original monotheism the "high gods" reported from various tribes, since for him these are data that indicate the survival of an original belief in a single deity. Lowie, the outstanding American antagonist of cultural evolutionism, entitled a work on the political organization of nonliterate peoples, *The Origin of the State;* one of his colleagues in the anti-evolutionist camp, Goldenweiser, called his first general book in anthropology, where prehistory is considered only in passing, *Early Civilization.*

This vitality of the concept of survival is in large measure due to the considerable validity it actually does possess. Whether or not it is possible to have a "survival" in the conventional sense of a meaningless element in culture—and opinion has moved to the position that there can be no element in culture that *is* meaningless—the fact that culture is a continuum that constantly changes implies a preponderance of the elements of any given culture that, at any given moment, will be carried over from an earlier period in its history. The real methodological difficulty arises when a living custom in one part of the world is accepted as the valid counterpart of a "cultural curiosity" in another part. It is on this basis that the concept of "social origins" was justified, and on this basis it fell into disuse. This is no reason, however, for permitting controversy to obscure for us the very real utility that the idea of cultural survivals—or retentions, as we shall call them—can have.

---

[20] M. T. Hodgen, 1936, p. 88.
[21] W. H. R. Rivers, 1913, p. 293; pp. 303–4.

4

WHEN we ask why evolutionism came to be rejected by so preponderant a number of students of man, we must not only phrase our answer in terms of methodology, but must also take fully into account the changing climate of opinion of the times in which the opposition flourished. As the European world moved out of the Victorian epoch, as the American frontier reached the Pacific, doubts began to appear concerning the validity of the overall conception of progress that dominated the thought of the period when evolutionism held sway. Under the influence of a developing, if unrecognized philosophy of cultural relativism that was based on a sense of the values in the lives of those who had been termed "savages," belief in progress gave way to recognition of the existence of a "problem of progress."

Writing in 1930, Boas phrased the prevalent anthropological point of view toward the question of cultural evolution in this manner: "While the general evolutionary scheme is no longer tenable, the problem of progress remains. Observation proves that the inventions and knowledge of man have extended with ever increasing rapidity, and it is possible to speak of progress in technique, in successful exploitation of natural resources and in knowledge, for every step taken is an addition to previous knowledge. Cases of loss of previous knowledge are comparatively rare and, for mankind as a whole, temporary. It is much more difficult to speak of progress in any other cultural activity, except in so far as those aspects of cultural life that contradict the advances of knowledge gradually disappear. The lack of change in fundamental ethical attitudes has been mentioned. Progress in social organization refers generally to a better adaptation to economic conditions and ethical requirements as understood according to the general state of knowledge."[22]

The doctrine of evolution was taken into the political field, where it hardened after the manner of any scientific hypothesis that becomes popular. Morgan's work was read by Karl Marx, and his notes on this book, almost unobtainable in Europe at the time, formed the basis of the Socialist classic, *The Origin of the Family, Private Property, and the State,* written by Marx' literary executor, Friedrich Engels. The hypothesis of stages was transmuted into a doctrine of hope for the underprivileged. In this political sense, social evolution meant that the path to the economic democracy of the socialist order was to be traced from savagery, through barbarism, and beyond the industrialized capitalistic societies of our day.

This episode in the history of social evolutionism seems, however, to have had few repercussions in anthropological thought. Anthropologists, like all scientists, continued the exploration of existing hypotheses on the basis of the new data derived from more intensive and more effective use of the techniques of field research. These findings, for example, tended more and more to invalidate the assumption of cultural inferiority and superiority.

[22] F. Boas, 1930, p. 103.

They thus struck at the root of the ethnocentrism that, as we shall shortly see, was fundamental in judging the "stage" which a given culture was held to have reached in its development. This is only one point we shall consider as we briefly review the grounds on which each of the three major postulates of the evolutionists was analyzed, and eventually abandoned by most anthropologists of the twentieth century.

1. The growing stress laid on the importance of cultural borrowing did much to undermine the postulate of unilinear evolution, a progression through which human culture, in all its aspects, was held to have passed. Diffusion, as this mechanism of cultural change was termed, was found to be responsible for so much more of all individual cultures than the inventiveness of any people could possibly account for, that to work out developmental sequences by comparing the ways of life of "untouched" societies came to be recognized as invalid from the point of view of method. What was an "untouched" society, it was asked? If borrowing was so universal in human experience, was it possible, by studying contemporary cultures of peoples assumed to have reached certain stages of their development, to be sure that the correspondences were not the result of diffusion rather than of independent development? When, for example, the couvade was found in different South American tribes, the question was at once posed whether it had not been diffused throughout the area by a process of cultural borrowing.

One misconception that has arisen as a result of the controversy over evolutionism must be corrected—that the early evolutionists were blind either to the existence of borrowing, or to its implications for their hypothesis. Morgan, at the outset of his book, says, "Some tribes and families have been left in geographical isolation to work out the problems of progress by original mental effort; and have, consequently, retained their arts and institutions pure and homogeneous, while those of other tribes and nations have been adulterated through external influence." [23] Tylor speaks of the "working analogy . . . between the diffusion of plants and animals and the diffusion of civilization." "The course of events which carried horses and wheat to America carried with them the use of the gun and the iron hatchet," he says, "while in return the old world received not only maize, potatoes and turkeys, but the habit of tobacco-smoking and the sailor's hammock." Tylor also recognized the difference in dynamics between the "distribution of culture in different countries" and "its diffusion within these countries." [24] That these scholars and others of the evolutionary school felt that they could discern the working out of the lines of human progress despite these borrowings may, from the point of view of the knowledge of later days, be recognized as methodologically ill-advised. This does not, however, justify a denial of the fact that they saw the problem and, in the light of their hypothesis, faced it.

As for the classical doctrine of the psychic unity of man, this could not stand against the growing realization that human behavior is so conditioned

---

[23] *Op. cit.*, p. 16.
[24] *Loc. cit.*, pp. 8–10.

that it is difficult, if not impossible, to discern innate from learned behavior. It fell, that is, not only because the fact of diffusion better explained the similarities in the cultural details that were crucial to the argument, but for the same reasons that the instinctivist school of psychology fell. We have seen that universals do exist in human culture, and that some of them— though not all—can be referred to the needs of the human organism. Yet we have further seen that because the manifestations of these universals of culture are so varied, the resemblances between the ways in which culture may be divided for purposes of study does no more than give us a framework on which to organize the behavior of peoples when we reify this behavior into the institutions and aspects we, as students, recognize. The psychic unity of man, as in this latter sense, is undoubtedly a valid concept. But this proposition leads us nowhere in the study of cultural dynamics, which was the use to which it was put by the cultural evolutionists.

2. The comparative method was given over because it came to be recognized that it was a denial of cultural reality. It consisted, in general, of comparing facts, torn out of their cultural context, with little reference to their meaning. The great volumes of Spencer's *Comparative Sociology* provide catalogues of fact from all parts of the world. But the meaning of a given cultural fact, that we have seen is critical in understanding it, is quite disregarded. If we but recall the controversy over totemism,[25] the point will become clear. For the phenomenon called "totemism" is so different in different societies that to compare instances except in full cultural context has come to be recognized as methodologically indefensible.

It must not be thought that the use of the comparative method was limited to the evolutionists. As in the concept of survivals, it was taken over by some of the strongest opponents of evolutionism. Lévy-Bruhl, who was no social evolutionist, used this method to document his hypothesis of primitive mentality. The extreme diffusionists, both English and German, employed it constantly, in many instances even less critically than some of the social evolutionists. As we shall see, however, it is as unsatisfactory in the hands of diffusionists as in documenting a presumed social evolutionary sequence. Any use of materials, that is, that fails to recognize cultural context and meaning must be rejected.

3. The culminating argument against cultural evolutionism derived from the refusal of the evolutionists to take into account those considerations of time and place that, as we have seen, are so important in any study of the dynamics of culture. Let us see how this worked out. According to Morgan, the system of matrilinear descent he associated with the gens (i.e., the mother-sib) was an attribute of middle savagery. As such, it characterized the Australians, and "remained among the American aborigines through the Upper Status of savagery and into and through the Lower Status of barbarism, with occasional exceptions." In middle barbarism, the Indians "began to change descent from the female line to the male, as the syndyasmian family of the period began to assume monogamian characteristics." With

---

[25] See above, pp. 300–01.

upper barbarism, "descent had become changed to the male line among the Grecian tribes." The monogamic family is held to have later developed because of the need to assure paternity so as to regularize the inheritance of property. "Between the two extremes, represented by the two rules of descent, three entire ethnical periods intervene, covering many thousands of years," Morgan concludes.[26]

The developmental series Morgan set up for this institution is as follows (reading from bottom to top):

Modern civilization (monogamy), with descent in the male line
↑
Grecian tribes, with descent in the male line
↑
American Indians, with change in descent from female to male line
↑
Australians (gens), with descent in the female line

But this series, from the point of view of an historical approach, is quite fictitious, since only the last two items in it are historically related. In terms of actual time, the series should be arranged in this way:

Modern Civilization   American Indians   Australians
↑
Grecian tribes

Placed in this fashion, it is at once seen to be no series at all, but rather a comparison of data existing on a given time plane, arranged according to a predetermined scheme of development.

Tylor understood this point better than Morgan. In discussing the criteria which are to be used in establishing "a means of measurement" of civilization, he dismisses the matter in terms of the common sense of his times. "The educated world of Europe and America practically settles a standard by simply placing its own nations at one end of the social series and savage tribes at the other, arranging the rest of mankind between these limits according as they correspond more closely to savage or to cultured life." [27] No critic of cultural evolutionism has ever phrased his criticism in terms more telling than this honest recognition by Tylor of the ethnocentric basis on which "progress" was to be noted. Once we eschew this ethnocentrism, the method derived from it is revealed in all its weighting.

5

It is important that we recognize the positive contributions made by the earlier evolutionists to the study of culture. These are too often so taken for granted that they tend to be lost sight of in the controversies that are waged over specific points of method, and over the philosophy of evolutionism.

[26] Op. cit., p. 67.
[27] Loc. cit., p. 26.

Cultural Origins and Cultural Evolution

Whatever the theoretical points at issue, however, it should not be forgotten that these early anthropologists achieved the following:

1. They developed the concept of *culture*, and advanced the principle that culture and race must not be confused in studying the ways of life of human societies;
2. They distinguished those subdivisions of culture we today call *aspects*, and showed the usefulness, in studying culture, of considering separately the problems that fall within these several subdivisions;
3. They established the principle of *continuity* and the orderly development of culture, a principle that must underlie any realistic approach to the analysis of cultural dynamics.

As the citation from Boas has indicated, the problems of human development the evolutionists broached were real problems, the answers to which have not as yet been found. The fact, for example, that an archaeologist of the competence of Childe has seen fit to apply the terms "savage," "barbarian," and "civilized" to the pre-Neolithic, the Neolithic, and the post-Neolithic periods of prehistory shows the viability of Morgan's scheme, however we may regret the resuscitation of words that carry the insidious connotations these worn designations do convey.

The revival of evolutionism, principally by White, is another index of the vitality of this hypothesis. White has waged a vigorous campaign to rehabilitate the evolutionist position. In the course of his discussions, he has also sharpened and refined the concepts of the evolutionists. The basic error of those who have attacked evolution, he maintains, is that they have failed to distinguish the *evolution of culture* from the *culture history of peoples*. "The evolutionists worked out formulas which said that a culture trait or complex B has grown out of trait or complex A and is developing into, or toward, trait or complex C. In other words they describe a culture process in terms of stages of development. They say nothing about peoples or tribes. They do not say that *a tribe* has to go through stages A and B before arriving at stage C. They know full well that a tribe can obtain the culture of stage C by diffusion without ever going through stages A and B." [28]

White denies the relevance of the psychological approach to the study of culture. He underscores the need, through a science of "culturology," of studying the ways of men in their own terms, without reference to psychological factors. Thus White, in reviewing one work, speaks of it as being notable because "it is a study of *culture*, not of the personality or reactions of the *human organism;* it is, in short, a culturological rather than a psychological study." [29] Thus excising the psychological aspects of culture from the concerns of cultural anthropology, he conceives of the processes of science, on the "level" of the cultural sciences, as divided into historical, evolutionary and functional techniques. The historical approach is temporal in its orientation, and includes the "history of customs, institutions, ideas, art forms, etc." The evolutionary method is temporal-functional, and treats of the "evolu-

---

[28] L. White, 1945b, p. 343.
[29] *Ibid.*, 1946, p. 85.

tion of traits, institutions, philosophic systems; evolution of culture as a whole." The functional technique is formal-functional and includes "studies of social structure and function; the 'anatomy' and 'physiology' of cultures or societies."[30]

These categories make explicit and clarify certain approaches to the study of culture that are implicit in any general study of human custom. That they leave out of account the psychology of culture follows from the position of White concerning the autonomy of culture. This position, it need not be said, is inacceptable as far as the hypothesis of the nature and functioning of culture advanced in this book is concerned. The question remains, moreover, what does the study of the evolution of culture hold for the student of cultural dynamics? Whether or not unilinear development is postulated, what light does the assumption of logical sequences throw on the processes of cultural change? It would be unrealistic in the extreme to deny the existence of specific past sequences, particularly in the field of material culture. But what is the logic or the fact that supports the hypothesis of a sequence that requires descent to have been originally counted on the mother's side rather than the father's? To take another instance, we may recall how, in our discussion of religion, we saw one hypothesis after the other of the development of religion along stated lines, from assumed origins, invalidated by subsequent findings.

A further point bearing on our present topic may also be mentioned here, though its exploration must await a later chapter. The end of scientific endeavor is analysis and prediction. One can but ask how the tracing of past events, divorced from the psycho-dynamic factors that we have seen condition them so deeply, can reveal trends of a given culture, or of human culture as a whole, and thus permit valid prediction. The newer approach to an evolutionary method, which denies relevance to the psychological mechanisms of man, and ignores considerations of space if not of time, would seem to be difficult to envisage as susceptible of very great use in terms of the ends of scientific anthropology.

It is, in every sense, regrettable that the study of culture was caught up in the controversies that centered about the word "evolution." This usage, by and of itself, has too often become a battle-cry rather than a research tool. Except in its historical meaning, it will therefore not be further used in this book. The word *development*, employed by Tylor as a synonym for "evolution," would seem to perform as useful a function, and to be free from the associations that make the analysis of possible sequences in cultural change on the broadest scale, so difficult a subject to discuss.

---

[30] *Ibid.*, 1945a, p. 243.

CHAPTER 28

Conservatism and Change in Culture

WE CANNOT too often emphasize the fact—we might say the axiom—that no living culture is static. Neither smallness in numbers, nor isolation, nor simplicity of technological equipment produces complete stagnation in the life of a people. Rules of conduct may be rigid; the strictest sanctions may be invoked to enforce these rules; acquiescence in them may be unquestioning. Yet the observer of a society where even the greatest degree of conservatism obtains will, over a long enough period of time, find that changes have taken place. They may be minute, but they will be there.

The evidence for cultural change is overwhelming. Archaeological findings have demonstrated how change consistently marks the remains left by peoples who have inhabited the same site. The materials from lower and earlier strata are invariably found to differ from those in the upper and more recent levels. In a given Indian mound, for example, a type of pottery found in profusion near the top will gradually diminish in quantity, and finally disappear, as the excavators work more deeply into the site. But the pottery itself will not disappear. At a particular level, a new type will be sparsely found, and this will eventually replace the one that dominated the topmost strata. This is reading the historic record backwards, which the archaeologist, as he works his way downward, must always do. What such finds mean is that the topmost sherds, profuse just under the surface, represent the dominant pottery types when occupation of the site was terminated. Their sparser incidence in lower levels represents their developing preponderance, and documents the changes in this cultural element that occurred over the period the site was inhabited.

Another kind of evidence for the ubiquitousness of change in culture can be drawn from our own everyday experience as well as from nonliterate societies. It is to be found in the differing attitudes the members of ascending generations show toward the accepted ways of behavior of their society. Observations of this phenomenon by anthropologists are common, even among groups whose conservatism is pronounced. There are few cultures where the elders do not register disapproval of the departures of the young from the traditions of an earlier generation, or where the young people do not voice their resentment at the restraints imposed on them, as they deviate in some respect from certain forms of behavior approved by the older people. "When we were young," goes the complaint of the elders, whether in literate or nonliterate societies, "things were different. Our generation knew how to respect old people, how to behave correctly, how to worship the gods properly. Today everything is changed. The young are unwilling to follow and to learn."

They will say this, even though, to the outsider, the change cited may involve no more than an innovation in the accepted manner of salutation, or a new dance, or an elaboration or simplification of a ritual. On their part, the young complain of the reluctance of the older generation to sense their needs. In Dutch Guiana, the term of address a young Bush Negro woman uses when she speaks to her grandmother or any woman of her grandmother's generation is *kambosa,* "She who makes trouble for me." This tugging of the young at the reins by which the old try to hold them on the cultural roadway they themselves have traveled, is a constant in human social life. What is rarely recognized by these elders is how successful they really are, for the stability of their culture escapes them, and they are irked by the relatively minor changes introduced by the oncoming generation. That their opposition to change is, however, ineffectual, is a lesson that seems never to be learned.

The fact of change is also documented by historic accounts, wherever these are available. This applies not only to the data bearing on the past of literate peoples, but is equally true where the evidence permits us to obtain a glimpse of the life of present-day nonliterate folk as it was lived in earlier times. Sometimes a cultural element that seems so deeply imbedded in the customs of the people that it is assumed to have existed there for years is found to be relatively recent in origin. Thus, for example, nothing could be more characteristic of the culture of Indians in the Pacific Northwest than the totem-pole. It is a kind of crest, and symbolizes the mythical past of the totemic group. Students of culture have been challenged by the intricate stylization of the animals it depicts, and have sought to understand its historical and social implications, while its artistry has appealed to those interested in its aesthetic qualities.

It seems inconceivable that early visitors to Northwest Coast villages could omit mention of these tall carved posts, but no account of them is found in such writings. Ethnologists who studied in the areas for many years assumed them to represent an ancient pattern, until research established that the totem pole, far from being a feature of these cultures since the early times of the people, is a development of the first part of the nineteenth century!

There seems today little doubt that this innovation originated from within the society and was made possible by virtue of contact with Europeans that introduced new technological devices, and that permitted a concentration of wealth and a standard of living not attainable in earlier times. "The growth of native technique," says Barbeau, who has given the subject most attention, ". . . hinged upon European tools—the steel ax, the adze, and the curved knife—which were traded off in large numbers to the natives from the days of the early circumnavigators—that is after 1778. The lack of suitable tools, of wealth, and of leisure in the prehistoric period precluded the elaboration of ambitious structures and displays. The benefits accruing from the fur trade at once stimulated local ambitions; they stirred up jealousies and rivalries and incited incredible efforts for higher prestige and leadership. The totem pole came into fashion after 1830 through the rise of these ambitions. The size of the pole and the beauty of its figures published abroad the fame of those it represented." [1]

We can also document change by considering its end-results as shown in regional variants of the same general culture. The argument here is simple. In their overall characteristics all the local groups of a given region have ways of life that are greatly similar. Each of them, however, differs from its neighbors in certain details of accepted behavior. These differences, that represent variations on the general theme, are end-results of a particular series of changes that had occurred in the locality where the deviation is to be observed. Local dialects offer a rich field for investigations of this sort. They supply many evidences of the changes that must have taken place over the years, by the accretion of minute, even individual differences that were handed down in one locality and not in another.

Art is an aspect of culture which also affords numerous examples of change. The instance of the Eskimo needle-cases, cited in an earlier chapter [2] to show how a particular art-style can grow, also illustrates how the end-results of change can be recorded in design, even where the exact story of the developmental process cannot be recovered. It will be recalled that on these tubular containers, the protuberances used to assure that the sinew cord holding them will not slip, form the basis of the embellishments with which the cases are decorated. In the variety of these decorations we have objective evidence of change. All the Eskimo make these needle-cases, which in form are much the same. But the individualizing imprints of at least some of the makers is demonstrated by the fact that over the total area inhabited by this conservative people, many variants in the decorative motifs are to be found.

Most new elements are introduced into a culture from outside the group. These borrowed cultural elements may be taken over and integrated into the life of the borrowers so completely as to baffle the most exacting student who seeks to determine what of the culture he is studying, is of foreign origin. The case of maize in Africa is much to the point. We have seen that the domestication of this plant was achieved in the Americas. We know that early European voyagers introduced it into Africa, after it came to Europe. The acceptance of maize by the Africans must have brought significant changes in their food economy and their diet, though we know that there are few phases of culture where conservatism is more likely to manifest itself than in the food habits of a people. Today, in many parts of Africa, maize is not only a staple food, but it also enters importantly into the food offerings given the gods. It has thus invaded a second aspect of culture—the sphere of ritual—where, again, changes tend to be adopted with reluctance.

With the spread of European culture over the world, and especially the

---

[1] M. Barbeau, 1930, p. 262.
[2] See above, pp. 395-6.

products of its machine technology, the acceptance of new ways of doing old things, or of modifications of old ways, or of innovations through borrowing has become increasingly accelerated. It must not be assumed, however, that indigenous nonliterate peoples have shown uncritical acceptance of what this expansion has presented to them, nor have they taken over European cultural elements without modification. On the contrary, they have done what all human groups do when presented with something new. They have responded to the innovation in terms of their prior experience, accepting what has promised to be rewarding, and rejecting what seemed unworkable or disadvantageous. Where changes have been imposed on them, they have again responded in terms of their experience, with seeming complacence and inner rejection, or with open intransigence, or with a reconciliation of new form to traditional meaning.

A point we must not overlook here is that it is of no special significance that so many examples of cultural change effected through borrowing are today the result of contact between Euroamericans and natives. The phenomenon of cultural borrowing is of itself neither unique nor new. It is only because borrowing by natives from Euroamericans can be better documented historically than can instances of intertribal borrowing, that we draw on examples of this particular type of contact as frequently as we do. Perspective may be somewhat corrected by considering the vast changes wrought in Euroamerican culture as a result of borrowing by Europeans and Americans from indigenous peoples with whom they have been in contact. Our dress, our food-habits, our language, our music—to name only some outstanding aspects of our life where these influences are at once apparent— have been greatly changed since the sixteenth century as a result of such contacts. But this, too, is of no singular significance—except to ourselves.

We recognize the ubiquity of cultural change when, beginning with the study of change in process and the analysis of existing nonhistoric cultures, we find that no two groups have exactly the same bodies of custom. Obviously, those peoples who live close together, or who, like the English and their descendants in modern Australia, have close historic contacts, will have more in common than those who live at a distance and rarely, if ever, come to know the cultures of each other. This is merely to say that groups who live in close contact have more opportunities to take over innovations from one another than to adopt new cultural elements from more distant societies. But since not everything introduced into a group will be taken over by it, we reach the basis of a dynamic explanation of the fact of local differences in culture, that will occupy us in the succeeding pages of this work.

Whether great or small, observed differences are but points in the historic chain of causation which has eventuated in a culture as it is to be seen at a given time. That in nonliterate societies scant documentation of actual sequences of events leading up to the end-results can be drawn upon, does not in any way controvert the fact that change has taken place. We have too much evidence from historic cultures, too many records of contact with nonliterate peoples by those who have left accounts of what they witnessed in earlier times that, when compared with present-day customs of the same people, document changes that have actually taken place, to question the presence of change even among peoples noted for their conservatism.

2

WE MAY say, then, that the process of change in culture is universal; that the significance of change must be faced in any study of the nature of culture; and, moreover, that the analysis of dynamics would patently be impossible without postulating change. This, however, does not imply that cultural change can be studied as an isolated phenomenon. It is only one side of the shield; for change, by and of itself, is meaningless, until it is projected against a baseline, measured in time and intensity and in terms of its extensiveness. Above all, it must be contrasted to the phenomenon that is always opposed to it, the phenomenon of cultural stability—a phenomenon which, in its psychological aspects, is called conservatism.

This proposition is not as simple as it appears. It is not difficult to see that since change is relative, any discussion of cultural change has significance only when approached in terms of cultural stability. The appraisal of either change or stability, however, not only depends on taking both into account, but it is dependent as well on the degree to which the observer achieves detachment from the culture in which he is studying change or evaluating stability. The closer the student is to a culture, the more blurred his perceptions in accurately identifying or isolating the changes that may be taking place in it. He reacts to the culture in a manner not unlike that of the members of the group he is studying. If conservatism is stressed as a prevailing pattern, he tends to gloss over the changes that may be occurring, often quite without being conscious of doing this. If the culture stresses change, as is the case in Euroamerican society, there is a tendency to slight the vast body of stabilizing elements that, lying beneath the changes that are actually in process, give continuity to the way of life.

The most striking expression of this limitation of perspective was illustrated by our example of the attitudes of elders, such as have been cited, toward the behavior of the younger generation, or the reaction of the younger members of a society to restraints laid on their innovations. From the point of view of the outsider, neither the old nor the young seem to direct their grievances toward matters of great importance. Often one is bewildered to understand why some innovation, that seems eminently logical when viewed from the outside, occasions so much debate and even distress among a people to whom it has been presented. Yet this reaction merely derives from the student's psychic distance from the culture. When viewed close up, minor distinctions loom large. When seen in more distant perspective, it is the overall picture that is obtained. But even with the psychic distance of the detached observer, the student faces many problems. It is no simple task, even for the trained ethnographer, to sense the differences in individual behavior found in a society new to him. What he sees are the consenses, the patterns. Recognition of deviations can only come later. Yet the student of culture, sensitive to change, must grasp variations as well as patterns. *For at a given moment, these variations are the expression of change in process.* As between conservatism and change, students of culture have devoted far more attention to the study of change than they have given to analyzing stability. There are two principal reasons for this. One reason, as we shall see, derives from the historical development of ideas about the extreme conservatism of nonliterate folk held by scholars in the earlier period of anthropological science—ideas that tended to persist even after the facts proved their untenability. The second reason, however, is inherent in the problem. For it is much easier, methodologically, to study change than it is to study such a negatively oriented phenomenon as stability. Both these reasons must be grasped if we are to understand the problems of cultural dynamics; and we shall consider them in turn.

Anthropologists have stressed—perhaps overstressed—change in nonliterate societies because change has so often been denied the culture of these peoples. "Primitive" man, that is, has been envisaged as a creature of habit, living a way of life so fixed that his culture, it was argued, holds him as in a vise, himself a passive, complacently imitative being. Emphasis on the extreme reluctance of nonliterate man to change his traditional modes of life has, for example, come to be a cornerstone of the theoretical structure erected by certain diffusionist schools in their attempts to reconstruct human history. "Primitive," moreover, has been held to be a term applicable to a way of life differentiated, as we have seen, from those cultures termed "civilized." The designation "civilized" has been used to mean cultures where progress is conceived as having been manifest, and the attainment of cumulatively higher goals to have been held as an ideal; whereas "primitive" ways of life were believed to be marked by adherence to older forms, without the aspirations that were believed essential to continuous improvement.

Some examples that appear in the older literature will the better aid us to understand why anthropologists came to feel the need to emphasize change in the "primitive" cultures with which they had first-hand acquaintance. Herbert Spencer puts the case as follows: "The primitive man is conservative in an extreme degree. Even on contrasting higher races with one another, and even on contrasting different classes in the same society, it is observable that the least developed are the most averse to change. Among the common people an improved method is difficult to introduce; and even a new kind of food is usually disliked. The uncivilized man is thus characterized in yet a greater degree. His simpler nervous system, soon losing its plasticity, is still less able to take on a modified mode of action. Hence both an unconscious adhesion, and an avowed adhesion, to that which is established." [3]

Sir Henry Maine expressed himself vigorously on this matter: "Vast populations, some of them with a civilization considerable but peculiar, detest that which in the language of the West would be called reform. . . . The multitudes of coloured men who swarm in the great Continent of Africa

---

[3] H. Spencer, *op. cit.*, Vol. I, p. 71.

detest it, and it is detested by that large part of mankind which we are accustomed to leave on one side as barbarous or savage. . . . To the fact that the enthusiasm for change is comparatively rare must be added the fact that it is extremely modern. It is known but to a small part of mankind, and to that part but for a short period during a history of incalculable length." [4]

Both these passages were cited by Lester Ward, who phrased the position taken by Spencer and Maine even more emphatically: ". . . at the beginning of this chapter it was shown that most savage and barbaric races . . . want no change and ask for nothing that does not exist; nay they detest and consistently oppose all change. If it were left to the initiative of such races there never would be any social progress." For, he says, a group of this kind has "reached such a complete state of equilibrium that it is incapable of performing any but the normal functions of growth and multiplication. It is reduced by the very principle that constructed it to the power of simple repetition." [5] These words were written at the beginning of the twentieth century. A few years later, this expression of the position we are considering, was penned: "The fact is that human nature remains fundamentally primitive, and it is not easy even for those most favoured by descent to rise above . . . primitive ideas, precisely because these ideas 'spring eternally' from permanent functional causes. Everyone would still be primitive were it not for education and environment. . . ." [6]

Statements such as these reflect the ethnocentrism that dominated the thought of Europe and America during Victorian times, on which we have commented in the preceding chapter. Such pronouncements were, of course, made in good faith. But those who set them down, like the lesser figures who repeated and rephrased their point of view, drew their inferences from information they gathered from books, not from first hand experience with native peoples. The "savage" that was portrayed was not a living being; he was an automaton, scarcely a man. Students who, in the field, had come to know "primitive" peoples as aggregates of individuals much like those they knew at home, understandably felt impelled to correct these distortions. Anthropology, in the early years of the twentieth century, it is true, had not reached the point where it was prepared to recognize differences in the behavior of individual members of the societies that were studied. Yet anthropologists, in studying cultural institutions and cultural processes, underscored the fact of change by pointing to the changes they knew had taken place because of variation in observed custom among a given people, or that were to be read in the variety of forms a given complex might assume as it was diffused over a given area.

What became important, then, was the need to emphasize the universality of change, and to challenge assertions that peoples of a "lower" order were not receptive to change in their habits of living. "Primitive" man was shown to be no automaton. "Primitive" societies were demonstrated to have undergone change, despite their remote habitat, their numbers, their technological

---

[4] Sir Henry S. Maine, 1890, pp. 132–4.
[5] L. Ward, 1919, p. 236.
[6] E. Crawley, 1927, Vol. I, p. 4.

resources. Gradually the evidence accumulated—instances of the kind that have been cited in the earlier pages of this chapter, and that are to be found in profusion in the earlier chapters of this book. It was an argument based on the results of field research among peoples all over the world. It was a development that comprehended only a portion of the broader theoretical position that holds culture to be the summation of individual behavior, and essentially dynamic; a part of the development of a relativistic point of view that studies each culture in terms of its own way of life, of its own values.

Granting that change is ubiquitous in culture, the fact that anthropologists have, in the main, continued to give little attention to the analysis of cultural stability, or conservatism, as such, remains to be analyzed. As has been pointed out, difficulties of a methodological order must be faced in studying a problem couched in negative terms, as is this one of cultural stability. If we accept change as ever present, then conservatism can be thought of as *resistance to change*. But unless an anthropologist happened to be on the spot when something new was presented to the nonliterate group he was studying—an idea, an object, a technique, an art-form—and he was thus in a position to observe how first one, then another, and another individual would have none of it, he could not know that the idea, the object, the technique, the art-form had been presented and rejected. How otherwise could he witness the force of conservatism at work, repelling the new, retaining the old?

On occasion it is possible to obtain native testimony on why innovations have been rejected. Among the Navaho, the Night Way Chant is one of an elaborate group of ceremonies that not only is used for curing, but also to bring rain and foster the well-being of the community. Certain Navaho do perform portions of the dance in the summer, or in disregard of its place in the cycle, altering words, or dancing softly, or changing its name. However, Hill, who has analyzed the reasons that changes are looked on with disfavor, quotes the following passage that explains why, in this ritual, "any tampering with the general ideology behind the ceremonial is not considered permissible":

You must be careful about introducing things into ceremonies. One chanter thought he could do this. He held a Night Chant. He wanted more old people so he had the dancers cough and dance as old people. He also wanted an abundance of potatoes so he painted potatoes on the dancers' bodies. He desired that there should be a great deal of food so he had the dancers break wind and vomit through their masks to make believe they had eaten a great deal. They surely got their reward. Through the coughing act a great many of the people got whooping cough and died. In the second change many of the people got spots on their bodies like potatoes only they were measles, sores, and smallpox. In the part, where they asked for all kinds of food, a lot died of diarrhea, vomiting and stomach aches. This chanter thought that he had the power to change things but everyone found out that he was wrong. It was the wrong thing to do and today no one will try to start any new ceremonies. Today we do not add anything.[7]

---

[7] W. W. Hill, 1939, pp. 259–60.

Conservatism and Change in Culture

The fact of the matter is that while culture-change offers many leads for study, cultural resistance, except in terms of testimony of this sort, yields few. It is quite true that resistance to change is revealed, at least by inference, in every study of change. Only minor differences are to be found between local Eskimo groups, or between different hordes of Australian aborigines or South African Bushmen or different tribes of Tierra del Fuego. These differences are slight, even when compared to the local differences found in varying degree elsewhere in the nonliterate world, and hence imply continued resistance to change. Yet when we go further, and ask why so little change occurred among these very conservative groups, phrasing our query in terms of what opportunities for change were presented them, and the reasons for their rejection of innovations, we are reduced to speculation.

Where historical documentation exists, cultural stability can, however, be analyzed, as has been done by certain sociologists interested in the resistance to ideas in our own culture. Thus Stern has considered the development of medical science, and has set down a long record of opposition to dissection as a medical technique, to vaccination, to the theories of Pasteur, to the doctrine of antisepsis—among others—that marked the reaction of medical practitioners to innovations in their field. Among the factors operative in this opposition seem to have been the interests of those committed to a procedure threatened by the innovation, devotion to the *status quo,* reverence for authority on the part of those lay persons not able to judge a medical innovation, the conservative force of the prevailing system of medical education, the resistances set up by established habit-patterns, and the adverse reaction of patients to new techniques that were painful when administered, like vaccination.[8] Many other studies of this kind could profitably be made in our own and other literate societies. If broadly conceived, the results would yield some measure of cross-cultural analysis of the phenomenon of resistance to change.

As for nonliterate peoples, it was not until the study of cultures in contact had come to have an adequate place in the anthropological repertory that the problem of resistance to change could be analyzed. Especially where nonliterate groups had been in contact with literate ones could the elements presented to them be discerned, and the fact of rejection established. With this in hand, the probing of the processes involved in the refusal to accept innovations could be initiated. This, however, is a matter we must leave for the moment, until we take up the study of acculturation. For the present, let us merely emphasize again that the study of resistance to change, that is, of cultural stability or cultural conservatism, is but a phase of the study of cultural change itself.

One further point, however, must be raised as we consider the balancing of change against stability. This has to do with the different rates of change that mark one aspect of a given culture as against another. The point poses the question whether we are justified in labelling one culture, *as a whole,*

---

[8] B. Stern, 1927, *passim.*

conservative, as against another, *as a whole*, which is held to be receptive to change. This is not the first time this methodological point has been raised in this book, nor will it be the last. The fact is, however, whether we document change and resistance to change historically, or infer it from distributions, we never find cultures that move at the same rate over the whole front.

Thus the Australian aborigines, who are held to be prime examples of a conservative people, seem to have been far more conservative in their material culture than in their social organization and religion. The simplicity of their material culture has been often noted in this book; it is apparent that the harshness of their habitat inhibited any drive to develop more effective ways of exploiting its potentialities. On the other hand, we observed the complexity of their system of kinship terminology, and the richness of their mythology and the ceremonial life based on those myths. We can only designate them extremely conservative as a whole if we ignore the receptivity to change that must have existed at some time in their past where ideas having to do with social structures and the supernatural world were involved. Conversely, our own culture, held to be "progressive" and hospitable to change, shows unsuspected resistances in the field of nonmaterial culture, when we view it objectively in terms of its aspects, rather than as a unit. Change thus differs with the time, the culture, and the aspect of the culture. It is a point to be borne constantly in mind in the study of cultural dynamics, no less than when we analyze the structure and forms of culture.

3

CONSERVATISM and change in culture are the result of the interplay of environmental, historical, and psychological factors. All must be considered when studies of cultural processes are made. The weighting given each of these factors, however, has tended to vary with the position of a given student and the emphasis his experience and training has caused him to lay on one or the other. Actually, generalizations as to the weighting to be given any one factor are as hazardous as are overall evaluations of total cultures. In some instances, habitat will be the predominating reason why resistance or hospitality to change is evidenced. Elsewhere, the circumstance of historic contact will most influence the development of a people. Always the psychological factor will be operative. At times we must seek psychological causes alone in explaining why some apparently advantageous opportunity for change, helpful in meeting the demands of the natural setting of a people, is rejected by them; or where something that, viewed from the outside as perhaps quite harmful, is accepted.

The influence of the habitat on the development of a culture has been implied in the chapter where the relationship between culture and its natural setting was considered in general terms. That is, the habitat offers possibilities that may or may not be utilized by those who live in a given region. It sets limits that are elastic in the face of an increasingly effective technology. Thus it is often stated that natural barriers to communication can act as forces militating against the changes that come readily to a people inhabiting an area of easy access. And it does seem to hold that the peoples who inhabit the most remote areas of the world are actually to be counted among the most conservative groups. Yet this does not mean that the converse is true. The civilizations of the Far East are often pointed to as examples of cultural conservatism, yet they are by no means isolated—that is, they are not isolated except as viewed from the perspective of a developing European culture.

Isolation, of itself, can explain very little. Are the cultures of the isolated peoples at the tip of South America, or in the Arctic, or in the depths of the Ituri forests in the Congo basin stable *because* these peoples are isolated; or because they are small in number, and have simple technological equipment that provides only a narrow base for change? Are the Eskimo conservative because they are isolated, or because a harsh habitat imposes limits that tend to suppress change? And what of the many opportunities for change peoples at the crossroads of the world, such as the Egyptians, have had presented to them, only to reject them?

Pertinent questions such as these are raised not to dispute the claim that geographical situation is to be considered in explaining cultural stability and change, but to assess this claim in perspective. Isolation is, at best, a difficult concept to work with, since it is only a relative term. The vast bulk of the Americas were isolated from the rest of the world for thousands of years. Yet from the point of view of the Americas, continents peopled with numerous Indian tribes who stimulated each other, it could as well be said that it was the Old World which was in isolation, not the new. Substantial proof was given of this after the fifteenth century, in the radical changes the discovery of the Americas by Europeans wrought in such important phases of European culture as food resources and dietary habits. Only after the stimulus of contact with the Americas did the European standard of living begin to rise.

We have seen how, to the inhabitants of the Pacific islands, the sea was a means of communication, not a barrier. Less recognized is how deserts can further contact between peoples. The Kalahari Desert of South Africa was a barrier between the Bushmen and the tribes to the north and east of them, though it did not by any means forbid communication. But trails across the Sahara Desert have for untold ages permitted interchanges between Negro Africa and the Mediterranean. It is only the fixed idea of Europeans, who approached Africa by sea and found few harbors and fewer seagoing natives, that has been responsible for the false notion of the isolation of Africa and the consequent cultural stagnation that has been held to mark African societies. Africa, however, is neither isolated, nor are her native cultures stagnant. Here the desert, not the sea, has afforded a means of communication with the other continents of the Old World, with all this implies for an exchange of ideas as well as commodities, and a consequent mutual change in the cultures that have been thus in contact.

As far as the question whether other elements of the habitat may induce or reduce cultural change—temperature, barometric pressure, humidity, altitude, for example—the evidence is too scanty and the point too controversial to permit discussion here. Certainly a very difficult habitat, to which a people have made an adjustment, does not encourage experimentation in the field of technology. Whether it be the Nuer who inhabit the swamps of the Upper Nile in East Africa, or the Siberians in their Arctic habitat, or the Paiute of the Great Basin deserts of Utah and Nevada, there is little encouragement under such aboriginal conditions to experiment with established modes of getting a living. Yet we need hardly repeat here that this is not necessarily a matter of cultural conservatism, but of conservatism in the technological aspect of culture. Where the habitat is less harsh, experimentation in this, or any other aspect, may or may not take place. Certainly it has proved difficult in the extreme, when all the available evidence is taken into account, to correlate any of the elements of the natural environment that have been named with universal or even consistent tendencies toward conservatism or change.

Within the limits set by the natural environment, access to the wide range of possible roads a culture may follow is given by historical circumstance. Here we must take into account two processes that will be discussed in some detail later, cultural drift and historic accident. Cultural drift is the working out of those sequences which seem logically to follow from the way in which a culture is organized, the interests of those persons who make up the society characterized by it, and the ends they seek in terms of the values and goals sanctioned by their culture. Historic accident is a phrase applied to those sequences of events in the life of a people, unforeseen and, from the inner logic of the culture unpredictable, that give new directions to the changes that mark the course of their history, so that sequences that might otherwise have been expected to occur are altered.

Such stimuli can come from within a group or from outside it. A chance discovery, recognized as useful, may induce change, or it may solidify opposition to change and be the instrument for emphasizing conservatism. A journey taken by an individual member of a society may reveal techniques or ideas that he brings back to his people with similar positive or negative results. Conquest may lead to an interchange of cultural elements; or conqueror and conquered, even when living side by side, may, in large measure, each continue his own way of life. Imposition of the institutions and standards of a dominant group on dependent peoples having different cultures may serve to rally them to forbidden earlier ways, and result in those contra-acculturative movements that often mark the course of foreign rule.

4

THESE circumstances of history make the development of every people a tale that is never exactly repeated, either by themselves or any other group. And it is these ever differing historic streams that at once reflect and shape the attitudes and points of view of societies that, in the final analysis, determine the degree to which each will be hospitable or hostile to innovations.

Conservatism and Change in Culture

This, then, is the third factor we must take into account in studying the dynamics of culture. It involves the consideration of the many psychological mechanisms that underlie human behavior in general, and as such constitutes a special aspect of the enculturative process we found to be so important in understanding the manner in which human beings are conditioned to the way of life of the society into which they are born, and the very nature of culture itself.

This enculturative process, it will be remembered, is the means whereby an individual, during his entire lifetime, assimilates the traditions of his group and functions in terms of them. Though basically involving the learning process, it was pointed out that enculturation proceeds on two levels, that of early life and that which marks the existence of the mature member of society. During early life, a person is conditioned to the basic patterns of the culture in accordance with which he is to live. He learns to handle the verbal symbols that make up his language, he masters accepted forms of etiquette, is inculcated with the ends of living recognized by his fellows, is adjusted to the established institutions of his culture. In all this, he has but little say; he is the instrument rather than the player.

In later years, however, enculturation involves reconditioning rather than conditioning. The learning process is one wherein choice can operate, wherein what is presented can be accepted or rejected. As was suggested, a change in recognized procedures of a society, a new concept, a reorientation of point of view can only come when people agree on the desirability of change. It is the result of discussion, of consideration by individuals who must alter their individual modes of thought and action if it is accepted, or argue preference for established custom in rejecting it.

Thus the mechanism of enculturation leads us to the heart of this problem of conservatism and change in culture. Its earlier conditioning level is the instrument that gives to every culture its stability; that prevents its running wild even in periods of most rapid change. In its later aspects, where enculturation operates on the conscious level, it opens the gate to change, making for the examination of alternate possibilities, and permitting reconditioning to new modes of thought and conduct.

ı⁊

Discovery and Invention as Mechanisms of Cultural Change

BROADLY considered, cultural change may be thought of as falling into two distinct categories. The first category comprises all change that stems from innovations originating from within a society; the second, all change that comes to it from outside. In this chapter we shall treat of the first category, change from within, which comprehends the processes of discovery and invention, leaving our consideration of the second category, borrowing, for later pages.

First, however, we may briefly consider certain basic problems that present themselves in the analysis of both categories. Thus, where the record is absent, we can but conjecture about the circumstances under which a given technique or system of concepts was invented, or a mechanical principle or a complex of pre-existing relationships was discovered, and the personal factors that were operative in furthering their acceptance by a given group. In like manner, we can only tentatively assume that widely distributed cultural elements indicate that there was, at one time, a prolonged and intensive contact over the region where they are at present found. We know enough about the psychology of fads to make us cautious in accepting unqualifiedly any assumption that because a cluster of cultural elements is found distributed over large areas, it must of necessity be of remote origin, or that the presence of many similarities between the customs of two peoples attests a prolonged and intimate connection between them. The probabilities, it is true, are with us in making such assumptions. But, as will be pointed out many times in succeeding pages, we must never lose sight of the difference between an historic probability, however high or however logical, and an historic certainty, that can be established only by means of observation and documentation.

Certain questions, principally of a psychological order, that recur when studying any form of cultural change, have been touched on in the preceding chapter. Outstanding here, we have seen, is the question of acceptance or rejection of an innovation, whether it originates from within the group, or is presented to it from outside. An invention that does not "take," or an innovation presented for borrowing that is rejected, vanishes without a trace among

Discovery and Invention as Mechanisms of Cultural Change

nonliterate peoples—and, in most instances, among literate ones as well, since few rejections in literate societies have claimed the attention of historians. Moreover, the mechanisms whereby an innovation wins acceptance by overcoming opposition are sufficiently difficult to discern, even where the facts are at hand, because of the complexity of motivations that come into play where choice is presented to human groups. Thus in the preceding chapter we saw how many hypotheses are advanced to explain why, in Euroamerican society, medical innovations were resisted on their initial introduction, and why they were finally accepted.

The greatest difficulty in studying the processes of invention and discovery, and of borrowing or diffusion as factors in cultural dynamics is that, as has been pointed out, we so seldom have the opportunity to make observations on the spot when new elements are introduced into a culture. But whatever the methodological obstacles, the problem is of first importance, and must be faced. For as has been stressed in this book from the very outset, change is a constant in every body of custom, and the analysis of the processes of change, achieved through discovery and invention on the one hand, and borrowing on the other, is essential for adequate comprehension of the subject of our concern, culture.

2

It is far simpler to name the first category of cultural change—those changes originating within a society as the result of discoveries and inventions—than it is to differentiate the two concepts expressed in the words we employ to phrase this proposition. The difficulty is essentially one of definition. Functionally, and as observed from the point of view of the results achieved, the distinction between an invention and a discovery is not too important, for both represent means of changing culture from within, in contrast to innovations that were already functioning elsewhere before they were borrowed.

Harrison, in a series of papers on the nature of invention as applied to material culture, analyzes the concepts of discovery and invention, while at the same time he emphasizes the difficulty of drawing sharp lines of distinction between them. "Discovery," he states, "lies at the root of all man's material activities, since he must know something of the everyday behaviour of material substances before he can apply or adapt natural objects to his purposes." He proposes that the discoveries of fundamental methods that result in the development of a body of activities, such as agriculture, or the domestication of animals, be called a "discovery-complex."

Such a discovery-complex, however, may stimulate the development of what he calls artifacts—tools, that is—to which the term invention is to be given. Yet there are difficulties in drawing distinctions even in these terms. For, as he points out, if weaving is a "discovery-complex," in which category does woven cloth fall? "We may perhaps best get out of the difficulty," he states, "by using the term discovery-product for all artificially extracted, prepared, and compounded materials which have no significant form imposed on them, but are merely the raw materials for the future production of shaped

493

artifacts." This being the case, the term "invention" remains to be applied "for general purposes, to all shaped or constructed artifacts, in spite of the fact that many simple types, such as hand-axes and clay pots, are in reality products of discovery rather than invention." [1]

In a later paper, this same student again faces the problem of defining terms. "It would be futile," he says, "to assign exact and arbitrary meanings to the word 'discovery' and 'invention.'" Discoveries "yield new knowledge of natural forces, and of the nature and reactions of material substances (including both natural objects and human artifacts) under varying conditions; and the process is not one of finding but of finding out." Invention, on the other hand, he leaves "for the moment with its current and vague popular meaning," which applies it "indiscriminately to a complex of human activities . . . and partly also because the expression is used in such a way as to place on an equality artifacts which are by no means comparable in their complexity and length of pedigree." [2]

Dixon, who has also probed this terminological difficulty, draws "a primary distinction" between the concepts of discovery and invention "on the basis of presence or absence of purpose." He points out that, "discovery would then be limited to the unpremeditated finding of something new, whereas invention might be defined as purposeful discovery." Yet, like Harrison and all others who have pondered the question, Dixon recognizes that, "the two forms grade into each other by imperceptible steps." They range, that is, between "the purely accidental stumbling upon something previously unknown, through a more or less painstaking search for the same, to the purposeful experimenting with existing materials leading to the creation of a wholly new thing, which would never have existed but for this conscious human endeavor. The accidental discovery of a new edible plant might serve as an example of the first; the search for a new and stronger kind of vegetable fibre would illustrate the second; whereas the utilization of the elasticity of wood in the construction of the bow would represent the third." In view of this, he refines his previous definition so as "more accurately" to "redefine discovery as the accidental finding of something previously unobserved, whereas invention is the purposeful creation of something radically new." [3]

Dixon differentiates discovery from invention not only in terms of the accidental finding of what already exists as against purposeful creation of the new; the processes that are involved in them are also distinguished. He assumes three antecedent conditions for discovery "in its purest form." These are, "(1) opportunity, (2) observation, and (3) appreciation plus imagination, in other words a measure of genius."

To these three, however, he adds, "for all but the simplest cases" two additional factors, curiosity and need. "The discovery of a new food—such as the oyster, for example—would be long delayed unless one had the curiosity and courage to taste it; the discovery of metals goes back doubtless to someone's curious experimenting with a new and peculiar sort of stone. Man, like other

---

[1] H. S. Harrison, 1930a, pp. 146–7.
[2] Ibid., 1930b, pp. 106–7.
[3] R. B. Dixon, 1928, pp. 34–5.

animals, is naturally curious, and to his inborn curiosity in aimless experimenting with new things the bulk of his discoveries are due." [4]

Need, however, for Dixon is paramount in both discovery and invention, and furnishes the bridge by which we pass from one to the other. Granted that something in the environment can be utilized for a given end ("opportunity") and its usefulness is recognized ("observation") by one with the imagination to understand its value ("appreciation," "genius"), the drive that carries man to new knowledge is necessity. Thus, "although the casual discovery of a new food or material may lead to its use, if the foods already utilized are insufficient and there is a need for new sources of supply, a powerful spur is added to curiosity, and purposeful search is likely to ensue. Necessity is indeed often the mother of invention, and is likewise the parent of discovery as well. With the strengthening of this factor of need we pass more and more definitely into the sphere of invention, in which the need is met, not by the appropriation to use of a hitherto unused thing, but by the creation of something new and fundamentally better." [5]

3

THESE analyses of the significance of the inventive process, as against that of discovery, pose a number of questions. For one thing, we perceive the need to re-examine the use of the word "invention." Its almost exclusive reference, in current speech no less than in the papers that have been cited, to the contrivance of new *material* objects raises a point of the first order of importance. Harrison, a student of material culture, explicitly restricts it to this field. Dixon, on the other hand, recognizes a broader meaning: "It must, of course, not be forgotten that both discovery and invention may have non-material as well as material results, for one may chance upon a new idea or invent a new philosophy." [6] Yet a scrutiny of Dixon's text, as the instances cited from it show, demonstrates that for him, invention, in effect, has the same limiting significance it holds for most people in Euroamerican society—the devising of some new *object*, some hitherto unknown *thing*.

As students of culture—as against specialists in its material aspects—we recognize how "the distorting mirror of the present," to borrow Harrison's phrase, affects our approach to the problem. In the climate of opinion of Euroamerican culture today, a thoroughgoing shift in orientation is necessary if we are to view the process of invention as operative over the whole of culture, rather than as applicable only to its tangible elements. We incline, with all ease, to overlook the role of the inventor of new ideas and new concepts; to disregard his function in contributing to the changes that mark the historical development of every culture.

The common use of the word "inventor" best exemplifies our thought concerning the matter. An "inventor," that is, is a person who "invents" a new

---

[4] *Ibid.*, p. 36.
[5] *Ibid.*, pp. 36–7.
[6] *Ibid.*, p. 35.

machine, a new mechanical process. One who develops suggestions for a new economic system, or devises a new political scheme, or works out a new conception of the universe is, for us, no inventor at all. We may call him a theorist, a philosopher, a visionary, or, with less complimentary connotation, a revolutionist.

Yet ideas are surely no less powerful than things in shaping the lives of men. It would be difficult to maintain that the "inventors"—and the word is here used in its ethnological and functional sense—who devised the method of counting descent on one side of the family, or who later developed classificatory systems of relationship terminology had less influence on the course of human culture than had the inventor of the skin tent, or of the outrigger canoe, or of the pump and bellows used in working iron.

This tendency to focus on material objects when discussing the introduction of new traits into a culture is not only bolstered by the climate of opinion of which this emphasis is a reflection. It also derives from the methodological fact that, in studying nonliterate cultures, it is easier to treat of the presentation of material than of nonmaterial cultural elements; while where the inventions of prehistoric man are involved, no other data are available. Leaving prehistory to one side for the moment, however, let us consider from this point of view Dixon's criteria—opportunity, observation and "a measure of genius"—as they might apply in nonliterate society.

These criteria are obviously far more applicable to the invention of material than of nonmaterial cultural elements. The processes by which, let us say, a modal progression in music, not hitherto employed in the songs of a people, might be discovered, would be difficult to fit to these specifications, except in a most general way. In homogeneous nonliterate societies, all have the opportunity to know the existing forms. Furthermore, where the degree of specialization is weak, musical talent is devoted to the rendition of accepted modes rather than to composition on new progressions. In Europe, despite the presence of specialists in the composition and performance of music, musical history does not show the "discovery" of new modes in the sense of the abrupt changes that would be expected with each discovery. Rather, over the centuries, each new, "modern," form has but brought into gradual use the next succeeding series of overtones of its predecessor.

The consistency of the musical styles of peoples inhabiting vast areas, which permits us to contrast Asiatic music, as a whole, with African and North American Indian music, suggests that the same process has been operative in these regions. Local differences in each of them reflect the accumulation of minor revisions of the dominant modal configurations of the region. It is, indeed, far more acceptable to conceive of musical discoveries in terms of one of Dixon's additional factors, curiosity. To postulate a sense of need, on the other hand, does not seem to help us at all. What, it may well be asked, is the "need" to discover a new musical mode?

The factor of need, in either discovery or invention, which is widely assumed to play a preponderant role, also seems to have more relevance for material than for nonmaterial cultural elements. Nevertheless, even as regards material culture, it is possible to overestimate the significance of need as dominant in the process of invention. It is easy to argue *a posteriori*, after the fact, and urge the necessity for having some tool, some weapon, some technique that seems indispensable to the way of life of a given people. Certainly those who enjoy its use would be the first to accept such an argument. Yet a need, even in the case of a material good, is subject to cultural interpretation. An invention, a discovery, which from the point of view of one society has filled an urgent need, frequently seems pointless or irrelevant to the members of a different group. Every field worker can find corroboration of this in the reaction of natives to items of his own field equipment. To the student, it seems self-evident that certain of these items should be of the highest utility to the natives, yet they bring forth no more than the curiosity that greets any novelty. This example, of course, concerns the phenomenon of diffusion rather than of discovery or invention; but the principle holds. Need, like so many other seemingly fixed concepts, is relative. There is no need, except in terms of the conception of necessity held by a people within the framework of their culture.

That need develops after the event of discovery or invention rather than before it, has seldom been better expressed than by Harrison:

> Foresight is a cultivated aptitude, not a human instinct. The men who began the growing of grain did not look forward to feeding a multitude—population increased with the food supply, and cornfields were enlarged to feed the growing numbers. The idea of a multitude of men evolved with the multitude itself. The plough was not invented as a means of more efficient tillage, but was the result of the discovery that a pick or hoe could be dragged through light soil so as to prepare a seed bed more rapidly than could be done by pecking up the soil; the implement got a new start in life by a change in the method of use, and it was improved as a result of discoveries arising out of its manufacture and employment, aided later by the adoption of modifications suggested by other contemporary devices or appliances. At no stage was there a premonitory vision of a method of agriculture, or a type of plough, having an origin in a mental conception cut off from its roots in the state of knowledge of the place and time. That kind of unconditioned foresight does not happen even nowadays, and we may assume it never will. It is only on the basis of his actual knowledge that man can reason and deduce, and though modern scientific learning may enable us to make predictions with some certainty, the result of experiment is either a confirmation of theory or it is a surprise—a true discovery; and the part played by chance in thrusting discoveries on man is well known to all of us.[7]

The widely cited proverb, "Necessity is the mother of invention," is thus seen, even in the material aspects of culture, to be only a partial truth. It is, however, no more true, and perhaps less so, than the inversion of it devised by Thorstein Veblen: "Invention is the mother of necessity." Once we move into the area of the intangibles of culture, and study the range of phenomena comprehended in the materials presented in our preceding chapters, the popular view that need governs invention is seen to be quite inapplicable. What is the "necessity" for a unilateral descent system that flies in the face of

---

[7] H. S. Harrison, 1930a, p. 141.

the biological facts of descent? What is the need that dictates the invention of a new art style, or a new dance step?

Only if we postulate some inner, quasi-mystical drive in man can we account, on the basis of need, for the invention or discovery of much of existing nonmaterial culture. Need may be uppermost in the minds of specialists in the devising of new objects who, in our culture, we call "inventors." But such specialists are unique to the machine age. They exist neither in the past of Euroamerican society, nor in any other contemporary group, literate or nonliterate. And even in their case, we may but give a moment's thought to the number of inventions that do not "take," to point the fact that what an "inventor" may conceive to be a need does not necessarily seem to be one to the other members of his group.

The ascription by Dixon of genius as a factor in discovery (and invention) likewise calls for consideration. It will be remembered that in his statement of the conditions necessary for a discovery, he lists as the third of his series "appreciation plus imagination, in other words a measure of genius." When he moves to consider invention, however, he places his whole emphasis on genius, stating that "this factor of genius is basic to all invention."

Genius, however, "cannot be independently measured," so that "any discussion of the correlation between inventions and genius" must at the outset meet this "almost insuperable difficulty." It is noted that "genius may vary in its character, its grade, and its frequency." That is, some persons may show genius in one field or another, as in the mechanical arts or in philosophy or in religion. "Only rarely do we get a da Vinci," whose genius lay in many aspects of his culture. In its character, genius may vary "from attainments but little above the average to the great geniuses of all times." Finally, some genius may rest with a single invention; the mind of another "seethes with new ideas" to make of him a prolific inventor.

Though individual genius cannot be measured, its incidence among a given people, Dixon holds, may be studied, though here again with some difficulty. "The opportunities which a given environment furnishes may be determined with considerable exactness; the needs of a people may be estimated with some degree of success; but no measure of a people's genius is yet possible save that afforded by those very inventions whose correlation with genius is what we seek." In pursuit of materials to document his hypothesis, Dixon turns to the products of various peoples as an answer to his problem. He compares the number of patents issued per thousand population in various countries, though when the validity of this procedure is considered, he finds its significance is small. Nonetheless, Dixon's discussion accepts invidious distinctions between peoples, as where we read that, while the genius of a people cannot be estimated, "there *seems* to be a very real and often very great difference between peoples, nations, and races, so that, for example, the inventive productivity of the Negro and other dark-skinned races is far inferior to that of the others." [8] It is but necessary to refer to the ethnocentrism that pervades our thought, and the resultant tendency to evaluate cultures in

---

[8] R. B. Dixon, *op. cit.*, pp. 39–40, 55–7.

terms of their achievements in the field of technological skills, to understand the reasoning that underlies these passages.

Quite aside from reference to racial differences, which we have seen to be scientifically inadmissible as a significant determining factor in cultural behavior, the use of the concept of "genius" in establishing qualitative criteria of inventions leads us into still other difficulties. It would be unrealistic to deny differentials in ability to different individuals who make various kinds of discoveries and inventions. Yet, aside from possible objective evaluations in the field of material culture, how the products of geniuses who live in different societies can be judged, poses an insoluble methodological difficulty. Here, as in many other instances where evaluation supplements the description and analysis of culture, the relativistic point of view must come into play. If only because no two cultures are the same, every people must be granted a measure of inventive genius. Among some peoples, material inventions may be paramount; among others, this creative drive will manifest itself in art, or religion, or social or political institutions.

That the situations needed for a discovery or an invention that have been set forth have a limited validity is not denied. But no one of them may take precedence, nor does their enumeration exhaust the list of possibilities, whether in the field of material or nonmaterial goods. Such an enumeration, indeed, is only a beginning. Both invention and discovery are basic in the dynamics of culture. Both are at once the result and the reflection of those processes of cultural change with which we are at the moment concerned. To a consideration of these processes, then, we now turn.

4

A QUESTION that has received much attention in anthropological theory has been that of independent invention *versus* diffusion. At this point, only the nature of this controversy will be indicated, for since the attack was, in the main, mounted by the diffusionists, its full treatment must wait until the problem of diffusion is considered in the next chapter. In essence, the matter turns on the inventiveness of man; whether, when in distant parts of the world we find similar artifacts or institutions or concepts, we must assume these to have been invented only once and diffused to the regions where they are to be observed, or whether we may deduce that they had originated independently in these several regions.

As far as most cultures are concerned, there can be little doubt that the elements that have been borrowed predominate over those that have originated from within. Man, it has been said, is a creature who finds it simpler to take over something someone else has devised than himself to work out solutions to his problems. Notwithstanding this human leaning toward dependence on what is already at hand, or near at hand, it is unlikely that the whole of any culture represents elements borrowed from other peoples. As we have seen, much of the controversy turns on what constitutes an invention. Assuming for the moment that the word applies to the less dramatic, smaller changes that mark the continuous reworking of every culture, as well as to the revolutionary changes that follow upon major innovations, then we cannot deny resourcefulness to any people.

Harrison, with his customary felicity, has, in a sentence, phrased the crux of the matter, which as we shall see certain diffusionists have found it necessary to treat in volumes. "The more complex the story," he says, "the more stages in the development, and the earlier its completion, the less likely is it that there would have been an independent repetition of the process in other areas."[9] This is apparent if we consider once more the principal stone-working techniques of prehistoric times. Core-tools and flaking are found both in western Europe and the Far East. Studied in detail, it is seen that characteristic differences between the two industries can readily be observed. Yet the discovery that stones could be put to various uses, that stones of certain kinds could be worked to heighten their effectiveness as tools, is of such a general nature, so lacking in complexity, that it is difficult to assume a single origin for this wide-spread complex.

Here we come upon a third possibility in accounting for cultural innovations. This is the mechanism that is termed *convergence*. Convergence was at one time the subject of considerable discussion. It was held to be significant for an understanding of the process of invention because it was described as comprehending a series of minor developments in two quite different manifestations of the same general phenomenon, that were believed to result in their having a similar outer appearance, on the basis of which common origin might reasonably be postulated. The principle is well known in the biological sciences. For example, desert plants develop thick integuments, and leaves tend to take the form of thorns. A classification "thorny plants" might conceivably be set up, but it would have none but the most superficial significance. For desert plants, having thorns, are not necessarily related to each other, but to many different species which, when found outside the desert, are quite different.

The concept of convergence was used by various anthropological theorists, notably Franz Boas and Paul Ehrenreich. It is, however, particularly associated with the name of A. A. Goldenweiser, who employed it in his classic study of totemism. Defining totemism as "the tendency of definite social units to become associated with objects and symbols of emotional value," he points out that the "totemic complex," whose "'origins' and historical fates . . . must be assumed to have been varied," nonetheless "reveal sufficient similarities in structure, content and psychic atmosphere, . . . to justify the designation of such complexes by one descriptive term."[10] That is, the relationship assumed to exist in so many different forms in various parts of the earth between a kinship group and an animal species is sufficiently general to have arisen—that is, to have been invented—quite independently in a number of different places. This would be especially true when we take into account the way in which any group of people who live close to nature tend to read hu-

[9] J. H. Harrison, 1926a, p. 118.
[10] A. A. Goldenweiser, 1933, pp. 316–18.

man characteristics into the animals of their habitat. We saw how, under stress, the sense of a relationship between animals and other natural phenomena developed quite independently among American soldiers during the first World War.[11]

Goldenweiser, in employing the concept of convergence, developed the accessory principle of *limited possibilities*. "A limitation of possibilities," he stated, "checks variety" in the development of a given cultural form. This means that the fewer the possibilities of development for a given cultural element, the greater the probability that changes occurring after its invention or discovery in different regions can be assumed to have taken the same course, independently of each other. That is, "Wherever a wider range of variability in origins and developments coexists with a limitation of end results, there will be a reduction in variability, decrease in dissimilarity, and increase in similarity or convergence." [12] One example is the oar which, though it can be made of many different kinds of materials and in varied shapes, must—"if you want a *good* oar"—be neither too long nor too short, must have a flat blade, must not be too unwieldy. In the face of these limitations, "sooner or later, in one way or another," oars had to develop as "a tool with certain relatively fixed features determined by conditions of effective use."

Other examples of this process can be thought of. There are but three possible ways of counting descent, for example—bilaterally, or on the father's side, or on the mother's. It would be rash to assume a single origin for any of these systems, especially when we find that in a relatively restricted area, such as West Africa, more than one patrilineal people has a matrilineal group as its neighbor. Or, again, the fact that many peoples decorate woven baskets with attempted representations of human or animal figures that turn out to be symbolic geometrical designs is, as has been indicated, dictated by the fact that the weaving technique cannot produce a curved line. Hence the desire of the artist who works in a basketry medium to reproduce these figures is restricted by the principle of limited possibilities, and the result is the geometric stylizations found in many parts of the world, which may be said to be the creative response expressed through convergence.

Convergence thus offered an alternative to the choice between diffusion and independent invention in accounting for similarities between cultures. Yet at best it only afforded a partial answer, for with the exception of a few historical instances, most of the examples lacked precise documentation, and were thus no more than statements of probability rather than fact. Nor did this principle, any more than the principles of diffusion and independent invention, tell us much about the nature of the processes by which an element introduced into a culture, whether from within or from without, came to be caught up in the never-ceasing stream of change that marks all bodies of tradition; or why it emerged as something quite different from the original innovation. What, we ask, returning to our principal problem, are the steps by which human beings recognize in some element in their habitat an intrinsic

[11] See above, p. 301.
[12] 1933, pp. 45–6.

worth they had never before perceived it to possess? Whence comes that surge which adds to existing knowledge and results in a new contribution to the cultural store of a people?

The answers we give to these questions depend on how far we are willing to go in designating the new as a discovery or an invention. Sayce, for example, in his treatise on material culture, says in one connection, "It has been said that the history of civilization is the history of the great inventions." [13] In this sense, no one would deny the use of the word, even though we may not agree with the suggestion that inventions occur *per saltum,* at one jump, so to speak, and without preparation. Most contemporary instances of this kind, as Harrison points out, turn out on analysis to be a "bundle of inventions of which one particular step is so decisive that to it is given the name invention." This is not only true of the complex machines of the industrial age, where this accumulative process is the rule, but, as he says, is also true of "the most primitive of true looms." In other words, the developments in culture resultant on changes introduced from within are in the nature of a collaboration, achieved through the accumulation of small changes in pre-existing elements, through the contributions of many persons.

It is reasonable to draw a distinction between great and small changes, if we recognize the role of the cultural base out of which all of them spring. Harrison speaks of "variations" and "mutations" in discussing the role of invention in the development of material culture. The "variation" results from a more or less random selection by man—especially by early man—in perceiving the elements in his surroundings he could put to his use, and in developing these beginnings once they had been perceived. This is termed "obtrusive" invention, such as occurred when Palaeolithic man "had his inventions thrust upon him"; a conclusion forced by the slowness with which cultural developments proceeded in prehistoric times.

On the other hand, "directional" inventions, which are the work of an inventor conscious of his function and seeking a new way to solve a problem, produce the single "inventive" steps that are called "mutations." A quotation will make the difference clear. "Mutations" in invention, says Harrison, "may be distinguished from variations on the one hand by the fact that, taken singly, they are considerably more important in their influence, and on the other, that they present an effect of abruptness, and even discontinuity—real in relation to the evolution of a particular appliance but . . . not so real if viewed from a wider standpoint." [14]

One treads on dangerous ground if, as is often the case, the word invention is reserved for some dramatic development, allowing the humbler day-to-day minutiae of change to be overlooked. Harrison's terminology is thus a distinct contribution toward clarifying our thought concerning the matter, particularly since he wisely refrains from drawing a line between variant and mutant, but leaves the distinction fluid, one that can be differently employed with reference to different cases. For in truth, there is no line. Man's inven-

[13] R. U. Sayce, 1933, p. 20.
[14] H. S. Harrison, 1926b, p. 155.

tive capacity plays over the whole of his culture, now striking deep into novelty, now merely changing some detail of accepted practice.

Kroeber, advancing the hypothesis of "stimulus-diffusion," has exposed another facet of our problem. By this term he means what occurs, "where a system or pattern as such encounters no resistance to its spread, but there are difficulties in regard to the transmission of the concrete content of the system." One example he gives is the invention of porcelain in Europe in the early eighteenth century. Chinese porcelain, Kroeber points out, had been known and admired in Europe for almost two hundred years. It was the desire to avoid the expense of importation that led to the experimentation that finally produced the desired product. "The consequence is that we have here what from one angle is nothing less than an invention. Superficially it is a 'parallel,' in the technical language of ethnology. However, it is equally significant that the invention, although original so far as Europeans were concerned, was not really independent. A goal or objective was set by something previously existing in another culture; the originality was limited to achieving the mechanisms by which this goal could be attained. If it were not for the preëxistence of Chinese porcelain, and the fact of its having reached Europe, there is no reason to believe that Europeans would have invented porcelain in the eighteenth century, and perhaps not until much later, if at all." [15]

Another example given by Kroeber is the invention of the Cherokee syllabary, about 1821, by Sequoya who, becoming impressed with the advantages writing gave the whites, determined to provide a system of writing for the Indians. He had no schooling, and since a syllabary fitted the patterns of Cherokee, his invention took that form instead of an alphabet. He used English letters plus many more signs. His system contained eighty-six symbols to represent such sound-clusters as "go," "ya," "tli," and others. He thus was stimulated by the diffused trait of writing to achieve what was, in Kroeber's words, a "primary invention" in terms of his own culture. A similar circumstance among the Vai of Liberia and Sierra Leone, West Africa, is also to be cited, where a native, having had contact with the missionaries, developed a syllabic writing system with over 200 characters, the result, we are told, of a divine inspiration in a dream. [16]

How complex are the processes of invention, discovery and subsequent change is apparent from these various approaches to the subject we have discussed. That man, viewed from the broad perspective we have taken, is seen to be more inventive than he is customarily accredited as being does, however, add to our comprehension of the dynamics of culture. For the sum of these changes, great *and* small, must be very large in any culture, even when compared with what has been borrowed from outside. Indeed, it is here that inventions, discoveries, and diffused elements meet, and can be grouped under the category of *innovations*. For whether discovered, invented or introduced, each innovation responds to the propensity for conscious human experimentation, and the play of human ingenuity. Small changes begin imme-

---

[15] A. L. Kroeber, 1940, pp. 1–2.
[16] *Op. cit.*, pp. 3–5.

diately on the introduction of an innovation, and the process of alteration never ceases. Sayce reproduces from a study of Spinden the steps by which a celt was modified into a stone amulet, each modification suggesting a further one, until a recognizable human figure was achieved.[17] This is merely another

FIG. 64   *Modification of stone celt into carved human figure, Mexico (after Sayce, 1933, fig. 6, from Spinden,* Ancient Civilizations of Mexico and Central America).

example of how men shape their cultures. In this instance, the artist, as virtuoso, has played with his technique. It is out of this ceaseless manipulation of all aspects of our way of life that the continuous process of change, of which discovery and invention are but one phase, proceeds.

---

[17] R. U. Sayce, *op. cit.,* p. 69.

CHAPTER 30

Diffusion and the Reconstruction of Cultural History

SYSTEMATIC investigation of the problem of cultural transmission, or cultural borrowing, dates from about the beginning of the twentieth century. Before that, as we have seen the theory of cultural evolution dominated the study of culture. It was not until the validity of this theory came to be re-examined that the significance of the mechanism of diffusion was fully recognized and its implications explored.

Three "schools" have made diffusion basic to their formulation and study of the problems of cultural history or cultural dynamics, or both. They are identified most often by the nationality of their principal proponents, though all have followers in more than one country, and two of them have had a world-wide influence on anthropological thought. We may first name the English group composed of Elliot Smith, W. J. Perry, and their followers. This is sometimes termed the pan-Egyptian, or the heliolithic school. It was last on the anthropological scene and first off it, despite the fact that the controversies it engendered were as heated as any in the history of anthropology. The next of these groups is the German-Austrian "culture-historical school." Founded by F. Graebner and E. Foy, of the Cologne Museum, it was continued by the scholars who, in the main, published their findings in the Austrian journal *Anthropos,* under the leadership of Pater W. Schmidt and his associates, W. Koppers and M. Gusinde. This has become one of the leading schools of anthropological thought on the continent of Europe, but has never achieved any degree of acceptance in English-speaking anthropological circles.

The third group, that may be termed American, can scarcely be called a "school" at all. It is historical in its approach, stressing field research and restricted reconstructions of history rather than the comparative studies, on a world-wide basis, that characterize the two preceding points of view. Most often associated with the name of F. Boas, its concepts have been developed and its field researches carried on by various of his students, such as Kroeber, Lowie, Goldenweiser, Sapir, Spier, and others. Closely allied to it in point of view and approach are the Scandinavian groups of Nordenskiöld and Lindblom in Sweden, and Thalbitzer and Birket-Smith in Denmark, while its methods have also been received sympathetically and effectively employed in France, Belgium, and Holland.

No discussion of diffusion would be complete without a review of the position taken by the anti-diffusionist functionalist school. This group, as we have seen, has been outstandingly identified with the name of B. Malinowski. The appellation, functionalist, is also given the Germans R. Thurnwald and W. Mühlmann and, in the literature, is sometimes applied to A. R. Radcliffe-Brown, who, however, has explicitly repudiated it. Diffusion studies, for this group, have little meaning. Insofar as they are made for the purpose of reconstructing the history of nonliterate peoples, such studies are rejected by them, and viewed as not only pointless, but actually harmful. As was indicated in our discussion of cultural integration, the exclusive interest of the functionalists is in the manner in which the institutions of a culture, operating on a single time plane, reinforce each other as part of a single cultural whole. Functionalists are thus concerned only with understanding how each aspect of a given culture is related to every other aspect; how each aspect, in functioning so as to satisfy human needs, gives point and meaning to the people who live in accordance with it. For them, time depth has no relevance.

Malinowski, like Elliot Smith, was a great polemicist, and his severest criticisms were directed against the study of diffusion, just as the critiques of the diffusionists have been directed against the evolutionists. The polemics of Malinowski effectively sought out the weak points of those he attacked, so that, with the positive contributions to method he made, his position was accorded wide acceptance. But Malinowski was a better critic of method than of theory. It was perhaps because of this that he rarely distinguished between the various diffusionist schools. In attacking "diffusionism," he coupled Graebner and Boas, or Kroeber and Schmidt, with utter disregard of the differences between them. Yet, as will soon be apparent, the area of disagreement between Boas and Graebner, or between Kroeber and Schmidt, was certainly as great as the differences between any of these scholars and Malinowski himself. Indeed, in most respects the position of the Americans differed from that of the functionalists but slightly. The real line of distinction was between these two groups, on the one hand—that is, the Americans and the functionalists—and the culture-historical school and the defunct position of Elliot Smith, on the other, despite the vast gap, in method as in concept, that separated the two extreme diffusionist schools.

2

THE rise and decline of the English diffusionist school constitutes one of the more ephemeral episodes of anthropological history. The founder of this "school," Sir Grafton Elliot Smith, was not a cultural anthropologist at all, but a distinguished anatomist whose work on the brain, and whose studies in palaeoanthropology, brought him great and deserved distinction. At one point in his career he embarked on a study of the brains of Egyptian mummies. His research took him to Egypt, where he became impressed with the quality of Egyptian civilization. As so many others have done, he began to note how the culture of ancient Egypt comprised many elements that seemed to have parallels in the cultures of other parts of the world. Unlike those who have noted such similarities in nearby regions, his daring theories transcended ordinary considerations of time and of space. He not only assumed that comparable cultural elements in the Mediterranean basin, Africa, the Near East and India were of Egyptian origin, but also that those of Indonesia, Polynesia, and the Americas were similarly derived.

The most elaborate presentation of the heliolithic theory of cultural history, as the hypothesis of this school came to be called, was given by Perry in his book *The Children of the Sun.* Its title was taken from one element in the complex of traits that was assumed to have originated in Egypt and, with such other elements as mummification, the erection of great monolithic monuments, the building of pyramids, high value set on gold and pearls, and a dual organization of society, to have diffused everywhere "civilization" is found in the world. The particular element Perry selected to symbolize this complex was the Egyptian belief that the ruler is descended from the Sun. This belief is widespread, though hardly as consistently as Perry and his associates in this "school" were wont to assume in trying to establish a continuous distribution for this and other traits.

Elliot Smith and his followers made of borrowing almost the sole means by which culture change could be achieved. That is, the inventiveness of mankind is reduced in his theory to a point where it is almost nonexistent. In a slight essay that gives the quintessence of his position, Elliot Smith states this very clearly. He first points out that most anthropologists believe that "in any community civilization can and did grow up and develop quite independently of similar events happening elsewhere in the world." He then poses as "a further consideration," the question why a community "acquires a multitude of features in its arts and crafts, customs, and beliefs that present a striking similarity to those of other communities, when all considerations of contact or prompting directly or indirectly are excluded." Another group of anthropologists, he says next, believe "that civilization has been developing during the whole of its history in very much the same way that we know it to be doing at the present time"—that is, by diffusion. "We know in the case of every modern invention, that it was made in one definite place and became diffused over a wider and wider area until everyone in any part of the world who is making use of this particular invention is indebted directly or indirectly to one man in one particular place who was originally responsible for initiating the process." [1]

Here is as clear a statement of extreme diffusionism as could be desired. That some traits of culture could be independently invented is explicitly denied. With this goes the denial of multiple origin and multiple diffusions, to say nothing of the possibility of convergence. Much of the argument of Elliot Smith and Perry depends on interpretation of data. The controversy Elliot Smith engaged in over the carvings on Mexican monuments offers a case in

---

[1] Sir Grafton Elliot Smith, 1927, pp. 9–10.

point. On the great Mayan monolith called Stela B, at Copan, are figures which students of the Maya have variously identified as tapirs or macaws. For Elliot Smith, however, these carvings represented elephants. They were held to be evidence of direct Mexican contact across the great distances of the Pacific, with Indonesia and southern Asia, and with India. Not only were these figures said to depict elephants, but they were held to have riders with prods, after the manner in which elephant-drivers control their charges in India. There is no question in the drawings of the figures as presented in the attractive wood-cuts of Elliot Smith's book, that these are elephants with their riders. Photographs of the originals, however, or casts, are unfortunately not so persuasive.[2]

This matter of interpretation may be further exemplified by citing the instance of pyramids. When, indeed, is a pyramid really a pyramid in the Egyptian sense? Is a pyramid used as a structure on which to place a temple (as the Mexican pyramids were) a cultural fact identical with a pyramid-shaped structure reared as a monument to a dead king, and designed to contain his body for eternity? Once a unity of origin for all pyramids is assumed, then the hypothesis is held to apply to more and more tenuous cases. The stone platforms of Polynesia, the earthen mounds of the Ohio valley are held to be vestigial or marginal forms of pyramids. And a similar interpretation is given when any other elements of the Egyptian "civilization" are discussed. The thigh-bone of a dead African king, preserved for ritual uses, represents for Elliot Smith a diffusion of Egyptian mummification. Any large single stone memorial is claimed as a megalithic monument that originated from the same source.

There is no question that every group borrows more elements of culture than it initiates; but this does not mean that mankind invents as little and copies as much as this extreme diffusionist position would hold. Conversely, because we accept the phenomenon of borrowing, this does not mean that it must be regarded as the sole mechanism whereby culture change is effected. It was the neglect to take into account the inventiveness of man, no less than the failure to recognize factors of time and space in assuming the world-wide diffusion of Egyptian culture, that caused the ultimate rejection of the heliolithic diffusionist position. Pressed by the gathering weight of the arguments levelled against him, Elliot Smith did attempt to show that there was time for elements of Egyptian culture, translated into phenomena of the life of India, to travel to America, so that in Peru the Inca as the Sun-god could be equated to Egyptian custom as could the Mexican pyramid; but here the element of distance intervened.

We must not, in considering the deficiencies in Elliot Smith's argument, be guilty of the fallacy of assuming that contact between Polynesia and the West Coast of the Americas could not have occurred. The Polynesians did reach Hawaii and Easter Island, and it is quite likely that some of their boats that missed the mark might have reached the continent to the eastward. Yet only by assuming so great a distinction between the "civilization" they carried

---

[2] Sir Grafton Elliot Smith, 1924.

and the crudeness of the pre-existing American Indian way of life that the culture of the newcomers, however few in numbers they may have been, was at once perceived as superior and adopted, can we postulate the effectiveness of such slight contact. The fact that all this is contrary to archaeological evidence is here beside the point. For the point is that acceptance of new cultural elements with such celerity and on such a scale goes contrary not only to the teachings of history, but to all our knowledge of the mechanisms of culture-contact.

It is on just this plane that any extreme diffusionist position tends to be vulnerable. For, in truth, it is only in terms of the total psycho-cultural setting that reasonable assumptions as to historical relationships between cultures whose elements seem to be similar can be reached. These psycho-cultural factors, and the likelihood of contact in terms of the channels of communication over the area where diffusion is assumed to have occurred, offer the only valid criteria for the establishment of the probabilities that a given contact did take place. Because the probabilities of Egyptian-Indian-Polynesian-American diffusion were so low when the data were considered from these points of view, then, the Elliot Smith hypothesis was rejected. Two decades after its enunciation, it was, as has been stated, but an episode in anthropological history.

3

THE point of view of the second "diffusionist" school we shall consider, the German-Austrian *kulturhistorische Schule,* is much more sophisticated than the one that has just been discussed. Its carefully drawn criteria for judging the value of assumed borrowings, its insistence on caution in the use of source materials, the care with which its definitions are drawn and the wealth of its documentation are fully in accord with the demands of scholarship. It is for these reasons that it has been so widely accepted. In consonance with the intellectual traditions of Central Europe, the insistence on ultimate ends and values of research marks this school off from the more pragmatic approaches of other groups.

This group is like the English diffusionist school in that it plots its lines of diffusion for world-wide areas, reconstructing presumed contacts between cultures so as to recover the total unwritten history of man. Like the English diffusionists, too, it disregards those psychological aspects of diffusion that we have seen to be so important in the rejection or acceptance of newly presented cultural traits. The proponents of this point of view, however, do not leave psychological considerations entirely out of account. Father Schmidt, for example, defines ethnology as "a science of the mind, of spatial and temporal relations." "Cultural causality," further, is divided by him into "external" and "internal causality," the former being those forces "which work upon man from without," the latter "those which he himself exercises from within." "Both kinds," we are told, "can only be received by human beings (external causality) and can only be effected by human beings (internal causality)." [3]

---

[3] W. Schmidt, 1939, pp. 7, 246–7.

Cultural Dynamics

These types of cultural causality, however, though phrased in psychological terms, are not related by him to such problems as were discussed in preceding chapters—the adaptation, by the individuals who comprise a society, of what is newly presented to them in the light of their previous ways of life. The categories set up by those who employ the culture-historical method are rather used by them as instruments in inferring probability of diffusion. This is to be seen when Schmidt discusses "external causality" in terms of culture changes effected by the habitat or by man. In both cases, he employs the concept of the "migrating culture," whose traces are to be seen as an overlay upon an indigenous one. The habitat will exert a greater influence in modifying the migrating culture in the realm of technology and its material aspects, he says, than in its non-material phases. In "external causality proceeding from man," the problem of modification over the total range of culture is to be attacked on the basis of the quality and number of similarities and differences, that permit judgments as to contact.

"Internal causality" on the other hand, which is held by Schmidt to be the psychological aspect of this process, "is not directly subject to observation." It can only be grasped "when it manifests itself by external works." The discussion of this postulate cannot be pursued here further, except to note one or two points. It is "internal causality," we read, that is the effective instrument in creating culture, both as regards its material and nonmaterial aspects, through its effect on man, the interaction between him and his habitat, and the relationships between him and his fellows. Under contact, it is this "inner causality," one gathers—though Schmidt does not clarify this rather obscure point—that makes for the assimilation by a people of cultural elements newly presented to them.

If these concepts as he presents them are found somewhat difficult to follow, it is because the system of the culture-historical school, as developed by Schmidt, who is recognized as its leader, is essentially based on a mystical approach to the nature of life and human experience. It has been developed within a frame of reference, and employs a terminology that differs fundamentally from the rationalistic point of view and vocabulary of most anthropological thought. How this invades the methodological approach of this school is to be seen in Schmidt's discussion of the techniques to be used in studying the various strata into which this school divides all cultures and which, through the diffusion of their elements, are held to have produced the cultures that today exist on the earth. Like all ethnographers, Schmidt recognizes the need to understand the meaning of "primitive life" to those who live it and, more importantly, to those who in past ages lived it. This we do, he tells us, by recourse to the psychological principle of empathy (*Einfühlung*), whereby one projects himself into the psychic state of the person with whom he is in relation.

This, of course, is what in some measure happens when any good fieldworker achieves rapport with his subjects. It is with some bewilderment, however, that we learn from Schmidt [4] that this permits the student to recon-

---

[4] *Ibid.*, pp. 263–5.

struct the earlier cultures which through their migrations produced the cultural strata held to yield the clues to historical reconstruction of the contact of present-day cultures. The Pygmies, for example, are held to represent the "primitive"—i.e., primeval (*Urkulturen*)—stratum of human experience. By studying them as they exist today, the economies, the social structures, and other aspects of this "primitive" stratum of human experience can, it is believed, be recovered. In these terms, however, it would seem that not *Einfühlung*, but the exercise of the imagination is the instrument Schmidt proposes to employ in determining the elements to be considered in studying cultural diffusion.

These overtones of mysticism were not present in the writings of the founder of this school, Fritz Graebner; or in the papers of others who, like B. Ankermann, were associated with Graebner in the task of forging the culture-historical method. The rigid objectivity in the approach of these men was, as a matter of fact, so extreme that it tended to defeat itself. Graebner, like Ankermann, as has often been pointed out, was a museum curator. The significance of this fact, though minimized by those who have defended their theories against attacks on their method, would seem undeniable. Museum workers must of necessity be concerned with objects. Sanctions, concepts, values, ideas cannot be exhibited in museum cases. It is significant that in Graebner's system nonmaterial culture played but a minor role.

Graebner's principal contribution, not only to the methodology of the culture-historical school, but to anthropology in general, was to sharpen and give objective expression to the criteria used in appraising the presumed diffusion of cultural elements from people to people. These criteria, called by him the criteria of form and quantity, are basic in all studies of cultural transmission. Their meaning is quite simple. When similarities are manifest in the cultures of two different groups, our judgment as to the probability that they have been derived from a single source depends on how numerous they are, and how complex. The greater the number of similarities, the more likelihood there is of borrowing having occurred; and the same is true regarding the complexity of a given element. This is why, for example, folktales can be used so effectively in the study of historical contact between nonliterate peoples. It will be remembered that a story is composed of independent variables, its characters, incidents and plot, each of which can travel separately. Therefore, when we find such a complicated cultural element as the Mother Holle story ("The Good Child and the Bad") widely distributed, the conclusion is inescapable that it must have been diffused, and not independently developed in each locality where it is told.

Goldenweiser has given an excellent example of how these principles are operative. He was accustomed to point out that if a Gothic cathedral was discovered in the heart of the Australian desert, there would be no denying the fact that Europeans had been there. Such a structure is so complicated, so distinctive, and composed of so many different elements, that it would be impossible to consider its hypothetical Australian counterpart as a duplication, independently developed, of the European form. The same would be true of any other complicated artifact or nonmaterial culture complex.

Cultural Dynamics

There are, however, certain pertinent reservations to his position that Graebner did not take into account. These reservations, that were paramount in the work of American diffusionists, are no more than the dictates of common sense, and stress the factor of accessibility in place and reasonable closeness in time. They have already been mentioned in connection with the postulates of the English diffusionists. Except in the most extreme hypothetical instances, such as those just given, the criteria of form and quantity, that is, are not of themselves sufficient to establish the case for diffusion in a given instance.

For Graebner, however, the principle of *ferninterpretation*—applied with certain cautions, to be sure—involved the disregard of these factors of time and distance. The term is difficult to render in English, for the phrase employed by Schmidt's translator, "distant interpretation," hardly conveys the meaning of the original. Perhaps "interpretation (of borrowing) despite distance" best renders Graebner's idea. In accordance with this Graebnerian principle, if two elements of culture, material or nonmaterial, are logically identical when their outward similarity is established, the factor of distance can be disregarded. That is, he holds that if these elements are established on the basis of the criteria of form and quantity and to the satisfaction of the student, to be the same, they must derive from the same source, wherever they may be found. Granting a preponderant tendency in man to borrow rather than to invent, the fact that similar "cultural complexes," as these bundles of traits are termed, must have a single origin follows logically, if not historically.

In Graebner's approach to the study of diffusion, the *kulturkomplexe,* or "cultural complexes" are quite different from those discussed in one of our earlier chapters, where the concept of the culture-complex was analyzed.[5] There, it will be remembered, it was pointed out that "each trait contributes to the larger unity which those groupings of elements we term culture-complexes always manifest within the context of a given culture." For Graebner, and others of the culture-historical school, the "complex" is composed of groups of individual traits that, while found together in various cultures, are themselves rather simple and have no functional relationship to one another.

An example will make this clear. Ankermann described the cultures of the Congo and West Africa in terms of the following "complex" of traits that were similar to those designated by Graebner to characterize the East-Papuan culture of Oceania: secret societies, masks, cannibalism, cane and wooden shields, xylophones, pan-pipes, bark-cloth, wooden drums, and carved human figures, among others. Since these elements are also present in certain Indian cultures of South America, the principle of *ferninterpretation,* operating in conjunction with the criteria of form and quantity, causes these "culture-complexes" to be referred to a single cultural stratum, from which it follows, for the Graebnerians, that they have resulted from the diffusion of a single historic stream.

Yet these traits, though numerous, are no more than separate items in three

---

[5] See above, pp. 176–181.

cultures located in widely distant regions. They constitute a "complex" only in the mind of the student; they have no functional association in the areas where they exist. The criteria of quantity and form thereby lose their effectiveness, and the probability of independent origin of the several functionally discrete units becomes much greater. Consider the trait of bark-cloth in the "complex" that has been named. As has been stated, bark-cloth comes from the inner bark of certain trees that grow only in the tropics. Since its manufacture is a relatively simple process, it is not difficult to conceive how it might have been come upon by different tropical peoples at different times. The same can be said for each individual component of a "complex" of this sort. Such "complexes" are therefore but a grouping of psychologically unrelated traits that, as complexes, exist only in the notebook of the student. As Sapir has put it, "a West Coast crutch paddle will not necessarily be heard to cry vigorously for its Melanesian mate." [6]

Cooper has shown that the position of the extreme diffusionists is untenable not only in terms of their method, but also where the facts concerning the area of his concern are taken into account. In his careful reconstruction of the development of South American cultures, to which we shall later refer in this chapter, he has commented tellingly on the conclusions of both the extreme diffusionist schools as far as Old World influence on the Americas is concerned. He says: "Our evidence regarding an element here and there, such as the sweet potato, the calabash, or the coconut, makes plausible—though far from proven—the assumption of sporadic pre-Columbian cultural contacts between Oceania and South America. But the inference that there has been notable or basic pre-Columbian Old World influence upon South American culture, as maintained by the Heliolithic and Kulturkreis schools, seems to rest on extremely weak positive evidence and furthermore to be in conflict at scores of crucial points with our massive ethnological and archaeological evidence. The resemblances on which these two schools mostly rest their respective cases seem far too few, too scattered, and too vague to justify conclusions of large-scale diffusion from the Old World to the New by the Oceanian or any other route. Apart from the initial 'palaeolithic' (in the sense of 'prehorticultural') inheritance, apart from a possible stray pre-Columbian accretion here and there, and apart from obvious post-Columbian influences, the culture of aboriginal South America gives every indication of being home-grown." [7]

It is because of these defects in its method of handling the ethnographic data, of its mystical approach to the fundamentals of human cultural experience, and the extremely hypothetical nature of its conclusions, that the position of the culture-historical school has been rejected by many anthropologists. Nevertheless, the criteria for assessing culture-contacts that have been drawn with such clarity in the writings of this group give this contribution significance, whatever position may be taken concerning its point of view as a whole. Furthermore, the stress laid by the culture-historical school on diffusion was, at the time of its initial formulation, a healthy reaction to the

---

[6] E. Sapir, 1916, p. 40.
[7] J. M. Cooper, 1942, p. 28.

evolutionist and sociological approaches to the study of culture, that predominated earlier. The rich documentation that Graebner and Schmidt afforded, and the field studies carried on by many members of the "school" as, for instance, the work of Koppers and Gusinde in Tierra del Fuego, also are reasons why this group has had the respect even of its most consistent opponents.

Yet it is apparent that more than clarity in definition, based on the assumption of regularity in historic development, is necessary, if we are to explain the processes of cultural change. Just as the reaction of man to culture is not rational, but rather rationalized, so the history of culture-contact has yet to be proved regular, despite all efforts to regularize it. Such an approach as that of the culture-historians, therefore, can at best but answer the question "what?" The "why?" of cultural dynamics, the reasons behind the acceptance or rejection of an innovation, lie as much outside the purview of this group as it did outside the concerns of the English diffusionists. Its objectives, in any case, thus comprise but a first step in the understanding of cultural change. Because of the hypothetical character of the results, this first step, as taken by the culture-historical school, can scarcely be said to have laid the ground for that analysis of cultural causation which must ultimately be the objective of the scientific study of the nature of culture and of cultural change.

4

THE studies of diffusion initiated by Franz Boas, the third approach to the problem of cultural borrowing, form a bridge to our consideration of acculturation. Boas recognized early in his career that the fundamental question toward which the study of culture must be pointed was not so much the fact of contact between peoples as the dynamic effects of such contact in making for cultural change. He was concerned with answering the question "what?" but only insofar as these answers led to that comprehension of process that is implied in the question "why?" It is, therefore, in the insistence on dynamics rather than on the recovery of descriptive fact, as the objective of diffusion studies, that the position of the American diffusionists, and those anthropologists of other countries who have accepted their point of view, differs most markedly from that of the two groups we have just considered.

"It is intelligible," Boas wrote in 1920, in one of his many papers devoted to the subject, "why in our studies the problem of dissemination should take a prominent position. It is much easier to prove dissemination than to follow up developments due to inner forces, and the data for such a study are obtained with much greater difficulty. . . . The reason why the study of inner development has not been taken up energetically, is not due to the fact that from a theoretical point of view it is unimportant, it is rather due to the inherent methodological difficulties."

A sentence that has been omitted in this quotation shows why the American position concerning diffusion studies may be regarded as a bridge to our discussion of acculturation. For in this sentence, Boas maintains that these phenomena of inner development—that is, the dynamic processes of culture —may "be observed in every phenomenon of acculturation in which foreign elements are remodeled according to the patterns prevalent in their new environment, and they may be found in the peculiar local developments of widely spread ideas and activities." [8]

In another discussion of diffusion, published four years later, Boas further clarified his position. "The importance of diffusion," he stated there, "has been so firmly established by the investigation of American material culture, ceremonies, art, and mythology, as well as by study of African cultural forms and by that of the prehistory of Europe, that we cannot deny its existence in the development of any local cultural type. It has not only been proved objectively by comparative studies, but the field student has also ample evidence showing the ways in which diffusion works. We know of cases in which a single individual has introduced a whole set of important myths. As an instance we might mention the tale of the origin of the Raven which is found in one single tribe on the northern part of Vancouver Island. It is still known to a few individuals that this tale was introduced by a man who had for many years been a slave in Alaska, and who was ultimately ransomed by his friends. Nevertheless, the myth is regularly told as part of the Raven cycle, although it is repudiated by all the neighboring tribes. . . . The introduction of new ideas must by no means be considered as resulting purely mechanically in additions to the cultural pattern, but also as an important stimulus to new inner developments. A purely inductive study of ethnic phenomena leads to the conclusion that mixed cultural types that are geographically or historically intermediate between two extremes, give evidence of diffusion." [9]

It is apparent from these quotations that the point of view taken by Boas differed from that of Elliot Smith, Perry, Graebner, Schmidt, and other more extreme diffusionists in the emphasis he laid on the following points:

1. The descriptive study of diffusion is a preliminary to the analytical study of process;
2. The study of diffusion must be inductive, in that associated traits of cultures (culture-complexes) held diffused must be considered in terms of their inner relationships rather than as groupings arbitrarily classified by the student;
3. The study of diffusion must work from the particular to the general, plotting distributions of traits in restricted areas before proceeding to the mapping of their distribution on a continental, to say nothing of a world-wide basis;
4. The approach to the study of the dynamic processes, of which diffusion is but one expression, must be psychological, and reach back to the individual for the comprehension of the realities of cultural change.

None of these points is given more than lip-service by adherents of the extreme diffusionist schools. As has been several times pointed out in discussing their work, one has difficulty in seeing any objectives in their research beyond the establishment of the facts about diffusion. Granted that to establish the fact of borrowing was important in the face of the belief that man everywhere

---

[8] F. Boas, 1920, p. 315 (reprinted in F. Boas, 1940, pp. 284–5).
[9] Ibid., 1924, p. 341 (reprinted in F. Boas, 1940, p. 291).

independently invented the elements of his culture, it is scarcely satisfactory to go to the other extreme and urge *a priori* that similar elements could never have been independently invented. Therefore, Boas held that a catalogue of similar traits in different cultures could never of itself afford adequate proof of historic contact. The similarities would have to include similar traits, similarly related, to afford proof of diffusion; and this, moreover, only within a restricted area, where communication between borrowers and lenders was not difficult to assume.

Above all, for Boas and those who agreed with him, it was of the greatest importance that the psychological factors underlying borrowing be continuously kept in mind. This, they held, must be done even where these factors could not themselves be studied, as among nonliterate peoples who had left no historic records. In such instances these cultures were to be analyzed individually, then compared in detail as to organization and structure as well as to their elements. Then only could conclusions be reached concerning such matters as acceptance and rejection of new traits, and the reshaping, in the light of pre-existing patterns of the borrowing culture, of what had been borrowed. Such conclusions, moreover, were regarded as applicable only to the extent that investigations in many areas of restricted scope justified setting them up as generalizations.

Because of their emphasis on a rigorous methodology, the positive contributions of this group to the theory of culture have tended to be obscured. The Jesup Expedition, conceived and directed by Boas, is only one of many research projects whose theoretical implications are quite as significant as their ethnographic return. This series of field researches, that established the historic unity of the cultures about the Bering Straits, was, as a matter of fact, from the first conceived in broad theoretical terms. Let us see how Boas expressed the objectives of this program in reporting on it to the Seventh International Geographical Congress, held in Berlin in 1899:

The thorough ethnological investigations which have been carried on during the last twenty years largely under the auspices of the Bureau of American Ethnology, and more recently also by other American institutions, have shown a considerable diversity of culture inhabiting the continent of North America. At the same time it was found that the displacement of tribes, the intertribal intercourse, had brought about a considerable dissemination of cultural elements.

The general trend of ethnological investigations suggests that at an early period there may have been a number of rather isolated centres, from which the peculiar forms of culture developed which we observe at the present time in different regions. This view is corroborated by the results of somatological investigation, which prove the existence of a number of well-defined types inhabiting limited areas of this continent.

One of the most striking phenomena disclosed by these inquiries is the distribution of languages and physical types on the Pacific coast. When we extend our view beyond the limits of America, and take into consideration the Pacific coast of northern Asia, we find similar conditions prevailing there. . . . Since this is at the same time the region in which Asia and America approach each other most closely, the question as to the cause of the similarity becomes particularly interesting.

Diffusion and the Reconstruction of Cultural History

With the problem stated in these terms, then, Boas set forth "the fundamental questions which the expedition has to solve":

1. The period of occupancy of various parts of the coast, and changes in the physical characteristics and culture of the inhabitants.
2. The geographical distribution of the types of man along the coasts, and their relationship to those of neighbouring areas.
3. The investigation of the languages and cultures of the coast tribes with particular reference to the question of the dissemination of culture.[10]

Here we have the essence of this approach. First all the weapons in the anthropological armory are employed—comparative analysis of physical type, archaeological investigation, the study of similarities and differences in language and culture. Second, the objective is restricted, the area well defined, its geographical unity respected. Finally, the investigation is pointed toward the solution of broader theoretical problems, and not limited to collection of data that merely establish the fact of contact.

5

IT CAN be seen that a primary aim of all diffusionist groups has been the reconstruction of history, and it was in terms of this aim that the ends of anthropological science were for a time almost exclusively defined. The heliolithic and culture-historical schools aspired to world-wide reconstructions; the American diffusionists sought to plot historic contacts on a more modest scale, with broader reconstructions held as a goal should the data justify them.

Perhaps the most systematic presentation of the ways in which the analysis of data designed to reveal the history of nonliterate peoples should be employed in this restricted fashion has been given by Sapir. He begins with the premise that, "so-called primitive culture consists throughout of phenomena that, so far as the ethnologist is concerned, must be worked out historically, that is, in terms of actual happenings, however inferred, that are conceived to have a specific sequence, a specific localization, and specific relations among themselves." Yet, since all the knowledge we have of these nonhistoric peoples are collections of data that lie mainly on a single time level, the question he seeks to answer is this: "How inject a chronology into this confusing mass of purely descriptive fact?" Sapir points out two limitations that must be recognized as modifying the validity of any answers given to this question. In the time perspectives of historical reconstruction, nothing like the absolute chronology of history can be achieved; while we must be content to deal with relationships between groups, and not in terms of the individuals who were the effective instruments of the processes we study.

In some cases, documents afford direct evidence which tell how nonliterate people appeared to early travellers. Accounts given by the old, and legends, which constitute native testimony, together with the testimony of stratified archaeological remains, are other kinds of direct evidence that can be used in drawing reconstructions of past events. For the most part, however, our evi-

---

[10] F. Boas, 1900, pp. 678-9.

dence must be indirect. According to Sapir, evidence of this sort is to be derived from physical anthropology, ethnology and linguistics. Here, however, we shall consider only the testimony ethnographic data can give.

The methods which yield inferential evidence from the data of ethnology take many forms, and involve many hypotheses. Thus, for instance, Sapir first of all advances the method of "cultural seriation" based on the hypothesis that the simpler elements of a culture are to be regarded as older than more complex ones. This principle, we are told, is to be used with great caution, and some pains are taken to give a specific instance from Iroquois and Wyandot social organization which demonstrates its tentativeness. However, "in spite of its inherent weaknesses as an historical method," it is nonetheless believed by Sapir to be of use if cautiously employed in the realm of material culture of a single tribe or a restricted area.

The consideration of how elements are associated in a culture, is a second method. The principle of "necessary presupposition," as for instance, that the bow-drill of the Eskimos must be regarded as older than the dot designs made by its use, is one example of this. Another point to be considered is the "relative firmness" of the association of traits in a culture as indicating relative age; as, for example, the lightness with which agriculture is set in the food economy of the Paiute Indians, as against its food-gathering aspects, which forces the conclusion that agriculture is "a borrowing of no great antiquity from the Pueblo Indians to the south." Other methods to be used include a consideration of the degree to which elements of a culture are fitted to its natural setting; the "frequency with which a particular culture element is associated with others"; the degree to which complexes in a culture are elaborated—the most elaborate being assumed to be the older; and the analysis of "survivals," or retentions, as we have called them, within a given culture.[11]

One cannot but be struck, in reading this discussion, by the extremely hypothetical character of this approach, and the tentativeness of any conclusions that may be derived from its use. The same is true for Sapir's presentation of how the facts of cultural distribution should be interpreted. Here we tread familiar ground, especially where the problems of convergence and of the use of "interrupted cultural distribution"—the type encountered in the writings of the extreme diffusionists—is discussed. However, Sapir also puts forward certain other principles to be applied in the study of restricted distributions that have been widely debated, and which we also must review briefly.

The most important of these is what Sapir terms the problem of interpreting "continuous distribution from a culture-centre,"[12] but which has come to be better known as the *age-area* hypothesis. Its most elaborate documentation has been given by Wissler, who used it to analyze the historic relationships between the tribes of North America. He stated it simply, as follows: "a distribution of narrow range may be suspected of being an innovation, whereas one of wide range would be of respectable age."[13]

---

[11] E. Sapir, 1916, pp. 5–25.

[12] Op. cit., pp. 25–37.

[13] C. Wissler, 1926, p. xv.

Diffusion and the Reconstruction of Cultural History

This proposition, which has been documented by archaeological and ethnographic distributions, is exemplified in the following diagram:

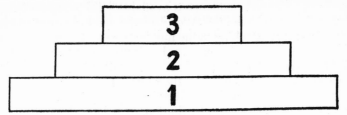

FIG. 65   *Diagram to illustrate basis of age-area concept.*

Let us say this represents the archaeological distribution of three related pottery types. In the center of the area where it is found, three strata are uncovered; over a wider range, two types will be present; while the distribution of
the type found at the bottom of each of the preceding two will be still wider.
The conclusion we reach, therefore, is that this kind of pottery originated in
region 3, and diffused to 2. In the meantime, the people of 3 were developing
a new type which later diffused to region 2, displacing the original kind,
which, during this time, had diffused to region 1. At the same time, however,
the people at the center developed a third type, which did not have time to
diffuse before the development in all the area came to an end.

Here the idea that diffusion occurs concentrically is basic, and it is on this
point that the theory has come in for the most criticism. Sapir, whose work
antedates Wissler's, enters three cautions to the idea of continuous distribution. He points out: 1) that spread may be more rapid in one direction than
another, 2) that the historically oldest form may have undergone such modification at the center that the actual point of origin will be wrongly determined, and 3) that population movements within the area of distribution may
have had repercussions that lead to a "misinterpreted type of culture distribution." [14]

Dixon, one of the most severe critics of the age-area hypothesis, has not
only challenged Wissler's basic assumptions, but has also challenged the validity of the mapping of the data from which his conclusions are derived.
Thus Dixon states categorically that traits diffuse "asymmetrically and errati-
cally, and at varying rates," while he also flatly asserts that "the area of origin,
the trait nucleus, is not usually the centre whence specializations spread, but
that these arise in the main marginally." He concludes by stating that while
the principles we term the age-area hypothesis may have a certain validity
within a culture-area, yet "just so soon . . . as . . . the trait passes into another environment and a different culture, the enormous and persistent
power of modification which both exert, comes into play, to the ultimate and
inevitable ruin of the principles hitherto active." [15]

To Dixon's cogent strictures on Wissler's use of data from the American
Indians are to be added instances showing where the principle is inapplicable

[14] Op. cit., pp. 26–7.
[15] R. B. Dixon, 1928, p. 145–6.

to facts concerning which we have the historic record. Wallis has found that "Wissler's 'principle' of centrifugal diffusion does not apply to traits of the Old World, where historic evidence is available." Taking as an example the "relative distributions in the Old World of the symbolism attaching to the number four and that attaching to the number seven," he shows that seven as a mystical number "for centuries . . . has been . . . more widely diffused . . . than the concept four, although . . . the latter is in these areas, as far as the historical record is available, the older." From this Wallis concludes that "the older trait is less widely diffused, and in neither case is the area of origin the center of the area of distribution." [16] A later demonstration of the fact that the age-area theory must be used with the greatest circumspection in making historical reconstructions is found in Hodgen's study of how the windmill achieved its present European distribution. Her research has proved that the spread of this item of culture was by no means in accordance with the hypothesis.[17] Many other examples that have been overlooked in considering this "principle" could also be adduced. Thus, the dog has long been held to be the oldest domesticated animal *because* of its world-wide distribution. Yet, this argument overlooks the fact that the chicken, which we know to have been domesticated in relatively recent times, also has a world-wide distribution.

Does all this, then, mean that attempts to reconstruct the historic contacts of nonliterate peoples and the historic developments of nonhistoric areas should be given over? Such a conclusion is hardly justified; certainly not if stress be laid on *probability* rather than on absolute recovery of historic fact.

In the paper of Cooper from which we have quoted, and in another contribution bearing on the subject,[18] this student has built up an impressive series of probable events in the historical development of South American Indian culture. He employs the concept of the "marginal"—that is, economically simpler—culture to develop, with the use of distributions of various traits and complexes, an historical scheme which, translated into culture areas, gives a workable understanding of how the present-day similarities and differences found between the cultures of that continent may have come into being.

A similarly skilful consideration of the Eskimo data by Collins affords another instance of how reconstructions, having a high degree of probability, can be built up when all the facts are utilized.[19] Collins uses archaeological data to test previous assumptions of relationships across the width of the North American continent; he utilizes the existing distributions of the ethnographic materials and takes into full account the geographic factor of the distance between North America and Asia across the Bering Strait as against that between the several Aleutian Islands to plot probable routes of migration and counter-migration. His conclusions do not concern us here, since we

---

[16] W. D. Wallis, 1930, pp. 75–6.
[17] M. T. Hodgen, 1942, pp. 351–68.
[18] J. M. Cooper, 1941.
[19] H. B. Collins, Jr., 1937, pp. 375–84.

are interested in the means students employ to achieve reconstructions of history that have a reasonable probability of being historically valid. It would seem, all things considered, that the effort is worth the return, provided 1) *that the area selected for analysis should be one whose historic unity can be assumed*, and 2) that *the probability, not the absolute fact of historic developments, be recognized as the aim.*

6

THE flowering of the positive elements in the approach of diffusionists who were interested in cultural dynamics rather than historical reconstruction *per se* is in reality, not to be sought in diffusion studies, but in the study of acculturation, which we will discuss in the next chapter. This is perhaps best exemplified in the researches into the Sun Dance of the Plains Indians, to which we have already had occasion to refer. The paper by Spier, which summarizes the findings and points their significance, is based on the field study of this rite among nineteen different Plains tribes. The particular elements that go to make up the total complex were noted as to their presence or absence in the dance as found in each tribe, as well as the manner in which each trait was integrated into the ceremony as a whole. Not only was the presence or absence of such material traits as the center pole of a dance lodge noted, but such items as the principles of organization of the dance, the factor of leadership in it, and other nonmaterial elements, were also included.

Having presented his distribution, Spier then moves to the analysis of the dynamic factors underlying the diffusion of the Sun Dance, that account for the similarities and differences between its manifestations in various tribes. The problem of differential borrowing is first attacked—why, for example, some tribes have taken over certain elements that others have rejected. Psychological factors are here held paramount—"We are surely justified in asserting that the discrimination" found in differential selection of traits "is due in large part to their mental content." Each dance is compared with the tribal system as a whole, in an attempt to understand the reasons for acceptance and rejection. The conclusion reached is that, "the agreement is greatest in organization and motivation, less in behavior, and least in material objects, regalia, etc. That is, the peculiar element injected into the mass of borrowed traits appears to have been largely determined by the ceremonial pattern." [20]

Yet this, and other conclusions of this study, insofar as they attempt to attain the historical and psychological heart of the problem of cultural transmission, could not but be tentative and hypothetical. As in all cases where the findings cannot be historically documented, it was the end-results of diffusion that had to provide the data. The processes by means of which these results had been attained were necessarily lost in an unrecorded past. Spier recognized this obstacle and faced it without equivocation. "The data on the

---

[20] L. Spier, 1921, pp. 504, 511.

sun dance are far from adequate to permit the full delineation of these developmental processes. The desideratum is a more precise knowledge of the function of the innovating individual, of his cultural equipment, the character of his milieu, and the extent of his contribution. . . . It is doubtful that data of this nature can now be obtained for the sun dance, but it is equally a requisite for any other study of cultural development. In fact, the consciousness of this is evidenced by the transformation of ethnographic works in recent years from presentations of culture as static, standardized products to their description as fluctuating, variable forms." [21]

[21] *Ibid.*, p. 522.

CHAPTER 31

Acculturation:
Cultural Transmission in Process

THE terms acculturation and diffusion have been used by anthropologists since the last decades of the nineteenth century. J. W. Powell employed *acculturation* to mean culture-borrowing as early as 1880. While the earliest use of *diffusion* has not been established, it is interesting to note that, as late as 1899, we find Boas writing of the *dissemination* of culture.

Shortly after the turn of the century, *diffusion* captured the stage, and *acculturation* was used rarely, if at all. Because the attention of students was fixed on establishing the fact of borrowing, diffusion studies, in effect, came to be the analysis of the distribution of particular cultural traits and complexes. We have seen how the realization grew that such studies could only be effective up to a point, and that students seeking to understand the dynamic phases of the processes involved turned for their materials to the analysis of cultures where change was actually to be observed. For such researches, the designation *acculturation* (or, in England, the phrase "culture-contact") studies came to be used.

The problem of defining the word *acculturation* and delimiting the scope of work to which the term can be applied came to the fore about 1935. At this time, a definition of acculturation was presented by a committee of the Social Science Research Council as part of a Memorandum designed to act as a guide in acculturation research. This definition and its accompanying delimitation of the field received wide acceptance and was employed in orienting many acculturation studies. It reads as follows: "Acculturation comprehends those phenomena which result when groups of individuals having different cultures come into continuous first-hand contact, with subsequent changes in the original cultural patterns of either or both groups." The reservations in the "note" appended to this statement show that the need to distinguish the term from others in use did not go unrecognized. "Under this definition," it says, "acculturation is to be distinguished from *culture-change*, of which it is but one aspect, and *assimilation*, which is at times a phase of acculturation. It is also to be differentiated from *diffusion*, which while occurring in all instances of acculturation, is not only a phenomenon which frequently takes place without the occurrence of the types of contact be-

523

tween peoples specified in the definition given above, but also constitutes only one aspect of the process of acculturation." [1]

Within five years of the publication of this definition, however, two of its three authors had entered reservations to its phrasing. In one instance, it was cogently indicated that, "the definition makes no attempt to specify the *nature* of the phenomena which are to be treated as a part of acculturation." The determinants under this definition, it was here pointed out, are "a) the particular situation under which the phenomena are present, and b) a suggested rather than clearly indicated limitation of the field of those phenomena which seem to be the results of a particular situation." The limitations imposed by the phrase "continuous first-hand contact" were also indicated —that of distinguishing "first-hand" from other contacts, and of delimiting "continuous" from intermittent relationships.[2]

The other critique was directed against the use of the phrase "groups of individuals." "It can be assumed, . . ." states this critique, "that where contact between cultures is mentioned a certain human contact must be taken for granted as the only means by which culture can spread from people to people or from generation to generation. Yet, while it is desirable to emphasize that culture is no mystical entity that can travel without its human carriers, it is also true that it is not a simple matter always to know when 'groups of individuals' are in contact. . . ."

An instance cited to make this point can be quoted. This example is taken from the South Seas island of Tikopia. Here "certain elements of European culture, especially in the fields of material culture and religion," have been "effecting an invasion of aboriginal patterns." The question is then raised: "Is the visit of the mission boat once or twice a year, and the work of a single missionary (a native of another island and not himself a European!) to be regarded as an acculturating force? Certainly this person is not a 'group of individuals,' nor can it well be maintained that recurring visits of those on the mission boat constitute 'continuous' contact." [3]

This reservation received later documentation from work among the Hausa of Northern Nigeria. This people, who live on the line of contact in West Africa between Mohammedanism and pagan religion, have effected a synthesis of these beliefs that affords highly significant materials for the study of cultural dynamics. "The main impulses which converted the bulk of the Hausa to Mohammedanism," we are told, "proceeded, not from Arab traders or elements of the white population of North Africa, but from the Negroes of the central Niger region in the West Sudan. This proselyting activity was carried out . . . by small parties or single individuals who either departed or became absorbed in the native population." A further point of importance in this discussion appears. "Because of this absence of prolonged contact with large bodies of other Moslem peoples, the essential acculturative agent has been the books in which Mohammedan teachings are contained. Amalgamation of Mohammedan and aboriginal belief has thus occurred as the end-

[1] R. Redfield, R. Linton and M. J. Herskovits, 1936, pp. 149–50.
[2] R. Linton, 1940, pp. 464–5.
[3] M. J. Herskovits, 1938a, pp. 11–12.

product of a process in which the native learned men, known as Malams, have adapted what they found in sacred texts to the native situation, retaining much of pagan culture at the same time, by fitting it into a Moslem framework." [4]

It is evident that neither duration nor intensity of contact can provide adequate criteria for differentiating acculturation from other mechanisms of cultural change. Here, as in many other instances where questions of definition enter, the problem of distinguishing between alternative terms must be held subsidiary to the need to analyze the facts in the most effective manner. Our concern is primarily with the processes of cultural change, and only secondarily with classifying the situations in which change occurs. From this point of view, it makes but slight difference whether a given case of cultural transmission is to be termed acculturation or diffusion. Only insofar as the circumstances in a particular instance affect the kind of reception accorded a given innovation do these circumstances, as such, come to be of consequence to us.

Terminology, however, is an essential tool in research, and terms must be as clear as possible. The distinction between the two designations can best be drawn on the basis of usage, rather than from the rigid delimitation of circumstances. We shall distinguish these designations, therefore, in terms of methodological considerations. Over the years, diffusion has come to mean the analysis of similarities and differences between existing nonliterate, and in this sense, nonhistoric, cultures. In such studies, the contacts that presumably took place between the peoples involved have had to be reconstructed, and the reshaping of the borrowed elements have had to be inferred from the variations in their forms as manifest in one culture after another. Acculturation, on the other hand, has most often been applied to the instances where transmission of cultural elements could be more fully documented, being thus susceptible of study on the spot, or by the use of documentary data, or both. In summary, then, diffusion, in these terms, is the study of *achieved cultural transmission;* while acculturation is the study of *cultural transmission in process.*

This usage rests on a real methodological distinction, wherein the difference between observation and inference are paramount. Diffusion studies, from this point of view, assume that contacts have taken place between peoples because of the similarities observed between their cultures at the time they are studied. The reconstruction of the processes by means of which transmission was made effective, as has been seen, must be a matter of inference, forced on the student by the nature of his materials. This was the case in the study of the Plains Indian Sun Dance cited in the preceding chapter. The studies of Wissler, who plotted the patterns of moccasins over the Plains and adjoining culture-areas, or Hallowell's researches into the regional variations in bear ceremonialism throughout northern North America and Asia give us a sense of how given cultural elements or complexes of elements were reworked as they moved from one tribe to another,

---

[4] J. Greenberg, 1941, p. 52.

or how a given complex incorporated varied elements as it was taken up in one tribe after another. Yet *how* all this happened, *when* it occurred, *where* it originated, and *by whom* the change was brought about, in such studies remain only for conjecture.

In acculturation studies, however, the historic facts are known or can be obtained. In most cases, acculturation research deals with contacts in the contemporary period. The conditions antecedent to the contact can thus be discovered, the pre-contact cultures of the peoples party to it can be ascertained, and the present condition of the cultures set down. In some cases, even the personalities involved in influencing the acceptance or rejection of varied elements can be reached. Where documentation is necessary, the welding of ethnographic and historical materials is merely a matter of cross-disciplinary research. This, indeed, has given rise to a special technique called the ethnohistorical method.

Where past contacts between historic peoples are the concern of the student, the acculturative situation can be studied by the use of documentary materials. These materials have not been used more because, as Hodgen has put it, "The scope of acculturation study has been unduly circumscribed by the tight but unrealistic boundaries of the formal academic disciplines." This student has shown what fruitful results can follow from breaking down these unrealistic boundaries by her own documentary study of the spread of glass making and paper in England.[5] The three steps in borrowing that she distinguishes are exposure, establishment, and dissemination. Treated as a continuous process, their application to studies of contact between contemporary peoples should yield valuable results. The study by Wittfogel of the social history of the Chinese Liao empire of the tenth and eleventh centuries, is another case in point. Cast in terms of "acculturation and relative, selective, and graded diffusion,"[6] it similarly demonstrates the results that can be gained from the study of historic documents which reveal, as process, the causes and effects of culture-change resultant on borrowing.

To differentiate diffusion from acculturation pragmatically as has been done here does not, however, fully delimit the meaning of the term "acculturation." It has been differently used by different disciplines, while certain equivalents for it found in the literature of anthropology itself have carried connotations that require clarification.

2

PSYCHOLOGISTS, educators, and child development specialists have found the word acculturation useful to describe the process of conditioning by means of which a child is habituated to the ways of life of its group. It will be obvious, however, that in this sense it is roughly the equivalent of the word enculturation that, in these pages, has been used to describe this same process. As far as can be ascertained, those who use the word acculturation in this way have

---

[5] M. T. Hodgen, 1945, pp. 466-7.
[6] K. Wittfogel, 1946, p. 5.

employed it without defining its meaning with any great degree of precision. In the case of child study reports, acculturation is often given the significance of several other terms, each of which carries slightly different connotations. It is a commonplace to find papers where *acculturation, socialization, education,* and *conditioning* are used, insofar as context would indicate, as synonyms, and without any attempt to distinguish shadings in their meaning.

It is not altogether surprising that acculturation has been so used by students of child development, for the word expresses their meaning well. There is certainly no justification for any discipline to insist on the exclusive right to the use of any technical term. However, as we must again repeat, knowledge is not bound by the various subjects into which it is conventionally divided. Problems must follow wherever the data lead, and the data have a habit of disregarding the intellectual fences that separate the concerns of one discipline from another. We can here, therefore, but note the difference between the anthropological use of "acculturation" and its employment in a different sense by students in closely related fields. No question of proper or improper usage intrudes, since in science there is no "right" or "wrong" in the non-evaluative use of a word, except by definition. It is essential, however, that different usages in science be made explicit in scientific analysis and that, above all, a term employed in any given work be consistently used. "Acculturation" in these pages then, will consistently signify the study of cultural transmission in process. Those who are accustomed to its use as comprehending either or all of the ideas expressed in such terms as *socialization, education, cultural conditioning,* and the like, will here find their equivalent in the phrase *early enculturation.*

The question of proper or improper usage does enter, however, where connotations of an evaluative character are injected into the study of acculturation, especially where research concerns contacts between what are termed higher or lower, or active and passive, bodies of tradition. For evaluations of this nature, injected into scientific study in any field, lessen objectivity and by this very fact increase the difficulty of obtaining the ends of scientific analysis.

Let us, for example, consider the position of Malinowski, that the study of African culture-contact is one of "an impact of a higher, active culture upon a simpler, more passive one." To the study of the resultant situation, he holds, "the conception of culture change as the impact of Western civilization and the reaction thereto of the indigenous cultures is the only fruitful approach."[7] His disregard of the fact that, in African culture-change the native exerts his influence upon the resultant borrowing, both intertribal and between Europeans and Africans, is difficult for those who take the position that under any contact all peoples party to it borrow from one another. A position that does not take this into account is psychologically untenable, also, since it is not easy to envisage any human being or group of human beings who, in any situation, are as passive as this approach would imply. Even slaves and prisoners react to their situations in ways that effectively change

[7] B. Malinowski, 1945, pp. 15, 17.

them, if only through passive resistance to measures they deem too oppressive. Africans, who are neither slaves nor prisoners, obviously do a great
deal to shape the course of their developing cultures under contact with
Europeans, to say nothing of how they influence the Europeans themselves.

Except for the German ethnologist, Mühlmann, no other student of cultural theory has laid such exclusive stress on what can best be described as
"cultural-imposition." Actually, Mühlmann's theory of the *kulturgefälle*, cultural decline (literally "culture-fall") that results from peoples with cultures
that are "unequal in content of civilization" (*Ungleichheit an zivilisato-
rischer Fülle*), would seem to be a kind of translation, in the sphere of culture, of the Nazi doctrine of racial superiority. The date of publication of
Mühlmann's work, 1938, is significant in this connection because of the climate of opinion in which he wrote. *Kulturgefälle*, which represents an extreme position in the theory of culture-contact, is mentioned here, however,
merely for the record. It is based on no field research, and lacks documentation to give it any validity.[8]

It is ironical that Malinowski's functionalist position should have been
called on to justify so arrant an ethnocentrism as that of Mühlmann. Both
explicitly and implicitly Malinowski's work stressed the values in the life of
nonliterate peoples and the necessity of studying every culture in terms of
its own orientations. We must, therefore, seek our explanation of Malinowski's point of view elsewhere than in any systematic exploitation of ethnocentrism. One reason for his position was the essentially anti-historical point
of view of functionalist theory, derived as it was from field-work in a single,
small, relatively static South Seas culture. Another reason is to be found in
the fact that Malinowski's concern with the phenomena of culture-contact
was to develop a basis for techniques that could be applied in solving the
practical problems of African colonial administration.

The first of these reasons caused Malinowski to evolve the concept of the
"zero-point" in culture, the point from which change in a static way of life
began. It is difficult to believe that he did not develop this concept merely
to be able to demolish it, for there is no "point" at which any culture is
static. What is done in studies of culture-contact is to take some period in
the history of a given culture, usually antecedent to the particular contact
being investigated, that can act as a base-line from which to triangulate
change, and thus provide the framework within which the resultant dynamic
processes can be analyzed. This technique Malinowski and his students, like
all others concerned with contact studies, were forced to employ; though his
ahistorical approach made it difficult for him to place change in Africa in its
proper perspective, as only one phase of the age-long process in human
experience of cultural transmission.

Malinowski's preoccupation with administrative problems led him to
overemphasize the weakness of African ways of life in the face of the impact
of European culture. The very works of his students, that he himself cites
to make his points, contain abundant proofs of the extent to which African
culture, despite the pressures brought against it, has withstood these on-

---

[8] W. Mühlmann, 1938, pp. 195–6, 202–3.

slaughts. It is this same preoccupation, too, that caused him to neglect the phenomenon of interchange of cultural elements under contact. In contact between Europeans and Africans, this interchange has at least been sufficient to make the life of Europeans living in Africa something quite different than it is in Europe, a fact that has theoretical, no less than practical, implications.

Far more acceptable than the evaluative phrasings we have just considered is the word transculturation, that first appeared in 1940. Ortiz, the Cuban scholar who devised it, gives these reasons for its use: "I am of the opinion that the word *transculturation* better expresses the different phases of the process of transition from one culture to another because this does not consist merely in acquiring another culture, which is what the English word *acculturation* really implies, but the process also necessarily involves the loss or uprooting of a previous culture, which could be defined as deculturation. In addition it carries the idea of the consequent creation of new cultural phenomena, which would be called neoculturation." [9]

The word transculturation, as described in this passage, is unambiguous with respect to the fact that every situation of cultural contact and the subsequent innovations that result from it implies cultural borrowing. The misapprehension of Ortiz concerning the use of the term acculturation is certainly not as serious as one which would ascribe to acculturation an ethnocentric quality which it has never had. Were not the term acculturation so firmly fixed in the literature of anthropology, "transculturation" might equally well be used to express the same concept. It is so used by some anthropologists who employ Spanish as their medium; but in Brazil, the Portuguese equivalent of acculturation, *aculturação,* is the accepted designation.

Aside from questions of terminology, what is important to understand is that the term acculturation in no way implies that cultures party to contact are to be distinguished from each other as "higher," or "more advanced," or as having a greater "content of civilization," or to differ in any other qualitative manner. As far as the evidence shows, the transmission of culture, a process of cultural change of which acculturation is but one expression, occurs when any two peoples have historic contact with one another. Where one group, because it is larger, or better equipped technologically than another, forces changes in the ways of life of a conquered people it rules, it can be called a "dominant" group.

Situations of this kind are no novelty, no unique attribute of the twentieth century. Mohammedan domination was of this character; so was that subsequent to the conquest of local groups by the Inca of Peru; so were the conquests of the autochthonous agricultural tribes of East Africa by the invading cattle-herding Nilotes. Contacts between Euroamericans and native nonliterate, nonindustrial peoples are taking place more widely over the world than in the past. It seems evident that present-day contacts are more demoralizing to the subject-peoples than the contacts of earlier times, if only because they have the sanction of a more fervent ethnocentrism than has in

---

[9] F. Ortiz, 1947, pp. 102–3.

the past marked the rule of one people by another. However, in these characteristics they differ in degree, not in kind, from the many instances in recorded history, to say nothing of unrecorded history, where one people have attempted to regulate the ways of life of another. The significant point is that whatever the nature of the contact, mutual borrowing and subsequent revision of cultural elements seem to result.

3

TYPES of contact between peoples differ in many respects. They can occur between entire populations, or substantial segments of these populations, or they may arise from contact between smaller groupings or even individuals. Where the representatives of one group bring to another a particular facet of their culture, the elements borrowed will self-evidently be those of the facet presented. When the men of two nonliterate groups meet periodically when following game, for example, one would not anticipate that the women's sphere of either culture might be much affected. Where the representatives of Euroamerican culture in contact with a native people are missionaries, relatively little change in native technology would be expected.

The conclusion, however, is not to be drawn that the more representative the segments of populations involved in an interchange, the more comprehensive the transmission of culture will be. As in other instances in the study of culture, deductions whose logic is impeccable are rendered invalid because of the nature of the particular historic circumstances of a given contact, and the ways in which the interests of the peoples concerned have, in a particular case, been pointed. Among the American Indians, the contacts between the sedentary Pueblos and the Spaniards never resulted in the Pueblo peoples taking the horse, though this animal became an integral part of Plains culture. In Africa, attempts to induce natives to improve their techniques of cultivation by changing from hoe to plow have met with great resistance. Yet in most of Africa, cotton prints for clothing have been taken over with avidity.

Contacts are also to be classified as friendly or hostile. So much stress has been laid on the more dramatic instances of hostile contact, that the less striking—but probably more numerous—examples of friendly association between peoples has tended to be lost sight of. An outstanding contribution that has effectively called attention to the importance of studying this latter type of contact is the analysis by Lindgren of the "culture contact without conflict," occurring between the Reindeer Tungus and certain Russian Cossacks in northwestern Manchuria. She defines the condition of this contact in terms of two salient facts: "1) I heard no Tungus or Cossack express fear, contempt, or hatred in relation to the other group as a whole or any individual composing it. . . . 2) No instance was recorded of the use or threat of force in the relations between these communities, although the reminiscences of the elderly cover most of the period of contact."[10]

[10] E. J. Lindgren, 1938, p. 607.

Acculturation: Cultural Transmission in Process

Redfield has sketched a similar situation in Guatemala, where contact has been continuous between the Spanish-speaking urban "ladinos" whose customs are European, and the "indios" who speak a native Indian language and whose culture is that of the native villages. Here again we have an instance of contact between peoples of different cultures—in the one case European, Christian, and literate, and in the other relatively non-European, relatively non-Christian, and nonliterate. Nonetheless, Redfield finds only, "benign ethnic relations: the absence of recent attempts by one group to dominate the other; the fact that there is little or no economic competition along ethnic lines; the circumstances that natural resources are plentiful; the individualistic character of the economy and the social organization; and the fact that both groups carry on some of the prevailing means of livelihood." [11] That neither in Manchuria nor Guatemala was prejudice felt by one group against the physical type of the other, must be accounted as significant. In both cases, too, no strong convictions of a religious or other nature seem to have stood in the way of a peaceful interchange of ideas.

It must be made clear that cultural interchange is not prevented by hostile contact between peoples. The mutual borrowing that has marked the contacts between Euroamericans and natives has often been achieved despite the absence of friendly relations between the parties to the interchange. Bushman "clicks" now characterize the language of the Zulu and other Bantu-speaking peoples of southeast Africa, whose cattle the Bushmen for many generations have systematically raided. The lesson to be drawn from examples such as these seems to be that cultural borrowing results from any kind of contact; that the factor of friendliness or hostility is of itself not crucial.

It is essentially out of contacts involving dominance of one people over another that contra-acculturative movements arise—those movements wherein a people come to stress the values in aboriginal ways of life, and to move aggressively, either actually or in fantasy, toward the restoration of those ways, even in the face of obvious evidence of their impotence to throw off the power that restricts them. The Ghost Dance that swept over various Indian tribes of Western United States in the latter half of the nineteenth century, and eventuated in the Indian wars of the period, afford one example of such a contra-acculturative movement. The rise of organized labor in various parts of Africa, and the association of the virtues of aboriginal, non-European life with the immediate economic ends in view, is another instance of this kind of reaction to contact. Of a similar type was the Gandhi movement in India, which stressed a return to the hand-loom as a part of a program whose essential aim was political independence.

One of the best documented instances of a contra-acculturative movement has been given by Williams, who has described the rise and subsequent career of what he termed the "Vailala Madness," naming it after the town on the Gulf of Papua, New Guinea, where the movement originated in 1919.[12] This cult arose as a reaction to the hopelessness of the situation in

[11] R. Redfield, 1939, p. 516.
[12] F. E. Williams, 1923 and 1934.

which natives found themselves under foreign domination, and was based on a doctrine of the early return of the dead. It had its prophets, and was marked by possession and violent dancing. Though it was anti-white, and predicted the day when olden times would return and the invaders would be wiped out, it led to the destruction of certain rituals and sacred objects of earlier times, and in the new cult substituted for them certain Christian and secular European elements. Twelve years later the Madness had abated, leaving only certain traditions that the miracles predicted by the prophets had actually taken place.

Three further types of contact are to be noted. One is where contacts are between groups about equal in size, or where groups are of different sizes. Another is where groups differ markedly in the complexity of their material or nonmaterial culture, or both; or where cultures are of an equal degree of complexity. Finally, we encounter those situations where a group having one way of life comes into the habitat of another, or where the receiving group achieves its contact with the new culture in the new habitat.

The significance of all these factors is readily apparent, though of the three situations it is likely that the first, where population size is involved, will prove to be of least importance. There are too many instances where small groups have influenced large ones, or where a large group has failed to influence a small one, for this to stand as a factor of any considerable significance. We may recall how few were the representatives of Moham- medan culture among the Hausa of Sudanese Africa, and yet how firmly entrenched the Moslem tradition has become there. Or we may consider how the sparse Pygmy populations of the Ituri forest have continued their own way of life despite the extended contact they have had, probably for centuries, with the more numerous Congo tribes among which they are in- terspersed.

Unequal complexity in various aspects of culture may, as we have seen, be referred to difference in population mass, and in this sense the size of the groups concerned may be accounted a factor in the resulting process, albeit a secondary one. The most important point to be held in mind in assessing the role of cultural complexity is that by and of itself, and aside from the prestige factor that may be introduced, greater complexity in a culture does not necessarily carry conviction to those whose traditional back- ground is of a simpler nature. A more complex culture can offer more things to be borrowed than a simpler one. But this very richness may confuse, or even remain unperceived, by a people whose ways of life are pitched in a different key. Though on first glance the spread of European dominance over the world seems to refute this, further analysis shows that such a con- clusion is premature. It is doubtful, as a matter of fact, if the native peoples of the world, by and large, have taken over much more of Euroamerican culture than the western world has borrowed from them.

More interesting is the problem presented by the third type of contact. Do a people who move into the habitat of another take over more of the culture they find, or does a migrating group give more of its culture to those among whom they settle? Many examples of both kinds of exchange are to be cited, so that the balance in a specific case must be struck in terms of the particular peoples involved, and the particular situation encountered. Europeans who migrated to the Americas took over much of Indian agricultural practice, foods, and clothing, but nothing of Indian social structure or religious beliefs. Europeans who migrated to the East Indies took over relatively little of the life of the natives. Euroamericans who migrated to Hawaii took over more of nonmaterial culture than of aboriginal foodstuffs or agricultural practices.

Negroes who were brought to Brazil influenced the culture of the dominant Portuguese, themselves migrants, and subject to Indian influence as well. These varied influences are to be seen merged in such widely differing aspects of modern Brazilian life as the cuisine, the social structure, beliefs of various sorts, current musical forms and linguistic usages, to say nothing of the extensive retentions of African belief and behavior that were maintained by the Africans themselves.[13] In North America, on the other hand, the Negroes took over far more of the dominant European patterns than they gave to the resulting culture. As a third example of differing results from the same forced migration, Haiti can be mentioned. Here, in spite of two centuries of early French domination, the present-day life of the peasants retains more African traits than French, and but little if anything that can be referred to the customs of the autochthonous Indians.

The situations in which acculturation occurs are, in a sense, but an aspect of the types of contacts that have been sketched. The first kind of situation to be envisaged is where elements of culture are forced on a people, or where acceptance is voluntary. The second situation is where no social or political inequality exists between groups. In the third situation, three alternatives are presented—that is, where there is political dominance but not social; where dominance is both political and social; and where social superiority of one group over another is recognized, without there being political dominance. Little can be added to the preceding discussion concerning these "situations." Political and social dominance are undoubtedly factors in accelerating or retarding cultural interchange. Where superiority of one group is acknowledged, a desire for prestige may act as a powerful stimulant to further the spread of the customs of the dominant group and to inhibit the masters taking over the traditions of those who are recognized as inferiors, or the rulers may act to prevent those they rule from adopting their customs. Prestige, however, can vest in the way of life of a politically impotent group. There is much reason to believe that the motive that brought the conquering Teutonic peoples to Rome was the prestige of Roman culture, which these "barbarians" were as eager to adopt as the Romans, in their turn, had been eager to take over the customs of the politically impotent Greeks.

In contacts between nonliterate peoples, it is to be doubted if considerations of this kind have been too important. In such cases, all parties to contact tend to be small and, because first-hand contacts are restricted in large part to neighboring peoples, borrowing is on a more modest scale. It is more a matter of taking over details of culture than of integrating many elements

---

[13] G. Freyre, 1946, passim; A. Ramos, 1940, Ch. I–VIII, passim.

that come from strikingly different ways of life. We have seen that the acculturation between Euroamerican and native peoples in the nineteenth and twentieth centuries is no more than a special instance of a process that is as old as man himself. Situations where political and social dominance play a principal role are therefore to be thought of as particularly applicable to this special case. The examples of contact without conflict indicate that more borrowing has probably occurred where dominance did not enter, than where it did.

4

SOME students of culture-contact have approached acculturative situations with the idea of analyzing the resultant cultures into their component parts, seeing which are borrowed and which represent retentions of older traits. Others have criticized this approach, holding that this treats borrowing as "a mechanical pitchforking of elements of culture, like bundles of hay, from one culture to another," as Fortes [14] has phrased it. To break down cultures of mixed origin into traits, they maintain, is to reduce the living reality of a way of life into lifeless and, what is worse, meaningless components. For them, the arithmetic of culture-contact is never a process of addition. The borrowed element is always merged with what was present before the contact. As a result, a culture of multiple origins is different from any of the bodies of tradition that have contributed to it. The dynamics of acculturation, they say, are creative. To study the results of acculturation by tracing traits to their origin is to distort the picture and falsify the results.

Similar reasoning has been encountered in our earlier discussion of the structure and integration of culture, where, for example, the concept of the validity of the culture-trait as a methodological device was considered. The point was made there that if we hold this concept of the culture-trait not too rigidly, and employ it flexibly as a tool, it can be of great usefulness in organizing the data about cultures, and can reveal facts about the structure and processes of culture that would otherwise be difficult to discern. The methods of all science, it was pointed out, involve isolating elements that actually exist only as components of larger unities that, of themselves, are so complex that they must be broken down for purposes of study. This same argument was seen to hold for the aspects of culture. These can be clearly marked off by the student, and employed to study significant problems, even though any aspect of culture is rarely if ever isolated in human experience, which comprises a continuum that merges these aspects with fine disregard of the anthropologist's classifications.

In acculturation studies, therefore, as in the study of any phase of cultural dynamics, cultures are analyzed into component elements only as a methodological device. There can thus be no conceptual disagreement with such a formula, typical of many that could be cited, as that advanced by Bateson for the study of the contact between peoples in terms of: "(a) The complete fusion of the originally different groups, (b) The elimination of

---

[14] M. Fortes, 1938, p. 62.

one or both groups, (c) The persistence of both groups in dynamic equilibrium within one major community." [15]

The ideal of studying the results of contact between peoples in terms of whole cultures is, without doubt, well worth pursuing. The principal difficulty in this approach lies in the fact that workable methods of achieving it have as yet to be devised. On the contrary, the really significant studies of culture-contact have been those where one aspect, even one trait, has been taken at a time, perhaps to be combined later into a comprehensive portrayal of the results of the acculturative experience.

One of the best examples of this flexibility in method is to be found in Parsons' study of the Mexican community of Mitla. This study had two ends in view. The first of these was to obtain comparative data to throw light on possible Spanish or Indian derivations of Pueblo Indian culture, far to the north. But it also had the broader objective of exposing "the patterns in Indian-Spanish assimilation and acculturation" and thus "add to the understanding of these fundamental processes of social change not only in Latin America but in society at large." The description of the life of the people of Mitla, with two exceptions that we need not name here, is drawn in terms of the accepted categories of the ethnographic monograph, while Parsons' summary chapter breaks down the institutions already described into their Indian or Spanish sources, and considers the amalgamations of custom that are seen to derive from both cultural streams. How telling this approach can be is to be seen if some quotations, given as "partial answers" to the "basic queries" of why the traits that have been studied survived, and why certain elements that might have been expected to be found are not present, are cited:

Traits may be preserved merely because of ignorance of anything different; in other words, certain parts of two contacting cultures may not be in contact at all.

Intermarriage is a more obvious factor in cultural breakdown or cultural assimilation, whichever way you look at it, particularly when the woman belongs to the dominant culture.

Ignorance of custom, whatever it is due to, is a great protection to custom.

. . . An old custom . . . [may survive] . . . because it is agreeable to the new one. [16]

The effectiveness of the study of a single cultural element is also to be seen in research that revealed much of the results of acculturation of the Pawnee Indians through the intensive study of one complex, the Ghost Dance hand-game. In studying this element, the background of aboriginal and later custom in which the hand-game was set was fully taken into account, and the subsequent acculturative experience of the Pawnee that provided the historic background for understanding the change in this game from a ritual to a gambling device was described. "The persistence of traits constitutes that body of cultural elements without which no identification of the two forms would be possible," says Lesser, discussing the changes in the

---

[15] G. Bateson, 1935, p. 179.
[16] Elsie Clews Parsons, 1936, pp. xii, 511–19.

hand-game. "There are first of all those traits which persist from the old game into the new form identically; these form the base. In addition there are persistences of phases of the pattern or form, into which similar but not identical cultural material has been filled." [17]

There are some situations in which the study of acculturative change can be made only in terms of how separate elements have fared in the interchange. Chinese migrants to the South Seas who return to their home, Hsü points out, "have not shown fundamental changes from the home culture but they have taken on many single items of the alien cultures. In addition, new ideas and ways of life have either been taken on by some emigrants in the South Seas or are being broadcast into the home communities by a few 'progressive' reformers. The latter insist on the abolition of the joint family, on the free choice of life partners, on the suppression of superstitions and so forth." [18] Obviously, the problem for study here is how each of these centers of change in Chinese communities is achieving acceptance or rejection of the changes in the particular elements where reform is being advocated. There would be little point, at the stage in the process indicated, to study the changing culture as a whole.

However desirable studies of changes in whole cultures may thus be, it seems most advantageous in practice for the student to analyze into its components the culture that has experienced contact, and the results of this contact that are the object of his research. One can no more study "whole cultures" than one can take as the subject for a specific research project the human body in its entirety, or a mountain chain, or "the mind." The study of New World Negro cultures, that we will refer to at some length in later chapters, shows this clearly. Here we find that the various aspects of culture differ significantly from each other in the degree to which they have responded to the acculturative situation; that in religion and music, for example, far more aboriginal African elements have been retained than in economics and technology.

It was only by analyzing a restricted cultural element that Hallowell [19] could demonstrate for the St. Francis Abenaki Algonkian Indians, or Eggan [20] could show for the Choctaw how kinship systems, long held to be one of the most conservative aspects of culture, could change under contact. Spoehr, building on this previous work and extending it to the comparative level, was able to utilize these analyses of this single phase of culture to yield a principle of still broader significance. For he found that while the kinship structures of the Southeastern Indians changed from one fundamental type to another, they nonetheless have preserved "characteristics of a 'system' despite radical changes in type." Thus, as always in science, we move from the particular to the general. [21] We agree with Parsons that to study borrowing and integration means the analysis of "one of the most subtle and

---

[17] A. Lesser, 1933, p. 309.
[18] Francis L. K. Hsü, 1945, p. 55.
[19] A. I. Hallowell, 1928.
[20] F. Eggan, 1937.
[21] A. Spoehr, 1947, p. 229.

elusive of social processes, which does not reveal itself by plucked threads, by isolated facts. . . ." [22] Yet it remains true that unless we pluck the threads, and analyze how they have been woven into the whole-cloth of culture, we will never understand the structural basis of the functioning unity that we seek to comprehend.

5

ONE of the most important reasons why the study of acculturation in terms of whole cultures is so difficult is that borrowing, even in the most intimate contacts, is selective. This principle of selectivity is so important that it is not only basic to a discussion of acculturation, but to the consideration of any phase of cultural change. It was the need to study the nature and processes of cultural selectivity that led anthropologists from the hypothetical reconstruction of presumed processes of change, to the study of changes actually taking place. The principle of selectivity is as important in understanding why innovations from within a society become a part of its culture or are discarded, as it is in helping us comprehend why elements of one culture presented to another are taken over or refused, or even give rise to contra-acculturative movements that seek to restore the sanctions of a pre-contact way of life.

Selectivity, moreover, accounts for the great variation in the degree to which peoples undergoing contact do take over elements of each other's culture. A variety of historic factors enter to facilitate acceptance or to steel resistance to innovations. Thus Willems has shown that the "horse complex," as he terms it, was taken over by the Germans who settled in southern Brazil not only because of the higher standing of *gaucho* [cattle-breeder] culture in the hierarchy of Brazilian regional cultures, but also due to certain cultural associations which the average German immigrant attached to the saddle horse. This latter point is illuminating. "It should be remembered," we are told, "that the German peasant cultures . . . do not have the horse as a riding animal. . . . The saddle horse represented and still represents one of the oustanding cultural traits of Germany's rural aristocracy. Here as elsewhere in Europe the large farmer . . . controls the activities of his field hands by using a horse from which he gives his commands. Landless fieldworkers and smaller landowners never own saddle horses." [23] As a result of this and other prestige factors centering about the horse, it has come about that, while the Brazilian Germans have retained many elements of the culture they brought with them, they have taken over the horse-complex of Southern Brazil, including the extensive Portuguese vocabulary that has to do with this animal.

Mandelbaum has described how, in the Nilghiri hills of India, four tribes have "lived in economic and cultural symbiosis . . . mutually interdependent, yet culturally distinct." The Toda are a pastoral people, the Badaga are

---

[22] *Op. cit.*, p. xi.
[23] E. Willems, 1944, pp. 156–7; see also *ibid.*, 1946, Ch. VIII.

agriculturalists, the Kota artisans, and the Kurumba food gatherers and sorcerers. Despite the fact that they inhabit the same area and have been continuously in contact for many generations, the four groups "were culturally and linguistically segregate." Though "there was some cultural give and take among the tribes; the great wonder is that it amounted to so little."

The different economic base of each culture provides one reason why so little borrowing between them took place. Another important reason is the kind of intercourse they did have; of this, one example may be given. The Kota are the musicians who play for the rituals of the Toda, a people we have already met, who are famous in anthropological writings because of the way in which the religion that dominates their life centers about the sacredness of their cattle. Therefore, though "Kota musicians have to be present at all major Toda ceremonials; yet if the band comes too close to a dairy, the place is polluted and can only be resanctified by elaborate purificatory rituals."

A third factor in inhibiting borrowing is the prestige symbolism of these people. "A unique tribal trait tends to be interpreted as a symbol of group status. Any attempt to imitate it by another group is violently resisted. For example, Badagas wear turbans, Kotas do not. When a few Kotas once took to wearing turbans, the Badagas felt that the Kotas were getting above themselves. Some of the Badagas ambushed and beat up the Kota offenders, tore off their headgear, and effectively blocked the borrowing of this trait." [24]

Another example of contact with a minimum of borrowing is found on the island of Trinidad, where British Indians and Negroes have lived in contiguity since the first half of the nineteenth century. The immigrants from India, brought as indentured workers on the plantations, settled in Trinidad, and their descendents now form a colony almost one hundred and seventy-five thousand strong. "They speak their own language, dress in the Indian manner, cultivate their irrigated rice patches, and otherwise follow the modes of life of the parts of India from which they derive." The Negroes, on the other hand, have become acculturated to many patterns of the Europeans who constitute the economically, politically, and socially dominant minority of the island's population. The Negroes, from the first, resented the importation of the "coolies" from India as an economic threat; the Indians looked on the Negroes as "savages," according to Charles Kingsley, who was on the scene in 1871. The Indians have taken over something of Negro magic, but the Negroes seem to have accepted nothing from the Indians. [25]

We contrast such situations with those in which peoples in contact take freely and even enthusiastically from each other, as is to be seen in the history of Europe; or where a people hold it desirable to borrow from another, but are restrained because a dominant group will not share a prestige symbol. An instance of this has already been cited from India. Another has been reported from Fiji, where the wearing of shorts by native men was in

[24] D. G. Mandelbaum, 1941, pp. 19–20.
[25] M. J. and F. S. Herskovits, 1947, pp. 19–20.

earlier times prohibited, since shorts were reserved for political officers and others of the dominant colonial power.

Contact, therefore, can result in minimum borrowing, with or without external pressure, or it can range to almost complete acceptance of the ways of life of another people. In any given case, the aspects of culture that are transmitted, or the transfer of the sanctions of an older custom to a new cultural form are the result of particular historical circumstances which influence the psychological motivations underlying the selectivity that comes into play.

It makes little difference that certain borrowings, objectively viewed, would be of advantage to a people to whom something new is presented, or even that something which seems attractive to a people is actually disadvantageous. Many European colonists in the tropics cling to habits of food and dress that are traditionally important to them, but are difficult, if not detrimental, in hot climates. Native peoples in these same areas often give prestige-value to sheet-metal roofs that conduct heat, and discard their cooler thatched roofs. Loeb has cited the case of the Mentawai Islanders near Sumatra, who have refused to borrow rice-cultivation from the neighboring Malay, despite the fact that this would raise their standard of living. Rice cultivation, however, entails continuous work, and Mentawai religion demands that all work stop for month-long periods. Therefore the Mentawai continue to grow their taro, that can be raised with intermittent care.[26]

The historical and psychological aspects of borrowing are, of course, only to be distinguished on the conceptual level. What we are saying, essentially, is that while all peoples are exposed to elements of cultures other than their own, what they will in a given instance take over and what they will reject is determined by their pre-existing culture and the circumstance of the contact. The enculturation of later life, as we have seen, is the mechanism through which change is achieved. The adult member of a group must make a decision as to whether or not he will accept something new; or, if something is forced on him, he must devise ways and means to retain what he has been taught are the right and proper kinds of belief or behavior. As Hallowell has put it, "readjustment on the part of individuals may influence the thinking, feeling or behavior of other individuals and perhaps lead to readaptation in the mode of life of the group." One of the least studied, but most important problems in acculturation research, as he points out, derives from "the drives that have motivated individuals toward readaptation and how these drives are rewarded." [27]

6

LET us turn once again to the points Spier raised in the concluding paragraphs of his study of the Sun Dance. These points, it will be remembered, brought to the fore questions that could only be solved by materials that,

[26] E. Loeb, 1935, p. 163.
[27] A. I. Hallowell, 1945a, pp. 177, 185.

though they were no longer available for that rite, were "equally a requisite for any other study of cultural development." These were, "a more precise knowledge of the innovating individual, of his cultural equipment, the character of his milieu, and the extent of his contribution." The nature of the circumstances in which "a novelty acquired by an individual and subsequently socialized by his fellows," was also pointed to as essential to an understanding of how a borrowed trait is taken over. Finally, the "mental conditions" that influence the incorporation of a new element into the preexisting cultural matrix, especially in terms of the dominant interests of the incorporating group, were held to be of significance.

As has been suggested, such questions could be no more than raised while anthropologists confined their researches to analyzing the results of assumed contact between nonhistoric peoples. Only after the study of cultural exchange in process could they be attacked on the basis of data gathered by direct observation, and by the use of written records. Spier himself recognized this, as was apparent in his statement that more data of the type presented by Radin in a preliminary statement of an early acculturation study entitled "A Sketch of the Peyote Cult of the Winnebago,"[28] was needed. The Peyote Cult, treated in this paper and in Radin's later work, is one of a series of revivalist movements that have marked the reaction of the Indians to white aggression. One of the most important of these, the Ghost Dance, had been studied by James Mooney, an army officer who realized its significance after the Sioux Indian outbreak of 1890. Its value in laying bare a pre-existing Messianic pattern in American Indian culture was soon recognized, and gave rise to a number of other studies of comparable movements.

The analysis of the Peyote Cult by Radin, however, came at a time when, as we have seen, the inadequacies of the hypothetical assumptions concerning the dynamics of culture that the diffusionist approach offered were becoming apparent to anthropologists. His study, therefore, pointed new possibilities in the investigation of the origin, development, and spread of specific cultural elements. This particular cult represented a reaction of the Winnebago against the frustrations of white domination. Radin came to know John Rave, the Winnebago who had brought the Mexican stimulant called peyote back from a visit to the Indians of Texas and Oklahoma. It was demonstrated how Rave had helped develop this religious movement of protest, that incorporated elements of Christian and Indian belief into a system centered about the values given by the physiological purging and the resultant vision experience which came after eating the peyote.

Here was diffusion in process—the antecedent situation, the "mental conditions," the selective taking over of foreign elements, the manner of their reworking into a new situation that became a part of the older culture. The observation of change in process that this represents, together with the use of relevant documents that give contemporary evidence of earlier conditions where change is an accomplished fact, have over the years afforded a

---

[28] P. Radin, 1914.

rich body of data that transcends the points Spier could but raise as questions desirable to answer.

Thus, in the case of the Teton-Dakota, Mekeel, utilizing documentary materials, has described the transition of this people from the buffalo hunting epoch to the reservation phase of their experience, showing the cultural changes that accompanied this process.[29] Goldfrank, extending the scope of this and other studies that analyze the differences in Dakota culture resulting from the transition from buffalo days to life on the reserve, has described "certain modifications within each period which . . . disturbed the inner balance between such factors as cooperation and competition, altered the social configuration and, in turn, the social character."[30]

How important historic depth can be in aiding the student to comprehend the dynamics of cultural change is similarly to be seen in studies of other tribes of this general region. Keesing has assessed the effects of three centuries of contact between Menomini Indians and the whites in the light of the present ways of life of these Indians;[31] Lewis, using the techniques of ethnohistory, has made a similar study of one group of Blackfoot, particularly as these people were affected by the fur trade;[32] while Goldfrank, here as in the case of the Dakota, has investigated the changes in the cultural configurations and basic incentive-drives of another subdivision of this people.[33] These and many other investigations that not only accept "adulterated" cultures as valid objects of study, but make their principal aim the search for an understanding of how such cultures arrived at the state in which they are to be observed, all reflect a profound reorientation in anthropological thinking.

In summary, then, the search for "pure" cultures, "uncontaminated" by outer contact, has been almost entirely given over, while the hypothetical nature of reconstructions of unrecorded history has come to be clearly understood as an exercise in probability. The use of historical documents and the field study of peoples whose cultures are changing under contact have, above all, demonstrated that culture-change is a single problem, whether studied in process, or through the consideration of accomplished cultural facts analyzed in terms of the distribution of variant forms of the same element. With this unity of the problem of cultural dynamics established, then, we may next take up certain aspects of the organization and the psychology of culture that, as part of the same problem, throw further light on the mechanisms of cultural stability and cultural change.

---

[29] S. Mekeel, 1943.
[30] E. Goldfrank, 1943, p. 67.
[31] F. Keesing, 1939.
[32] O. Lewis, 1942.
[33] E. Goldfrank, 1945.

CHAPTER 32

Cultural Focus
and Reinterpretation

Cultural focus designates the tendency of every culture to exhibit greater complexity, greater variation in the institutions of some of its aspects than in others. So striking is this tendency to develop certain phases of life, while others remain in the background, so to speak, that in the shorthand of the disciplines that study human societies these focal aspects are often used to characterize whole cultures.

An example of this is the changing emphases to be discerned in the various cultures that were the forerunners of modern Euroamerican ways of life. We characterize Egypt by saying that here economic and politico-religious concerns predominated. Athens of the classical period is described as a democratic society wherein the quest for truth and the search for a balanced view of the universe prevailed. In Rome, the principle of organization, particularly as manifested in political organization, but pervading other aspects of the culture as well, was outstanding. During the Middle Ages, the emphasis shifted to regard for the other world, with a hierarchical concept of the universe shaping modes of life as well as belief. The Renaissance again marked a change in stress, with emphasis on secular matters, learning, and the arts. The Industrial Revolution initiated a period that, in the twentieth century, has produced a society patently centered about the technological and economic facets of life.

This progression is a commonplace in the writing of history, and has been expressed in various ways. It has been ascribed to changes in a kind of mystical "spirit of the times" (*Zeitgeist*). With pseudo-biological analogy, as in the writings of Oswald Spengler, it has been ascribed to the fact that every culture is born, flowers, and decays, so that "the decline of the West" that he envisaged was believed to be an inevitable result of the operation of these inner forces. Flinders-Petrie, who at about the same period wrote of the "revolutions of civilization" expressed the same concept, though his position was philosophically less sophisticated, and his findings documented in a far less monumental fashion. Toynbee and Kroeber have continued the quest for a clue to the puzzle. The former, with the ethnocentrism we have seen to mark his approach, seeks to comprehend the reasons for the rise and fall of the cultures he designates as "civilizations"; the latter attempts to develop generalizations about the causes of cultural growth.

All these studies, it should be pointed out, are characterized by a tendency to disregard the psychological factors involved in cultural change. Phrasing this somewhat differently, we find that the concern in all of them is exclusively with institutions. The human element in the process, the reactions of the masses of individuals that make or made up the societies whose cultures are analyzed do not appear at all. These researches, in White's terminology, are thus purely "culturological" studies.

Here we shall indicate a different, and far less sweeping approach to the problem. The hypothesis of cultural focus refers the dynamics of culture to the only instruments through which change in culture can be achieved—the individuals who compose a society where a way of life is undergoing change. It is people who believe in one way at one historic period and in another way at a later time. The emphasis they lay on the sanctions, the values, the goals that comprise the motivating drives to their behavior gives meaning to what they do at a given moment. We must thus turn to these changing emphases and drives if we are to comprehend more adequately the changes in the artifacts, the institutions, the organized systems of belief that characterize a culture at a given time, and mark it off from what it was at a different time or from the other cultures that exist coterminously with it.

We have already pointed out how in any culture much more will be taken for granted than is given purposeful thought or articulate expression. It has been seen, for example, how great a proportion of a people's linguistic resources lie dormant at any particular moment, to be called on only when it is necessary to use a given word, or to phrase an unusual shading of meaning. Analogously, though from a slightly different point of view, it can be said that human beings learn their cultures so well that they react almost automatically to the most varied kinds of situations, some of which present themselves quite seldom. When the time comes, however, this back-log of learning is called on, just as the needed words are produced to convey on occasion an idea not often expressed.

Though he may possess a wide range of cultural responses, we have seen that no individual, even in the most stable, conservative culture, knows all the elements in the mode of life of his group. "Not every musician is a virtuoso, nor does he control the full range of orchestral instruments; and in the same manner no one individual controls his culture or is even conscious of its total resources, and no group, as a group, places the same emphases on all facets of the entire body of custom of which its members are the carriers."[1] That is, the differences we perceive in cultures, that allow us to designate a given culture by its outstanding concerns, merely convey the fact that the concerns of the persons who go to make up the group at a given time are more centered in some aspects of their culture than in others.

The fact that no two individuals have exactly the same interests, and respond to differing possibilities offered by every culture for satisfying dif-

---

[1] M. J. Herskovits, 1945a, p. 164.

ferent kinds of interests, will occupy us when we consider in detail the importance of variation in culture. We are, in essence, treating of the nature and role of cultural "alternatives," as they have been termed by Linton,[2] except that it is their overall character, as consenses of behavior, rather than as manifestations of individual differences in behavior, that concern us here. Though it may seem paradoxical, it will become evident that it is out of these consenses that the alternatives arise and grow, and thus open the way to change. This is what is meant when it is stated that the phenomenon of cultural focus is a factor of far-reaching significance in understanding the dynamics of culture.

Of the varied aspects that go to make up the body of custom of a people, those that dominate are the least apt to be taken for granted. That is, those aspects will be most often talked about, and will thus be closest to the levels of consciousness for a greater part of the time than are elements that are of less interest. From the point of view of culture, objectively considered, these aspects of a culture will be found to manifest the greatest degree of variation. Or, as it has been phrased, "a people's dominant concern may be thought of as the focus of their culture; that area of activity or belief where the greatest awareness of form exists, the most discussion of values is heard, the widest difference in structure is to be discerned."[3]

If we follow this line of reasoning a step further, the relevance of these points in the analysis of cultural dynamics will become clear. The things that outstandingly mark the culture of a people—technology (present-day Euroamerican culture), supernaturalism (Mediaeval Europe), or economics as directed toward the attainment of prestige (Melanesia)—also tend to dominate their lives. Because such matters are important to them, people will think and talk a great deal about personalities, events, and possibilities lying in this aspect of their culture. As a result of this interest and the concomitant discussions that are carried on, possibilities for realignment will emerge, and emerge with enough frequency so that resistance to the idea of something new will be lessened. It is apparent that a suggestion of change in a phase of life that is taken for granted and seldom discussed will meet with greater resistance than in one where the phenomenon is under common discussion, and various possibilities in its form and function are thus constantly being suggested. In the former instance, the seed falls on barren ground; in the latter, the soil is fallow. Therefore, we can state that the greatest variation in custom, manifest in the greatest complexity of form, can be looked for in the focal aspects of a culture, and that this represents either potential or achieved cultural change.

2

THE fact that the interests of a people tend to concentrate on a given phase of their culture has been established by studies reported in many monographs, whose emphasis on certain institutions as against others reflect the

[2] R. Linton, 1936, pp. 273–4.
[3] M. J. Herskovits, 1945a, pp. 164–5.

emphases laid by the society itself. We do not refer here to monographs which are restricted to consideration of a particular phase of a given culture. It is rather in the rounded presentations of culture that we find the expression of concentration of a people's concern that we are considering here. It is not too much to say that almost any anthropologist, asked to identify the most important aspect of aboriginal Australian life, would without hesitation reply by naming its social organization. But, it may be asked, is this not the reflection of a tradition among anthropologists rather than of the focal concerns of the Australians themselves? The very fact, however, that stress was laid independently by various early observers on this aspect of culture, suggests that they were reacting to an emphasis of the culture. The internal evidence is even more convincing. For in aboriginal Australian culture, the primacy of its social structures is shown in the way these orientations tend to dominate the forms taken by economic and religious and other institutions. These others, so to speak, feed into the social organization. We have seen, for example, how important it is that a man's place in the kinship structure of his own group be indicated when he falls in with a new horde. Or, again, it has been made very apparent that the key to the Australian world-view is to be sought in sanctions of the totemic system.

We may take, as another instance, a people whose religion we have had occasion to consider, the Puyallup-Nisqually of the northern Pacific Coast of the United States. A quotation already given from a general survey of the life of this people is to the point. "Every individual characteristic and every cultural complex, except those related to sexual life, was understood and thought to operate through power. Adult life without power was inconceivable and childhood was viewed as a period of preparation for the reception of power." [4] Here the ethnographer was influenced by no body of previous writing that had established a tradition of emphasizing this particular aspect of the culture of these Indians. Nor is this a report by an early explorer. It is, rather, a systematic analysis of a culture by a trained scientist. This analysis, even the discussion of its religious aspects in these pages, leaves little question that this portion of the total body of custom of this tribe is dominant in the life of these people.

The culture of the Todas of India offers perhaps as striking an instance of cultural focus as that of any people that has ever been studied. Here, as has been noted, the particular institution that orients the culture and gives meaning to life is the buffalo dairy. We can with profit re-examine this case in somewhat greater detail. The report on this culture by Rivers, deservedly an anthropological classic, was written to be "not merely a record of the customs and beliefs of a people, but also a demonstration of anthropological method." [5] Therefore, though Rivers' concern was primarily with social organization and religion, this book presents a rounded portrayal of the culture, and reflects the meticulous preparation and execution of his methodological attack.

In addition to Rivers' study, moreover, we are aided in examining Toda

---

[4] See above, pp. 357–8.
[5] W. H. R. Rivers, 1906, p. v.

culture in the light of the hypothesis of cultural focus if we have recourse to the later studies of these people, on which we have already drawn in discussing the problem of acculturation. For in them we can perceive the significance of focus as a dynamic force. We can discern how the focussing of a people's concerns influences the course of their lives when they are in contact with other folk having different cultures.

"The daily life of the Toda men is largely devoted to the care of their buffaloes and to the performance of the dairy operations," says Rivers at the outset of his work.[6] "The milking and churning operations of the dairy form the basis of the greater part of the religious ritual of the Todas. The lives of the people are largely devoted to their buffaloes, and the care of certain of these animals, regarded as more sacred than the rest, is associated with much ceremonial. The sacred animals are attended by men especially set apart who form the Toda priesthood, and the milk of the sacred animals is churned in dairies which may be regarded as the Toda temples and are so regarded by the people themselves. The ordinary operations of the dairy have become a religious ritual and ceremonies of a religious character accompany nearly every important incident in the lives of the buffaloes."[7]

Buffaloes and dairies are held to have various degrees of sanctity. "The dairies," says Rivers, "form an ascending series in which we find increasing definiteness and complexity of ritual; increasing sanctity of the person of the dairyman-priest, increasing stringency of the rules for the conduct of his daily life, and increasing elaboration of the ceremonies which attend his entrance upon office. There are also certain dairies in which the ritual has developed in special directions, and there are special features of the organization of buffaloes and dairies not only in each of the two chief divisions of the Toda people, but also in many of the clans of which each division is composed."[8]

The buffaloes are ubiquitous, figuring in all aspects of life. They form the economic base of the culture. They, or their milk, play prominent parts in the rituals of birth, childhood, marriage, and death, especially in funeral rites. The gods are thought of as having dairies and buffalo herds as do mortals, and buffaloes have an important place in Toda mythology. As we read Rivers' account, there is little question that the buffaloes, and the religious complex centering about them, give point and meaning to the Toda men and to a lesser extent women in whose lives they function so incessantly. That religion is the motivating drive of the Todas is further clarified in Rivers' extended discussion of the religious beliefs and rituals which occur in the dairy. The dairy is therefore to be thought of as the central point of the focal aspect of culture, where, if our hypothesis were valid, we should expect greatest variation. And that this is what is actually found is quite evident from the "comparison of procedure of different dairies" given by Rivers. The "increasing elaboration and complexity from the lowest to the

---

[6] *Ibid.*, p. 31.
[7] *Op. cit.*, p. 38.
[8] *Op. cit.* pp. 38-9.

highest grade of dairy," he says, is "one of the most striking features of the ritual in all its branches." [9] Likewise, the milk from buffaloes of various grades, that belong to different dairies, has different degrees of sanctity. Various villages have special rites; the groupings into which the two Toda sibs are divided are distinguished by the different degree of complexity of their dairy rituals.

As always in scientific procedure, the test case is the one where a special condition alters the customary situation. This permits us to understand and evaluate the role of elements whose functions are lost sight of in the ordinary, undisturbed course of events. In this sense, therefore, it is instructive to consider what happened to the one Toda sib-village, the site of whose sacred dairies was taken over to be a part of the parade-ground of a British cantonment. This unfortunate group, alone of the Toda villages, experienced the destruction of what is described as "the heart of the Toda cult." They alone were deprived of access to the all-important places that, for a sib, are "one, inalienable and irreplaceable." The case is the more significant because the other sibs were undisturbed in the process, and thus form a contrast which tests the statement that, "Toda culture is so highly integrated, so tightly knit about the care and cult of the buffalo, that unless the buffalo cult breaks down, other influence can hardly penetrate." [10]

The sib whose territory was needed for military purposes were able to keep buffalo in the new location, but they could not maintain rituals associated with the buffalo cult. Because of this, the statement that, "only this solitary settlement has taken to raising potatoes, only they keep cattle as well as buffalo," takes on special importance. "Deprived of the hub of their ritual," we learn, "this group has lost its zest for buffalo care and has taken over certain non-buffalo traits." In contrast to this, "the other Toda sibs continue to maintain their ritual, retain the old economic pattern, remain impervious to foreign ways." [11]

Another instance of cultural focus comes from the study, made by Bascom, of the Micronesian island of Ponape, in the Eastern Carolines. The inhabitants of this island have lived under the control of four foreign powers —Spain, Germany, Japan, and the United States. They are primarily agriculturalists. In addition to yams they raise coconuts, from which copra is derived, breadfruit, taro, and bananas. They have pigs, and gather wild foods, while fishing adds to their subsistence resources. Of all these, coconuts are the most important from an economic point of view—they are "the primary agricultural crop in the commercial economy of Ponape." Yams, however, which "have never had a real place in the commercial economy," are "because of their importance in both the prestige economy and subsistence" to be regarded "as the primary agricultural crop. . . ."

Ponape social organization is made up of exogamous matrilineal sibs, that function in the economic as well as in the social system. Socially, they regulate marriage and affect status; while as economic institutions they operate

[9] *Ibid.* p. 232.
[10] D. G. Mandelbaum, 1941, p. 22.
[11] *Ibid.*, p. 23.

as mutual-aid groupings. Ponape is divided into five districts, within which the sibs actually function. Because of the importance of political orientations, these districts are the effective organizing mechanisms of native life. Each district is ruled by two parallel sets of chiefs, with distinctive titles and order of rank. Heading these sets of chiefs are two principal rulers. One, sometimes spoken of as "the king," was so surrounded by ritual restrictions (of the type previously mentioned when the religious phenomena of *mana* and *tapu* were discussed) that he could not carry on the administrative work of the district. This was therefore done by a kind of "speaking chief," who, in theory, ruled in the name of his superior, but in practice was the effective head of the government. Districts are today divided into sections, each headed by its Section Chief. These sections, in turn, are subdivided into farmsteads.

As in all Micronesian and Polynesian islands, rank and prestige are so important that they must be regarded as focal. Just as among the Todas the focus on ceremonialism was seen to be pointed up by a concern with buffaloes and the dairy, so in Ponape the yam is the instrument that symbolizes the rank-prestige preoccupation of the people. This was suggested when it was pointed out that the yam, rather than the coconut is the primary agricultural crop; despite the fact that, under the acculturative situation of contact with four ruling powers whose economy was on a money base, the principal cash crop, coconuts, might *a priori* be expected to dominate. This, however, is not the case. Rather, as far as the interests of the Ponapeans go, yams are the most important crop, because only through his yam-growing ability can a man better his status. Yams thus become the prime mover in Ponapean motivation.

It has been stated that one expects greater range of variation, more content, in focal elements of culture than in those outside them. A crude measure of this comes immediately to hand in the Ponapean data. Fourteen different native varieties of coconuts are recognized and named. One hundred and fifty-six varieties of yams, however "were recorded, with descriptions as to size, shape and color and, for most varieties, the period of their introduction" into the island—that is, under what regime they had been imported or developed. "The total number of native varieties planted on Ponape probably runs well over two hundred." The reason why botanical identification of these varieties is difficult—why, indeed, it is so hard to arrive at any accurate figure regarding their number—is because of the secrecy that surrounds yam-growing.

The reason for this secrecy is that the prestige competition, which "is a fundamental factor to the understanding of the Ponapean's motivations and his attitudes toward work" centers about yams. So strong is this that families will go hungry rather than touch the large yams that may be in their gardens. When the Section feasts are given, these large yams are displayed. The man who consistently brings the largest yams is not only respected and praised by his fellows, but is selected to assume a Section title that may be vacant, or is promoted to a higher title, if he already has one.

The secrecy about yam-growing is reminiscent of the American businessman's attitude toward the technical and financial details of his organization. Larger operations bring him prestige and enhance his position, and he resents an outsider "prying into his affairs," as the saying goes. So on Ponape, as concerns yams. "A Ponapean may speak openly about the number of coconut trees or the amount of money he has, or even boast about them; but his answers to questions about the number and kind of yams he has planted are evasive and often deliberately falsified. He conceals this information so that he may surprise the others when he produces his yams at a feast, in the hope that he may be able to surpass them." More than this, "It is impolite to look at another man's yams, and any one caught doing so will be shamed by gossip and ridicule." How successful as yam-growers the Ponapeans are is evident from the criterion of size they use—that is, the number of men it takes to carry a given yam. This makes its point when it is realized that a yam weighing 100 kilograms (220 pounds) has been produced.

A few other indications of how yam-growing claims the interest of this people can be given. One of Bascom's informants was able to name ninety native varieties of yams without stopping. Many Ponapeans are able to name the man who first planted a given variety of yam, and in what District and Section he lived. The contrast with bananas in this regard is impressive. The banana worm destroyed all the older native varieties of bananas, and new types were introduced, during the period of Japanese rule. Though this was only a comparatively short time before the research described here, the name of the man who introduced them had been quite forgotten. A new variety of yam, brought to a feast, however, occasions much excitement, and the man who exhibits it obtains even more prestige than if he had brought a very large tuber. He usually gives it his own name. He grows it in secrecy so that when he "unveils" it he will have cuttings to present to the many persons who will want them.[12]

In modern American life, the focussing of the culture on technology and the associated phases of business activity needed to promote technological change is evident to anyone who will give the matter a moment's thought. We can see this in our readiness to accept technological changes, when contrasted to the resistance to changes in economic theory—even though this is a field closely related to technology—or in social institutions or in religion. The lad who tinkers with a broken-down automobile until he has a workable vehicle, or plays with a set of chemicals is prepared to welcome "improvements" when he grows up. In this, he is merely responding to a deep-seated enculturative drive. But nothing comparable exists outside the focal aspect; it is in these other phases that our cultural conservatism is most manifest.

3

THESE examples are sketched to demonstrate that the greatest variation in form is to be found in the aspect of a culture that is focal to the interests of

---

[12] W. R. Bascom, 1947, *passim.*

a people. This variation, by implication suggests that the focal aspect has undergone greater changes than other elements, a point we may now examine by considering several cultures where the process can be observed in operation as a result of the circumstance of acculturation. In such cases, we find that where cultures are in free contact, the focal aspect will be likely to be the one where the new elements are most hospitably received. On the other hand, in situations where one people is dominated by another, and pressure is brought against customs lying in the focal aspect, retention will be achieved by devious ways, the importance of which we shall consider shortly.

For an example of how cultural focus affects borrowing under free interchange, we may turn to a description of the mutual influence exerted by the indigenous Arab culture of Palestine, and the European ways of life of the Jewish groups who settled there. Patai, who has analyzed the course of this acculturation [13] shows how, at first, the early Jewish settlers adapted themselves to prevailing Arab patterns, in dress, house-types, and other aspects of culture. The swelling flood of newcomers from Europe after the first World War, however, gradually tipped the balance, so that Palestine came to take on a European character. Then, because of various social and economic reasons, the Arabs came to borrow from the Jews.

Patai demonstrates how attitudes toward agriculture, which is focal in Jewish but not in Arab concerns, have affected the degree of conservatism or change in this aspect of culture among the two groups. The Arab agriculturalists, the *fellahin*, occupy an inferior place in Arab society. They inherit their position from their fathers, but are much more interested in life in the towns than on the farm. Those who remain in the country continue to live much as their ancestors did. For the *fellah* "his agricultural work . . . is . . . an amount of inevitable toil, necessary for his subsistence, but neither a matter of ideological enthusiasm, nor of as much interest as carried by many other aspects of his life." [14]

The *fellah* therefore moves to the towns when he can, there to enjoy the higher economic reward and greater prestige that accrues to the townsman. Where *fellahin* villages have been in contact with Jewish settlements that employ improved agricultural methods, a certain degree of modernization has resulted. "But even in these cases it was only the superior technical equipment of the Jewish village which was adopted, and not its types of social system, or its methods of work, such as the division of labour, which were at least as much responsible for its prosperity and success as its technical equipment." In Arab villages farther removed from Jewish settlements, westernization has taken the form of acceptance of products imported from the towns—clothing, shoes, implements, furniture—while village industries, such as weaving, have declined. "Thus it came about that the material objects used by the fellah, and at times even his house itself, became westernized and modernized, and at the same time his methods of tilling his soil

---

[13] R. Patai, 1947, *passim*.
[14] *Ibid.*, p. 31.

and of taking care of his few animals, underwent practically no change." [15]

In contrast, agriculture is the center of Jewish interest. "To be a farmer in Palestine was from the very beginning the highest ideal." New Jewish villages are made up of recruits from the towns, and of immigrants who have had prior agricultural training. "Members of the second generation leave the village for the town very rarely, while they much more often take the contrary course and, leaving the town-homes of their parents, go to the land." The foundation of a village is as important to the Jews of Palestine as the news of a new variety of yam is to the Ponapeans. To be a member of a village from its founding is to attain great prestige, and many young people are strongly motivated by this honor. Conversely, it is resented when a member of a village community leaves the group.

As might be anticipated, granting the validity of our hypothesis, the Jews show far greater receptivity to change in agriculture than do the Arabs. Initially, the Jews took over Arab methods of farm ownership and operation, and cultivated the same crops. Then came experiments that led to transition from wheat farming to mixed crops, while the social distance between farm-owner and laborer, imported from Europe, began to disappear. In 1908 the first communal village, a social form that has come to be widespread, was founded.

Thus among the Jewish group, since "the ideal of 'back to the land' occupies a central position . . . the forms of agriculture and of rural community life underwent a constant change"—in this case, induced from within rather than from without. However, "no corresponding changes can be observed in Jewish urban life," which is removed from the focal aspect of Jewish Palestinian culture. And by the same token, "no corresponding changes were found to have taken place in Arab agricultural life, which does not occupy a comparable focal position in Palestinian Arab culture." [16]

A similar result is noted by Patai in the case of language. For the Jews, this has been a matter of interest and debate as a result of the many problems incident on the utilization of Hebrew in a modern setting. The Arabs, however, have had to give language little thought. Thus we find rapid change, and the incorporation of Arabic words in Palestinian Hebrew; little change, and few Hebrew words in Palestinian Arabic. In the one case, language is a focal concern, as against the manner in which the Arab has taken his mode of speech for granted. [17]

West African cultures and their New World derivatives afford an instance of retention of an original focus under forced acculturation. These West African societies, unlike those other nonliterate groupings considered previously in this chapter, are among the largest in the nonliterate world. Their technological equipment is advanced, their economies complex, their political systems sophisticated and their social structures well organized and administered. Their art has become famous, their folklore is noted for its subtlety, and their music is at the base of the reorientations in Euroamerican

---

[15] *Ibid.*, p. 31.
[16] *Ibid.*, pp. 32–4.
[17] *Ibid.*, pp. 37–9.

musical style that has manifested a shift from exclusive emphasis on melody to stress laid on rhythm. The focus of these cultures, however, is on religion in all its manifestations—belief-systems, world-view, and ritual. The greatest stimulus to thought and creative expression lodges here, and the greatest variety of form is found.

The emphasis in these West African cultures on the elements of the focal aspect is apparent to anyone doing field-work in West Africa. It has been indicated how Rattray, among the Ashanti, had to study the religion of these people before he could intelligibly analyze their political structures. Here the ancestral cult, in addition to the beliefs in the gods and magic, was crucial, as it is elsewhere in the area. Similar sanctions give meaning to other aspects of West African life. The gods of the market-place must be properly served if the trader is to prosper. The spirits of the earth must be propitiated if the fields are to yield. The god of the forge must be properly worshipped by the ironworker if he is not to be injured by flying sparks, and if the tools he produces are to be effective. Art functions principally in the service of religion, whether in graphic or plastic forms, or in the musical arts. Similarly, the most important body of folk literature treats of the gods and their adventures in the world of men.

Native psychology, as revealed in discussions of their culture with West Africans themselves, underscores the interest these people have in the aspect of their culture we have termed focal. A conversation concerning kinship terminology turns on the place of the ancestors in directing the lives of their living descendants. A description of agriculture inevitably entails a discussion of how the farmer assures himself that no places sacred to supernatural beings are violated when he breaks the ground for a new field. This does not mean that these people do not give full consideration to the problems of the workaday world, for they are practical and hardheaded. But it is the "why" of the universe that intrigues them, that captures their imagination.

In the New World, this focus of concern in religion stood the Africans and their descendants in good stead. Perhaps because belief was focal, and thus encouraged experimentation and the acceptance of innovations, an adaptation was achieved that eventually surmounted and conquered the tragedy of slavery as in the case of almost no other people that has experienced so far-reaching a disruption of their culture. For while their religion gave meaning to life, their belief was not committed to any rigid dogma. In West Africa, tribal gods had been freely borrowed, and there was no reason why the Christian concept of the universe and the powers that rule it, which the Negroes encountered in the New World, could not equally well be incorporated into their system of belief.

West African gods are often described by the members of a tribe as having been taken over from another people, and one native explanation why this was done shows such insight into the psychology of the matter that it should be noted here. When one group conquered another, the superior power of the gods of the conquerer was self-evident, and it was thus to the advantage of the conquered to appease them. But the conquerors also took over the gods of their foes. It was reasoned that defeated gods are especially to be feared; that it was, therefore, wisest to placate them and lessen the frustrations of their defeat. Conquest thus became a mechanism for the interchange of gods, which not only accelerated the diffusion of religious belief and concept in Africa, but cushioned the impact of the New World experience of the Africans.

In the New World, the recognition of the value of taking over the gods of other folk thus made for significant psychological and institutional adaptations. These adaptations, which retained African belief while taking over European forms, or which added the beliefs of the masters to aboriginal belief, exist today everywhere in New World Negro societies. That the changes in aboriginal religious custom did not come about only in deference to the superior power of the European's deity is to be seen where Africans had contact with Indians, as in Brazil and Guiana, Cuba, and Haiti. Here full attention is paid the autochthonous spirits who ruled the new land, despite the fact that in these countries full-blown African religious forms have been retained. This is to be seen in the Caboclo (Indian) cult of the Brazilian *Africanos*, or the "Indian spirits" (*ingi winti*) of the Dutch Guiana Bush Negroes, or the "indigenous spirits" (*loa créole*) of the Haitian *vodun* worship.

The changes which were made in African forms of religion in this process of survival under the harsh regime of slavery, and which to a lesser degree permitted the retention of Africanisms in other than religious aspects of life, bring us to a second hypothesis regarding cultural change. This has to do with the process of reinterpretation, to which we now turn.

4

Reinterpretation marks all aspects of cultural change. It is the process by which old meanings are ascribed to new elements or by which new values change the cultural significance of old forms. It operates internally, from generation to generation, no less than in integrating a borrowed element into a receiving culture. But it is in the latter process that the phenomenon is most easily to be studied.

Syncretism is one form of reinterpretation. It is most strikingly exemplified by the reconciliations that have been effected by New World Negroes in the focal aspect of aboriginal African culture, religion. Outstanding here is the identification, in Catholic countries of the New World, of African deities with the saints of the Church. This phenomenon is so well documented that it has been established beyond any doubt. The means whereby the identification has been achieved varies. In Haiti, for example, Legba, the trickster of the West African Dahomeans and Yorubans, is identified with St. Anthony. This saint is depicted in the chromolithographs acquired by the devout as the patron of the poor, while Legba is conceived as an old man who wanders about, clad in tatters. Damballa, the Dahomean rainbow-serpent, is identified with St. Patrick, who is portrayed in his familiar role, and therefore has serpents about him. Erzulie, a goddess of the water who is believed to control riches, is identified with *Mater Dolorosa*, a manifestation of the Virgin Mary, shown with many rich ornaments.

Many other instances of religious syncretism are to be cited. Thus it was established that among the Hausa of West Africa, where aboriginal belief is in contact with Mohammedanism, the pagan *'iskŏkĭ* are identified with the *jinn* of the Koran.[18] In the New World, where Africans came into contact with Protestantism, retention of individual gods was impossible, since no identification with subsidiary beings could be effectuated, as was the case under Catholicism. Reinterpretations thus took the form of emphasis on the power of the Holy Ghost; or stressed the importance of the River Jordan, the equivalent of the rivers that, in Africa, the spirits must cross to reach the supernatural world. In ritual, spirit possession continued, but by the Holy Ghost, while the place accorded baptism in running water reinterpreted the significance in Africa of the river and sea cults. In organization, the function of the "mourning groun'" became that of the initiatory rites of African cult-groups.

Let us see how this last retention was achieved in the Shouters (Baptist) groups on the island of Trinidad. "The head of the Shouters group, the 'teacher' or 'leader,' who has the highest degree of spiritual power and control, is the equivalent of the African cult-head, the priest. The more important church officials correspond to the principal assistants of such a cult-head, who in Africa are initiates of long standing and of proved capacity. . . . Instruction before baptism, revelation of the hymn, psalm, and chapter, binding the eyes of the novitiate, baptism in 'living' water and the ensuing possession . . . are comparable in New World practice to the preinitiation African custom of washing the head to dedicate it to the god. . . ." In the "mourning ground," the fact that "the novitiate is reborn and, as a child, has all his wants cared for, that muscles, tired from holding a single position over long periods, are ritually massaged; the fact that inattention is punished by the spirit, and that one learns to 'talk language'—these are all details to be found in the initiatory rites not only in West Africa, but . . . in the African cults of Brazil and Haiti and, in all likelihood, in Cuba as well. Other details are that one takes a new name after mourning, and that at the ritual which marks the emergence of a group from their initiatory experience, each novitiate demonstrates his spiritual power and ability. In Africa and the New World countries mentioned, . . . this takes the form of performance in the dance. That in the Shouters temples it is expressed in testimony given, or in the spiritual hymn that has been revealed only to the initiate, indicates the form that this particular reinterpretation of aboriginal custom has taken under Protestant concepts of the universe and Protestant modes of worship." [19]

The fact that retentions of aboriginal African custom achieved through reinterpretation bulk so large in the focal aspect of New World Negro religions does not mean that substantial numbers of reinterpretations are not found in other elements of these cultures. "Bury leagues," with their elab-

---

[18] J. Greenberg, 1946, pp. 60–1.
[19] M. J. and F. S. Herskovits, 1947, pp. 305–8.

Cultural Focus and Reinterpretation

orate funerals, conceptions of the place and role of the dead, forms of kinship nomenclature, the economic and social position of women, traditions of polite behavior, lodge organization—these are but a few of the phases of New World Negro cultures that have persisted in reinterpreted form in various parts of the Americas. In the field of social organization these reinterpretations have been so far-reaching as to change a culture that, in Africa, was dominated by men, to one in which the women play the dominant role.[20]

·Language offers a broad documentation of the process of reinterpretation. Among New World Negroes, the vocabulary of the masters was taken over by the newly arrived Africans, the words were pronounced as best they could be in view of the pre-existing phonemic patterns, but the words, as pronounced, were cast into the mold of African grammatical structure. When a Gulla Negro of South Carolina in a folk-tale, says "Rabbit tell Fox, said," for "Rabbit told Fox," he is expressing an African idiom with English words. When he says "Man, don' you see all dis fresh meat standing in dis lot?" or "Rabbit lie in de sun on he so' skin," or "an' all her people died out an' leave her one," he is reinterpreting with English words the African expression of the following ideas: "Man, don't you see all these animals in this pasture?"; "Rabbit lay with the sun on his body"; "and all her family died and left her alone." Other instances of similar reinterpretations in the English of Negroes in the West Indies and the Guianas, in the Créole (Negro-French) of Haiti and the French New World possessions, of Papiemiento (Negro-Spanish) of Curaçao might be given, to show that in most areas of the New World, linguistic Africanisms are present.[21]

Linguistic reinterpretations of a comparable sort are found everywhere. Indeed, much of philological research, broadly interpreted in cultural terms, can be regarded as the study of the phenomenon. One or two examples of Indo-European reinterpretations can be given to make the point. It is recounted how, during the Napoleonic wars, the French soldiers were greatly feared by the Russian peasants. The French troops, wanting to make friends with the people, would go about repeating the phrase *bon ami*, "good friend." Because of this, the French became known as *bonamicheski*, "bonamis," a word that for the Russians took on the meaning "scoundrel." In Europe generally, the word "smoking" is used for a man's dinner coat. In the nineteenth century, at formal dinners, men did not smoke when women were present, while at all-male parties, where a dinner coat rather than full evening clothes were worn—"smokers," as they were called in English—smoking was the rule. In France, therefore, to be invited to an affair *en smoking*—with no accent on the first syllable—means that dinner clothes are to be worn.

The Maya Indians who live in the territory of Quintana Roo in Yucatan, Mexico, have syncretized native gods and various beings worshipped in Catholic rituals in a manner analogous to that in which Christian Negroes of the New World, and the Mohammedanized Hausa of West Africa have achieved a similar reinterpretation. Among these Maya, the role accorded

---

[20] Cf. *ibid*, pp. 5–17, for a discussion of this process.
[21] For elaboration of these points, see M. J. and F. S. Herskovits, 1936, pp. 117–35, and M. J. Herskovits, 1941, pp. 143–275.

the cross represents the most striking aspect of the phenomenon. "The cross is the most sacred symbol of the group," writes Villa. "It acts as an intermediary between God and man, for wherever stands a cross, there are the eyes of God. The cross does not, however, communicate directly with God, but through His Son, Jesus Christ, also called John of the Cross." Crosses have power to work miracles, are blessed and sprinkled with holy water, decorated, and dressed. Certain kinds of wood, which are held to have especially great power, are particularly important, and there is a hierarchy of crosses. Domestic crosses, that hold the "lowest rank and sanctity" protect the immediate family. These humble protectors have no shrines, except when a family cross gains prestige by the wonders it comes to have the reputation for working, whereupon this miraculous cross then becomes public, so to speak. Village crosses have greater powers, and on occasion may come to act in their own right. La Santísima (The Most Holy) is the name of the most sacred of these crosses. It has its own altar, cult, and votaries, and masses are said for it. It has become "the guardian of the moral and religious order of the subtribe and the protector of its people from danger and distress." [22]

Innumerable cases, from all parts of the world, of still other instances where cultural elements have been reinterpreted under contact come to mind as soon as the concept is elucidated. The reasons why regional variations are found in the same trait or complex of traits in a given area, the problem that occupied students of diffusion, become clear in principle, if not in detail, in the light of the hypothesis of reinterpretation. The differences that Spier found between the various tribal forms of the Plains Indian Sun Dance, for example, represent the end result of a process whereby, under contact, each tribe reinterpreted in its own way the elements it borrowed from its neighbors. That is, each tribe placed the new element in a pre-existing setting, sometimes retaining, sometimes changing its meaning.

From another area, a specific example shows how unpredictable the reinterpretation of a specific cultural element can be. When Europeans came to East Africa, they brought their guns with them. But the BaTswa (Ba-Thonga) of Portuguese East Africa took the stock and trigger-guard traits of what we may call the gun-complex, and reinterpreted them as the handle of a gravy-ladle, as is shown in the illustration on the opposite page. To complete the story, the linguistic reinterpretation that accompanied it must also be given. For these people call this kind of ladle by the word *shipúne*, a three-syllable modification of the English word "spoon."

The concept of reinterpretation, however, has a broader applicability than just to change in culture under contact, for the internal development of a culture in large measure also consists of a process of reinterpreting pre-existing elements in terms of new cultural reorientations. Originally, for example, the French word *chauffeur* meant a stoker, a fireman; but its use as the driver of an automobile has not only taken a full place in French, but in this sense is a full-fledged member of the vocabulary of English and other languages. A "factory" in earlier English was a place where a "factor,"

---

[22] Alfonso Villa R., 1945, pp. 97–9.

the agent of a business concern, carried on his work. It then became a "manu-factory," where goods were made. We still have the word "manu-facture," but a "factory" is today reinterpreted as the place where a business concern fabricates the articles it sells.

The principle of reinterpretation sharpens certain propositions regarding the dynamics of culture that are well established in anthropological thought. Linton has suggested that "every element of culture has qualities of four distinct, although mutually interrelated kinds: i.e., it has *form, meaning,*

Fig. 66   *BaTswa ladle (courtesy C. E. Fuller).*

use and *function.*" [23] Barnett, building on this formulation, points out that each of these qualities can vary independently as cultural elements change. New meaning can be read into an old form, or a new principle can be ap-plied despite the retention of a previous function. He exemplifies this with the instance of the application of the principle of the screw to the automobile jack in which a lever and ratchet mechanism was long used. "This, it seems evident, was suggested by a different form (a vise or compressor) serving entirely different functions." Thus, as he indicates, "On the one hand this was a principle departure and a functional substitute, and on the other it was a reapplied principle and a functional departure." That is, "from the viewpoint of the automobile mechanic it was a new way to do the same thing, from the viewpoint of the bookbinder or carpenter it was an old way to do something different." [24]

In the terminology used in this book, these changes may be called cultural reinterpretations, the reading of old meaning into new forms, or the retention of old forms with new meanings. It is apparent, in this connection, that the concept of reinterpretation is also of significance for the hypothesis of "stimu-lus diffusion" that has been advanced by Kroeber.[25] In many of the cultural changes that fall under such a category the principle of reinterpretation is fundamental.

Fenton provides still another example of reinterpretation, showing how it

[23] R. Linton, 1936, p. 402.
[24] H. G. Barnett, 1942, pp. 15–16.
[25] See above, p. 503.

can act as a mechanism in the retention of a custom under changing conditions, in his study of the patterns of suicide among the Iroquois Indians. In early days of European contact, the attitude of these people toward suicide was ambivalent, but under the influence of Christianity it came to be condemned. This hardening of attitude was enhanced by "a definite concept of allotted life and exclusion from the land of the dead," the former a belief introduced by the outsiders, the latter a development of indigenous beliefs. Yet, though attitudes toward self-destruction have changed, the "fundamental suicide patterns" have remained stable. "The same motives, the same methods, and similar beliefs concerning the fate of souls prevail. Danger of capture and torture ceased with the wars, and blood revenge is giving way to white law enforcement on the reservation: The onus is shifted but throughout avoidance remains the dominating motive." Fenton then concludes: "Pattern then serves as a cultural continuant for custom, antecedents have already defined the situation for the individual, and once a fundamental pattern becomes established it tends to persist despite substitution within its framework." [26] That is, the earlier pattern, with the passage of time, is reinterpreted so as to be in accord with change in the total setting of the culture as a whole.

5

THE significance of the concepts of cultural focus and reinterpretation become apparent when we consider the answer usually vouchsafed the question, "Why do a given people take over one new idea or new thing presented to them, and reject another?" Customarily it is stated that those elements that are in accord with the preceding patterns of the culture will be accepted, while those that are not will be rejected. Sometimes the answer is differently phrased. It will be expressed in terms of the cultural base, with the implication that when a culture is ready for an innovation, the innovation will make its appearance. This, it will be recalled, is the answer of the cultural determinists to the problem of the acceptability of inventions, and is usually documented by reference to the fact of multiple independent inventions in our own culture.

The question, however, is by no means answered by any of these formulations. It is quite true that, looked at after the fact, a given historic development that has made for the favorable reception of a series of innovations seems clear, or can at least be given a rational explanation. This is why we hold that every culture does have an internal logic, that determines the course of its own particular development. But for a surer understanding of the process, we must couch our explanation in psychological terms, and turn to the later enculturative experience for explanations of cultural change, on the level of the reactions of the individual members of a group to novelties presented to them. We may phrase this in terms of learning, as broadly conceived, or reconditioning, or rehabituation. In any case, we recognize that,

---

[26] W. N. Fenton, 1941, pp. 134–5.

as with all cultural processes, this is fundamental, since it is the individual who decides whether he wants a given novelty or not. In these terms, then, a cultural innovation is one which enough members of a society accept to make of it a recognized element in the range of traditions and modes of behavior to be found among the group.

The problem, we need not repeat, comprehends all phases of cultural change—whether these originate from within the group as discoveries or inventions, or whether they are transmitted from outside. As has been stressed in preceding chapters, the methodological problem of studying, in nonhistoric cultures, the processes whereby internal innovations are accepted or rejected, is a most difficult one. Because the broad range of comparative materials—which we know to be essential if generalizations are to be reached—is lacking, the fact that almost all our data bearing on discoveries and inventions come from the literate cultures, particularly from Euroamerican society, must fully be taken into account in evaluating hypotheses regarding the operation of all mechanisms of cultural change. We do, of course, use these data, just as we must employ the technique of studying the end-results of change, external or internal, that are manifest in comparative studies of variation in form of the same element in nonliterate societies. But, in truth, we have in the past learned most of what we know about the processes of change by analyzing the end-products of change rather than from the study of change in process.

It is apparent, however, that the answer to the question posed at the beginning of this section must, in the final analysis, be obtained from such study of change in process. Data derived from distribution studies can be used to test our hypotheses. It cannot be too greatly emphasized, however, that the hypotheses themselves, as instruments of scientific investigation, must arise out of the direct observation of the changes, whether internal or stimulated by contact, that are actually taking place.

We have not, in this chapter, answered the question raised concerning the differential selectivity of a people faced with a cultural innovation. It is doubtful if the answer will be given, except in general terms, for many years to come. This is the ultimate quest of most social scientists, as well as of many students whose concerns are entirely of a practical nature. The problem presents itself every time a new commodity is placed on the market, for the market survey is but one attempt to study this problem of acceptance or rejection of an internal change. In every attempt to introduce, in a foreign society, a new idea, a new technique, a new kind of goods, the question must be faced.

Manchester-made copies of Ashanti cloths, for instance, lay on the shelves of Gold Coast shops for want of buyers, despite the fact that these exact replicas were far less expensive than the native weaves. The reason for their rejection was a puzzle to those who charted their course in terms of economic theory based on concepts of price and value. Prestige and position, however, mean more to the Ashanti than an advantageous price. These cloths are marks of rank, and a man who appeared wearing one to which he was not entitled was subjected to unmerciful ridicule. Those upper-class persons who were entitled to wear them, on the other hand, had no need to take price differentials into account, even if considerations of their rank did not dictate their obligation to have cloths made by native weavers.

If our question cannot be answered, however, it can be refined and clarified. It is toward this end that the discussion in this chapter has been directed. The hypotheses of *cultural focus* and of *reinterpretation*, that have been derived from the study of cultures where change in process has been under observation, have a significance that transcends their applicability only to the situations in which they have been studied as such. These concepts reorient the approach to the fundamental problem of cultural change. The answers to the question, "Why do a given people take over one new idea or new thing presented to them, and reject another?" are customarily phrased only in terms of culture itself. Its formulation in terms of focus and reinterpretation introduces a needed psychological perspective. This approach, it should once more be emphasized, is essential if the motivations that cause a people to accept or reject a possible innovation are to be comprehended, and the process of cultural change is really to be understood.

PART VII

CULTURAL VARIATION

CHAPTER 33

The Significance of Variation
in Culture

THAT individual differences which mark off the behavior of one person from that of another can be discerned only when one becomes familiar with the way of life of a people, has been noted in earlier pages.[1] It has been pointed out how, on first acquaintance, these differences are so submerged in a flood of new impressions that they recede into those least common denominators of behavior we have called cultural patterns. It takes time and experience to comprehend what are the limits set for approved deviations rather than the similar ways in which, broadly considered, the members of a particular society react to a given situation.

It was out of the difficulties in perceiving individual differences in strange cultures, that the idea arose that "primitive man" lived in a cultural straitjacket. The quotations given in an earlier chapter [2] from Spencer and others bearing on this point will be remembered. It is not too much to say that this conception dominated anthropological thought until well after the nineteenth century. Not only did students who employed the comparative method draw on the accounts of travellers, missionaries, and others, who invariably wrote in terms of generalized custom, but early field-workers tended to be blind to the existence of individuals, as such, in the societies they studied. Much early field-work, it will be remembered, aimed at recovering cultures that were in process of disintegration, often under Euroamerican contact, as in the case of the American Indians. Here, understandably, individual differences were lost in the reminiscences of the survivors who acted as informants. But because of the tradition of field-work thus established, even in functioning cultures reliance too often was placed on statements of informants rather than on first-hand observation. Though a living culture might be had for the observing, the informant in many cases was summoned to the ethnographer's residence, frequently removed from the native habitations, there to answer generalized questions about the customs of his people.

Still another cause for the neglect of individual differences in earlier an-

---

[1] As, for example, pp. 483–4.
[2] See above, p. 485.

thropological writing was the feeling that anthropology, as the science of custom, was to be opposed to psychology, which was regarded as the discipline that studied the individual. As has been seen in preceding chapters, there is some truth in this assertion; yet it was carried to an extreme that could scarcely be justified. Sapir phrased the point very well, when he described how the province of anthropology, under these terms, was held to emphasize "those aspects of behavior which belonged to society as such, more particularly societies of the dim past or exotic societies whose way of life seemed so different from that of our own people that one could hope to construct a generalized picture of the life of society at large, particularly in its more archaic stages of development."

He continued in this vein: "The whole temper of cultural anthropology was impersonal to a degree. In this earlier period of the development of the science it seemed almost indelicate, not to say indecent, to obtrude observations that smacked of the personal or anecdotal. The assumption was that in some way not in the least clearly defined as to observational method it was possible for the anthropologist to arrive at conclusive statements which would hold for a given society as such. One was rarely in a position to say whether such an inclusive statement was a tacit quotation from a primitive 'John Doe' or a carefully tested generalization abstracted from hundreds of personal observations or hundreds of statements excerpted from conversations with many John Does." [3]

Names of informants were given, it is true, but there was little attempt to indicate how the statements they may have made about a given point differed. "I remember being rather shocked than pleased," says Sapir, "when in my student days I came across such statements in J. O. Dorsey's 'Omaha Sociology' as 'Two Crows denies this.' This looked a little as though the writer had not squarely met the challenge of assaying his source material and giving us the kind of data that we, as respectable anthropologists, could live on. It was as though he 'passed the buck' to the reader, expecting him by some miracle of cultural insight to segregate truth from error." But Dorsey, as Sapir points out, was ahead of his time. He knew his Indians well, and recognized that they, as individuals, differed in their behavior and in the interpretations they gave of this behavior like the members of any human group. "Apparently Two Crows," says Sapir, "a perfectly good and authoritative Indian, could presume to rule out of court the very existence of a custom or attitude or belief vouched for by some other Indian, equally good and authoritative." [4]

A demonstration of how valid is the point raised by Sapir in this passage is to be found in Roberts' study of variants in the songs of the Negroes of Jamaica. With the precision that the analysis of musical forms lends to the investigation of cultural phenomena, she shows how, both in melody and words, individual songs differ in their rendition not only from district to district of the same part of the island, but from singer to singer.

---

[3] E. Sapir, 1938, p. 7.
[4] *Ibid.*, pp. 7–8.

The Significance of Variation in Culture

From the several series of variants presented, we may take the "Jim Crow" (or "Cyam Crow") song, as recorded in the northwestern part of Jamaica. John Crow is the vulture, the turkey-buzzard. The name given him is, in all likelihood, an Anglicized version of the African name Yankoro given this same bird; his other name is probably derived from "carrion-crow," pronounced in the manner of the Jamaican Negroes. The point of the song, which is of a common African and New World Negro type, is that it ridicules the greed of the ungainly bird who in his haste to get the food from "Missa Wright's cow," fell rather than flew, and "broke his diaphragm ['diagram' in the song], or wind, as it was explained." [5] The author goes on: "From this small incident has sprung all the train of happenings that may be found in the different versions, and doubtless many more."

I. JOHN CROW
Sung by Mathilda Kerr, Harmony Hall

John Crow fall- in' off a tree top, lose him di- a-
gram[1]. Mis-sa Wright did ha' one co', an' Mis-sa Wright did kill da
co', an' John Crow fa' downg off a tree top fe go h'eat de tripe.
[1][diagram=diaphragm.]

II. JOHN CROW
Sung by Ada Smith, Whitehall

Mis- sa Wright ben ha' one cow. Mis- sa
Mis- sa Wright ben go to shop. Mis- sa

Wright ben kill de cow. But a John Crow tum- ble downg
Wright ben buy a drink. But de John Crow tum- ble downg

off a tree top, los' him di- a- gram.
out a dry tree, los' him di- a- gram.

---

[5] H. H. Roberts, 1925, p. 178.

Cultural Variation

III. JOHN CROW
Sung by Charles William, Retirement

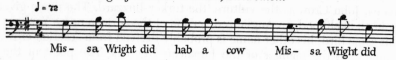

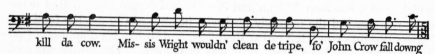

Mis- sa Wright did hab a cow Mis- sa Wright did kill da cow. Mis- sis Wright wouldn' clean de tripe, fo' John Crow fall downg off a dry tree top, los' him di- a- gram.

IV. JOHN CROW
Sung by Lydia White, Christiana

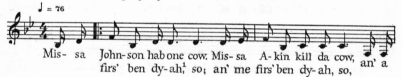

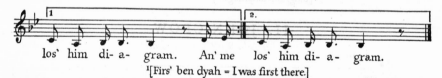

Mis- sa John-son hab one cow. Mis- sa A- kin kill da cow, an' a firs' ben dy-ah,[1] so; an' me firs' ben dy- ah, so, John Crow fall down off a wil- low tree, him los' him di- a- gram. An' me los' him di- a- gram.

[1][Firs' ben dyah = I was first there.]

V. JOHN CROW
Sung by Ivy Lewis Grant, Brownstown

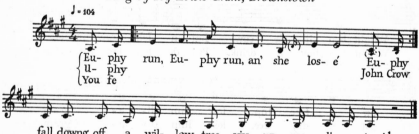

Eu- phy run, Eu- phy run, an' she los- é Eu- phy
U- phy   John Crow
You fe
fall downg off a wil- low tree, viv up me di- a- too!![1]

[1][Vomit up my diaphragm.]

566

The Significance of Variation in Culture

VI. JOHN CROW
Sung by Agatha Christie, Brownstown

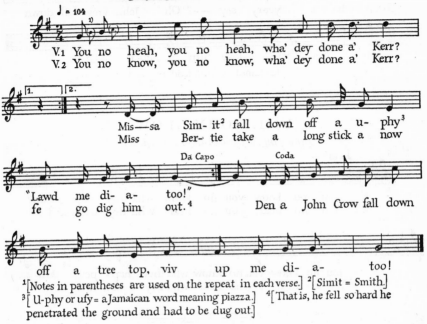

V.1 You no heah, you no heah, wha' dey done a' Kerr?
V.2 You no know, you no know, wha' dey done a' Kerr?

Mis—sa Sim-it[2] fall down off a u-phy[3]
Miss Ber- tie take a long stick a now

"Lawd me di- a- too!"
fe go dig him out.[4] Den a John Crow fall down

off a tree top, viv up me di-a- too!

[1] Notes in parentheses are used on the repeat in each verse.] [2] [Simit = Smith.]
[3] [U-phy or ufy = a Jamaican word meaning piazza.] [4] [That is, he fell so hard he penetrated the ground and had to be dug out.]

VII. JOHN CROW
Sung by Emanuel Johnson, Brownstown
(Orange Hill)

You no heah, you no heah wha' me yer-ry say—? Oh
(hear)

John Crow fall down off a tree top, viv up me

di-a-to! Oh di- a- to! You no heah, you no

heah wha' me yer-ry say——? You no heah, you no

567

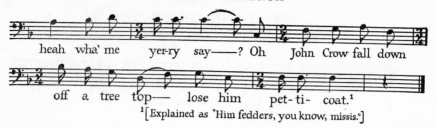

heah wha' me yerry say——? Oh John Crow fall down

off a tree top— lose him pet-ti- coat.[1]

[1][Explained as "Him fedders, you know, missis."]

VIII. JOHN CROW

Sung by Adinah Mills, Brownstown

V.1 You no know, you no know wha' they hap- pen?
V.2 You no hear, you no hear wha' dey done a' Kerr?

You no know, you no know wha' they hap- pen? Mis- sa
You no hear, you no hear wha' dey done a' Kerr?

Sim- it fa' downg off a u- phy. Los' him di- a-
Ce- les ha' one lit- tle brown boot an' she whit-en
Variant: "Lawd, me di- a-

gram. Mis- sa Sim- it fa' downg off a u- phy
gram."
it. Ce- les ha' one lit- tle brown boot

Los' him di- a- gram.
"Lawd, me di- a- gram."
an' she whit-en it. John Crow fa' downg off a tree top,

"Lawd, me di- a- too!" John Crow fa' downg

off a wil- low tree, viv up me di- a- too!
Variant: Los' him ped- al- mount[1]
[1][Pedalmount = Balance.]

The Significance of Variation in Culture

IX. CYAM CROW (JOHN CROW)
Sung by Winifred Leach, Brownstown

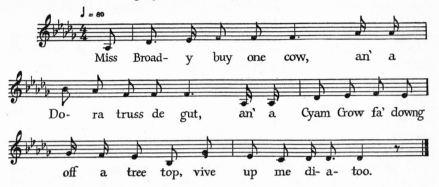

Miss Broad- y buy one cow, an' a Do- ra truss de gut, an' a Cyam Crow fa' downg off a tree top, vive up me di- a- too.

X. CYAM CROW (JOHN CROW)
Sung by Calvin Emmins, Brownstown
(Orange Hill)

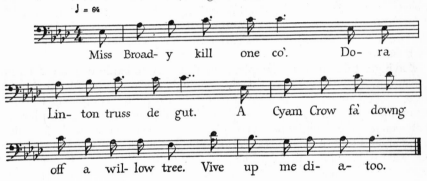

Miss Broad- y kill one co'. Do- ra Lin- ton truss de gut. A Cyam Crow fa' downg off a wil- low tree. Vive up me di- a- too.

XI. JOHN CROW
Sung by Guendolyn Sertin, Brownstown

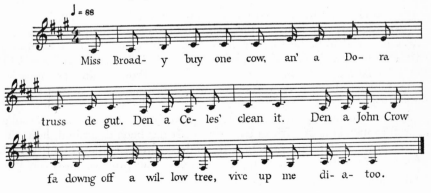

Miss Broad- y buy one cow, an' a Do- ra truss de gut. Den a Ce- les' clean it. Den a John Crow fa downg off a wil- low tree, vive up me di- a- too.

569

Cultural Variation

The first three songs were recorded in neighboring settlements. "Harmony Hall, Whitehall and Retirement," says the author, "are not far apart, perhaps within a radius of three miles. The same church ministers to all three districts and the people see one another frequently." Yet it is apparent that, despite similarities in melodic line and rhythm, and in the motifs of the verses, even here variants are to be observed. The other songs, which show wider dissimilarities, are from communities farther removed. They demonstrate how a single cultural item can continue to extend its limits of variation as the region in which it is studied is widened. We do not take up here the matter of variation in the performance of an individual. The rendition of this song by each singer, we are told, was quite constant. Yet Roberts gives other instances that demonstrate how differences are present in repetitions of a given song by the same singer.

Where, then, does ethnographic "truth" lie? There is scarcely any need to repeat here what has been often stated in earlier pages concerning the problem of establishing truth when describing cultural phenomena. The methodological aspects of this point have been considered in connection with our discussion of field methods, while its theoretical implications have been indicated as they bear on the problem of cultural relativity. We need only emphasize here once again that ethnological truth is not fixed, but variable. What the ethnographer must ascertain, then, is *the limits within which a culture recognizes and sanctions variations* in a given belief or a given mode of behavior.

Having set down this principle, it is necessary to explore some of its implications. As in the case of so many seemingly obvious principles that guide research and analysis in the field of culture, unsuspected complexities appear as an apparently simple point is probed. It is essential that the difference between *ideal* and *actual* behavior be held very clear in the mind of the field student, and that this distinction also be held in mind in reading accounts of the ways of life of any people. The principal difficulty is that the members of a society unfortunately do not necessarily agree as to what constitutes ideal behavior. Different members of the same community will give different versions of what is sanctioned by their group, while actual observation will reveal broad differences in behavior that reflect the variety of accepted sanctions.

An example of how this search for ethnographic truth is complicated by the deviations found in actual practice will both clarify the problem and indicate how it is to be faced. Our instance may be taken from the acculturative syncretisms between African belief and Catholicism in the culture of the Brazilian Negroes. As in other New World Catholic countries, ancestral African beliefs have been reconciled with Christianity, as a result of the forced conversions of slavery times. Today, the descendants of these Africans, who worship the African gods, are professing and practising Catholics as well as members of African cult-groups. It has been described, how, due to the process of reinterpretation through syncretism, they identify their African gods with the saints of the Church.[6] The process, however, goes

[6] See above, pp. 553-4.

570

much farther. A hollow-log drum that has not been "baptized" will not call the proper deities to the dance, since it does not have the disciplined spiritual control that goes with baptism. In Salvador, Bahia, a novitiate, after a long period of initiation into cult-practices in the cult-house of her group, will immediately on emerging from her training make one pilgrimage to the shrine of the principal saint of the city, and another to worship at the altar of the saint that is identified with the African god to whose worship she is vowed. Bastide, however, has shown that even in a single city, one cannot flatly say that a given African deity is always identified with a given Catholic saint. In Recife, for example, though the African water-goddess named Yemanja was identified by the members of four cult-centers with Our Lady of the Immaculate Conception, Shango, the African thunder-god was held by one group to be the same as St. Jerome, by another as St. Anthony, and by a third as St. John the Baptist.[7]

As in all Catholic countries, Lent is a period of great importance, and so is Shrove Tuesday (Mardi Gras), the culmination of the annual Carnival. Now almost everyone in this Brazilian city of Salvador, Negro or white, cult-member or not, will tell the visiting ethnographer, with perfect good faith, that Lent is no time to study cult-ceremonies, since cult-houses are closed for the observance of Lent and the cycle of public rites is suspended. Statements to this effect are to be found in the literature describing the Afro-bahian cults, and the student is advised to plan his research so that during this period investigations of other than the religious aspects of the culture can be carried on. As one pursues his inquiry he is told, with comparable unanimity, that Holy Saturday (*Sábado da Aleluia*) is the day when, with elaborate rites, these African cult centers reopen after their Lenten suspension of activities. Some persons are even more specific. They say that these cult rites are timed to begin at 11 a.m. when, on the day before Easter, the bells of all Bahia's many churches peal to mark the moment of the Resurrection.

Yet, as far as could be ascertained, in actual practice many cult centers continue the worship of their African gods well into Lent. Not a single center could be found in the year 1942 that suspended its activities at the beginning of that period. All cult-houses were closed during Holy Week. Even the people who live in these centers went elsewhere then, since this is regarded as a time of spiritual danger, when the gods have departed. But again by no means all these centers reopened on Easter Saturday. In actuality, the rites that reopen them may be witnessed for a month or more after Easter Sunday. It depends largely on the plans of the priest who heads the cult-house, or on the wishes of the gods themselves, as revealed by divination, or on other circumstances.

The gods, which as we have said are believed to be absent while the cult-house is closed, are thought of as being "off to the wars" during the period. The rite of closing the house, called *lorogun*, is one whose essential purpose is to speed these beings on their way. This ceremony is obviously an important one, and is given with as much elaborateness of display as the resources

[7] R. Bastide, 1946, pp. 18–19.

of a given cult-center permit. In it the deities are "called," possess their devotees, and in some centers stage a dance which, with the intricate choreography of a mock combat, determines which spirits will "rule" the center during the ensuing year. The gods then shoulder their food-sacks, visit in turn the shrines of the center to say their good-byes, and then finish the dance in the cult-house, proffering their favorite foods to the spectators before they depart.

Here, in outline, is an abstract of this *lorogun* rite taken from least common denominators in the descriptions of it given by three different informants, plus observations of six actual ceremonies that were witnessed and recorded. Each informant reported, in considerable detail, the sequence of events, and the reasons why each element in this rite was carried out. But each was, in all likelihood, thinking of a particular instance of the ceremony as performed in the cult-center with which he was affiliated. Among some groups, for example, the "combat" was described as between male and female deities, to see which would "rule" for the year. Among others, it was said to be between gods of different pantheons. In one center, at an actual ceremony, it was the god that first "came" to a devotee when the drum-rhythms called—that is, in whose name the initial possession occurred—that was to be paramount for the year. On occasion, an informant would say, "In our center we do it this way, but in others they don't do this," or, when presented with the conflicting statement of another informant, would shrug his shoulders, and say, "They probably do it that way in his house."

What is the "truth" of Afrobahian cult practices as regards the identification of Catholic saints and African gods, or in connection with Lent? Here, it is apparent, there is no single truth. There are many truths. But it is equally apparent that there are limits beyond which statements are not true, while there is a core of common behavior wherein a minimum of deviation is to be found. The fact that practically all cult-houses are closed during Holy Week is one such core element; the common items given in our general outline of the *lorogun* rite constitute others; yet about this core are the numerous variants, all of which have an ethnological validity that is beyond dispute. It is the same when, in other cultures, and in an entirely different realm, a person in good faith tells how in his group men show respect for their mothers-in-law by avoiding them—specifically, by not speaking to them in face-to-face conversation. More than one ethnographer has been nonplussed later to observe this same informant talking to his own mother-in-law, only to be told that here was a special instance—a child was ill, or the man's wife was in need of advice she herself could not come to get.

"Circumstances alter cases" is as good a rule of thumb in ethnography as it is in guiding everyday conduct. For it is circumstances that make for differences in individual behavior that are reflected in the variability found in the patterned sanctions that permit deviations from the norm of approved conduct, or in the recognized forms of institutions. The problem of ascertaining the range of accepted variation in custom, then, is the essence of the question of ethnographic truth. We may, therefore, now consider the importance of this fact in furthering our understanding of the forms, functions, and processes of culture.

2

THE concept of variability is a statistical one, and the difficulty of applying statistical methods to the study of many phases of culture is self-evident, particularly among peoples where measurement is minimal. We can measure certain phenomena in the economic field, such as hours of labor or agricultural yield. But even in the field of economics, as we have seen, measures of value in a society that bases its exchange of goods on barter, and has no least common denominator of worth in the form of money, are still to be worked out. It is scarcely necessary to point out how this difficulty increases as we move away from material things into the realm of the intangibles of culture, and try to measure variation in religion, or in family structure, or in the ideals that motivate men and women as they carry on the activities of everyday life.

Some attempts have been made to utilize certain statistical methods in studying culture, but these have been more in the nature of efforts to make use of the concept of correlation in reconstructing historical processes and the contacts between peoples. In the early days of anthropology, Tylor attempted to show that certain conditions found in association with others are caused by them, as, for example, matrilineal descent and matrilocal residence. Much later, Kroeber and Driver utilized the trait-element list, discussed in an earlier chapter, as a basis for correlating traits and thus reconstructing historic contacts between the peoples involved in their studies.

Perhaps because cultural anthropologists have not been taught to think statistically, but operate in terms of a humanistic tradition, they have not formulated their problems so as to study cultural variation by means of techniques that involve a quantitative approach. Much research can, however, be carried on in these terms, once the foundation has been laid in the form of a monograph which gives a rounded portrayal of patterns that represent the consenses of the cultural behavior of a given people. From the point of view of statistical theory, these consenses are the equivalent of norms or modalities, which lay the ground work for investigations into the extent to which deviations from behavior norms are manifest.

More measuring can be done than seems possible at first glance; and once measurements have been gathered, the computation of statistical constants, of which variability is but one, is a simple matter. Hours of labor, or output of craftsmen and agriculturalists, or expressions of value where some form of money is present have been studied and, in rough fashion, as we have seen, have been presented as variables. But in music, for example, recordings of the same song sung by different persons, or by the same person at different times can, when analyzed in the laboratory, yield measurements that are to be described in terms of differences in wave-length of the same note—differing tones—or in volume, or in tempo. Recordings of speech

573

would yield similar mathematical indices of variation, far more precise than even the careful study of dialectic differences by the linguists have been able to achieve. Designs in weaving or basketry likewise afford materials that are susceptible of measurement and statistical treatment. It is apparent that this list could, with a little ingenuity, be continued indefinitely.

But, it will be pointed out, these are but details of culture. Even if such studies were available, would they not leave the problem, in its broad outlines, untouched? This is, however, scarcely a valid objection. If the inductions of scientific method have taught us anything, it is that the great problems are solved only after the intensive study of minutiae has revealed fundamental processes. To assess the variability of a note, of a unit of value, of a phoneme is to reduce to exactitude the study of an element of culture. Given a series of measurements, and the theoretical concept of variation applied in the analysis of a number of such elements, and we begin to arrive at a comprehension of how variable culture can be.

This is why, for example, it was held that the three steps that have marked the study of the relationship between culture and the individual represent clear gains in the move to attack this complex problem in more precise ways. The concept of personality norms is more easily handled than that of personality type. The attempt, in turn, to reduce these norms to measurable terms by referring them to the results of study based on the use of projective tests, still further promotes the desired end. The instruments used in this latter process may be subject to differing interpretations, but the interpretations themselves can be expressed quantitatively. It is reasonable to assume that the same student will interpret his instrument in the same way; that different students who can work together will interpret findings not dissimilarly. Hence the statistical constants to be derived from the measurements can be compared, as evaluations drawn on a broad impressionistic scale in terms of institutions or drives cannot be.

This is something analogous to the situation in physical anthropology when comparisons of skin-color by means of reference to a color-chart were made more precise by using a color-top. The color-top is a crude instrument, but it does yield quantitative expressions of differences in skin-color, and hence more precise statements of differences in this trait between populations are made possible. It is one of the most important truisms of science that once a workable method of *measurement* has been achieved, its refinement is only a question of time.

3

THE concept of culture-pattern that was advanced earlier in this book defined this phenomenon as the consensus of differing individual behavior patterns. The point, however, was further made that the term, in all discussions except those that are concerned with describing and analyzing a particular pattern, should be used in the plural sense. This conclusion was reached because we found that, even in the most homogeneous group, *institutionalized* variants in ways of meeting the same situation are always to be encountered.

574

The Significance of Variation in Culture

These differing sets of patterns seem to reflect the fact that every society is an aggregate of sub-groups, whose particular ways of life are to be distinguished within the general sanctions of the group as a whole. The fact that these lines cross and recross, in the sense that a given individual belongs to a number of sub-groups, was seen to complicate the problem presented by the pattern-phenomenon. At the same time it was pointed out that a recognition of this complexity tends of itself to clarify certain problems in the study of culture that otherwise present serious difficulties.

Let us recall some of the sub-groupings which, in a given society, can be expected to exhibit different characteristic behavior-patterns. Two of these, that are everywhere present, are based on sex and age. In small aggregates, a third category, based on occupation, will be closely related to the preceding two. That is, even in the most homogeneous societies, men and women will perform different kinds of tasks. In larger societies, however, occupational patterns will go farther, since within each sex various specialized callings will have patterns that mark off the behavior of those who follow them from the behavior of men or women who are specialized in other ways. In larger societies, too, class differences will produce different patterns, while everywhere local groupings within a larger population aggregate will have their special kinds of patterns, whether in language, or industry, or belief, or any other aspect of culture.

Underlying all these differences, however, are those that mark off individual from individual, and intermediately, family from family. This is why the nature of any pattern, no matter how minute or particular, or how broad, as a *consensus* of behavior, was stressed. The larger the number of persons who react to a given situation in similar—not identical—ways, the wider its effectiveness over the society where it is found. It follows that to deny the element of consensus on the ground that not all members of a particular society participate in all its patterns, is in essence to deny unity and coherence to culture.

Consensus of cultural behavior is but another expression of cultural variation. For since each culture is different from every other, and no two individuals belonging to the same society react in exactly the same manner to the same situation, it follows that variation in patterns themselves make up a factor to be taken most carefully into account in the study of culture. A culture, considered in this way, becomes an aggregate of differing individual patterns which, in their totality, reflect the fact that the behavior of any member of a particular society will be more like that of any fellow-member, than it will be like the behavior of any outsider.

Linton has suggested a useful series of concepts to denote certain degrees of similarity and difference in behavior to be found in a culture. The first of these he calls "universals," which are those beliefs and forms of behavior to be expected of any normal member of a society. Language, types of clothing and housing, the ways a group orders its social relationships fall within this category. The second category comprises the "specialties," which are composed of those particular aspects of behavior that characterize the members of specialized groups within the larger social whole. Here are placed those differences we have indicated as marking off the activities of one sex from those of the other, or of different kinds of craftsmen. Specialties thus fall mainly in the field of economic and technical fields, as, for example, the skills of the smith, or the doctor, or the priest.

Next come the "alternatives." These forms of behavior are recognized by a society as valid but cut across class or occupational or sex lines. They represent the different ways of doing the same things that are sanctioned by the group. They are present in all aspects of culture. A man may choose one color or another in decorating a basket he is making, or may phrase an assertion with one set of words or another; a game may be played in various ways, marriage may be sanctioned by observing different forms. The number of alternatives thus conceived is a measure of the homogeneity of a society and its way of life. Small nonliterate groups have fewer alternatives—and also fewer specialties—than larger ones, while the literate cultures have the greatest number of all.

The fourth category is that of "individual peculiarities." These are the experimental forms of behavior, so to speak. They represent the contribution of the individualist. Linton points to these as the source of innovation in culture. Every contribution to a way of life, as he says, must have been started by someone. At the outset, it is an individual peculiarity which, regarded benevolently by the members of the society when it is introduced, passes into more general use.[8]

In a sense, however, these categories overlap. Redfield has pointed out, for example, that the concept of "alternatives" stands for two different kinds of cultural phenomena. The first includes those elements shared by some persons, but not by all members of a society or even of its sub-groups. The second includes those elements in the culture that are alternatives in the strict sense, wherein the individual may exercise choice between various recognized ways of alternate behavior in a given situation. To these, Redfield says, the term "alternatives," strictly speaking, should be applied. Where elements are shared by some but not by others in a society, without regard to group or sub-group, Redfield accepts the term "variants," which had been advanced by Tax. "Alternatives," in this sense—the example given by Redfield is whether one should, in our culture, use a bus or a train—are thus "a kind of Universal," since they are shared as alternative possibilities by all the members of a group or sub-group, and thus come under Linton's definition of universals.[9]

If we apply the concept of variability to Linton's series, we find that there are levels of difference not unrelated to these categories. Thus the variations that mark off the belief and behavior of every member of any group from that of any other are, in a sense, the "individual peculiarities" of Linton's scheme. However, as a statistical concept, this most general level of variation defines the limits of acceptable behavior permitted by a group rather than the extreme deviants that are stressed by Linton in describing his category. From the point of view of cultural variability, an extreme deviation,

---

[8] R. Linton, 1936, pp. 272–5.
[9] R. Redfield, 1941, pp. 347–8.

The Significance of Variation in Culture

if accepted, merely widens the range of variation in a culture. If it does not "catch on," or is suppressed, it is to be put down as an innovation that departed too widely from accepted custom.

Individual variation, however, may exist without involving innovation. The nearer the individual's particular kind of behavior is to the normative forms, the less marked it will be from that of his fellows. But no two persons, even those who do not question their culture at all, will perform the same operation, or conceive the same accepted belief, in identical terms. It is just as important for a comprehension of cultural form and process to understand this fact as it is to recognize the role of the individual idiosyncrasy that constitutes an extreme departure from the norm. It is the range of permitted deviation that marks off the complexity of one culture in a given aspect from another—what Linton terms alternatives, in the sense of Redfield's use of the word. In its totality, this range of permitted deviation is an index of cultural homogeneity or heterogeneity. To recognize that in no culture do all members of a group react the same way to a given situation is but to say that variation is a universal in culture, no less than any of its other aspects. This means that variability must be taken into account, however imperfect the instrument for analyzing it, in all studies of culture. The recognition of the fact of variation in cultures, no matter how expressed, thus becomes one of the most significant steps in the development of anthropological science.

As we move from the total group to sub-units, the range of variation becomes more restricted. The smaller the unit, the greater the degree of homogeneity likely to be present. A family group will comprise persons whose individual enculturation is so similar that deviations from the norms of behavior that may mark off the members of that family group from each other will be at a minimum. The local group will, in general, be composed of individuals whose reactions are more alike than are those to be noted among the members of a tribal or wider social grouping. Specialists, however, will differ from each other in accordance with the patterns of variation sanctioned for their specialty. This suggests the hypothesis that specialists, because of the technical proficiency they attain through specialization, will be prone to experiment and thus extend the range of variation of their group without as much regard for its size as is the case among the population at large.

4

THE points that have thus far been made concerning variation in culture may be summarized in the following propositions:

1. Culture is an expression of the behavior of a people, and of the sanctions that underlie behavior.

2. The behavior and belief of no two individuals is identical; hence these must be thought of, and studied, as variable rather than rigidly structured.

3. The total range of variation in individual belief and behavior found among the members of a given society, at a given time, thus defines the culture of that society, and this holds true for the sub-cultures of smaller units within the social whole.

Cultural Variation

However,

4. Belief and behavior in any society are never haphazard, but vary about established norms.

5. These norms are to be derived inductively from the consenses of the observed beliefs and modes of behavior of a given group, and comprise the patterns of a culture.

Finally,

6. Other things being equal, the smaller the group, the more homogeneous its patterns of belief and behavior will be.

7. Specialist groups, however, may be expected to exhibit a greater range of variation in the field of their specialties than groups of equivalent size among the population as a whole.

The approach to the problem of the nature of culture and its organization suggested by this formulation, though conceived in statistical terms cannot, in view of the methodological problems involved, be treated in mathematical form. What is important to recognize, as one reads the ethnographic literature and discussions of anthropological theory, is the significance of the problem of *cultural homogeneity* and *cultural heterogeneity*. Furthermore, the student must be prepared to utilize data bearing on this problem despite the fact that, in most cases, their meaning is not recognized or is expressed in other ways. We have seen how concepts of patterning, of area differences, of the role of the individual in culture turn on different conceptions of the degree of variation to be taken into account. It will only be necessary to recall our discussion of field methods to understand how important the recognition of individual variability is in orienting any approach to the problems of field research. We shall see to what an extent attempts to classify total cultures in graded series of various sorts is based on the ascription of differing degrees of homogeneity to cultures assigned to different categories.

It may be that, for the present, it would be best to employ the methods of quantitative analysis only in the study of those aspects of culture, such as certain elements in musical style, in the graphic arts, or in the economic life of a people, that have been indicated as susceptible of mathematical treatment. The student must always be on his guard against the spurious sense of accuracy that arises from the unwarranted use of statistical method. There is much in culture where qualitative description, as against a quantitative analysis, can be employed quite effectively to give a lively and significant sense of the range of differences found in one group or sub-group as against another. It is hardly necessary, for example, to resort to counting to know that the cultures of the tribes of the Mackenzie basin are more homogeneous than those of Java. But, as we shall see when we consider the nature of cultural laws and the problem of prediction, it is important to conceive of their differences in homogeneity as comprising differing degrees of variation in the expressions of belief and behavior that characterize the life of the members of such groups.

It should be evident that the conception of a culture as the summation of the variables in belief and behavior of a people is of importance in approaching almost any problem of cultural dynamics. As in so many fields of science, the fact of difference between the individual units of any category of phenomena must in the study of culture be recognized as a primary mechanism of change. The role of the extreme deviant in widening the range of variation in a culture has been mentioned. This, in turn, may set up a dynamic reaction that leads to other deviations which push the frontiers of accepted convention ever farther. This is at the base of the process of cultural drift, to a discussion of which we shall turn shortly.

Propensities to change in culture can, indeed, be envisaged as a function of the variable attitudes toward innovation that are found in a given society or in different societies. This idea is inherent in the concept of a culture as being oriented differently from other cultures in terms of its different cultural focus, that aspect of culture wherein the range of institutional manifestations is great because there is a greater readiness on the part of people to accept new forms than in other aspects of their culture. Thus when we say that religion is the focal aspect of West African culture, we are not only expressing the fact that the concerns of the people center in this more than in other aspects of their experience. We also imply a patterned receptivity to change in the focal aspect that is not present where social organization, for example, or technology are concerned. The recognized family or sib structures, the kinds of hoes used in agriculture are taken for granted. There is consequently no patterned encouragement of change in these cultural elements. Therefore, as we shall see, when we speak of one aspect of culture, or even one whole culture as being more "fluid" than another, we mean that there is a greater degree of patterned acceptance of variation in it than in another we call "conservative."

CHAPTER 34

Cultural Drift
and Historic Accident

A STUDY of documentary and historical materials reveals two kinds of cultural change. The first kind are those changes that represent the accumulation of small variations, whose total effect, over a period of time, is to bring about alterations that, viewed from day to day, are scarcely noticeable. The other kind is more abrupt, more dramatic. Here short-term effects, of far-reaching consequence, impress themselves on members of the group and outside observers alike. In this category come those innovations that are inspired by events initiated by circumstances not foreseen by members of the society experiencing them. They result in innovations which, whether voluntary or enforced, so considerably alter the character of a culture, or certain of its aspects, that it soon becomes appreciably different than it was prior to the introduction of these new elements.

The fact that these two kinds of cultural change are to be distinguished has important implications for culture theory. This becomes apparent when it is considered how different the concept of culture and the theories of cultural process eventuate when either of these kinds of change is emphasized to the neglect of the other. The theory of cultural evolution, for instance, was based essentially on the first of these approaches, stress being laid on the steady and regular introduction of new elements. As a result, human civilization was envisaged as a kind of stream, moving down the ages with an irresistible force, that, following the contours of history, would eventually reach its ordained end. The stream had rapids, as when striking novelties disturbed its calmness; it was split into varied channels by the islands of particular circumstance that distinguished the history of one people from another. But despite these, it was held that its course could be mapped and that its destiny was secure.

The underlying postulates of the cultural determinists similarly stress the inevitability of cultural change through the accumulation of small variations. An invention, or a discovery, in these terms, is made only when the times call for it. Conversely, this hypothesis maintains that when the times do call for it, it will be made. Thus we recall the independent discoveries by Darwin and Wallace of the evolutionary hypothesis; or on the other hand the case of Gregor Mendel. It will be remembered how, in the writings of the cultural determinists, it was stated that if the principle of biological evolution had not been discovered by Darwin or Wallace, it would have been come on by some other student. On the other hand, in the tenets of the cultural determinists, a discovery made too soon will be disregarded and play no role in the life of the people. Here Mendel's discovery of the mechanism of heredity, as evidenced in the principle of the inheritance of unit characters, is pointed as evidence. We may again recall how Mendel announced his discovery in a scientific journal of wide circulation, only to have it neglected until, some decades later, biological science was ready for it; whereupon its original statement was discovered and various students, again working independently, came on it.

Stress laid on the more abrupt developments in culture brings us to quite different conclusions regarding the factors in culture change, and the ways in which change manifests itself. The role of the great man in history is one expression of this point of view. In these terms, the geniuses of history, the Alexanders, the Caesars, the Rousseaus, the Voltaires, the Farradays, the Edisons are not regarded as exponents of their cultures and the periods in which they lived but rather as embodying the forces that are held to bring about the conquests, the revolutions, the technological changes associated with their names. In anthropological writings where the individual does not figure, this point of view is given a somewhat different expression. As an obvious example we may take the English diffusionist school. Here, the discovery of "civilization," as expressed in the various elements of the heliolithic complex, was believed to have occurred in a relatively short space of time, as the counting of human history goes, and in the relatively restricted area of Egypt, with later modifications in India. Yet such was the assumed effect of contact with this "civilization" that pre-existing "simpler" ways of life were held to have given over in favor of it, with the presumed far-reaching results we have sketched.

It should be apparent that no adequate study of culture can afford to neglect either of these kinds of change. What must be sought is an understanding of the nature of both gradual and abrupt cultural alterations, why they occur and the forms they manifest. The complexity of culture is such that both may be operative, in different aspects of culture, at the same time; in which case we may have an explanation for the abrupt shifts in cultural focus that present so puzzling a phenomenon.

To the first process—that is, where minor alterations slowly change the character and form of a way of life, but where the continuity of the event is apparent—we shall apply the term *cultural drift*. The more abrupt innovations, whether arising from within a culture or coming from outside a given society, we shall call *historic accidents*. Together, they act to give a culture at a given moment in its history the forms it manifests, and endow it with the sanctions that give these forms meaning and permit them to function in the lives of the people. First the one process, then the other will be considered; after which we will see whether a synthesis of them can be reached.

2

THE concept of *cultural drift* follows logically from the idea of a culture as the consensus of the variables in the beliefs and modes of behavior of a people. As we have seen, the presence of deviations from norms of concept and conduct, most of them so small as to go largely unrecognized, is important in giving to a culture an inner dynamic that, in the long run, results in alterations that may be of the most profound character. These variants, however, do not all have the same dynamic significance. They tend to be random variations, in the sense that they represent all kinds of departures from all sorts of norms. They are dynamically significant only when they begin to accumulate, and thus give direction to cultural change.

As an instance, we may take the habit of men, in Euroamerican culture, to wear about their necks strips of cloth, or neckties, as these strips are termed. This is the norm. Some of these ties are longer than others, some are tied as bows and others as slip-knots. Some are more brightly colored than others. Different kinds of neckties will be in order on different occasions. A person who has suffered the death of a near relative will, ordinarily, wear a dark-colored tie tied in a slip-knot. He will not wear a bright-colored one, nor wear a bow-tie. On the other hand, a man wearing formal clothes will wear only bow ties, though degrees of formality of the occasion will be indicated by whether the bow is black or white. If it is black, this has no reference to mourning, but denotes a lesser degree of formality than a white one.

If we revert to commonest custom, we find a recognizable swing in fashion, over the years, from knotted ties to bow ties. At a given time one type or the other will predominate. Yet the fluctuations have had to do with the type of tie, not with the incidence of wearing ties. The variations concerned color and form; the question whether or not to have neckties was not raised. Lurking in the background of this consensus, however, was a more radical deviant—the tieless man. The fact that the necktie had a status association was of some significance here. Persons of substance and respect have been notably reluctant to discard this symbol of their position. However, it began to be noted that the lower-class individual, the workman, gained a certain measure of comfort by the absence of need to conform to the wearing of additional widths of constricting cloth about his neck.

Some men of status came to veer toward this particular deviation. As more and more men did this, especially during the summer heat, clothing manufacturers began to take cognizance of this tendency and to design shirts that could be worn open at the neck or closed, with or without a necktie. Whatever the final outcome of this tendency toward "necktielessness"—which has been part of a still wider dress complex that need not be detailed here, but that includes brighter colors in clothing, and greater informality of clothes in general—it provides a good example of how at one time a particular deviation will be of greater significance than another. That is, we see, in this minor and perhaps frivolous detail of Euroamerican culture, a manifestation of *that process of cumulative variation we mean when we speak of cultural drift.*

The term drift represents an adaptation of Sapir's concept of linguistic drift, a concept that, despite its usefulness for the study of culture, has been strangely neglected by most cultural anthropologists. It should be indicated, in passing, that this concept affords still another example of how, in the broad field of cultural theory no less than in the documentation of cultural detail, the anthropological study of language can reveal processes and data of the greatest importance. Sapir moves to his discussion of linguistic drift from a consideration of variability in linguistic expression. Every person, he observes, manifests idiosyncrasies in his particular speech-habits. Yet in a social class, or in a local area, the speakers of a common language form "a compact, relatively unified group" in contrast to other such groups. "The individual variations are swamped in or absorbed by certain major agreements —say of pronunciation and vocabulary—which stand out very strongly when the language of the group as a whole is contrasted to that of the other group."[1]

If we translate this into the terms of our discussion of variability in culture as a whole, we would say that the individual differences in belief and behavior of persons who belong to one sub-group or local community within a particular society are submerged in the consenses that characterize the sub-cultures of the two groups, and thus make it possible to distinguish them from each other in terms of their typical patterns of thought and conduct. In language as in the rest of culture, however, not all of the idiosyncrasies, the random deviations from the norm are of the same consequence. "If individual variations 'on a flat' were the only kind of variability in language," says Sapir, "I believe we should be at a loss to explain why . . . it is that a linguistic prototype gradually breaks up into a number of mutually unintelligible languages. But language is not merely something that is spread out in space, as it were—a series of reflections in individual minds of one and the same timeless picture. Language moves down time in a current of its own making. It has a drift."[2]

Linguistic change is brought about, then, by a process whereby certain deviations from established norms are taken over by a number of people, thus initiating and continuing a tendency that becomes a trend. In the case of culture, too, this process may be true of entire societies or of any of their sub-groups. Where societies are small and isolated, the accumulated changes mark the life of the group as a whole. Where a population mass is large and the territory which it inhabits is of considerable extent, change may go in one direction for one sub-group and another in the case of a different sub-group.

In language, this process results in dialectic differences. In culture as a whole, it results in local or class traditions that, operating within the confines of the entire society, mark off the typical or characteristic ways of life of one class or local group from another. It will be recalled how, in discussing the pattern phenomenon in culture, the significance of differences of this order was considered—how between sex and class and generation and local groupings different consenses of behavior are to be discerned.[3] These are but the end-results of the process of selective emphasis on variants, within the predominant patterns that represent consenses for the society to which they all belong. The differences in the consenses of total cultures, in turn the end-

---

[1] E. Sapir, 1921, pp. 157–8. Reprinted by permission.
[2] *Ibid.*, p. 160.
[3] See above, pp. 207–212.

results of selectivity of variations on a more comprehensive scale, are what make it possible to distinguish the ways of life of one people from another.

The criticism has sometimes been made in discussing Sapir's concept of linguistic drift, that it has a mystical quality which places it outside the range of scientific investigation. It is apparent that if this point has validity for the hypothesis as applied to language, it is equally valid when lodged against the postulate of drift in culture as a whole. Sapir, however, anticipated this criticism. It is worth while to see how he did this. "If the historical changes that take place in a language," he asks, "if the vast accumulation of minute modifications which in time results in the complete remodeling of the language, are not in essence identical with the individual variations that we note on every hand about us, if these variations are born only to die without a trace, while the equally minute, or even minuter, changes that make up the drift are forever imprinted on the history of the language, are we not imputing to this history a certain mystical quality? Are we not giving language a power to change of its own accord over and above the involuntary tendency of individuals to vary the norm?" In answering his own question, he refers again to the fact of individual variations, from which change must come. For, he states, "it by no means follows that the general drift of a language can be understood"—or "apprehended," as he says in a footnote—"from an exhaustive descriptive study of these variations alone." For these are "random phenomena, like the waves of the sea, moving backward and forward with purposeless flux."

On the other hand, drift is not haphazard. "Only those individual variations embody it or carry it which move in a certain direction." "The drift of a language," he therefore concludes, "is constituted by the unconscious selection on the part of its speakers of those individual variations that are cumulative in some special direction." As in language, so in culture as a whole, though here the phenomenon is more complex. Just as we cannot study cultures as wholes, so we cannot study change in culture without considering the different rates and forms of change that characterize its different institutions. The necktie trend moves toward lesser formality, and it is a part of a drift that marks many aspects of our life. But there are other phases of our culture, such as religion, or conceptions of morality, that it does not invade at all.

The concept of drift, the piling up of minor variations that are in accord with pre-existing tendencies, must be considered as associated with the idea of cultural focus. We have advanced the hypothesis that because there is a lively interest in the focal aspect of a culture, change is more likely to occur in the institutions lying here than in those found in other of its aspects. Granting that change is not haphazard, but directional, then the increased range of variation in the focal aspect of a culture would not only continuously tend to produce a wider range of variants in line with the direction in which the institutions were moving, but would also make for more decided change than in other aspects. If, further, the focal aspect was the one which gave a culture its "flavor," then the outstanding changes that marked the development of cultures in terms of the succession of focal interests manifested by it over long periods could be referred to the fact that drift is not a simple unilinear phenomenon. This would further reflect the fact that the broad stream which comprises any culture has varied currents, of which now some, now others will be the more rapid.

Drift is a difficult concept to grasp because every culture, from the short-term view, seems to have a high degree of stability. Here again language offers an excellent case in point, though any of the aspects of culture whose sanctions tend to lodge deep beneath the level of consciousness, such as musical or art styles, could also be called on for instances. "As we look about us and observe current usage," Sapir says, "it is not likely to occur to us that our language has a 'slope,' that the changes of the next few centuries are in a sense prefigured in certain obscure tendencies of the present and that these changes, when consummated, will be but continuations of changes that have been already effected. We feel rather that our language is practically a fixed system and that what slight changes are destined to take place in it are as likely to move in one direction as another. The feeling is fallacious. Our very uncertainty as to the impending details of change makes the eventual consistency of their direction all the more impressive." [4]

It will become apparent when the problem of prediction of cultural change is discussed, how significant this concept of Sapir's potentially is. For though the phenomenon of cultural drift can, as yet, only be studied in terms of its past manifestations, it is nonetheless easier to project lines of established developmental drift than if the concept were not present to sharpen our perceptions. In the main, this can only be done for details of culture, rather than for its larger subdivisions or for a culture as a whole. Sapir's demonstration of the drift, in English, toward the use of the pronoun "who" for "whom" is a telling case in point. "Whom did you see?" he observes, though actually "correct," may seem "incorrect" to many who feel uncomfortable when they employ the phrase. They prefer the "colloquial" usage "Who did you see?" and their preference marks the drift that will characterize this as the "correct" usage of the future. This, it is shown, is only part of a broader trend that makes it possible to predict that English of the future, in this detail as in certain other aspects—as "Come quick!" for "Come quickly!"—will but embody the continuation of tendencies that the discerning backward look can isolate, see in present usage, and project into the future.

3

In 1934–35, Eggan made a field study of culture change among the Tinguian of the northern Philippines. The documentation for such a study is rich, since not only are early records available, but in the first decade of the twentieth century field research by the Coles [5] resulted in a detailed description of Tinguian culture as it existed at that time. In addition comparative materials on the neighboring peoples had in the meantime also been amassed.

---

[4] E. Sapir, op. cit., pp. 165–6.
[5] F. C. Cole, 1922.

Cultural Variation

Added to this is the fact that before the period of Spanish rule that antedated American conquest, the Tinguian were subjected to earlier Hindu influences from Sumatra and Java, and had contact with the Chinese and even the Japanese.

The study of culture change among the Tinguian must, obviously, thus involve many elements in a highly complex relationship. It was therefore found best, in seeking to understand the developments that had taken place, to study changes in the culture of this people in relation to the changes that had occurred in the cultures of their neighbors. As Eggan put it, "culture change among the Tinguian could not be satisfactorily studied without projecting it against the larger outline of culture change in the region as a whole." [6] These tribes, "with similar basic cultures" are the Ilocano, Apayao, Bontoc, Ifugao, and Igorot. They all inhabit villages and their economies are based on rice cultivation; but on this pattern "considerable variations" are to be seen as one group after the other is studied.

The differences between them, however, when plotted on a map, reveal interesting regularities. "As one goes from the interior down to the coast," we are told, "from Ifugao through Bontoc, Tinguian and Ilocano, a regular series of changes takes place in social, political, economic and religious institutions, a series of changes which has a definite direction." To this series of changes Eggan applies the term cultural drift. He emphasizes that this concept "is essential to a proper understanding of changes in Tinguian culture." For, as this research developed, it became apparent that "changes, which on the surface seemed to be the results of Spanish or American contacts, turned out on closer inspection to be native cultural changes. Resistance to change, on the one hand, or rapid acceptance, on the other, seemed explicable in many cases in terms of this 'drift.' "

The regularity of change in social, political, and religious institutions as one moves from the interior tribes to those of the coast or from the coast to the interior, can be sketched here. In the farther interior, village organization is simpler than among the tribes nearer the coast. Ifugao villages are small and scattered in the valleys, without institutionalized political structures. Bontoc villages are large, but are not of themselves units; they are divided into wards, each "with its own council and a considerable degree of independence of action." Next come the Tinguian with still larger villages, each composed of a central nucleus about which cluster a number of *barrios*, under the rule of a village headman. The large villages of the coastal Ilocano are grouped, two or more, under a single political authority—or were so grouped during pre-Spanish times, according to early accounts of this people, for the outside controls along the coast have made the retention of aboriginal political institutions difficult.

Kinship structures show a similar kind of directional variation, from the sib system of the Ifugao to the European-like family forms of the Ilocano. There is a corresponding reduction in the range of obligations one must ful-

---

[6] This, and following quotations on this study of drift in culture, are from F. Eggan, 1941, pp. 11–18.

fill to kinsmen, and a consequent increase in the importance of social units based on the territorial ties of ward, *barrio*, and village itself. Controls shift from the family heads of the Ifugao to the ward and *barrio* and village heads or councils, while "customary law decreases in complexity and development until it practically vanishes." Class lines, based on economic resources, are the more sharply drawn as one moves from the interior to the coast and the per capita wealth increases. Marriage customs show similar regularity in the differences to be observed as one moves from tribe to tribe. These vary from the relatively free choice exercised by the Ifugao and Bontoc to the arranged marriages of the Tinguian and the Ilocano. As might be expected, the ease with which separation or divorce is achieved shows a similar series of differences, as do their frequency.

It is apparent that the acculturative process has figured in establishing this series, and that other factors such as population density, based in turn on different environmental factors and different degrees of technological control, have also been operative. Here, as in the many other cases where this methodological principle has been stressed, we must understand that a single—to say nothing of a simple—explanation of such a complex phenomenon as culture, is likely to be fallacious, or at best partial and therefore misleading. Eggan fully recognizes this when he says, "The factors responsible for certain of these variations are both external and internal. Long continued contacts with Asiatic and European peoples have brought about both direct and indirect changes; these have affected the coastal peoples more profoundly but have also penetrated into the interior. But certain of these changes seem based upon internal socio-economic factors which vary from one region to another and which operate relatively independently. Thus the shift in village organization seems more closely related to topography and water distribution than to acculturation phenomena. Likewise, the variations in social organization which we have noted seem to represent a series of correlated phenomena which has an internal consistency and which is related to factors such as population density, relative wealth per capita, and the like, rather than to external contacts."

What, then, of cultural drift? The case of the presumed instance of Spanish repression of head-hunting among the Tinguian is to the point. This is supposed to have made trade and other kinds of relations possible in a wider area than had previously been the case. Yet, according to Eggan, "a closer examination of the situation among the Tinguian and their neighbors . . . suggests that the Tinguian had themselves developed an effective mechanism for stopping head-hunting." In the days preceding Spanish rule, this people had not only compacted to maintain the peace with neighboring villages but had also developed agreements, validated and strengthened by intermarriage, with the peoples inhabiting villages over the mountains eastward. "These were rigidly enforced by the headmen and made trade and travel possible over a wide area. The relative ease with which head-hunting was stopped in the Tinguian region, compared with the difficulties encountered in the Ifugao and Bontoc areas, seems as much a result of the shift in type of local integration as of the efforts of the Spanish authorities."

Cultural Variation

In terms of the concept of cultural drift, this would seem to imply that where the policy of the dominant political power was in accord with a pre-existing tendency, the success of the effort was not difficult to achieve. On the other hand, it proved much more difficult where no tendency had been established. This is apparent in the other aspects of these cultures. "The Spanish worked in vain to christianize the Tinguian, while the Americans have struggled to break down the class system through the introduction of free public education and universal suffrage." The Spanish succeeded best in the coastal area, the Americans best in the interior.

In both regions, each unwittingly was building on pre-existing custom. Their successes or failures were due to the fact that they were able to utilize a pre-existing momentum of prevailing patterns that was the end-result of established drift, or that they had to counteract the unsensed, but nonetheless powerful force of these cumulative drives. On the coast, where class lines long existed, the Spanish had but to superimpose a new class, their own, atop the ones they found, and thus a pre-existing system was continued. On the other hand, the democracy of the interior peoples resisted this innovation, but was amenable to the efforts of the Americans which, in turn, were not acceptable to the coastal peoples.

Here we are presented with an interaction between established drift and outer compulsions, which means that an additional factor has to be taken into account. This factor is the one we have called historical accident. Therefore it is well for us, at this point, to turn to a consideration of the nature and significance of this concept. With our analysis in hand, we may then assess the manner in which accidental happenings act to reinforce or counteract the drifts already present in the cultures where they occur.

4

Historic accident, it has been indicated, is the term to be applied to abrupt innovations that arise from within a culture or result from the contact of peoples. It must be made clear, at the outset, that the use of the word "accident" in no way implies an absence of causation. It is, rather, that happenings of this kind occur outside any sequence of events that might ordinarily have been anticipated. In this sense, the concept in no way begs the question of causation, as some writers have claimed. Rather it recognizes the multiplicity of factors that can act as causes, and phrases an acknowledgment of the fact that no causal sequence is self-sufficient.

The word "accident," as commonly used, has precisely this meaning. When it is said that a person "accidentally" fell down the stairs and broke his leg, this does not imply that the possibility of falling downstairs was not previsioned, or that such a consequence of this occurrence was not conceived as a possibility. It merely means that this happening was outside the run of events ordinarily to be expected when people go up and down stairs. In this case, for instance, the person suffering the "accident" had a child who left a ball, or a roller skate, or a stick on the stairs. It was dark, and the man, who had walked up and down these particular steps many times, had no reason to anticipate the presence of any object that might impede or accelerate his descent. Once the "accident" took place, the chain of causation that led to it could be ascertained, thus enabling us, after the event, to tell why it happened. The child who was the responsible agent could thus be recognized and dealt with accordingly. The point is that the chain of causation was outside the expected and ordinarily predictable succession of events.

We call such a happening an "accident" even though, in a statistical sense, it is quite predictable. Statisticians concerned with public and private safety can, with reasonable certainty, not only predict that in the next twelve months, a given number of accidents will occur in the United States, for instance, but will also be able to predict reasonably well how many people will break their legs by falling down steps. In other words, the accidental is sufficiently within a chain of causation that its incidence, in the large, can be foretold.

This may be cold comfort to the man who lies in the hospital with a broken leg, or the child who has been punished for leaving his playthings where his father could slip on them. It is, however, important for the student of society, since it demonstrates the regularity with which events that are outside a given pattern may be expected to occur. From this point of view, it brings into high relief the importance of taking into account those occurrences which tend to be dismissed as "exceptions," especially when, as is often the case, they stand in the way of explanations of sequences that are envisaged as unfolding in culture as a whole, or within a given culture. They cannot be ignored, however, especially since, as we shall see, without taking them into account our understanding of the dynamics of culture will be inadequate.

It is unfortunate, in a sense, that the commonly accepted use of the word "accident" brings to it the connotation that the unforeseen event is one having undesirable consequences. In applying it to the study of culture, it must be made clear that no such evaluative meaning is to be attached to the word. Many happenings outside the range of probability, which we would term historical accidents, have operated to make more effective the efforts of a people to live their lives more adequately, with better inner adjustment, and on a higher material plane than would otherwise have been possible. The many food plants that were introduced into Europe after the discovery of the New World, from the point of view of the people of Europe, and even from the point of view of the motivations that led to the discovery of the Americas, are to be thought of as a series of cultural accidents. It would be difficult to argue that their effects were other than beneficial. And if, as will soon become apparent, we apply the term historical accident to unlooked-for results of developments that take place within a culture, then the number of such beneficent happenings increases apace.

Except for Goldenweiser, the concept of historical accident has been generally taken for granted where it has been used at all, for there has been little attempt to analyze and assess its implications. In Goldenweiser's discussion, the idea of "accident" has been used as one of a series of three paired categories he employs to classify "social facts or events." The first of these pairs considers the data from the point of view of what Goldenweiser calls their "level"—whether they are external or whether they "occur in our minds," and this dichotomy yields the classes "objective" and "psychological." The second pair concerns the time factor, and are "historical" (i.e., "chronologically successive") and "contemporaneous." The third pair classify the data as to their "deterministic" or "accidental" character.

It is important to understand Goldenweiser's idea of the meaning of these last two words. "Deterministic," for him, describes cultural phenomena "more or less definitely determined within a relatively closed system of historic (or cultural) relations." To this statement, however, he adds the caution that, "the term as used has no relation to any philosophical view of the universe." "Accidental," in contrast, signifies impulses "coming into a system a from without, from another system, b; hence, from the point of view of system a relatively undetermined and unforeseeable." He again cautions that, as in the case of the preceding term, it has "no wider philosophical implications"; and he adds, "nor does it mean 'uncaused.'" [7]

The problem of determinism in culture need not concern us here, for it has been treated at various points in preceding chapters of this work. It need merely be pointed out that Goldenweiser's use of it stresses the chain of causation that marks the development of custom in terms of the interrelation between differing aspects of culture, and the mutual and perhaps limiting influences they exert on each other. It is rather his concept of accident that interests us. "An accidental event," he first says, "is one normally belonging to a different system from the one in which it makes its appearance in the particular instance: from the standpoint of the latter system the event or thing is accidental." This, it need not be repeated, is the conception of accident we hold here.

The next step in the development of his theme, however, requires some analysis. Here, he says, "It thus becomes clear that all phenomena pertaining to intertribal, international, inter-culture-area contact, will fall into this category. From the standpoint of the north African natives the advent of Mohammedanism was an accident; so also was the Spanish introduction of the horse among the Indians of the Plains; the appearance of white man's iron among the American Eskimo was an accident, as well as 'fire-water' among all primitive tribes which were suddenly thrown open to the blessings of civilization. . . . In all of the above and innumerable similar instances the 'accidental' events or things did not grow out of the preferential connexions of events within the recipient systems . . . but came from without, from other systems; not only were the time and place of emergence of these events or things adventitious, but their particular contents came as chance accretions to the systems that received them." [8]

Where the concept of historical accident has been used by anthropologists, it has had the meaning given it in this passage signifying those abrupt, un-

[7] A. A. Goldenweiser, 1933, pp. 7, 9.

[8] Ibid., pp. 24–5.

Cultural Drift and Historic Accident

foreseeable changes in a culture that have been introduced from outside. This is quite understandable, since occurrences of this kind offer much clearer examples of the nature and consequences of historic accident than do internal changes. Outer influences making for abrupt change can be richly documented in instances of culture-contact, where the acceptance of new elements by a people shifts lines of development, and moves them into new channels. Internal accidents of history are exemplified, however, in the unforeseeable consequences of a given discovery or invention, and are much more difficult to study; and this is the case whether or not a chain of antecedent developments can later be discerned as leading to the particular discovery or invention.

An example of how the unanticipated impact of a foreign culture effected changes of the kind we call accidental, that is often cited and that merits some consideration here, is that of Japan. The visit of Commodore Matthew C. Perry in 1852, which, as Euroamerican terminology has it, "opened the door" of Japan to the rest of the world, let a great flood of ideas and material objects into this hitherto isolated country. The subsequent changes in the culture need only be mentioned for their significance to be recognized.

It is important, of course, to understand that these impulses did not affect all aspects of Japanese culture equally. Some it altered so fundamentally that older forms went into the discard. This was especially true where technology, urbanization and industrialization were concerned. Some —certain basic sanctions of family structure, aspects of rural economy and technology, religious life, and status orientations—were altered very slightly, if at all. What did occur was that, given the initial happening and subsequent impulses from other cultures, the course of development of Japanese culture was deflected into channels that, as has been stated, no one in Japan could have foreseen.

As far as those outside Japan were concerned, it is quite conceivable that certain predictions of possible coming events in her history could have been made. A student of 1850, with a profound knowledge of world history, might well have seen that the expansion of Euroamerican control, motivated by the quest for markets to satisfy the demands of a profit economy based on the ever increasing productivity of a machine technology, would ultimately reach Japan. The times being what they were, he might in all likelihood have predicted, however, that Japan not having the requisite military equipment to resist the superior armaments of European Powers, would go the way of India and other colonial areas. And, in all truth, had Commodore Perry been a European rather than an American, this probably would have happened. But by circumstance he represented a Power concerned primarily with the development of its own territory and with little interest in empire; one which, therefore, preferred economic penetration and assured markets to political controls. This circumstance, too, was in the nature of a happening that could not have been predicted. For, in the Philippines the Spanish, in the Indonesian Islands the Dutch, in Siam the French, in Malaya the English—all had established, or were pressing for the hegemony that might have been anticipated in the case of Japan. But these Powers did not take over. It was the United States that was the historic instrument that brought about changes in Japanese ways of life.

After the fact, it seems strange that the events could not have been foreseen by our scholar of 1850. But we cannot imagine that, even with a knowledge of all the facts that might have been available to him, the best Japanese scholar of 1850 could ever have even approximated the subsequent course of development of his society and the subsequent changes in his culture. And this is paralleled over all the world, where an outside force has impinged on an unsuspecting people. As far as they are concerned, this kind of circumstance and its consequences are unforeseeable; these historic accidents must be taken fully into account in understanding the nature and functioning of their culture.

As has been stated, the accidents of history that occur within a culture are far more difficult to document than those unpredictable results of contact that are everywhere to be perceived merely for the looking. Historians, however, recognize the fact of such "accidental" happenings in their writings; especially where a powerful individual makes decisions whose consequences, often affecting the lives of multitudes, could not have been foretold. Of a somewhat different type are the unforeseen consequences that have followed on discovery or invention, a point we have already made.

Consider, for example, the invention of the automobile. As we have seen in discussing the problem of the nature of invention, this in itself is to be regarded as the cumulation of a long series of minor developments that flowered in the "horseless buggy" of the initial stage of the motor-car. This sequence can be readily treated within the conceptual framework of Goldenweiser's "deterministic" category. It would include the change in form from a true horseless carriage to a vehicle that was designed for higher speeds in the light of aerodynamic principles. The linguistic lag implicit in the statement, "I *drive* a car," a carry-over of the idiom "to drive a horse" is matched by the reluctance of car-users to accept cars where the motor is at the rear, something that is functionally far more reasonable than to have it in front. With facts such as these we are not concerned, however. Both they, and other aspects of the technical development of the motor-car encompass parts of a series of events that represents a regular sequence in the history of our culture, a logical working out of the impulses that began with the invention of this particular machine. Nor is prediction too difficult as regards the automobile, provided the factor of probability be taken into account. Thus it should surprise no one when cars with motors installed at the rear actually do become current.

What was unpredictable in the development of the motor-car were some of the consequences of its invention that lay entirely outside the technological field. The tendency toward the concentration of people at the center of cities diminished and eventually ceased, and the ensuing rise of the suburb and the satellite town took place because of the greater distances that the automobile made it possible to traverse. Change invaded other spheres of life in unexpected ways. A process of secularization that took men and women out of the churches onto the golf links was accelerated. The effect on competing transportation media was another unlooked-for consequence, since the ability to cover long distances in reasonable time by routes of one's own choosing and at relatively low cost made this kind of travel appealing. As a result, the railways were hard put to it to survive, and were forced to consider new ways and means of meeting this unanticipated onslaught on their business.

These are only a few of the more obvious repercussions of the invention of the automobile. Many more, some of them affecting details of the moral code, of family life, of the inner organization of cities, for instance, could be given. From the point of view of the people living in 1900, they were as unpredictable as were the changes wrought in the lives of Africans since 1900 as a result of the impact of European culture. In terms of the criteria that have been advanced, however, all must be thought of as historic accidents. That one originates within a society, another outside it, is not important as far as the results of such occurrences are concerned. Their effect is to shift the lines along which the development of a culture had been taking place, so that an established trend—a "drift"—is deflected in a new direction.

That in nonliterate societies historical accidents arising from events within the group are more difficult to document than in literate ones is likewise aside from the point. The discovery of fire, or the domestication of animals must have been occurrences that were of the order of historic accidents; so were the discovery of iron-working, or the wheel, or the loom. The chicken, domesticated in southeast Asia for purposes of divination, became primarily a factor in the food-producing economy of many peoples. The invention of powder, used in China for fireworks, became in western Europe an instrument of destruction. Within a society or through diffusion, a discovery, an invention, a borrowing that is incorporated into a culture may have effects that seem quite outside the range of probability. It thus initiates a series of events that we call accidental. In these terms, then, the accidents of history become prime factors to be taken into account in our search for a comprehension of the nature and processes of culture.

5

THE concepts of cultural drift and historic accident bring us one step further in attaining an understanding of how cultures develop, especially as this concerns the selective nature of change. If we recognize the importance of differential variation in providing a basis both for change and selection, then drift is to be regarded as the expression of the process whereby some variants come to be of more importance than others to a particular people at a given time. If this were the whole story, the study of culture would be much simpler than it is. Given the analysis of drift, it would be possible to plot future growth within far more restricted limits of probability than is actually the case.

Historic accidents, whether originating from within or without, intervene in the process. Yet the established drift must not be thought of as a passive element in change. Even where historic accidents of far-reaching consequence emerge, the selective tendencies that are in existence exert their influence. Sweeping changes imposed through conquest are met by reinterpreting older values in terms of new forms, or old forms may be carried on in secret if the demands of the conqueror involve too great changes in earlier custom.

Drift, whose outstanding expression is in the focal aspect of a culture, thus influences what is to be taken into a culture, whether the innovation arises out of inner variation or is introduced from outside the group. Likewise, drift, together with focus, offer an explanation of why diffused elements are reinterpreted so as to assume forms and meanings in accord with established patterns. Finally, these two concepts aid us in perceiving how the unpredictable events of history, even though their initial shock is such as to demoralize a people who experience them, are eventually assimilated, and an adjustment to them is ultimately achieved.

The significance of these concepts, however, transcends just these points in the study of culture. They have a bearing on questions that tap the fundamental assumptions of anthropological science. They are pertinent to problems of the organization of data and to the problems of law and prediction in history, to a consideration of which we now move.

CHAPTER 35

Classification and Process in the Study of Culture

WITHOUT classification, data are merely gatherings of fact. Unless they are organized according to some scheme, they are not susceptible of systematic treatment. Schemes of classification may vary, and do vary in accordance with the problem that is being analyzed. As Dobzhansky has put it, "Books in a library may be classified according to contents, name of the author, year of publication, size, or color of the cover; which of these methods is selected depends on convenience." [1] This same principle, he points out, applies to the classification of animals; and it applies with equal force to culture as well.

The classification of data, and the drawing of definitions on which classifications are to be based, are of such importance that it has taken science a long time to shake off the tradition that classification is an end in itself, rather than something to be used as a means to an end. The Aristotelian approach, that is, dominated the search for an understanding of the universe from the time of the Greeks until the Renaissance. This means that we are the heritors of an age-long tradition which stressed an understanding of form to the comparative neglect of process. To recognize and describe classes of phenomena was the aim of scientific inquiry, and the classes that scholars did establish were regarded as fixed and rigid. The factor of variation, which alone could lead to an understanding of the importance of process, was overlooked to such a degree that not until the time of Gauss and LePlay, toward the end of the eighteenth century, were the mathematical formulae for the expression of variability worked out.

Once discovered, however, variation became of increasing importance in scientific thought until, eventually, it dominated scientific research. No result of this shift in emphasis has been more significant than that which was instrumental in changing the earlier, static approach to phenomena of the most diverse kinds, to a dynamic one. As a result of this, classification has moved into its proper place, as an essential first step toward the analysis of process.

Yet in science, no less than in any other aspect of culture, tradition is

---

[1] Th. Dobzhansky, 1941, p. 362.

tenacious. A convention that held truth to be absolute, and that had been maintained for centuries, required much time to be replaced by so revolutionary a concept as that which holds truth to be evolving, relative, and continuously changing. The weight of past convention has made it difficult to regard facts not as fixed entities, but rather as points on a scale of variability.

Anthropology, like all the other sciences, has steadily moved toward this point of view. Classification, that is, has come to be regarded as the essential first step toward analysis, and discussion of classifications turns rather on their value as guides toward the understanding of processes than in terms of their validity by and of themselves. This has been made apparent in preceding chapters, where various classifications of ethnographic data have had to be discussed and definitions clarified before other problems could even be approached.

Culture, in the large, has been classified as to distribution, in terms of culture areas; according to content, in terms of its aspects; according to dominant interests, in terms of focus. Whole cultures have been classified in accordance with the presence or absence of writing, as to whether they are literate or nonliterate; economies in accordance with the use of money or other means of exchange; art in terms of the stress laid on realism or conventionalization. These are only a few of the sets of categories that have had to be discussed in this book. In almost every chapter, additionally, it has been necessary to consider alternative classifications, and to indicate why the ones used are more acceptable—that is, more useful in terms of an understanding of the dynamics of meaning and function—than others that have been proposed or have been current at one time or another.

The difference between a scientific description of a culture arranged in accordance with a well defined system, pointed toward the clarification of a problem, and the descriptions contained in travellers' diaries, has several times been pointed out. The ethnographic presentation by the trained anthropologist is scientific in the sense that it is based on established categories that are either implicit and reflected in the organization of the data, or are explicitly drawn in terms of the problem to be attacked. In the case of the traveller's diary, however, observations are strung along the thread of time, which is the only principle of organization. Facts about the culture of a people—no matter how interested in their ways of life the traveller may have been, or how good his understanding of the people he describes—are presented in the order in which they were encountered. One day our traveller will go fishing with his native friends; he observes a wedding procession on his way home; that evening there is a dance for the gods; and during it he acquires a mask that is then described. These facts may all be pertinent to an understanding of the culture; even their meaning to the people may be made clear. Yet this is not science. The scientific student of culture who turns to such materials—as is increasingly done, especially where the writings of earlier travellers are consulted to document a nonliterate people's past—must himself organize the facts in accordance with the system he uses to classify his data.

Classification and Process in the Study of Culture

Classification becomes an obstacle to scientific analysis, however, when it is conceived as an end in itself. This danger always exists when a classification, especially an established one, is under review, or where it has been used so long that it is taken for granted. The history of the study of race offers a striking instance of how this can come about, especially as concerns the classical delimitation of peoples on the basis of their head-form. Head-measuring became almost the characteristic mark of the physical anthropologist, as he worked to ascertain the "racial" category to which a given people might be held to belong. So taken for granted did these categories come to be that they were in themselves eventually held causal factors in the racial equation. As a result, the long-headed Nordic, for example, came to be regarded as warlike because he was Nordic—that is to say, because he was long-headed. That the category "Nordic" existed only as a part of the conceptual apparatus of the student of human physical type, was so lost sight of that it became a matter for argument among scientists, to say nothing of the unfortunate role this system of classification played in establishing the basis for racist philosophies.

The change in outlook that has marked the development of work bearing on the problem of classification is perhaps best illustrated by reference to the field of animal biology. Taxonomy, as the classification of living forms was called, has come to be a technique for the solution of problems of form and function and process, rather than an end in itself, which it once was. Mayr has effectively contrasted the "old systematics" with later methods of classifying data. "The old systematics," he says, "is characterized by the central position of the species. No work, or very little, is done on infraspecific categories (subspecies). A purely morphological species definition is employed. Many species are known from a single or at best a very few specimens; the individual is therefore the basic taxonomic unit. There is great interest in purely technical questions of nomenclature and 'types.' The major problems are those of cataloguer or bibliographer, rather than those of a biologist."

In contrast to this are the newer methods of classification, the "new systematics," as they are called. "The importance of the species as such is reduced," in this approach, "since most of the actual work is done with subdivisions of the species, such as subspecies and populations. The population or rather an adequate sample of it, the 'series' of the museum worker, has become the basic taxonomic unit. The purely morphological species definition has been replaced by a biological one, which takes ecological, geographical, genetic, and other factors into consideration. The choosing of the correct name for the analyzed taxonomic unit no longer occupies the central position of all systematic work and is less often subject to argument between fellow workers. The material available for generic revisions frequently amounts to many hundreds or even thousands of specimens, a number sufficient to permit a detailed study of the extent of individual variation." [2]

---

[2] Ernst Mayr, 1942, pp. 6–7.

These statements, though couched in terms of another discipline, describe very well the changes that are taking place in the study of culture as this has moved from an emphasis on classification to an emphasis on dynamics. The importance of variation in culture is the equivalent of the emphasis laid by the "new systematics" of biology on the need to study adequate samples of the populations of forms to be analyzed. In the study of culture, too, the way of life of a people, in all its variety, shapes investigation rather than the pre-conceived class to which their culture is *a priori* held to belong; just as the population, rather than the "type specimen" has become the unit for the biological taxonomist. Most striking of all is the analogy to anthropological methods found in Mayr's statement that "the choosing of the correct name no longer occupies the central position of all systematic work. . . ." Terms and definitions, that is, must be here subordinate to problems. This point, whose importance has been increasingly recognized as science has developed its methods and refined its objectives, thus merits further probing as it bears on the study of culture.

2

WHEN a phenomenon has been described and named, an important step in the scientific process has been taken since, as we have seen, data must be recognizable and capable of delimitation before they can be systematically studied. However, experience has taught that as soon as a description or a definition becomes the statement of a position, it may come to be a major preoccupation of scholars and thus defeat the end for which it was devised. When classes that represent a system of terminology and a set of definitions harden into dogma, they become an obstruction rather than an aid to scientific analysis.

The danger-point in this process is not difficult to find. It is reached when cases that are not fitted by the definition are brushed aside as "exceptions." The method of science, however, which is to test hypotheses by ascertaining the extent to which the facts verify postulates, admits of no "exceptions." For, in science, "exceptions" are the critical cases, and constitute the real challenge to the research-worker. If they are numerous enough, they negate the hypothesis. If they are not so numerous, they must be studied with special care to determine how the hypothesis is to be revised in accordance with the facts. In the laboratory, controls can be manipulated until recalcitrant data of this kind can be explained. The problem of coping with the "exception" is therefore the technical one of employing instruments at hand, or devising new instruments, to alter the conditions under which the experiment has been carried on. But such experimentation is impossible in the disciplines where the data cannot be manipulated in the laboratory, as is the case in the study of culture.

Where the controlled experimentation of the laboratory sciences cannot be achieved, historic controls must be sought. That is, situations of various kinds must be found where differing circumstances make it possible to test hypotheses in terms of achieved results that are to be referred to differing series of ascertainable historic events. Above all, in applying the methods of science to the study of culture, it is essential to investigate the "negative" manifestations of a phenomenon. If we would understand totemism, for example, we must be careful not only to describe, classify and analyze as many examples of it as are to be found, but also to study as carefully as possible cultures where totemism is not present.

It has been seen how controversial this issue was in the period between 1910 and 1920, and how important was Goldenweiser's analysis, which established the broad criteria under which totemic phenomena of varied kinds were to be comprehended. What gave rise to the controversy was the familiar problem of classification. The customs of the Australians had come to be set up as the essential criteria of totemism. But many "exceptions" to totemic forms of this sort began to be manifest elsewhere in the world. What, then, were these "exceptions"? They either were phenomena of a different order, or the definition of totemism was in error. The definition was broadened—but this has not settled the question why, though many groups have totemic beliefs, by no means all societies have them; or why these beliefs can function so differently in the many societies where they are found. Only minute analysis of data from societies in varied settings, with historical backgrounds of differing degrees of similarity, including those where totemism is absent as well as where it is present, can yield answers to the basic problem of the development and functioning of totemism in human society.

Other instances of this sort may be recalled from earlier discussions in this book. Consider, for example, the four-fold classification of economies that at one time gained wide acceptance. Arranged in a presumed order of development, these are food-gathering, hunting, herding, and agriculture. Quite aside from the validity of this developmental series, which is not at issue here, we have seen how these categories break down as useful tools in economic analysis when an adequate range of data are inspected. That is, it has become amply apparent that few if any cultures have economies that do not partake of elements falling in more than one of these categories. It is difficult to envisage any period in the history of mankind when men did not hunt as well as utilize such foodstuffs as roots, or wild fruits, or nuts which are the staples of an assumed "food-gathering" economy. Obviously, these kinds of economic activities must have preceded the domestication of animals and plants. But this does not mean, as we have seen, that peoples who have great herds do not plant gardens, or that agricultural peoples are without domesticated animals. Nor, moreover, does it mean that food-gathering activities, and hunting, are entirely superseded by these later forms of food production.

The terms food-gathering, hunting, herding, and agriculture describe *activities*, not *economies*. Once this reorientation is achieved, definitions of these categories become available as tools for further investigation. Cultures become bodies of tradition in which, to varying degrees, activities of these several kinds are carried on. The degree to which one of these activities is found in association with another, to which they complement one another or tend to be mutually exclusive, can thus be studied. The manner in which any of these types of food-economies can be thought of as influencing institutions lying in other aspects of culture can also be probed—such a question, for example, as the kind of political system that might be expected to order the lives of sedentary peoples who practise agriculture, as against migratory bands whose food economy is based on herding.

For many years, problems of classification dominated the study of language. The common designation of language as "isolating," "agglutinative," and "inflectional" that continues to be encountered, has already been considered in connection with our discussion of linguistics. As was seen, this classification has proved no more satisfactory than other classifications drawn on the basis of types of grammatical forms, or complexity of structure, or any other single criterion. For such classifications, as Sapir puts it, "do not so much enfold the known languages in their embrace as force them down into narrow, straight-backed seats." He notes four reasons why attempts to classify languages have been unrewarding. First, to find a satisfactory basis of classification is most difficult: "A language shows us so many facets that we may well be puzzled." In the second place, to generalize from "a small number of selected languages," even so varied as Latin, Arabic, Turkish, Chinese and "perhaps Eskimo or Sioux as an after thought," is "to court disaster." Yet most classifications are drawn on the basis of just such limited materials. Third, "The strong craving for a simple formula," such as that which gives to word-structure the importance we have noted, has motivated those who are confronted with the many varieties of linguistic expression speech-forms are found to manifest. Finally Sapir notes the biases that have crept in as a result of an ethnocentrism that has caused students of language to judge languages different from their own as inferior tongues, and classify them accordingly.[3] Sapir's conclusions regarding what kinds of classifications can aid in linguistic study are of great interest when they are read in terms of the objectives of such an approach as that of the "new systematics" of biology. For as was seen in this revised taxonomy, it is dynamics, rather than the inert forms themselves, that make for given forms, that dictate significant linguistic classification.

In the field of religion, to take another example, we are wont to read of entire belief-systems that are described as "animistic" or "monotheistic," or dominated by "fetishism." Experience, however, has taught us that such simplifications are barriers rather than aids to comprehension. Not only do designations of this sort give false perceptions, but they also mask the variation in world-view and ritual that marks the religious life of all peoples. Animistic beliefs are indeed wide-spread, but what do we mean when we categorize a people as "animistic"? Does this mean they have no conception of deities? That they do not practise magic? That they have no idea of impersonal power operating in the universe?

Our discussion of the complexities of religion, and of the difficulties present in drawing a definition of the phenomenon makes the answer we

---

[3] E. Sapir, 1921, pp. 129–31.

must give to questions such as these self-evident. As categories to describe any religion, they are too simple. Their validity derives only from the fact that they do designate certain kinds of belief and behavior that we call religious. The problems we seek to solve in this aspect of culture, however, concern the nature of the religious experience, the way in which its many manifestations are interrelated, its function in the total life of a people. These are dynamic problems, that look beyond mere classification. It was in such dynamic terms, indeed, that the definition of religion as a process of "identification with a greater force or power" was drawn. The forms in which this process manifests itself must, as in every aspect of culture, afford the basis for analysis. The first step must be to reduce their variety to some kind of order. But, as we saw in considering this aspect of culture, the classification of religious forms is only a first step. Beyond form lies process, and here, as in all phases of the study of culture, it is in dynamics, not descriptions, that the key to understanding is to be sought.

This tendency to employ a single criterion, even to the classification of whole cultures, is found in systems where entire ways of life of differing peoples are designated in terms of the dominant psychological and personality types they are held to develop. The classification of cultures as extroverted or introverted is one such we have considered, and so is the related pair of appellations that calls them Dionysian and Apollonian. The positive contributions of such classifications in aiding us to understand the relationship between culture and personality, as well as the respect in which they have been found less satisfactory, have been discussed in earlier pages, and need not be treated again. What may be pointed out here is that such categories have been superseded because, while challenging as concepts, they have not led to the development of more precise methods of studying the dynamic mechanisms of personality formation as influenced by culture.

Other classifications of cultural phenomena have proved unsatisfactory because they have arisen out of an ethnocentrism that dictates the lines along which they are drawn. One such type has been cited in the case of language where, as we have seen, divergence from Indo-European forms has been the basis for classifying speech-systems as "higher" or "lower" in a scale of value. Such classifications, however, run counter to the postulate of scientific method that precludes value-judgments as bases for classification, and are thus by that very fact rendered inacceptable. "Better" and "worse" are designations that, in scientific research, can only be defined in terms of specific ends. One chemical may be worse than another in that it kills while the other does not; as a chemical, however, it is to be analyzed as any other compound, not judged. In the field of culture, as long as a cultural institution, a linguistic system or any other item functions satisfactorily in the lives of those who employ it, its position as a valid datum in the study of culture is established. It can only be "better" or "worse" in the mind of the student, and his patterns of thought will inevitably reflect the value-system inculcated in the course of his own enculturative experience.

It is not necessary, however, that classes of cultural phenomena that derive from ethnocentrism be couched in evaluative terms. Ethnocentric classification can be quite colorless insofar as evaluation is concerned. We have encountered one such in discussing folklore categories. Here the distinction has been drawn between myth and fable and *märchen*, or fairy-tales. These distinctions have validity when applied to various sorts of tales recounted by Euroamerican peoples and their forerunners, but they only lead to confusion when they are used to classify the folk-literature of peoples in other cultural streams. There, as we have seen, a story that in one culture deals with supernatural beings, and is thus a myth in terms of this classification, will in another be told to amuse children or as an educational device, and thus comes into the category of the *märchen*. Animal-stories told in Europe are identical with sacred tales of Africa and Asia. From any functional point of view, the system of classification of myth, fable, and *märchen* breaks of its own weight. But it has really been discarded because, again, it masks rather than furthers an understanding of the creative processes by which tales arise and develop, and are altered as they move from place to place. It is, in short, not only ethnocentric, but static. It carries no recognition of those dynamic aspects of folklore that are basic to scientific analysis and thus to ultimate comprehension.

3

THUS far, our discussion has made the following points:

1. that classification is an important first step in the study of data, but may not be regarded as an end in itself;
2. that the factor of variation must be taken into account when classifying data, so that the resulting classifications will have a flexibility that those based on the concept of "type" cannot have;
3. that to devise a series of categories of a complex phenomenon, based on a single criterion, is to over-simplify the data and thus vitiate the validity of the resulting classes;
4. that to base classifications on value-judgments is to employ criteria that will not stand the test of scientific analysis which takes into account all the facts.

These propositions describe the limits within which acceptable classifications of data can be achieved. In turn, they lead us to the crucial point that classifications of the materials of culture, based on *form*, are but a step in achieving an understanding of *process;* that is, in achieving a comprehension of dynamics. As we shall see, this has implications of the greatest significance for the problems of cultural law and the prediction of change in culture, which are to be taken up in the next chapter.

At the moment, however, we will consider this point as it bears on another characteristic of the many classificatory systems that have been advanced in the study of culture, their *polarity*. In most classifications, that is, concepts are contrasted as extremes of a scale on which differing manifestations of a phenomenon may be placed. This was basic in all classificatory systems that developed out of attempts to place data in an evolutionary sequence. The economic sequence of food-gathering, hunting, herding, agriculture was held to represent a change from simpler to more complex methods of gaining a livelihood. For Tylor, animism was contrasted to monotheism as ends of a series between which were placed what he held to be the earliest and latest forms. When the concept of impersonal power called mana was discovered among the Melanesians, it was given precedence in this sequence under the name "animatism," since it was held to exemplify an even earlier "stage" in the development of religion. In the same category is the continuum that has as its poles cultural extroversion or introversion, or designates the extremes of cultural "types" as Apollonian and Dionysian, even though it is recognized that no cultures, as actually found, represent more than the most pronounced examples of the polar types, but are rather farther along the implied scale toward one end or the other.

This brings up the question of the *ideal type*. Is it essential in classifying materials to confine oneself to actual manifestations of the data in setting up series of classifications that are arranged from simple to complex, let us say, or from inward to outward orientation, or from large to small, or on the basis of any other paired opposites? Classes of data arranged in series of this kind, it is true, have in the past clarified problems, revealed relationships, and thus furthered the ends of investigation. As such, they are a part of the methodological armory of science, and are as useful in the study of culture as in research in any other field. It is when the arrangements of these classes become an end rather than a means, when emphasis is on the validity of the series as formulated, rather than on the utility of the classification in revealing dynamic processes, that valid objections can be raised to them.

Classifications arranged on a scale between two polar extremes are, on analysis, found in most cases to derive essentially from conceptualizations of the data by the student. A culture that is officially monotheistic may on investigation reveal animatistic beliefs, a belief in magic, and animistic beliefs as well. There is every advantage to be gained in separating such data in terms of these categories as a first step toward furthering our understanding of their nature and functioning. But to place a culture where all are present on a scale ranging from animatism to monotheism is to reflect the position of the student rather than to describe the orientations and inner relationships of the data themselves in the culture being studied.

We are here on familiar ground. The argument advanced is the same as was earlier employed in considering the position of the extreme diffusionists, for example. These schools developed "complexes" that were constructs of the students, and whose elements were seen to have no necessary relationship to each other in the cultures where they actually exist. The so-called heliolithic culture was indeed the culture of Egypt. But when bits of it were projected as Egyptian (or Indian) into South Seas or American Indian cultures, they became culturally unreal. Or, again, it was stressed that, while the Graebnerian culture-complexes do include items that are found in a series of cultures, these gatherings of cultural items are complexes only for the Graebnerians, since their elements have no inner functional relationship to each other in the cultures where they are found. Or, as another instance, we may consider the practices in museums devoted to exposing the presumed cultural evolution of items of material culture. Here, as we have seen, arrows, or clothing, or house-types will be arranged in terms of an assumed scheme of development that moves from the simplest to the most complex manifestations of a given artifact. Yet in this instance, too, we must recognize that such series derive not from historical documentation of an actual succession of cultures, but from an assumption made by the student, that such an arrangement reveals a logical progression that must reflect an historic developmental sequence.

The appeal of series arranged between polar conceptions lies just in this fact of their logical character; for they are always logical. But if this is their strength, it is also their weakness. As has been stressed many times in earlier pages, the historical development of every culture has its own logic. The logic of history, however, does not admit of the neat arrangement of data between the opposites that classifications of this kind presuppose. Historical logic differs from culture to culture, from historic stream to historic stream. It is an inner logic that, to the observer who marks only the forms it takes, may seem untidy, even illogical. It is, in short, a logic of process, that because of the factor of variability, is manifest in many forms. And since we here again encounter a point that is crucial for the comprehension of the nature of law in the study of culture, we will leave it for the moment, to return to the problem of classification in terms of cultural phenomena ranged on a scale between two polar concepts.

4

LET us consider, from this point of view, one of the most carefully drawn and best documented examples of this kind, in which all of the four criteria for a valid system of classification indicated in the preceding section are complied with; the system that opposes the concept of the "folk society" to that of the "modern urbanized society." This mode of classifying cultures has been documented by first-hand investigation in Yucatan. The research has been carried out in terms of careful field method, and has yielded important ethnographic data. The system is set up as a framework within which problems of dynamics can be attacked; it takes into full account the fact of cultural variation; it does not rely on a single criterion; no value-judgements are implicit in it. It is, however, based on criteria of form, and arranges the data on a scale between the polar concepts of differing types of societies. It thus affords an excellent opportunity for analyzing the aspect of the problem of classification in terms of polar types with which we are concerned at the moment.

The problem, as stated in the work in which it was first given full expression[4] is as follows: "The chief objective of this investigation is . . . to define differences in the nature of isolated homogeneous society, on the one hand, and mobile heterogeneous society, on the other, so far as these kinds of societies are represented in Yucatan." The documentation is drawn from four communities in the region, which vary in size and complexity as one

---

[4] R. Redfield, 1941, pp. 17–18.

moves from the city to sections where Euroamerican culture has least penetrated. The statement of the problem is expanded in these terms: "It is hoped
that questions of more general interest will arise out of consideration of
these materials. Are some of the differences among these four communities
instances of what often happens when an isolated homogeneous society
comes in contact with other societies?"

Here, obviously is a problem in dynamics, even though its expression in
terms of degrees of isolation and of homogeneity already indicate a reference to opposable extremes. This is made explicit in the sentences that
follow those just quoted: "Stated as though the comparison represented a
process illustrated at four stages of its course, the chief of these general
differences . . . are the disorganization of the society, and the individuali-
zation of the society. So stated, the comparison may be converted into a
hypothetical description of any contrasting isolated-homogeneous and
mobile-heterogeneous pairs of societies. . . . The formulation makes it possible to ask a number of general questions which the analysis of new facts
and the further analysis of the facts from Yucatan might answer, or perhaps
reformulate. The important question may be asked whether, if regular
changes of the kind noted result from the contact of the isolated-homogeneous society with another society, the changes would result from contact
with any other society or only from contact with a more heterogeneous, less
isolated, society, or perhaps only from contact with some recent Western
society." [5]

It is evident that the concepts of the folk society and the modern urban
community are susceptible of use so as to facilitate the investigation of
dynamic problems in the study of culture. Yet the question remains as to the
validity of these, *as polar concepts*, whatever their usefulness in orienting the
investigation of cultures in general. For once an ideal sequence, ranged between two poles, has been set up, certain questions inevitably arise to which
answers must be given. To what extent does the proposed sequence correspond to the facts? To what extent may we disregard, or explain data that are
not in accord with the scheme? Why will not a dichotomy that cuts through
the data on a different plane do equally well? And, above all, how are
human cultures in general to be ranged on the scale that presumably moves
from one extreme type to the other?

The characteristics held to mark a folk society are as follows: A folk
society is small and isolated. In contrast with its isolation from other groups
is the intimacy of communication among its members. The people who make
it up are much alike in physical type, no less than in their customary modes
of behavior; they have a "strong sense of belonging together." There is not
much division of labor in folk societies, but it is a group economically self-
sufficient. It is "a little world off by itself." It has still other traits. The basic
sanctions of life are understood by all, and there is a minimum of criticism
levelled against accepted modes of conduct; abstract thinking is not found
to any extent. The social structures are tightly knit and family relationships

---

[5] R. Redfield, 1941, p. 18.

are clearly distinguished. There is little legislation; custom is king. The sacred quality of life is outstanding and extends to such cultural items as food or utensils, which in urban culture are regarded as secular. Magic is another reflection of what is termed the folk mind. "The man of the folk society tends to make mental associations which are personal and emotional, rather than abstractly categoric or defined in terms of cause and effect." Finally, "there is no place for the motive of commercial gain. . . . There is no money and nothing is measured by any common denominator of value." [6]

It is apparent that these traits in many respects parallel those ascribed in the literature to peoples called "primitive." They are what has been meant, in the large, in this book where the word "nonliterate" has been used, especially when to the absence of writing is added the factor of nonindustrialization and an absence of mechanization. What, then, is the point at issue? It lies in the fact that while terms such as "primitive" or "nonliterate" are used to indicate, in a kind of anthropological shorthand, a condition that marks off some peoples from others, nothing more than this is connoted. It is important to seek to understand why some peoples have writing and others do not; but we do not set up an ideal category of the nonliterate society in order to contrast it with a literate one. The function of writing, in making for elaboration of culture, is a problem on which we have touched; but so is the problem of population size and its relationship to specialization, which we have seen to be so important a factor in differences between cultures in one aspect after another.

There are small and large literate and nonliterate societies, wherein the degree of specialization varies greatly. Even in Guatemala, a country that is relatively close to Yucatan, as Redfield himself notes in the best tradition of scientific method, Tax has shown that "a stable society can be small, unsophisticated, homogeneous in beliefs and practices" and yet have "relationships impersonal, with formal institutions dictating the acts of individuals, with familial organization weak, with life secularized, and with individuals acting more from economic or other personal advantage than from any deep conviction or thought of the social good." [7] It is also to be noted that in discussions of the folk society, African data are nowhere taken into account. In West Africa, however, many urban communities are to be found that range from one hundred thousand inhabitants (the approximate size of Merida, Redfield's Yucatan "city") to over three hundred and fifty thousand. These populations have complex specialized economies exhibiting, as we have seen, the use of money and the presence of profit motivation. Yet in these cities relationships are as personal as in any "folk society," and religion is the focal aspect of the culture. In short, here we have the anomaly—anomaly, that is, in terms of the concept of the folk society—of urban, *sacred*, communities.

The ideal type of any phenomenon, as most of those who work with such concepts point out, cannot by definition fit any particular case. The greater

[6] R. Redfield, 1947, pp. 296–306.
[7] S. Tax, 1939, p. 467.

Classification and Process in the Study of Culture

the number of criteria, the more difficult will be the applicability to any given instance. We must again indicate that this follows from the fact that in such systems the orientation is in terms of categories based on *form*, rather than problems phrased in terms of *process*. Herein lies the real difference between the concept of "folk society" and of "nonliterate" peoples. The first is a category which dominates the data; the second is merely a convenient handle to describe materials destined to be examined in the light of differing situations that have arisen out of the historic process. Let us again emphasize that this particular polar ideal form of the "folk society" is only one instance of this approach to the data of culture; that it has been used here because it is one of the most sophisticated and carefully documented of any of this kind that has been advanced. That it, like others, leads to the difficulties indicated in the light of the facts only strengthens the point that has been made, that classification must not be accorded too prominent a place in scientific study.

CHAPTER 36

Cultural Law and the Problem of Prediction

THE history of cultural anthropology can be thought of as a striving toward an ever greater degree of historic control over its data, by refining its methods of attacking the problem of universals in culture. The comparative method used by the early anthropologists sought to discover similarities in human behavior over the world that would chart the evolution of civilization from a savage state to its present high condition. The realization of the importance of cultural borrowing was an initial refinement of the comparative method, and revealed the futility of merely comparing elements of culture that are similar only in outer form. The emphasis laid on detailed rather than generalized world-wide historical reconstructions represented a further step in attaining comprehension of the processes involved.

The functionalist approach, with its stress on investigating the inner relationships between aspects of culture, sharpened our understanding of the nature of culture and the interplay of its various parts. Similarly the study of how a culture influences the personalities of those who live in terms of it, with the reciprocal influence of the individual on the culture in which he lives, marked still another refinement in effectively assessing the nature and processes of culture. The development of acculturation studies called on all these later approaches. It utilized observation as against hypothetical reconstruction. It added the element of ascertained time depth to the intensive study of whole cultures. Finally, it pointed the way toward a surer documentation of the psychological problem of the individual in his culture, in terms of motivations that lead to retentions and reinterpretations of cultural elements through the mechanisms of focus and drift.

It is apparent that this continuous refinement of method has been made possible through the more adequate utilization of historically valid data. World-wide diffusion studies gave way to analysis of the problem in areas where contact could be assumed. These, in turn, led to researches on cultures where historic relationships were a known factor in the equation. In every instance, the tendency has been to move from the hypothetical to the verifiable. Archaeological evidence is called on to support findings inferred from the study of distributions. Historic documents are employed to so great an extent that a welding of historical and ethnographic materials in what has come to be known as the ethnohistorical method has become a commonplace in anthropological research.

In earlier years, an ethnographic report was confined strictly to the data collected by the anthropologist. Such "history" as was found in it consisted of recollections of old people, and the current traditions of past events. But little attempt was made to go to the written records, often reaching back two or three centuries and more, to give time-depth to the presentation. That this ethnohistorical procedure has come to be so widely accepted is a further indication of how the need for valid historic controls has gained recognition.

2

ONE reason why culture cannot be studied in the same way as organic and inorganic phenomena, as we have seen in the preceding chapter, is the difficulty of obtaining laboratory controls. But it is just in the use of these controls that the scientific method has realized its greatest achievements. It can well be said that only as scientists have perfected their laboratory techniques has their knowledge of the nature and functioning of the materials with which they have been concerned become more precise and more tenable. In the laboratory, the scientist is able to manipulate his data so that, of the many variables that enter into the chain of causation, all but one is held constant. Out of this procedure comes his law—that given certain conditions, certain results will follow. Checking, testing, verifying—these are but incidental to the factor of control. For when the conditions under which an experiment is carried on are repeated, the results must check with earlier tests. If they do not, then the conditions are assumed to have varied—or, in other words, the controls have been changed.

In the disciplines that deal with historic phenomena, controls of this kind cannot be exercised. This is true not only of the study of culture. The astronomer or the historical geologist also deals with data that cannot be manipulated. One can no more take a star or a mountain into the laboratory than one can take a human society. Recourse must be had in such disciplines to historic controls that manifest themselves in sequences of related events. In the case of astronomy and geology, the sequences are more regular than in the case of culture. But the difference is one of degree, and not of kind; just as is the greater difference—again, of degree and not kind—between historic controls and those that are set up in the laboratory of the physicist or the zoologist.

The difference between the student of culture and the laboratory investigator is not that the former is a kind of historian and the student who works in a laboratory is a scientist. It is, rather, that the laboratory of the student of culture *is* an historical one. It is the circumstance of historical happenings that, over the world, sets up situations which are used by the anthropologist to test his hypotheses in a way quite analogous to that in which the chemist sets up his test-tubes or the physicist his balances, or the geologist seeks out stratified outcroppings of rock to ascertain the facts about the development of the earth. The anthropologist, it is true, deals with far more variables, and with variables much less subject to control, than do his fellow-scientists. But crude as they may be, the controls—the historic situations in which at least a number of variables are held approximately constant—are there. To the extent these historic controls reduce the number of variables, to that degree they permit the anthropologist to use the circumstances of history to investigate, as any other scientist, the data with which he is concerned.

The distinction between science and history has long figured in discussions of anthropological theory, turning largely on the question whether anthropology is an historical or a scientific discipline. Such a formulation at once raises the problem whether the aims of anthropological study should be to recover the story of the development of human culture and of given cultures, or whether the ends of research should be to disclose broad principles of form and structure and interrelationships that will lead to the enunciation of valid "laws" of culture.

The degree to which these two approaches are held to be mutually irreconcilable alternatives, or to which they are regarded merely as facets of a single objective, has varied from time to time, from scholar to scholar, even from one time to another in the writings of the same scholar. The case of Boas is instructive. "If we found that ethnology as an historical science is intimately related to the history of culture," he wrote in 1888, "this connection appears still closer when we turn to the second important task of our science. A comparison of the social life of different peoples proves that the foundations of their cultural development are remarkably uniform. It follows from this that there are laws to which this development is subject. Their discovery is the second, perhaps the more important aim of our science. There is no fundamental contrast between these aims, for the general law is expressed in the individual phenomenon just as much as the individual phenomenon is interpreted as an exemplification of the general law." [1]

Eight years later, in 1896, he formulated the point as follows: "The immediate results of the historical method are . . . histories of the cultures of diverse tribes which have been the subject of study. I fully agree with those anthropologists who claim that this is not the ultimate aim of our science, because the general laws, though implied in such a description, cannot be clearly formulated nor their relative value appreciated without a thorough comparison of the manner in which they become manifest in different cultures. But I insist that the application of this method is the indispensable condition of sound progress. . . . When we have cleared up the history of a single culture and understand the effects of the environment and the psychological conditions that are reflected in it we have made a step forward, as we can then investigate in how far the same causes were at work in the development of other cultures." [2]

This is perhaps as clear an expression of the inductive method in its con-

---

[1] F. Boas, 1940, pp. 633–4.
[2] Ibid., pp. 278–9.

ventional sense, as applied to the search for laws of culture, as has ever been given. The historic development of one culture after another is to be traced. The factors and forms common to all are to be worked out, and the analysis of these least common denominators will then lead to the formulation of "laws" of culture. In actual practice, however, the pursuit of this ideal proved to be a discouraging business. Reconstruction of culture yielded only hypothetical results that themselves were open to debate; intimate knowledge of the range of cultural forms only revealed how great the differences that are to be discerned in the ways men employ to achieve the same ends. It is thus understandable that more than a quarter of a century later, in 1930, we find Boas writing in one place, "The attempts to reduce all social phenomena to a closed system of laws applicable to every society and explaining its structure and history do not seem a promising undertaking,"[3] while elsewhere he states, "The complexity of cultural development is so great, and the conditions that determine the course of historical happenings are logically so entirely unrelated, that the attempt to give an adequate explanation of the history of any individual society in regard to biological type, language and culture seems hopeless."[4]

Radcliffe-Brown has approached the problem of history *versus* science in a different manner. "Using the word science to mean the accumulation of exact knowledge," he says, "we may distinguish two kinds of scientific study, or two kinds of method. One of these is historical. The other method or type of study I should like to call the inductive, but there is a chance that the word might be misunderstood. I will therefore call it the method of generalization. This distinction between the historical and generalizing sciences was emphasized long ago by Cournot. It is one of great importance in any question of scientific methodology." Because of this, he suggests that, in effect, anthropology must be thought of as encompassing two subdisciplines. One he calls "ethnology," the other "comparative sociology."

The first of these, he states, "is concerned with the relations of peoples," and is "a historical and not a generalizing science." "It is true," he says, "that in making their historical reconstructions the ethnologists often assume certain generalizations, but as a rule little or no attempt is made to base them on any wide inductive study. The generalizations are the postulates with which the subject starts, not the conclusions which it aims to attain as the result of the investigations undertaken." On the other hand, comparative sociology is "a science that applies the generalizing method of the natural sciences to the phenomena of the social life of man and to everything that we include under the term culture or civilization."

This field of comparative sociology, says Radcliffe-Brown, is different from the older discipline of social anthropology in that it rejects "all attempts at conjecturing the origin of an institution when we have no information based on reliable historical records about that origin." The "newer social anthropology" or comparative sociology rather "endeavours to give precise descriptions of social and cultural phenomena in sociological terms.

---

[3] *Ibid.*, p. 268.
[4] F. Boas, 1930a, p. 109.

and to this end seeks to establish a suitable exact terminology, and seeks at the same time to attain to a systematic classification of those phenomena. . . . It applies to human life in society the generalizing method of the natural sciences, seeking to formulate the general laws that underlie it, and to explain any given phenomena in any culture as a special example of a general or universal principle. The newer anthropology is therefore functional, generalizing and sociological." [5]

It is apparent from the preceding discussion that the question of whether anthropology is history or science does not present us with two mutually exclusive alternatives. Our task, therefore, is to weigh the two possibilities in terms of methods and achieved results, rather than to go to either extreme of the scale that moves from description to generalization.

3

LET us see how historic controls are to be used in our search for generalizations, by following one of a number of problems that might be cited, wherein the resources of the laboratory of history are utilized. This concerns the investigation of the ways of life of Negro societies in varied parts of Africa and the New World where historical relationships can be ascertained. The "laboratory" is of vast geographic scope, and has a time-depth of from three to four centuries. It comprises the western part of Africa south of the Sahara, and the western part of the Congo basin; it includes the eastern coastal strip of North America, most of the southeastern part of the United States, the West Indies, Central America and most of South America.

From the regions of Africa just named, great numbers of Negroes were brought to these reaches of the New World, where they made lives for themselves in accordance with the possibilities of their condition of servitude. They were not passive agents in the process, but the limits imposed on them in making their adjustment were of a special kind, that laid more specific and more severe restrictions on them than are ordinarily operative in contact between peoples. In this fact, then, we have a first of those "controls" that permits us, after the manner of science, to be more precise in analyzing the ensuing cultural changes than would otherwise be possible.

The cultures of Africa from which the Negroes derived, like the cultures of any area, differ from each other to varying degrees. Beneath this variation in detail, however, are certain broad patterns in which they are quite similar. In some New World countries, for reasons that can be isolated and analyzed, certain of these specific African cultures came to predominate, and recognizable retentions of these customs are present. Elsewhere, especially where tribal conventions became increasingly difficult to maintain, the underlying patterns came to the fore. Under such conditions, generalized Africanisms, blended with the patterns of the dominant groups so subtly that only the most careful dissection can reveal historical derivations, are

[5] A. R. Radcliffe-Brown, 1932, pp. 143–4, 154.

to be found. Yet despite all this, there is to be discerned an African base-line from which degree, direction, and type of cultural change are to be plotted.

The African retentions in New World Negro societies are found to vary in accordance with the dominant social, political, economic, and religious patterns of the European group with which the Negroes in a given New World area came into contact. In Brazil it was a Portuguese culture; in the rest of South America, in Central America, and in Cuba, a Spanish one; in Haiti and other islands of the Antilles and in Louisiana, a French way of life—all predominantly Catholic in religion. In most of the United States and much of the West Indies, the English predominated. In the Virgin Islands Danish traditions, in part of the West Indies and in Dutch Guiana the culture of the Netherlands, prevailed. All these latter countries are pre-dominantly Protestant in religion. Each group, whether Catholic or Protestant, had its own set of attitudes toward the Negroes. The economic situation, though principally based on a plantation system, was by no means a constant. Not only did skilled Negro artisans everywhere constitute an elite, but in some regions of South America the Negroes did not work on plantations at all, but were imported to labor in the mines.

It is not necessary here to specify the many other, more detailed, his-toric controls that are provided by this "laboratory." Enough have been in-dicated to make it apparent how the existence of such controls renders it possible to analyze the manner in which cultural elements vary when one or another aspect of this complex is held constant. What differences, for example, are to be found in the linguistic adaptation of the Negroes to English, to French, to Spanish, to Portuguese, to Dutch? What are the simi-larities and differences to be found between the ways of life of Negroes in these different settings who belong to the same socio-economic classes? How has living under Catholicism influenced the development of present-day religious patterns of these Negro groups as against exposure to Protes-tant tradition? In which aspects of culture, over the whole New World, have African ways proved to be most tenacious? Wherein have they most changed? What are the adaptations that have been made to fit them into these differing cultures of the New World? What are the mechanisms by which they are achieved?

The basic apparatus we set up for the researches that lead to answers to such questions is the apparatus of an integrated program of historical and ethnological investigation. The base-line of African culture for our analysis had first to be established. This was done in two ways. Studies of the cul-tures of New World Negroes pointed to certain regions of Africa because they were found to have the same or similar institutions, conventions, often details of custom, such as specific names of places, persons, and deities found among specific African tribes. Field research in these regions of Africa provided further leads, which brought to light Africanisms hitherto over-looked in the New World. At the same time, the historical documents deal-ing with the slave trade and the writings of travellers and others who re-corded their impressions of life in the New World during the days of slavery, made it possible to establish the historical validity of the relationships that the comparison of ethnographic findings in African and New World Negro communities had revealed. These documents also were found to give a firm historical record of the ways of life of the Europeans who came to the New World. In telling of their customs, and particularly in their accounts of plantation life, these documents yielded much insight into the nature and mechanisms of the early phases of those adjustments to the New World setting that have become established in the present-day scene.

With the base-line from which to plot cultural change established, the next step was to organize the materials according to some comprehensive scheme of classification. In accordance with the principles stated in our preceding chapter, the scheme employed in classifying the materials of New World Negro cultures was drawn in terms of the historical framework of the problem. That is, a *scale of intensity of Africanisms* was set up on which the data were ranged, country by country, from most African to least—that is, to most European. That American Indian elements had to be taken into account in analyzing the New World scene in general was recognized, but those were found to enter significantly only in restricted instances.

As in all scientific research, however, a continuous refinement of procedure resulted from the collection of new data and the consequent revision of working hypotheses. Initially the scale of intensity of Africanisms was set up in accordance with the presence or absence of retentions in entire countries of the New World. Research soon made it apparent that such a classification, involving the alignment of whole cultures, was unsatisfactory. It masked differences between degrees of retention in different aspects of culture—as, for example, in religion, where there are numerous retentions, and in economic life, where they are few. Furthermore, it masked differences in the degree and kind of retentions that marked various socioeconomic classes within the Negro communities of various countries of the New World. For whether it was in the United States or Haiti or Guiana or Brazil, those in the more favored strata were found to have far fewer Africanisms, most often manifest only in terms of the subtlest kind of reinterpretations, than among the underprivileged majority. Factors of accessibility to means of learning the ways of the dominant group of European descent, or of prestige, had to be taken into account, in understanding the processes that had brought about acceptance of European ways by the upper-class groups, and the retention of traditional affirmations of status and psychological worth which the Western cultures denied, by those less favored.

These refinements led to the classification of the data shown in the accompanying table. This table reflects the working hypotheses and methodological devices out of which it derives. The fact that the degree of retention is given by aspect of culture rather than in terms of whole cultures represents a recognition of the variability of cultural elements not only in form, but in the extent to which, in a given historical situation, they are subject to change. This is the hypothesis that was explored in discussing the problem of cultural focus and cultural drift. It derived, in turn, from the assumption, considered in an earlier chapter, that culture can be studied as the series of related but independent variables we term aspects. Again, in this table the fact is recognized that in the New World, local differences must be taken into account; that larger regions must be treated in terms of their sub-areas. This is a reflection of the ecological approach to culture,

SCALE OF INTENSITY OF NEW WORLD AFRICANISMS [6]

(Only the greatest degree of retention is indicated for each group.)

	Tech-nology	Eco-nomic Life	Social Or-gani-zation	Non-kin-ship Insti-tutions	Reli-gion	Magic	Art	Folk-lore	Music	Lan-guage
Guiana (bush)	b	b	a	a	a	a	b	a	a	b
Guiana (Paramaribo)	c	c	b	c	a	a	e	a	a	c
Haiti (peasant)	c	b	b	c	a	b	d	a	a	c
Haiti (urban)	e	d	c	c	b	b	e	a	a	c
Brazil (Bahia)	d	d	b	d	a	a	b	a	a	a
Brazil (Porto Alegre)	e	e	c	d	a	a	e	?	a	c
Brazil (north—urban)	e	d	c	e	a	b	e	d	a	b
Brazil (north—rural)	c	c	b	e	c	b	e	b	b	d
Jamaica (Maroons)	c	c	b	b	b	a	e	a	a	c
Jamaica (general)	e	d	d	d	c	b	e	a	b	c
Trinidad (Toco)	e	d	c	c	c	b	e	b	b	d
Trinidad (Port-of-Spain)	e	d	c	b	a	a	e	b	a	c
Cuba	e	d	c	b	a	a	b	b	a	a
Virgin Islands	e	d	c	d	e	c	?	b	?	d
Gulla Islands	c	c	c	d	c	b	e	a	b	b
United States (rural south)	d	e	c	d	c	c	e	c	b	e
United States (north)	e	e	c	d	c	c	e	d	b	e

a: very African
b: quite African
c: somewhat African

d: a little African
e: trace of African custom, or absent
?: no report

as worked out in the many distribution studies that have established the importance of the local variant out of which the larger units are conceptually to be built up.

Finally, and perhaps most important of all, is the fact that this table represents a scale of intensity of Africanisms only insofar as the *greatest degree of retention* is concerned. This derives from the acceptance of the hypothesis of individual variability within a culture. The caution concerning this point, as phrased in the original presentation of this table, may

[6] Adapted from M. J. Herskovits, 1945b, p. 14.

be repeated: "It cannot be too strongly emphasized that in every area of the New World, except in the Guiana bush, variation in African forms of behavior stretches from the point of greatest intensity indicated in our table to almost complete conformity with European ways of life. The problem thus becomes one of accounting for differing degrees of variability in the different populations studied. But since the variation does in almost every case extend to the limit set by the conventions of European custom, it can be seen how significant is the analysis of retentions of African convention if we are to discover how far the distribution extends toward the patterns that made up the cultural endowment of the ancestors of present day Negro populations . . ." of the New World.[7]

The broad attack on the particular problem of New World Negro acculturation that has been sketched is thus seen to afford a method whereby accepted postulates can be tested, and new hypotheses devised on which to base further investigation. In this latter category are the hypotheses that bear on the dynamics of cultural change as this is implemented in the behavior and attitudes of the individuals who are the heritors of these varying bodies of tradition, and the instruments through which the retentions and reinterpretations that have been analyzed were effectuated. The problem, as it has been outlined, has in the main been concerned with the cultural matrix out of which the observed cultural variations from the basic patterns have arisen. The resulting data thus set the stage for a further attack, in terms of the new constants that can be employed as further controls in the analysis of the differential behavior patterns, and differing degrees of individual variation to be found in these Negro societies of the New World. The investigation can also proceed to the study of similar historically related sets of cultures elsewhere, so as to test in these situations the comparability of the dynamic processes, and the generalizations derived from them, found in the historic cultural sequence examined here.

4

THE framework for the analysis of the mechanisms of cultural change and their expression in new cultural forms that has been employed in the study of the relationship between African and New World Negro cultures can be paralleled in other "laboratory" situations, elsewhere in the world. The value of such an approach has been demonstrated in various studies. The Jesup North Pacific Expedition not only studied the historic relationship between the cultures bordering on the North Pacific, but had also as its purpose a comprehension of how the elements common to the area had been changed as they travelled from people to people. The study of the Plains Sun Dance, to which we have referred a number of times, treated of tribes living in a restricted area, between which diffusion could be assumed, so that the resulting variation in cultural elements could be analyzed—the fundamental hypothesis thus being that the phenomena under examination derived from a single historic stream.

---

[7] *Ibid.*, p. 15.

Cultural Law and the Problem of Prediction

That later acculturation studies could be carried on with assurances of the historic relationships involved rather than assumptions of them, only meant that the conclusions drawn could be the more securely based on historic fact. Redfield's study of cultural differentials in four related communities, though conceived in terms of the establishment of ideal classifications of culture, may be thought of as falling in this category. We have seen how Eggan's study in the Philippines had to do with a series of historically related groups. Of a similar nature is Hunter's analysis of the Pondo in southeastern Africa, consisting of comparative studies of the life of this people on the reserves, as farm-workers, and in the towns.[8] In the field of the relationship between personality and culture, the analysis by Hallowell combines the use of ethnohistory with projective psychological techniques, in assessing the underlying similarities between related Algonkian and neighboring peoples.[9]

Still another study is that of Barnett, who investigated the Yurok, Hupa and Karok of northwestern California with reference to the reaction of these people to "the different modes and degrees of Caucasian impingement upon this common cultural background." The problem here was to "discover an empirical basis for defining the changes to which a newly introduced trait or complex is subject, and the character of the readjustments following upon its acceptance." "The idea," he says, is "to ascertain what uniformities and consistencies of pattern underlie the acceptance and integration of new elements into a culture."[10] In this study the history of the contact these three tribes had with the incoming whites, and their varied reaction to the differing circumstances of contact is first sketched. Examples are then given of how the new has been reinterpreted in terms of established patterns, as well as instances showing how the substitution of the new for the old has been resisted. An hypothesis of "functional equivalence" is thus reached, whereby older functions may be retained when achieved by new forms, with the corollary that where no functional equivalence can be achieved, this leads to demoralization of a recipient group that cannot resist the imposition of these new ways by the donor society.

It is important that in most of the studies made of cultures where the historic factors are under control, the resulting generalizations are of a dynamic character. They are, indeed, to be differentiated in just this way from the generalizations derived from the use of the older comparative method wherein similarities between cultural elements or relationships were studied without reference to whether they eventuated from the play of like historic forces or not. Such earlier generalizations are preponderantly concerned with cultural forms.

It has been just such generalizations that have given the anthropologist the unwelcome task of repeatedly questioning the conclusions of his fellow social scientists by reference to cross-cultural data. It has been this use of cross-cultural materials, more than anything else, that has sounded the

---

[8] Monica Hunter, 1936.

[9] A. I. Hallowell, 1947, pp. 195–225.

[10] H. G. Barnett, 1940, pp. 22–3.

death-knell of theories about "human nature." "Human nature" was that chameleon-like force in man that was variously held to cause him to seek profits, or to be a monogamist or to have polygamous tendencies, or to strive to better his standard of living or to do any of those things that seemed ob-viously basic to students of Euroamerican society. The anthropologist, how-ever, beginning, "But, in Kamchatka . . ."—or in Senegal or Ecuador or Pukapuka—would proceed to give instances where men and women, pre-sumably activated by this same "human nature," eschewed profits, or were polygamist or monogamist, or seemed to be content with their lot. It can, indeed, be said that the philosophy of cultural relativism, that has come to dominate most anthropological thought and, indeed, social science in gen-eral, had its beginnings in the refutations of "human nature" that mark the literature of cultural anthropology.

The case of the classical evolutionists offers a good example of the use of cultural forms as the basis for generalization. The "stages" through which mankind was held to have evolved were described as a series of forms that succeeded each other in the history of the development of culture as a whole. Yet how were we to know that this presumed series, based on the arrangement of data from contemporary peoples all over the world, actually represented a sequence that was in fact a chain of causation? Even when archaeological materials are employed as skilfully as they have been by so competent an archaeologist as Childe, and he limits this discussion to the facts of material culture where sequence can be established, how can we know that his series is a generalization of the type we term "law," and not a description of a succession of events that were the result of a particular series of historic happenings?

The argument *post hoc, ergo propter hoc,* has great appeal in the study of man. This is precisely because we cannot vary conditions at will. Our laboratory of history can only be used when the test cases that comprise our apparatus come to hand, set up and ready to be utilized. We say the wheel must have been discovered before the wagon, and the conclusion is drawn that an evolutionary sequence leading to the motor-car has been established. What we are really saying is that the wheel *did* come before the wagon, and this, in turn *did* precede the motor car. It is possible to have the concept of the wheel, and never make the connection between its form and transport. This was what happened, for example, in the "high cultures" of Central and South America, where the form of the wheel was used as an ornament. Or, for instance, transport on the island of Madeira is achieved by the use of sledges, even though wheels would be more useful in pulling loads up the steep hills than the unwieldy vehicles that are not inefficient in sliding down them.

5

IF THE actual course of events in human history represents only one of a series of possible developments, can we encompass the alternatives in any formulation that will permit the study of culture to achieve the end of scientific research, prediction? Answers to this question have ranged from an insistence that the regularities in culture already to be discerned justify the development of those generalizations that are a first step toward prediction, to an emphasis on the unique historical character of every culture, and the conclusion that to discern regularity in the diversity of custom is a hopeless task.

Yet is this dichotomy, a kind of rewording of the problem of science versus history in the study of culture, really an accurate statement of the alternatives? The fact that we have found, in the case of history as against science, that there is no opposition, but that the scientist can use historical sequences as an aid in developing his generalizations, indicates other possible resolutions of the difficulty. It was seen that classification is an essential step in the analysis of data; and that, as long as the classes of data hold to the facts, and do not go beyond them, they are an aid in clarifying materials and preparing the way for further analysis. In the same manner, we have seen how history provides the laboratory in which the scientist of culture works, and how basic insights into the nature and processes of culture have been obtained by utilizing these resources.

The resolution of the apparent dilemma that arises when we stress the uniqueness of each culture can, therefore, be formulated in the following terms: *Cultural forms are the expression of unique sequences of historical events, but they are the result of underlying processes that represent constants in human experience.* This means that "laws" of culture must be statements of process. Their results are expressed in the most diverse forms, which are alike only insofar as they represent the end-results of the play of similar processes. Thus we may say that borrowing will result from contact between peoples. But what in a given case will be borrowed—whether material objects or ideas, whether technology or religion—and in what amount, will differ from one case to the next. We can, of course, go farther than this. Calling on such concepts as focus and reinterpretation, we can generalize that, in a particular case, borrowing will be selective, and that elements taken over by one people from another will assume new forms that are determined by the pre-existing cultural matrix.

The essential point in formulations of this sort is that they make full use of the fact of cultural variation. Generalizations follow the scientific principle of recognizing that a change in the total situation will make for differing results in the phenomenon under observation. "Other things being equal," is a phrase that has a profound significance in scientific research. The history of the development of scientific controls can be thought of as a succession of attempts to make "other things"—the conditions under which experimentation is carried on—more and more equivalent. To the degree that antecedent conditions are thus rendered equivalent, results will be comparable. But the fact that the conditions of the experiment, when varied, will produce different results, gives to the search for cultural "laws" a dynamic quality that is summated when we understand that cultural form is but the expression of cultural process, and that any generalizations about form must, in the final analysis, derive from hypotheses regarding process.

Cultural Variation

Problems of dynamics, it should be made clear, are not the exclusive domain of cultures in contact. They may be studied within a single culture, analyzed at a given period in its history, as well as by research into the results of contacts between cultures, or of the factors that have operated to make for retentions and reinterpretations of cultures lying within a given historic stream. Herein are to be found the most important contributions of the functionalist approach, and of the modern use of the comparative method. The interrelation between the institutions of a culture, and the manner in which they function so as to affect the totality of a culture are not inert, fixed, and static. Inner relationships are as dynamic as outer ones. There is no more important approach to an understanding of the nature and processes of culture than the analysis of how one element in culture, by its very form, affects other elements with which it is in association.

The number of "laws" which govern the research of anthropologists is actually very considerable. Many of these are so fundamental in anthropology that they are largely taken for granted. Such a "law" is that which holds culture to be learned and not inborn. The fact that culture is learned leads to the generalization of cultural borrowing which, when taken together with its subsidiary refinements, has played so important a role in the study of culture. From this principle, also, has been derived the hypothesis of enculturation as the mechanism whereby cultural stability and change is achieved. That culture responds to its natural setting in accordance with the forms of its technology is another such generalization; or, in the field of economics, that specialization increases as does the surplus represented by the degree of production in excess of subsistence requirements of a people. When we say kinship structure influences behavior toward blood and affinal relatives, or that religion is the reflection of a world view—that man makes his gods in his own image—or that folklore functions as an educational device, we are again only setting up generalizations that guide our approach toward the study of culture and our conception of how human beings respond to it.

Once full account is taken of the fact of variation, then the reconciliation of range in cultural form with regularity in process is well in hand. It submits the phenomenon of culture, whatever its manifestations, to scrutiny after the manner of the established methodological procedures of all science. Even such a concept as historic accident is seen to fall into place as one of the armory of weapons employed by the student of culture. For the accidental occurrence that alters the course of the development of a given body of tradition is, from this point of view, no accident. It is but another expression of the fact that the experience of no people duplicates that of any other—that is, that the course of history varies as it is expressed in the way of life of one group after another. It may be suggested that it is in terms such as these, rather than in the description of cultural forms, that the study of how "civilizations" develop and decay can best be attacked. The problem of the relation of population mass to complexity of institutions is a very real one. But as posed by such students as Flinders-Petrie, Spengler, Toynbee, and Kroeber, it leads to no more than a debate concerning the number and complexity of cultural forms that can be regarded as constituting a way of life of higher or lower quality.

Just as we study culture in terms of accepted generalizations that are in reality more numerous than we make explicit, so prediction has been achieved to a greater extent than is commonly suggested. The postulate of the enculturative process leads to the concept of the regularity of behavior within a society. Where a degree of regularity is present, to that degree prediction can be achieved. Therefore, the generalization that through the learning process the developing human organism becomes a being whose behavior is overwhelmingly in consonance with the sanctioned patterns of his culture, leads to an acceptance of the further postulate that we can predict the behavior of the individual conditioned to live in accordance with these patterns. This does not mean that every detail of behavior can be predicted; the fact of probability and the resulting variation must always be taken into account. We can, however, not only say that an Australian aborigine will, in a given familial situation, react differently than a Crow Indian or a Mushongo of the Congo Basin, or a banker in any city of the Western world, but we can also predict, within fairly narrow limits, what his behavior will be.

The degree to which prediction can be envisaged with reasonable accuracy becomes appreciably less as we move into those situations where cross-cultural factors enter. Yet even here, workable propositions can be stated. Given two cultures in contact, for example, it is apparent that borrowing will not go beyond the limits of form described by the differences between the elements and institutions of the cultures concerned. Moreover, it should be possible to predict, with some degree of validity, wherein the two particular cultures will give way, and where they will resist change the most. Such predictions depend largely on how precise is our knowledge of the situation being studied, not only as concerns the outer forms of the cultures involved but also the inner sanctions that activate the dynamics of each culture party to the contact. Thus it is not too speculative to anticipate that, in West Africa, the acceptance of European technological and economic patterns will proceed apace; that the response in the field of non-material culture will show a good measure of plasticity in outer form, and a resistance to inner change, especially in such aspects of West African culture as kinship structure and religion, that will withstand severe pressures.

For a time, however, prediction of cultural change will undoubtedly be more successful within cultures than cross culturally. Predictability will only become greater as we are able to increase the degree of probability that a given process, operating within the framework of a particular situation, will eventuate in certain forms rather than in others. But, in the final analysis, the forms themselves, as noted by the student, will always be variable. It is thus the task of the scientist concerned with culture to probe beneath form to process. To this end, he must utilize the laboratory situations provided by the many sequences of unique historic events to search out those generalizations that, as process, reveal the regularities in culture that make of it a subject for scientific analysis.

PART VIII

SUMMARY

CHAPTER 37

A Theory of Culture

In this chapter, the concepts of the nature, forms, and functioning of culture presented in the preceding pages of this work will be brought together, to present the theory of culture that has formed the basis of our discussions. In briefest form, the propositions that can be abstracted from these discussions are as follows:

1. Culture is learned;
2. Culture derives from the biological, environmental, psychological, and historical components of human existence;
3. Culture is structured;
4. Culture is divided into aspects;
5. Culture is dynamic;
6. Culture is variable;
7. Culture exhibits regularities that permit its analysis by the methods of science;
8. Culture is the instrument whereby the individual adjusts to his total setting, and gains the means for creative expression.

The many implications these propositions hold have been explored in earlier chapters. Here we will take up each in turn, recalling these implications, and indicating again which among the various hypotheses concerning them that have been advanced seems most justified by the facts.

2

Culture is learned.
Defined as the man-made part of the environment, culture is essentially a construct that describes the total body of belief, behavior, knowledge, sanctions, values, and goals that mark the way of life of any people. That is, though a culture may be treated by the student as capable of objective description, in the final analysis it comprises the things that people have, the things they do, and what they think.

When we ask how people come by the forms of belief and behavior that mark their way of life, we find the answer in the learning process, broadly conceived. It includes both those responses to conditioning on the uncon-

625

Summary

scious level, whereby the basic patterns of the group are impressed on the developing infant, and those more consciously received forms of instruction that we call "education."

This process of learning one's culture we have called enculturation, and it is enculturation which permits us to account for the fact that a culture maintains a recognizable form generation after generation. This is because every human being is born into a group whose customs and beliefs are established before he arrives on the scene. Through the learning process he acquires these customs and beliefs; and he learns his cultural lessons so well that much of his behavior in later years takes the form of automatic responses to the cultural stimuli with which he is presented. Enculturation is achieved in large measure by the symbolism of language, which comes to be an "index to culture" in a more profound sense than is customarily recognized. The process is extraordinarily subtle, and affects even such aspects of behavior as various kinds of motor habits or emotional reactions to stress situations. So far-reaching is the process that it has become apparent that the very personality of the individual is to a considerable extent the result of his enculturative experience.

The common elements in the enculturation of the members of succeeding generations of a group give to their culture the appearance of such continuity that a kind of independent existence has come to be attributed to culture. This position is strengthened by a consideration of such a phenomenon as cultural drift, which has caused some students to ascribe to the regularity of cultural change an inevitability that is deemed to arise out of the inner drives of a culture, without reference, or with but small regard for the human beings whose behavior constitutes the culture. Such is the position that holds culture to be a superorganic phenomenon; that treats problems of the forms of culture and the processes of culture change as having an existence and a dynamic of their own. Yet one comes eventually to the individual and his accommodation to the accepted traditions of the group, when seeking an explanation of the nature of culture. Therefore, while culture can be treated as a phenomenon susceptible, through reification, of study in terms of its own structures and processes, it must be concluded that the reality of culture is psychological.

There are no human beings who are not functioning members of some society; for man is a social animal. But it must be remembered that while man is a social animal, he is by no means the only social animal. On the other hand it is important to stress that he is the only culture-building animal. Such aggregates as the family, the local group, are present among many of the lower forms. Socialization is a process that many animals experience, as the peck-order among fowls demonstrates, or the regulation of relationships within a community of hamadryad baboons. All these processes man shares with his fellow-members of the biological series. But because he is the only speaking animal, he alone has the power of continuously changing his way of living through the invention and accumulation of new habits, that are passed on from one generation to the next by the verbal symbols of language.

A Theory of Culture

Early enculturation is a process which, during infancy and childhood, makes for the conditioning of behavior that gives stability to culture. The reconditioning process we call later enculturation, however, provides the mechanism that makes possible the changes that mark the history of every body of custom. Culture, being learned, can be relearned. Hence when an individual has reached maturity and some new mode of behavior, some new technique or concept is presented to him, he reacts to it in terms of his previous experience. If he accepts it, he must to that extent recondition his responses. In other words, he must to that degree reenculturate himself. Thus the process of enculturation, which signifies conditioning to the totality of a culture and not a segment of it, also aids us in resolving the apparent dilemma that culture is stable and yet, at the same time, is in continuous change.

Though a culture can be reified into a body of traditions susceptible of objective study, and without regard for the people whose lives are ordered in accordance with it, it has become increasingly apparent that no fundamental comprehension of culture can be achieved that leaves the individual out of account. We have seen how true this is in the study of cultural change. It is apparent that all changes in culture, whether large or small, must be the result of some act by an individual who initiates some kind of behavior that deviates from the established customs of his society. How wide-spread this process is becomes evident when we examine in detail the ways of life of the members of a given community. Even though it be small, isolated, and conservative, no two of its members will behave in exactly the same way, or react to any situation in an identical manner. This is why the examination of this interaction between the individual and his culture, that has taken the form of investigations into the cultural mechanisms that shape personality structures, assumes an important place in the anthropological repertory. Students of individual psychology have demonstrated how deeply the early experiences of the human being lodge in his psychological makeup, and students of culture have followed through with a demonstration of the significance of the fact that these earliest experiences, like those of later life, are culturally determined.

A final implication of the fact that culture is learned is the conclusion that the many differing ways of life that are found over the earth must each be accorded worth and dignity in its own terms. We have seen that no logical or factual bases for the evaluation of cultures can be found, except as these are dictated by ethnocentrism. Ethnocentrism, however, is a widespread attitude of human groups. Men are ethnocentric either because they know no other forms of behavior than those of their own group, or if they are acquainted with the customs of foreign peoples, are driven by the force of their cultural conditioning to judge their own practices more favorably than those of another society.

Anthropology has gradually moved from more to less ethnocentrism. Because the historical development of the sciences left to the anthropologist the task of studying peoples outside the Euroamerican cultural stream, the early literature was replete with analyses of "savage," and "barbarous" ways of life. These later were subsumed under the term "primitive," which, though in its scientific sense came to have the meaning of being without writing, yet retained a cluster of evaluative connotations that blunted its effectiveness as an instrument of scientific investigation. Studies that tended to contrast "primitive" man, despite the great variety of cultures falling in this category, with "civilized" peoples, or to ascribe to "primitives" special mental processes such as particular forms of reasoning, further lessened the usefulness of the term. It has become apparent, moreover, that the unity of human culture is such that anthropologists can no longer take unlettered man as an exclusive field for study. Hence the term "nonliterate" has been employed as a purely descriptive, non-evaluative word to be applied to the peoples whose cultures the methods of anthropology have been shown best fitted to understand.

3

Culture derives from the biological, environmental, psychological, and historical components of human existence.

Man is a member of the biological series, and it therefore follows that the existence of human culture, *as a whole,* must be referred to abilities that inhere in man's physical constitution. That is, the development of such fundamentals of culture as the use of tools and language are to be traced to the character of man's anatomical and physiological makeup.

This becomes clear when the evolution of *homo sapiens* from the time of his earliest appearance on earth is traced. The story of his development, in broadest outline, is one in which man moves steadily away from anthropoid and toward human characteristics. This is particularly apparent in the case of the two most critical traits, upright stature and brain size, that differentiate man from the other primates. The fact that man came to walk on his hind legs made it possible for his anterior extremities to be converted from organs of locomotion to grasping organs. The same fact made possible adjustments in the structure of the cranium that permitted the brain-case to become enlarged and the size of the jaw to diminish, thus affording the basis for the development of an ability to speak. The earliest types that have been recovered have cranial capacities much closer to those of the apes than do later forms. Where long-bones have been recovered, it is evident that upright posture was achieved early, though a stooping position marks protohuman forms as against the completely upright stance of present-day man.

It should be made clear, however, that to accept the fact that culture has a biological basis in no way implies acceptance of the hypothesis that holds physical differences between present-day sub-types of *homo sapiens* to be related to differences between the cultures of groups belonging to these sub-types. Race has never been satisfactorily proved to influence culture. Theories of culture that do not recognize this fact tend to take the form of racist philosophies, and these have repeatedly been demonstrated to have no scientific validity. The fact that culture has the quality of being "contagious," and that elements of culture are readily taken over and successfully carried on by societies of individuals having the most diverse physical forms, is one evidence of the fact that racial type is irrelevant as a causal factor in determining cultural behavior. Another demonstration of this is the fact that any child of ordinary capacity, whatever his racial affiliation, can be enculturated to any way of life. Finally, the fact that man, a domesticated form, comprises a single species all of whose sub-types are mutually fertile, and that extensive crossing has brought it about that there is no pure human race, stresses the futility of looking to race as an explanation of cultural differences.

This does not mean that there is no relationship between *physical type* (as against race) and cultural behavior. Populations, because of inbreeding, may differ markedly from each other, and it is at least hypothetically possible that aptitudes of various kinds, in generalized form though not in their specific manifestations, may, by this process, have been intensified within such inbred groups. Less hypothetical, however, and more apparent is the fact that culture does influence physical type. As one of the domesticated animals, man lives a life that is quite different from that he would have to live under natural conditions. This means that natural selection is replaced in large part by social selection. Social selection is most apparent in the operation of those traditions that govern mating within a group, especially whereby there is inbreeding or free mixture. Aside from this, such factors as diet, occupation and traditions of child-rearing affect the adult form of the members of a given group, and may result in characteristics that, actually the result of extra-biological factors, have been uncritically regarded as the expression of genetic endowment.

In considering the relation between culture and the environment, it is necessary to distinguish between the natural setting (which is meant here) and the social setting of an individual or a group. These are often confused, especially in the literature of psychology and education, but also, on occasion, by anthropologists as well. Because of this confusion, it seems advisable to adjust our terminology, so that the word *environment* can stand for the total setting of an individual or a group, *habitat* can be used to indicate the elements of the natural setting, and *culture* can be applied to those aspects of the environment that are the work of man.

Though controversy has long existed regarding the role of the habitat in influencing culture, no critic of environmental determinism has gone so far as to deny that it does play some role. Environmental determinism, which holds that the habitat dictates the forms culture takes, represents an extreme position that is as easily refuted as is an extreme position regarding racial determinism. The real problem, that has occupied both geographers and anthropologists, is to discover and describe, in as precise terms as possible, the nature of the relationship between the characteristics of specific regions and the cultures found in them. Here both culture and habitat must be taken into account, as is done in the general formulation that the natural setting prescribes limits which the culture cannot exceed. Such instances as that of rice grown by irrigation on mountain sides through the medium of

Summary

terracing, however, shows that societies do succeed in going beyond what would seem to be "natural" limits.

The most satisfactory resolution of the problem, in general terms, is that the limits set by the environment vary in accordance with the technological equipment of any given culture. Improvement in technology thus means that limits previously set are thereby extended. Culture may therefore be envisaged as a buffer between man and his habitat. The greater the technological resources of a society, the more effective the buffer and the wider the range of alternatives. Furthermore, it must be understood that habitat does not influence all phases of culture to an equal degree, but that as we move from its more material aspects to the intangibles, the effect of habitat becomes more difficult to discern. It thus becomes clear that the original simple formulation of this problem must be replaced with one that is complex indeed, varying not only from culture to culture but from one aspect of a given culture to another.

The story of the development of culture, as an expression of growing innate human capacity and of more effective techniques of coping with the habitat, is a long one. The study of prehistory, the counterpart in the study of the development of culture to the researches in palaeoanthropology that have recovered the story of the evolution of human physical type, has yielded much information bearing on this problem. That prehistory can but partially recover the facts about the development of culture, in no way lessens the brilliance of the achievements of prehistorians. By the use of scientific imagination, they have done much to fill out the picture, which otherwise must have been restricted to the stone artifacts and such other elements of material culture that have been preserved in the earth.

Earlier prehistorians failed to perceive that the learned character of culture removes it from the order of natural phenomena, but later work has stressed the need to classify prehistoric cultures in terms of the materials found in given areas, and not on the basis of a nomenclature and typology derived from the sites of southern and central France. Two principal areas in the Old World are recognized; the European, marked by "hand-ax" and "blade" cultures, and the Asiatic, marked by "chopping-tool" cultures. In addition, the problem presented by prehistoric remains in the Americas differs from both these, since the migration of man to the New World, though the precise period when it occurred is disputed, took place after the basic inventions of human culture had been achieved in the Old.

The long span of developing human culture has shown man to have gained a continuously better command of resources, and a continuously more efficient technology. Except for these elements of culture, and perhaps the art of certain restricted areas, no comparable development in the field of nonmaterial culture can safely be charted. Early forms of social and political life, religion, language, and music, for example, are hidden from us. The technique of equating living "primitive" peoples with early man has been found methodologically inacceptable, given the known propensity of all cultures to change. Perhaps the most striking advance in describing the course of man's development, at least for the Mediterranean and adjacent areas, is Childe's concept of the three revolutions. His hypothesis that earliest man lived in small groups, subsisting on a hunting and food-gathering economy seems incontrovertible. The first "revolution," the Neolithic, made for stable agricultural societies; the second, or "urban revolution," saw the development of cities, dynasties, trade, economic specialization, and slavery; the third, or Industrial Revolution is a matter of recent history. The theoretical implications of this hypothesis—particularly its applicability to cultures outside the area where it has been applied—are yet to be explored. Whatever the findings may be, the data available on the prehistoric development of culture shows that this has gone along with the increased potential of the physical form of *homo sapiens,* and that it has involved a continuous adjustment to the changing habitat of mankind through the utilization of increasingly effective technological equipment.

4

Culture is structured.

The regularity of culture is nowhere better exemplified than in the way in which the most diverse bodies of custom can be broken down into comparable units. One set of structures into which culture may be analyzed is in terms of traits and trait-complexes. Despite the contention that this is too mechanical a scheme, and destroys the living reality of culture, it has nonetheless proved its usefulness as a tool in the study of certain problems, particularly where detailed comparison of the objective aspects of cultural elements among different peoples is desirable. The concept of the trait as the basic element in culture has also been employed usefully in attempts to encompass, in detail, the units that go to make up culture after culture in a restricted region, as in the case of the study of California Indian tribes. Here a trait-list has served as a basis for recording in objective form as many elements as possible in the culture of tribe after tribe, and has had results that point to the worth of further use of this method. It has shown how complex even a "simple" culture can be, in addition to making possible statistical studies which are held to reveal historical relationships between the peoples of the area.

More difficult to meet is the assertion that the concepts of trait and complex can at best only be vaguely described; what is a trait in one context becomes a complex in another. That this is true emerges from the ever growing size of the trait-element lists from California, where greater knowledge of the culture and continued use of the trait-list resulted in the student setting down as elements many subdivisions of complexes he earlier treated as units. The criticism that these concepts can never be more than loosely defined is not a serious one, however, since a certain flexibility in their use is by no means undesirable. The important fact is that where culture is to be studied objectively, especially as regards those problems where psychological considerations do not enter, such as in mapping distributions, it is impossible to operate without some concepts such as traits and complexes.

Summary

That a trait in one context is a complex in another merely means that the basis of judgement shifts in terms of the requirements of the problem.

The concepts of trait and complex, which have been found especially useful in distribution studies, are basic when the mapping of culture-areas is undertaken. Culture-areas have been distinguished in North and South America, Africa and Asia, and can be thought of as comprising the principal divisions recognized in the common groupings of the Pacific Islands— Polynesia, Micronesia and Melanesia. The ability of students to localize bundles of complexes in the cultures of a given region, so to speak, has many implications for cultural theory. It demonstrates the universality of borrowing, it indicates an ecological base for culture, and it has been used in an attempt to show how, in each area, the characteristic culture comes to a "climax" among the tribes that manifest its most typical and concentrated forms. In general, however, the concept of the culture area has been found most useful in descriptions of cultures that lie on a single time-plane. It has not been employed with any great success as a means for the study of dynamics of culture, where time-depth is essential.

Culture areas, like traits and complexes, are constructs. They are not recognized by the persons who live in them, for to an individual the way of life of his group seems quite different from the customs even of neighboring peoples. This, however, is a matter of perspective. The closer one is to a culture, the more important to him are the minor differences between it and other cultures that may be found nearby. To the student who takes a view that is continental, however, these differences merge in the broader similarities that mark off bodies of custom that occupy vast regions. Two auxiliary concepts mark the culture-area as ordinarily employed, the culture-center and the marginal region. These, again, are aids to the student and their use does not imply that the culture of the tribes who are at the center is any "richer" than those in the margins of the area. It is rather a question of typicality. This means that as one moves in space away from the districts where the tribes are located that can be regarded as most typical of the area, different traits and complexes begin to appear until peoples are reached whose customs are sufficiently different that they can be thought of as belonging to another area.

Whatever the position of a culture in an area, and despite the fact that it can be broken down for purposes of study into traits and complexes, every way of life follows patterns that are integrated so as to make up a functioning whole. The concepts of pattern and integration are thus essential for any workable theory of culture. By patterning is meant the characteristic forms taken by the institutions of a culture, forms which represent the consenses of the differing individual behavior patterns of the members of the society whose traditions are being described. It is essential to recognize that even the simplest culture has many patterns. These represent differences in typical behavior between groups based on age, on sex, on status, and on occupation, to name but a few. They overlap, as do all other cultural phenomena. Yet, when isolated, they show an amazing regularity. They are, in a very real sense, the guides that all persons use in their day-to-day intercourse. For though abstractions, they are nevertheless sufficiently real so that they can be and indeed are used, all unconsciously, to predict the behavior of the fellow-members of one's society. As such, their importance in the science of culture is patent.

Traits, complexes, and patterns, which describe the structure of culture, are in every case so closely integrated that, as far as the members of a group are concerned, their existence moves as a unit in a continuum of time. The individual, as he lives his life, goes from one phase of his culture as distinguished by the student, to the next, quite unconcerned with how his behavior is determined by the patterning of the customs he accepts with so little awareness of them. So closely interwoven is the texture of a culture that a description of a way of life can begin anywhere. If the relationships of an object, a custom, an institution are followed to their ultimate associations within the culture of which they are a part, all, or almost all elements of that culture will have been brought into the picture.

This fact of the integration of culture gives to a body of custom meaning for those who live in accordance with it. More importantly, this characteristic of culture makes for the adjustment of the individuals whose lives are shaped in accordance with its patterns. Demoralization can be thought of as resulting from the severe disturbance of the balance achieved in the integration of a culture.

The concept of the integration of culture has given rise to various hypotheses concerning culture as a totality to be studied in terms of this underlying unity. The approach of the functionalists, who stressed the interrelationship of all elements of culture, is one such point of view. Concepts such as cultural configuration, or of the covert culture, or of cultural themes or cultural sanctions have been devised as instruments with which to reach and analyze this most subtle facet of culture. These directions, that underlie much of the conduct of a people, are found among every group. To what extent it is possible to describe and assess them on the basis of objectively verifiable criteria is a question that only much research will answer. What is important for any theory of culture is that no matter how a culture may be analyzed into component elements, the fact remains that it is integrated and meaningful, and is the supreme expression of the process of adjustment essential to every people if they are to survive.

5

Culture is divided into aspects.
The universals that mark off all bodies of custom are not only to be found in the structures of culture. They are also to be discerned in the groupings of institutions, termed cultural aspects, which are divisions of culture that cut across the categories comprised in the trait-complex-pattern-area approach. These universals represent different ways of accomplishing the same ends that every people seem to have felt essential to their adjustment in the world as they experience it.

633

Summary

Various types of categories have been devised to describe the divisions of culture we term aspects. These categories differ principally in their inclusiveness, or in the degree of detail with which they mark off universals in culture. The series of categories that has been employed in this work proceeds from those parts of culture that meet the physical wants of man, through those that dictate social relations, then to the institutions that explain the universe and regulate individual conduct, and finally to those that provide creative satisfactions of an aesthetic order. The "culture-scheme" that emerges from this approach is as follows:

Material Culture and its Sanctions
Technology
Economics
Social Institutions
Social organization
Education
Political structures
Man and the Universe
Belief systems
The control of power
Aesthetics
Graphic and plastic arts
Folklore
Music, drama and the dance
Language

From the postulate of the unity and integration of culture, that is basic to our theory, it follows that the aspects of culture are distinguished more by the student of human behavior than by those who live their daily lives in terms of the accepted patterns of their culture. Life, we must recognize, moves as easily from one aspect to another as it does from one culture-complex to the next. In a sense, however, the aspects do have a certain inner psychological validity. People do distinguish a religious rite from a purely secular commercial transaction. They will associate the rite with their belief-system, and the purchase they make with the business of getting a living. This does not mean that gods of the market-place do not exist, or that servitors of the supernatural do not have to take economic factors into account in providing the goods and services needed in religious ceremonies.

The question of whether the aspects of culture can be treated separately or not, or whether analysis must center about institutions that cut across aspects, is largely a matter of problem and point of view. To the extent that people within a culture think of certain kinds of activities as pertaining to a given area of experience, aspects have cultural reality. To the extent that the student finds problems that are essentially to be analyzed within the confines of a given aspect, to that extent it is possible to say that it should be set off from others. The examples that have been given suggest that aspects have a certain psychological validity. The fact that whole disciplines treat of the problems of economics, or social structures, or politics, or religion or art or language indicates that many questions can profitably be studied that do not require the student to move outside a given aspect of culture.

How many problems of this kind exist has been amply indicated in the chapters where one aspect of culture after another has been treated. Problems concerning the character of a given kind of cultural phenomenon, the variety of its forms, the lines along which it has developed, its distribution, are only some that are to be considered for aspect after aspect. This is not an argument for over-specialization, however. The experience of all science teaches that no phenomenon can effectively be sealed off in a separate compartment. In the case of culture, which moves in an historic stream that inextricably mingles all elements in the everyday life of the individual, this is a paramount consideration. Nonetheless many problems have been fruitfully studied in terms of a single aspect of culture.

Here again, then, we must conclude that though aspects have reality and utility, they must not dominate the study of culture. They are important because they point to universals in human experience and thus help us understand the nature and functioning of culture as a whole. They cannot, of themselves, give us the answers we seek in the study of culture. Too great a reliance on them, like a disregard of them, will give a partial picture of what culture is and how it operates. Used in perspective, and as one of a number of approaches, their actuality comes alive, and thereby affords numerous insights that would otherwise be denied us.

6

Culture is dynamic.

Change is a constant in human culture. It is, however, always to be studied against a background of cultural stability. Even though changes may appear to be far-reaching to the members of a society where they occur, they seldom affect more than a relatively small part of the total body of custom by which a people live. The problems of cultural dynamics thus are seen to take on a positive and at the same time a negative aspect. Change, that is, must always be considered in relation to resistance to change. People who accept new ways of doing some things are reluctant to agree to innovations where other facets of their way of life are concerned. The problems of cultural dynamics are thus seen to involve an analysis of the conditions under which conservatism and change dominate a given cultural scene, how these attitudes toward the old and the new develop, what conditions the acceptance of innovations, and how innovations, once accepted, are molded by the cultural matrix into which they are fitted.

Change can come about from within a society, or from outside it. Internal development results from discovery or invention. Changes introduced from outside result from a process of borrowing, or cultural transmission. Far more attention has been given the latter process, if only because of the fact that much more of the culture of any given people has been taken over from

Summary

the ways of life of other societies than has originated from within the group. The processes of discovery and invention are obscure. In some cases, pure chance must be postulated as having led an individual to hit upon a new technique, a new concept, a new belief. In some instances, need may have dictated a search for some method of resolving a want, but this seems to have been overemphasized. The calculated inventions of Euroamerican industrial culture must, in the history of man, be regarded as exceptional instances of the process. For the same reason, the identification that is often made of the word invention with material cultural elements must be considered as out of perspective, since some of the most significant innovations of a nonmaterial character must be recognized as belonging, psychologically, to this category.

Change has been taken into account from the earliest days of scientific anthropology. The evolutionists postulated a unilateral order of development in culture, which laid stress on the psychic unity of mankind and thus emphasized internal factors making for change. Later, in reaction to this position, the diffusionists underscored the propensity of man to borrow elements of culture rather than to invent them. A more reasonable position, however, was that neither independent origin nor diffusion could in themselves account for the changes found in every culture, but that both processes must be allowed for in accounting for the forms a given culture manifests at a given time. Too great stress on either distorts perspective rather than aids understanding. In like measure, such a distorted emphasis invalidates hypotheses of culture that fail to take both processes into account.

The fact of cultural transmission has been amply established, so that controversy over diffusion tends to be pointless except insofar as specific ways of the borrowing of particular elements by given nonhistoric—that is, nonliterate—peoples, are under consideration. The technique that established the fact of cultural borrowing beyond dispute was the analysis of the distribution of culture-traits and complexes over restricted areas. This consideration showed plainly what has already been pointed out in our discussion of the culture-area—that cultures found closer together present more similarities than those farther removed from each other. Such findings can be accounted for in no other way than on the assumption that similarities are due to diffusion; and that the greater the opportunity for borrowing, the more the cultures that have been in contact will resemble each other. This is scarcely to be wondered, granting the postulate that culture is learned. Nonetheless the history of anthropological theory testifies that much controversy preceded the realization and acceptance of borrowing as a factor in cultural change.

Until the study of change in process was undertaken, all theories of cultural dynamics were of necessity hypothetical. With acceptance of the fact of cultural change, anthropology, having reached the limit of hypothesis in analyzing distributions and reconstructing unrecorded history, turned for further enlightenment to those situations where peoples were actually in contact. If investigations of the end-results of cultural change, through the analysis of the distribution of cultural elements, are termed diffusion studies, then those researches which take change in process as their subject may be

636

called acculturation research. These researches represented a substantial step toward the realization of a scientific approach to the study of cultural dynamics. The method of science, which involves first-hand observation of process no less than the study of end-results, was obviously much more closely approximated when hypothetical reconstructions of change gave way to the observations of changing cultures.

Studies of cultural transmission in process have demonstrated that borrowing is never indiscriminate, but is selective. In some contact situations, elements may be taken over wholesale; elsewhere, resistance may be very strong to any borrowing. Two of the most important mechanisms in determining what and how much will be borrowed are the mechanisms of cultural focus and of reinterpretation. The hypothesis of cultural focus derives from the observed fact that different cultures show a more luxuriant growth in some aspects than in others. It is apparent that these focal aspects are those in which people are more interested, which they therefore discuss, and where they are thus more hospitable to innovations than in other aspects, where cultural forms and particularly their sanctions tend to be taken for granted. This being the case, under free contact, elements from outside will be more readily accepted if they fall within the focal aspect than if they do not; and the same principle is applicable to innovations that originate from within the culture.

On the other hand, where the situation is one in which a people have elements of a foreign culture forced on them, reinterpretation permits the retention of earlier ways in changed form. This same process of reinterpretation, under free borrowing, causes a newly accepted cultural element to take on a form that accords with the pre-existing patterns of the culture. This, however, only describes what happens. For an explanation of this process we turn again to the psychological phenomenon of enculturation—in this instance, the enculturation of later life where choice must be exercised by the adult members of a community. It is the reactions of individuals to any innovation that determine what will be taken over and what will not, and the forms in which the reinterpretative process will shape innovations. These reactions, however, stem from the cultural conditioning of the individuals who are the agents of change. We have here, then, a psychological mechanism that validates the earlier customary formulation of the borrowing process, couched in terms of culture alone, which held that new cultural elements are taken over to the degree they are in accord with pre-existing patterns, but are modified to fit their new cultural setting.

7

Culture is a variable.

Variability in culture is at once an expression of its dynamic quality; and the means whereby cultural change is achieved. Cultural variation manifests itself in two ways. The first is obvious, and can be dismissed with brief comment. This refers to the variation in human culture as a whole, manifest in

Summary

the many ways different peoples have devised to achieve the same ends. This kind of variation has been discussed in connection with a number of questions that have been treated in this book, and, as a matter of fact, is not so much an expression of variation, as it is an expression of the variety of custom. Why the great number of these varieties that exist have come to be, why they persist and how they change, are among the basic questions that the science of anthropology seeks to answer.

The answers we give such questions, must, as a matter of fact, and in larger measure than has been realized, derive from the analysis of the second kind of cultural variability, the variation that is expressed in the differences in behavior of individual members of the same society. It is not always easy, when studying exotic cultures, to see that no two persons behave in exactly the same way, even though the group be small, isolated, and conservative. It was not until perfected methods of field investigation permitted anthropologists to break through the concept of the extreme conservatism of "primitive" peoples that this factor of variation could be recognized, and made an instrument of field research. This achievement, however, made possible one of the principal advances in anthropological science.

The smaller the social unit, the less variation will be found in the behavior of its members. A family aggregate exhibits less variation than a local group, and this, in turn, tends to be more homogeneous than a regional grouping. This indicates the importance of gross population size, as a factor in making for cultural complexity. The greater the range of variation in culture, the more opportunity is afforded for the development of new facets of the pre-existing body of custom. How significant population size can be is further attested by the way in which it is found to be correlated with the economic productivity of a group, so that the larger the society the greater its economic surplus over subsistence needs, and the greater its possible degree of specialization in all aspects of culture.

Certain variations, however, are more significant than others. Each individual deviation from accepted modes can be thought of as a potential force to influence the direction of change in a culture. These variations can, in fact, be thought of as minute innovations, which may be taken over by a society, or discarded, as the case may be. If such a variation is taken over, to that extent it alters a pattern that existed before it came on the scene. It can either replace an earlier habitual type of reaction, or supplement it, or provide a new alternative form of accepted behavior. Here the hypothesis of cultural focus re-enters our discussion, since this explains why the greatest variation in custom is present in the aspects of life where interests are most acute, and enter most often in the conscious thought of a people.

Because variations are random, and because it is impossible to predict the historical events that will shape the course of a given culture, the factor of accident must be taken into account. Accidental developments in culture do not mean those that occur outside the broad cycle of cause and effect. They are rather those happenings that could not be foreseen, even if all available information about a given culture at a given moment in its history were at hand. In the main, the accidents of cultural development are to be referred to contacts between peoples that bring to one party cultural elements quite new to them, and which affect their way of life in a manner that could not be predicted by them. In this sense, however, inventions and discoveries that alter a way of life to an appreciable extent and come unexpectedly to the members of a society, can also be regarded as cultural accidents. All these broaden the base of the culture, introducing new variables. This is perhaps the reason for the common observation that cultural contact stimulates cultural growth.

Given a relatively undisturbed culture, certain random variations in individual behavior take on more significance than others because of the factor of cultural focus. The resulting process is expressed in the concept of cultural drift. First recognized in the study of language, the phenomenon is found equally discernible in culture as a whole. Most of the random variations in culture disappear with the individual who manifests them. Those that do not disappear, that are taken up by other members of a society, tend to be cumulative. This is especially true in the focal aspect of a culture. Cultures that have been observed with this point in mind have been found to exhibit greatest change—that is, to manifest the greatest degree of variation and the most decisive instances of drift—in those phases of life that are uppermost in the interests of the people.

8

Culture exhibits regularities that permit its analysis by the methods of science.

That generalizations of the sort set forth above can be drawn about culture points a way toward resolving the controversy over whether culture is to be studied as history or science. The first approach stresses the unique character of the historical development of every culture. The second lays emphasis on classification and analysis of the similarities and differences between cultural forms, to the end that valid generalizations about culture as a whole, that permit prediction, can be achieved. The two positions, however, are not mutually exclusive. The historical development of each culture is admittedly unique, in that a particular sequence of events is never repeated, and no two sequences issue in identical cultural forms. It is from this fact that the assertion that anthropology is an historical discipline derives its validity.

Nonetheless it remains true that, as in the case of other historical sciences such as astronomy and geology, generalizations have been achieved through following the procedures of scientific method. In the science of culture, therefore, history is not to be opposed to science. Rather historical developments are to be looked to to provide the anthropological counterparts of the laboratory situations through which scientists working in physics or chemistry or zoology achieve their controls over the data they study. Through analysis of how unique historical sequences have developed, and an understanding of the forms of culture in which they have eventuated, ample and

Summary

adequate generalizations can be put forward for testing after the manner of science. The laws, however, must be laws of process; the cultural forms which represent their end-results must be regarded not as fixed, but as variables whose limits are set by the probabilities that a given type will emerge from a given concatenation of circumstances.

In these terms, prediction is quite possible. It is achieved in everyday life when, all unconsciously, we predict within fairly narrow limits how a man or woman of a given society will behave in a given situation. Prediction of a broader sort can be made with considerable confidence about how certain dynamic processes will operate under cross-cultural contact. Given the characteristics of the cultures of two peoples who meet, we at least have a fairly good idea of the limits within which the resulting amalgam of cultural traits will manifest itself. The challenge of anthropological science is thus to cope both with historical and scientific factors. Through the study of culture on both fronts, techniques and concepts are emerging that are permitting us, ever more surely, to assess and comprehend both the general laws of cultural dynamics, and the particular historical sequences that make of each body of custom the unique complex of patterned systems of belief and behavior that gives it its identity as a recognizable way of life.

9

Culture is the instrument whereby the individual adjusts to his total setting, and gains the means for creative expression.

The enculturative process includes the whole of that aspect of the adjustment of the newly-born individual to the group of which he is to become a member, and more. Those adjustments a person must make to the fellow-members of his group, beginning with his family, and later including aggregates of many different kinds, are important in making him a fully functioning member of society. They are what is commonly designated as the process of socialization. The enculturative experience, however, also includes those reactions to aspects of life that, as expressions of the creative drive, are only secondarily reactions to the social structures which make of society an organized unit. The individual is enculturated to patterns of music and art and dancing, where self-expression is accorded freer play than in other aspects of culture; speculation about the universe and the powers that govern it, also come under this broader category.

The institutions that mark the sanctioned behavior-patterns of human groups may be regarded as the outward expressions of the deeper, often unrecognized series of motivations underlying the forms of behavior that encompass the range of culture on the descriptive level. There has been considerable discussion of whether these institutions, which go to make up the aspects of culture, represent patterned methods of meeting the needs of human beings. Some students stress the way in which culture fulfils the biological needs of man, while others emphasize the large proportion of the content of any culture that can only with difficulty, if at all, be thought of as fulfilling this function.

Those who argue for a biological base for culture, in this broad sense, point to such phenomena as the innate drives of the human animal that must be satisfied through the maintenance of the food supply and the regulation of sexual conduct. They point to the function of social structures in providing for rearing the young, and training them to become full-fledged members of society; to political structures as a means to assure the internal order, and the protection from dangers from without, that every society must have. Yet in much of all these aspects, and to an even greater extent in the creative activities of human beings, particularly in the arts, it becomes difficult to ferret out the biological needs that are satisfied. A culture, too often, seems to be a system that makes the attainment of a desired end more difficult than need be. The refusal of peoples to recognize what seems obviously efficient to the outsider cannot be forgotten in considering this problem.

Every culture functions as importantly in fulfilling the psychological needs of those who live in accordance with it as in meeting the demands that are to be referred to the physical constitution of man. Such a position in no way rules out the satisfaction, by culture, of needs that are dictated by man's inborn characteristics, or the nature of human society, or the requirements of the habitat. But it also takes into full account needs that may not only not be related to the requirements of the organism, but in their urgency may even run contrary to them. The drive for prestige, for example, is one such; and it would be as difficult to deny its far-reaching consequences in ordering cultural forms as it would be to deny the force of the need to have an assurance of a constant and adequate food supply. No valid theory of culture, therefore, can fail to take these needs into as full account as the primary requirements of food, shelter, and the like when explaining the function of culture in adjusting the individual to the way of life of his group.

Yet though culture is the instrument whereby human beings adjust themselves to their total setting, it must never be conceived as reducing the individual to a passive or inert status in the process. Actually, the process of adjustment is circular and never-ending; it is a process of interaction between the individual and his group in terms of his enculturation to its pre-existing patterns. This adjustment is furthered by the creativeness which, as a fundamental expression of the restlessness of the individual in the face of the ways of his group, permits him to exercise various modes of self-expression, and thus to extend the scope of his culture without breaking down its basic orientations.

CHAPTER 38

Anthropology in a World Society

DURING the century that anthropology has existed as a recognized discipline, it has developed from a study of the quaint and unusual in human custom as seen from the point of view of Euroamerican culture, to the scientific analysis of the ways of life of man, and of the psycho-social drives that underlie the cultural forms which are the expressions of behavior of all human groups. Whether bodies of tradition are simple or complex, whether peoples live relatively undisturbed by outside influence or their cultures are in a state of flux, they furnish materials for the anthropologist to study, compare, understand. In these terms the prosaic and the exceptional, the familiar and the exotic have no special significance except as they throw light on the nature and processes of custom. They are alike in that they are treated as a part of the totality of culture into which they fit, as a part of the scientifically conceived matrix in which they function.

We have in this book seen how comprehensive is the mandate under which the study of man must be conducted, and how, over the years, this mandate steadily broadened. Problems close at hand were investigated by specialists who could take the historical, social, and environmental setting of the subjects they studied much for granted. But the anthropologist, to whom was left the task of studying the cultures of peoples outside the historic stream of Euroamerican society, had to develop methods that not only permitted systematic observation of these many different bodies of tradition, but also techniques which would allow him to gain comprehension and insight. With these methods, he gradually forced the recognition of the degree of variety in human culture. Himself impressed with the dignity and maturity of the peoples with whom he worked, he labored incessantly to make known the fact of the basic unity of human behavior, to broaden the conceptual boundaries of those whose investigations were confined to a single culture, their own.

Because there were so many peoples to be studied, and so few students to conduct cross-cultural research, the earlier anthropologists perforce confined their efforts to studying nonliterate peoples, who came to be regarded as special subjects for anthropological investigation. This was logical for the period, though the reasons variously given for exclusive preoccupation with the study of these peoples have not stood the test of time. Thus, for example, the assumption that we must study "savage" folk so as to recover the history of our own development, is, as we have seen, quite untenable. Nonliterate man, we recognize, is not a contemporary ancestor, but like the peoples who have developed writing and a machine technology, stands on his own historical feet. He has travelled a different path, but not one that is on a different level from those trod by the literate folk.

Later reasoning, that the study of "primitive" peoples was important because their cultures were simpler than those of literate societies and could therefore be studied in their entirety as the more complex bodies of convention could not, has greater validity. Yet continuing research has shown that this argument must similarly be taken with considerable reservation. The data, yielded from intensive investigation among nonliterate folk over all the world, made it apparent that the cultures, even of small groups whose customs, on the surface, show what proves to be a deceptive simplicity, can in some respects be most complicated. Involved systems of "primitive" social conventions, of concepts of the universe, of musical forms, of law, have been described. It has become an anthropological truism that no culture can be encompassed by any student; that the way of life of any people can ever be probed deeper and deeper to reveal new facets, or show new values. This is as true when the same student returns again and again to study a given culture, as when different students go at different times to study it.

Nonetheless, the preoccupation of anthropologists with nonliterate peoples has been richly justified by the contributions these researches have yielded. The resultant knowledge of their ways has given depth and perspective to the understanding of human social life. It has afforded new perceptions concerning the character and meaning of the creative process. It is difficult to imagine how the very concept of culture could ever have been developed without a comprehension of the functioning existence of many different bodies of custom, all directed toward the attainment of the same ends. In the same way, cross-cultural research has provided an understanding of the plasticity of man as a social animal, by pointing the degree to which human behavior represents an intricate series of learned responses to the particular setting in which every human organism lives.

Without a knowledge of the possible variants in this setting—that is, of the range of cultures—the earlier view that much of what actually is learned behavior represents instinctive, inborn reactions, a view that did dominate psychological thought at the turn of the century, would have persisted longer than it did persist. In the same way, the lessons taught by the study of nonliterate peoples in stressing the learned nature of culture, has done much to supplement and reinforce the work of the physical anthropologists in reducing the concept of race to its proper dimensions. It afforded a final demonstration, if such was needed, that all human beings, members of the single species we term *homo sapiens,* are one in their ability to take on new ways of life.

As time went on, however, it became apparent that if man is one, and cultures, however complex, are compounded of aspects and elements that achieve the same ends, then to restrict the study of man to peoples without

Summary

writing, was to restrict its findings and limit its usefulness. The story has been traced, in recent chapters, of how anthropology turned from the analysis of "uncontaminated" societies to the study of all nonliterate groups, no matter what the conditions under which they might be living. The concept of literate as against nonliterate, in this context, came to have only secondary significance. An American Indian tribe, living on a reservation in European-type houses, using implements obtained from mail-order concerns, wearing the clothing of their non-Indian neighbors, numbering college graduates among their membership, were seen to be quite as rewarding subjects for study as peoples living in accordance with aboriginal patterns. But the life of these reservation Indians could not be understood in terms of their past customs alone. The ways of their neighbors of European derivation, the social and political relationships between these people and the Indians, the attitudes that determined the contacts between Indian and white, all these had to be taken into account in understanding Indian life as it unfolded under the probing of the investigator.

In the same way, the need to consider the results of contacts between native peoples, and Europeans and other literate folk everywhere in the world, stressed the unity of the study of culture no less than it emphasized the unity of culture itself. Anthropologists found themselves analyzing the ways of New Zealand Maori who had long taken over the outer aspects of the modes of life of their English neighbors. They investigated the living habits of colonies of South African tribesmen in Johannesburg, the customs of Mexicans of Indian descent living in Chicago, the religious beliefs of the descendants of Africans in Rio de Janeiro, where the total setting of the life of these peoples, whether native or intrusive, had to be taken fully into account. It came to be realized that what the dominant culture offers such groups, and what it withholds from them, equally affect their modes of existence and cannot be ignored.

Thus the wheel has come a full turn. Euroamerican culture, the sole subject of investigation for many disciplines, from which anthropologists turned in their quest for comparative materials, has again come into the anthropological field. This time, however, it takes its place as but one of a vast number of ways of life that must be studied by the same methods if the full tale of man's adaptation to his natural setting and to his fellow-men, in terms of his psychological and biological endowment, is to be told. This has operated in two ways. To the student of culture, it has opened the way to achieve full perspective on culture, by studying without the handicap of artificial barriers all forms of custom, whether near at home or in remote regions of the world. To students who are concerned with one aspect of their own culture, or with tracing the events of a single historical stream, it has revealed new vistas, and offered alternatives to explanations that otherwise might be accepted as universals. Other effects of the realization that human culture is a single phenomenon, whose wide range of variation must be considered in generalizing about any phase of human existence, is to be seen in institutional economics, cultural history, in the comparative study of the arts, in new approaches to linguistic phenomena. More than realized, it has provided a philosophical basis for cross-cultural cooperation in a world where space has shrunk and communication spans greater distances than ever before.

The science of man has not achieved this of itself. It has been but a part of a larger movement to which it has responded even as it has exerted its influence in shaping the tendencies present in the total culture to which it belongs. The growth of science, the discovery of new frontiers of knowledge, the development of new values, the establishing of new goals, have all contributed to this movement, in which anthropology has played but one part. What this part has been, and what it may be expected to be in the future, we may next consider.

2

For most of its existence, the problems that anthropologists studied were remote from the concerns of everyday life. Theoretical preoccupation with cultural evolution, or diffusion, or the description of cultural curiosities could hardly be reconciled with problems of conflict and adjustment that were pressing for attention both within expanding cultures and where cultures were in contact. The desire of anthropologists to study only "uncontaminated" ways of life, and a consequent obliviousness to the manifestations of cultural change that went on about them, gave to their findings an esoteric quality not unlike that which characterized the work of laboratory investigations in the exact and natural sciences.

This was science at its purest. Those who studied nonliterate man, and those others who had daily dealings with him, not only had no contact with each other, but avoided one another. Policy regarding native peoples was determined, often with the best intent, without any consultation with anthropologists who were in a position to indicate what the effects of a given measure might be. On the other hand, the anthropologists, the only persons who might speak for the native, or who might by public pronouncement insist that the living habits of native peoples be respected when policies affecting them were being drawn, remained silent. Their search for the fundamental principles of human civilization kept them far removed from the hubbub of public debate, even though, as individuals, they might resent the effects of procedures that were detrimental to the natives they knew.

Thus, for example, two agencies of the United States government concerned with the Indians, both in the city of Washington, were for long years quite out of contact with each other. The Office of Indian Affairs, charged with administering the "wards" of the government, could not understand, much less use the detailed anthropological monographs that issued from the Bureau of American Ethnology, whose mandate was the scientific study of Indian life. The scientists in the Bureau, reciprocally, whose contacts with the Indians were on a human rather than an official basis, resented such policies of the Indian Office as those which took Indian children from their families to place them in boarding schools, where, their tribal language forbidden, they were required to speak only English so that the process of "civilizing" them could be accelerated.

Summary

A similar tale of lack of communication between administrators and students of native affairs obtained elsewhere—between the British Colonial Office and the Royal Anthropological Institute, the French Ministry of Colonies and the Institute of Ethnology, and so on. The anthropologists felt frustrated in the face of the demoralization of natives by ill-advised administrative measures that not only demoralized, but failed to achieve the practical ends for which they had been instituted. Administrators, on the other hand, equally frustrated by the way in which procedures they had been trained to regard as proper proved inapplicable when used in governing peoples of different cultures, reacted against what they regarded as unwarranted attempts of scientists, unschooled in the solution of practical questions, to interfere in what were at best difficult, and at times dangerous, situations.

Anthropological training for Dutch colonial officers destined for service in the East Indies had long been customary, and was the outstanding exception to the picture just drawn. The French, also, in time drew anthropology into the curriculum of their advanced work in the School of Colonial Studies. It was not, however, until the decade between 1925–1935 that "practical anthropology," as it was called in England, or "applied anthropology," as it was called in the United States, began to take on definite form in English speaking countries. In English colonies, especially in Africa, this was encouraged by the enunciation of the doctrine by Lord Lugard of "indirect rule." In the United States, increasing criticism, over a decade, of the blindness of the Indian Service to the human problems of Indian Administration resulted, in 1933, in a revision of existing policy that introduced new measures calculated to preserve, rather than destroy Indian ways of life in achieving the adjustment of these people to the demands of the larger society of which they formed a part.

It became increasingly understood that to implement policies of this kind required knowledge of native customs, and insights into the sanctions of native life, that only experts in the field of cross-cultural investigation could attain. Indirect rule, which placed the immediate direction of tribal affairs in the hands of tribal rulers, under the supervision of Colonial officers, called for knowledge of native law, native rules of land tenure, native political institutions, native social structures that the anthropologically untrained political officer was unequipped to obtain. At first, such officers were "seconded" as government anthropologists after a period of special training, so that they could devote their time to getting the requisite information. Thus men like R. S. Rattray and C. K. Meek and P. A. Talbot were enabled to study the peoples of the Gold Coast and Nigeria, or F. E. Williams to study the peoples of New Guinea. Later, C. E. Mitchell, in East Africa, tried the experiment of creating a team of an academically trained anthropologist and a political officer as a step to the utilization of practical anthropology, after a series of articles in the journal *Africa* in which he debated the problem with Malinowski.

Similarly, in the United States, the conventional anthropological mono-

646

graph afforded but a beginning in amassing the information needed to implement the new policy of the Indian Office. Committed to a program of respect for Indian tribal patterns while integrating Indian societies into the socio-economic matrix of American life in general, the need for information of a kind not available in previous studies took on paramount importance. Here, again, new researches were necessary. The established methods by which anthropologists had been able to penetrate beneath cultural form to cultural sanction were called on to provide the base for implementing policies which tended to place the ordering of Indian affairs in the hands of the Indians. These studies came more and more to be made by professional anthropologists, who either joined the Indian Service, or were attached to it for varying periods of time as consultants and research experts. They encompassed a wide range of topics, far beyond the analysis of those social, economic, and political studies that are the primary interest of the administrator. They ranged into the fields of religion and art, of the effect of the changing milieu on personality structures, as well as studying native patterns of education and other social controls.

This approach spread farther over the Americas. In Mexico, Central America, and South America, government officers in charge of departments touching on the lives of the vast Indian populations there introduced policies of training and using experts in cross-cultural study to an ever-increasing extent. In Mexico, a center was established for the express purpose of furthering the study of indigenous peoples of the Americas, and perfecting techniques of integrating these peoples into the total life of the countries where they live. This movement not only consciously aimed to weld scientific findings and administration, but it took the further step of incorporating the natives in it as well. This has been evidenced by the appointment of Indians as reservation superintendents in the United States, and the growing number of Indian members of government departments dealing with Indian affairs in Latin America.

In the United States, the application of the findings of anthropology to matters of practical concern did not stop with the use of anthropological concepts, techniques, and points of view in attacking the Indian problem. It was argued, rather, that anthropological methods might also be applied to problems of the literate majority groups as well as to those arising out of the adjustment of nonliterates. Problems of personal relations in industry, for example, were studied in an initial effort stimulated by the introduction of anthropology into the Harvard University Graduate School of Business Administration. In 1941, those interested in the study of problems of this kind formed a Society for Applied Anthropology, having as its ends, "The promotion of scientific investigation of the principles controlling the relations of human beings to one another, and the encouragement of the wide application of these principles to practical problems." The journal published by the Society, *Applied Anthropology,* is devoted to "articles having to do with the solution of practical problems of human relations, organization and culture in the fields of political and business administration, psychiatry, social work,

Summary

agriculture, community and regional rehabilitation, and administration of dependent areas."[1]

This approach has been concerned primarily with social relations between individuals who are identified with various strata of contemporary American society. It attempts to assess the manner in which the differing backgrounds of each group contribute to their characteristic reaction to a situation, such as that of labor-management relations within a given plant. Certain techniques derived from cross-cultural analysis are utilized in such studies, especially as they relate to social structures and the interaction between the individuals concerned. In some of these applied anthropological studies, the lines between cultures are crossed, as where problems raised by the presence of immigrant groups receive attention, or situations incident on the evacuation of Japanese to relocation camps at the outset of World War II were analyzed.

On the whole, however, the problems studied by these applied anthropologists are in most cases indistinguishable from those that are conventionally the preoccupation of students in social psychology, sociology, personnel research and related fields. This is of no importance in itself, except insofar as it underscores the concern of this approach to social problems with what, to all intent, is the exclusion of those other cultural phenomena that are included in the total range of human learned behavior. This is understandable, for, as has been pointed out, studies conducted in a single culture permit the student to take for granted much that must be made explicit in other cultures. The danger in such studies is that, as anthropological projects, the lessons of method and the conceptual postulates that derive from cross-cultural research will be lost sight of amid the complexities of the problems within our own society that are under consideration. Nor can we overlook the dangers that the anthropologist concerned with interpersonal relations in industry may fail to take into account the economic stresses that those who deal with industry as a whole accept as primary, and which have long been elementary considerations of specialists in this field.

The development of applied anthropology along all the lines sketched above was accelerated by the circumstance of global warfare. The Axis powers, during the tense pre-war years of the nineteen-thirties, were quite alive to the potentialities of using anthropological techniques in the colonial situation, and were prepared to employ them should hoped-for events bring native peoples under their rule. They therefore instituted training centers for future colonial rulers, in which ethnology and comparative linguistics had a prominent place. The racist dogmas of the Nazi political creed also brought physical anthropologists into the arena of public debate as never before.

That anthropological science was put to use in all these cases is an historic fact that must, however, be placed beside the complementary fact that these distortions were fought by the majority of anthropologists everywhere, in many cases at the expense of liberty and even life. The uses to which those who control power put the findings of science are, unfortunately, beyond the

---

[1] These passages are quoted from a statement of purpose carried in most issues of *Applied Anthropology*.

648

control of scientists. The findings of scientists, when published, are a matter of public record. How to obviate the misuse of these findings, as was done here in the instance of anthropology, or as is done in utilizing the work of the physical scientists for destructive rather than constructive purposes, is a major problem of our society. We can here but note that it applies to anthropology no less than to any other discipline.

Among the powers opposed to the Axis, it was not until the actual onset of war brought problems that anthropologists alone could cope with, that they were called to active participation. Especially in the United States, where experience in large-scale contact with peoples of greatly different ways of life was relatively slight, was it essential to have expert aid in lessening the frictions that would inevitably ensue without the advice of those who were specialists in these matters. Conquest brought the need to govern peoples with differing cultures, whose conventions could not be flaunted. Occupation officers had to be trained to respect customs far different from any, perhaps, they had even heard of. Anthropological linguists were called on to devise methods of teaching men, who had never spoken any language but their own, how to handle a foreign idiom. Native peoples in tropical countries unaffected by the war, as in South and Central America, had to be induced to work to provide raw materials when normal sources of supply were cut off. At home, the problem of adapting the people to unaccustomed items of diet had to be faced, and was faced as a problem of the type which, in this book, is called reenculturation.

The growing sense of urgency at the necessity for instituting some form of supernational control as a measure to prevent future wars but extended the call for anthropological participation in practical affairs. But the implications of this participation are many. They have by no means been realized; the questions they raise are far more numerous than the answers that have been given them. We thus, then, finally turn to some of these questions in assessing the contributions anthropology can be expected to make in a world society.

3

IN MOST of the exact and natural sciences, the realization of the social responsibility of the scientist to see to it that his findings are not misused has added a third tier to the existing structure whose base is fundamental research and teaching, and whose second story is the application, in the engineering sense, of the results of scientific investigation to the solution of practical problems. Anthropologists, together with other scientists, have newly awakened to this sense of social responsibility. But in their case the second story that did not exist for them in earlier years has likewise been added to the single-storied structure of fundamental research they had erected. It follows, then, that the questions raised in this chapter take a special form, and that debate over the issues they present involves the clarification of points that in other disciplines have come to be taken for granted.

Insofar as the basic contribution of anthropology to our knowledge of man

Summary

and his works is concerned, there is little argument except over questions of method and theory. All who accept the fundamental postulates of science and admit the need for scientific analysis of all aspects of the natural world and human experience in it take this for granted. That anthropologists have not studied more peoples, or have not encompassed in their research a greater range of cultures and problems inherent in their study is a matter of lack of available personnel, not of a failure to realize the need, or a desire to study the problems. That the efforts of anthropologists have been effective is apparent in the steady development of the resources of the discipline. This is to be seen in all phases of anthropological science—in the increase in the available data, in refinements in method, and in the constantly growing number of anthropologists equipped to carry on the necessary researches. Quietly, without debate, in centers of learning, in museums over the world, this process goes on. New cultures are under investigation, new problems are being studied, while the training of students in the basic concepts of anthropology makes these known ever more widely, and leads to the more intensive disciplining in anthropological method and theory necessary for those who contemplate making anthropology a career.

This, it must be repeated, is fundamental. But the issues whether or not anthropology should be applied to the solution of practical problems, and how the use of its findings should be controlled, have been the subject of much discussion. The problem of applying anthropology has been made the more complicated by the fact that, as has been indicated, this issue posed for anthropologists, for the first time, the question of pure as against applied science. Now this is a commonplace in the natural and exact disciplines. The biologist does not attempt to do the work of the physician who draws on his laboratory findings. The builder of bridges uses the work of physicists, but would not attempt to carry on their researches. Anthropologists, however, have attempted to do basic research and applied anthropology at the same time, with resulting confusion not only as regards the division of labor, but also as concerns fundamental values, ultimate aims, and the ethics of anthropological science.

Pertinent comment on this last point has been made by Evans-Pritchard, who may be quoted to advantage regarding the problem:

"I cannot see what objection there can be to an anthropologist advocating a policy or helping frame an administrative measure in the light of present anthropological knowledge. In those cases where a considerable amount of anthropological knowledge is required to make a sound judgement about what ought to be done, or how it should be done, he is likely to be the person best qualified to make it. It has been objected that judgements about what ought to be done imply moral values. Naturally they do; but it is surely not required of an anthropologist that he shall have no moral values or shall refrain from using them in situations which demand an ethical standard. What is objectionable is for an anthropologist to allow his particular philosophy to determine his observations, to influence his deductions, and dictate his problems within the field of his own science. Within the anthropological field the anthropologist is, like any other scientist within his particular field of study, bound to exclude moral values because they are methodologically irrelevant. In practical affairs, where they are relevant, he is equally bound to include them. Personally I do not find that any acrobatics are necessary to speak sometimes as an anthropologist within the anthropological field, sometimes as an anthropologist within other fields, such as those of politics and administration, and at most times not as an anthropologist at all. Misunderstandings and self-deception can alike be avoided by making clear not only in what capacity one is speaking but also in what field." [2]

Anthropological contributions to the solution of practical problems can take various forms. Anthropologists can advise, as official members of a government organization, regarding the solution of problems of immediate concern. Questions of native rules of land ownership, or of status prerogatives, or of religious customs may be analyzed by them so as to permit an administrator better to comprehend the complexities of a situation with which he must deal in reaching a decision. Of broader scope is the evidence anthropologists can assemble as regards larger questions of policy, such as the degree to which, in a world economic and political system, varied cultures can be integrated so that a minimum of friction will follow when cultures that have quite different orientations are in intimate contact. On the broadest plane of all, the most immediately related to the cross-cultural research that yields the basic data of anthropology, is the investigation of those general principles of cultural form and dynamics without which the controls needed for world-wide adjustment of different peoples are impossible to achieve.

All these, of course, involve a weighing of ends by the anthropologist— as Evans-Pritchard points out, not as anthropologist but as citizen. There are few anthropologists who work with organs of government who do not have a conviction that in this way they can lessen friction and minimize the demoralization that has too often marked the history of native peoples under Euroamerican rule. The anthropologists who have felt that anthropology has no place in such a system point to the palliatives that take the place of reorientations they feel will alone restore a sense of dignity and worth to natives who have lost the freedom to determine their own destiny. Those who take this position hold that the expropriation of land, the lack of adequate economic return for labor, the reduction of free peoples to conditions of degradation resulted from the play of historical factors, especially of an economic order, that no amount of expert advice could alter. They point, for example, to the spread of the American frontier with the ruthless wiping out of large portions of the Indian population as a prelude to the beggary to which the remaining tribesmen have been reduced.

On the other hand, where policies toward native peoples and minority groups with whom the anthropologist works support the ends in which he can believe, it is understandable that he often feels that he can not only respond when called on by administrative agencies for advice, but is under obligation to make his expert knowledge available to them. Thus in the United States, anthropologists gave their aid to the Indian Bureau when an earlier policy of calculated demoralization of Indians gave way to a policy of building on pre-existing patterns so as to integrate these people into

---

[2] E. E. Evans-Pritchard, 1946, p. 92.

Summary

American life by restoring to them economic independence and cultural autonomy. In similar fashion, the policies of the Mexican government, pointed toward achieving comparable ends, have received similar anthropological support.

It is in the nature of the case that the anthropologist is best fitted to see the strains and stresses of underprivileged groups, or of natives who no longer control their own lives. He sees these stresses and strains from the less pleasant, under-side of the situations in which they live. He sees the problems of the native as no administrator, however gifted, can possibly see them. Where, then, he is in a position to aid in obtaining for the natives he knows some reinstatement of the human rights they have been deprived of, he customarily welcomes the opportunity. As one who has the relationship to native peoples that is peculiarly his by reason of the nature of his work among them, his biases as a human being are usually what they would be expected to be. He is their friend and, where possible, their spokesman in the high places where their voices would not otherwise be heard.

A further objection that is raised to the participation by anthropologists, as such, in the solution of practical issues, must be considered before we leave this aspect of the matter. This concerns the significance, for anthropology itself, of the development of practical or applied anthropology. Does not the diversion of anthropologists to the doing of the tasks applied anthropology has come to have assigned to it take them away from the study of problems of the nature and functioning of culture that should be a first charge against anthropological effort? Evans-Pritchard, who argues for the appointment of anthropologists on the staffs of colonial administrations, leaves no room for doubt as to the relative place of pure as against applied anthropological science: "How should an anthropologist best employ his knowledge and, which comes to very much the same thing, his time?" he asks. "I would suggest that he can best use his knowledge for the purpose for which it was collected, namely the solution of scientific problems. . . . An anthropologist within his own scientific field will use the knowledge he acquires by research to solve anthropological problems and these may have no practical significance whatever. It may be held that it is laudable for an anthropologist to investigate practical problems. Possibly it is, but if he does so he must realize that he is no longer acting within the anthropological field."

He then comes to the heart of the matter: "Of one thing I feel quite certain: that no one can devote himself wholeheartedly to both interests; and I doubt whether anyone can investigate fundamental and practical problems at the same time. Moreover, there is a grave danger that the pressure of political and administrative interests, and the allurements that accompany them, may draw away so many of our small band from the investigation of purely scientific problems that the advance of the science may be seriously retarded."[3] That is, granting that we separate the study of scientific problems from the solution of practical issues, without prejudice to either, it is argued that it is the long view, the research seemingly removed from issues of the day, that will really yield the richest reward to society.

[3] *Op. cit.*, p. 93.

Anthropology in a World Society

"Both administration and science recognize that the more knowledge there is available for use, the better can be its application," runs another discussion of the topic. "Science consists of a graded series of abstractions from the more particular to the more general; it attempts to become more and more general, supposing that the more general a proposition is, the more it takes into account all phenomena, the more valid it is. . . . For example, if one wishes to apply anthropological knowledge to a given Indian tribe, science would hold that knowledge about that tribe is less important than knowledge about all Indians, or generalizations about human nature and society. . . . It is a misapprehension that . . . the anthropologist is primarily concerned with the community he is studying. Typically, and ideally, he is not. He studies that community to gain understanding of all communities, and of culture and society in general." [4] In a word, as a scientist, the anthropologist must achieve that detachment toward his data that is the mark of the scientific search for truth. In this search he must realize, as it has been stated elsewhere, that "the search for truth must come before all else. The debt we owe the society that supports us must be made in terms of long-time payments, in our fundamental contributions toward an understanding of the nature and processes of culture and, through this, to the solution of some of our own basic problems." [5]

4

It is from this point of view that the greatest contribution of anthropology must be envisaged. If a world society is to emerge from the conflict of ethnocentrisms we call nationalism, it can only be on a basis of live and let live, a willingness to recognize the values that are to be found in the most diverse ways of life. [6] Surely, though at times slowly, anthropology has moved toward documenting this position. The fact of cultural variability, the existence of common values expressed in different modes of behavior, the devotion of every people to its way of life—these, and many other aspects of human existence have gradually fallen into place to form a pattern for tolerance and understanding. Just as the physical anthropologists have ceaselessly combatted the concept of racial superiority, so cultural anthropology has, both explicitly and implicitly in the presentation of its data, documented the essential dignity of all human cultures.

Problems of world-wide scope, such as are presented by the need to integrate nonindustrial peoples in a world economic order, must be attacked in terms of cross-cultural analysis. To dismiss a nonindustrial tribal group as incompetent to direct their lives because their ways are different from those of the peoples who dominate the world scene, is to generate resentments that may be resolved only with future bloodshed. Anthropologists are in a position to demonstrate how a people react to foreign control, even as they lie

---

[4] S. Tax, 1945, pp. 26–7, 28.

[5] M. J. Herskovits, 1936, p. 222.

[6] Cf. the "Statement on Human Rights" submitted to the United Nations by the American Anthropological Association, 1947.

Summary

inert and powerless. They can see, all too clearly, how quickly customs can go underground or, if they do not, how demoralization can be the lot of those who experience the frustrations that go with impotence in the face of an assault on deep-seated, accepted values and goals.

Almost a laboratory study of this was afforded in the assault on democracy launched by the fascist powers during the 1930's. Democracy, it was held, was decadent, outworn. The doctrine that the individual is paramount, that the state is the servant of the citizen, was declared to be false and perverted. Rather the individual was held to exist for the state, which had no need to respect the integrity of the personalities of those who did not obey when summoned. Thus the very bases of democratic society were assailed—loudly, tauntingly, and with a challenge to the ultimate test of force. Heavily armed, the totalitarian powers continuously extended their scope, and with concentrated and calculated derision pointed to the indecision of the democracies.

Now it is of the essence of democracy that it is an essentially peaceful way of life; that war is not glorified, but something abhorred, and to be avoided save as a last resort, in self-preservation. How could a democratic philosophy, however, maintain itself in a world where war, not peace, was the declared aim of the most heavily armed nations, with governmental systems geared efficiently to a work of destruction that is the antithesis of the democratic ideal? It was a question insoluble in terms of accepted values, as the resulting bewilderment about proper courses of action revealed. Debates concerning pacifism and nonintervention aligned persons of widely differing points of view on the same side against those with whom ordinarily they would be in agreement. Only the onset of war, the resolution to put conviction to the test of force, cleared the air, and answered the doubts of millions.

This experience gave Euroamericans a taste of the kind of demoralization that had come to be the portion of untold millions of native folk caught in an expanding world polity and world economy. Even the tactics that marked German expansion in Europe paralleled the mechanism by which the spread of Euroamerican political controls in the far parts of the earth were achieved. The Sudeten Germans or the Germans in Poland were the equivalent of the missionary, the trader whose mistreatment by natives brought the army or the warships of the Power that henceforth was to impose its rule on the offending tribesmen. The exercise of force in demonstrating the ability to impose controls impresses any people; just as it did impress the democracies when they were confronted with the fascist nations. Those who are the victims of the exercise of force find it difficult to resist the argument that power represents superiority, just as the democracies found it difficult not to draw a comparable conclusion with respect to those who lost no opportunity to point out that their way of life was superior because it was stronger.

In this instance, the reaction had enough power to repel the threat. Native peoples, opposing cannon with bows and arrows, have had no choice but to submit. Yet the anthropologist, as one who studies the meaning of a way of life to those who live it, need not depart from his devotion to pure science when he points out the dangers to world peace that are inherent in repressed resentments, in the force of rising native nationalisms that are a reaction to

654

the depreciation and suppression of a people's culture. It is his contribution, as the scientific student of cultures other than his own, to underscore the need, in a world society, to give every people cultural autonomy. It is he who must point out that customs foreign to one society may be treasured by another, or stress the importance of the fact that cultural differences are not indications of cultural inferiority. Recognizing that the processes of history are not reversible, he can nonetheless, by his data, demonstrate the psychocultural mechanisms that make inevitable the devotion of every people to their culture, and make plain to statesmen that it is possible to reconcile cultural autonomy with participation in a world economic and political order.

Anthropology can make another, even more far-reaching contribution to this end. The quotation that opens this book, though cast in retrospect, is as true when applied to the present or projected into the future. "Each fresh start on the never-ending quest of *Man as he ought to be*," it will be remembered it runs, "has been the response of theory to fresh facts about *Man as he is*. . . . Meanwhile, the dreams and speculations of one thinker after another—even dreams and speculations which have moved nations and precipitated revolutions—have ceased to command men's reason, when they have ceased to accord with their knowledge." Irresistibly, the knowledge about man and his works that anthropologists have amassed has continued to force the revision of our ideas about the value of human ways of living, and to reorient policy and the implementation of policy.

Cultural relativism, which whether in implicit or explicit form dominates the thinking behind moves toward building a world society, exemplifies the point made in our quotation. It is a philosophy out of which arises mutual respect based on the facts that throw into bold relief the hard core of *similarities* between cultures that have been consistently overlooked in favor of the emphasis laid on cultural differences. These facts show that every society has values and imposes restraints that are worthy of appreciation, even though they differ from one's own. Cultural relativism, which stresses the universals in human experience as against ethnocentric concepts of absolute values, in no wise gives over the restraints that every system of ethics exercises over those who live in accordance with it. To recognize that right, and justice, and beauty may have as many manifestations as there are cultures is to express tolerance, not nihilism. As anthropology's greatest contribution, this position puts man yet another step on his quest of what he ought to be, in the light of the facts, as we know them, about what in his unity, no less than in his diversity, he is.

BIBLIOGRAPHIES
AND INDEX

Literature Cited

THE following list contains the titles of those books and papers that have actually been cited in the preceding pages. For each item the name of the author, date of publication, title of book or article, and the place of its publication are given. Where more than one title published by the same author in a given year is included, the items are to be identified by the letter following the year, as "1942a," "1942b," etc.

ACKERKNECHT, ERWIN H., 1942: "Primitive Medicine and Culture Pattern." *Bulletin of the History of Medicine*, Vol. XII, pp. 545–74.
ALLEE, W. C., 1938: *The Social Life of Animals*. New York.
AMERICAN ANTHROPOLOGICAL ASSOCIATION, EXECUTIVE BOARD, 1947: "Statement on Human Rights." *American Anthropologist*, Vol. XLIX, pp. 539–43.

BACON, ELIZABETH, 1946: "A Preliminary Attempt to Determine the Culture Areas of Asia." *Southwestern Journal of Anthropology*, Vol. II, pp. 117–32.
BACON, ELIZABETH and HUDSON, A. E., 1945: "Asia (Ethnology)." *Encyclopaedia Britannica*, Vol. II, pp. 523–5.
BALFOUR, H., 1895: *The Evolution of Decorative Art*. London.
BARBEAU, M., 1930: "Totem Poles, a Recent Native Art of the Northwest Coast of America." *Geographical Review*, Vol. XX, pp. 258–72.
BARNETT, H. G., 1940: "Culture Processes." *American Anthropologist*, Vol. XLII, pp. 21–48.
   1942: "Invention and Culture Change." *American Anthropologist*, Vol. XLIV, pp. 14–30.
BARRETT, S. A., 1925: "The Cayapa Indians of Ecuador." *Indian Notes and Monographs, Heye Foundation*, No. 40, Parts I and II. New York.
BARTLETT, F. C., 1937: "Psychological Methods and Anthropological Problems." *Africa*, Vol. X, pp. 401–20.
BARTON, R. F., 1919: "Ifugao Law." *University of California Publications in American Archaeology and Ethnology*, Vol. XV, No. 1, pp. 1–186.
   1922: "Ifugao Economics." *University of California Publications in American Archaeology and Ethnology*, Vol. XV, No. 5, pp. 385–446.
BASCOM, W. R., 1939: "The Legacy of an Unknown Nigerian Donatello." *London Illustrated News*, Vol. CIV, pp. 592–4.
   1944: "The Sociological Role of the Yoruba Cult-Group." *Memoir 63, American Anthropological Association*.
   1947: *Ponape* (MS.)
BASTIDE, ROGER, 1946: "Contribuição ao Estudo do Sincretismo Católico-fetichista." *Estudos Afro-Brasileiros* (Sociologia No. 1), Vol. LIX, Fac. de

Bibliographies

Filosofia, Ciencias e Letras, Univ. de São Paulo, pp. 11–44. São Paulo, Brazil.

BATESON, G., 1935: "Culture Contact and Schismogenesis." *Man,* Vol. xxxv, *199,* pp. 178–83.

1936: *Naven.* Cambridge.

BEALS, R. L., 1946: "Cherán: a Sierra Tarascan Village." *Smithsonian Institution, Institute of Social Anthropology,* Publication No. 2.

BENEDICT, R., 1923: "The Concept of the Guardian Spirit in North America." *Memoir 29, American Anthropological Association.*

1934: *Patterns of Culture.* Boston and New York.

1938: "Continuities and Discontinuities in Cultural Conditioning." *Psychiatry,* Vol. i, pp. 161–7.

BIDNEY, D., 1944: "On the Concept of Culture and Some Cultural Fallacies." *American Anthropologist,* Vol. xlvi, pp. 30–44.

BLACKWOOD, B., 1935: *Both Sides of Buka Passage.* Oxford.

BLEEK, D. F., 1929: "Bushman Folklore." *Africa,* Vol. ii, pp. 302–12.

BLOOMFIELD, L., 1933: *Language.* New York.

BOAS, F., 1897: "The Social Organization and Secret Societies of the Kwakiutl Indians." *Report of U. S. National Museum for 1895,* pp. 311–738.

1898: "The Northwestern Tribes of Canada, Twelfth and Final Report." *British Association for the Advancement of Science, Proceedings,* pp. 40–61.

1900: "The Jesup North Pacific Expedition." *Verhandlungen des VII. Internationalen Geographen-Kongressen in Berlin,* 1899, pp. 678–85. Berlin.

1908: "Decorative Designs of Alaskan Needle Cases." *Proceedings, U. S. National Museum,* Vol. xxxiv, pp. 321–44. (Reprinted in F. Boas, *Race, Language and Culture,* pp. 564–92.)

1909–10: "Tsimshian Mythology." *31st Annual Report, Bureau of American Ethnology,* pp. 27–1037.

1911: "Introduction." *Handbook of American Indian Languages,* Bulletin 40, Part 1, Bureau of American Ethnology, pp. 5–83.

1914: "Mythology and Folk-tales of the North American Indians." *Journal of American Folklore,* Vol. xxvii, pp. 374–410. (Reprinted in *Race, Language and Culture,* pp. 451–90.)

1916: "On the Variety of Lines of Descent Represented in a Population." *American Anthropologist,* Vol. xviii, pp. 1–9.

1920: "The Methods of Ethnology." *American Anthropologist,* Vol. xxii, pp. 311–21. (Reprinted in *Race, Language and Culture,* pp. 281–9.)

1924: "Evolution or Diffusion?" *American Anthropologist,* Vol. xxvi, pp. 340–4. (Reprinted in *Race, Language and Culture,* pp. 290–4.)

1927: *Primitive Art.* Oslo.

1930a: "Anthropology." *Encyclopedia of the Social Sciences,* Vol. ii, pp. 73–110.

1930b: "Some Problems of Methodology in the Social Sciences," in *The New Social Science,* (L. D. White, Ed.), pp. 84–98. Chicago.

1936: "Die Individualität primitiver Kulturen," in *Reine und Angewandte Soziologie* (volume in honor of F. Tönnies). Leipzig.

1938: (Ed.), *General Anthropology.* New York.

1940: *Race, Language and Culture.* New York.

BOGORAS, W., 1904–09: "The Chuckchee." *Memoir* xi, *American Museum of Natural History.*

1918: "Tales of Yukaghir, Lamut and Russianized Natives of Eastern Siberia."

Literature Cited

Anthropological Papers, American Museum of Natural History, Vol. xx, Part I, pp. 3–148.

BOTKIN, B. A., 1944: *A Treasury of American Folklore.* New York.

BREUIL, L'ABBÉ H., 1936: "Oeuvres d'Art Magdaléniennes de Laugerie Basse (Dordogne)." *Actualités Scientifiques et Industrielles,* No. 382.

BRITISH MUSEUM, 1910: *Handbook to the Ethnographical Collections.* Oxford.

BROWN, J. F., 1936: *Psychology and the Social Order.* New York.

BUCK, P. H. (Te Rangi Hiroa), 1934: "Mangaian Society." *Bulletin 122, B. P. Bishop Museum.*

1938: "Ethnology of Mangareva." *Bulletin 157, B. P. Bishop Museum.*

BUNZEL, R., 1929: *The Pueblo Potter.* New York.

BURKITT, MILES C., 1933: *The Old Stone Age.* New York and Cambridge.

CAMERON, NORMAN, 1938: "Functional Immaturity in the Symbolization of Scientifically Trained Adults." *Journal of Psychology,* Vol. VI, pp. 161–75.

CAMPBELL, A. A., 1943: "St. Thomas Negroes, A Study in Personality and Culture." *Psychology Monographs,* Vol. LV, No. 5 (Whole No. 253).

CARPENTER, C. R., 1934: "A Field Study of the Behavior and Social Relations of Howling Monkeys." *Comparative Psychology Monographs,* Vol. X, No. 2 (No. 48).

CARTER, ISABEL GORDON, 1928: "Reduction of Variability in an Inbred Population." *American Journal of Physical Anthropology,* Vol. XI, pp. 457–77.

CASSIRER, E., 1944: *An Essay on Man.* New Haven.

CHAPPLE, E. D., 1940: "Measuring Human Relations." *Genetic Psychology Monographs,* Vol. XXII.

CHILDE, C. G., 1946: *What Happened in History.* New York.

CODRINGTON, R. H., 1891: *The Melanesians, Studies in their Anthropology and Folk-Lore.* Oxford.

COLE, F. C., 1922: "The Tinguian." *Publication 209, Field Museum, Anthropological Series,* Vol. XIV, No. 2.

COLE, F. C. and DEUEL, T., 1937: *Rediscovering Illinois.* Chicago.

COLE, G. D. H., 1933: "Introduction" to K. Marx, *Capital,* pp. xi–xxix, London (Everyman's Library).

COLLINS, H. B., JR., 1937: "Culture Migrations and Contacts in the Bering Sea Region." *American Anthropologist,* Vol. XXXIX, pp. 375–84.

COOPER, J. M., 1941: "Temporal Sequences and the Marginal Cultures." *Catholic University of America, Anthropological Series,* No. 10.

1942: "Areal and Temporal Aspects of Aboriginal South American Culture." *Primitive Man,* Vol. XV, pp. 1–38.

1946: "The Yahgan." *Handbook of South American Indians.* Bulletin 143, Bureau of American Ethnology, Vol. I, pp. 81–106. Washington.

COX, MARIAN ROALFE, 1892: *Cinderella.* Publications of the Folk-lore Society, Vol. XXXI. London.

CRAWLEY, E., 1927: *The Mystic Rose* (new ed.). New York.

DALZEL, A., 1793: *A History of Dahomy.* London.

DANIEL, G. E., 1943: *The Three Ages.* Cambridge.

DAVIDSON, L. J., 1943: "Moron Stories." *Southern Folklore Quarterly,* Vol. VII, pp. 101–4.

DEACON, A. B., 1934: *Malekula, a Vanishing People in the New Hebrides.* London.

DE LAGUNA, G. A., 1927: *Speech, its Function and Development.* New Haven.

Bibliographies

1942: "Cultural Relativism and Science." *Philosophical Review*, Vol. LI, pp. 141–66.

DENNIS, WAYNE, 1940: *The Hopi Child*. New York.

DEWEY, JOHN, 1939: *Freedom and Culture*. New York.

DIGBY, ADRIAN, 1938: "The Machines of Primitive People." *Man*, Vol. XXXVIII, 50, pp. 57–8.

DIXON, ROLAND B., 1916: *Oceanic Mythology* (*The Mythology of All Races*, Vol. IX.). Boston.

1928: *The Building of Cultures*. New York.

DOBZHANSKY, TH., 1941: *Genetics and the Origin of Species*. New York.

1944: "On Species and Races of Living and Fossil Man." *American Journal of Physical Anthropology*, Vol. II (n.s.), pp. 251–65.

DRIBERG, J., 1930: *People of the Small Arrow*. New York.

1935: "The 'Best Friend' among the Didinga." *Man*, Vol. XXXV, 110, pp. 101–2.

DRIVER, H. E. and KROEBER, A. L., 1932: "Quantitative Expression of Cultural Relationships." *University of California Publications in American Archaeology and Ethnology*. Vol. XXXI, No. 4, pp. 211–56.

DRUCKER, PHILIP, 1939: "Rank, Wealth, and Kinship in Northwest Coast Society." *American Anthropologist*, Vol. XLI, pp. 55–65.

DU BOIS, C., 1936: "The Wealth Concept as an Integrative Factor in Tolowa-Tututni Culture," in *Essays in Anthropology Presented to A. L. Kroeber*, pp. 49–65. Berkeley.

1944: *The People of Alor*. Minneapolis.

DUNDAS, C., 1913: "History of Kitui." *Journal of the Royal Anthropological Institute*, Vol. XLIII, pp. 480–549.

DURKHEIM, E., 1915: *The Elementary Forms of the Religious Life*. London.

DYK, W. (Ed.), 1938: *Son of Old Man Hat*. New York.

EGGAN, F., 1937: "Historical Changes in the Choctaw Kinship System." *American Anthropologist*, Vol. XXXIX, pp. 34–52.

1941: "Some Aspects of Culture Change in the Northern Philippines." *American Anthropologist*, Vol. XLIII, pp. 11–18.

EINSTEIN, CARL, 1920: *Negerplastik*. Munich.

ENGELS, FRIEDRICH, 1909: *The Origin of the Family, Private Property, and the State*. Chicago.

ERIKSON, E. H., 1943: "Observations on the Yurok: Childhood and World Image." *University of California Publications in American Archaeology and Ethnology*, Vol. XXXV, No. 10, pp. 257–302.

ESSENE, F., 1942: "Culture Element Distributions: XXI. Round Valley." *Anthropological Records*, Vol. VIII, No. 1, pp. 1–96.

EVANS-PRITCHARD, E. E., 1937: *Witchcraft, Oracles and Magic among the Azande*. Oxford.

1940: *The Nuer*. Oxford.

1946: "Applied Anthropology." *Africa*, Vol. XVI, pp. 92–8.

FENTON, WILLIAM N., 1941: "Iroquois Suicide: A Study in the Stability of a Culture Pattern." *Anthropological Papers*, No. 14 (Bureau of American Ethnology, Bulletin No. 128) *Smithsonian Institution*, pp. 80–137.

FIRTH, RAYMOND, 1929: *Primitive Economics of the New Zealand Maori*. London.

1939: *Primitive Polynesian Economy*. London.

Literature Cited

FIRTH, ROSEMARY, 1943: "Housekeeping among Malay Peasants." *Monographs on Social Anthropology, University of London,* No. 7.

FLIGELMAN, F., 1932: "Moral Vocabulary of an Unwritten Language." *Anthropos,* Vol. XXVII, pp. 213–48.

FORDE, C. D., 1934: *Habitat, Society and Economy, a Geographical Introduction to Anthropology.* London.

    1937: "Land and Labour in a Cross River Village, Southern Nigeria." *Geographical Journal,* Vol. XC, pp. 24–51.

FORTES, M., 1938: "Culture-Contact as a Dynamic Process." *Memorandum* XV, *International Institute of African Languages and Cultures,* pp. 60–91. London.

FORTES, M. and S. L., 1936: "Food in the Domestic Economy of the Tallensi." *Africa,* Vol. IX, pp. 237–76.

FORTES, M. and EVANS-PRITCHARD, E. E. (Eds.), 1940: *African Political Systems.* London.

FORTUNE, R. F., 1939: "Arapesh Warfare." *American Anthropologist,* Vol. XLI, pp. 22–41.

FOSTER, G. M., 1942: "A Primitive Mexican Economy." *Monographs of the American Ethnological Society,* Vol. V.

FRAZER, SIR J. G., 1910: *Totemism and Exogamy.* (4 vols.) London.

    1935: *The Golden Bough: The Magic Art and the Evolution of Kings.* (2 vols.) (3rd ed.) New York.

FREYRE, G., 1946: *The Masters and the Slaves.* New York.

FREUD, S., 1919: *Totem and Taboo.* London.

GARROD, DOROTHY A. E., 1938: "The Upper Palaeolithic in the Light of Recent Discovery." *Proceedings of the Prehistoric Society,* Vol. IV, pp. 1–26.

GATES, R. RUGGLES, 1944: "Phylogeny and Classification of Hominids and Anthropoids." *American Journal of Physical Anthropology,* Vol. II (n.s.), pp. 279–92.

GAYTON, A. H., 1946: "Culture-Environment Integration: External References in Yokuts Life." *Southwestern Journal of Anthropology,* Vol. II, pp. 252–68.

GIFFORD, E. W. and KROEBER, A. L., 1937: "Culture Element Distributions: IV. Pomo." *University of California Publications in American Archaeology and Ethnology,* Vol. XXXV, No. 4, pp. 117–254.

GILFILLAN, S. COLUM, 1935: *The Sociology of Invention.* Chicago.

GIST, NOEL P., 1940: "Secret Societies: A Cultural Study of Fraternalism in the United States." *University of Missouri Studies,* Vol. XV, No. 4.

GLUCKMAN, MAX, 1943: "Essays on Lozi Land and Royal Property." *Rhodes-Livingstone Papers,* No. 10.

GOLDENWEISER, A. A., 1910: "Totemism, an Analytical Study." *Journal of American Folklore,* Vol. XXIII, pp. 179–293. (Reprinted in Goldenweiser, 1933, pp. 213–332.)

    1922: *Early Civilization.* New York.

    1933: *History, Psychology and Culture.* New York.

GOLDFRANK, E., 1943: "Historic Change and Social Character: A Study of the Teton Dakota." *American Anthropologist,* Vol. XLV, pp. 67–83.

    1945: "Changing Configurations in the Social Organization of a Blackfoot Tribe during the Reserve Period." *Monographs of the American Ethnological Society,* No. VIII.

Bibliographies

GOODENOUGH, FLORENCE L. and ANDERSON, JOHN E., 1947: "Psychology and Anthropology: Some Problems of Joint Import for the Two Fields." *Southwestern Journal of Anthropology*, Vol. III, pp. 5–14.

GOODWIN, G., 1942: *The Social Organization of the Western Apache*. Chicago.

GREENBERG, J., 1941: "Some Aspects of Negro-Mohammedan Culture-Contact among the Hausa." *American Anthropologist*, Vol. XLIII, pp. 51–61.
　1946: "The Influence of Islam on a Sudanese Religion." *Monographs of the American Ethnological Society*, Vol. X.

GREGORY, WM. K., 1929: *Our Face from Fish to Man*.

HADDON, A. C., 1894: *The Decorative Art of British New Guinea*. Dublin.
　1914: *Evolution in Art* (new ed.). London and New York.
　1925: *The Races of Man and their Distribution*. New York.

HAINES, C. G. and B. M., 1926: *Principles and Problems of Government*. New York.

HALLOWELL, A. I., 1928: "Recent Changes in the Kinship Terminology of the St. Francis Abenaki." *Atti de* XXII *Congresso Internationale degli Americanisti* (Rome), pp. 97–145.
　1942: *The Role of Conjuring in Saulteaux Society*. Philadelphia.
　1945a: "Sociopsychological Aspects of Acculturation," in *The Science of Man in the World Crisis* (R. Linton, Ed.), pp. 171–200. New York.
　1945b: "The Rorschach Technique in the Study of Personality and Culture." *American Anthropologist*, Vol. XLVII, pp. 195–210.
　1947: "Some Psychological Characteristics of the Northeastern Indians." *Papers of the Peabody Foundation for Archaeology*, Vol. III, pp. 195–225.

HAMBLY, W. D., 1937: "Source Book for African Anthropology." *Publication Nos. 394 and 396, Field Museum, Anthropology Series*, Vol. XXVI (2 parts).

HARRIS, J. S., 1944: "Some Aspects of the Economics of Sixteen Ibo Individuals." *Africa*, Vol. XIV, pp. 302–35.

HARRISON, H. S., 1925: "The Evolution of the Domestic Arts." *Handbook of the Horniman Museum, Part 1* (2nd ed.). London.
　1926a: "Inventions: Obtrusive, Directional and Independent." *Man*, Vol. XXVI, 74, pp. 117–21.
　1926b: "Variations and Mutations in Invention." *Man*, Vol. XXVI, 101, pp. 154–8.
　1930a: "Evolution in Material Culture." *Report of the Ninety-Eighth Meeting, British Association for the Advancement of Science*. London. pp. 137–59.
　1930b: "Opportunism and the Factors of Invention." *American Anthropologist*, Vol. XXXII, pp. 106–25.

HERSKOVITS, F. S., 1934: "Dahomean Songs." *Poetry*, Vol. XLV, pp. 75–7.
　1935: "Dahomean Songs for the Dead." *The New Republic*, Vol. LXXXIV, No. 103, p. 95.

HERSKOVITS, M. J., 1924a: "A Preliminary Consideration of the Culture Areas of Africa." *American Anthropologist*, Vol. XXVI, pp. 50–63.
　1924b: "On the Negro-White Population of New York City: The Use of the Variability of Family Strains as an Index of Heterogeneity or Homogeneity." *Proceedings*, XXI International Congress of Americanists, pp. 5–12. The Hague.
　1926: "The Cattle Complex in East Africa." *American Anthropologist*, Vol. XXVIII, pp. 230–72, 361–80, 494–528, 633–64.

Literature Cited

1928: *The American Negro, a Study in Racial Crossing.* New York.

1930: "The Culture Area of Africa." *Africa,* Vol. III, pp. 59–77.

1934: "Freudian Mechanisms in Primitive Negro Psychology," in *Essays Presented to C. G. Seligman,* pp. 75–84. London.

1936: "Applied Anthropology and the American Anthropologists." *Science,* Vol. LXXXIII, pp. 215–22.

1937: *Life in a Haitian Valley.* New York.

1938a: *Acculturation, the Study of Culture Contact.* New York.

1938b: *Dahomey, an Ancient West African Kingdom* (2 vols.). New York.

1940: *The Economic Life of Primitive Peoples.* New York.

1941: *The Myth of the Negro Past.* New York.

1945a: "The Processes of Cultural Change," in *The Science of Man in the World Crisis.* (R. Linton, Ed.), pp. 143–70. New York.

1945b: "Problem, Method and Theory in Afroamerican Studies." *Afroamérica,* Vol. I, pp. 5–24.

1945c: *Backgrounds of African Art.* Denver.

1946: "Folklore after a Hundred Years: A Problem in Redefinition." *Journal of American Folklore,* Vol. LIX, pp. 89–100.

HERSKOVITS, M. J. and F. S., 1934: *Rebel Destiny, among the Bush Negroes of Dutch Guiana.* New York.

1936: *Suriname Folklore.* New York.

1947: *Trinidad Village.* New York.

HERZOG, G., 1938: "Music in the Thinking of the American Indian." *Peabody Bulletin,* May, pp. 1–5.

HILL, W. W., 1939: "Stability in Culture and Pattern," *American Anthropologist,* Vol. XLI, pp. 258–60.

HOBHOUSE, L. T., WHEELER, G. C. and GINSBERG, M., 1915: *The Material Culture and Social Institutions of the Simpler Peoples.* London.

HODGEN, M. T., 1936: *The Doctrine of Survivals.* London.

1942: "Geographical Distribution as a Criterion of Age." *American Anthropologist,* Vol. XLIV, pp. 345–68.

1945: "Glass and Paper: an Historical Study of Acculturation." *Southwestern Journal of Anthropology,* Vol. I, pp. 466–97.

HOEBEL, E. A., 1940: "The Political Organization and Law-Ways of the Comanche Indians." *Memoir 54, American Anthropological Association.*

1946: "Law and Anthropology." *Virginia Law Review,* Vol. XXXII, pp. 835–54.

HOGBIN, H. I., 1937–38: "Social Advancement in Guadalcanal." *Oceania,* Vol. VIII, pp. 289–305.

1938–39: "Tillage and Collection, a New Guinea Economy." *Oceania,* Vol. IX, pp. 127–51, 286–325.

1946–47a: "Puberty to Marriage: a Study of the Sexual Life of the Natives of Wogeo, New Guinea." *Oceania,* Vol. XVI, pp. 185–209.

1946–47b: "A New Guinea Childhood: from Weaning till the Eighth Year in Wogeo." *Oceania,* Vol. XVI, pp. 275–96.

HOIJER, HARRY, 1944: "Peoples and Cultures of the Southwest Pacific." *The Southwest Pacific and the War,* pp. 31–68. Berkeley and Los Angeles.

HOLMES, W. H., 1886: "Origin and Development of Form and Ornament in Ceramic Art." *4th Annual Report, Bureau of American Ethnology,* pp. 443–65.

HSÜ, FRANCIS L. K., 1945: "Influence of South-Seas Emigration on Certain Chinese Provinces." *Far Eastern Quarterly,* Vol. V, pp. 47–59.

Bibliographies

HUNTER, M., 1936: *Reaction to Conquest*. London.
HUNTINGTON, ELLSWORTH, 1945: *Mainsprings of Civilization*. New York.

JENKS, A. E., 1900: "The Wild Rice Gatherers of the Upper Lakes." *19th Annual Report, Bureau of American Ethnology*, pp. 1019–1137.
JUNOD, HENRI A., 1927: *The Life of a South African Tribe*. 2nd ed., 2 vols. London.

KARDINER, A., 1939: *The Individual and his Society*. New York.
   1944: "Elaboration" of "The Problem," in *Alor*, by C. Du Bois, pp. 6–13.
KEESING, F., 1939: "The Menomini Indians of Wisconsin." *Memoirs, American Philosophical Society*, Vol. x.
KLIMEK, S., 1935: "Culture Element Distributions: I. The Structure of California Indian Cultures." *University of California Publications in American Archaeology and Ethnology*, Vol. XXXVII, No. 1, pp. 1–70.
KLUCKHOHN, C., 1941: "Patterning as Exemplified in Navaho Culture," in *Language, Culture and Personality; Essays in Memory of Edward Sapir*, pp. 109–30. Menasha (Wisc.).
KLUCKHOHN, C. and MOWRER, O. M., 1944: " 'Culture and Personality': a Conceptual Scheme." *American Anthropologist*, Vol. XLVI, pp. 1–29.
KÖHLER, W., 1925: *The Mentality of Apes*. New York.
KRIEGER, H. W., 1932: "Design Areas in Oceania." *Proceedings, U. S. National Museum*, Vol. LXXIX, pp. 1–53.
KROEBER, A. L., 1917: "The Superorganic." *American Anthropologist*, Vol. XIX, pp. 163–213.
   1919: "On the Principle of Order in Civilization as Exemplified by Changes of Fashion." *American Anthropologist*, Vol. XXI, pp. 235–63.
   1923: *Anthropology*. New York.
   1928: "Sub-Human Cultural Beginnings." *Quarterly Review of Biology*, Vol. III, pp. 325–8.
   1931: "The Culture-Area and Age-Area Concepts of Clark Wissler," in *Methods in Social Science, a Case Book* (S. A. Rice, Ed.), pp. 248–65.
   1936: "Culture Element Distributions: III. Area and Climax." *University of California Publications in American Archaeology and Ethnology*, Vol. XXXVII, No. 3, pp. 101–16.
   1939: "Cultural and Natural Areas of Native North America." *University of California Publications in American Archaeology and Ethnology*, Vol. XLVIII, pp. 1–242.
   1940: "Stimulus Diffusion." *American Anthropologist*, Vol. XLII, pp. 1–20.
KROEBER, A. L. and RICHARDSON, JANE, 1940: "Three Centuries of Women's Dress Fashions, a Quantitative Analysis." *Anthropological Records*, Vol. v, No. 2.
KROGMAN, W. M., 1945: "The Concept of Race," in *The Science of Man in the World Crisis* (R. Linton, Ed.), pp. 38–62. New York.
KROPOTKIN, P., 1916: *Mutual Aid, a Factor of Evolution*. New York.
KUO, Z. Y., 1930: "The Genesis of the Cat's Response to the Rat." *Journal of Comparative Psychology*, Vol. XI, pp. 1–30.

LANG, ANDREW, 1887: *Myth, Ritual, and Religion*. London.
LEAKEY, L. S. B., 1934: *Adam's Ancestors*. New York.
LEIGHTON, DOROTHEA and KLUCKHOHN, C., 1947: *Children of the People, the Navaho Individual and his Development*. Cambridge, Mass.
LESSER, A., 1933: *The Pawnee Ghost Dance Hand Game, a Study of Cultural Change*. New York.

666

Literature Cited

Lévy-Bruhl, Lucien, 1923: *Primitive Mentality*. New York.
    1926: *How Natives Think*. London.
Lewin, K., 1936: *Principles of Topological Psychology*. New York.
Lewis, Oscar, 1942: "The Effects of White Contact upon Blackfoot Culture, with Special Reference to the Role of the Fur Trade." *Monographs of the American Ethnological Society*, No. VI.
Li An-Che, 1937: "Zuni: Some Observations and Queries." *American Anthropologist*, Vol. XXXIX, pp. 62–76.
Lindblom, K. G. (Ed.), 1926—: *Smärre Meddelanden*. Stockholm, Statens Ethnografiska Museum.
Lindgren, E. J., 1938: "An Example of Culture Contact without Conflict: Reindeer Tungus and Cossacks of Northwestern Manchuria." *American Anthropologist*, Vol. XL, pp. 605–62.
Linton, R., 1924: "Totemism in the A. E. F." *American Anthropologist*, Vol. XXVI, pp. 296–300.
    1928: "Culture Areas of Madagascar." *American Anthropologist*, Vol. XXX, pp. 363–90.
    1936: *The Study of Man*. New York.
    1940: (Ed.), *Acculturation in Seven American Indian Tribes*. New York.
    1945: *The Cultural Background of Personality*. New York.
Llewellyn, K. N. and Hoebel, E. A., 1941: *The Cheyenne Way*. Norman (Okla.).
Loeb, E. M., 1935: *Sumatra, its History and People*. Vienna.
Lowie, R. H., 1920: *Primitive Society*. New York.
    1924: *Primitive Religion*. New York.
    1927: *The Origin of the State*. New York.
    1935: *The Crow Indians*. New York.
Lundborg, H. and Linders, F. J., 1926: *The Racial Characteristics of the Swedish Nation*. Stockholm.
Luomala, Katherine, 1946: "Polynesian Literature." *Encyclopedia of Literature* (J. T. Shipley, Ed.), pp. 772–89.
von Luschan, F., 1919: *Die Altertümer von Benin*. Berlin and Leipzig.
Lynd, Robert S. and Helen M., 1929: *Middletown, a Study in Contemporary American Culture*. New York.

MacCurdy, G. G., 1924: *Human Origins* (2 vols.). New York.
MacGregor, G., 1935: "Notes on the Ethnology of Pukapuka." *B. P. Bishop Museum, Occasional Papers*, Vol. XI, No. 6.
Maine, Sir H. S., 1888: *Lectures on the Early History of Institutions*. New York.
    1890: *Popular Government*. London.
Maitland, F. W., 1911: "The Body Politic," in *Collected Papers*, Vol. III, pp. 285–303.
Malinowski, B., 1922: *Argonauts of the Western Pacific*. London.
    1926: Article "Anthropology." *Encyclopaedia Britannica*, supplementary Vol. I to 13th edition, pp. 131–42.
    1927a: *Sex and Repression in Savage Society*. London.
    1927b: *The Father in Primitive Psychology*. New York.
    1929: *The Sexual Life of Savages* (2 vols.). London.
    1944: *A Scientific Theory of Culture, and Other Essays*. Chapel Hill (N.C.).
    1945: *The Dynamics of Culture Change*. New Haven.
Mandelbaum, D. G., 1936: "Friendship in North America." *Man*, Vol. XXXVI, 272, pp. 205–6.

Bibliographies

1939: "Agricultural Ceremonies among Three Tribes of Travancore." *Ethnos,* Vol. IV, pp. 114–28.

1941: "Culture Change among the Nilghiri Tribes." *American Anthropologist,* Vol. XLIII, pp. 19–26.

MARETT, R. R., 1912: *Anthropology.* London.

1914: *The Threshold of Religion.* New York.

MARTIN, PAUL S., QUIMBY, GEORGE I. and COLLIER, DONALD, 1947: *Indians before Columbus.* Chicago.

MARTIN, R., 1928: *Lehrbuch der Anthropologie* (3 vols.). Jena.

MASON, J. A., 1927: "Eskimo Pictorial Art." *Museum Journal,* Vol. XVIII, pp. 248–83.

MASON, OTIS T., 1894: *Woman's Share in Primitive Culture.* New York.

1895: *The Origins of Invention.* London and New York.

MAUSS, MARCEL, 1923–24: "Essai sur le Don, forme archaique de l'échange." *L'Année Sociologique* (n.s.), Vol. I, pp. 30–186.

MAYR, E., 1942: *Systematics and the Origin of Species.* New York.

McGREGOR, J. H., 1938: "Human Origins and Early Man," in *General Anthropology* (F. Boas, Ed.), New York, pp. 24–94.

McKERN, W. C., 1922: "Functional Families of the Patwin." *University of California Publications in American Archaeology and Ethnology,* Vol. XIII, No. 7, pp. 235–58.

MEAD, MARGARET, 1928: *Coming of Age in Samoa.*

1939: *From the South Seas.* New York.

1940: "The Mountain Arapesh. II. Supernaturalism." *Anthropological Papers, American Museum of Natural History,* Vol. XXXVII, Part III, pp. 317–451.

MEKEEL, S., 1943: "A Short History of the Teton-Dakota." *North Dakota Historical Quarterly,* Vol. X, pp. 137–205.

MENGHIN, O., 1931: *Weltgeschichte der Steinzeit.* Vienna.

MÉTRAUX, A., 1946a: "Ethnography of the Chaco." *Handbook of South American Indians.* Bulletin 143, Bureau of American Ethnology, Vol. I, pp. 197–370.

1946b: "South American Indian Literature." *Encyclopedia of Literature* (J. T. Shipley, Ed.), pp. 851–63.

MILLER, N. E. and DOLLARD, J., 1941: *Social Learning and Imitation.* New Haven.

MOFOLO, THOMAS, 1931: *Chaka, an Historical Romance.* London.

MONTAGU, M. F. ASHLEY, 1945: *An Introduction to Physical Anthropology.* Springfield (Ill.).

MORANT, G. M., 1939: *The Races of Central Europe.* London.

MORANT, G. M. *et al,* 1938: "Report on the Swanscombe Skull." *Journal of the Royal Anthropological Institute,* Vol. LXVIII, pp. 17–98.

MORGAN, L. H. *Ancient Society.* Chicago, n.d.

MORRIS, B., 1943: *The Aesthetic Process.* (Northwestern University Studies in the Humanities, No. 8). Evanston, Ill.

MORTON, DUDLEY J., 1927: "Human Origin. Correlation of Previous Studies of Primate Feet and Posture with other Morphologic Evidence." *American Journal of Physical Anthropology,* Vol. X, pp. 173–203.

MOUNTFORD, CHARLES P., 1946: "Earth's Most Primitive People." *National Geographic Magazine,* Vol. LXXXIX, pp. 89–112.

MOVIUS, HALLAM L., JR., 1942: *The Irish Stone Age.* Cambridge.

1944: "Early Man and Pleistocene Stratigraphy in Southern and Eastern Asia." *Papers of the Peabody Museum,* Vol. XIX, No. 3.

MÜHLMANN, W., 1938: *Methodik der Völkerkunde.* Stuttgart.

668

Literature Cited

MURDOCK, G. P., 1945: "The Common Denominator of Cultures," in *The Science of Man in the World Crisis* (R. Linton, Ed.), pp. 123–42. New York.

MURDOCK, G. P., *et al.*, 1939: *Guía para la investigación etnológica* (A. Ramadés, tr.). Tucumán.

1945: "Outline of Cultural Materials." *Yale Anthropological Studies*, Vol. II (2nd ed.).

MYRES, SIR J. L., 1916: "The Influence of Anthropology on the Course of Political Science." *University of California Publications in History*, Vol. IV, No. 1.

NADEL, S. F., 1942a: *A Black Byzantium. The Kingdom of Nupe in Nigeria.* London.

1942b: "The Hill Tribes of Kadero." *Sudan Notes and Records*, Vol. XXV, pp. 37–79.

1945: "Notes on Beni Amer Society." *Sudan Notes and Records*, Vol. XXVI, pp. 1–44.

NELSON, N. C., 1932: "The Origin and Development of Material Culture." *Sigma Xi Quarterly*, Vol. XX, pp. 102–23.

1938: "Prehistoric Archaeology," in *General Anthropology* (F. Boas, Ed.). pp. 146–237. New York.

NORDENSKIÖLD, E., 1919: "An Ethno-Geographical Analysis of the Material Culture of Two Indian Tribes in the Gran Chaco." *Comparative Ethnographic Studies*, I. Gothenburg.

O'NEALE, L. M., 1932: "Yurok-Karok Basket Weavers." *University of California Publications in American Archaeology and Ethnology*, Vol. XXXII, No. 1, pp. 1–182.

OPLER, M. E., 1938: "Personality and Culture: a Methodological Suggestion for the Study of their Interrelations." *Psychiatry*, Vol. I, pp. 217–20.

1941: *An Apache Life-Way.* Chicago.

1945: "Themes as Dynamic Forces in Culture." *American Journal of Sociology*, Vol. LI, pp. 198–206.

1946: "An Application of the Theory of Themes in Culture." *Journal of the Washington Academy of Sciences*, Vol. XXXVI, pp. 137–66.

ORTIZ, F., 1947: *Cuban Counterpoint: Tobacco and Sugar.* New York.

OSGOOD, CORNELIUS, 1940: "Ingalik Material Culture." *Yale University Publications in Anthropology*, No. 22. New Haven.

PARSONS, E. C., 1918: "Nativity Myth at Laguna and Zuñi." *Journal of American Folklore*, Vol. XXXI, pp. 256–63.

1936: *Mitla, Town of the Souls.* Chicago.

1939: *Pueblo Indian Religion* (2 vols.). Chicago.

PATAI, RAPHAEL, 1947: "On Culture Contact and its Working in Modern Palestine." *Memoir 67, American Anthropological Association.*

PECHUËL-LOESCHE, E., 1907: *Volkskunde von Loango.* Stuttgart.

PERISTIANY, J. G., 1939: *The Social Institutions of the Kipsigis.* London.

PERRY, W. J., 1923: *The Children of the Sun.* London.

PETRIE, W. M. FLINDERS, 1912: *The Revolutions of Civilization.* New York.

PETTITT, GEORGE A., 1946: "Primitive Education in North America." *University of California Publications in American Archaeology and Ethnology*, Vol. XLIII, pp. 1–182.

POWDERMAKER, HORTENSE, 1933: *Life in Lesu.* London.

Bibliographies

PROVINSE, J. H., 1937: "Cooperative Ricefield Cultivation among the Siang Dyaks of Central Borneo." *American Anthropologist,* Vol. xxxix, pp. 77–102.

RADCLIFFE-BROWN, A. R., 1931: "The Social Organization of Australian Tribes." *Oceania Monographs,* No. 1.
    1932: "The Present Position of Anthropological Studies." *Report of the Centenary Meeting, British Association for the Advancement of Science.* London. pp. 140–71.
    1940: "Preface" to *African Political Systems* (M. Fortes and E. E. Evans-Pritchard, Eds.), London.

RADIN, P., 1914: "A Sketch of the Peyote Cult of the Winnebago." *Journal of Religious Psychology,* Vol. iii, pp. 1–22.
    1937: *Primitive Religion, its Nature and Origin.* New York.

RAMOS, A., 1940: *O Negro Brasileiro* (2nd ed., rev.). São Paulo.

RATTRAY, R. S., 1923: *Ashanti.* London.
    1929: *Ashanti Law and Constitution.* Oxford.

RATZEL, FRIEDRICH, 1896: *The History of Mankind* (2 vols.). London.

RAUM, O., 1940: *Chaga Childhood.* London.

RAY, VERNE F., 1942: "Culture Element Distributions: xxii. Plateau." *Anthropological Records,* Vol. viii, No. 2, pp. 99–257.

REDFIELD, R., 1939: "Culture Contact without Conflict." *American Anthropologist,* Vol. xli, pp. 514–17.
    1941: *The Folk Culture of Yucatan.* Chicago.
    1947: "The Folk Society." *American Journal of Sociology,* Vol. lii, pp. 293–308.

REDFIELD, R., LINTON, R. and HERSKOVITS, M. J., 1936: "Memorandum on the Study of Acculturation." *American Anthropologist,* Vol. xxxviii, pp. 149–52.

REICHARD, G. A., 1933: *Melanesian Design* (2 vols.). New York.
    1943: "Imagery in an Indian Vocabulary." *American Speech,* Vol. xviii, pp. 96–102.

REISNER, G. A., 1923: *Excavations at Kerma.* (Harvard African Studies, Vols. v and vi). Cambridge.

RICHARDS, A. I., 1939: *Land, Labour and Diet in Northern Rhodesia.* London.

RIVERS, W. H. R., 1906: *The Todas.* London.
    1910: "The Genealogical Method of Anthropological Inquiry." *The Sociological Review,* Vol. iii, pp. 1–12.
    1913: "Survival in Sociology." *The Sociological Review,* Vol. vi, pp. 293–305.
    1914: *The History of Melanesian Society* (2 vols.). Cambridge.

ROBERTS, H. H., 1925: "A Study of Folk Song Variants Based on Field Work in Jamaica." *Journal of American Folklore,* Vol. xxxviii, pp. 148–216.
    1936: "Musical Areas in Aboriginal North America." *Yale University Publications in Anthropology,* No. 12.

ROQUETTE-PINTO, E., 1925: "On the Ñanduti of Paraguay." xxi *Congrès International des Americanistes,* pp. 103–12. Gothenburg.

ROSCOE, J., 1911: *The Baganda.* London.

SAIT, EDWARD M., 1938: *Political Institutions: a Preface.* New York.

SAPIR, E., 1916: "Time Perspective in Aboriginal American Culture, A Study in Method." *Memoir 90* (No. 13, Anthropological Series), *Canadian Geological Survey.* Ottawa.
    1921: *Language.* New York.

Literature Cited

1927: "The Unconscious Patterning of Behavior in Society," in *The Unconscious, a Symposium* (E. S. Dummer, Ed.), pp. 114–42. New York.

1933: "Personality." *Encyclopedia of the Social Sciences*, Vol. XII, pp. 85–8. New York.

1934: "The Emergence of the Concept of Personality in a Study of Culture." *Journal of Social Psychology*, Vol. V, pp. 408–15.

1938: "Why Cultural Anthropology Needs the Psychiatrist." *Psychiatry*, Vol. I, pp. 7–12.

SAPIR, E. and SWADESH, M., 1939: *Nootka Texts*. (Wm. Dwight Linguistic Series, Ling. Society of America). Philadelphia.

SAYCE, R. U., 1933: *Primitive Arts and Crafts*. Cambridge.

SCHAPERA, I., 1930: *The Khoisan Peoples of South Africa*. London.

1938: *A Handbook of Tswana Law and Custom*. London.

1940: *Married Life in an African Tribe*. London.

SCHJELDERUP-EBBE, T., 1935: "Social Behavior of Birds," in *A Handbook of Social Psychology* (C. Murchison, ed.). Worcester (Mass.), pp. 947–72.

SCHMIDT, W., 1931: *The Origin and Growth of Religion*. New York.

1939: *The Cultural Historical Method of Ethnology* (S. A. Sieber, tr.). New York.

SCHNEIRLA, T. C., 1946: "Problems in the Biopsychology of Social Organization." *Journal of Abnormal and Social Psychology*, Vol. XLI, pp. 385–402.

SCHULTZ, A., 1936: "Characters Common to Higher Primates and Characters Specific for Man." *Quarterly Review of Biology*, Vol. XI, pp. 259–83, 425–55.

SELIGMAN, C. G., 1932: "Anthropological Perspective and Psychological Theory." *Journal of the Royal Anthropological Institute*, Vol. LXII, pp. 193–228.

SHERIF, M., 1936: *The Psychology of Social Norms*. New York.

SKINNER, H. D., 1921: "Culture Areas in New Zealand." *Journal of the Polynesian Society*, Vol. XXX, pp. 71–8.

SMITH, SIR G. ELLIOT, 1924: *Elephants and Ethnologists*. London.

1927: "The Diffusion of Culture," in *Culture, the Diffusion Controversy*, pp. 9–25. New York.

SMITH, J. RUSSELL, 1925: *North America*. New York.

SMITH, M. W., 1940: *The Puyallup-Nisqually*. New York.

SPECK, F. G., 1914: "The Double-Curve Motive in Northeastern Algonkian Art." *Memoir 42* (No. 1, Anthropological Series), *Canadian Geological Survey*. Ottawa.

1935: *Naskapi*. Norman (Okla.).

SPENCER, B. and GILLEN, F. J., 1904: *The Northern Tribes of Central Australia*. London and New York.

SPENCER, HERBERT, 1896: *The Principles of Sociology* (3rd ed.). New York.

SPENGLER, O., 1927: *The Decline of the West*. New York.

SPICER, E. H., 1940: *Pascua, a Yaqui Village in Arizona*. Chicago.

SPIER, L., 1921: "The Sun Dance of the Plains Indians: Its Development and Diffusion." *Anthropological Papers, American Museum of Natural History*, Vol. XVI, part 7, pp. 451–527.

SPOEHR, A., 1947: "Changing Kinship Systems." *Anthropological Series, Field Museum of Natural History*, Vol. XXXIII, No. 4, pp. 159–235.

STAYT, H. A., 1931: *The Bavenda*. London.

STERN, B. J., 1927: *Social Factors in Medical Progress*. New York.

STEWARD, JULIAN, 1947: "American Culture History in the Light of South America." *Southwestern Journal of Anthropology*, Vol. III.

Bibliographies

STEWART, OMER C., 1942: "Culture Element Distributions: XVIII. Ute-Southern Paiute." *Anthropological Records*, Vol. VI, No. 4, pp. 231–360.

STURTEVANT, E. H., 1947: *An Introduction to Linguistic Science*. New Haven.

TAX, S., 1939: "Culture and Civilization in Guatemalan Societies." *Scientific Monthly*, Vol. XLVIII, pp. 463–7.
    1945: "Anthropology and Administration." *América Indígena*, Vol. V, pp. 21–33.

TEGGART, F. J., 1941: *Theory and Processes of History*. Berkeley.

THOMPSON, STITH, 1929: *Tales of the North American Indians*. Cambridge (Mass.).
    1932–36: *Motif-Index of Folk-Literature*. (F F Communications Nos. 106–9, 116–17; Indiana University Studies, Vols. XIX–XXIII)

TOYNBEE, A. J., 1934–39: *A Study of History* (6 vols.). London.

TREMEARNE, A. J. N., 1912: "Notes on the Kagoro and other Nigerian Head-Hunters." *Journal of the Royal Anthropological Institute*, Vol. XLIII, pp. 136–99.

TSCHOPIK, H., JR., 1946: "The Aymara." *Handbook of South American Indians*. Bulletin 143, Bureau of American Ethnology, Vol. 2, pp. 501–73.

TUETING, LAURA T. (Thompson, Laura), 1935: "Native Trade in Southeast New Guinea." *B. P. Bishop Museum, Occasional Papers*, Vol. XI, No. 15.

TURNEY-HIGH, H. H., 1942: "The Practice of Primitive Warfare." *University of Montana, Publications in Social Science*, No. 2.

TYLOR, E. B., 1874: *Primitive Culture* (2 vols.). (1st American, from the 2nd English ed.). New York.
    1881: *Anthropology*. New York.
    1889: "On a Method of Investigating the Development of Institutions . . ." *Journal of the Royal Anthropological Institute*, Vol. XVIII, pp. 245–69.

VAN GENNEP, A., 1920: *La Formation des Légendes*. Paris.

VEBLEN, THORSTEIN, 1915: *The Theory of the Leisure Class*. New York.

VILLA R., ALFONSO, 1945: *The Maya of East Central Quintana Roo* (Publication 559, Carnegie Institution of Washington). Washington.

VOEGELIN, C. F., 1935: "Tübatulabal Grammar." *University of California Publications in American Archaeology and Ethnology*, Vol. XXXIV, No. 2, pp. 55–190.

VOEGELIN, ERMINIE W., 1942: "Culture Element Distributions: XX. Northeast California." *Anthropological Records*, Vol. VII, No. 2, pp. 47–251.
    1946: "North American Native Literature." *Encyclopedia of Literature* (J. T. Shipley, Ed.), pp. 706–21. New York.

WAGLEY, C., 1941: "Economics of a Guatemalan Village." *Memoir 58, American Anthropological Association*.

WALLIS, W. D., 1930: *Culture and Progress*. New York.

WARD, L., 1919: *Pure Sociology*. New York.

WARNER, W. L. and LUNT, PAUL S., 1941: *The Social Life of a Modern Community*. New Haven.

WATKINS, M. H., 1943: "The West African 'Bush' School." *American Journal of Sociology*, Vol. XLVIII, pp. 666–74.

WEIDENREICH, F., 1943: "The Skull of Sinanthropus Pekinensis." *Palaeontologica Sinica*, new series D, No. 10, whole series 127.

Literature Cited

1945a: "The Puzzle of Pithecanthropus," in *Science and Scientists in the Netherlands Indies*. New York, pp. 380–90.

1945b: "Giant Early Man from Java and South China." *Anthropological Papers, American Museum of Natural History*, Vol. XL, Part 1, pp. 1–134.

1946: *Apes, Giants and Man*. Chicago.

WERNER, A., 1930: *Structure and Relationship of African Languages*. London.

WHITE, L., 1945a: "History, Evolutionism and Functionalism: Three Types of Interpretation of Culture." *Southwestern Journal of Anthropology*, Vol. I, pp. 221–48.

1945b: "Diffusion vs. Evolution: an Anti-Evolutionist Fallacy." *American Anthropologist*, Vol. XLVII, pp. 339–56.

1946: "Kroeber's Configurations of Culture Growth." *American Anthropologist*, Vol. XLVIII, pp. 78–93.

WHITING, J. W. M., 1941: *Becoming a Kwoma*. New Haven.

WILLEMS, EMÍLIO, 1944: "Acculturation and the Horse Complex among German-Brazilians." *American Anthropologist*, Vol. XLVI, pp. 153–61.

1946: *A aculturação dos Alemães no Brasil*. São Paulo.

WILLIAMS, F. E., 1923: "The Vailala Madness and the Destruction of Native Ceremonies in the Gulf Division." *Territory of Papua, Anthropological Report No. 4*, Port Moresby.

1930: *Orokaiva Society*. London.

1934: "The Vailala Madness in Retrospect," in *Essays in Honour of C. G. Seligman*, pp. 369–79. London.

1936: *Papuans of the Trans-Fly*. Oxford.

1940: *Drama of Orokolo*. Oxford.

WISSLER, C., 1922: *The American Indian*. 2nd ed. New York.

1923: *Man and Culture*. New York.

1926: *The Relation of Nature to Man in Aboriginal America*. New York.

WITTFOGEL, F., 1946: "General Introduction" to "History of Chinese Society, Liao (907–1125)" by K. Wittfogel and Feng Chia-Shêng. *Transactions, American Philosophical Society*, Vol. XXXVI, pp. 1–35.

YERKES, R. M. and A. W., 1935: "Social Behavior in Infrahuman Primates," in *Handbook of Social Psychology* (C. Murchison, Ed.). Worcester (Mass.). pp. 973–1033.

YOSELOFF, T. and STUCKEY, L. (Eds.), 1944: *The Merry Adventures of Till Eulenspiegel*. New York.

ZEUNER, F. E., 1944: "Review of the Chronology of the Palaeolithic Period." *Conference on the Problems and Prospects of European Archaeology* (*Occasional Papers, No. 6, University of London Institute of Archaeology*), pp. 14–19.

ZUCKERMAN, S., 1932: *The Social Life of Monkeys and Apes*. New York.

A List of Selected Titles

THIS list is in three parts. In the first part are given the titles of anthropological periodicals which carry articles wholly or partly in English. They are important because it is in such journals that announcements of new discoveries, discussions of theory, and reviews of books are found. The second part is comprised of American and English monograph series, wherein are contained much of the working materials for comparative studies, particularly reports of the results of field-work, presented in the detail necessary for scientific analysis. Finally, there is given a suggested list of readings from the literature of anthropology in English. This is a series of books that might be regarded as a good working library for those interested in doing further reading on the subject. Some of the titles are also in the first bibliography, since they have been cited in the pages of this book; there are others, however, which have not been used there, but should find a place in any list such as this.

I. PERIODICALS

Journal of the Royal Anthropological Institute (1872)
Folklore (1878)
American Anthropologist (1888)
Journal of American Folklore (1888)
Journal of the Polynesian Society (1892)
Journal de la Société des Américanistes (1895)
Man (1900)
Anthropos (1906)
International Journal of American Linguistics (1917)
American Journal of Physical Anthropology (1918)
Sudan Notes and Records (1918)
Man in India (1921)
Africa (1928)
Primitive Man (1928)
Human Biology (1929)
Oceania (1930)
American Antiquity (1935)
Ethnos (1936)
Applied Anthropology (1941)
América Indígena (1941)
African Studies (1942)
Acta Americana (1943)
Southwestern Journal of Anthropology (1945)
Afroamérica (1945)

A List of Selected Titles

II. MONOGRAPH SERIES

American Anthropological Association, *Memoirs*
American Folklore Society, *Memoirs*
American Ethnological Society, *Monographs*
American Museum of Natural History, New York, *Anthropological Papers*
Bernice P. Bishop Museum, Honolulu, *Bulletins* and *Memoirs*
Columbia University, *Contributions to Anthropology*
Chicago Natural History Museum, *Fieldiana, Anthropology* (earlier entitled *Anthropological Series*, Field Museum of Natural History)
International Congress of Americanists, *Proceedings*
International Congress of the Anthropological and Ethnological Sciences, *Reports*
Peabody Museum of American Archaeology and Ethnology, Harvard University, *Papers*
Philadelphia Anthropological Society, *Publications*
Public Museum of the City of Milwaukee, *Bulletins*
Rhodes-Livingstone Institute, *Papers*
Royal Anthropological Institute, London, *Occasional Papers*
Smithsonian Institution, Bureau of American Ethnology, *Annual Reports* and *Bulletins*
University of California, *Publications in American Archaeology and Ethnology*
University of California, *Anthropological Records*
University of London, *Monographs on Social Anthropology*
University of Washington, *Publications in Anthropology*
Viking Fund, *Publications in Anthropology*
Yale University, *Anthropological Studies*
Yale University, *Publications in Anthropology*

III. BOOKS AND MONOGRAPHS

1. GENERAL WORKS

BOAS, F., *Race, Language and Culture*, New York, 1940
BOAS, F. (ed.), *General Anthropology*, New York, 1938
GOLDENWEISER, A. A., *Early Civilization*, New York, 1922
HADDON, A. C., *History of Anthropology*, London, 1910
LINTON, R., *The Study of Man*, New York, 1936
LINTON, R. (ed.), *The Science of Man in the World Crisis*, New York, 1945
LOWIE, R. H., *The History of Ethnological Theory*, New York, 1937
MARETT, R. R., *Anthropology*, London, 1912
MURDOCK, G. P., *Our Primitive Contemporaries*, New York, 1934
TYLOR, E. B., *Anthropology*, New York, 1881
WISSLER, C., *Man and Culture*, New York, 1923

2. BIOLOGICAL BACKGROUNDS

ALLEE, W. C., *The Social Life of Animals*, New York, 1938
HOOTON, A. E., *Up From the Ape* (2nd ed.), New York, 1947
HOWELLS, W. W., *Mankind So Far*, New York, 1944
KÖHLER, W., *The Mentality of Apes*, New York, 1925
WEIDENREICH, F., *Apes, Giants and Men*, Chicago, 1946
ZUCKERMAN, S., *The Social Life of Apes and Monkeys*, New York, 1932

3. PREHISTORY (OLD WORLD AND NEW)

BURKITT, M. C., *The Old Stone Age*, New York, 1933
CHILDE, V. G., *The Dawn of European Civilization*, New York, 1939

675

Bibliographies

COLE, F. C. and DEUEL, T., *Rediscovering Illinois*, Chicago, 1937
MacCURDY, G. G., *Human Origins* (2 vols.), New York, 1924
MARTIN, PAUL, QUIMBY, GEORGE I. and COLLIER, DONALD, *Indians Before Columbus*, Chicago, 1947
SHETRONE, H. C., *The Mound Builders*, New York, 1930

4. RACE AND PHYSICAL TYPE

BARZUN, JACQUES, *Race, A Study in Modern Superstition*, New York, 1937
BOAS, F., *The Mind of Primitive Man* (2nd ed.), New York, 1938
DUNN, L. C. and DOBZHANSKY, TH., *Heredity, Race and Science*, New York, 1946
HADDON, A. C., *The Races of Man and Their Distribution*, New York, 1925
KLINEBERG, OTTO, *Race Differences*, New York, 1935
MONTAGU, M. F. ASHLEY, *Man's Most Dangerous Myth: The Fallacy of Race* (2nd ed.), New York, 1925

5. LINGUISTICS

BLOOMFIELD, L., *Language*, New York, 1933
SAPIR, E., *Language*, New York, 1935
STURTEVANT, E. H., *An Introduction to Linguistic Science*, New Haven, 1947

6. THE ORDERING OF SOCIETY

FIRTH, R., *Primitive Polynesian Economy*, London, 1939
FORDE, C. DARYLL, *Habitat, Society and Economy*, London, 1934
FORTES, M. and EVANS-PRITCHARD, E. E., *African Political Systems*, London, 1940
HERSKOVITS, M. J., *The Economic Life of Primitive Peoples*, New York, 1940
LLEWELLYN, K. N. and HOEBEL, E. A., *The Cheyenne Way*, Norman, Okla., 1941
LOWIE, R. H., *Primitive Society*, New York, 1920
RATTRAY, R. S., *Ashanti Law and Constitution*, Oxford, 1929
RICHARDS, A. I., *Land, Labour and Diet in Northern Rhodesia*, London, 1939
RIVERS, W. H. R., *Kinship and Social Organization*, London, 1914
SCHAPERA, I., *A Handbook of Tswana Law and Custom*, London, 1939

7. THE INDIVIDUAL IN HIS CULTURE

DENNIS, W., *The Hopi Child*, New York, 1940
DU BOIS, C., *The People of Alor*, Minneapolis, 1944
DYK, W. (ed.), *Son of Old Man Hat*, New York, 1938
KARDINER, A., *The Individual and his Society*, New York, 1939
LEIGHTON, DOROTHEA and KLUCKHOHN, CLYDE, *Children of the People*, Cambridge, Mass., 1947
MALINOWSKI, B., *Sex and Repression in Savage Society*, London, 1927
OPLER, M. E., *An Apache Life-Way*, Chicago, 1941
RAUM, O. F., *Chaga Childhood*, London, 1940
SACHS, WULF, *Black Hamlet*, London, 1937; New York, 1947

8. RELIGION

EVANS-PRITCHARD, E. E., *Witchcraft, Oracles and Magic among the Azande*, Oxford, 1937
HOWELLS, W. W., *The Heathens, Primitive Man and his Religions*, New York, 1948
LÉVY-BRUHL, L., *The "Soul" of the Primitive*, New York, 1931
LOWIE, R. H., *Primitive Religion*, New York, 1924
MARETT, R. R., *The Threshold of Religion*, New York, 1914

676

A List of Selected Titles

PARSONS, E. C., *Pueblo Indian Religion* (2 vols.), Chicago, 1939
RADIN, PAUL, *Primitive Man as Philosopher*, New York, 1927
RIVERS, W. H. R., *Medicine, Magic and Religion*, London, 1924
UNDERHILL, RUTH, *Papago Indian Religion*, New York, 1946

9. THE ARTS

BOAS, F., *Primitive Art*, Oslo, 1927
DIXON, R. B., *Oceanic Mythology*, Boston, 1916
LANG, ANDREW, *Myth, Ritual and Religion* (2 vols.), New York, 1887
THOMPSON, STITH, *Tales of the North American Indians*, Cambridge, Mass., 1929
THOMPSON, STITH, *The Folktale*, New York, 1946
WERNER, ALICE, *Myths and Legends of the Bantu*, London, 1933
WILLIAMS, F. E., *Drama of Orokolo*, Oxford, 1940

10. CULTURAL DYNAMICS—EVOLUTION, DIFFUSION, ACCULTURATION

DIXON, R. B., *The Building of Culture*, New York, 1928
GOLDENWEISER, A. A., *History, Psychology and Culture*, New York, 1922
HERSKOVITS, M. J., *Acculturation*, New York, 1938
HERSKOVITS, M. J., *The Myth of the Negro Past*, New York, 1941
KROEBER, A. L., *Configurations of Culture Growth*, Berkeley, Cal., 1944
LINTON, R. (ed.), *Acculturation in Seven American Indian Tribes*, New York, 1940
MALINOWSKI, B., *The Dynamics of Culture Change*, New Haven, 1945
MORGAN, L. H., *Ancient Society*, Chicago, n.d.
PARSONS, E. C., *Mitla, Town of the Souls*, Chicago, 1936
PERRY, W. J., *Children of the Sun*, London, 1923
REDFIELD, R., *The Folk Culture of Yucatan*, Chicago, 1941
SCHMIDT, W., *The Cultural Historical Method of Ethnology* (S. A. Sieber, tr.), New York, 1939
TEGGART, F. J., *Theory and Processes of History*, Berkeley, Cal., 1941
WISSLER, C., *The American Indian* (2nd ed.), New York, 1923

11. DESCRIPTIVE WORKS

A. NORTH AND SOUTH AMERICA

BIRKET-SMITH, K., *The Eskimos*, London, 1936
JENNESS, DIAMOND, *People of the Twilight*, New York, 1928
KLUCKHOHN, C. and LEIGHTON, D., *The Navaho*, Cambridge, Mass., 1946
LOWIE, R. H., *The Crow Indians*, New York, 1945
MEANS, P. A., *Ancient Civilizations of the Andes*, New York, 1931
SMITH, MARIAN, *The Puyallup-Nisqually*, New York, 1940
SPECK, F. G., *Naskapi*, Norman, Okla., 1935
STEWARD, JULIAN H. (ed.), *Handbook of South American Indians*, Bulletin 143, Bureau of American Ethnology, Washington, Vols. 1 and 2, 1946
THOMPSON, ERIC, *Mexico Before Cortez*, New York, 1933
WISDOM, C., *The Chorti Indians of Guatemala*, Chicago, 1943

B. AFRICA

CULWICK, A. F. and G. M., *Ubena of the Rivers*, London, 1935
EVANS-PRITCHARD, E. E., *The Nuer*, Oxford, 1940
FORTES, M., *The Dynamics of Clanship Among the Tallensi*, London, 1945
HERSKOVITS, M. J., *Dahomey* (2 vols.), New York, 1935
NADEL, S. F., *A Black Byzantium*, London, 1942

677

Bibliographies

ROSCOE, J., *The Baganda*, London, 1911
SCHAPERA, I., *The Khoisan Peoples of South Africa*, London, 1930
STAYT, H. A., *The Bavenda*, London, 1931

C. OCEANIA AND AUSTRALIA

BLACKWOOD, BEATRICE, *Both Sides of Buka Passage*, Oxford, 1935
FIRTH, R., *We, the Tikopia*, New York, 1936
KABERRY, PHYLLIS, *Aboriginal Woman*, London, 1939
MALINOWSKI, B., *Argonauts of the Western Pacific* (2 vols.), London, 1922
SPENCER, B. and GILLEN, F. J., *The Arunta*, London, 1927
WILLIAMS, F. E., *Papuans of the Trans-Fly*, London, 1936
WILLIAMSON, R. W., *Social and Political Systems of Central Polynesia* (3 vols.),
    Cambridge, England, 1924
WILLIAMSON, R. W., *Religious and Cosmic Beliefs of Central Polynesia* (2 vols.),
    Cambridge, England, 1933

D. ASIA

BOGORAS, W., *The Chuckchee* (3 vols.), New York, 1904–09
COLE, F. C., *The Peoples of Malaysia*, New York, 1945
ELWIN, V., *The Baiga*, London, 1939
HUTTON, J. H., *The Sema Nagas*, London, 1921
RIVERS, W. H. R., *The Todas*, London, 1906
SELIGMAN, C. G. and B. Z., *The Veddas*, Cambridge, England, 1911

Index

Abevillian period of prehistory, 121–2
Abnormality, concept of, as culturally defined, 66–7
Absolutes, philosophical, distinguished from universals, 76–7
  stress laid on, in enculturation of Euro-americans, 77–8
Acceptance, into animal societies, conditions for achieving, 35
Accident, definition of, 588
Accident, historic, see Historic accident
Acculturation, and diffusion, delimitation of, 636–7
  Arab-Jewish, in Palestine, 550–1
  as re-enculturation, 539
  as synonym for enculturation, 527
  defined, by Social Science Research Council Committee, 523
  in methodological terms, 525
  early use of, 523
  of Philippine tribes, regularity of changes under, 587
  reservations to definition of, 524–5
  situations of, in which borrowing occurs, 533–4
  studies of, among American Indians, 540
  use of, with evaluative connotations, 527–8
  varied meanings assigned to, 527
Acculturation studies, place of, in analysis of cultural dynamics, 525–6
Acculturation study, of California Indian tribes, 617
Accuracy, spurious, need to guard against, in studies of cultural variation, 578
Ackerknecht, E. H., quoted, 224
Acting, of West Indians, in telling folktales, 433
Adaptation, linguistic, of Africans, 613
Adhesion, cultural, hypothesis of, 264
Adjustment, achievement of, through spirit possession, in African and New World Negro societies, 67
  function of religion and art in furthering, 347

Adjustment (*continued*)
  individual, role of early enculturation in, 44
  of individual, to culture, need for study of, 56–7
  to group, circular character of, 641
  social setting of, 45
Administrators, earlier lack of communication by, with anthropologists, 646
Admiralty Island art, analysis of stylistic aspects of, 399
Africa, complexity of political institutions of, 332
  culture-areas of, 191–2
  differences in area distributions of cultural aspects in, 185
  importance of rhythm in music of, 437
  power-concept in religions of, 358–9
  protohuman remains recovered from, 107, 108
  relations between wives in polygynous households of, 295
  ubiquity of iron-working among tribes of, 264–5
  variation in native political structures of, 338–40
Africa, West, reflection of basic sanctions of cultures of, in folklore, 420
African deities, identification of, with Catholic saints, by New World Negroes, 553–4
Africanisms, scale of intensity of, as used in classifying New World Negro cultures, 614–15
Africanthropus njarasensis, 107
Age-area hypothesis, validity of, in reconstruction of history, 518–20
Agriculture, as focal aspect of Palestine Jewish culture, 550
  of natives of Wogeo, 269–71
  of Siang Dyak, 269
Alaskan Eskimo needle-cases, analysis of designs on, 395
Algonkian Indians, design elements of, 409–10
  psychological study of, as "laboratory" approach to cultural analysis, 617

Index

Allee, W. C., cited, 32
quoted, 31, 32, 33, 34
Allied powers, use of anthropology by, 649
Alternatives, cultural, as expression of cultural variation, 544
concept of, 576
Ambivalence, derivation of concept of, from anthropological data used by Freud, 47
America, problem of Polynesian contacts with, 508–9
American Anthropological Association, "Statement on Human Rights," 653
American Folklore Society, categories of folklore to be studied in America as set up by, 422
American Indians, see Indians
Americas, special archaeological problems of, 129
Anatomy, relationship of, to physical anthropology, 12
Anderson, J. E. and Goodenough, F. L., cited, 58
Animal tales, Old World, variation in forms and functions of, 414–15
Animatism, hypothesis of, as earliest form of religion, 349
Animism, as "minimum definition of religion," 348
as part of world-view of peoples, 353
forms of, in machine culture, 350
incidence of, in human societies, 350
persuasiveness of belief in, 353
phenomena held to substantiate belief in, 350–1
Ankermann, B., cited, 512
Anthropogeography, development of, 156
Anthropological methods, use of, in study of problems of industry, 647
Anthropologists, basic tasks of, 652–3
contributions of, to solution of practical problems, 651–2
earlier emphasis by, on technology as against economics, 268
Anthropology, and psychology, interdisciplinary training in, 58
as historical science, 461, 639
as pure and applied science, 653
basic contribution of, 655
changes in orientations of, 642
cultural, development of, 5–6
non-validity of definition of, as study of "primitive" peoples, 80
relationship of, to history, philosophy, and psychology, 12
to humanistic disciplines, 10–12

Anthropology (continued)
to social sciences, 9–10
scope of, 1–3
special techniques in study of, 6–7
customary differentiation of, from psychology, 564
defined, 5
diminution of ethnocentrism in, 627–8
divisions of, 1
early, as pure science, 645
growth in scientific resources of, 650
historical and generalizing sub-disciplines of, 611
impersonality of approach of, to culture, 564
nature of problems studied by, 6
physical, relationship of, to biological sciences, 12
place of classification in, 596
primary aims of, 653
relationship of, to psychology, 45
social, 9
special methodological problems of, 643
synthesizing character of, 12–13
unity of, 2, 5, 13
Apache, educational methods of, 315–17
extended family among, 302
monogamy and polygamy among, 293–4
reaction of women among, to polygyny, 294–5
themes in culture of, 225
Apes, anthropoid, present distribution of, 99
Apollonian, as culture-type, 51
Apo rite, of Ashanti, psychological significance of, 59
Applied anthropology, acceleration of development of, by World War II, 648
debate concerning, 651–2
Applied Anthropology, 647
Arapesh, warfare among, 51–2
Archaeologists, reconstruction of prehistory by, 116–17
Archaeology, American, use of historic documents by, 131
as social science, 113
of North and South America, particular problems of, 129
prehistoric, relationship of, to other disciplines, 12
scope of, 1
special fields of, 5
special techniques of, 7
Armies, of nonliterate peoples, 344
Army, organization of, in Ashanti Kingdom, 337

Index

Art, and religion, universality of, 347
  definition of, 380
  degree of integration of, in Euroamerican and nonliterate cultures, 378–9
  development of, in Palaeolithic, 386–8
  elements of, as affording evidence of cultural change, 481
  evolutionary approach to study of, 390–2
  formal aspects of, 405
  graphic and plastic, relation of, to cultural anthropology, 11
  influence of habitat on, 160–1
  non-utilitarian, rarity of, in nonliterate societies, 380–1
  Palaeolithic, realism and conventionalization in, 385–8
  philosophical, problems of, 378
  "pure" and "applied," as categories in Euroamerican culture, 379
  relation of form and function in, 410–11
"Art for art's sake," as concept unique to Euroamerican culture, 411–12
Artist, experimentation of, as factor in creative process, 405
  role of culture in creative drive of, 419
Arts, graphic and plastic, forms of, 380
  of European Upper Palaeolithic, 124–6
  synthesis of, in nonliterate drama, 433–4
Art-style, function of, in directing work of artist, 403
  use of, in identification of art-forms, 399
Aryan, as racial designation, 148
Asafoche, Ashanti men's communal organization, 181
Ashanti, apo rite of, 59
  dramatic elements in ritual dance of, 429–30
  dual exogamy among, 299–300
  governmental forms of, 333–8
  Kwasidae rite of, 432–3
  men's communal organization of, 181
  prayer of, quoted, 364
  preferential mating among, 299–300
  rejection of Manchester-made cloths by, 559
Asia, as point of derivation of American Indian, 130
  culture-areas of, 193
Aspects, aesthetic, of culture, disregard of, in functionalist hypothesis of "cultural imperatives," 235
  as universals in human culture, 633
  of culture, as listed, by E. B. Tylor, 229
    by C. Wissler, 230
    in cross-cultural survey, 231–3

Aspects (continued)
  as responses to basic needs, 234–5
  categories of, 634
  differential intensity of Africanisms in, among New World Negroes, 614–15
  differential rates of change in, 20–1
  hypothesis of derivation of, from basic human needs, 234–5
  justification for use of concept of, 239–40
  nature of, 229
  outlined, 19
  significance of differences in, 579
  significance of hypothesis of, 635
  special problems lying in, 238
  study of, 238
  validity of distinctions between, 634
  universal, of culture, system for presentation of, 239
Assimilation, differentiation of, from acculturation, 523
Associations, degrees of formal structure in, 306–7
  early theories of, 303
  functions of, 306
Astronomy, use of historic sequences by, 609
Attitudes, toward supernatural, in Euroamerican and other cultures, contrasted, 362
Aurignacian period, of prehistory, 124
Australian aborigines, adaptation of, to habitat, 155
  conservatism and change in different aspects of culture of, 488
  education in kinship usages among, 320
  educational functions of tribal initiation among, 325
  focal aspect of culture of, 545
  relation of children to mother in patrilineal families of, 293
  totemism of, as basis for classification of totemic phenomena, 599
  use of fire by, in adapting to habitat, 254
Australoid race, geographical distribution of, 136
Authority, lines of, among Ashanti, 334–7
Autobiographies, collection of, 92
Autocracy, incidence of, among American Indians, 341
Automatic responses, as basis for cultural behavior, 46
Automobile, nontechnical results of invention of, as internal historic accidents, 592

iii

Index

Autonomy, cultural, of peoples, need for, in world order, 655

Axis powers, use of anthropology by, 648

Aymara, animistic beliefs of, 352
extended family among, 302

Azilian, Mesolithic culture of Southern France, 127

Azande, forms of magic of, 366-7
method of conducting field-work among, described, 84

Bacon, E., cited, 193

Baganda, sharing of resources among, 267

Bahia, variation in cult-practices of Negroes of, 570-2

Balfour, H., cited, 391

Bantu languages, 453

"Barbarous," inferiority implied in use of, 71

Barbeau, M., quoted, 481

Bark-cloth, as material for clothing, 258

Barnett, H. G., quoted, 557, 617

Barter, in nonliterate societies, 276

Barton, R. F., cited, 163, 345
quoted, 277

Bascom, W. R., cited, 385, 549
quoted, 306

Base-line, of cultures of New World Negroes, 612

Basic personality structure, concept of, in study of relationship between individual and culture, 52-4

Basketry, techniques of making, 260-2

Bastide, R., cited, 571

Bateson, G., quoted, 307-8, 535

BaTswa, reinterpretation of European gun-stock by, 556

BaVenda, power-concept of, 358
schools of, 323

Beals, R. L., cited, 238
quoted, 368

Beauty, as universal in human experience, 76
search for, 378

Behavior, cultural, automatic nature of, 46
deviation from norms of, as related to group size, 577
human, symbolic character of, 27
ideal and actual, 570
social, of hamadryad baboon, variations in, 35
varieties of, permitted by culture, 44-5

Behavioral world, of individual, 165

Behaviorism, and psychoanalysis, use of, in study of individual in society, 49
concepts of, used by anthropologists in study of culture, 45-6

Beliefs, and superstitions, differentiated, 360

Bemba, cycle of food production and consumption of, 281
integration of various aspects of culture of, 221
rhythm of work among, 271-2

Benedict, R., cited, 50, 51, 59, 222
quoted, 177, 181, 199, 221-2

Beni-Amer, variety of kinship structures among, 301

Benin, bronze and ivory figures of, stylistic elements in, 401

Billingsgate dialect, as evidence of linguistic change, 456

Biographies, collection of, 92

Biological series, man as component of, 99

Biology, human, dynamic problems in study of, 138-47

Biometrics, as technique of physical anthropology, 12

Blackwood, B., cited, 205-6

Blade, as primary tool of prehistoric man, 120
perfection of, in Upper Palaeolithic, 123

Bleek, D. F., quoted, 365

Bloomfield, L., quoted, 442, 443, 448

Boas, F., cited, 45-6, 51, 140, 407-8, 418, 425, 500
quoted, 142, 175, 185, 237, 278-9, 395, 396, 413, 437, 446, 447, 473, 515-16, 517, 610-11

Bogoras, W., cited, 252, 417

Bollaert, W., cited, 151

Borrowing, as mechanism of change in culture, 508, 635-6
as source of new elements in culture, 481-2
between Euroamerican and nonliterate cultures, need for perspective on, 482
cultural, absence of logic in determination of, 539
evidence for, 636
preponderance of, 499-500
recognition of, as factor in refuting evolutionary hypothesis, 474-5
historical and psychological aspects of, conceptual distinction between, 539
selective, nature of, 537
psychological mechanisms of, 637

Botany, relationship of, to prehistoric archaeology, 12

Botkin, B. A., quoted, 423

Index

Brain, human, size of, as concomitant of attainment of upright structure, 102–3

Brazil, influence of Africans on culture of, 533

Brazilian Negroes, cult-practices of, as example of cultural variation, 570–2

Bronze Age, of prehistory, 128

Brown, J. F., cited, 46

Brünn finds, 110

Buck, P. H. (Te Rangi Hiroa), quoted, 275, 363–4

Budgeting, of resources, in nonliterate cultures, 281–2

Bunyan, Paul, as creation of frontier society, 419

Bureau of American Ethnology, earlier disregard by, of problems of Indian administration, 645

Burin (graver) method of making, 119–20

Bushmen, South African, absence of constructed shelters among, 253
absence of economic surplus among, 284
adaptation of, to habitat, 155
monogamy and polygamy among, 293
political controls of, 338–9
prayer of, 365

Bush Negroes, ethnocentrism among, 68
integration of culture of, 217–20
methods of field research among, 81–3
name-magic of, 368
wood-carving of, 383

Business activities, in nonliterate societies, 278–9

California Indians, culture-element lists from, 172–4
money tokens used by, 278

Cameron, N., quoted, 406

Cameroons, forms of divining in, 371

Campbell, A. A., cited, 58

Capital goods, forms of, in nonliterate societies, 282–3

Carpenter, C. R., quoted, 35

Case-method, use of, in comparative study of law, 345

Cassirer, E., quoted, 27

Categories, of culture, advanced by A. A. Goldenweiser, 590
of European prehistory, restricted applicability of, 128–9
of primary tools used by prehistoric cultures, 119

Catholic saints, identification of, with African deities, by New World Negroes, 553–4

Cattle, dominating role of, in East African culture-area, 195–6

Caucasoid race, 136–7

Causality, external and internal, in theory of culture-historical school, 510

Causation, varied conceptions of, in "primitive" societies, 73

Ceremonialism, definition of, 361
theories of role of in society, analyzed, 372

Chaco, tribes of, political forms among, 331

Chaga, education in use of kinship terminology among, 320–1

Chaka, scientific utility of biography of, 92

Chamberlain, Houston Stewart, early racist, 150

Change, cultural, *see* Cultural change
in art-styles of nonliterate peoples, 403–4
in focal aspect of culture, receptivity to, 544
in nonliterate cultures, universality of, 484
rate of, in written and unwritten languages, compared, 455–6

Chapple, E. D., quoted, 308–9

Charm, use of, as magic device, 367

Charms, categories of, 368–9

Chatelperronian period of prehistory, 124

Chellean period of prehistory, 122

Cherokee Indians, ethnocentrism of, as shown in creation myth, 68–9

Cheyenne Indian law, aims of, 330

Cheyenne Indians, medical patterns of, 224
political institutions of, 342

Child development experts, meaning given "acculturation" by, 527

Childe, C. G., cited, 132
quoted, 120

Children, in nonliterate societies, early education of, 312
position of, in Dahomean polygynous household, 62
reactions of, to inanimate objects, difference of, from animistic beliefs, 350

Chimpanzees, integration of, into group, 36

Chinese, acculturative changes in customs of, 536

Chinook, "word-sentence" in language of, 447

Choice, as factor in reenculturation of later life, 41

Index

"Chopping-tool culture," of Asiatic Palaeo-lithic, 117

Christianity, animistic components of, 352–3

Chronology, prehistoric, geological basis of, 117

Chukchi, and other Siberian tribes, adaptation of, to habitat, 157–8

"Cinderella," combination of, in Dutch Guiana, with other tales, 418

Cinderella tale, as example of combination of traits into culture-complexes, 177

Civilization, as synonym for culture, 17
investigation into nature and processes of, 71–2
"revolutions" of, as basis for cyclical theory of history, 542

"Civilized" as cultural evaluative term, 70

Clactonian, early prehistoric culture, 121

Clan, definition of, 299

Class, and sex, differences in patterned behavior of, 575

Class differences, role of clothing in marking, 260

Class structure, as instrument of cultural specialization, 23
of Philippine coastal tribes, cultural drift of, 588

Classes, of data, use of, in science, 598

Classification, and analysis of process, relationship between, 595–6
and dynamics, in study of language, 600
as principle of Bantu languages, 453
conventional, of prehistoric culture, 117
of prehistoric cultures, revision of, 117–20
danger-point in, 598
of cultural facts, in terms of evolutionary hypothesis, 470
of data, in history of science, 595
of economies, 599–600
of finds, in North American archaeology, 131
of forms of totemism, 599
of personality types, 601
of prehistoric cultures, changes in, 630
of races, difficulties in, 133
utility of, 138
systems of, concept of ideal type in, 603
polarity as characteristic of, 602–3

Classifications, of various aspects of culture, 600–2

"Clicks," phonemic nature of, 445

"Climax," as dynamic concept in culture-area analysis, 200

Cloth, manufacture of, 256

Clothing, materials used in making, 256
reasons for wearing, 259–60
types of, 255–6, 259

Codrington, R. H., quoted, 355–6, 362

Coiling, as basketry technique, 261–2
as pottery technique, 263

Cole, F. C., cited, 585

Cole, F. C. and Deuel, T., cited, 131

Collier, D., cited, 262

Collins, H. B., Jr., cited, 520

Colonial administration, use of "practical anthropology" in, 646

Color scheme, racial, invalidity of, 133

Communication, and language, differentiated, 454

Communism, primitive, 283

Comparative data, from "primitive" peoples, reasons for gathering, 80

Comparative method, difficulties in use of, 475
ignoring of individual variation in, 563
use of, by cultural evolutionists, 469–70

Comparative musicology, value of anthropological approach to, 11–12

Comparative religion, relationship of, to anthropology, 10–11

Competition, between wives, in Dahomean polygynous household, 62

Complexes, cultural, of diffusionists, as subjective classifications of data, 603

Complexity, in primitive cultures, 72
of cultures, influence of, on borrowing, 532

Concealment, of data, by informants, 88

Concordance, in Bantu languages, 453

Conditioning, as mechanism for acquisition of culture, 26
cultural, as basis of learning process, 46
in process of socialization, 38–9
linguistic, 441
of men and women, to different patterns of behavior, 208–9

Configuration, of culture, as exemplified in study of medical practices, 223–4

Configurational psychology, use of, in study of relationship between individual and culture, 46–7

Configurations, cultural, study of, 222

Consensus, cultural, as expression of cultural variation, 575

Conservatism, and change, as phases of cultural dynamics
in culture, relation between, 483
rates of, need of distinguishing, for different aspects of culture, 487–8

Index

Conservation (*continued*)
of nonliterate peoples, in early statements concerning, 484–5
cultural, as resistance to change, 486
relative nature of, 20
Consistency, of phonemic systems of languages, 446
Consonants, range in, 445
Conspicuous consumption, theory of, 286–7
Consumption, economics of, in nonliterate societies, 279–82
Contact, with minimal borrowing, 538
Contacts, between friendly and hostile groups, cultural borrowing resulting from, 530–1
between groups of differing size, 532
"Contemporary ancestor," derivation of concept of, 71
"Contemporary ancestors," hypothesis of nonliterate peoples as, 469
Continuity, of culture, causes for, 626
Contra-acculturative movements, derivation and types of, 531–2
Control, as factor in scientific analysis, 609
Controls, historic, 598–9, 608
scientific, establishment of, by ethnographer through field-work, 79–80
Conventionalization, and realism, in art, problem of, 381
of designs, examples of, 383–5
Convergence, cultural, hypothesis of, 500–2
Cooper, J. M., cited, 520
quoted, 293, 513
Cooperation, between wives, in Dahomean polygynous household, 62
Cooperative, work, efficiency of, 271
Coquetry, as factor in use of clothing, 260
Core tools, method of making, 119
Correlations, of data of prehistory, 118–20
Cosmology, as theological system, 361
Cour d'Alène Indians, imagery in vocabulary of, 456–7
Courts, functioning of, in Ashanti Kingdom, 337–8
incidence of, in nonliterate societies, 345–6
Covert culture, of Navaho, 224
Cowry-shell, as monetary unit, in Africa, 278
Cox, M. R., cited, 177
Craftsman, place of, in machine and non-machine societies, 241
Cranial capacity, in study of human evolution, 111
Crawley, E., quoted, 485

Credit, use of, in nonliterate cultures, 278–9
Cree Indians, institutionalized friendship among, 304
Crises, sexual, at adolescence, as culturally defined, 44
Criteria, of form and quality, 511
of invention, of R. B. Dixon, 496
Cro-Magnon man, 109–10
Upper Palaeolithic cultures of, 124–6
Crops, rotation of, by nonliterate gardeners, 249–51
Cross-cousins, relationship between, 299
Cross-cultural data, utility of, 617–18
Cross-cultural survey, universals in culture indicated by, 231–3
Crossing, between human types, universality of, 139
Crow Indians, guardian spirit concept of, 178
political institutions of, 342
prayers of, quoted, 364
Cultivation, techniques of, 249–51
Cultural accident, as reflection of regularity of process, 620
concept of, 591
as factor in cultural dynamics, 638–9
Cultural and linguistic drift, empirical basis of, 584
Cultural anthropology, *see* Anthropology, cultural
Cultural aspects, *see* Aspects, of culture
Cultural base-line, African, as historic control, 613
Cultural borrowing, *see* Borrowing
Cultural change, acculturation as one aspect of, 523
accumulation of small variables as factor in, 583
and conservatism, relation between, 483
approach to study of, 635
archaeological evidence for, 479
attitudes toward, in different societies, 614
of old and young, 479–80
categories of, 492
conceived as impact of higher on lower cultures, 527
documentation of, in prehistory, 630–1
enculturation of later life, as making for, 491
evidence for, 479–81
factors in, 488
function of later enculturation in making for, 40–1
hypothesis of inevitability of, 626
influence of habitat on, 488–90
internal and external, 635–6

Index

Cultural change (*continued*)
opportunities of individuals to achieve, 64
phenomenon of drift in, 581–5
place of study of, in history of anthropology, 636
principle of convergence applied to, 500
psychological mechanisms for, 491
psychological problems underlying, 21
reenculturation as mechanism of, 627
regional variants, as evidence of, 481
relative character of, 20
significance of, for relativistic approach to culture, 77
stress on, in anthropological studies, 484
ubiquity of, 20, 479, 482–3, 485–6
variation in individual behavior as mechanism of, 578
variation in stimuli to, 490
variations in behavior as expressions of, 483
Cultural changes, large and small, significance of, 502
Cultural configurational approach, to relation between individual and culture, 50–2
Cultural conservatism, problems in study of, 483
Cultural continuities and discontinuities, significance of, 59
Cultural determinism, arguments for, 22–5
Cultural determinists, role of small variations in theories of, 580
Cultural drift, as adaptation of concept of linguistic drift, 582
as expression of selective change in culture, 639
as process of cultural change, 490
changes in Euroamerican men's clothing as example of, 582
deflection of, by historic accident, 593–4
hypothesis of, 581
relation of, to hypothesis of cultural focus, 584–5
Cultural dynamics, approaches to study of, 461–2
concept of reinterpretation as aid in analysis of, 557
drift and accident as factors in, 593–4
positive and negative aspects of study of, 635
significance of hypothesis of cultural focus for, 544
study of, as exemplified in analysis of New World Negro culture, 616
Cultural evolution, stress on small changes in theory of, 580

Cultural focus, as dominant in interests of people, 544
as dynamic force, in Toda culture, 545–7
as psychological explanation of cultural change, 560
defined, 542
hypothesis of, 637
illustrations of, 545–9
psychological mechanisms of, 544
relation of, to concept of cultural drift, 581–5
to concept of cultural variability, 579
to hypothesis of variation in culture, 638–9
retention of, under forced acculturation, 553
role of, in selective borrowing, 637
variation of customs in, under free and forced acculturation, 550
Cultural form, range of, as related to regularity in process, 620–1
Cultural growth, neglect of psychological elements in hypothesis of, 543
"Cultural imperatives," hypothesis of role of, 235
Cultural integration, dual aspect of, 215–16
hypothesis arising from study of, 633
Cultural "laws," exemplified, 620
Cultural pattern, *see* Pattern, cultural
Cultural relativism, as aid in understanding differing conceptions of habitat, 165
as applied to culture-area concept, 198–9
as exemplified by reactions toward foods, 70
as philosophy of tolerance, 76
as resulting from availability of ethnographic data, 78
beginnings of, in critiques of "human nature," 618
in comparative study of art, 378
need to distinguish, from relativism of individual behavior, 77
philosophy of, as basic contribution of anthropology, 655
questions raised, concerning philosophical validity of, 75–8
statement of principles underlying, 63
"Cultural seriation," as method in historical reconstruction, 518
Cultural similarities, emphasis laid on, by relativistic philosophy, 655
Cultural stability, function of early enculturation in making for, 40–1
relative nature of, 20

"Cultural strait-jacket," of "primitive" man, concept of, 563

Cultural structures, regularity of, 631

Cultural symbiosis, in tribes of Nilghiri Hills, India, 537–8

Cultural transmission, selective character of, 637

   systematic study of, 505

Cultural universals, biological interpretation of, 233

Cultural variation, *see* Variation, cultural

Culture, analysis of, in behavioristic terms, 45–6

   and ecology, correlation of, in culture-areas, 188

   and individual, relationship between, alternative methods of studying, 59

      relationship between, in terms of gestalt psychology, 46–7

   and personality, approaches to study of, 49–55

   approaches to study of, by modern evolutionists, 478

   approaches to unified study of, 644

   as complement of habitat in total human environment, 629–30

   as construct in mind of individual, 21

   as distinguished from habitat, 153–4

   as factor differentiating human from infra-human societies, 37–8

   as inborn human drive, 234

   as independent variable, 149

   as instrument in achieving individual adjustment, 633

   as reification of individual behavior into institutions, 43

   as superorganic phenomenon, hypothesis of, 626

   as tradition embodying past of a people, 19

   as unique attribute of man, 29–30

   aspects of, *see* Aspects, of culture

   categories of, as indicated in cross-cultural survey, 231–3

   concept of, as summation of variables, 578–9

   conformity of individuals to, 64

   contribution of comparative musicology to study of, 435

   covert, 222–4

   cumulative character of, as unique human attribute, 626

   definition of, as man-made part of environment, 17

      by A. Kardiner, 52

      in psychological terms, 25

   development of concept of, from study of nonliterate peoples, 643

Culture (*continued*)

   differentiation of, from society, 29

   difficulty of obtaining laboratory controls in study of, 609

   "discovered" by infant, 49

   dynamic character of, 20, 479

   functionalist approach to study of, 216–17

   generalizations concerning dynamics of, from historical studies of, 617–18

   historical sequence of approaches toward, 462

   history as laboratory of student of, 609

   human, basic contributions of prehistoric man to, 131–2

   hypothesis, of flowering and decay of, 542

      of independent existence of, 626

      of relative richness of at center and margins of area, 198–9

   importance of study of processes of, 461

   influence of, in shaping behavior, as demonstrated by results of field research, 80

      on formation of physical types, 148

      on physical type, 143–5, 629

   influence of habitat on, 162, 164

   institutions as components of, 229

   integration of, 221–3

      as illustrated, by cultural forms of Bush Negroes, 217–20

      in terms of gestalt psychology, 46–7

      with habitat, problems raised by, 166

   knowledge of, held by individual, in specialized and unspecialized cultures, 22–3

   learned character of, as basis of culture-area, 183

   material, *see* Material culture

   meaningful character of, 27

   modes of classifying, 596

   nature of, 625

   need for historic controls in scientific study of, 609

   objectivity of, as construct of student, 28

   overt, 222–3

   paradoxes in study of, 18

   place of individual in, 627

   prehistoric, classifications of, 117–120

      difficulties in reconstructing development of, 114

      relation of, to physical development of *homo sapiens*, 628

   "primitive," difficulty of defining, 72

   propositions concerning nature and functioning of, listed, 625

Index

Culture (*continued*)
psychological mechanisms for acquisition of, 25–6
psychological reality of, 25–7, 626
psychological unity of, difficulty in studying, 221
psychology of, 45
realization of learned nature of, as result of cross-cultural study, 643
reasons for dividing into aspects, 239–40
reflection of, in folklore, 418–19
rejection of psychological approach to, by modern evolutionists, 477
relation of, to habitat, 159–62, 629–30
to human biological endowment, 628
to physical type, 143–8
relation of individual to, approaches to study of, 49–55
status of study of, 55–7
relationship to, of individual, as revealed by study of enculturative process, 44
restricted study of, by aspects, reasons for, 239–40
role of, in fulfilling psychological and biological needs of human organism, 641
in distinguishing man from other social animals, 17
role of ethnocentrism, in development of evaluations of, 627–8
role of language in, 440
rounded study of, illustrated, 238
scientific and popular use of term, contrasted, 18
selective character of, 221–2
structure of, 169
as construct of student, 214
study of, as history or science, controversy over, 639
as objective phenomenon, 21–2
theory of habitat as limiting factor in, 159
unities, in approaches to study of, 215
unity of, as evidenced in contacts between Euroamericans and natives, 644
hypotheses concerning, 633
need to comprehend, 214–15
universal aspects of, system for presentation of, 239
universality of, among human groups, 19
universality of ends of, as basic postulate in anthropology, 233
universals in, as indicated by Crosscultural Survey, 231–3

Culture (*continued*)
problem of explanation of, analyzed, 237–8
reasons for, 233–4
utility of comparative musicology, in study of, 439
value of study of language, for understanding of, 454–7
various aspects of, differing influence of habitat on, 160–2
various procedures employed for study of different problems of, 215
whole, methodological difficulty in studying, 239
"Cultured," meaning of, 18
Cultures, as wholes, described in terms of cultural focus, 542
classification of, in terms of evolutionary stages, 468–9
degree of unity of, in culture-areas, 185
difficulty of classifying as wholes, 185
evaluation of, criteria for, 61
role of ethnocentrism in encouraging, 68
evaluative classifications of, 601
homogeneity of nonliterate, as factor in educational process, 315
integration of, 632
literate and nonliterate, anthropological concern with, 642–4
prehistoric, conventional classifications of, 117–20
"pure," search for, value of, 541
"uncontaminated," as main concern of early anthropologists, 643
Culture-area, as dynamic concept, 199–200
definition of, 183
determination of "typical" cultures in, 195
East African, characteristics of, 196
invalidity of conception of, as "incipient nationality," 198
lack of psychological validity of concept of, 198
Plains, characteristics of, 194–5
uses of, 196
value of trait concept in delimiting, 176
Culture-area concept, development of, 183–4
geographical character of, 199
inapplicability of, to cultures with class stratification, 199
Culture-areas, as constructs in study of culture, 632
degree of unity of cultures in, 185
divisions of Pacific considered as, 193
mapping of, 186–93

Index

Culture-areas (*continued*)
  of Africa, 191–2
  of Asia, 193
  of Madagascar, 193
  of New Zealand, 193
  of North America, 186–8
  of South America, 189–90
  relative nature of differentiations drawn between, 197–8
  technique of mapping, 194–6
  use of, in reconstruction of culture-history, 190
  utility of concept of, 632
Culture-center, cautions in use of concept of, 198
  concept of, 195
"Culture-circle," contrasted to culture-area, 199–200
Culture-complex, and culture-trait, differences between, 181–2
  as exemplified in guardian spirit of North American Indians, 177–8
  differentiated from *Kulturkomplexe*, 512
  heliolithic, of English diffusionists, 507
  integration of, 179–81
  nature of, 176–9
  utility and validity of concept of, 631–2
Culture-complexes, in Pueblo Indian religion, 176–7
  integration of traits in, 177
  Melanesian trading as example of, 178–9
Culture-contact, contemporary resemblances in, to contacts of earlier times, 529–30
  formula for study of, 535
  influences of administrative problems on study of, 528–9
  study of, in terms of traits borrowed, 534–7
  types of, 530–4
Culture-element, definition of, 172
  in study of acculturation, 535–6
Culture-element list, logic of, 182
Culture-element lists, mode of collecting, 173
  growth of, 172–4
Culture elements, correlation of, in study of cultural development, 174
  differences in distribution of, 185
  number of, listed for various California Indian tribes, 172
Culture-historical school, approach to psychological problems of culture by, 510
  criteria of form and quantity used by, 511–12

Culture-historical school (*continued*)
  definition of ethnology by, 509
  methodology of, 511
  position and contribution of, 513–14
"Culture-scheme," as indication of cultural universals, 634
  of C. Wissler, 230
Culture-trait, and culture-complex, differences between, 181–2
  as conceptual tool, 174
  criteria for, 170–1
  defined, 170
  independence of, 172
  limitations on use of, 176
  problem of delimitation of, 170–1
  relative character of, 172
  use of, in archaeology, 174
  use of in comparative ethnographic studies of Swedish school, 175
  utility of concept of, 631
Culture-traits, hypothesis of concentric distribution of, 519–20
  integration of, in culture-complexes, 177
  of California Indians, 172–4
  of Tsimshian Indians, as used in analyzing mythology, 175
"Culturology," 21, 477
Custom, and law, problem of differentiating, 345
Custom, cultural determination of, 22–3

Dahomey, applique cloths of, as illustrating change in art-forms, 404
  brass figures from, 385
  categories of magic charms used in, 368–9
  conception of soul in, 352
  cooperative work-groups of, 179–81
  description of religious thrill in, 376
  institutionalized friendships in, 305
  ritual poetry from, 434
  sibs of, 301
  sub-cultural patterns, in, 210–11
  values in polygynous family of, 61–3
Dakota Indians, acculturation of, 541
  institutionalized friendships among, 304
Dalzel, A., quoted, 278
Dance, methodological problems in study of, 437–8
Daniel, G. E., cited, 124
Data, esoteric, value of, 88
Davidson, L. J., quoted, 423
Dawson, C., as discoverer of Piltdown man, 107
Deacon, A. B., cited, 352
  quoted, 304–5
de Laguna, G. A., quoted, 76, 442

Index

Democracy, of American Indians, 341
Demoralization, psychological, from foreign domination, 654
Dendrochronology, as archaeological technique, 12, 131
Dennis, W., cited, 58
Descent, form of, psycho-social relationship within family, influenced by, 291
  mode of counting, in unilineal descent system, 296
  types of, 290
Design, as factor in art, 381
Determinism, and accident, in culture, 590
  cultural, arguments for, 22–4
  alternatives to, in explaining culture, 27–8
  nature of, 22
  environmental, 156
  racial, 148
Deuel, T. and Cole, F. C., cited, 131
Development, as synonym for evolution, 478
  human, complexity of, 111
Deviations, cultural, difficulty of discerning, 563
  random, from cultural norms, dynamic quality of, 582
Dewey, J., quoted, 64
Dialect, as expression of linguistic drift, 583
Dialects, phonemic variations in, 443
Didinga, institutionalized friendship among, 305
Differences, between literate and non-literate cultures, as basis of classification, 75
  individual, in behavior, as mechanism of cultural change, 579
  in behavior, difficulty of discerning, 563
  and family, in cultural behavior, 575
  physical, within race, as between races, 135
Diffusion, American approach to study of, 505, 514–17
  and acculturation, delimitation of, 636–7
  as basis of culture-area, 183
  assumed, of Old World traits to New World, hypotheses of, 513
  defined, in methodological terms, 525
  early use of term, 523
  folklore as aid to study of, 424
  hostility of functionalists to, 506
  of Plains Indians Sun Dance, significance of study of, 521–2

Diffusion (continued)
  recognition of, by evolutionists, 474–5
  versus independent invention, controversy concerning, 499
Diffusion studies, place of in analysis of cultural dynamics, 525–6
Diffusionism, extreme, statement of, 507
  criticisms of, 509
  English, place of abrupt cultural changes in theory of, 581
  use of comparative method by, 475
Digby, A., quoted, 242
Digging-stick, utilization of, in cultivation, 249
Diplomacy, problem of, in nonliterate societies, 343–4
Direction, cultural determination of perception of, 64–5
Discipline, in spirit-possession, among African and New World Negroes, 67
Discoveries, of prehistoric man, used in modern cultures, 131–2
Discovery, and invention, problem in the study of, 492–3
  as mechanism of internal cultural change, 635–6
  conditions antecedent to, 494
Discovery-complex, concept of, defined, 493
Discovery-product, defined, 493
Distribution, of goods, in societies of differing degrees of specialization, 274–5
  of New World Negroes and ancestral cultures, 612–13
Divination, forms and functions of, 370–1
Division of labor, types of, in nonliterate societies, 272–4
Dixon, R. B., cited, 425
  quoted, 494, 495, 498, 519
Dobjhansky, T., cited, 110
  quoted, 595
Dobu, inhabitants of, as example of cultural type, 51
  medical patterns of, 224
Documents, use of, in study of New World Africanisms, 613–14
Dokpwe, Dahomean cooperative work-group, 179–81
Dollard, J. and Millar, N. E., cited, 39
Domesticated animals, special traits of, 145–6
  and plants, number and distribution of, 248–9
Domestication, as factor in formation of racial types of man, 145
  criteria of, 146

Index

Domestication (*continued*)
of animals or plants, problem of primacy of, 251
of man, significance of for hypothesis of social selection, 629
Dominance, and submission, in animal societies, 32–4
Dorsey, J. O., cited, 564
Drachenloch, cave of, inhabited during Mousterian period, 122
Drama, degree of participation in, in literate and nonliterate societies, 427
differentiation of, from everyday life, 429
forms and functions of, in nonliterate societies, 427
hypothesis of derivation of, from ritual, 432
integration of, in life of nonliterate societies, 429
nonliterate, as synthesis of arts, 433–4
"primitive," difficulty of defining, 428
relation of, to cultural anthropology, 11
ritual, in nonliterate societies, 427–32
secular, forms of in nonliterate societies, 432–3
Driberg, J. H., cited, 305
quoted, 196
Driver, H. E. and Kroeber, A. L., quoted, 171–2
Drawing, development of, in European Upper Palaeolithic, 125–6
Dress designs, study of, 24–5
Drift, cultural, *see* Cultural drift
Drucker, P., quoted, 302
DuBois, C., cited, 53
Dubois, E., as discoverer of *homo wadjakensis*, 106
as discoverer of *pithecanthropus erectus*, 97, 104
Dundas, C., cited, 345
quoted, 195
Durkheim, E., cited, 349, 372
Dutch colonial service, anthropological training of members of, 646
Dutch Guiana Negroes, concept of *fiofio*, held by, 59–60
drama in ritual dance of, 431
Dyk, W., quoted, 73
Dynamics, and classification, in study of languages, 600
as against description, in study of diffusion, 514

Earth sciences, relationship of, to prehistoric archaeology, 12
East Africa, examples of formal education in, 322

East African Cattle area, cultures of, 195–7
Ecology, and culture, correlation of, in culture-areas, 188
human, field of, 153
Economic determinism, hypothesis of, analyzed, 288
Economic life, of early Palaeolithic peoples, assumptions concerning, 122
of Neolithic, Bronze and Iron Ages, 128
Economic principles, cross-cultural relevance of, 266–7
Economic stages, hypothesis of, 247
Economic surplus, nature and functioning of, 284–7
relation of, to political forms, 327–8
Economic systems, classifications of, 599–600
Economics, of nonliterate cultures, aspects of, subject to statistical treatment, 573
of machine and nonmachine societies, contrasted, 266–7
relationship of, to cultural anthropology, 10
Economists, concern of, with historic cultures, 268
Education, as aspect of enculturative process, 325–6
as directed learning, 318–19
contrasted to schooling, 310
differing emphases on, in different cultures, 319
ethnological definition of, 325
for marriage, methods of achieving, in nonliterate societies, 322
in kinship usages, 320–1
in nonliterate societies, effectiveness of, 311
varied techniques of, 313
influence of specialization in, 310–11
religious, special character of, in nonliterate societies, 325
universal, elements in, 319
Educational techniques, used by Apache, 315–17
Educators, meaning given "acculturation" by, 527
Egypt, as source of civilization, postulated by English diffusionists, 507
Eggan, F., cited, 536
quoted, 586–7
Ehrenreich, P., cited, 500
Einstein, C., cited, 400
Elders, importance of data obtained from, 88
Elema, of New Guinea, *hevehe* rites of, 427–8

Index

Elements, of California Indian cultures, listing of, 172–4
  universal, in culture, as indicated by cross-cultural survey, 231
Empathy, as methodological principle of culture-historical school, 510–11
Enculturation, as basis for relativistic judgements, 64
  as continuing process in lifetime of individual, 41
  as factor in shaping artistic creativeness, 403
  as force in molding individual to patterns of group, 43
  as primary mechanism of cultural conservatism and change, 491
  as psychological mechanism for perpetuation of cultural forms, 625–6
  differentiated from socialization, 40
  early, as factor making for cultural stability, 491, 627
  nature of, 40
  passive role of individual in, 41
  role of, in influencing personality of individual, 44–5
  in America, to patterned ideal of equal opportunity, 44
  later, as explanation of cultural change, 558
  as making for cultural change, 491
  as reconditioning process, 41
  musical, as factor in analysis of musical styles, 435–6
  role of education in, 310
  study of, as revealing relation between individual and culture, 44–5
Ends, of applied anthropology, weighting of by anthropologists, 651
Engels, F., cited, 473
Engineering, relation of, to pure science, 649
English diffusionist school, postulates of, 507
Environment, definition of, 154, 629
  differing relation of, to various elements of culture, 630
  natural, as against social environment, 153
    theory of, as limiting factor in influencing culture, 159
Environmental determinism, arguments against, 157
  status of hypothesis of, 629
Eoanthropus dawsoni, 107
Eolithic period of prehistory, controversy over, 121
Erikson, E. H., quoted, 58

Eskimo, adaptation of, to habitat, 155–6
  contrasted with adaptation of Siberian natives, 157–8
Eskimo culture, reconstruction of historical affiliations of, 520
Eskimo needle-case designs, as evidence of cultural change, 481
Essene, F., cited, 172
Ethical content, in religions of nonliterate peoples, 353
Ethics, as factor in religion, 375
Ethnocentrism, as primary mechanism in evaluation of cultures, 68
  concept of absolute values arising out of, 655
  curbing of, by relativistic concept of culture, 78
  derivation and forms of, 627–8
  Euroamerican, reflected in statements of "primitive" conservatism, 485
    sanctions of, in technological achievement, 69
  implicit in classifications of ethnographic data, 601
  in writings of A. J. Toynbee, 71–2
  nature of, in cultures outside Euroamerican area, 68–9
  need to eliminate, in conduct of field research, 81
  values in, 69
Ethnographer, reaction of, to different personalities of members in group under study, 86–7
  restraints to be exercised by, in conducting field research, 85
  special techniques in field research of, 92–3
Ethnographers, approach of, to study of political institutions, 329–30
Ethnographic studies, emphasis on institutions in, 43
Ethnographic truth, problem of ascertaining, 570–2
Ethnography, definition of, 9
  human problem in, 93
  reflection of, in folklore of people, 418–20
Ethnohistory, as technique of acculturation research, 526
  increase in use of, in analyses of cultures, 608–9
  use of, in analysis of American Indian acculturation, 541
Ethnology, as historical science, 611
  relation of, to social anthropology, 9
Euroamerican culture, as field for anthropological study, 644

xiv

Index

Euroamerican culture (*continued*)
  forerunners of, as series of cultural reorientations, 542
  nature of ethnocentrism in, 69
  "prelogical" patterns of mentality in, 74
  rapidity of change attributed to, 20–1
Europe, prehistoric cultures of, 118–20
  protohuman forms recovered from, 106–10
Evaluation, of cultures, bases of, 61, 627–8
Evaluations, as relative to given cultural backgrounds, 63
Evans-Pritchard, E. E., cited, 196
  quoted, 84, 302–3, 339–40, 366–7, 650–1, 652
Evans-Pritchard, E. E. and Fortes, M., quoted, 332
Evolution, biological, importance of variations in, 99
  conception of, as development, 478
  cultural, role of doctrine of psychic unity of man in, 474–5
  hominid, consistency in patterns of, 103
  human, lack of correlation of, with development of human culture, 113
  of culture, distinguished from culture history, 477
  of human form, with attainment of upright posture, 99–103
  physical, of man, fragmentary nature of materials bearing on, 97
Evolutionary process, in nature, as aid in reconstruction of development of human physical type, 98
Evolutionism, cultural, absence of racism in theories of, 465
  approaches to, 466
  contribution of, to cultural dynamics, 478
  ethnocentrism in, 476
  origins of, 464–5
  political use of, 473–4
  reasons for rejection of, by anthropologists, 473–6
  revival of doctrine of, 477–8
  of H. Spencer, lack of flexibility in, 469
  social, assumptions of, 463–4
Evolutionists, cultural, basic postulates of, listed, 467
  contributions of, 477
  recognition of diffusion by, 474–5
  use of comparative method by, 475
  developmental series of, disregard of time factor in, 475–6
Exceptions, to systems of classification, importance of, 598

Exchange, of goods, theories of origin of, 275
  ritual, economic significance of, 275
  in Solomon Islands, 205–6
Exogamy, defined, 299
Expansion of Europe, effect on development of anthropology of, 5
Experience, as culturally defined, 27
  enculturative, as force molding individual, 43
Experimentation, pre-marital, as technique of assuring adjustment in marriage, 295

Family, biological and social, distinction between, 290
  constancy of, in human societies, 296
  educational role of, in nonliterate societies, 314
  extended, distribution of, 301–2
  immediate, types of, 293
  monogamous and polygamous, values in, compared, 62–3
  nuclear, universality of, 292–3
  polygynous, of Dahomey, mode of life in, 61–2
  primary, basis of evaluating different forms of, 61
  primeval, role of, in Freudian explanation of individual and culture, 48
  relationship between members of, under various descent systems, 292
Family life, difficulty in reconstructing prehistoric development of, 116
Family lines, in study of human physical type, 139
Fantasy, social, as revealed in folklore, 421
Fashions, changes in, as evidence of culture as "superorganic" phenomenon, 24
Father, role of, in patrilineal and matrilineal descent systems, compared, 291–2
Fear, as factor in religion, 374
Femur, human, changes in, with assumption of upright posture, 101–2
Fenton, W. N., quoted, 558
Ferninterpretation, principle of, 512–13
Fertility, mutual, of human groups, 139
Fertilizers, use of, by nonliterate cultivators, 250
Fetichism, validity of concept of, 368
Field methods, importance of explicit presentation of, 81
Field research, need for relativistic approach to, 80–1

Index

"Field-theory" psychology, significance of, for study of culture, 46–7

Field-work, advantages and disadvantages of use of interpreter in, 91–2
aims of, 79–80
among various peoples, described, 81–4
collection of biographies and autobiographies during, 92
general rule for conducting, 84
importance of "sorting-out" process in, 86–7
procedures of, 86–8
significance of, in ethnography, 79
techniques employed in, 89–93

Field-work techniques, extension of, to literate cultures, 80

Field-worker, essential characteristics of, 93

Fiofio, concept of, held by Negroes of Dutch Guiana, 59–60

Fire, as domesticating agent for man, 146–7
role of, in adapting man to habitat, 253–4

Fire-making, distribution of knowledge of, 246
prehistoric knowledge of, 113
techniques of, 253–4

Fire-screen, of Australian aborigines, 253

Firth, Raymond, cited, 275
quoted, 280

Firth, Rosemary, quoted, 281

Flake, category of primary tools of prehistoric man, 119

Flaking tools, development in prehistoric times of skill in making, 121

Flexibility, in delimiting culture-traits, 170–1

Fligelman, F., quoted, 457

Folk-custom, study of, 422

Folklore, as contrasted to folk-custom, 422
as ethnography, 418–21
as literary arts of a culture, 11, 421, 425–6
classifications of, 602
compensations afforded by, 421
history of development of, as discipline, 421–2
forms and functions of, 414
in literate cultures, 423–5
problems in classification of elements of, 414–15
stylistic elements of, difficulty of studying, 425–6

"Folklore," early definitions of, in Europe and America, 421–2

Folklore areas, characteristics of, 424–5

Folk-society, characteristics of, 605–6
concept of, as classificatory device, 604
differentiated from "nonliterate," 606–7

Folk-tale, as complex of traits, 177
difficulty of adapting, to mechanized culture, 419

Folk-tales, ease of diffusion of, 416
drama in telling of, 433
significance of distribution of, in study of culture, 424

Food, consumption of, in nonliterate society, as related to physiological need, 280–1
relativistic nature of attitudes toward, 70

Food-gathering, technological problems of, 248

Food-gathering peoples, distribution of, 248

Foodstuffs, classification of types of, 247

Foot, human, changes in, with upright posture, 101

Forde, C. D., cited, 272
quoted, 153, 247

Form, artistic, elements of, 405
and process, in study of religion, 601
resolution of dichotomy between, in development of cultural laws, 619
role of, in analysis of culture, 602
criterion of, in culture-historical method, 511–12
in drama, 429
relation of, to function, in art, 410–11

Fortes, M., quoted, 534

Fortes, M. and Evans-Pritchard, E. E., quoted, 332

Fortes, M. and S. L., quoted, 280–1

Fortune, F., cited, 51–2

Foster, G. M., quoted, 271

Frame of reference, psychological concept of, 65

Frazer, Sir J. G., cited, 300, 359, 367

Free mating, as mechanism in formation of population type, 141

"French," varied meanings of, as physical type, language and culture, 149

French Colonial service, use of anthropology in, 646

Freud, S., influence of, on anthropological study, 47
lack of understanding of cross-cultural materials by, 47–8

Freyre, G., cited, 533

Friendship, institutionalized, nature of, 304–6

Fulani, moral vocabulary of, 457

Index

Function, relation of, to form, in art, 410–11

Functional equivalence, hypothesis of, as dynamic principle in culture-contact, 617

Functionalism, opposition of, to diffusion, 506
theory and methods of, 216–17

Functionalist school, hypothesis of cultural aspects held by, 234–6

Functionalists, English and German, 506

Gandhi movement, in India, as contra-acculturative reaction, 531

Garrod, D. A. E., quoted, 117–18

Gates, R. Ruggles, cited, 110

Gayton, A., quoted, 166

Gebauer, P., cited, 371

Gender, varieties of, in various languages, 452–3

Genealogical method, in field-work, 89–91

Generalizations, dynamic, of historical studies of culture, 617

Genetic approach, to study of human physical type, 139

Genetics, human, problems in study of, 143
relationship of physical anthropology to, 12

Genius, as factor in discovery and invention, hypothesis of, 498–9

Geniuses, of history, theory of abruptness of changes introduced by, 581

Gens, definition of, 299

Geographers, study of relation between culture and habitat by, 159–60

Geography, relationship of, to cultural anthropology, 9–10

Geology, relationship of, to prehistoric archaeology, 12
use of historic sequences by, 609

Gestalt psychology, in study of relationship between individual and culture, 46–7

Ghost, differentiation of, from soul, among Keraki, 351–2

Ghost Dance, of Indians, as contra-acculturative movement, 531

Gifford, E. W. and Kroeber, A. L., cited, 172

Gift exchange, economic significance of, 275–6

Gigantopithecus blacki, 104

Gillen, F. J. and Spencer, B., cited, 325

Gist, N., quoted, 207

Gliddon, G. R., as early American racist, 151

Gluckman, M., cited, 285

de Gobineau, Count Arthur, as early racist, 150

Gods, hypothesis of derivation of, from belief in souls, 353–4

Goldenweiser, A. A., cited, 45, 54, 300, 472
quoted, 375, 500, 501, 590

Goldfrank, E., quoted, 541

"Good Child and the Bad," distribution of motifs from, 416–18

Goodenough, F. L. and Anderson, J. E., cited, 58

Goods, capital, controls of, in nonliterate societies, 267

Goodwin, G., quoted, 294, 302

Government, aboriginal, in North and South America, 341–2
Ashanti, complexity of, 333
role of, in life of individual, 338
difficulty in defining concept of, 340

Government anthropologists, use of, in British colonies, 646

Governmental institutions, nature of, in terms of ethnological approach, 330

Graebner, F., cited, 511–12

Grammar, nature and subdivisions of, 450

Grant, M., cited, 151

Gravettian period of prehistory, 124

"Great man" theory of history, 45, 580

Greenberg, J., cited, 554
quoted, 524–5

Gregory, W. K., cited, 99

Grimaldi finds, 110

Group, social, relation of size of, to degree of cultural variation, 577

Group mind, as analogy to concept of "superorganic," 25

Guadalcanal, conspicuous consumption in, 287

Guardian spirit, concept of, among North American Indians, as culture-complex, 177–8

Guatemala, cultural borrowing in, between Indians and "ladinos," 531

Günther, H. F. K., German racist, 151

Habit formation, influence of, on cultural behavior, 236

Habitat, adaptation to, of various tribes, 154–6
as factor in limiting culture, 159, 163
conception of, as relative to culture, 165–6
definition of, 154, 629
influence of, on clothing-types, 259
on cultural change, 488–90

Index

Habitat, influence of, (*continued*)
 on shelter, 252–3
 on various aspects of culture, 160–2
influence of technology on, 164
of southwestern United States, differing reaction of tribes to, 159
reflection of, in folklore, 418–20
relationship of, to technology, 246
Southeast African, differing reactions of various tribes to, 158–9

Habituation, as mechanism for acquisition of culture, 25

Haddon, A. C., cited, 391

Haines, C. G. and B. M., cited, 329

Haitian Negroes, tale of Jesus and the mule told by, 415

Hallowell, A. I., cited, 536, 617
 quoted, 54, 57, 58, 371, 539

Hamadryad baboon, social behavior of, 35

Hambly, W. D., cited, 192

"Hand-ax cultures," as type-form of Palaeolithic epoch in Europe, 117

Hand-axes, development of, in prehistoric times, 121

Harris, J. S., quoted, 282

Harrison, H. S., quoted, 253–4, 493–4, 497, 500, 502

Hausa, nature of acculturation among, 524
 syncretism of Mohammedan and pagan spirits in culture of, 554

Head, human, changes in, with attainment of upright posture, 102–3

Hebrews, name-magic of, 367–8

Heidelberg man, 107–8

Henry, John, as hero of mechanized culture, 419

Heredity, of intelligence, West African explanation of, 73–4

Herskovits, F. S., quoted, 434

Herskovits, M. J., cited, 61, 147, 181, 192, 285
 quoted, 85, 273, 305, 352, 368–9, 376, 543–4, 615–16, 653

Herskovits, M. J. and F. S., cited, 217, 417, 555
 quoted, 39, 81–3, 538, 554

Herzog, G., quoted, 439

Heterogeneity, of human physical types, significance of, 140–2

Hevehe rites, cycle of, among New Guinea Elema, drama in, 428–9

High gods, of nonliterate cultures, varied nature of, 353
 theory of primacy of, analyzed, 354

Hill, W. W., quoted, 486

Historic accident, as process of cultural change, 490
 basis of hypothesis of, 581
 connotations of, 588–9
 role of, in deflecting cultural drift, 593–4

Historic accidents, arising within cultures, 592–3

Historic controls, employment of, in study of New World Negro cultures, 612–16

Historical data, use of, in acculturation studies, 526

Historical documents, use of, by American archaeologists, 131

Historical materialism, hypothesis of, 288

Historical method, in anthropology, 610

Historical reconstruction, methodological problems of, 517–18
 utility of, in study of cultural dynamics, 520

Historical reconstructions, principles making for utility of, 521
 use of culture-traits in formulating, 176

History, and science, distinctions drawn between, 610–11
 as laboratory for study of culture, 609
 increasing use of, by anthropologists, 608–9
 reconstruction of, as end of diffusion studies, 517
 relationship of, to anthropology, 12
 role of, in anthropology, 461
 significance of concepts of accident and drift for problem of law in, 593–4
 use of, in acculturation studies of North American Indians, 541

Hobhouse, L. T., Wheeler, G. C., and Ginsberg, M., cited, 175

Hodgen, M. T., cited, 520
 quoted, 472, 526

Hoe, use of, in agriculture, 249

Hoebel, E. A., quoted, 345

Hoebel, E. A. and Llewellyn, K. N., quoted, 330, 345

Hogbin, H. I., quoted, 269–71, 274, 287, 305, 312

Hoijer, H., cited, 193

Holmes, W. H., cited, 391

Homeostasis, condition of adjustment comparable to enculturation, 40

Homo heidelbergensis, 107–8

Homo modjokertensis, 105

Homo neanderthalensis, 108–9

Homo sapiens, biological endowment of, as basis for human culture, 628

Index

Homo sapiens fossilis (dawsoni), suggested name for Piltdown man, 107

Homo soloensis, 106

Homo wadjakensis, 106

Homogeneity, cultural, problem of, 577-8
in human physical types, significance of, 140-2

Hopi potter, experimentation of, in creating decorative designs, 404-5

Hopi snake dance, drama in, 432

Horse-complex, of Brazilian Germans, as selective borrowing, 537

Houses, psychological associations with, 255

House-types, distribution of, 254-5

Hottentots, modelling of pottery by, 263
utilization of economic surplus among, 284

Hsü, F. L. K., quoted, 536

Hudson, A. E., cited, 193

Human biology, as physical anthropology, 12

Human forms, early, controversy over sequence of, 103

Human nature, use of cross-cultural data in analyzing concept of, 618

Human organism, plasticity of, as revealed by study of enculturation, 44

Hunt, J., as early English racist, 150-1

Hunter, M., cited, 617

Hunting peoples, distribution of, 248

Huntington, E., quoted, 157

Iatmul, social relations among, 307-8

Ibo family, budget of, 282

Ideal type, the, concept of in systems of classification, 603

Identification, of individual with group, as factor in social life, 36
with greater force or power, role of, in religion, 377

Ife, realism of bronze heads from, 385

Ifugao, money-barter among, 277

Imagery, linguistic, as reflection of cultural values, 456-7

Imitation, as factor in integrating primates into social groupings, 36
as mechanism for acquisition of culture, 26

Implements, agricultural, distribution of, 249-50

Inbreeding, significance of, for formation of human types, 140

Inca, governmental forms of empire of, 343

Incest, cultural definition of, 66

Incest lines, drawing of, in unilineal kinship systems, 298-9

Independent discoveries, as argument for culture as "superorganic" phenomenon, 23-4

Independent origin, disavowal of, by English diffusionists, 507
and diffusion, role of, in cultural change, 636

Index, between head length and height, of human and protohuman forms, compared, 112

Indian Office, use of anthropologists by, 647

Indians, migration of ancestors of, to Americas, 130
American, plants domesticated by, 249
range of governmental forms among, 341-2
reflection of cultural sanctions in folklore of, 419-20
North American, forms of divination among, 371
influence of, on culture of Europeans in New World, 533
power concepts in religions of, 357-8
of North Pacific Coast, extended family among, 302
of Southwest, differing utilization of common habitat by, 159

Indirect rule, doctrine of, and "practical anthropology," 646

Indirection, as sanction of Negro culture, 226

Individual, and culture, influence of psychoanalysis on study of, 47
relationship between, alternative methods of studying, 59
in terms of gestalt psychology, 46-7
behavioral world of, influence on perception of habitat by, 165
denial of role of, in cultural change, by cultural determinists, 22
enculturation of, as factor in establishing behavior patterns, 207-8
place of, in culture, 627
relation of, to culture, 21, 44, 49-54, 55-7
role of, in acculturative process, 44-5
role of government in life of, among Ashanti, 338

Individual behavior, as basis for reified institutions studied by ethnographers, 43

Individual differences, ignoring of, by early students, 563-4

Individual peculiarities, in cultural behavior, 576-7

Index

Individuals, psychological study of, 45

Industries, study of, by prehistorian, 118

Industry, anthropological studies of social relations in, 648

Inference, use of, in prehistory, 114–16

Infixes, uses of, 449

Informants, advantages and disadvantages in use of, 87–8
  attitude of early anthropologists, toward disagreement between, 564

Ingalik Indians, material culture of, 245

Initiation, tribal, at puberty, educational functions of, 325

Innovations, problem of acceptance and rejection of, 493
  borrowed, role of, in cultural change, 482
  cultural, as designation for new elements, 503
  role of reinterpretation in facilitating, 558–9

Instinct psychology, inadequacy of, for understanding of culture, 25–6

Instincts, inadequacy of theory of, in explaining cultural behavior, 46
  role of, in influencing cultural behavior, 236
  social, of animals, role of, in achieving integration into groups, 35–6

Institutions, as basis of ethnographic studies, 43
  as components of cultural aspects, 229
  as subject for anthropological study, 45
  cultural, functionalist approach to, 216–17
  political, range of variation of, in nonliterate cultures, 327
  role of, in formation of basic personality structure, 52
  social, dynamic approach to problem of, 307–9
  influence of, on group life, 289–90
  intermediate between family and sib, 301–3

Instruction, methods of, among various nonliterate groups, 313–19

Intangibles, as property, 283–4
  of culture, difficulties in reconstructing prehistoric development of, 116

Integration, cultural, as factor in individual adjustment, 633
  of Bemba culture, 221
  of Bush Negro culture, 217–20
  of cultural traits, as factor in study of diffusion, 516
  of culture, as conceived by R. Benedict, 221–2
  as expressed in themes, 223

Integration, of culture, (continued)
  aspects of, 215–16
  in study of acculturation, 534
  significance of, 632–3
  of experience, with habitat, 166
  of traits, in Kulturkomplexe, absence of, 513
  Trobriand Kula ring, as example of, 221

"Intensity," as dynamic concept in culture-area analysis, 200

Interaction, social, study of, 308–9

Interpretation, as factor in realism in art, 381

Interpreters, advantages and disadvantages in use of, in field research, 91–2

Invention, and discovery, factors antecedent to, 494
  difficulty of differentiating, 493
  as mechanism of internal cultural change, 635–6
  as "mother of necessity," 497
  definition of, 494
  hypothesis of genius as factor in, 498–9
  of material objects, methodological considerations leading to emphasis on, 496
  rarity of, postulated by English diffusionists, 507

Inventions, and discoveries, difficulty in designating innovations as, 502
  in realm of ideas, 496

Inventor, concept of, as innovator in material culture, 495–6

Iron Age, of prehistory, 128

Iron-working, distribution of, in nonliterate world, 264–5

Iroquois, League of, political institutions in, 341–2
  reinterpretation of aboriginal patterns of suicide among, 558

Irrigation, use of, by nonliterate cultivators, 251

Isolation, as factor in cultural conservatism or change, 489

Jamaica, variation in songs of, 565–9

Japan, recent history of, as exemplifying concept of historic accident, 591–2

Javanese, of Dutch Guiana, sex division of labor in mat-making among, 273

Jenks, A. E., cited, 272
  quoted, 248

Jessup North Pacific expedition, as study of cultural "laboratory" situation, 616

Index

Jew, lack of validity of term, as racial designation, 148

Judgement, of values, danger of drawing, in field research, 81

Judgements, basis of, in cultural experience, 63

Junod, H. A., cited, 322–3

Kardiner, A., quoted, 52

Karma, reconstruction of culture-contacts of, by use of pot-sherds, 262

Keesing, F., cited, 541

Kelautan, relation of food production and consumption among fishermen of, 281

Keraki, delimitation of political institutions among, 331

Kgatla, range of educational methods employed by, 317

Kinship, preciseness of terms of, in various descent systems, 296–7

Kinship aggregates, variety of, among Nuer, 302–3

Kinship system, classificatory, illustrated, 298

Kinship systems, changes in, under acculturation, 536

cultural determination of, 66

Kinship usages, stress on education in, among nonliterate peoples, 320–1

Kipsigis, educational aspects of circumcision rites among, 322

Klimek, S., cited, 172

Kluckhohn, C., quoted, 223, 224

Kluckhohn, C. and Leighton, D., quoted, 321

Kluckhohn, C. and Mowrer, O. H., quoted, 57

Köhler, W., quoted, 32, 36

Kroeber, A. L., cited, 24, 37, 183, 188, 542

quoted, 23, 24, 172, 200, 503

Kroeber, A. L. and Driver, H. E., quoted, 171–2

Kroeber, A. L. and Gifford, E. W., cited, 172

Krogman, W. M., cited, 133

quoted, 136–7

Kropotkin, Prince Peter, quoted, 31

Kru, proverbs of, 420

verb-forms of, 450–1

Kula ring, of Trobriand Islands, as example of cultural integration, 221

as prestige economic system, 279

Kulturhistorische Schule, see Culture-historical school

Kulturkomplexe, of culture-historical school, 512–13

Kunu, as manifestation of power-concept among Bush-Negroes, 359

Kuo, Z. Y., cited, 39

Kwakiutl Indians, conspicuous consumption among, 287

credit system of, 278–9

cultural type attributed to, 51

guardian spirit, concept of, 178

Kwoma, educational methods employed by, 318

Labor, hours of, in nonliterate societies, 69–71

sex division of, as affected by invention of potter's wheel, 264

sustained, need for, by nonliterate peoples, 268–9

Labor-market, absence of, in economies of nonliterate peoples, 267

Laboratory, historical, for study of culture, in Negro societies of Africa and New World, 612

Laboratory situations, for study of culture, illustrated, 616–17

Laboratory techniques, use of, in verification of hypotheses, 609–10

Land, ownership of, 283

Lang, A., cited, 349, 354, 421

Lango, poetry of, quoted, 196

Language, and communication, differentiated, 454

as independent variable, when considered with race and culture, 149

as "index to culture," 457

as mechanism for enculturation, 626

changes in, under Arab-Jewish acculturation, 551

classification of, in terms of word-structures, 448–9

definition of, 440

elements of, 441

examples of, as documenting cultural conditioning, 26

native, knowledge of, in field research, 92

nonliterate, aspects of, subject to statistical treatment, 574

reinterpretations of, under borrowing, 555

symbolism of, as agent in culture-building, 27

value of, in analysis of culture, 454–7

Languages, classifications of, 600

historical relation between, study of, 443

pidgin, varieties of, to be used in field-work, 91

Index

Law, definition of, 345
  formal character of, 330
  of nonliterate societies, study of, 344–6
Laws, cultural, as statement of process, 619
  factor of process encompassed in, 640
  general, of culture, establishment of, as aim of anthropology, 610–11
Learning, as factor in enculturation, 39–40, 625–6
  as factor in socialization, 38–9
  attitudes toward, in nonliterate societies, 312–13
  importance of, for definition of culture, 25
Learning process, relationship of, to cultural conditioning, 46
Leighton, D. and Kluckhohn, C., quoted, 321
Leisure class, theory of, 286
Lent, variation in cult-practices of Brazilian Negroes during, 571
Lesser, A., quoted, 535–6
Lesu, educational methods in, 317–18
  institutionalized friendship in, 305
Levalloisian period of prehistory, 122
Levirate, 296
Levy-Bruhl, L., cited, 73
Lewin, K., cited, 46
Lewis, O., cited, 541
Li An-che, cited, 51
  quoted, 314
Limited possibilities, hypothesis of, 501
Limits, of variation within culture, need to ascertain, 570
Lind, R. and H., cited, 80
Lindblom, G. K., cited, 175
Lindgren, E. J., quoted, 530
Lineages, types of, among Nuer, 302–3
Linguistic change, accumulation of small variables as factor in, 583
Linguistic drift, concept of, as applied to cultural change, 582–4
Linguistic elements, integration of, 442
Linguistics, comparative, fields of, 5
  scope of, 1–2
  special techniques of, 7–8
Linnaeus, classification of man with anthropoid forms by, 99
Linton, R., cited, 52, 301, 544, 576
  quoted, 56, 193, 524
Literate societies, study of, by anthropologists, 80
Literature, derivation of, from experience of creators, 419
  relationship of, to cultural anthropology, 11

Llewellyn, K. N. and Hoebel, E. A., quoted, 330, 345
Loango, power-concept in religion of, 358
Loeb, E., cited, 539
Logic, historical and classificatory, compared, 604
  in West African explanation of inheritance of intelligence, 73–4
  of culture-trait list, and culture-complex, differentiated, 182
  of structure, as aid in reconstructing early human forms, 98
  relativistic nature of patterns of, in different societies, 73–4
Looms, use of, 256–7
Lorogun, rite of Brazilian Negro cults, variation in, 571–2
Loss of ancestry, as mechanism in formation of population type, 140
Lowie, R. H., cited, 472
  quoted, 298, 303, 304, 306, 329, 341, 360, 364
Luck, concept of, as form of mana, 355
Luomala, K., cited, 425
  quoted, 324–5

MacCurdy, G. G., quoted, 107, 126
MacGregor, G., cited, 164
McGregor, J. H., quoted, 108, 110
McKern, W. C., cited, 302
Machine societies, relative complexity of economic processes in, 266
Machine technology, of Euroamerica, uniqueness of, 241
Machines, classification of, 242
Madagascar, culture-areas of, 193
  study of basic personality types of peoples of, 52
Magdalenian period of prehistory, 124
Magic, among Azande, 366–7
  as explanation of Upper Palaeolithic art, 126
  as part of religion, 360
  as "primitive science," 359
  classification of forms of, 367
  logic of presuppositions underlying, 73
  relationship of, to religion, 359–60
  techniques of, 366–70
  universality of belief in, 359–60
  "white" and "black," validity of categories of, 369–70
Magic charms, forms and functions of, 368
"Magic Flight" tale, distribution of, 416
"Magic Whip," combination of, with other tales, in Dutch Guiana, 418
Maglemosian, Mesolithic culture of Denmark, 127

Index

Maine, Sir H., quoted, 328, 484–5

Maitland, F. W., quoted, 461

Maize, diffusion of, to Africa, 481

Maladjustment, of individual in culture, stress on study of, 56

Malekula, concept of soul held by people of, 351–2
  institutionalized friendship in, 304–5

Malinowski, B., cited, 48, 179, 221, 237, 292
  quoted, 83–4, 216, 234–5, 320, 527

Man, as component of biological series, 99
  as "culture-building animal," 18–20, 626
  as domesticated animal, significance of, in study of race, 145–7
  as social animal, differentiated from man as culture-building animal, 29–30, 37–9
  contemporary, unities in culture of, 629
  evolution of, role of erect posture in achieving, 99–103
  plasticity of, as social animal, 643
  prehistoric, basic discoveries of, 131–2

Mana, as generic term for power-concept in religion, 355
  as power, forms of belief in, among various peoples, 356–9
  classical incidence of, in Melanesia, described, 355–6
  significance of concept of, for theories of origin of religion, 349

Mandelbaum, D. G., quoted, 288, 304, 538, 547

Mangaia, ritual exchange in, 275

Mangareva, prayers of, quoted, 363–4

Manitou, power-concept of Algonkian Indians, described, 357

Maori, food consumed by, at feasts, 280
  stylistic elements in art of, 400–1

Marett, R. R., cited, 354
  quoted, 348, 375

Marginal culture, cautions in use of concept of, 198

Marginal cultures, of areas, concept of, 195

Market, differing degrees of complexity of, in machine and non-machine societies, 267

Marquesan Islands, study of basic personality structure of people of, 52

Marriage, definition of, 296
  relationships in, to family of spouse, 295–6

Martin, P. S., cited, 262

Martin, R., cited, 125

Marx, K., influence of L. H. Morgan on, 473
  quoted, 288

Masai, sanctioned pre-marital relations among, 295

Mason, O. T., quoted, 261

Material culture, as affording data for study of prehistory, 116
  autonomy of, 245
  defined, 241
  evolutionary stages of, as subjective classifications, 603–4
  unequal distribution of elements of, 245–6

Mathematics, relationship of, to physical anthropology, 12

Mating, factors governing choice in, 296
  patterns of, in Euroamerican society, 203–5
  in Solomon Islands, 205–7
  preferential, types of, 299
  selection in, significance of, in formation of human types, 147

Matrilocal residence, place of male in societies having systems of, 291–2

Mauss, M., cited, 275

Maya Indians, religious reinterpretations in culture of, 555–6

Mead, M., cited, 44, 50–1, 52, 93

Meaning, as function of language, 456
  devices employed to shade, 449
  in culture, as function of cultural integration, 633
  new, of old forms, as factor in cultural reinterpretation, 557

Meanings, of cultural facts, as revealed by informants, 87–8

Measurement, in development of scientific methodology for study of culture, 573, 574

Medicine, study of, as example of cultural configurational approach, 223–4

Medium, relation of, to art forms, 405

Meek, C. K., studies of, as government anthropologist, 646

Meganthropus palaeojavanicus, 104

Mekeel, S., cited, 541

Melanesia, absence of religious specialization in, 362
  concept of mana found in, 355–6
  forms of trade in, as culture-complexes, 178–9
  media of exchange used in economies of, 278
  political structures of, 340
  prayers addressed to ghost in, 365

Melody, as accompaniment to rhythm, in African songs, 437

Index

Menghin, O., cited, 123

Menomini, ethnohistorical analysis of acculturation among, 541

Mentality, prelogical, inapplicability of use of, as criterion of "primitive" peoples, 73

Məntú, power-concept of Algonkian Indians, described, 357

Mesolithic period of European prehistory, 126–7

Metal-working, types of, among nonliterate peoples, 264

Method, alternatives in, in study of relation between individual and culture, 59

    ethnographic, principles of, stated by B. Malinowski, 83–4

    inductive, in search for cultural laws, 610–11

    of American anthropologists, in study of diffusion, 517

    refinement of, in history of anthropology, 608–9

    statistical, of studying homogeneity and heterogeneity of human populations, 140–1

    used in study of diffusion of Plains Indian Sun Dance, 521–2

Methods, anthropological, as distinguishing anthropology from related sciences, 6

    field, rarity of descriptions of, 81

    in study of historical reconstructions, 517–21

    of prehistory, use of fact and inference in, 114–16

    specialized, employed in study of American archaeology, 130–1

    varied, need to employ, in study of culture, 215

Métraux, A., quoted, 331, 425

Mexico, applied anthropology in, 647

    calabash dishes from, as illustrating relation of realism and conventionalization in art, 397

Migration, effect of, on cultural borrowing, 532–3

    forced, of Negroes to New World, 612

    of man to America, probable date and path of, 130

Millar, N. E. and Dollard, J., cited, 39

Miolithic, term suggested to include Upper Palaeolithic and Mesolithic, 123–4

Mitchell, C. E., work in "practical anthropology" under auspices of, 646

Mitla, results of culture-contact in, 535

Mixture, of physical types, significance of study of, 140

Modal personality, concept of, 56

Modesty, as factor in use of clothing, 260

Molding, as technique of pottery-making, 263

Money, characteristics of, 278–9

Money-barter, nature and forms of, 277

Money-economy, restricted incidence of, in nonliterate cultures, 278

Money-symbol, unique character of, in Euroamerican culture, 267–8

Mongoloid race, distribution and physical characteristics of, 136–7

Monkeys, howler, social organization of, 35

Monogamy, and polygamy, economic bases of, 293–4

    practice of, in various nonliterate societies, 293–4

Monoliths, Mexican, interpretation of carvings on, 507–8

Montagnais-Naskapi, məntú as power-concept of, 357

    nature of belief in soul held by, 351

Montagu, M. F. A., quoted, 103, 107

Morals, relativistic approach to, questions raised by, 76

Morant, G. M., cited, 110, 148

Morgan, L. H., cited, 233, 328, 463, 473

    quoted, 463, 465, 468, 470, 474, 476

"Moron" stories, derivation of, 423

Morpheme, definition, and types of, 448

Morphology, human, as aid in reconstructing evolution of man, 97–8

Morris, B., quoted, 378

Morton, D. J., cited, 101

"Mother Holle," as variant of "Good Child and Bad" tale, 416

Mother-in-law taboo, significance of, 295

Motifs, importance of study of, 415

Motivation, Freudian approach to study of, by anthropologists, 47

    social setting of, 45

Mountford, C. P., quoted, 254

Mousterian culture of prehistory, 122

Movius, H. L., Jr., quoted, 113, 117, 127, 129

Mowrer, O. H. and Kluckhohn, C., quoted, 57

Mühlmann, W., quoted, 528

Murdock, G. P., quoted, 231, 236

Muscles, relation of, to skeletal structure, 101

Museums, ethnological, role of, in establishing culture-area concept, 184

Music, African, importance of rhythm in, 437

Index

Music (*continued*)

of nonliterate peoples, aspects of, subject to statistical treatment, 573

complexity of, 439

methodological problems in study of, 435–6

patterned reactions to, variations in, 209

use of, in study of cultural variation, 564–70

Music theory, of nonliterate peoples, 439

Musical instruments, classification of, 438

Musicology, comparative, as branch of cultural anthropology, 11–12

significance of study of, for analysis of culture, 435

use of recording phonograph in study of, 435

Müller, F., quoted, 148

"Mutations," in invention, defined, 502

Mutual aid, as factor in evolution, 31

Myres, Sir J. L., quoted, 332, 655

Mysticism, religious, 376

Myth, of Cherokee Indians, of origins of human races, 68–9

Mythology, function of, as sanction for belief and ritual, 373

in providing sanctions for sib, 300

Nadel, S. F., cited, 285

quoted, 301, 331

"Name-magic," forms of, 367

Naskapi, absence of prayer among, 305–6

Natchez, political structures of, 341

Nationalism, ethnocentrisms of, as hinderance to world society, 653

Native language, use of, in field-work, evaluated, 91

Nativity tale, as found among Zuñi Indians, 415–6

Navaho Indians, common-sense reasoning of, exemplified, 73

covert culture of, 224

drama in rituals of, 431–2

education in kinship usages among, 321

example of cultural conservatism from, 486

Nazism, racial doctrines of, 148

Neanderthal man, Mousterian culture of, 122

remains of, 108–9

"Necessary presupposition," as principle in historical reconstructions, 518

Necktie, as example of cultural drift, 582

Need, as factor in discovery and invention, 494–5

problem of, in study of cultural determinants, 640–1

Needs, basic, as source of cultural institutions, 234–5

derived, role of in formation of cultural institutions, 236

"Negro," sociological and biological definitions of, in various countries, 144–5

Negroes, American, color values in selection of mates by, 147

New World, power-concepts of, 359

retention of African cultural focus by, 553

societies of, as laboratory for study of culture, 612

New World and African, normal character of spirit possession among, 66–7

of Suriname, change in written and unwritten dialects of, compared, 455

sanctions of, as expression of integration of cultures of, 225–6

Negroid race, 136–7

Nelson, N. C., quoted, 244

Neolithic period of European prehistory, 127–8

"Neolithic revolution," hypothesis of, 132

New England community, investigation of social structures in, 308

New World, introduction of food plants of, into Europe, as historic accident, 589

New Zealand, culture-areas of, 193

Nilghiri district, of India, cultural symbiosis in, 537–8

"Noble savage," influence of concept of, on political philosophy, 332

"Non-historic," as synonym for "primitive," reasons for rejecting use of, 74–5

Nonliterate, as classificatory device, contrasted to folk-society concept, 606

as synonym for "primitive," 75

derivation and utility of, as descriptive term, 628

secondary significance of concept of, 644

Nonliterate peoples, reasons for conducting research among, 80

practical approach of, to problems of technology, 246–7

problems in conducting field research among, 79

values in study of, 643

Nordenskiöld, E., cited, 175

Norm, social, of experience, experiments establishing validity of, 65–6

Normality, concept of, as culturally defined, 66–7

Index

North America, characteristics of folklore in, 425
culture-areas of, 186–8
Northwest Coast Indians, totem-poles of, as evidence of cultural change, 481
Notes-and-Queries, as approach to field-work, 89
Nott, J. C., cited, 151
Nuba, ends of political institutions of, 330–1
Nuer, forms of political control among, 339–40
method of conducting field-work among, described, 84
variety of kinship aggregates among, 302–3

Oberholzer, E., quoted, 55
Obia, power-concept among West Indian Negroes, 359
Objective reality of culture, argument for, 21–2
Objectivity, need of, in conducting field research, 81
Observation, first-hand, place of, in field-work, 87
Œdipus complex, analysis of, by B. Malinowski, 48
Office of Indian Affairs, early disregard by, of scientific anthropology, 645
Olbrechts, F. M., cited, 69
Old World, characteristics of folklore of, 424
Opler, M. E., quoted, 59, 223, 225, 315–17
Organism, human, requirements of, role of culture in fulfilling, 641
Organization, in animal societies, variation in degree of, 34–5
Origin, of *homo sapiens*, locality of, unknown, 97
of religion, search for, 353–4
Orokolo, drama of, in Papua, 427–8
Ortiz, F., quoted, 529
Osgood, C., quoted, 245
Overlapping, as phenomenon studied in differentiation of races, 134–5

Pacific islands, divisions of, as culture-areas, 193
Painting, in European Palaeolithic, 125–6, 388
Paiute Indians, "word-sentence" in language of, 447
Palaeolithic, art of, realism and conventionalization in, 385–8

Palaeolithic (*continued*)
evidence for religious customs during, 347
in Europe, cultures of, 121–6
Palaeontology, relationship of, to prehistoric archaeology and physical anthropology, 12
Palestine, role of cultural focus in Arab-Jewish acculturation in, 550–1
Pan-Egyptian diffusionist school, 505
Papuans, Keraki, marriage patterns of, 213
Parallel cousins, relationship of, 299
Parsons, E. C., quoted, 88, 176–7, 415–6, 535, 537
"Participant observer," doctrine of, 83–4
Patai, R., quoted, 550–1
Paternity, physiological, lack of recognition of, in Trobriand Islands, 290
Pattern, cultural, as psychological phenomenon, 201
as used in configurational approach to study of culture, 222
definition of, 223
Patterning, cultural, nature of, 632
of African and New World Negro spirit possession, 66–7
of American secret societies, 207
Patterns, artistic, role of, in influencing work of artist, 403
behavior, individual variation in, 208–9
cultural, as consenses of individual behavior patterns, 202–12, 575
definiteness of, 202–3
forms of, as manifest in cultural institutions, 201
need for comprehension of, in cross-cultural understanding, 211
plural nature of, 212
predictive value of, 213
variations in, with occupational or class lines, 209
of mating, in Solomon Islands and Euroamerican culture, contrasted, 203–7
plurality of, in cultures, significance of, 575
sub-cultural, in Euroamerican culture, 208–9
knowledge of, by members of other sub-cultures, 212
of Dahomey, 210–11
role of specialization in forming, 210
Patwin, "functional family" of, as extended family, 302
Pawnee Indian Ghost Dance hand-game, study of, as acculturation, 535–6
Pawning, in West Africa, 279
Peck-order, of fowls, 32–3

Index

Pei, W. C., discoverer of *sinanthropus pekinensis*, 105
Percussion instruments, of nonliterate peoples, 438–9
Peristiany, J. G., quoted, 322
Perry, Commodore M. C., visit of, to Japan, as historic accident, 591
Perry, W. J., cited, 507
Personalities, in foreign cultures, reaction to, of ethnographer, 86–7
status, hypothesis of, 56
Personality, and culture, approaches to study of, 49–55
components of, 56–7
of individual, influence of enculturation on, 626
role of early enculturation in influencing, 43–5
Personality norms, influence of culture in formation of, 52–4
Personality types, modes of classifying, analyzed, 601
of those experiencing spirit possession in African and New World Negro societies, 66–7
Peschuël-Loesche, E., cited, 358
Petrie, Sir W. M. Flinders, cited, 542
Pettitt, G. A., cited, 314
Peyote cult, influence of analysis of, on study of cultural processes, 540
Philippines, cultural drift as exemplified in cultures of tribes of, 585–7
irrigated rice cultivation in mountainous country of, 163
study of native cultures of, as "laboratory" approach to cultural analysis, 617
Philosophical problem, of reality of culture, 21
Philosophy, of cultural relativism, as basic anthropological contribution, 64
positive contributions of, 76, 655
Phonemes, definition of, 443
range of variation in, 445
Phonemic symbols, use of, 444
Phonetics, definition of, 443
Physical anthropology, scope of, 1
special techniques of, 6–7
stress on classification in, 597
Physical characteristics, of races, 137
Physical type, relation of, to culture, 143–8, 629
Pidgin dialects, utility of, in field research, 91
Pigmentation, importance given to, in differentiating human races, 133
Piltdown man, 107
Pitch, absolute, problem of, 65, 435–6

Pithecanthropus erectus, 97, 104–5, 113
Pithecanthropus robustus, 104
Plains Indians Sun Dance, *see* Sun Dance
Plot, in drama of nonliterate societies, 429–30
Plow, influence of, on patterns of sex division of labor, 251–2
Poetry, Dahomean, 434
nonliterate, relation of, to song, 434
of Lango, 196
of Mangareva, 363–4
of South African Bushmen, 365
Polarity, as characteristic of classificatory systems, 602–3
in folk-society concept, 605
Political forms, range of, in nonliterate societies, 327
Political institutions, lack of comparative study of, by political scientists, 329
of Philippine tribes, differences between, as examples of cultural drift, 586–7
scope of, 330
universality of, 328
Political organization, influence of habitat on, 161
Political organizations, native, of West Africa, complexity of, 332
Political philosophers, early, influence of concepts of American Indian life on, 332
Political science, relationship of, to anthropology, 10
Political structures, of Melanesia, 340
Polyandry, restricted distribution of, 294
Polygyny, incidence and nature of, 294–5
problem of assessing values in, 161
Polynesia, complexity of ritual drama in, 430
formal education in native cultures of, 324
political institutions of, 340
power-concept in religions of, 356
question of contact of, with Americas, 508–9
reflection of cultural sanctions in mythology of, 419
Polyphony, in Euroamerican and nonliterate music, 436
Polyrhythms, in African music, 437
Ponape, cultural focus of, 547–9
Pondo, study of, as "laboratory" approach to cultural analysis, 617
Popoluca Indians, cost of cooperative and hired work among, compared, 271
Population, as unit for study of biological processes in man, 139

Index

Population size, relation of, to political forms, 328
relation of, to production of economic surplus, 284
Poro schools, of Liberia and Sierra Leone, 323–4
Portuguese, stories of, told in Brazil, 423
Possession, spirit, forms and functions of, 371–2
in African and New World Negro societies, 66–7
Posture, upright, role of, in giving man present capacities, 99–103
Potlatch, of Kwakiutl Indians, as example of conspicuous consumption, 287
Potters, nonliterate, motor skill of, 263
Potter's wheel, restricted distribution of, 263–4
Pottery, factors governing distribution of, 262–3
techniques of making, 262
Powdermaker, H., cited, 305
quoted, 317–18
Power-concept, nature and manifestations of, 355–9
Practical anthropology, development of, in England, 646
Practical problems, anthropological contributions to solution of, 651
Prayer, forms and functions of, 363–6
relation of, to magic, 366
Pre-Chellean period of prehistory, 122
Predictability, of cultural behavior, as argument for cultural determinism, 22
Prediction, cross-cultural, status of, 621
of individual behavior, in terms of culture-patterns, 213
problem of, in terms of cultural laws, 640
within culture, as reflection of regularity of behavior, 621
Předmost finds, 110
Preferential mating, among Ashanti, 299–300
Prefixes, use of, in Bantu languages, 453
Prehistoric cultures, classification of, 117–20, 630
Prehistory, European, special character of categories of, 128–9
geological basis for chronology of, 117
of Old and New World, problems of, contrasted, 129–31
use of inference in, 114–16
welding of to history, in New World archaeology, 131
world-wide sequences of cultures in, difficulty of establishing, 117

"Pre-literate," as synonym for "primitive," reasons for rejecting, 75
"Prelogical" mentality, as pattern of human thought, 74
Prestige, and subsistence, derivation of dual economies from, 279
as incentive to work, 274
in cultural borrowing, 533
role of yam cultivation in giving, among Ponapeans, 548–9
Prestige economy, mechanisms of, 284
nature of, 287
Priests, and diviners, support of, as factor in economic aspect of religion, 374
utilization of economic surplus by, 286
Primates, as category including man and anthropoid forms, 99
complexity of processes of integration of, into social groups, 35
"Primitive," as evaluative term, 70–1
concept of, contrasted to folk-society concept, 606
non-scientific connotations of, 628
synonyms for, reasons for use or rejection of, 74
use of, in sense of "primeval," by evolutionists, 469
"Primitive" cultures, difficulties in defining, 72
rejection of hypothesis of simplicity of, 643
variation in, 74
Primitive man, conception of, as "contemporary ancestor," 71
Probability, as critical factor in historical reconstruction, 520
Problems, nature of, studied by anthropology, 6
of world order, anthropological contributions to solution of, 653–4
sociological, studied by use of genealogical method, 90
Process, and form, role of, in analysis of culture, 602
as basis of cultural laws, 619–20
Productivity, of labor in nonliterate societies, 272
Progress, concept of, in evolutionary thought, 464, 473
Euroamerican concept of, as reflection of ethnocentrism, 69
Projective tests, use of, in study of culture and personality, 54–5
Pronunciation, standardization of, in language, 446
Pronouns, variations in use of, 452
Property, forms of, 283

Index

Protection, as primary criterion of domestication, 146

Protestantism, and Catholicism, differing influence of, on retention of Africanisms in New World, 613

Protohuman forms, earliest, 103–4

Proverb, in Africa, utilization of, 420

Proverbs, as expressions of cultural sanctions, in Negro cultures, 226

Provinse, J. H., quoted, 269

Psychiatry, contributions of, to study of relation between culture and individual, 56

Psychic unity of man, doctrine of, 474–5

Psychoanalysis, and behaviorism, in study of individual in society, 49
contributions of, to study of relation between individual and culture, 47, 56

Psychological factors, in culture, disregard of, in theories of cultural growth, 543
in diffusion, importance of, 516

Psychological formulations, of cultural unity, 215

Psychological mechanisms, for acquisition of culture, 25–6

Psychological tests, of First World War, use of, by racists, 151–2

Psychological reality of culture, arguments for, 25–7

Psychologists, meaning given "acculturation" by, 527

Psychology, and anthropology, interdisciplinary training in, 58
influence of various schools of, in study of individual and culture, 45
relationship of, to anthropology, 12, 45

Psychology of culture, interdisciplinary bases for, 45

Psychopathology, misapplication of concepts of, to African and New World Negro possession, 67–8

Pueblo Indians, religion of, combination of elements into complexes in, 176–7

Pueblo Indian pottery, as art-form reflecting virtuosity of potter, 382
changes in decoration of, 404

Pukapuka, mode of making land for agriculture in, 164

Puyallup-Nisqually Indians, power-concepts of, 357–8
"power-demonstrations" of, as form of prayer, 365
power-quest of, as cultural focus, 545

Pygmies, Congo, suspension bridges erected by, 246

Pyramids, Mexican and Egyptian, fallacy of comparing, 508

Quantity, criterion of, in method of culture-historical school, 511–12

Quimby, G. I., cited, 262

Race, and culture, problem of relationship between, 143–8, 628–9
as independent variable, when considered with language and culture, 149
definition of, 133
genetic basis of, 138–9
repudiation of, by evolutionists, as factor in establishing cultural differences, 465

Races, classification of, 133, 136–7
controversy over early appearance of, 103
controversy over taxonomic status of, 110
genetic reality of, 136
importance of study of variation in delimiting, 134–5
principal, geographical distribution of, 136

Racial classifications, types falling outside of, 138

Racial differentiation, human, possible early appearance of, 106

Racial superiority, difficulty of establishing criteria for, 150

Racial traits, similarity of, to traits of domesticated animals, 145

Racism, American, early manifestations of, 150–1
definition of, 148

Radcliffe-Brown, A. R., cited, 331
quoted, 293, 320, 329, 611–12

Radin, P., cited, 376, 540

Ramos, A., cited, 533

Rattray, R. S., cited, 59, 285
quoted, 333–7, 364
studies of, as government anthropologist, 646

Ratzel, F., cited, 156
early mapping of African culture-areas by, 190

Raum, O. F., cited, 325
quoted, 310, 320–1

Ray, V., quoted, 173, 174

Readjustment, of individuals, under culture-contact, 539

Realism, and conventionalization, in art, problem of, 381
relation between, as shown in Mexican calabash designs, 395

Index

Realism (*continued*)
defined, 382
in art of nonliterate peoples, 385
in paintings of Upper Palaeolithic, analyzed, 393–5
relative character of, as illustrated by Yoruban masks, 382
Reality, cultural relativistic problem of, 63–4
sense of, among "primitive" peoples, 73–4
Reasoning, logical character of, among nonliterate peoples, 73–4
Reconditioning, as mechanism for adaptation of behavior to new conditions, 26
function of, in cultural change, 627
Redfield, R., quoted, 531, 576, 604–5, 606
Redfield, R., Linton, R., and Herskovits, M. J., quoted, 523–4
Reduplication, uses of, 449
Reenculturation, as factor in cultural reinterpretation, 637
as mechanism of cultural change, 627
Reichard, G. A., cited, 401, 456
Reinterpretation, as process of cultural dynamics, 553, 556–7
as psychological explanation of cultural change, 560
cultural, role of reenculturation in, 637
linguistic, 555
Reinterpretations, of African customs, by New World Negroes, 553–5
Reisner, G. A., cited, 262
Relationship, between culture and habitat, reciprocal nature of, 164–5
Relationships, perception of, experiments on, 65–6
"Relative firmness," as principle in historical reconstruction, 518
Relativism, cultural, as applied to culture-area concept, 198–9
as curb on ethnocentrism, 78
as exemplified in attitudes toward foods, 70
importance of conception of, for field research, 80–1
principle of, defined, 63
questions raised concerning philosophical validity of, 75–78
Relativity, of culture-traits and complexes, 172
Religion, African, varied degrees of retention of, in New World, 613
and art, universality of, 347
as focal aspect of West African culture, 551–2

Religion (*continued*)
as philosophy, of nonliterate peoples, 362–3
comparative, relationship of, to cultural anthropology, 10–11
definition of, 377, 601
difficulty in defining, analyzed, 374–5
early development of, in prehistoric times, 347
economic factors in, 374
Freudian explanation of, 376
function of, 360
inferences regarding prehistoric manifestations of, 115–16
"minimum definition of," by E. B. Tylor, 348
non-supernaturalistic manifestations of, 377
problem of discovering origins of, 349
relationship of, to magic, 359–60
special education in, among nonliterate peoples, 325
special features of, in Euroamerican culture, 361
theory of mana as basis of, 348
Religions, classifications of, 600–1
Religious life, of Mousterian man, assumptions concerning, 122
Religious phenomena, types of, 349–50
Religious thrill, description of, by Dahomean, quoted, 376
theory of, as basis of supernaturalism, 375
Research, in field, by ethnographers, 79–91
Residence, in marriage, types of, 291
Resources, capitalization of, 282–3
maximization of, as universal trait of culture, 266
Responses, automatic, in cultural behavior, 46
to cultural stimuli, 625
cultural, to basic needs, as explanation of institutions, 235
"instrumental," in formation of cultural institutions, 236
Restorations, of early human types, techniques used in making, 98–9
Restraints, to be exercised by ethnographer, in field-work, 85
Retention, as measurement of intensity of Africanisms in New World, 613–16
Revenue, modes of collecting, in Ashanti kingdom, 337
"Revolutions," of prehistory, 132, 631
Rhythm, and melody, differing roles of, 437

XXX

Index

Rhythm (*continued*)
  complexity of, in certain nonliterate musical styles, 436–7
  decorative, as reflection of technical competence, 382
Rice cultivation, in mountainous country, as example of relation between culture and habitat, 163
Richards, A. I., cited, 221
  quoted, 271–2, 281
Richardson, J., cited, 24
Rivers, W. H. R., cited, 90, 294
  early interest in psychology of, 45
  quoted, 90, 472, 545, 546
Ritual, and belief, complementary character of, 361
  forms of, 363
Rituals, mythological sanctions of, 373
Roberts, H. H., quoted, 185, 565–9
Roquette-Pinto, E., quoted, 385
Rorschach tests, use of in cross-cultural study of personality and culture, 54–5
Roscoe, J., quoted, 267
Rulers, power of, among Ashanti, 333
  utilization of economic surplus by, 285–6

Sait, E. M., cited, 329
Sanctions, as unifying principle in culture, 222
  in Negro cultures, 225–6
  social, revelation of, in folklore, 420–1
Sande schools, of Liberian and Sierra Leone tribes, 324
Sapir, E., approach of, to problem of relation between individual and culture, 50
  cited, 184
  quoted, 49, 50, 211, 442, 447–8, 453, 513, 517–18, 564, 583, 584–5, 600
Sapir, E. and Swadesh, M., cited, 284
Saulteaux Indians, percentages of adjusted and maladjusted individuals among, 57
  shamanistic conjuring of, 371
"Savage," caricature of, in writings of A. J. Toynbee, 72
Sayce, R. U., cited, 504
  quoted, 502
Scale of intensity of Africanisms, use of, in classifying New World Negro cultures, 614–15
Scepticism, in nonliterate societies, 376
Schapera, I., cited, 276, 285, 338–9
  quoted, 263, 293, 317
Schismogenesis, as sociological process, 308

Schjelderup-Ebbe, T., quoted, 32
Schmidt, W., cited, 349, 354, 472
  quoted, 509, 510
Schnierla, T. C., quoted, 37
Schooling, contrasted to education, 310
  in nonliterate societies, examples of, 322–5
Schultz, A., cited, 99
Science, as system of thought relative to Euroamerican concepts, 76
Scientific findings, lack of control over use of, by scientists, 648–9
Secrecy, in yam cultivation, in Ponape, 548
Secret societies, American, patterning of, 207
Security, role of early enculturation in giving, 44–5
Selection, social, as domesticating agent for man, 146
  role in formation of human racial types, 145
Selective factor, habitat as, in limiting culture, 163
Selectivity, differential, of cultural innovations, 559
  in cultural borrowing, significance of, 537
Seligman, C. G., early interest in psychology of, 45
  quoted, 47
Sequences, of cultural evolutionists, 467–9
Sex, and class, differences in patterned behavior of, 575
Sex behavior, education in, in nonliterate societies, 321–2
Sex differences, in behavior, as basic cultural phenomenon, 22–3
  patterns of, in Euroamerican society, 208–9
Sex division of labor, hypotheses of, 273
  influence of plow on, 251–2
  universality of, 272
Shamanism, distribution and functions of, 371
Shasta Indians, guardian spirit concept of, 178
Shelter, relation of, to habitat, 252–3
Shelters, distributions of types of, 254–5
Sherif, M., cited, 65
  quoted, 66
Shouters, of Trinidad, religious reinterpretations of Africanisms by, 554
Shuswap Indians, version of "Ant and the Grasshopper" tale tole by, 415
Siang Dyak, work done by, 269
Sib, derivation of sanctions of, 300
  definition, types and functions of, 299

Index

Silent trade, nature and examples of, 276

Simplicity, of "primitive" cultures, rejection of hypothesis of, 643

Sinanthropus pekinensis, 105, 113

Skin-color, invalidity of differentiation of races by, 133

Skins, preparation of, for use as clothing, 257–8

Skinner, H. D., cited, 193

Skull, human, changes in, with attainment of upright posture, 102–3

Slang, significance of, for study of linguistic change, 456

Slavery, Negro, justification of, as source of American racism, 150

Smith, J. R., quoted, 156

Smith, M. W., quoted, 358

Smith, Sir G. E., quoted, 507

Smithfield dialect, as evidence of linguistic change, 45–6

Social anthropology, relation of, to ethnology and ethnography, 9

Social contract, theory of, as deriving from conception of primitive political institutions, 328

Social institutions, common to man and subhuman forms, 626

human, range of variation in, 38

of Philippine tribes, differences between, as examples of cultural drift, 586–7

Social leisure, relationship of, to economic surplus, 284

Social life, as domesticating agent for man, 146–7

Social norms, hypothesis of, 65

Social organization, delimitation of, 289

of howler monkeys, 35

scope of, 29–30

"Social origins," early currency of, 466

Social relations, in American industry, study of, by applied anthropologists, 648

Social selection, role of, in formation of human physical types, 629

Social structure, reflection of, in kinship systems, 298

Socialistic, as term used for Inca empire, 343

Socialization, as part of enculturative experience, 640

differentiated from enculturation, 40

nature of, 38

Societies, animal, forms of, 31–2

human and infrahuman, common elements in, 37

Society, concept of, as aggregate of subgroups, 575

Society (*continued*)

differentiation of, from culture, 29

distinguished from culture in terms of process, 37–8

"Society," as conceptual construct of student, 30

Society for Applied Anthropology, aims of, 647–8

Sociology, animal, study of, 30–37

comparative, as generalizing science, 611

relationship of, to cultural anthropology, 9

Sollas, W. J., cited, 129

Solomon Islands, patterns of mating in, 205–7

problem of value, as expressed in barter, in, 277

Solutrian period of prehistory, "laurel-leaf" flints of, 124

Song, predominance of, in nonliterate music, 437

"Sorcerer," of cave of Trois Frères, validity of assumptions concerning, 114–15

Sororate, 296

"Sorting-out" process, importance of, in field work, 86–7

Soul, as source of concept of deity, 354

conception of, in various cultures, 351–2

phenomena substantiating belief in, 350–1

Sound, cultural determination of patterning of, 65

South America, characteristics of folklore of, 425

culture-areas of, 189–90

programs of applied anthropology in, 647

South American Indian culture, reconstruction of history of, 520

South Seas, characteristics of folklore of, 425

Southeast Africa, differing reaction of tribes in, to habitat presented by, 158–9

Specialists, utilization of economic surplus by, 285

variation in behavior of, 577

Specialization, absence of, in Melanesia, 362

artistic, in nonliterate societies, 379

as factor in education in machine societies, 315

degree of, in cultures with differing economies, 241–2, 267

economic, relationship of, to production of economic surplus, 284

Index

Specialization (*continued*)
types of, in nonliterate societies, 272–4
in culture, influence of, in forming subcultural patterns, 209
of Euroamerican culture, as factor in production and appreciation of art, 378–9
relation of, to education, 310–11
religious, in Euroamerican culture, 361–2
sex, as universal in culture, 22–3
social, significance of, for study of drama, 429
variation in, as factor in shaping legal institutions, 345–6
Specialties, cultural, 575
Speciation, dynamic character of, 139
Speck, F. G., quoted, 351, 357, 366, 410
Spectators, role of, in drama of literate and nonliterate societies, contrasted, 427
Speech, functional units of, 447–8
Speech-community, concept of, 442–3
Spell, use of as magic device, 367–8
Spencer, B. and Gillen, F. J., cited, 325
Spencer, H., as originator of term "superorganic," 23
cited, 233
quoted, 469, 484
Spengler, O., cited, 542
Spicer, E. H., quoted, 307
Spier, L., cited, 521–2, 539–40
Spinden, H., cited, 504
Spinning, techniques of, 256–7
Spirits, conception of, among Aymara, 352
Spoehr, A., cited, 536
Stability, cultural, as relative to culture-change, 20
early enculturation as making for, 491
factors inducing, 488
psychological explanation of, 26
Stages of development, evolutionary, hypothesis of, 463
methodological problem of, as seen by evolutionists, 476
Standards, moral, relativistic approach to problem of, 63
State, concept of, distinguished from tribe and nation, 331–2
Statistics, use of, in study of culture, 573–4, 578
Stayt, H. A., cited, 285
quoted, 323, 358
Stereotype, as psychological mechanism in fixing "racial" types, 148–9
Stern, B., cited, 487
Steward, J. H., cited, 190

Stewart, O. C., cited, 172
Stimulus-diffusion, hypothesis of, 503
role of cultural reinterpretation in, 557
"Stock" as alternative term for "race," 133
Stoddard, Lothrop, cited, 151
"Stone age complex," basic discoveries constituting, 131–2
String instruments, of nonliterate peoples, 438
Structure, of culture, as framework of behavior, 214
Style, artistic, analysis of, 398
literary, of folklore, difficulties in studying, 425–6
musical, elements of, 436
Stylistic elements, artistic, tenacity of, 400–1
Stylization, in woodcarving of Africa and Marquesas, contrasted, 300
Stuckey, L. and Yoseloff, T., quoted, 423–4
Sub-cultures, as expressions of differentials in cultural drift, 583
Sub-groupings, social, cultural patterns of, 575
Submission, and dominance, in animal societies, 32–4
Sub-races, concept of, 133
of principal races, differentiated, 137
Suicide, among Iroquois Indians, changing patterns of, as reinterpretation, 558
Sun Dance, as "laboratory" approach to cultural analysis, 616
problems posed by, as subjects for acculturation study, 539–40
study of distribution of, 521
variants in, as reinterpretations, 556
Supernatural forces, special attitudes toward, in Euroamerican culture, 362
Supernaturalism, definition of religion in terms of, analyzed, 375–7
Superiority, racial, as non-scientific question, 150
Superorganic, doctrine of, 22–5
Superstition, definition of, 360
Suriname Negroes, folk-tale of, as illustrative of animal learning, 39
proverbs of, 420
Surplus, economic, role of, in establishing prestige economic system, 284–7
Survival, cultural, validity of concept of, 472
Survivals, cultural, differing approach to study of, in Europe and America, 471
in folklore, interpretation of, by early folklorists, 421

Index

Symbolism, dream, in Freudian system, inacceptability of, to anthropologists, 47

linguistic, as factor in shaping culture, 456–7

role of, in defining cultural experience for individual, 27

Syncretism, as cultural reinterpretation, 553–4

Syncretisms, religious, of Brazilian Negroes, variation in, 570–2

Systematics, science of classification, 597

Swadesh, M. and E. Sapir, cited, 284

Swanscombe man, 109–10

Swedish school, use of culture-trait concept, in comparative ethnographic studies of, 175

Talbot, P. A., studies of, as government anthropologist, 646

Tales, elements of, as independent variables, 416

Tallensi, cycle of food production and consumption of, 280–1

Tarascan Indians, magic spell of, quoted, 368

rounded study of, 238

Tardenoisian, Mesolithic culture of Central France, 127

Tax, S., cited, 576

quoted, 606, 653

Taxation, systems of, in Africa, 285

Taxonomy, earlier and modern approaches to, 597–8

Teaching, attitudes toward, in nonliterate societies, 312–3

Techniques, brought to Americas, by original migrants, 130

complexity of, in nonliterate societies, 241

special, used by anthropologists, 6

specialized, of ethnographic field-research, 92–3

Technology, as cultural focus of modern American life, 549

differentiated from material culture, 241

influence of, on habitat, 164

of nonliterate peoples, as arising from observation of cause and effect, 246

relation of, to political institutions, 328

results of development of, in Euroamerican society, 241–2

Teeth, giant, of fossil hominid form, problems posed by, 97

human, changes in, with attainment of upright posture, 102

Teggart, F. J., quoted, 464

Tenaciousness, of folktales, illustrated, 423–4

Tensions, between wives in polygynous household, 62

Terminology, of prehistory, 118, 123–4

political, difficulties in use of, as applied to nonliterate governmental forms, 342–3

Teton-Dakota, acculturation of, 541

Themes, cultural, as expressions of cultural integration, 223

of Apache culture, 225

Thompson, L. (Tueting, L. T.), cited, 179

Thompson River Indians, guardian spirit concept of, 178

Thompson, S., cited, 424, 425

Thoms, W. J., cited, 421

Thonga, medical patterns of, 224

Till Eulenspiegel, cycle of, as source of modern tales, 423–4

Tinguian, cultural change among as cultural-drift, 585–7

Todas, cultural focus of, 545–7

polyandry of, 294

relations of, with neighboring tribes, 538

use of genealogical method in study of, 90

Tolowa and Tututni Indians, subsistence and prestige economies of, 279

Tone, significant, as factor in linguistic expression, 449–50

Tools, of Upper Palaeolithic, profusion of, 124

prehistoric, primary, categories of, 119

stone, modern implements derived from, 244

Torres Straits, crocodile arrows from, use of, to document evolutionary theory of art-style, 390–2

use of genealogical method in, 90

Totem and Taboo, anthropological reaction to, 47

Totemism, defined, 300

in American Expeditionary Forces, 301

logical nature of presuppositions underlying, 73

problem of classification as illustrated by, 599

psychological basis of, 301

Totem-poles, recency of, 480–1

Toynbee, A. J., cited, 542

ethnocentrism in study of "civilization" by, 71

quoted, 72

Trade, in nonliterate societies, 276

XXXIV

Index

Trading, in Melanesia, as example of culture-complex, 178–9

Tradition, as synonym for culture, 17

Traits, number of, used to differentiate races, 133

objective nature of discrete treatment of, 214–5

of California Indian cultures, listing of, 172–4

positive and negative, use of in mapping culture-area, 194, 196

use of, in study of acculturation, 534

Trait-list, logic of, 182

Transculturation, as synonym for acculturation, 529

Traveller's reports, lack of classification of data in, 596

Trees, ownership of, 283

Tribe, concept of, distinguished from state and nation, 331–2

definition of, for Papua, 340

Trinidad, reinterpretations of African customs by Negroes of, 554

reluctance to borrow, between Hindus and Negroes of, 538

Trobriand Islands, brother-sister avoidance among, 320

Kula ring of, as example of cultural integration, 221

relationship of father to children in, 292

Trois Frères, cave of, 114

Truth, standards of, as universals in human society, 76

Tschopik, H., Jr., quoted, 302, 352

Tsimshian Indians, life of, as reflected in mythology, 418–19

Tübatulabal, verb-forms of, 451–2

Tungus, borrowing resulting from contacts of, with Cossacks, 530–1

Tuomoto, "word-sentence" in language of, 447

Turney-High, H. H., cited, 330

quoted, 344

Twilling, as basketry technique, 261

Tylor, E. B., cited, 174, 229, 233

dissociation of, from Darwin and Spencer, 464–5

quoted, 348, 354, 465, 469, 470, 471, 476

Uniqueness, historical, of cultures, problem of drawing generalizations from, 618

Urban society, concept of, as classificatory device, 604

Unilineal descent, kinship orientations in, 296–8

Unity, psychological, of culture, difficulty of studying, 221

Universal aspects, of culture, system for presentation of, 239

Universality, of religion and art, explanations of, 347–8

Universals, as distinguished from philosophical absolutes, empirical derivation of, 76–7

cultural, 575

in culture, as basis of philosophy of cultural relativism, 655

problem of explanation of, 237–8

reasons for, 233–4

Upper Palaeolithic, of Europe, art-forms of, 124–6

"Urban revolution," hypothesis of, 132

Use, of land, as conferring title, 283

Utility, of art-forms, in nonliterate cultures, 380–1

Vacation, uniqueness of concept of, in Euroamerican culture, 274

Vailala Madness, of Papua, as contra-acculturative movement, 531–2

Value, relativistic approach to problem of, 63

problem of determination of, in non-pecuniary economies, 276–7

Values, absolute stress on, as barrier to comprehension of relativistic philosophy, 77

in culture, utility of informants in revealing, 87–8

in polygynous family structure, 61–3

Van Gennep, A., quoted, 415

Variability, cultural, principle of, 570

differing levels of, 576–7

propositions concerning significance of, in study of culture, 577–8

family and fraternal, of various populations, 142

significance of, in analysis of physical types, 140–1

in study of race, 134–5

of Africanisms, in New World Negro cultures, problem of accounting for, 615

statistical concepts of, in study of culture, 573–4

Variables, cultural, differential significance of, 582

Variants, cultural, 576

importance of study of, 416

regional, as evidence of cultural change, 481

Variation, as factor in development of material culture, 502

Variation (*continued*)
as reflection of cultural homogeneity and heterogeneity, 577
cultural, as expression of differences in individual behavior, 638
as expression of principle of cultural consensus, 575
as mechanism of cultural change, 26
demonstration of, in Jamaican songs, 565–9
hypothesis of, 577–8
in cult-practices of Brazilian Negroes, 570–2
manifestations of, 637–8
psychological factors in, 579
relation of, to size of group, 577, 638
importance of, in evolutionary process, 99
in cultures of African societies ancestral to New World Negroes, 612
in focal aspect of Ponopean culture, 548
in governmental forms of North and South American Indians, 341–2
in modes of administering justice, in nonliterate societies, 345–6
in native political structures of African peoples, 338–40
in population, as index of homogeneity or heterogeneity, 140
individual, as related to cultural innovation, 577
principle of, in development of laws of cultural processes, 619–20
range of, in cultural behavior, as basis of ethnographic truth, 572
in human social institutions, 38
within culture, degree of, 64
Variations, in behavior, within culture, as expressions of cultural change, 483
cultural, difficulty of discerning, 563
random, in culture, differing significance of, 583
small, importance ascribed to, by cultural determinists, 580
Veblen, T., quoted, 287, 497
"Venuses," Aurignacian, of European Upper Palaeolithic, 124–5, 393
Verb-forms, variety of, 450–2
Villa R., A., quoted, 556
Village mapping, as technique of field research, 91
Virtuosity, artistic, specialized character of, 405–6
as factor in art, 382, 403
restriction of, to medium used by artist, 408–9

Vocabulary, concepts reflected in imagery of, 456–7
Voegelin, C., quoted, 452
Voegelin, E. W., cited, 173, 425
von Koenigswald, J. H. R., as discoverer of various protohuman forms, 104
Vowels, range in, 444–5

Wagley, C., quoted, 281
Wallis, W. D., quoted, 520
Wants, psycho-cultural, immediacy of, 266
relationship of, to subsistence, in technologically simple societies, 266
War, of nonliterate peoples, fewness of data concerning, 344
Ward, L. F., quoted, 485
Warfare, constant elements in, 330
Warner, W. L., quoted, 308, 309
Watkins, M. H., quoted, 324
Wealth, non-monetary symbols of, in nonliterate societies, 278
Weaving, as basketry technique, 261
Weidenreich, F., cited, 103
quoted, 105, 106, 107, 110, 112
Werner, A., quoted, 453
West Africa, applicability of folk-society concept to, 606
education in sex behavior in, 321
religion as focal area of cultures of, 551–2
West Indies, drama in telling of folktales in, 433
White, L., quoted, 477–8
Whiting, J. M. W., cited, 318
Whole cultures, study of contact in terms of, 535–6
Wild rice gatherers, of Great Lakes region, productivity of, 272
varied food resources of, 248
Willems, E., quoted, 537
Williams, F. E., cited, 428, 531
quoted, 213, 331, 340, 351, 427–8
studies of, as government anthropologist, 646
Wind instruments, of nonliterate peoples, 438
Wissler, C., behavioristic approach to study of culture of, 46
cited, 80, 169, 194, 237, 377
quoted, 170, 184–5, 186, 195, 230, 234, 518–19
Wittfogel, K., quoted, 526
Wogeo, attitude of children in, toward learning, 312
incentives to work in, 274
institutionalized friendship in, 305

Index

Wogeo (*continued*)
natives of, amount of labor performed by, 269–71

Women, position of, in Dahomean polygynous household, 62

Word, definitions of, 446–8

Words, types of, 448

"Word-sentences," examples of, 447

Work, incentives for, varied nature of, 274
patterns of, in nonliterate societies, 268–9
rhythm of, among Bemba, 271–2

World, physical, mediation of perception of, by ideas, 64–5

World society, anthropological contributions toward, 653–5

World-view, animism as forming part of, 353

Writing, letters used in, as phonemic approximations, 443
presence or absence of use of, as criterion to designate cultures, 75
relation of, to linguistic change, 455–6

Xylophone, as tonal and percussion instrument, 439

Yahgan, monogamy and polygamy among, 293

Yakö, productivity of, 272

Yam-cultivation, as focal point of Ponape culture, 547–9

Yap, symbols of wealth in, 278

Yerkes, R. M. and A. W., quoted, 35

Yoruba, nature of secret societies among, 306
realism of masks made by, 382

Yoseloff, T. and Stuckey, L., quoted, 423–4

Young people, value of obtaining information from, 88

Yucatan, study of Indian cultures of, as "laboratory" approach to cultural analysis, 617

Yurok Indians, psychoanalytic study of, 58

Yurok-Karok Indian basketry, conventionalized designs of, 382–3

Zeitgeist, mysticism in concept of, 542

"Zero-point," in culture, 528

Zuckerman, S., cited, 31, 35
quoted, 37

Zuñi Indians, as example of cultural type, 51
changes in decorative art in pottery of, 404
educational methods of, 315
nativity tale, as told by, 415–16
ritual dances of, as drama, 432
role of group in educating child among, 314

A NOTE ON THE TYPE

The text of this book is set in CALEDONIA, *a Linotype face designed by* W. A. DWIGGINS, *the man responsible for so much that is good in contemporary book design and typography. Caledonia belongs to the family of printing types called "modern face" by printers—a term used to mark the change in style of type-letters that occurred about 1800. It has all the hard-working feet-on-the-ground qualities of the Scotch Modern face plus the liveliness and grace that is integral in every Dwiggins "product" whether it be a simple catalogue cover or an almost human puppet.*

The book was composed, printed, and bound by KINGSPORT PRESS, INC., *Kingsport, Tennessee. Typography by Sidney R. Jacobs; binding based on designs by W. A. Dwiggins.*